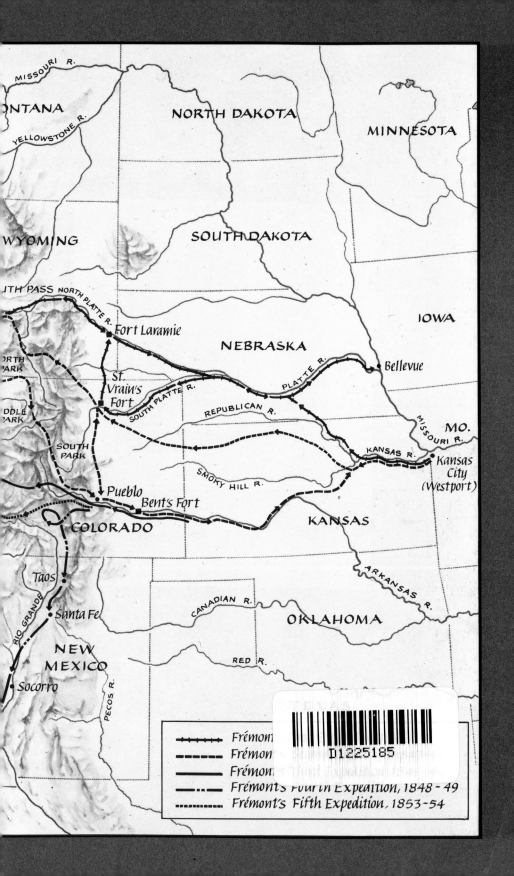

MONTANA

MISSOURI R.

YELLOWSTONE R.

NORTH DAKOTA

MINNESOTA

WYOMING

SOUTH DAKOTA

IOWA

SOUTH PASS

NORTH PLATTE R.

Fort Laramie

NEBRASKA

Bellevue

NORTH PARK

St. Vrain's Fort

SOUTH PLATTE R.

PLATTE R.

MIDDLE PARK

REPUBLICAN R.

MO.

MISSOURI R.

SOUTH PARK

KANSAS R.

Kansas City (Westport)

Pueblo

SMOKY HILL R.

Bent's Fort

COLORADO

KANSAS

Taos

ARKANSAS R.

Santa Fe

CANADIAN R.

OKLAHOMA

RIO GRANDE

NEW MEXICO

RED R.

PECOS R.

Socorro

TEXAS

D1225185

Frémont's
Frémont's
Frémont's
Frémont's Fourth Expedition, 1848 – 49
Frémont's Fifth Expedition, 1853-54

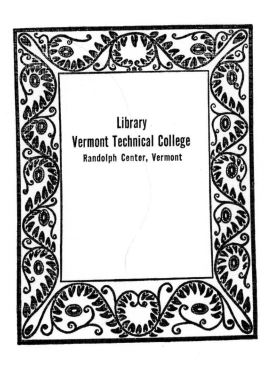

Backward amid the twilight glow
Some lingering spots yet brightly show
    On hard roads won;
Where still some grand peaks mark the way
Touched by the light of parting day
    And memory's sun.

From "Recrossing the Rocky Mountains, After Many Years"
by JOHN C. FRÉMONT

BOOKS BY FEROL EGAN

*Nonfiction*

The El Dorado Trail: The Story of the Gold Rush Routes
Across Mexico
Sand in a Whirlwind: The Paiute Indian War of 1860
Frémont: Explorer for a Restless Nation

*Edited Works*

GEORGE D. BREWERTON: Incidents of Travel in New Mexico
JOHN YATES: A Sailor's Sketch of the Sacramento Valley in 1842
J. MÜLLER: California, Land of Gold or Stay at Home and Work Hard
J. ROSS BROWNE: A Dangerous Journey
HOZIAL H. BAKER: Overland Journey to Carson Valley and California
THOMAS SALATHIEL MARTIN: With Frémont to California
and the Southwest 1845–1849

# ❧ Frémont ❧

## Explorer for a Restless Nation

FEROL EGAN

Doubleday & Company, Inc.
Garden City, New York
1977

Library of Congress Cataloging in Publication Data

Egan, Ferol.
  Frémont, explorer for a restless nation.

  Bibliography: p. 559.
  Includes index.
  1. Frémont, John Charles, 1813–1890.   I. Title
E415.9.F8E33    979'.02'0924 [B]
ISBN 0-385-01775-8
Library of Congress Catalog Card Number 76–2770

For A. B. Guthrie, Jr., Richard Dillon,
and James Schevill—good friends in a lonely craft

# Acknowledgments

MOST OF THE SOURCES for this book are indicated in the Notes. A few other key items are listed in the Bibliographic Essay, and I have used all the primary sources available. John Charles Frémont's published government reports and his *Memoirs* have been very helpful in tracing the path of his life. Also, I have had access to the extensive collection of unpublished letters, business papers, and manuscripts that make up the *Frémont Papers* in The Bancroft Library, University of California, Berkeley.

Another major ingredient that forms the fabric of this biography is the land itself. Wherever possible, I have tried to trace the various routes that Frémont and his men followed, tried to see these places in the different seasons of the year, and tried to capture something of the flavor of the landscape as he knew it.

The major portion of my research was done in The Bancroft Library, University of California, Berkeley. For all the help that this great institution gave me, I wish to thank Dr. James D. Hart, Director of The Bancroft Library; and I especially wish to thank Ms. Irene Moran, Head of Public Services, for her thoughtfulness and valuable aid. Other staff members who were helpful as I tracked various leads were Mr. Robert Becker, Mrs. Susan H. Gallup, Mr. Peter E. Hanft, and Mr. William M. Roberts. A particular debt is owed to Mrs. Alma Compton, who cheerfully and carefully placed my many orders for illustrations. Finally, I owe a lasting debt of thanks to Dr. George P. Hammond, Director Emeritus. Whenever I was in need of a guide to point me in the right direction, he was willing to take time away from his own work and give me the benefit of his wide knowledge of the history of the American West.

Other institutions which helped me in this project were the California State Library, Sacramento; the Sutro Library, San Francisco; the California Historical Society, San Francisco; the Society of California Pioneers, San Francisco; and the Southwest Museum, Los Angeles.

Among friends and fellow authors, the following persons deserve special thanks: Mr. Richard Dillon, Head of Sutro Library, not only for helping me secure hard-to-find books but also for taking on the task of reading my manuscript for errors—a task that only a true friend would accept; the late Dr. Charles L. Camp, who carried a vast knowledge of the American West with grace and wit, and whose warm and friendly presence I shall always miss; Dr. George R. Stewart, who asked the right questions at the right moments; Mr. Warren Howell, of John Howell—Books, who gave me permission to use a rare painting by Lieutenant James W. Abert; Dr. Carl Schaefer Dentzel, Director of the Southwest Museum, who gave me permission to reproduce the T. Buchanan Read portrait of Jessie Benton Frémont; Mr. Lawton Kennedy, who gave freely of his time as I plied him with questions about various illustrations; Mr. Luther Nichols, of Doubleday & Company, for his understanding in his role as editor, and Mr. James E. Ricketson for his excellent copy editing and penetrating questions; and Mr. T. H. Watkins, who shared his research on early Washington, D.C., with me.

The illustrations for the book are used through the courtesy of the following: The Bancroft Library, University of California, Berkeley; Chicago Historical Society; Denver Public Library; The Detroit Institute of Arts; John Howell—Books; Library of Congress; and the Southwest Museum.

As in all my books, the work has been made lighter by my wife, Marty. She encouraged me at the low moments; made the field trips with me; listened to the progress of the book and made excellent editorial comments; copy edited, typed the final manuscript, and went through the whole production of the book with me; and backed me above and beyond the call of love.

FEROL EGAN

Berkeley, California
September 1975

# Contents

# Introduction

THE ULTIMATE CURSE of being a national hero is that once the fires of acclaim go out, only the ashes of criticism remain. This was the fate of John Charles Frémont, for he climbed the peaks of glory only to endure the deserts of despair.

Few men in the period of Manifest Destiny—that time when the nation began to flex its muscles, stretch its limbs, and take the giant strides that would shape the essential boundaries of the land—ever approached Frémont's heroic role as a spearhead of the way West. In his five expeditions between the years 1842 and 1853, Frémont mapped and described much more of the American West than the famous expedition headed by Meriwether Lewis and William Clark in their grand reconnaissance of what President Thomas Jefferson had acquired through the Louisiana Purchase.

John Charles Frémont and his men crossed and recrossed great areas of the trans-Mississippi West. They followed the early scratchings of trails to Oregon and California when this vast land was known only to Indians, mountain men, and the few parties of hardy emigrants who had heard tales of Mexican California and British Oregon from returning sailors and mountain men. Yet Frémont and his men made their way beyond South Pass to cross the Rocky Mountains, worked their way over the lava-covered Snake River Plain, followed the Columbia River to the Hudson's Bay Company's Fort Vancouver, doubled back into the void of the Great Basin, crossed the Sierra Nevada in the middle of winter, stopped at Sutter's Fort, and then traveled the length of California's Sacramento and San Joaquin valleys before they headed back into the Great Basin again by way of the Mojave Desert to work their way to the Rockies and Bent's Fort to hit the Santa Fé Trail and strike out for St. Louis.

High adventure with all the qualities of an epic odyssey is one way of putting it. And to add to what he had accomplished, Frémont shared his knowledge with the nation and most of the countries of Europe through his magnificent government reports. The flora, fauna, and geology were carefully described. Not only were routes for would-be emigrants mapped, but also instructions were included for the proper season of travel, the supplies and equipment to take, and the location of waterholes and grass for livestock. He described the various Indian tribes and their cultures, and gave advice on how to treat them according to their mores. In general, his view of the Indians was one of compassion and understanding. His reports served as a survey of the economic potentiality of the West. But it was his writing style which appealed to the reading public; and with the resolute aid of his father-in-law, the powerful Senator Thomas Hart Benton of Missouri, the publication and dissemination of these reports served as publicity for the making of a Two Ocean Nation.

Frémont's overall contribution to an expanding nation, to a people reaching out for control of the Pacific shoreline, was a dream put into words —a dream that made the course of empire seem to be within easy grasp for anyone willing to pull up roots and transplant them in the rich soil of the West. Because of his reports and maps, the boundaries of the United States took on a new meaning to empire builders and common men in search of a share of the bountiful wealth of a new land, a land ready and open for a people on the move. To such people, John Charles Frémont stood out as a man who combined all the best traits of the Founding Fathers.

As a romantic hero, Frémont was outstanding. Here was a man who had explored a country as strange as some undiscovered continent. Here was a man whose close companions on the trail had been such fabled mountain men as Kit Carson, Broken Hand Fitzpatrick, Joseph Walker, and Alexis Godey. Added to this group of guides were such artists and cartographers as Charles Preuss and Edward Kern. Making up the rest of these parties were Frémont's faithful French-Canadians and the ever-loyal Delaware Indians. For the men who traveled with Frémont were a mixture of the American frontier—a breed well trained in the art of survival in the wild country across the wide Missouri.

To add even more to Frémont's place as an epic figure, there was the knowledge that he was supported in whatever he did by his beautiful and talented wife, Jessie Benton Frémont. Without doubt, the only other couple in this period of America's history who even approached their popularity in the public's imagination were George Armstrong Custer and his wife, Elizabeth. And there is much to be said about the resemblance of the two couples in the loyalty and love shown between husband and wife in each case.

Handsome as Lord Byron, mysterious as Sir Richard Burton, a figure of dash and romance—all these images apply to John Charles Frémont. He was a man of courage and conviction, and he went against the establishment of his time. Lacking a degree from West Point, he became the outstanding officer in the Army Topographical Corps. Yet he was in constant difficulty because of his inability to go along with the red tape of regulations. Time and again he ignored orders that he considered to be wrong or a waste of his time. Eventually the regular military managed to catch him out of line during the Mexican War in California. When they did, they decided to make an example of him.

The court-martial of Frémont only proved the pettiness of other officers and added to his fame in the eyes of the public. He had been caught in a power struggle between Commodore Robert Stockton of the U. S. Navy and General Stephen W. Kearny of the U. S. Army. Part of the blame can be placed upon Frémont for his refusal to obey General Kearny and give up his position as U.S. military governor of California. But the orders handed down by both Kearny and Stockton were confusing at best, and without logic at worst.

Serving as his own defense with the counsel of Senator Benton and William Cary Jones, Frémont proved a worthy foe in the dimly lighted Washington Arsenal. But he was found guilty by the court on three counts of mutiny. Then the court admitted that the older officers had been at fault, and requested that President James Knox Polk set aside the punishment. Yet when this was done, when Frémont was told to report back to duty, he refused. He was not guilty, and he was not going to give the impression that he had been wrong. With his pride intact, he resigned his commission.

Determined to prove his worth and to show up the blindness of the government, Frémont made his ill-fated fourth expedition, in search of an all-year railroad route across the San Juan Mountains in the southern Rockies. But this privately sponsored expedition came to a tragic end in one of the worst winters in the Rockies. Before the survivors stumbled into Taos, ten men had died. There was talk of cannibalism, and criticism of Frémont for having failed to heed the warning of mountain men. Still, he had two of the greatest mountain men as guides in Old Bill Williams and Alexis Godey.

Never a man to quit, as many of his enemies hoped he would, Frémont remained in Taos just long enough to regain his strength to move on to California, where he struck it rich in gold mines on his Las Mariposas property near Yosemite Valley. Overnight he rose from poverty and despair to riches and glory. He entered the first political race for the United States Senate from the new state of California. When he returned to Washington, beautiful Jessie had the joy of watching Senator Frémont take his oath of office.

Though he was only a short-term senator for one session of Congress, his political career was not over. For after he had successfully crossed the San Juan Mountains in the winter of 1853–1854 on his fifth expedition, he was once again the figure of adventure and the symbol of freedom. A man ahead of his time, Frémont forcefully demonstrated his opposition to slavery by taking free blacks with him on his expeditions and by speaking out against the dreadful institution. To the founders of the liberal Republican Party, John Charles Frémont was the natural candidate for President of the United States in their first campaign of 1856.

"Free Speech, Free Press, Free Soil, Free Men, Frémont and Victory" was one of the slogans of the Republican Party. Poet John Greenleaf Whittier; newspaperman Horace Greeley; and a host of antislavery Northerners backed him in his bid for the highest office in the land. But Frémont became the victim of one of the dirtiest smear campaigns in the history of American politics.

His illegitimate birth became part of the daily news. He was accused of being a Catholic, even though he was an Episcopalian. His court-martial and the tragedy of the fourth expedition were used against him. Yet, the major factor that caused his defeat by the Democratic candidate, James Buchanan, was his antislavery stance. Even so, the contest was close. Frémont lost by only sixty electoral votes in a three-party contest. Still, he had accomplished one major thing by running for office. He had set the stage for the victory of Abraham Lincoln in the election of 1860.

The irony of the latter event came about at the beginning of the Civil War. In his position as General of the West, headquartered in St. Louis, Frémont issued the first emancipation proclamation. This upset President Lincoln so much that he sent written instructions to General Frémont in which he ordered him to retract his proclamation in the interest of keeping the Border States within the Union. In the long run, Lincoln's reasoning proved itself. Yet there is the nagging question as to how much sooner the Civil War might have ended if Frémont's move had been allowed to stand.

His attempt to free the slaves was not the only failure he endured as a Union general. Though he was a splendid leader of men in his exploration of the West, he did not succeed as a military man. In part, his failure can be attributed to a lack of supplies and a shortage of troops. But it is doubtful that he would have had much success even if his command had been adequate and properly supplied. He was no military match for the likes of Stonewall Jackson and other Southern military men. He had not had their training, nor did he possess their natural talent as tacticians on the field of battle.

Caught up in a quarrel with President Lincoln and the politically powerful Blair family of St. Louis, Frémont resigned his commission before the war ended. Though he was asked to run against Lincoln in the election of 1864, he turned the offer down when he realized that he would not receive enough support to make his candidacy practical.

Once again, Frémont turned to the West for his future. Unfortunately, his California property had been entrusted to the care of shady speculators who who ran up such great debts in his name that he was almost stripped of his great fortune. To add the final blow to his financial woes, he invested in unsuccessful railroad schemes. By the 1870s, Frémont had come full circle from poverty to riches to poverty.

In the remaining years of his life, the great explorer of the American West lived, for the most part, off the writings of his wife, Jessie. He was territorial governor of Arizona for the period from June 8, 1878, to October 11, 1881. Then by 1890 he managed to get Congress to grant him a pension at his highest military rank. But only shortly after he received his pension, Frémont died of peritonitis in a New York hotel room, with only his son John C. Frémont, Jr., and his physician and friend, Dr. William J. Morton, standing by his bedside.

After Frémont's death, two aspects of his life were stressed in articles and biographies. His detractors refused to credit him with anything, and they constructed an elaborate picture of a self-seeking egotist whose claim to fame rested upon the works of others. At the opposite pole, his defenders made him into a romantic legend, an epic hero whose every deed was surrounded with glory.

In between these value judgments is the real John Charles Frémont. Like any other leader, he was not without flaws. But overall, his place in our history is secure because of his great success in making the American West known to the world. His scientific approach to exploration, his mapping of poorly defined trails and of uncharted wilderness, and his ability to make his government reports as readable as adventure novels served as the come-on for a restless nation looking for growing space.

Today, as the exploration of the moon proved to all of us, the explorer-hero with an antiestablishment attitude and a gift for describing that which others have not seen has been replaced with a new breed. Instead of men like Frémont, we see a bureaucracy of civil servants, technicians, computerized and controlled astronauts, and public relations officers holding forth with diagrams and a jargon of terms created out of compounded first letters.

Now, more than at any other time, we need to be able to look back at the full-of-life men who made this country. Better to endure human flaws than a faulty transistorized panel in the control system. Better to know what one man felt as he explored part of the Great Salt Lake, or as he struck out across the Great Basin in search of a mythical river. For these reasons, it is time to see a man like Frémont once again before we forget our national roots and give in to a millennium of machine-controlled mediocrity.

Part of the story of this quiet, introverted intellectual has been told before, but previous biographers have not had full access to all the journals and letters of men who traveled through the wilderness with Frémont; nor have they had access to all the other papers and government documents that round out the full picture of this man who gave so much to his country and received so little in return.

John Charles Frémont and his striking wife, Jessie Benton Frémont, were something new for this nation. They were symbols of a national identity that no longer had to look back toward Europe for its cultural heroes. In Frémont, a restless nation on the move had its epic figure astride the wild horse of the plains. His name was associated with freedom and open land, and his deeds as an explorer of the American West gave him a lasting place in our history. As Jessie put it, "From the ashes of his campfires have sprung cities."

# The Nomad Strain

MOVING SLOWLY, a steady column of black smoke curling from its stack and rising upward to drift with the wind, the train looked like some extinct and unclassified animal as it climbed the grade toward South Pass and the Continental Divide. Inside one of the sooty parlor cars, a handsome and distinguished looking white-haired man peered out the window at the passing landscape. The light covering of wind-blown snow made the sagebrush into frosted, miniature trees in a country dominated by broken ground and low hills that gave no indication the pass was over seven thousand feet. Years before, on his first expedition into the West, he had noted that South Pass did not give the feeling of crossing from the Atlantic to the Pacific watershed, nor did it give any more sense of height than the climb up Washington's Capitol Hill.

Even with the steady chugging of the locomotive, the memory of that first summer in the West stirred in his mind. He got out his writing pad and let his thoughts drift back to that earlier time. Then there had been no train tracks, no streamer of black smoke drifting with the wind. There had been the steady beat of hooves on the hard earth, the constant wind, and the glare of an endless sky. Now, only the land and sky remained the same. Slowly, he began to write a poem of what was etched in his memory of that first expedition and all the other adventures that were the final tally of his years of exploration. When he finished the poem and jotted down its title, he put it away. It was a recounting of that special knowledge that only a man who has known the thrill of an untouched wilderness carries with him, and he carries it with him for the rest of his life.

Yet the memories of hard roads won, of men who had traveled with him and shared the daily measures of excitement and hardship, must have been very near the surface of his inner thoughts. For the vision of a well-mapped trail, a cleared wagon road, and then a railroad to the West had been driving forces that had sent him forth to the wilderness. All those lonely days and nights, those moments of near death, those terrible times of disaster had been endured for the very thing he was now doing—riding westward in the comfort of a railroad car. This was Senator Thomas Hart Benton's "road to India."[1] But Senator Benton was gone. And John Charles Frémont must have wondered what the great champion of Manifest Destiny would have thought of this westbound train. For that matter, what would all the other ghosts of the past have thought of this wagon train riding the ruts of steel rails? All this, and more, must have been in his mind as he wrote of hard traveling in hard places. And in back of it all, there was the memory of his initial taste of adventure in the first five years of his life as his father and mother moved by wagon from one southern town to another in search of a livelihood. On such trips, he may have heard his father speak of earlier travels among the Indian tribes of the South—the tales of an amateur anthropologist, tales to stir the boy's imagination. Ghosts of his own past, ghosts of the American wilderness dream were all part of those first years for young Frémont—years of training, years of developing a feeling for the land, and years that kindled the lasting fires of curiosity and wonder.

2

A CHILD OF LOVE, a child who knew the meaning of discrimination before he knew the word, Frémont came from a background with all the trappings of a Charles Dickens novel. The boy entered the world without benefit of wedlock. This birthright gave him a choice of two roads to follow: accept the scorn and defeat accorded a child of illegal love and live a life of obscure failure; or accept the challenge of his inheritance, endure, and become a magnificent survivor. Thanks to the courage and love of his parents, Frémont chose the role of proving that the fixed ideas of a closed culture were open to question and change.

None of the beginning was easy for the boy as he carried the dual heritage of scandal and the blunt label of bastard. Family background, no matter how proper, made no difference. Even though one of his later biographers, John Bigelow, tried to present a background of legitimate parentage, the facts surrounding the boy's birth point in only one direction.

Though Frémont's mother, Anne Beverley Whiting, came from a family which proudly traced its roots to the Founding Fathers, this made no difference to Tidewater Virginians, who were properly shocked when she deserted her elderly, gouty husband and ran off with a mere teacher of French. No one bothered to consider why she had decided to go against the mores of her community. Yet there were reasons of terrible unhappiness—as well as her love for a younger man—that resulted in her decision to make such a move.

She was the youngest daughter of a family that had known much better days. But her father, Colonel Thomas Whiting, was dead and buried; and she had been forced into a marriage with a man old enough to be her grandfather. She was simply a financial burden to the rest of her family. Worst of all, Major John Pryor was well past the point of being able to carry out the role of husband for such a young bride. All these emotional factors were overlooked by local rumor mongers. None of them bothered to mention that even Anne's husband had recognized the failure of their marriage and had unsuccessfully appealed to the Virginia legislature for a divorce.

All that mattered was local pride. After all, Major Pryor had fought under the command of George Washington, had acquired a respectable amount of money, slaves, and land, had become a fixture among the landed gentry of horse breeders and horse racers, had become well known for his wit, and had occupied a prominent position in Richmond society for many years. In short, young Anne was fortunate to be married to such a man. For even though Major Pryor was much too old to fulfill his role as husband, he was not some French dandy who had drifted in from God-knows-where with an empty purse and a roving eye for another man's wife.

But there was much more to Frémont's father-to-be than gossip indicated. A native of a small French village near Lyons, Jean Charles Frémon had the misfortune of being on the losing side during the French Revolution. To save his life, he fled his native land and took passage on a ship bound for Santo Domingo. Here, he knew he would have safe refuge with an aunt. But the ship carrying him to safety was stopped at sea by an English man-of-war, and all the French citizens aboard were taken as captives to the British West Indies.

Here Charles Frémon remained a prisoner for some time. During his internment, he was given the opportunity to add to the small allowance given prisoners by making use of his talents as a fresco painter, cabinetmaker, and basket weaver. But the days ran into weeks and months before a change in British policy played a key role in his future. Called before the officers in charge, Frémon was given the choice of remaining in captivity or sailing to the United States as an immigrant. Seeing this as a potential way of returning to France once the political climate had changed, he accepted the offer. Not long after, he arrived free but without means at Norfolk, Virginia.

A man of charm, the fine-featured, dark-haired Frémon obtained a position as a teacher of French at William and Mary College. After teaching there for a time, he left in the spring of 1808 for a better offer from Louis Girardin's outstanding private school in Richmond. Girardin was a brilliant man and a close friend of Thomas Jefferson, and he headed the academy that he owned in partnership with David Doyle. And it was while Frémon taught at this academy that he began his association with Anne Pryor.

At first, Girardin and Doyle heard only the rumor that Frémon was seeing some woman. This was easy to dismiss as the sort of gossip one was apt to hear about a young, single instructor who was both charming and handsome. Then word came to the owners of the academy that their new teacher not only was seeing some woman but was living with her, or at the very least having some affair. By itself, this was reason enough to dismiss him. The academy could not afford this sort of scandal.

Public talk about the love affair became much more dramatic as the details began to surface. Friends of Anne Pryor—including her niece, Kitty Cowne—became more and more open. They were much too obvious in their dislike of Major Pryor, the rather vulgar horse breeder, and they became careless with regard to their approval of what was taking place between Anne and Charles.

The inevitable day of reckoning occurred at Major Pryor's home during the first part of July 1811. In front of Kitty Cowne, the angry and hurt husband allowed all his suspicions, all his knowledge of town talk to come to a head. He lost his composure and openly accused the lovers of taking advantage of his trust, of carrying on behind his back, and of making him into an object for gossip and whispered conversations. Then, as his temper exploded from the many months of not knowing whether or not his wife was being unfaithful, the old man threatened to kill her for having dishonored his name and home.

This was the breaking point. In no uncertain terms, Anne made clear to the major that she would not allow Frémon to become involved in any violent action against him. Then she served Major Pryor the final blow. There was to be no reconciliation, and no begging for forgiveness. To the contrary, Anne told him she fully intended to elope with her lover the very next morning.

With everything out in the open, it was impossible for Anne and Charles to continue living in Richmond. Local society would not tolerate this open insult to traditional behavior. Knowing this, and knowing they were outcasts, the lovers departed from Richmond on a stage bound for Williamsburg. Anne took her personal belongings and two slaves, and Charles his limited amount of money and personal effects. But though they were free of Richmond and the censure of Major Pryor and his friends, they were not out of Virginia. They knew that the news of their deed would travel as fast as the horses that pulled their stagecoach.

The couple passed through Williamsburg and Norfolk, where they made brief stops to gather other property that belonged to Anne. Then they headed southward on what was to be a combination honeymoon and tour of the Indian tribes. Frémon was interested in studying and observing the cultures of these people. The small amount of money which Anne had inherited from her father's estate gave them the means to indulge in this romantic interlude before the money ran short and Charles had to seek employment again.

The few months of summer passed very quickly, and as the frosty mornings of October arrived, Anne and Charles had already become residents of Savannah, Georgia. They lived in a house back of the mansion belonging to Charles Howard, a prominent man of Savannah. Money was running short.

To add to their dwindling resources, Anne advertised for boarders, and Frémon took a position as a teacher and dancing master in the J. B. LeRoy academy. During the next two years, the couple made their home in Savannah, but moved from the Howard residence to a red brick, two-story house in the Yamacraw section. This home belonged to the Gibbons family and was located on a land grant from George II in 1760. It was in this setting that John Charles was born on January 21, 1813. From his first cries of life, the baby boy was the product of the Old and New worlds.

## 3

THE BOY was only a few months old when his parents left Savannah to seek better opportunities. At the City Hotel of Nashville, Tennessee, a moment of violence crossed his path with that of a man who would one day play a key role in his life.

Thomas Hart Benton had not yet moved to Missouri, where he was to begin his own career as a famous U.S. senator. At this time, he was a young frontier lawyer and legislator in Tennessee. A striking figure of a man, he was noted for his loyalty to friends, and for a disposition that allowed no room for any improper conduct by persons he considered to be dependable and trustworthy. But he was forced to face the apparent lack of these qualities in a man who had been his patron when he had been admitted to the bar, and who had been his commanding officer when he had served as a colonel in the early campaigns of the War of 1812. This was none other than General Andrew Jackson, who had just won a battle in his campaign against the Creeks and was reported to be marching from Natchez to Nashville in this first week of September 1813.

The difficulty between Thomas Hart Benton and "Old Hickory" was over a duel which had taken place between his younger brother Jesse Benton and William Carroll. Thomas had not been present at this affair of honor, but he knew two things about it: Jesse had received a slight flesh wound, and Jackson had acted as second for Carroll. To Thomas this was a betrayal of friendship. To compound the makings of a feud, Benton even went so far as to accuse Jackson of behaving in a savage, uncivilized manner. This remark was reported to Jackson, who took offense and said that the next time he caught sight of Benton he would horsewhip him.

News of the break in friendship between the Bentons and Jackson was among the key topics of daily conversation in Nashville, for the anticipation of violence at the next meeting of these men provided a vicarious excitement that broke the normal flow of day-to-day activities. There was no doubt in the mind of anyone who knew about the Bentons and Jackson that when they ran into each other there was bound to be a showdown.

Soon after the Bentons had stopped at the City Hotel, Jackson and his party arrived and took rooms at the Nashville Inn. Word of this spread quickly among the townsfolk, as Jackson was located within easy strolling distance from the man he had sworn to horsewhip. All that separated the former friends was the public square.

There are many variations in the accounts of how Jackson and the Benton brothers ran into each other. One story has Jackson and Thomas Benton meeting each other outside the post office. Another tale pictures Jackson striding over to the City Hotel with his pistol and horsewhip in hand. Rumors, fiction, and the passing of time make it impossible to know exactly how the men became involved in a common brawl. Jackson and a few of his companions did encounter the Bentons in the lobby of the City Hotel.

Words were exchanged. Tempers flared, and the fight began. Jackson and Jesse Benton drew their pistols, aimed, and fired. Jackson stumbled backward from the impact of a pistol ball and fell to the floor. His left shoulder was shattered, and he was losing a lot of blood. Seeing their leader sprawled out like a broken doll, Jackson's supporters joined in the fray. As they did, Thomas began to move into a position to aid his brother, stepped backward, and tumbled headlong down a full flight of stairs into the hotel basement. While he was picking himself up, the shooting continued in the lobby. The excited men were wild in their aim, and none of the shots hit any of the other combatants. Then, as Jackson's men realized the seriousness of his wound, the shouting and gunplay ceased. The fallen warrior was carried to a room and placed on a bed. For a time Jackson was close to death. His steady bleeding soaked two mattresses, but Old Hickory was too tough to kill.

Once the excitement ended, the participants and curious spectators discovered that stray shots had very nearly caused another casualty. To the horror of the men involved, wild shots had penetrated the thin walls of the room in which the Frémons were staying, shots which narrowly missed the sleeping baby, John Charles. Anne was so upset she fainted. When the father returned to the hotel and learned what had happened, he confronted the responsible men. Without tempering his language, he let them know that he considered the pursuit of a personal feud in a public place a mark of barbarism. Still shocked by what might have happened, the men took Frémon's criticism as something they deserved and offered their apologies. Yet apologies did not remove the fact that a frontier quarrel had almost killed the infant who was to become a key figure in Thomas Hart Benton's concept of America's destiny.

4

AFTER THE EPISODE OF VIOLENCE at the City Hotel, the Frémons remained in Nashville long enough for Anne to give birth to a daughter. When she was able to travel, the family moved back to Norfolk, Virginia. Sometime during this period of their lives, Major Pryor died, and his death made it possible for the lovers to be legally married.

The next few years of the family's life remain rather vague. It is known that another son was born, that they continued to move from one community to another, and that Charles Frémon's brother—Francis—appeared on the scene with his wife and children. About this time, the Frémon brothers decided it was safe to return to France. As they talked about this and made plans to end their exile, Charles became ill and within a short time died. Only seven years had passed since Anne and Charles had made the hard decision to go against the grain of Southern society. Now, in 1818, she was left without husband, without sufficient means, and with three children to support. While she could have gone to France with her brother-in-law, she could not imagine herself living anywhere but in the United States. She loved her native land and always would.

Grief-stricken and lonely, Anne decided that she and the children would remain in Norfolk. She felt comfortable in this city where she had so many friends. But after a short time, this feeling of comfort gave way to despair. There was no escaping her situation. She was a widow who was somewhat beyond the desirable age for marriage. She had no fortune to insulate her against the tightness of her budget. She was not in a financial position to return the hospitality she had received from others, and she must have known that behind her back there were always the whispered memories of the scandal that her love for Charles Frémon had caused. Caught in this web, Anne decided to move to Charleston. There, at least, she would not be reminded of her lot in life, nor would she have the feeling that she was a part of the past the community would rather forget.

The move to Charleston was a major turning point for the eldest of Anne's three children. Here John Charles came to know something of stability. Called Charley by friends and adults, the boy at last knew the feeling of belonging. True enough, his mother had to take in boarders in order to support the family, and she was a poor widow in an affluent community whose cultural and social life was for the wealthy. Yet, being without money or any real status did not bother Charley. He moved with equal grace among all classes of people—ranging from rich families to French Huguenots to slave families. Along with his mobility among the various classes, the boy also had a chance for an education and the training of his brilliant mind. Young John Charles was in the right place at the right time; and he learned the feeling of planting roots, of not moving from place to place, and of identifying with a single community and its people.

Handsome Charley made friends easily. He was a favorite among the young girls, and it was no wonder. He was a boy of fine features topped by a beautiful mass of curly, dark hair; and his light blue eyes and olive-colored skin made him stand out in any group of young people. His imagination, wit, and friendly nature made him popular among all his peers. But these days of youth were all too short. To a much older Frémont writing his *Memoirs*, these were days that "went by on wings."[2]

At fourteen, young Frémont (the *t* was added about eleven years later) had to contribute to the family's limited income. To accomplish this and to continue his education seemed impossible. Yet, the door of hope opened when his mother accepted the offer of a clerkship for him in the law office of John W. Mitchell. This was another turning point in Frémont's life, a fork in the trail where he was guided in the right direction. For Mitchell recognized the young man's native ability to grasp difficult concepts, to reach out for knowledge, and to approach other people with a refinement and courtesy that was most unusual for his age. Though Mitchell knew Frémont was well suited for a career in law, he also realized that the young man's desire to train for the pulpit in the Episcopal faith was confirmed by his obvious love of logic, philosophy and classical literature. Here was a future leader of the community, and Mitchell was willing to foot the cost of sending John Charles to a first-rate preparatory school run by Dr. Charles Robertson, a scholar from the University of Edinburgh and a teacher noted for preparing boys for Charleston College.

The association with Professor Robertson was a major influence on Frémont's life. From this classical scholar he received his introduction to Greek and Latin, to the works of such men as Homer and Virgil, and to the power of the written word. As the young student wrote his essays, Professor Robertson saw that he had a way with words, a talent for imagery and expression that was very rare. It was this talent that was to be brought into full use in Frémont's future writing of reports about his explorations—reports that were to serve as models for other government explorers and surveyors of the American West.

After two years of studying under the guidance of Professor Robertson, John Charles was ready to enter Charleston College as a junior. Though he was behind his classmates in some disciplines, he overcame this because of his intellectual curiosity and his fondness for study. But he was still young and restless, and he lacked the ability to settle down to the routine and requirements of the college. Part of his mind was on his work, but another part of it was committed to a deep affection he felt for a beautiful Creole girl whose family had escaped from Santo Domingo during the violent revolt of Toussaint L'Ouverture and Dessalines.

Cecilia's dark eyes and blue-black hair were an intrusion in the thoughts of John Charles. For days at a time he was absent from the college. In his passionate state of mind, he paid no heed to warnings about expulsion. Even when the warnings became a fact, he gave no thought to the possibility that he was throwing aside his chances for a career.

Drawn toward Cecilia of the dark hair, Cecilia of the clear complexion, he enjoyed an interlude of love and friendship that only youth can know. Along with the companionship of the fair Cecilia, John Charles also enjoyed his days with the other young people of the family.

> In the summer, [he wrote] we ranged about in the woods, or on the now historic islands, gunning or picnicking, the girls sometimes with us; sometimes in a sailboat on the bay, oftener going over the bar to seaward and not infrequently when the breeze failed us getting dangerously near the breakers on the bar. I remember as in a picture, seeing the beads of perspiration on the forehead of my friend Henry as he tugged frantically at his oar when we had found ourselves one day in the suck of Drunken Dick, a huge breaker that to our eyes appeared monstrous as he threw his spray close to the boat. For us it really was pull Dick pull Devil.[3]

Yet even these days of love and youthful freedom were not enjoyed without a feeling of guilt. In moments of remorse, in those times when Cecilia's grandmother scolded her grandchildren and John Charles with an outburst of French, he tired of his relationship with Cecilia and felt guilty about having been expelled from college and not pursuing his own career. For he was well aware of his mother's need for his help.

Having already done a short stint as a country teacher, he decided to abandon his days of love and self-indulgence to accept another teaching position in John A. Wooten's private school. While carrying out his duties as a teacher, John Charles turned back to quiet moments with books he found in the library. He was fascinated with a chronicle about the lives of famous and infamous men. But the book which challenged his imagination most of all was a Dutch publication on practical astronomy. Though he couldn't read the language, he was intrigued by the maps of the constellations and the examples of astronomical calculations. Through this volume he came to know the sky of night and learned the fundamentals for the calculation of latitude and longitude.

The years of Frémont's youth were drawing to a close. While he worked as a teacher, his sister died, and his young brother left home to pursue a career on the stage. Now, at seventeen, John Charles had crossed the invisible line that separates the boy and the man.

## 5

WHEN FORTY-NINE-YEAR-OLD JOEL ROBERTS POINSETT returned to Charleston after four and a half years as the first United States minister to Mexico, it was Frémont's good fortune to meet and come under the guidance of this man of great gentleness and cultured refinement.

John Charles was invited to attend the weekly breakfasts which Poinsett gave at his home. Here, during three formative years, young Frémont met other bright young people as well as men of learning and stature. He heard the give and take of intellectuals and the wide range of fascinating stories which Poinsett told. Through these tales of travel, of the world ready to be explored by men with curiosity, the skills of observation and the disciplines of learning, Frémont was smitten with the urge to escape the narrow confines of Charleston. He was anxious to move outward and begin his own travels in distant places and to add to his limited store of knowledge.

Poinsett helped John Charles secure an appointment as a teacher of mathematics aboard the sloop of war *Natchez*, which was ready to sail on a cruise down the coast of South America. But though he helped him, Poinsett didn't think that a potential naval career was shooting for the stars and believed that Frémont should not take a position which offered so little future. Yet, at the same time, he realized it was vital for the young man to enlarge his sphere of experience. At the very least, this voyage would accomplish that much.

For the next two years, Frémont was under the command of Captain John P. Zantzinger as the *Natchez* sailed the coast of South America. During this period John Charles met young officers such as Lieutenant David Farragut, and Midshipmen Lovell of South Carolina and Parrot of Massachusetts. And it was Frémont and another young officer, Decatur Hurst, who were responsible for preventing a possible tragedy when Lovell and Parrot got into a quarrel while their ship lay at anchor in the harbor at Rio de Janeiro. Hotheaded, prideful, and afraid to lose face—even though their disagreement was not that important—the two midshipmen challenged each other to a duel. Hurst and Frémont agreed to be their seconds in this affair of honor. Unknown to either duelist, the seconds had also agreed to fill the weapons with powder only. But if the two men insisted on another shot after the first round, the seconds knew they would then have to put lead in the pistols, as each man would be watching.

> Leaving the boat, we found a narrow strip of sandy beach about forty yards long between the water and the mountain. In such a place men could hardly miss each other. The few preparations made, we placed our men twelve paces apart and gave the word. Both looked sincerely surprised that they remained standing upright as before. Going up each to his man, we declared the affair over; the cause of our quarrel in our opinion not justifying a second shot. There was some demur, but we insisting carried our men triumphantly back to the ship, nobody hurt and nobody wiser. Hurst and I greatly enjoyed our little *ruse de guerre*.[4]

This adventure at Rio de Janeiro proved to be one of the most memorable experiences for Frémont during the voyage of the *Natchez*. All the other days flowed into each other in the day-to-day teaching of mathematics, watching the changing colors of the sea from daybreak to nightfall, reading books from the ship's library, and exchanging ideas with the young officers aboard the ship. For John Charles it was a quiet, introspective period—a time to think, a time to dream, a time to consider the years ahead and wonder what to do with his life.

6

WHEN THE TWO-YEAR VOYAGE of the *Natchez* ended at New York on June 13, 1835, twenty-two-year-old Frémont received his discharge from the ship and returned home to Charleston. He visited his mother, talked to old friends, and began to consider a possible naval career. For during his voyage along the coast of South America, Congress had created a number of professorships of mathematics in the navy. These positions paid a beginning salary of $1,200 per year, and examinations for the commissions were to be given at Norfolk, Virginia.

Frémont decided this was an opportunity that he should not overlook. He sent in his application, and by return mail he received instructions to appear before the examining board at Norfolk within a month. To prepare for the examination, he devoted most of his time to study. "All day long," he wrote, "I was at my books, and the earliest dawn found me at an upper window against which stood a tall poplar, where the rustling of the glossy leaves made a soothing accompaniment."[5]

He had no difficulty in passing the examination, and not long after, he was offered an appointment as a professor of mathematics. But the young man turned down what could have become a naval career. Another opportunity had presented itself through the influence of Joel Poinsett. Captain W. G. Williams of the United States Topographical Corps needed another assistant engineer to help in making a survey of a projected railroad route from Charleston to Cincinnati. This appealed much more to John Charles.

Assigned to the detail of men under the command of Lieutenant Richard M. White, a West Point graduate from South Carolina, John Charles found that being in the wilderness and working long hours was more than agreeable. From the beginning of the first light until the sun had set, they tramped through the wild country and ran experimental lines. Then before nightfall they would return to the nearest farmhouse or inn. If their quarters happened to be a farmhouse, and this usually was the case, they were treated to the fare of the farm. There was fresh milk to drink, homemade bread, vegetables and fruit that were in season, chicken or wild game, and whatever else the woman of the house could bring to the table to feed the appetites of men who had been walking through the woods all day. Then when they had finished their hearty supper, the men sometimes worked until midnight by lamplight and candle as they plotted their field notes.

To John Charles it was a great experience and one he never forgot. "The summer weather in the mountains was fine, the cool water abundant, and the streams lined with azaleas. As often is with flowers of that color the white azaleas were fragrant."[6] To a young man who loved nature and whose feeling for plants and animals was always one of curiosity and deep appreciation, the job he had taken for the summer really wasn't work at all. It was a calling. And when the summer came to an end, when the days in the woods were over, when the survey notes were all finished and the last farmhouse meal had been eaten, he was sorry the time had been so short. For the survey "had been a kind of picnic with work enough to give it zest."[7]

Unemployed once again, Frémont received another offer from Captain Williams. This time he was to serve as an assistant to the captain on a government survey of the Cherokee land. Following its policy of moving Indian tribes ever westward to make room for white settlers, the government was getting ready to take over the Cherokee country.

In that autumn of 1836, Frémont traveled with Williams and his men into the area where the boundaries of North Carolina, Tennessee, and Georgia cornered together. Here they were to make a rough survey that was to serve a twofold function: give the military some idea of the region in case it became necessary to use troops against the Cherokees, and give the government some information about this land that would be of use when the time arrived for its division and distribution to white settlers once the Cherokees had been pushed to the west on what was to become the infamous Trail of Tears.

To Frémont this experience in the Cherokee country was the beginning of a path he was destined to walk. And when he looked back on this time in the wilderness, he realized that the scenes of the autumn and winter of 1836–37 were repeated in variation in other places during the many years of his exploration in the American West. As he summed it up: "Here I found the path which I was 'destined to walk.' Through many of the years to come the occupation of my prime life was to be among Indians and in waste places."[8]

Captain Williams divided his party into smaller groups to cover as much of the Cherokee country as possible in the short time allotted for the survey. When they entered the Indian country, Frémont traveled with two other young men, Archie Campbell and Hull Adams. The first Cherokee village they reached was beside the Nantahéylé (now Nantahala) River. Fortunately for the men it was dark when they arrived, for the Cherokees were having a feast and drunken party. Some of the women thought it would not be safe if the men caught sight of the white surveyors, and they hid them in a log corncrib. Here, on a bed of shucked corn, the men rested for the night as best they could, but it was not a night for a quiet sleep. All night long they heard the shouts of the drunken men and were bothered by rats that kept running over them. In the morning they were cold and dirty. But despite the thin coating of ice along the banks of the river, they dove in to clean themselves of the smell of the corncrib and the droppings of rats.

After their experience at the first Cherokee village, Frémont and his fellow members of the survey team moved deeper into the heavily wooded and mountainous country. To these young men, the whole reconnaissance was an outdoor adventure that brought them in contact with the Cherokees and with the thinly settled and unspoiled woods. While the work required good physical condition, a toleration for roughing it, and the ability to learn the art of survival in the wilderness, it also offered a rare frontier experience.

Interested in anything and everything that he saw in the country of the Cherokees, Frémont observed that it was a region of forest land, fine streams, and beautiful valleys of excellent soil for crops. Here, for the first time, he had the services of a guide who knew the country and the Cherokees from having lived in this area for many years.

The man, Laudermilk, and his wife lived in an isolated log cabin in the woods. They grew their crops, knew the Cherokees as their neighbors, and developed a personal relationship with the natural environment that only people who live beyond the boundaries of towns and cities ever know. From this gentle, quiet frontiersman, Frémont learned many of the arts of living in a wild country: the ways of living off the land and making good meals from natural plants and game animals; the proper way to pack a mule to avoid losing the pack or giving the animal a sore back; and the techniques of setting up camp for the night in all kinds of weather—of erecting a half-faced tent and building a fire with wet hickory logs while the first sleet and snow of winter swept across the land in driving wind.

During one of the jobs assigned to him, he made a reconnaissance of the Hiwassee River. This survey required traveling over country where the going was so rough that he had trouble in getting over the trunks of old trees that had fallen because of lightning strikes or heavy rains and severe winds. Yet, even in this isolated region, he came upon a Cherokee farm that greatly impressed him as he and his companions stayed with the family for the night.

It was a handsome specimen of forest architecture; a square-built house standing on a steep bank of the Hiwassee, with glass-paned windows. But the striking feature in such surroundings was that all the logs were evenly hewed so that they laid solidly together and presented a smoothly even surface. Its finish, in its own way, made quite an agreeable impression from its unexpectedness in such a place. Below, the river banks fell away, leaving a little valley, in which he had made his cornfield.[9]

But while he saw many Cherokee farms that were being taken care of in a manner that would do honor to any region of agricultural people, he also saw other Cherokees who were debased by their close proximity to whites who had introduced them to liquor. To Frémont, this negative influence upon some of the Indians was a tragedy. Though these instances were the exception and not the rule, it left a lasting impression on his mind. For he saw the brutal results of such debasement in bloody fights among drunken men.

Still, even though he saw the Cherokees at their best and their worst, he never mentioned that he considered the proposed removal of these people a bad thing. To the contrary, he thought the government policy both wise and humane. A man of his times, Frémont failed to see that the Cherokees were living in peace with their white neighbors and that they were making great efforts to adapt to white civilization.

As the survey and reconnaissance of the Cherokee country came to a close, John Charles returned to Charleston to stay with his mother for a while, to visit old friends, and to give some thought to the direction of his life. Of all the things he had done up to now, he was convinced that his work on the two surveying expeditions had given him the most pleasure and offered the greatest challenge. This was especially true of his last experience in the Cherokee country, where he had traveled into an unmapped wilderness and had seen a land that still remained very close to its natural state. And in his thoughts of this reconnaissance, he became fully aware of how much he had enjoyed this work.

During his absence his friend and mentor Joel Poinsett had been appointed Secretary of War by President Martin Van Buren. Thinking he might have a chance to continue working for the Topographical Engineers, Frémont applied for a commission; and a letter of recommendation was sent to Washington by Captain Williams in December 1837. As the year ended and January passed into February, Captain Williams received orders to come to Washington and bring Frémont with him. The long road that John Charles was to follow lay just ahead. He bid his mother good-bye and left for Washington; and while he knew he was beginning a career, he could not have known that he was about to begin a life of exploration and adventure, or that by going east he was heading west toward the setting sun.

## ·❧ II ❧·

# An Explorer's Apprenticeship

THE TOUCH OF WINTER remained in the wind when John Charles arrived in Washington. March 1838 was much like the same months for other years in the nation's capital. Trees had the chilled look of snow and ice, and the green of spring awaited the warm rains of April. All this added to his disappointment in Washington. For what he saw was anything but beautiful and exciting. This was a raw, unfinished city which awaited some kind of spring of its own to give it the look of a proper seat of government. The White House and the Capitol seemed to be the only buildings that could be measured by any sense of taste, and the only street that deserved the name was Pennsylvania Avenue. Thanks to the foresight of Thomas Jefferson, this street was lined with rows of Lombardy poplars. All the rest of the town presented a dreary spectacle to young Frémont, and none of it measured up to Charleston.

But he wasn't the only first-time visitor who saw Washington as an uninspired, uncomfortable, and unhealthy seat for the central government of the United States. And it was small wonder that visitors were not impressed. With the exception of the government buildings, structures ran the scale from cheaply constructed buildings to outright shacks. The street lighting, except in the immediate area around the White House and the Capitol, was so bad that travel after nightfall involved the risk of stumbling into a chuckhole, crossing a vacant lot that might be filled with all sorts of refuse, or becoming the victim of a crossman with a pistol or knife in his hand.

Poor housing, bad lighting, and thieves weren't the only drawbacks to Washington. Creeks that flowed into the Potomac River carried raw sewage and gave off a sickening odor from rows of overused privies. These same creeks often became accidental swimming pools for stumbling drunks; and during rainstorms, open sewers would overflow the banks and flood Pennsylvania Avenue. In addition, heavy rains turned the streets into muddy quagmires. When the weather turned warm, the same streets became the breeding ground for dust storms whipped across the city by hot summer winds. As

Charles Dickens remembered it, Washington was no more than a "city of magnificent intentions." But the intentions had never been realized. In their place were a series of misguided plans, accidents of vision, and an obvious display of bad taste carried to its ultimate height in this collection of incomplete villages that ran into each other in a helter-skelter manner but failed to produce anything other than chaotic ugliness. Another touring English novelist, Captain Frederick Marryat, saw the city the same year Frémont did.

> Everybody knows that Washington has a capital, but the misfortune is that the capital wants a city. There it stands, reminding you of a general without an army, only surrounded and followed by a parcel of ragged little boys, for such is the appearance of the dirty, straggling, ill-built houses which lie at the foot of it.[1]

It is no small wonder Frémont saw the city as a dismal and lonely place. Even though he realized that his possible future might be decided here, he longed for company of friends and for surroundings of beauty. This period of his life, this time of waiting for something to happen remained strong in his memory.

But his stay in Washington was fortunately short. At the request of Secretary of War Poinsett, the Bureau of Topographical Engineers had employed the distinguished French scientist Joseph Nicolas Nicollet to make a survey of the northern territory lying between the Mississippi and Missouri rivers. But Nicollet needed a sturdy, young assistant to help him in this task—one who had some knowledge of surveying, mathematics, and wilderness experience. Of all the possible young men available for the position, John Charles appeared to be tailored for the job. Accordingly, he was offered the post of civilian assistant to Nicollet.

Official word of his future employment reached Frémont in the latter part of April. The letter from Lieutenant Colonel John James Abert of the Bureau of Topographical Engineers was short and to the point. Frémont was to report for duty at St. Louis, where he would meet Nicollet. His rate of pay was to be four dollars per day, and he was to receive an allowance of ten cents per mile for expenses incurred in traveling to St. Louis. As to his duties, he was to relieve Nicollet of all unnecessary tasks, and act as disbursing agent for the expedition.

This was the kind of position Frémont had been hoping for, and he wasted no time in leaving Washington. Here, at last, was an opportunity that promised great things. Not only would he be working with a scientist of great acclaim, but also he would be heading beyond the line of settlements into the country of buffalo herds and Indian tribes.

Moving as quickly as possible, he traveled by stagecoach across the Alleghenies. Then when he reached the Ohio River, he took passage on a steamboat bound for St. Louis. The paddlewheeler steamed downriver to the confluence of the Ohio and Mississippi rivers. Here the vessel changed its course and headed up the Mississippi to St. Louis. As the steamboat pulled alongside the levee of this bustling waterfront, young Frémont gathered his gear, walked down the stageplank, and hurried into the heart of this busy city that served as a supply center and jumping-off point for men heading west.

2

JOSEPH NICOLAS NICOLLET was already a seasoned explorer when Frémont met him at St. Louis. Having lost most of his personal fortune in failing business speculations in France, he had come to New Orleans in 1832 to pursue a dream. He had been fascinated by the pioneer explorations of La Salle and Champlain, and it was his intention to add to their body of knowledge about the West. By the time Frémont was sent to be his assistant, Nicollet had explored the southern Appalachians; had traveled up the Red River and the Arkansas River; and, with the aid of the famous fur trading house of Chouteau and Company, had toured the Upper Mississippi, made extensive notes regarding the customs and languages of the Indian tribes that he met, wintered at Fort Snelling (located at present Minneapolis and St. Paul)—on the frontier fringe of the Northwest fur country—and traced the source of the Mississippi River and determined its location with astronomical accuracy.

All this, together with many other attributes of learning, made Nicollet the very right man for Frémont to meet at this formative stage of his career. Nicollet introduced him to both the scientific approach to exploration and the proper areas of study for any young man who wished to be something more than an amateur in the world of knowledge. For Nicollet was a polished scholar and a first-rate scientist. He had the proper background of a Parisian intellectual, but in the tradition of such a person, he remained quiet about his accomplishments. Yet his credentials included membership in the Legion of Honor and a reputation of high standing as a mathematician, and he was a former secretary of the Observatory in Paris and a former professor at the Collège Louis-le-Grand. He was known as a talented musician, a gourmet, a conversationalist of keen wit, and a gentleman with highly cultivated social graces.

For young Frémont, the chance to learn from such a giant was a piece of good fortune. Not only did he become a student of scientific exploration under the guidance of a remarkable teacher, but also he found himself being introduced to an ever-widening social circle.

Nicollet had many friends in St. Louis. They ran the range from old French residents to young Captain Robert E. Lee, who was in charge of government improvements of the harbor at St. Louis and the shipping waterways of the Upper Mississippi and the Missouri rivers. In addition, Nicollet was intimate with Pierre Chouteau of the fur trading house of Pierre Chouteau, Jr., and Company, and was an acquaintance of other businessmen in

the community and a close friend of the Catholic clergy. Through intro-
ductions to such persons, Frémont was included during evenings of pleasure
at various homes; and he joined Nicollet and the Catholic priests in suppers
at the refectory, where the food on the table was more than complemented
by food for the mind. Such gatherings in various settings left a lasting impression.

The short stay at St. Louis wasn't all pleasure. During the days, there was
plenty of hard work to get the expedition ready to travel. Frémont was responsible for making sure that all the necessary details were followed to the
letter, so at some later date in the wilderness the expedition would not be
without necessary supplies. In this task, he was fortunate to have the advice
and services of P. Chouteau, Jr., and Company. From these seasoned men, he
learned how to plan for a field expedition. True enough, the Nicollet party
was going to make its principal headquarters at St. Peter's (now Mendota)
close to Fort Snelling, but this was to be no more than a base to start from
and to come back to when the expedition had ended. Beyond St. Peter's and
Fort Snelling, there were other posts that belonged to Chouteau's American
Fur Company,[2] but these were not close to each other, and they carried only
enough goods and supplies to take care of their own men and any Indians
who came to these outposts with furs to trade. None of these wilderness stations could be counted on as places to offer more than minimal supplies.

As a result of what was known about the great sweep of country the expedition planned to explore, the matter of purchasing enough supplies to carry
the party along during its time in the field was vital. By being placed in
charge of this aspect of the outfitting, Frémont gained the kind of knowledge
that an explorer needed. The degree of preparation was quite extensive as a
sampling from the government vouchers indicates. Foods ran the range from
such common items as dried beef, barreled pork, ham, bacon, pemmican,
flour, salt, butter, rice, potatoes, sugar, tea, and coffee to such rarities as
tablettes de bouillon, sardines, and imported French chocolates. Added to this
were necessary items for scientific work: barometers, chronometers,
magnifiers, microscopes, thermometers, compasses, a sextant, paper, notebooks, pens, pencils, ink, and tools for geological surveys.

Yet food and scientific equipment were only the beginning. Firearms—
including Hawken rifles and double-barreled fowling pieces—were purchased at no small expense, as one Hawken fowling piece alone cost forty-six
dollars. Then there were the everyday items that had to be purchased: frying
pans, pots, tin plates, and cups, knives and forks, blankets, mosquito netting,
lanterns, candles, matches, soap, India rubber coverings for the instruments, a
medicine chest containing drugs to combat illnesses and infections, material
for bandages, thread and needles, and what must have seemed like an endless
list of things to young Frémont. But all the supplies were not so practical.
There were some things which were brought along to make life on the trek a
bit easier. Into this category fell such products as tobacco, port wine, claret,

and bottles of cognac. One other category of goods to be purchased and packed were trade items such as knives and cloth to be used for gifts to the various Indian tribes the party would meet. Finally, arrangements were made to hire horses, carts, canoes, and other baggage carriers.

The most important task was the selection of men. Pierre Chouteau helped Nicollet and Frémont select seasoned voyageurs who had grown up beyond the frontier. Most were part French and part Indian. They spoke a mixture of French, English, and various Indian languages. They tended to have long hair and beards which made them appear much older than they were, and wore buckskin clothing and beaded moccasins. These men were a tough breed who had learned to live with danger on an intimate basis. They had developed the necessary sense of humor to cope with days and nights when a man's life might depend upon the mood of a given Indian, the correct aim at an enemy or a fast-moving buffalo, and an overnight change in the weather from the first warm days of spring to a sudden cold snap that saw the temperature drop well below zero. These were men of the wide open spaces and the endless sky, men who had learned to survive food shortages, arrow wounds, broken bones, fever, and diarrhea even though they traveled in a country so far beyond the last smoke of a settler's cabin that they might as well have been exploring the canyons and mountains of a far-distant planet.

With voyageurs hired and supplies purchased, the time had arrived for the Nicollet expedition to leave the friendly atmosphere of St. Louis. From this day on until their return, there would be no more grand parties and dinners in the warmth of French households, nor would there be suppers with the Catholic priests and evenings of challenging intellectual conversation. Their friends and hosts bid them farewell. Many of them came down to Front Street to see them board the steamboat *Burlington* for the long voyage up the Mississippi to Fort Snelling.

At Front Street all the activity of loading and unloading the steamboats lined up beside the levee left a lasting impression. There were so many boats at the river port that the steamers were doubled up, side by side, waiting for attention. There was the constant sound of shouted commands as the movements for arrivals and departures took place, the work songs of the black cargo handlers, and a steady stream of smoke curling upward from the double stacks of the steamboats—smoke that was caught by the breeze and drifted over the roofs of offices and warehouses on the waterfront like a series of passing storm clouds.

Then as other steamboats appeared in sight—coming up- or downriver— the first man to see an approaching paddlewheeler would sing out, "Steamboat a-coming! Steamboat a-coming!" Mixed in with these cries, the shouts of command, and the work songs, was the steady chatter of pitchmen who greeted incoming passengers with claims of grandeur for their respective hotels, restaurants, and boarding houses. Above all this came the ringing of the last bell, the call from a deck hand for all who were not sailing to get ashore.

There was a flurry of activity in the pilot house above the texas deck; the stageplanks were pulled in; then the smoke from the two stacks increased, and the sound of the engine dominated all other sounds save the slap-slap of the paddlewheel blades against the water, the last shouts of farewell, the creaking and groaning of the contracting and expanding hull and deck, and the last lonely cry of the departing whistle as the steamboat moved away from the levee and into the yellow, rushing water of the mainstream of the Mississippi.

Ahead of the men lay a voyage into the heartland of America and the prospects of a frontier adventure. For Frémont and nineteen-year-old J. Eugene Flandin—the son of a New York merchant friend of Nicollet—this was to be a crossing over from the tame country of the South and the East to the wild lands of the unsettled West. And for another young man in the party, Charles Geyer,[3] a twenty-nine-year-old botanist who had come from Dresden, Germany, in 1834 to explore North American plant life, this was to be yet another opportunity to add to his knowledge. For the other men of the expedition it was a return to the wilderness, a leave-taking of town life and town men, to see once again the endless horizon stretching before them like a new life always waiting for the vitality of renewal in the warm days of spring.

## 3

THE *Burlington* MADE HER WAY UPRIVER. Frémont saw the steady traffic of steamboats, keelboats, and rafts bound for St. Louis. They rode low in the water, the heavy weight of cargo causing them to draw a deep draft in the fast current. Along the shoreline, villages became smaller and smaller. By day and by night, close watches were kept to prevent collisions with logs, branches, tree trunks, and other debris that made its way on the heavy, rushing spring runoff.

Twice a day—usually at morning and evening—the *Burlington* was obliged to stop for wooding. Such an event usually took place at an isolated farm or woodyard on the shoreline where enterprising men or families had stacked cord upon cord of wood for steamboats plying the river. Upon nearing such a place, the captain rang a bell for a wood stop. The engineer cut the speed of the steamboat, and she eased toward the bank, pier, or waiting wood raft. Lines were tossed to hands ashore to secure the steamboat; steam pressure in the engine was cut to a minimum; and when the vessel was secure, stageplanks were passed from deck hands to the waiting wood merchants. Then a frantic procession of men darted from the lower deck, crossed the stageplanks to the stacks of firewood, and quickly loaded the decks of the waiting steamboat with fuel. Then a bell rang for departure. Once more, the engine began to build up pressure; the stageplanks were pulled aboard; the whistle echoed into the vast stretch of lonesome country while the wood merchants and their families waved farewell. Then the paddlewheel slap-slapped against the onrushing current, and the boat creaked and groaned as she began to move. Aft of the boat, the paddlewheel churned a wake of curling whitecaps that marked the boat's passage away from the shore.

The hours of travel grew into days and nights of movement for Frémont and all the other men aboard the *Burlington*. They watched the shorelines for something to break the monotony of earth, sky, and water; and the memory of days and nights in St. Louis grew more important as the boat moved ahead.

Then came the day when a deck hand sang out, "Fort Snelling, dead ahead!" This was the end of the voyage up the Mississippi River. Here at the confluence of the Mississippi and St. Peter's (now Minnesota) rivers was the outpost of adventure.

Over five hundred miles northwest of St. Louis, Fort Snelling stood on a promontory overlooking both rivers. To men coming into the steamboat landing below, the fort loomed over everything in sight. From the river landing a road was cut into the bluff to allow passage upward toward walls that were ten feet high and two feet thick. Towering above the walls were a three-story hexagonal tower on the south side, a round tower at the rear with a cannon platform that stood twenty-two feet above the ground, and a pentagonal tower commanding the north view across the Mississippi. When Frémont first saw this post, on May 25, 1838, it was the most outstanding military installation between the Mississippi and the Pacific.[4]

But the Nicollet expedition stopped only for an exchange of greetings at Fort Snelling. Their destination was across the narrow channel of the Minnesota River at the nearby hamlet where Henry Sibley ran the field headquarters for Chouteau's American Fur Company. This collection of log cabins, corrals, a blacksmith shop, a Sioux Indian village, and Henry Sibley's house was called by three different names. Sibley referred to it as New Hope; others called it St. Peter's; and some used the Sioux name Mendota, which means "meeting of waters."[5] Arrangements already had been made for Sibley to provide Nicollet's party with two-wheeled Red River carts,[6] horses, and drivers to help them carry their supplies as they moved across the rolling plains country.

At Mendota the party was greeted by Henry Sibley. Only twenty-seven years old, Sibley was a striking figure. He was a tall, rangy man who was completely at home on the frontier. His face was almost like that of the Sioux he associated with: dark complexion, high cheekbones, an aquiline nose, deeply set dark-brown eyes, black hair, and a closely trimmed mustache. Addicted to hunting, Sibley often made long trips with the Sioux to the buffalo country. On such journeys he wore buckskins, let his beard grow out, and was always accompanied by his favorite hunting dogs. Sibley was much more than a romantic adventurer who had crossed over from white to Indian ways. He ruled the outposts of Chouteau's American Fur Company with a strong will, and was highly respected by settlers, trappers, and Indians. He was known as a man who liked the benefits of civilization; and whenever a steamboat came upriver from St. Louis, there were books, liquor, cigars, and other items of town living for this man who ruled a vast region that stretched north to the Canadian border from Mendota and Fort Snelling.

To Frémont, life at Sibley's headquarters was unlike anything he had ever known. The house was very much like a hunting lodge, and Sibley's Irish wolfhounds, Lion and Tiger, had the run of the place. Indians always were near the house, and it was among these Sioux that Frémont saw one of the most beautiful Indian girls he had ever seen.

The pleasant interlude at Mendota was not just a time of becoming acquainted with this new world; there was work to be done. All the equipment had to be checked for the trek beyond this last major outpost, and the days and nights were also periods for taking both geological and astronomical observations. Then, on June 9, the time for departure arrived. In a letter to his mother Frémont explained that the expedition would travel part of the distance by boat up the Minnesota River to a rendezvous with the Red River cart drivers. There they were scheduled to go ashore and take to the prairies.

4

THE FIRST LEG OF THE JOURNEY was a trek of 115 miles toward the northwestern prairies. The expedition followed the Minnesota River. From sunrise to sunset, observations were made of the geology, the rich and fertile soil, and the varieties of plant and animal life. And at night, Frémont and Nicollet made astronomical observations to chart the course of the river.

As they moved along their way, they passed several Indian camps. These passings always served as breaks in the endless stretch of sky and earth and were welcomed by the travelers. They noted that the lodges were always pitched in locations that took advantage of the morning sun, and as they neared these camps, the dogs barked and scurried from lodge to lodge. Children stopped their play momentarily, saw that these passing men rode the Red River carts of the fur traders, and then went back to their games. Indian ponies, picketed on rawhide ropes and feeding on the lush wild grass near the skin lodges, neighed and pulled at the ropes holding them. Men and women standing near campfires watched the passing carts and shouted greetings to the voyageurs. The color and drama of these scenes were etched in the memories of Frémont and the others who had never seen an Indian encampment far beyond the settlements.

Beyond these camps, the expedition arrived at its first destination. This was a fur trading post at Traverse des Sioux, a crossing place of the Minnesota River stretching nearly thirty miles long. In the elbow of the river was a body of water called Big Swan Lake, and close to the shoreline was a large summer encampment of Sisseton Sioux. They had selected an excellent campsite, and their tepees were pitched under large trees. Through the services of an interpreter, Nicollet received permission from the Sioux for his party to camp beside them at the mouth of the Cottonwood River.

Nicollet made further use of his interpreter to converse with the Sioux about the lake and the origin and direction of the streams flowing into the Minnesota River. Then in his scholarly fashion, he slowly repeated the Sioux term for streams and other landmarks, and entered these names in his notebook. While he did this, Frémont made sure that all the instruments for mapping the country were in proper order, and he observed the customs of the Sioux. He noticed that they also were observing the customs of the explorers and that as Charles Geyer gathered plants for specimens, he was followed by some Indians who were curious as to why he was digging up plants and placing them in individual containers.

As they rested and got ready for the next move in their survey, Nicollet took precautionary steps to insure their safety as they were bound for reputedly hostile Indian country. In a later letter to Joel Poinsett, he wrote that a messenger was sent ahead to pass the word that the expedition would be passing through the territory of these Indians. When the messenger returned, he was accompanied by a Sioux chief who was almost seven feet tall.

Though suffering from a wound, the chief had traveled a considerable distance to welcome Nicollet and his friends to his country. He even offered to go with them as they passed beyond his country and entered the territory of his enemies. Nicollet thanked him for this courtesy but suggested he was not well enough to make such a long journey. At this, the chief offered his son to go in his place and to fight against these enemies if they dared to attack his white friends.

That evening Frémont was part of the council around the campfire, and he listened as Nicollet referred to the earlier times when the Great French had come as friends among the Sioux, and said that he now came as a representative of their Father at Washington to visit their country, count their lodges, and bring them something to eat.

John Charles was intrigued with the natural eloquence of the chief's reply as he related how his nation had known happier days, when hunger was not always a companion and when their enemies were few and far away. With a stylized speech that had the ring of poetry, the chief recalled those earlier times when the specter of starvation was not always with them:

"Then, the Buffalo covered the plains. Our enemies fled before us & the blaze of our Fires was seen from afar, but they have dwindled away until their light is almost extinguished. There is no more game & my people are few & our enemies press on every side. We thought that we were to die when the snow comes but you come & bring us life. Our sky was covered with clouds & dark with storm, but you came & again the sun shines bright in the blue heavens & we are happy."[7]

After warning the chief not to make war against his enemies and to pay his debts to the traders, Nicollet presented him with a gift of gunpowder and food. What Frémont learned from this evening around the campfire was a very important lesson for an explorer venturing into Indian country. Nicollet's dealings with the Sisseton Sioux demonstrated how consideration, compassion, and tact represented the difference between safety and danger in leading an expedition into tribal territories.

Leaving the company of the Sisseton Sioux and the parklike surroundings beside the mouth of Cottonwood River, the expedition moved on its way. The first phase of their work was to spend some days mapping the country around the Pelican Lakes as well as "the lower spurs of the *Coteau des Prairies,* a plateau which separates the waters of the Mississippi and Missouri Rivers."[8] Fascinated by the beauty of this country, John Charles wrote to Henry Sibley that the country around the Pelican Lakes was so beautiful that no English words did it justice, but that the French term *gracieux* came closer to describing it.

Named by the voyaguers, the "Prairie Coast" was so called as this plateau separates the waters of the Missouri and Mississippi rivers, and resembles a sea coast because the blue line of its wooded ravines "contrasts with the green prairie which sweeps to its feet. . . ."[9]

Beyond the Coteau des Prairies, the expedition headed toward the Red Pipestone Quarry. As they moved in the direction of this area, they became aware that they were being followed by a party of Indians. Taking the necessary precautions, the explorers established a night guard. To Frémont this was an added task after a day's work of traveling and sketching the country. To make up for lack of sleep from having to stand his turn at night guard, he took advantage of the noon halts to sleep in the shade of one of the Red River carts. But their precaution turned out to be a waste of energy, for, as they later learned, the Indians behind them were friendly Sioux who were on their way to the quarry to gather stone for the making of images and pipes.

As the expedition reached the valley of the Red Pipestone, a sudden summer storm shattered the peace of the country. To the Sioux who were traveling with them this was a good sign, for it was their belief that "the Spirit of the Red Pipe Stone speaks in thunder and lightning whenever a visit is made to the Quarry."[10] But the storm vanished as quickly as it had arrived, and the sunlight on the red bluff outlined the expanse of red sandstone and gave it a highly dramatic quality, which Frémont thought made it appear like the ruins of an ancient and deserted city that once had been a center of great villas and splendid farms.

The two groups had three friendly days together, and Nicollet's men helped the Indians gather red pipestone by using gunpowder to blast away portions of stone. The ridge of stone "was in a layer about a foot and a half thick, overlaid by some twenty-six feet of red-colored indurated sand-rock; the color diminishing in intensity from the base to the summit."[11]

After their stay at the quarry, and after having carved their names in the stone, the Nicollet expedition moved on and headed north toward the trading post of Lac qui Parle. Here, Frémont met Joseph Renville, Sr.–the father of their guide and interpreter. Half Sioux and half French, the elder Renville had worked as an interpreter for Zebulon Pike in 1805–6. He had fought for the British in the War of 1812, then worked for the Hudson's Bay Company, and had assisted in the organization of the Columbia Fur Company. When this company was sold, Renville moved to the area controlled by the American Fur Company and built his trading post. To John Charles, Renville was very much like a border chief. And there was a good deal of truth in this assessment, as he did exercise a tremendous influence in the region between his place and the British border. The various Indian tribes in this vast region had great respect for Renville and his son, and their word was a passport through this land.

The expedition's stay at Lac qui Parle was a considerable treat for the weary men. Hospitality was freely given by the Renvilles, who enjoyed seeing visitors as much as the visitors enjoyed a change from guarded movement through Indian country.

While at this outpost they watched a skillful and fast-moving game of lacrosse; among the players was a relative of the Renvilles who was very tall, fast on his feet, and one of the roughest players on the field. Yet the stay was not just an interlude of pleasure. The explorers used Renville's as a base for surveying the nearby lakes and making notes on the nature of the country and the cultures of the various Indians who inhabited this region.

This was as far northwest as Nicollet and his men had time to travel without risking the coming of the first snows. On the return trip to Henry Sibley's post and Fort Snelling the expedition was divided into two groups. Nicollet headed one, and he and his party surveyed the Lesueur River area. Frémont and the other group of men examined the Mankato or Blue Earth River country.

When the two parties next met at Sibley's, there was a pleasant surprise awaiting them. During the wilderness trek, a list of army promotions and appointments had reached the fort and its commandant, Major Joseph Plympton. Among the names on the list was Frémont's. This was his first knowledge of his appointment as a lieutenant of the Bureau of Topographical Engineers.

While preparations were made for the return trip to St. Louis, all the scientific data were put into proper order. Notebooks were reviewed and packed; maps were gone over; and the collections of specimens were checked and made ready for the return trip.

John Charles took time out to go on a November hunting trip with Henry Sibley and all of the members of Red Dog's village. The weather was cold, and the hunters killed only the best and fattest animals. When they shot deer, they avoided killing any bucks because the meat would be rank from the rutting season. But young, fat does were choice targets for tender meat. At the end of a day's hunt, the camp was a scene of "bright fires, where fat venison was roasting on sticks . . . or stewing with corn or wild rice in pots hanging from tripods; squaws busy over the cooking and children rolling about over the ground."[12]

By December, Frémont and Nicollet were back in St. Louis. Once again they worked with Pierre Chouteau and his men as they made the first preparations for the next year's expedition, which would take them into the distant country of the Upper Missouri River. Then, at the end of 1838, Nicollet sent Frémont on ahead to Washington with official letters and a verbal account for Poinsett. Prior to Nicollet's arrival, the handsome lieutenant enjoyed the limelight of a returning explorer in the off-duty hours when he was not caught up in the mundane business of trying to straighten out the accounts to the satisfaction of Colonel Abert.

5

NICOLLET SPENT ONLY A BRIEF TIME IN WASHINGTON. There was much work to be done in St. Louis to get things in order for the next wilderness survey, and he soon left Frémont to head back to Chouteau's. In the latter part of February, Frémont sent a letter to Colonel Abert in which he outlined the plans for the coming expedition.

The extent of this proposal called for a "Military and Geographical Survey of the Country West of the Mississippi and North of the Missouri." In order to accomplish these goals, Nicollet had made arrangements with Chouteau to use his company's distant outpost at Fort Pierre (present site of Pierre, South Dakota) as their base camp. But while this would place the expedition close to regions they wished to explore, it also meant that all the supplies and men would have to go by steamboat up the Missouri River, which flows into the Mississippi just above St. Louis, to Fort Pierre—a voyage of over a thousand miles against the heavy current of the spring runoff. At best, the going would be slow; and it called for a departure time at the beginning of April.

In the first week of March, Colonel Abert sent two letters to Lieutenant Frémont regarding the expedition. In one he directed him to complete his business in Washington as quickly as possible and to get on his way to St. Louis. In the same letter he also authorized the hiring of botanist Charles Geyer and workman J. Eugene Flandin at two dollars per day. In addition, he notified Frémont that the expedition would be allowed to draw up to five thousand dollars to cover its expenses. The second letter dealt specifically with money and the handling of it. It consisted of two detailed paragraphs instructing the lieutenant in the proper handling of accounts and vouchers with regard to all expenditures. For Colonel Abert was trying his best to train

Lieutenant Frémont in the army method of keeping accurate accounts and records of every transaction, no matter how small or large it might be.

But Colonel Abert had more than met his match, and one can only surmise that he hoped that somehow Frémont would recognize the need to adjust to governmental red tape. For, even though Frémont tried, the business of keeping books was something that he did in a haphazard way even at his very best. And as he departed from Washington, bookkeeping must have been something that he placed way down the list of things to worry about. Ahead of him was something a good deal more exciting and important than worrying about vouchers and accounts.

## 6

FRÉMONT AND THE MEN worked at a frantic pace. They packed supplies and loaded them aboard the *Antelope,* a Missouri River steamboat that belonged to Chouteau's American Fur Company. Caught up in the mood of getting ready for a long journey, John Charles immediately set to work at trying to keep his accounts and vouchers in order for the supplies that had been purchased and the men who had been hired.

Among the new men were two unusual characters: Louis Zindel, who had served nineteen years as a noncommissioned artillery officer in the Prussian Army and who was clever at making rockets and fireworks, and Etienne Provost, or *l'homme des montagnes,* a legendary figure among mountain men, a man who had managed to stay alive in an occupation not noted for contributing to long life. Provost had trapped in the Rockies as early as 1815–17, traveled clear to the Great Basin, and may have been the first white man to see the Great Salt Lake when he passed that way in the fall of 1824. No expedition could have had a better guide. Frémont could not have had a better teacher. As an indication of the high value placed upon Provost's services, he was paid $778 for his tour of duty, more than seven times the amount paid to Louison Frenière, a half-breed Sioux who was noted for his knowledge of the wilderness.

The plan for the expedition called for one stop at the mouth of the James River. At this tributary of the Missouri River the party would pick up additional men from the outpost at Lac qui Parle. Knowing that this connection would be made, Frémont wrote to Henry Sibley on April 4, 1839, the date of their departure from St. Louis, and informed him that if he could be at Lac qui Parle at the end of June they should be happy to see him. Then as he finished his short letter, he wrote that there was a case being sent to him in which he would find two boxes of cigars.

As Frémont boarded the *Antelope* that early morning, he might well have compared her to the regular steamboats that sailed up and down the Mississippi River. For the boats that were used for the Missouri River run at this time were not the most graceful vessels afloat. Roughly built, clumsy in appearance, these steamboats were 100 to 130 feet in length, twenty to thirty feet in beam, and drew about three to five feet of water. The bow was spoon-shaped, so that the boat could run onto a sandbar and not become stuck. When she hit such an obstruction, two spars near the bow would be lowered like giant stilts into the sand. Then cables would be tightened on the capstan, and, in a fashion resembling the movements of a grasshopper walking along a puddle's surface, the steamboat would be "grasshoppered" over the sandbar and out of the shoals into deeper water.

Walking across sandbars, dodging snags, fighting the fast, downriver current, and pulling ashore for the crew to cut a supply of wood as well as to make camp for the night added hours and days and weeks and months to the upriver voyage. To Frémont and the other men who had not made this voyage before, it became almost a dreamlike state once the *Antelope* moved beyond the sparse settlements near the mouth of the Missouri River. All noises seemed to take on a special quality: The lonely whistle of the steam pipe echoed and re-echoed into the never-ending horizon; the swish of the water against the paddlewheel blades beat a steady pulse that was picked up in counterpoint by the chug-chug of the steam engine; the captain and crew called back and forth in voices of warning as jagged snags rushed toward the boat; and all the passengers aboard talked quietly as they stared upriver for the half-submerged tree that might well mean total disaster. Beyond these sounds, the land was a silent land, almost a brooding land, and John Charles found it intriguing.

> The stillness was an impressive feature, and the constant change in the character of the river shores offered always new interest as we steamed along. At times we travelled by high perpendicular escarpments of light colored rock, a gray and yellow marl, made picturesque by shrubbery or trees; at others the river opened out into a broad delta-like expanse, as if it were approaching the sea. At length, on the seventieth day we reached Fort Pierre, the chief post of the American Fur Company. This is on the right or western bank of the river, about one thousand and three hundred miles from St. Louis. On the prairie, a few miles away, was a large village of Yankton Sioux. Here we were in the heart of Indian country and near the great buffalo ranges. Here the Indians were sovereign.[13]

Here in the land of the Sioux, the expedition made final preparations for its journey of exploration. Additional supplies were purchased from Chouteau's outpost at Fort Pierre. All the scientific equipment was checked over to make sure things were in proper working order. Then to add to the complement of the party, other men were hired from the force at Fort Pierre. Among these new hands were Louison Frenière, half French and half Sioux, a man whose reputation as a hunter and scout ranked him among the very best; Dorion, son of the fort's interpreter, whose knowledge of Indian languages and customs made him a good man to have along; and William Dixon, an interpreter whose knowledge came from his father Robert Dixon, an early fur trader in this country. All these men were highly experienced in dealing with Indians, and all of them knew this plains country as well as a town man knows the limits of his backyard.

By the first part of July all the equipment was in traveling shape, and the party of nineteen men was ready to strike out and head northeast toward the British line and the rising sun. But before the journey began, it was necessary to visit the nearby Sioux encampment to bring gifts and to ask permission to pass through their territory in peace.

A few days after this meeting, one of the chiefs came to the fort. With him was a young, beautiful girl who was no more than eighteen. The chief greeted Nicollet and Frémont. Then through an interpreter, he offered his daughter as a woman for Nicollet. As Frémont watched this situation unfold, he found it highly amusing and waited to see how Nicollet would get around a problem that had to be handled with great delicacy in order to avoid any slight to the good-hearted chief. But Nicollet had a ready reason for not being able to accept such a generous offer. He explained that he already had a woman and that the Great Father would not allow him to have more than one. Then, to Frémont's embarrassment, he suggested that his young assistant was not committed to any woman and might, indeed, like to have this lovely woman as his wife. Put into a hard corner, John Charles politely informed the chief that as much as he admired his daughter, it would not be proper for him to take her as his woman. He was going to go far away, and this would not be good for his daughter as she would be lonely for her people.

Then to make sure he did not insult the chief, he told him he "was greatly pleased with the offer, and . . . would give the girl a suitable present. Accordingly, an attractive package of scarlet and blue cloths, beads, a mirror, and other trifles was made up, and they left us; the girl quite satisfied with her trousseau, and he with other suitable presents made him."[14]

All the proper conferences and exchanges of gifts having been made with the Yankton Sioux, the Nicollet expedition gathered its horses and Red River carts and began its journey. Twenty-six years old, full of life and excited by everything he saw, Lieutenant Frémont rode with the mountain men and scouts and saw the wind-swept and lush prairie country—a region colored by the burst of summer wild flowers, by the great thunderheads riding oceans of wind in the endless blue sky like some wondrous mountain ranges that had learned the secret of flight, and by the sudden sight and sound of a vast herd of buffalo thundering across the plains as the hunters shouted, "La vache! La vache!"

On his first buffalo hunt, he learned the complete thrill of riding his horse at a gallop and charging into the running herd. For as they topped a rolling hill, the grunting and feeding herd was alerted by their presence and began to move in a headlong rush. The hunters cried out and began their wild chase. They rode at a full gallop, and in the deep grass the ground seemed to vanish and the ride was like floating above waves of water.

The young lieutenant learned more than the thrill of the chase and kill. In the wild ride across the rolling high plains, he became separated from the other hunters. When the chase ended, he looked around for his companions. Not one was in sight. Still, he was not concerned until he tried to find his way back to camp. Hours later, as the sun dropped in the western sky, he realized he was lost. The discovery came as a shock to him. He dismounted and, leading his tired horse, he walked on for hour after hour. "Toward midnight, I reached the breaks of the river hills at a wooded ravine, and just then I saw a rocket shoot up into the sky, far away to the south."[15] Zindel was sending out a signal for the lost hunter; but Frémont was so far from camp, he decided it would be wiser to wait for daybreak. He removed the saddle from his horse, picketed the mount, and, using his saddle as a pillow, settled down for a lonely sleep until the first light of day. But before he did any of this, he had the good sense to place his rifle on the ground facing in the direction in which he had seen the glare of the rocket.

At dawn he checked the direction indicated by the rifle, saddled his horse, and began to ride. Before he got very far from his night's camp, he saw three riders approaching at a full gallop. Obviously, these horsemen had seen him, so he realized it would do no good to make a run for it. He hoped they were not hostiles but men from the camp. To his relief, they were men Nicollet had sent out to find him and there was a reward for the first man to touch the wayward hunter—a bounty which was collected by Louison Frenière. Frémont's reward for this experience was the knowledge of how easy it was to become lost in the rolling sea of grass that stretched into the horizon.

Still heading northeast, the expedition struck the area between the James and Sheyenne rivers (in present North Dakota). Vast herds of buffalo grazed along the plains; and when the lieutenant was not busy making sketches or working on maps with Nicollet, he made other hunting trips with the hired hunters as they killed buffalo for camp meat. Even on these exciting excursions, he learned more and more about the art of survival in the vast country of the West. He observed how these men of the plains and mountains watched every movement on the horizon, how they could tell what caused the slightest movement of dust, and how they could read trail sign as though the marks of a passing Indian or game animal were carefully worded passages from a guidebook.

As mid-July grew warmer day by day, the traveling became that much harder. The men grew tired of the constant glare of the sun during the middle hours of the days; and though the evening breezes offered a rest from heat, these cool hours were also the time when deer flies and mosquitoes were a plague for men and horses. They left the James River region and approached the Sheyenne River. As they neared this tributary to the Red River of the North, they passed through great herds of buffalo, working their way carefully and slowly to keep the herds from stampeding. Then as they reached the Tampa, a small stream flowing into the Sheyenne River, Dixon and Frenière rode into camp with three Sioux who had been watching the movements of the expedition.

The warriors said that nearby was an encampment of nearly three hundred lodges, or almost two thousand people from various Sioux tribes. Through the intrepreters, they learned that the Indians were about to make a surround of the herds and take a large supply of meat. The Indians invited the members of the expedition to make camp next to their lodges until the big hunt was over. The leaders of the expedition were treated to a series of feasts at the lodges of the various chiefs. To show how grateful the party was for such hospitality, Nicollet invited the chiefs to eat at the expedition's camp. The feast began with all the best intentions in the world.

The chiefs sat around in a large circle on buffalo robes or blankets, each provided with a deep soup plate and spoon made of tin. The first dish was a generous *pot-au-feu*, principally of fat buffalo meat and rice. No one would begin until all the plates were filled. When all was ready the feast began. With the first mouthful each Indian silently laid down his spoon, and each looked at the other. After a pause of bewilderment the interpreter succeeded in having the situation understood. Mr. Nicollet had put among our provisions some Swiss cheese, and to give flavor to the soup a liberal portion of this had been put into the kettles. Until this strange flavor was accounted for the Indians thought they were being poisoned; but, the cheese being shown to them, and explanation made, confidence was restored; and by the aid of several kettles of water well sweetened with molasses, and such other tempting *delicatessen* as could be produced from our stores, the dinner party went on and terminated in great humor and general satisfaction."[16]

On the day after the near disaster with the Swiss cheese, the Indians made their grand surround. This was their principal summer hunt, and the slaughter of fat cows went on all during the day. As the animals were killed, the meat was brought into camp, where the women cut it into strips and placed it on low scaffolds for sun drying. This would be the major supply of meat for the winter months when hunting would be poor, and it was vital to cure as much meat as possible for the lean months ahead. Then when the surround ended, there was a grand feast and celebration throughout the large encampment for the whole night. To add to the joy of the event, Nicollet had presents of cloth, trade beads, finger rings (three gross had been taken for such an occasion), and tobacco.

During the next two days, the party moved north even closer to the British line on their trek to Devil's Lake, which the Indians called "Heart of the Enchanted Water." This short trip was not a pleasant one, as mosquitoes swarmed about men and horses in great clouds of torment. While the men got some protection by covering their faces with long green veils, the horses were bothered so much that at night they would quit feeding "and come up to the fires to shelter themselves in the smoke."[17]

At Devil's Lake the expedition found traces of a large camp that had been abandoned only recently. From the wheel marks on the ground and from other familiar signs, the guides knew this had been a large camp of hunters from the Red River of the North. During the buffalo season these so-called Free People of the North, who were métis or a mixture of French and Indian, would come south of the British line. Here they would make their hunting camp and take what they needed from the herds feeding in the area. Each of their Red River carts would carry the meat of ten buffalo made into pemmican. The pemmican consisted of meat dried by the fire or the sun and then pounded, mixed with melted fat, and packed into skin sacks. The pemmican came in two different qualities: "the ordinary pemmican of commerce, being the meat without selection, and the finer, in small sacks, consisting of the choicest parts kneaded up with the marrow."[18]

For a period of more than a week the explorers surveyed Devil's Lake and the region around it. While they found the water was brackish, there was no shortage of fish. During one of his excursions around the lake, John Charles learned that making camp near water in buffalo country was not the wisest thing to do. Despite the years of experience of Dixon and Frenière, the three men set up camp near the lake shore. All went well until they bedded down for the night. Then they were aroused by the sound of moving, grunting buffalo. Quickly they threw more wood on the fire to ward off the herd coming to the lake for water. The men shouted, fired their guns, and made as much noise as they could. It forced the herd to move around them and make a little room, but it was close quarters until the animals had drunk their fill and moved back onto the plains.

By the middle of August the expedition had moved southeast from Devil's Lake and crossed the region between the Sheyenne and Red rivers. From the head of the Coteau des Prairies, they traveled south toward Lac qui Parle and a meeting with the Renvilles. Frémont continued to fill his notebooks with sketches of the lake region of western Minnesota. What impressed him most of all was the change in the look of the plains country as the first cold nights and mornings of autumn came on. The green of early summer and the brown grass of the middle summer no longer dominated the landscape. Groves of aspen were turning orange and golden and shimmering with the slightest breeze, and the cottonwoods looked like burnished silver.

At Renville's post, the men relaxed and talked about their journey. Then they made short trips to explore the nearby lakes before the coming of winter. Even as they bid farewell and started toward the Minnesota River and the trail to Fort Snelling, Indian summer was already gone and autumn was well advanced. To Frémont the colors he now saw possessed a rare beauty.

The prairie flowers had been exceptional in luxuriance and beauty. The rich lowlands near the house were radiant with asters and golden-rod, and memory chanced to associate these flowers, as the last thing seen, with the place. Since then I have not been in that country or seen the Renvilles; but still I

John Charles Frémont as he looked in 1850. He was thirty-seven years old, and he had been elected as one of the first two senators from the new state of California. (*Courtesy of The Bancroft Library, University of California*)

This portrait by T. Buchanan Read captures the striking beauty of young Jessie Benton Frémont. (*Courtesy of the Southwest Museum*)

Senator Thomas Hart Benton was an imposing figure when he posed for this daguerreotype. *(Courtesy of the Library of Congress)*

Washington, D.C., was still an unfinished city even though twelve years had passed since John Charles Frémont had first seen it. (*Courtesy of the Library of Congress*)

never see the golden-rod and purple asters in bloom, without thinking of that hospitable refuge on the far northern prairies.[19]

The Nicollet expedition hurried along its way once it left Lac qui Parle, for the feel of winter was in the wind. Some cursory exploration of the Minnesota and the Mississippi rivers took place, but the main object was to get to the steamboat landing near Fort Snelling before the river iced over.

In the darkness of nightfall, Frémont reached the steamboat landing in a bark canoe with a small detachment of the party. It was the first of November 1839, and a steamboat lit up the dock with the fire from its engine as it built up steam for its departure to St. Louis. Nicollet, who had reached Fort Snelling before Frémont, was already on his way downriver. But the lieutenant was tired of hurrying, and he thought it would be a pleasant break to stop over for a couple of days. It would be good to see his friend Sibley once again, to have a glass of brandy with him and talk about the travels of the expedition, and to sleep in a real bed for a change. Another steamboat would be coming upriver before winter, and a few days wouldn't make any great difference.

But a lesson in making the right move at the right time was brought home to him on the following morning. During the night the first storm of winter had blown in. The ground was already covered with snow, and it was getting deeper even as he watched it swirl in white clouds. Then he looked at the river and realized there would not be another steamboat until spring. The river was frozen over. So, while Nicollet was well downriver aboard a comfortable steamboat, the young lieutenant made preparations for a cold overland trek southward.

With the two expeditions under Nicollet's tutelage behind him, Frémont was becoming an explorer. He had learned to make astronomical observations, record topography, observe botany, soils, and minerals, and make careful sketch-maps. This was a scientific approach to exploration that would serve him well in a field that had few professionals and a good many amateurs. He had learned a great deal from such mountain men and scouts as Frenière and Provost, and from experienced traders such as Sibley and the Renvilles. These masters of the plains had taught him how to set up a proper camp, how to find game, how to avoid the dangers of getting lost in the rolling grasslands, and most of all, how to meet the Indians in their own country and make friends. Without this ability, all the scientific knowledge in the world was without value once a man journeyed beyond the last outpost and moved into the frontier country of the Indians.

All these lessons from these two expeditions had been an explorer's apprenticeship for John Charles. Now, he would return to Washington as a young man with more than talent and some possible promise for the future. He was no longer Mr. Nicollet's young assistant. He was homeward bound as Lieutenant Frémont, an American explorer.

## ·❧· III ·❧·

# A Fork in the Trail

TURNING POINTS IN A MAN'S LIFE cannot be anticipated. Sometimes a slight and seemingly inconsequential event can mark a new departure, another starting point that results in a different outcome in the long run. At other times, the path a man's life will follow is charted by a series of events. For John Charles Frémont both currents of change flowed together to form his fork in the trail, his path to follow. And the first steps that he took on this trail happened not long after he had returned to Washington toward the end of 1839.

When he had gone as Nicollet's assistant in the survey of the Northwest frontier between the Upper Mississippi and Missouri rivers, he was already known around Washington as a young man of talent and definite possibilities. These same compliments were applicable to other young men who were waiting around the city to get a chance to prove themselves. Still, after his second successful tour of duty with the distinguished Nicollet, the lieutenant was looked upon as a man with great promise. He had proved himself in the field and had been trained by one of the finest scientific explorers in the world. All this added up to one thing: Frémont was a potential American explorer who might carve a new destiny for the nation in the wilderness country beyond the last boundaries of civilization.

The first indication of things that might break open occurred when Nicollet asked him to accompany him on an official visit to President Van Buren and Secretary of War Poinsett. Not only was Lieutenant Frémont received with cordiality and interest as he added his comments about the expedition to the Northwest, but he was complimented by Poinsett, who informed him that he was highly gratified with the report of his performance on the expedition which had been delivered to him by Nicollet.

This reception should have convinced John Charles that something was in the wind with regard to his future. Yet he failed to see that this meeting with the President and the Secretary of War was anything more than a normal interest in the results of the expedition. He was, of course, pleased with Nicollet's praise of his work to Poinsett. Still, he must have felt like any bright student who is complimented by his professor, but who knows that he has much more to learn before he can count himself an equal of the master.

A vacation was in order for the explorers, and Nicollet needed a good rest. He was exhausted from the long frontier journey, and he looked forward to good beds, savory cuisine that would remove the taste of camp cooking, fine wines, and evenings of intellectual conversations. As in St. Louis, Nicollet relied upon his close friendships with Catholic scholars and priests. Again, he invited Frémont to accompany him, and the two men traveled to Baltimore, Maryland. Here, they stayed at the Sulpician seminary at St. Mary's College. Bishop Chance, president of the college, was a very close friend of Nicollet's, and he always kept quarters for him at the institution. This was Nicollet's refuge from the wilderness, and in his rooms he had the garments of civilization carefully stored in his wardrobes: fine linen suits tailored for the drawing room and not a skin lodge, and all the other items to outfit a gentleman for evenings of stimulating conversation and excellent dining.

Just as Frémont began to enjoy this break from life on the trail, as he became accustomed to wearing tailored suits and dining with the congenial priests on one night and in a splendid Baltimore home on another, his taste of the good life was cut short by a personal tragedy. He received a letter from his mother informing him that his brother had died. Frank had gone to Buffalo, New York, to pursue his career as an actor. While there he was accidentally shot while observing a riot—an injury that finally resulted in his death. This came as a shock to John Charles as it had been only eight years since the unexpected death of his sister, Elizabeth. Knowing his mother's anguish, he caught a train to Charleston to be by her side and to take care of all the arrangements and numbing details that follow a death in a family.

2

AFTER THE BURIAL OF HIS BROTHER, John Charles remained with his mother for a short period until she had recovered from her initial grief. During this time, he tried his best to help her adjust to the loss of another child. For a while he managed to make the days seem like those past years of happiness. But the need for his return to Washington came much too quickly, and he was well aware of his mother's lonely burden of sadness. To help her get over this time of mourning, he prevailed upon his mother's old friend Kitty Cowne to stay with her for a month's visit. Then feeling despondent from the knowledge that only he and his mother remained, he caught the train that would take him back to a world of much-needed work that would help him to forget.

Upon his return to Washington, he was depressed even more by the look of the city. With the exception of the mansions around Capitol Hill, the city struck him as something raw and unfinished. The idea of residing there until the final work was completed on the notes and maps of the regions they had explored was not pleasing to contemplate. While he knew the work would be interesting and that he would continue to broaden the scope and depth of his knowledge, there was no escaping the surroundings. The ever-present stench of open sewers filled the air on warm days; the unfinished streets remained as choking dust in dry weather and as quagmires in wet weather; and the view of barren ugliness seemed like some vision of a filthy hell in comparison to the open plains country with its natural beauty, or to Charleston with its combination of gardens, cobblestone streets, and handsome buildings that enhanced the natural setting.

But Frémont was to be spared the kind of dwelling and working quarters he assumed he would have to endure. Instead, Nicollet informed him that both of them were to live with Nicollet's old friend Ferdinand R. Hassler, superintendent of the United States Coast Survey. This was a welcome bit of good fortune, for the seventy-year-old Hassler's home was one of the finest in the city. It was located on Capitol Hill and overlooked the Potomac River. To make things even more convenient, it was within easy walking distance of the Coast Survey building, where Hassler agreed to provide several workrooms for the two explorers.

For Frémont the acquaintance with Hassler was another stroke of good luck. Trained in mathematics, Hassler also had considerable knowledge in such fields as anthropology, astronomy, physics, jurisprudence, and political science. Abrupt and prickly in temperament, he had had an impressive though difficult and uneven career in teaching and geodetic work in his native Switzerland and in America.

By the time Frémont met this remarkable man of science, Hassler traveled into the country on surveying trips in a large, specially designed carriage nicknamed "the ark," which never failed to draw attention. It was constructed to carry scientific instruments, including a big theodolite, without jarring them on rough roads. It was also built to accommodate him in comfortable quarters while he traveled. Mounted on huge C springs, the carriage had places in the front and back for instruments. The square shape of the carriage also allowed space for a spirit room where Hassler kept his favorite German wines; and beneath the seats there were lockers for his baggage, stationery, and books. While this wasn't the best-looking carriage ever pulled by four horses, it was comfortable and provided Hassler a traveling house and office where he had a proper bed for the nights and plenty of work room for the days.

Even in Washington, Hassler traveled about in "the ark." And it was not unusual to see his tall, thin figure, clothed in a fine suit, emerge from the carriage. If he were on his way to a dinner party, he carried his own wines, as he had no intention of being served something of an inferior quality. Despite his innate ability for rudeness, Hassler provided the best of quarters and food for Nicollet and Frémont.

Evenings in the Hassler home consisted of good rousing talk about scientific methods and problems, after a superb dinner of French cuisine. The latter was provided by a newly arrived chef from France, an excellent master of the kitchen, who had been turned down by President Van Buren because he thought the chef's salary request much too high. The excellent dinners the chef prepared at Hassler's were not limited to the three men alone. Hassler knew most of the eminent people in Washington, and he often gave dinner parties which included fellow scientists, congressmen, appointed government officials, and other guests whose intellectual background brought them into the circle of his friends and acquaintances. Through such gatherings Frémont developed an ever-widening circle of persons who saw him as something more than the usual run of bright, young men to be found in Washington.

Not all the time at Hassler's was devoted to the pursuit of pleasure. In the offices provided for them at the Coast Survey building, Nicollet and Frémont worked long hours on refining their astronomical observations, translating their field notes into official reports, and constructing maps of the areas they had explored. To aid them in their tasks, Lieutenant Eliakim Scammon of the Corps of Topographical Engineers was assigned to their project. Frémont liked him very much and found that, in addition to their mutual facility with figures, both enjoyed a good game of chess. Scammon also was a man of wide interests and an avid reader in many fields. This, along with his pleasant disposition, made him a fine companion as well as a valuable assistant in the daily work of organizing and completing the final data and maps of the expedition's findings.

To add to the refinement of their work, Nicollet was allowed to build an observatory on top of Hassler's house. Here many a long night was spent in making astronomical observations.

Sometimes during these hours of watching the stars, Frémont would become restless. During one such evening, he became bored while jotting down his observations. A beetle lit on the book in which he was making his entries, and before it flew away he made a lifelike sketch of it. Nicollet came over to his desk to use his lantern while he read his instrument. Seeing the sketched bettle, he tried to brush it away. Frémont couldn't contain himself, and broke out in laughter. To Nicollet this was not a laughing matter, and he reproached him for what he considered to be frivolity. "Instead of occupying your mind with these grand objects you give your attention to insect things."[1]

This kind of conflict between age and youth, however, was not a typical thing for the two men. On the contrary, Frémont was quite capable of carrying on a very close and friendly relationship with older men. This was a trait that was to help in the pursuit of his career.

As the work progressed, important visitors stopped by to see the unfolding results of their expeditions into the Northwest frontier. Colonel Abert was a frequent caller, but two other men of great influence also stopped to talk and to watch the growth of the maps and reports. One was the senior senator from Missouri, Thomas Hart Benton, and the other was the junior senator from Missouri, Lewis F. Linn. Both men were firm believers in the idea of western expansion, but it was Senator Benton who carried the greatest weight in the Senate, and ultimately he would manage to get enough backing for the exploration of the West.

At first Senator Benton was disappointed at the slow progress in the making of maps, but he was extremely interested in the material for the reports. Frémont was fascinated with Benton's grasp of the nature of the frontier country. And as he got to know him, he learned that the idea of expanding the nation to the Pacific was an old one in Benton's mind—an idea that had been part of his own background on the frontier, part of his admiration for Thomas Jefferson, and part of his grasp of the knowledge he had obtained through his friendship with the Chouteaus and General William Clark of St. Louis.

From his first meeting with Senator Benton, the direction of Frémont's life began to take a major change. Though the young lieutenant knew that the expeditions with Nicollet had given him the proper training for a fine career as an army engineer, he had never considered greater paths to follow. But as he listened to Senator Benton point out the ultimate importance to the nation of a complete exploration of the lands beyond the Mississippi River, Frémont caught the fever to become part of a grand design that would push the boundary of the nation toward the setting sun. And this urge to explore new country, to make proper descriptions of the natural wealth of the land and to make maps and reports that would be of use to emigrants became major factors in his life as he joined the Benton family for frequent dinners and heard the senator and his friends expound upon grand plans for a westward course of empire.

## 3

To YOUNG FRÉMONT, the Benton home became the family home that tragic events had prevented his knowing for a long time. Night after night he joined the family for dinner. He came to know Senator and Mrs. Benton as a couple who were devoted to each other and to their children. Two of the daughters and the boy, Randolph, were at home, and the older girls were attending Mrs. English's boarding school in Georgetown. But the family life appealed to him. It combined great affection and love with respect for social grace and disciplined work habits. At the center of all family activities was the constant example of proper living that was set by Senator and Mrs. Benton. The children were encouraged to pursue learning, to know music, to practice good manners, to appear at the dinner table in good dress, and to present a pleasing disposition and avoid disagreeable topics during dinner.

Dinner was generally served at five o'clock, and then the men—and there were quite often guests—would retire from the table to discuss their favorite topic. At these gatherings Frémont heard the views of Senator Linn, of his half brother, Delegate Augustus C. Dodge of Iowa Territory, and of Senator John M. Robinson of Illinois. All these men from the edge of the frontier were caught up in the excitement of opening the Far West. All of them supported the idea of sending a government exploring expedition beyond the Mississippi and the Missouri. To these men, the Lewis and Clark expedition had been the beginning, but too many years had passed without expanding the work of the explorers who had been sent into the wilderness by Thomas Jefferson. Now, at a time when the nation was restless, when it needed new breathing space, when it needed to consider what the British might be up to on the Pacific Coast, there was all the reason in the world to break the steady delays in Congress and to send forth another expedition to follow up the work of Lewis and Clark.

Even as Senator Benton and his friends talked of the Far West and of what should be done, the man who was the natural leader for a government expedition was suffering from poor health. As Nicollet's physical condition declined, so, too, did his usual driving energy. He found it difficult to continue the project. Frémont watched his friend grow weaker and weaker and became quite concerned about him. Under the strain of illness, Nicollet was restless. He made frequent visits away from Washington and away from his work. During these times, he usually traveled to Baltimore to visit many friends and to see his physician.

To Senator Benton and the others who were laying the groundwork for an expedition that would have the scientific solidity about it that had been the quality of Nicollet's work in the Minnesota-Dakota country, the presence of Lieutenant Frémont was a stroke of good fortune. If Nicollet did not become well enough to head such a party of exploration, then the next best man appeared to be the personable young lieutenant.

While talk of western exploration took the center stage at the Benton home, music also played its role as John Charles listened to Susan and Sarah perform in the family music room. And it was music that created a new and major drama in his life and in the lives of Senator and Mrs. Benton. One evening he was asked to accompany Sarah to a concert at Georgetown as the parents were not able to attend. To Frémont this was a pleasant way to spend an evening, and he gladly accepted the family's request.

But the concert at Mrs. English's select private school turned into much more than an evening of listening to music and enjoying Sarah's company. This was his first meeting with Jessie, and from the moment he saw her, he knew that this was much more than the beginning of a friendship. Jessie was only fifteen years old, but she already had many suitors—far too many for the Bentons, and this had been one of the reasons for sending her to Mrs. English's school. The first sight of Jessie was all that he needed. Her oval face, her thin and classic nose, her dark hair, and her deep-set brown eyes added the right touches to highlight her full and beautifully shaped lips, and flawless complexion. Along with her physical beauty, she was gay and witty, and had Senator Benton's "grasp of mind, comprehending with a tenacious memory; but with it a quickness of perception and instant realization of subjects and scenes in their complete extent . . . and a tenderness and sensibility that made feeling take the place of mind. . . ."[2]

Frémont was smitten with an immediate love for this beautiful young girl who made the evening vanish as though time had found a new sense of speed. Jessie, too, saw much more than a young army officer that night. Dark curly hair, clear blue eyes, a man whose movements were graceful, and who was "slender, upright, elastic and tough as fine steel."[3] Later that night, after Frémont and Sarah had returned to the Benton home, Jessie confided in her sister Eliza that at long last, she had met the handsomest man in all of Washington. Then, in a burst of excitement, she said, "I'm so glad I wore the pin candy-stripe with the rose sash instead of the dotted muslin with the blue. It made me look much older."[4]

This first meeting was the beginning of a classic love affair, the kind of relationship which carries throughout a lifetime without diminishing, without losing that first glance of recognition that tells them they are to be together for their span of years. To Frémont, beautiful Jessie was all he could ever hope to find in any woman. She was warm, compassionate, beautiful, and possessed of a keen mind. To Jessie, the handsome explorer had all the qualities she so admired in her father, but along with them he had the dash and imagination of a man on his way to great deeds.

Some months passed before the love-stricken couple saw each other again. When Jessie returned to Washington for a vacation from Mrs. English's school, the attraction between the couple bloomed. The Bentons gradually noticed that there was more than friendship between Jessie and John Charles, and this upset Mrs. Benton.

To her, the idea of Jessie seeing so much of an army officer was something to worry about. She had never approved of the limitations an army career placed on a man, and she had even postponed her own marriage because Thomas Benton was an army officer. As Jessie wrote in later years: "My mother had at first refused to marry my father and it was seven years before she did so—when he was quite forty. She said she would never marry a red haired man, a democrat, or a western man, all of which were in fuller force than ever when at last she consented."[5]

Jessie was subjected to lectures by her father which consisted of detailed explanations of the difference in age, the meagerness of John Charles's income, and the slow process of promotion within the army. And Jessie wasn't the only one to hear the negative arguments against this growing courtship. Senator Benton also spoke to Frémont about the situation. There was the matter of his future. Not that he did not think the lieutenant had a future. But it was the kind of prospect his life would hold for any young woman of

Jessie's background that concerned the senator. Not only was the life of an officer in the service a poor way to earn a decent income, but also it promised constant movement, all of which would be subjected to the orders of the military. There would be times when it would not even be possible for man and wife to be together for months, perhaps, years at a time.

The concern of the Bentons cut sharply into the meetings between Jessie and John Charles. The lieutenant was not turned away from the Benton household. Yet for a time the young lovers saw each other only on "an occasional weekend during which Frémont was asked to dinner at the request of Grandmother McDowell, who pronounced him 'a highly superior young man.'"[6] But the nearness caused the lovers to be careless in their obvious feeling: They looked too longingly at each other, and more than once the Bentons had seen them whispering as though a conspiracy of secret courting might be taking place somewhere out of sight of parental gaze.

All this was more than either parent desired, but it was Mrs. Benton who objected the most. Behind all her arguments against John Charles as a suitor for her daughter lurked her true ambition. Martin Van Buren, who was just completing his first term as Democratic President, had indicated more than a passing interest in Jessie. Van Buren was thirty-two years older than Jessie, and had four sons who were beyond her age. Yet Mrs. Benton let it be known that the widower President of the United States would be a proper match for Jessie. Little did she realize that Van Buren was due to lose his bid for a second term in office to the elderly Whig candidate, the hero of Tippecanoe, William Henry Harrison. For the nation was still suffering from the economic panic of 1837, and "Little Van" was to bear the brunt of a voting public looking for any change which might promise something better.

The closeness of Jessie and John Charles reached a climax in the minds of the Bentons at the termination of Van Buren's term of office as the eighth President of the United States. On March 4, 1841, Harrison's inauguration ceremony took place. During this event it became obvious that the vivacious Jessie was quite openly in love with Lieutenant Frémont. When the occasion ended, Jessie was called into the library for a family talk. The senator spoke softly, but he left no room for argument when he said, "We all admire Lieutenant Frémont, but with no family, no money, and the prospect of slow promotion in the Army, we think him no proper match for you. And besides, you are too young to think of marriage in any case."[7]

After talking to Jessie, Senator Benton made it a point to have another conversation with Lieutenant Frémont. This time the senator made it quite clear that it would be much better for everyone concerned if he did not see Jessie so often. Benton the father replaced Benton the senator as he told John Charles that any thoughts of marriage would have to wait for at least a year. There had to be time for Jessie to mature. Mrs. Benton and he had talked it over, and that was their decision. If after that time they still felt the same way, they could discuss it then. Stunned and hurt, Frémont had no other choice, and he agreed to the senator's wishes.

As John Charles faced the prospect of his agreement with Senator Benton, an unforeseen event gave him the chance to entertain Jessie. This was the unexpected death of President Harrison just one month after the inauguration ceremony. While the death of the President did not appear to present an opportunity for the lovers to see each other, it so happened that the quarters which Frémont and Nicollet were using for their work also offered a convenient place from which to view the funeral procession. Seizing this opportunity, Frémont invited the Benton family to see it from the comfort of his place. Senator Benton thanked him but told him that he and Mrs. Benton would have to be elsewhere during the ceremony. Not to be deprived of seeing Jessie, Frémont suggested that his workroom would be a most comfortable place for Grandmother McDowell, and that perhaps Jessie might be allowed to escort her.

When Jessie and Grandmother McDowell arrived at the appointed time, Jessie was amazed at the transformation of the working area, where there were usually papers, maps in various stages of completion, and all the clutter of a considerable project under way. Now, it was entirely different.

The working tables had been carried up to another floor (lots of trouble that) and this best room made charming by many flowers and plants in pots. A cheerful woodfire made a good contrast to the chill gray day, and there was a pretty tea-table with cakes and ices and bonbons. It was for my grandmother's special pleasure that we were there, and only a few of our friends had been added. These wise elders were troubled that their young host should have made such graceful preparations for them—expensive to a "poor army man" —but this was one of the unforeseen chances for meeting. . . . Outside in the raw cold of early spring was the heavy tramp of a great crowd, and the waiting of funeral marches; within, our friendly group excited and amused (and two entirely content).[8]

While the ceremony of death passed by in the cold day, the pleasures of life carried forth at Lieutenant Frémont's expense. He had managed to obtain sick leave for the day, and put his personal budget into debt in order to make this an affair to remember. He built a roaring fire, served tea and cakes, waited on his guests as though he were a headwaiter, and nursed the slight cold which allowed him to be off duty for the day.

Everything was just as he wished it to be, and once again the young couple enjoyed the chance to be close to each other. But the day came to an end much too swiftly. John Charles allowed the joy of seeing Jessie once more to betray him. On the day following the party, Frémont—in a gesture of good will—had geraniums and roses delivered to Jessie's mother.

While Mrs. Benton may have been suspicious about the reason in back of the gift of flowers, events were shaping up to remove John Charles far away from Jessie. The need to survey the lower reaches of the Des Moines River in Iowa Territory was crucial. A steady tide of farmers was moving into this region, and it was vital to have boundaries marked off and maps made of the frontier area between the territory and the state of Missouri. Only by doing this would years of confusion and law suits be avoided. The logical man to replace the very sick Nicollet for this expedition was Frémont.

On June 4, 1841, the lieutenant received his orders from Colonel Abert. The orders were right out of a military handbook, minced no words, and made it clear that the lieutenant was to form his expedition to survey the region, and to strike out for the Raccoon Fork of the Des Moines River, *without delay*, to survey the topography of this frontier land. For the time being, Jessie and John Charles would have to wait.

4

DUTY CALLED LOUDER AND STRONGER THAN LOVE, and the growing closeness of Jessie and John Charles came to a halt for the summer months. Jessie traveled with her family to Virginia for a family wedding. It was not an affair to be carried out in a day or two. Rather, it was a gathering of Mrs. Benton's side of the family. The McDowells and all their relatives came for the meeting of the clan as much as they did for the wedding. While great tables of food fed the throng, there was constant talk of other times. All the tales of past deeds by those long departed filled the days of this special occasion. But while this festive affair entertained Jessie and took her mind off her love, such joy was not the lot of John Charles.

The expedition was quite important, and Frémont did not treat it lightly. Once again he returned to St. Louis, where he had the help of Chouteau's American Fur Company in making preparations for his journey. While here, he received a letter from Joseph Nicollet that made him keenly aware of his mentor's health and state of mind. This had been an expedition Nicollet had wished to head to complete his work on the Northwest frontier. Not being able to make this trek, he had also been forced to part with his key assistant at a time when his services were needed for the completion of the reports and maps of their other expeditions.

The task of surveying the Des Moines River as far upstream as the mouth of the Raccoon Fork was vital. Already, there were some 45,000 settlers in Iowa Territory. This number of migrating farmers was putting the Sauk and Fox tribes on edge as they were being pushed out of their tribal territories. Then to the south, Missourians were concerned about the southern border of the Iowa country. If it were not properly surveyed soon, the inevitable struggle over who owned what piece of land was bound to cause trouble.

In addition to the men he hired from Chouteau, Frémont once again hired botanist Charles Geyer to identify and make drawings and collections of the various plants. But the expedition was operating on very limited funds, and Frémont was only able to pay Geyer the rate for an engagé, or $1.50 per day. This was hardly enough for a man of his talent and experience, and to make matters worse, the botanist was in desperate need of money. Frémont wrote to Nicollet about this situation, and Nicollet contacted Chouteau's and had them draw one hundred dollars against his own account to give to Geyer.

After outfitting at St. Louis, the expedition traveled up the Mississippi River to the settlement of Churchville, Missouri. From this point, the men departed on June 27, 1841. They traveled through wooded country where blackjack oaks and shingle oaks were the dominating trees, and by the end of their first day of travel they had crossed a flat prairie that marked the ridge line between the Fox and Des Moines rivers. They stopped for the night at an isolated farmhouse where the nearest smoke of settlement was a day's journey to Churchville to the southwest or an equally long trip to the northeast where the little town of Portland bordered the Des Moines River.

Twelve miles above Portland, they reached the tiny settlement of Iowaville. Here, they were on the thin line between the farming settlements of the emigrants and the Indian country. Beyond this region, they met Indians on horseback and came to camps beside the river where the men smoked and talked as the women made baskets, cooked, cared for the children, and did all the other chores that kept the camps in order.

Frémont made sketches, took astronomical observations, and jotted notes about the various changes in the course of the Des Moines River. Geyer collected specimens of plants in the region, made his own sketches and notes, and observed the excellent soil that produced the lush growth of wild quinine, blazing star, coneflower, and hackberry. Both men were amazed and fascinated by the varied growth of trees: white oak, black oak, bur oak, shagbark hickory, pignut hickory, pecan, basswood, American elm, slippery elm, river birch, ironwood, Kentucky coffee tree, eastern cottonwood, and dense forests of willows along the riverbanks.

At the trading post of Chouteau's American Fur Company located near a village of Sauk and Fox Indians, they picked up a guide and additional supplies. It was now the end of June and the weather was becoming warm. On July 3, they began the tedious work of surveying the river valley.

The instruments and provisions were carried by a canoe, manned by five men. But the nature of the river made the upstream voyage a slow one. Frémont forded the river to its southern bank and walked through the woods to make his survey sketches, write his notes, and take astronomical readings. Because the canoe was not able to make many miles during a day, he was usually able to find the camp before nightfall. Six days later they reached the Raccoon Fork.

The next phase of their assignment was to follow the Des Moines River from that point to its mouth. This part of their journey took until July 22, as the river meandered 203 miles through a rich valley that was 140 miles long and varied in width from three to four miles.

On the downstream trip Frémont and Geyer observed the fine soil for farming, the lush growth of native plants, the thick forests which presented an easy access to timber, and the construction of earthen dams and mills which white settlers had built or were building. From William Phelps, who headed Chouteau's post near the Sauk and Fox tribes, Frémont learned that, even though the Des Moines River tended to be shallow, steamboats which drew four feet of water were able to come within eighty-seven miles of Raccoon Fork between the first part of April and the middle of June, that keelboats drawing two feet were able to come upstream until July, and that keelboats drawing twenty inches could make the voyage as late as November. With additional work on the river channel, Frémont thought it would become a fine artery of navigation into Iowa Territory and this heartland of growing farms.

By the second week of August, Frémont was back in Washington. This tour of duty in Iowa Territory was a good indication of how well Nicollet had trained John Charles in the art of exploration, but it also showed that the combination of youth and love drove him with as much ardor as his passion for knowledge. Now, the weeks and months of completing the final work on the maps and reports were to come. But most important of all, he was back where he could see Jessie once again, back where the wishes of his heart might, this time, come true.

5

FRÉMONT WASTED NO TIME in paying a call to the Benton home. On the surface, his excuse was to give Senator Benton a personal account of the Des Moines River survey. The explorer was not fooling either of Jessie's parents. Plainly and simply, he had come to see Jessie. His greeting to her, her obvious excitement at seeing him once again, and the muffled giggles of her younger sisters made all this only too clear and did not ease parental worry. There was no denying Jessie's feelings about the lieutenant, and now the success of the Des Moines expedition had served to make him much more glamorous. Absence had done more than make Jessie's heart grow fonder; it had added more stature to Frémont and made him a young man of the moment in Washington—a young man who was everything that Jessie's romantic dreams pictured as the proper man to become her husband.

But the combination of Joseph Nicollet's ill health and the concern of the Bentons about this affair added to the difficulty of arranging meetings for John Charles and Jessie. Frémont had assumed the task of completing the map work which Nicollet had been doing, and this consumed much of his time. Following all the teaching of Nicollet, Frémont pursued the best scientific methods of the time. He consulted their notebooks for the expeditions, and made sure that his own work was carefully based upon what was indicated within these field journals. This meant going over the figures for barometric determination of altitudes, checking all the astronomical observations, and taking into consideration the daily magnetic bearings which had been used to estimate distances in the drawing of field sketches.

Visits to the Benton home became more and more limited. Restrictions were placed upon how much the young couple could see of each other, and Mrs. Benton was determined to see that the agreed-upon waiting period of a year should be observed before any talk of marriage could even be considered. Though the time limit was due to expire within six months, there was no guarantee that the match that Jessie and John Charles desired would ever be allowed.

What neither one had counted on was the service of a natural matchmaker. One turned up in the person of Mrs. J. J. Crittenden, wife of the senator from Kentucky. She allowed them to have secret meetings at her home, and when John Charles and Jessie decided to elope but could not find a Protestant clergyman who would marry them—even with the aid of the ill Nicollet—it was Mrs. Crittenden who became their champion. While the Protestant ministers were much too fearful of arousing the potential wrath of Senator Benton to risk performing such a marriage, Mrs. Crittenden interceded for them with Father Van Horseigh. He agreed to carry out the services, and with the guiding hand of Mrs. Crittenden, Jessie made careful plans so that neither Senator or Mrs. Benton would become the slightest bit suspicious.

On the day of their marriage, Jessie asked permission of her father and mother to visit the Crittenden home. She had done this before, so there was no reason to suspect that anything unusual was taking place. Approval was given for the visit. If Jessie appeared at all nervous, apparently it was not noticed by her parents or her sisters.

On the evening of October 19, 1841, Frémont also appeared at the Crittenden home. He was greeted by Senator and Mrs. Crittenden and was introduced to Father Van Horseigh. This was to be the wedding party: Senator and Mrs. Crittenden were the witnesses; John Charles and Jessie were the principal actors; and Father Van Horseigh was the representative of God and the civil laws of marriage. Here, in an atmosphere of cordiality and excitement, seventeen-year-old Jessie Benton became the wife of twenty-eight-year-old John Charles Frémont.[9] After the wedding ceremony, the couple parted. John Charles returned to his quarters, and Jessie went to her family home. While they hated this separation, it was all they could do until they felt Jessie's parents were in a more receptive mood for the news of their marriage.

While waiting for the proper moment, John Charles and Jessie lived apart as though they were still single. Whenever they could, they arranged to see each other—either under the watchful eyes of Jessie's mother or at some prearranged clandestine tryst. During one of their meetings outside the gaze of

Mrs. Benton, they traveled to Baltimore to visit Nicollet, whose illness kept him confined to his room.[10]

Nicollet was quite concerned about their situation and told them it would be far wiser to get the truth out into the open. If they continued to postpone the day of facing Senator and Mrs. Benton, they would simply make it that much harder ever to tell them. They were running the constant risk of having the news reach the family by means of gossip.

The couple agreed that Nicollet's suggestion was the logical one to follow. There was no point in trying to find the right moment. The truth of the matter was that there was not going to be a right time. No matter how long they waited, Jessie's parents were going to be shocked and very likely angry. Turning toward Jessie, Frémont said, "The sooner the better, but as to that Mrs. Frémont must decide."[11]

During their return to Washington, the couple must have talked at length about what now needed to be done to bring about a speedy resolution of their problem. By the time they were back in the city, Frémont suggested that he should go to see the senator. There would be no hedging, no dodging around the issue. It would be a man-to-man talk, straight to the point. Surely, the senator would accept the fact of their marriage. After all, he was a man who always searched for facts to get at the heart of any matter.

Jessie did not think this was a good idea. It was a sure way to court disaster. She was not going to allow her husband to face her father with this news all by himself. The elopement was as much her doing as it was his. Taking charge of things, she arranged the whole matter by saying, "We will explain together. Come to the house tomorrow morning before ten o'clock. I will ask for an interview."[12]

On the next morning Lieutenant Frémont arrived at the Benton household just before the appointed hour. While he was ushered into the house as a friend of the family, there must have been some curiosity as to what he was doing there so early in the morning. But before questions were asked, Jessie took him to the senator's library. What had seemed to be a good idea lost much of its zest as Frémont looked at the large figure of Senator Benton sitting at his desk. Frémont became pale, then turned red as he finally managed to blurt out the news of their marriage.

The reaction of the senator was immediate, loud, and not at all what the couple had thought would happen. Looking at Frémont as though he were a stray dog in the yard, the senator bellowed, "Get out of my house and never cross my door again! Jessie shall stay here."[13]

In his flash of fatherly anger, Senator Benton had forgotten that his daughter was not one to obey an order simply because he had issued it with a sharp tone. Jessie was the most independent of his children and the one who would stand up against anything in a time of adversity. All of this must have come rushing back to his mind as he watched her hold her husband's arm and very coolly quote the pledge of Ruth. "Whither thou goest, I will go. Where thou lodgest, I will lodge. Thy people shall be my people, thy God my God."[14]

Senator Benton had created his own corner. Now he was backed into it without any room for maneuvering. The choice was up to him. He could reject the marriage and lose his favorite daughter, or he could accept the marriage and gain a son-in-law. Without any attempt to play on Jessie's emotions, without pointing out that her mother would be greatly disappointed and hurt, the senator did the only thing that would keep peace between Jessie and himself, he accepted their marriage. Still, he was not about to have his daughter leave the Benton home. His years in politics had taught him the art of compromise and survival. He had given up his daughter. Now he would dictate where the couple should live. Without asking for any opinion, without expecting any opinion, he told Frémont, "Go collect your belongings and return at once to the house. I will prepare Mrs. Benton."[15]

All the months of waiting to become man and wife, all the secret meetings before their marriage, all the deception had come to an end with a suddenness that was typical of Senator Benton's decision-making process. Frémont left the house to collect his gear, and during his absence the shocked Mrs. Benton saw to it that the guest suite was prepared as a combination bedroom and study for the newlyweds. Whether Frémont knew it or not, the major fork in the trail of his life had been taken. From this point on his destiny was to be linked with one of the most powerful men in the United States Senate. The Benton home became the family home he had never really had during his life. He truly had no people for Jessie to join, and the pledge of Ruth applied more to him than to Jessie as he became an important member of the Benton family.

## ·❦· IV ·❦·

## Toward the Setting Sun

SUPREMELY HAPPY AS JESSIE'S HUSBAND, caught up in his work on maps and reports, Frémont might well have lived out his life as a career officer in the Bureau of Topographical Engineers. But the vision of the American West, the call of a vaguely charted land beyond the Mississippi River, and the symbolic theme of Senator Benton's "road to India" created an excitement that came to Frémont like some strange mission spoken to him during his sleep. Exploration was not to be his escape from the world; it was to become his world.

Around his office in the Coast Survey building and at meetings in Senator Benton's library, Frémont had heard the conversations of his father-in-law and Senator Linn. He had heard the litany of what had taken place in the past and of what remained to be accomplished. These men spoke of the West as though they were recalling the joys of a lost love affair. To them, the Lewis and Clark expedition was a memory to be cherished as a grand design that had sprung from the genius of Thomas Jefferson. But the trek into the wilderness, the incredible journey all the way to the mouth of the Columbia River had taken place in 1804–6. Now, it was almost 1842. Much had taken place in the intervening years.

In 1806, right after Lewis and Clark had completed their journey, Lieutenant Zebulon M. Pike had headed into the Southwest to locate the Red River and find the boundary between what Americans had bought in the Louisiana Purchase and what the Spanish still owned. To try to escape a streak of bad weather, Pike and his men strayed into Spanish territory, built a fort, were captured by the Spaniards and taken to Santa Fé and Chihuahua for a time. Some knowledge of the Southwest came out of Pike's experience, but it was too limited to be of much value.

Following the Pike experience, Major Stephen H. Long headed an expedition that went all the way to the base of the central and southern Rocky Mountains in 1820. Again, this western penetration didn't come back with much in the way of solid information.

Along with these official expeditions, knowledge of the West came from such fur trappers as Jedediah Smith and other mountain men who ranged the unexplored high country and the low deserts as they looked for beaver streams that had not yet been heavily trapped. In their travels, they saw more of the vast land than any of the early government explorers; and they came back with wild tales of salt lakes, jagged mountain peaks that punctured the clouds, a valley of a Thousand Smokes, where hot water shot skyward from geysers, deserts of alkali and endless sagebrush flats, rivers that vanished into the earth, and soil to make a farmer weep for joy in those faraway lands of Oregon and California. But the knowledge that mountain men carried with them was too often a tale told in such places as Pierre Chouteau's headquarters or a St. Louis tavern. These reports of what lay west of the Mississippi were tantalizing, but they didn't provide proper maps and all the necessary details that were needed if Senator Benton and his colleagues were to convince the government of the need for a national role in these distant places.

The same could be said for Captain Benjamin Louis Eulalie de Bonneville's crude exploration of the country between Independence, Missouri, and the Great Salt Lake in 1832–35. For though Bonneville saw mountain man Jim Bridger's "ocean" (the Great Salt Lake) and then traveled as far north as the headwaters of the Missouri and Yellowstone rivers, his 1837 map of western America was not even as reliable as Albert Gallatin's 1836 map of the same area. The only contribution that Bonneville made was to turn his journals over to Washington Irving for rewriting and publication.

This was the state of affairs with regard to western exploration, as Frémont learned in discussion after discussion. The key push had been that of Lewis and Clark. But Meriwether Lewis was long dead, having come to a violent end while traveling the Natchez Trace, and General William Clark was growing old as he traveled out of his St. Louis headquarters to watch over the Indian tribes for whom he was responsible as Indian Agent for the western tribes. Still, Senator Benton and William Clark were good friends. From the aging explorer Benton had heard what the Oregon country was like, had listened to word pictures of rich soil, of great forests, of an endless supply of water flowing into the Pacific, of the bounty of salmon and other fish that made their spawning runs up these rivers, of the great game herds, and of the clear air that let a man see until the curve of the earth cut off his view at the horizon. This was the land of promise, but the way West was not mapped. And while some farmers with enough get-up-and-go were willing to risk the lives of their families to make the long journey to this Eden of the Pacific slope, the best they could ever hope for in the way of directions was to hire an old mountain man to guide them through that easy pass in the Rocky Mountains—the one called South Pass—ease them through the Great Sandy Desert or skirt it along the rocky rim, avoid hostile Indian tribes, and get them to the new land before the first snowfall.

The flaw in the western dream was the need for knowledge. True enough, the Spanish had drifted north from Mexico to settle in the Southwest and California long before there was such a nation as the United States. And news of where the Mexicans were now located and what they controlled had come back to the States from mountain men and Santa Fé traders. But that didn't hand over maps to guide farmers toward the setting sun.

There was talk of a growing British stronghold in Oregon. With the Hudson's Bay Company's major post at Fort Vancouver alongside the Columbia River, there was always the possibility that the British might look upon the weak Mexican control of Alta California as an invitation to conquest. It was well known that the British had a large naval force cruising up and down the Pacific Coast, and this was just the kind of help that any invasion force would need. Senator Benton and his friends fretted about this situation, and they talked at great length about the need to stretch American influence all the way to the Pacific.

Frémont heard all these discussions, heard them time and again until they were as much a part of his thinking as they were to the men who gave voice to this belief. But the need for more information about this horizon country was paramount, and Frémont listened with great interest as Benton and the others talked of sending a government expedition to map the Oregon Trail properly—an expedition that would go as far as South Pass under the leadership of Joseph N. Nicollet and Lieutenant Frémont. The flaw in this grand design was Nicollet's failing health, and there was no avoiding the fact that he was not getting any better as the days passed.

Added to Nicollet's physical condition was the realization that there wasn't enough time to wait for an improvement in his health. There were already rumors of a possible war with Mexico, and there was no way to overlook one inescapable fact: Americans were already in the West; more were on their way, and still more would follow. Restless men on the edge of the frontier were not going to wait for the government to act. Instead, by their own actions they were forcing the government to consider the voices of western advocates and pointing out that it was time to turn away from the Atlantic seaboard, time to look toward the West and to think about becoming a Two Ocean Nation with a distant promised land just waiting for the taking.

2

To FRÉMONT, whose bride was already expecting a child, the idea of being second-in-command on an expedition was an exciting prospect. But all plans were up in the air.

As John Charles and Jessie sat and talked before the warm glow of the fireplace on a stormy evening in the latter part of December, a stranger appeared at the front door with a note of introduction from Ferdinand Hassler. He was a short, stocky man with a shock of light curly hair—a bit on the homely side—and his round face was reddened by the cold. As Frémont heard the man stammer nervously and look about with anxiety, he was not at all sure this man was not some wayward patron of a local tavern who had come to the wrong door.

Momentarily he stepped outside to make sure this stranger was all that he claimed to be. Charles Preuss stammered, and his German accent made it even harder to understand him. But he did manage to explain that he was a skilled cartographer who had once worked for Hassler on the Coast Survey, and that his old position was no longer open as there had been a cut in the Survey's budget by Congress.

Frémont invited him into the house, and they sat and talked beside the fireplace. There was no doubt about the man's credentials. A native of Germany, he had studied the science of geodesy during the early part of the nineteenth century when this science was just coming into its own. He had worked as a surveyor for the Prussian government; and on a trip to Switzerland in 1829, he met Ferdinand Hassler, who was already Superintendent of the United States Coast Survey. Five years later, Preuss and his family emigrated to the United States, and he worked for the Coast Survey until 1839. He resigned his position to become engineer and superintendent for a British mining company. This advancement did not prove very appealing to him; so on this stormy night in December 1841 he sat and talked to Frémont about the possibility of working for him.

Embarrassed by his situation, Preuss insisted that Frémont come to his home so that he could see for himself that it was vital for him to have employment in order to provide for his family. To the lieutenant, this was not at all necessary. Yet, because Preuss insisted, he went with him to verify the family's desperate straits. Then after he made sure that all of them were taken care of for the Christmas season, he talked to him about the possibility of employment.

> There were astronomical observations remaining unreduced. That work, I told him, I could get for him. This he said he was not able to do. His profession was topography—in this he excelled, but that was all. The only thing I could devise was to get for him this astronomical work and do it myself, which I could by working in the evenings. It troubled him greatly that I should have to do this for him, but it was the only way I could come in aid; and so it was done.[1]

## 3

As THE END OF 1841 DREW CLOSER, John Charles and Jessie were fully aware of two opposing forces that would determine their future. Since the death of President Harrison—a devoted campaigner for the opening of the West—the cause of western expansionism had suffered greatly. President John Tyler was fearful of any potential clash with England over the destiny of the Oregon country and only interested in the annexation of Texas. He was strongly supported in his position by Secretary of the Treasury John Spencer, who was extremely vocal in his opposition to any government-sponsored move into the trans-Mississippi West. The fact that farmers were already following the traces of such earlier Oregon pioneers as Nathaniel J. Wyeth and Dr. Marcus Whitman did not make any difference to Tyler or Spencer. If an occasional wagon train of families headed for the Willamette Valley because they had heard talk about the great soil, then these families would have to take their chances without any support from the government of the United States.

Yet there was opposition to official government policy, and it was composed of such Western men as Senators Benton and Linn, who had gathered as many supporters for their vision of a westward-moving nation as they could convince. But their hole card, Joseph Nicollet, was not able to raise himself from his sickbed to aid in convincing President Tyler that the future of the nation was tied into an expansionist push to the Pacific shoreline. Nicollet did let it be known that he backed Lieutenant Frémont as his successor to head an expedition that would make the first decent map of that leg of the Oregon Trail that ran northwest from Westport Landing (present-day Kansas City) on the Missouri River to the Platte River, to Fort Laramie and South Pass.

New Year's Day 1842 came like a good omen from the gods for the Frémonts and the Western men. Washington was treated to springlike weather. All who were invited to the White House reception could go in style and not have to endure either snow or rain. Before noon all the streets near the White House were crowded with private and public carriages. Spectators crowded about waiting for a glimpse of somebody famous as they watched this passing show of Washington society. John Charles and Jessie were the center of attention. Hassler had insisted that they use his "ark" on this very special day; and when they arrived in the London-built carriage, all eyes watched to see who would step out.

Sightseers pressed closer for a good glimpse of this exciting young couple. When they saw them, they gave a loud cheer for their youth and good looks. "Frémont was in dress uniform and Jessie in a formal gown of dark blue velvet, full straight skirt over narrow hoops, the close-fitting bodice outlined at neck and sleeves with frills of Mechlin lace. A tiny cape of blue velvet, strapped slippers, lemon-colored gloves, and a blue-velvet bonnet adorned with three lemon-colored ostrich tips completed her costume."[2] Here was the youth of America all dressed for the occasion; and to many who watched on that warm New Year's Day, the glimpse of Lieutenant Frémont and his beautiful Jessie was much more than the passing of a handsome young couple.

They represented the essence of America. They were the living proof, the symbolic forms of America's promise to anyone who had enough energy and courage to grasp for the magic ring on Democracy's merry-go-round of chance.

As John Charles and Jessie walked from the "ark" to the Executive Mansion, the music of the Marine Band was clearly audible all the way from the vestibule to the out-of-doors. When they entered, they joined a throng of people who seemed to fill every nook and cranny. Dignitaries were everywhere. Senator Benton was holding forth with Senator Daniel Webster and a host of other Democrats. General Winfield Scott was imposing in his full-dress uniform, and sunken-cheeked Senator John C. Calhoun looked like a haunted figure that might have been chiseled from Vermont granite. It was the greatest crowd to grace the White House at a social affair since President Jackson's time.

Inside the White House, Senator Linn was quick to spot the entrance of the young couple, and, with another of his colleagues, he escorted them to President Tyler, who was receiving guests in the East Room. "Tyler glanced approvingly at the radiant couple and paused for a few pleasant remarks before turning to the next in line."[3] Then after John Charles and Jessie exchanged greetings with many friends and well-wishers, Jessie excused herself from this scene of talk, music, and excitement. She was needed at the family home to assist in all the last minute details of preparation for the guests who would come to visit her father. She especially wanted things to be just right for the dinner that would follow the open house.

That evening after the dinner was finished, Senator Benton and other senators and congressmen who believed in the future of the West sat and talked over the preparations that needed to be made if an expedition was to become a reality. All were aware of the $30,000 dollars which had been budgeted by the Topographical Corps. But this appropriation had to be handled wisely in order to avoid arousing President Tyler's suspicion as to the real intent of the expedition. That evening was more than the beginning of a New Year for John Charles Frémont. It was the open door to his life's work.

# 4

THE CONCEPT of Oregon for the Americans ran deep in Senator Benton's background, and his son-in-law was to be the key figure in his design of expansion. To Benton, the idea of holding back for the right political moment, of negotiating a treaty with Great Britain over the division of the Oregon country was a notion fraught with foolishness. The British were already established there, and they had the advantage of having the strong arm of the Hudson's Bay Company entrenched at Fort Vancouver. It was all too obvious that the longer Congress debated the idea of sponsoring an expedition to map the way to the Pacific and plant the American flag in Oregon soil, the less there would be for the taking without risking a direct conflict.

As Senator Benton later put it in his *Thirty Years' View*, "The title to the country being thus endangered by the acts of the government, the saving of it devolved upon the people—and they saved it."[4] In a large measure, he was correct, for by 1842, "upwards of a thousand American emigrants went to the country, making their long pilgrimage overland from the frontiers of Missouri. . . ."[5] But even though Benton and other Western men offered one bill after another in the Senate for the granting of land to Oregon settlers and for the guarantee of government protection, they were not successful in arousing enough support for their cause. Still, there was more than one way to get what they wanted. The fact that Colonel John James Abert was dependent upon Congress for his annual budget for the Topographical Corps gave Senator Benton and the others a means by which they could ease around both the legislative and executive branches of the government and achieve their goal without official sanction. In this manner, the appropriation was made for Lieutenant Frémont's first expedition.

Knowing he was taking Nicollet's place as the leader, Frémont decided that the orders from Colonel Abert did not include anything more than for him to proceed to the frontier beyond the Mississippi. This, according to Senator Benton, did not meet with Frémont's approval. On his own Frémont spoke to Colonel Abert and convinced him that the order should be changed so that the Rocky Mountains and South Pass would be the objective of the expedition. It was this important pass that was already serving as the major Rocky Mountain crossing for emigrants bound to Oregon. What was needed was a thorough exploration of this region that would have "the double effect of fixing an important point in the line of the emigrants' travel, and giving them encouragement from the apparent interest which the government took in their enterprise."[6]

Whether this is actually what took place cannot be documented other than through what Benton and Frémont wrote many years after the fact. Frémont indicated that his secret movements were to avoid arousing suspicion on the part of President Tyler, who had no desire to back a project that might well endanger relationships with Great Britain. He also stated that the expedition's real purpose was quite definitely to aid the flow of migration to Oregon.

The question as to Colonel Abert's knowledge of what was taking place remains a missing factor either because he wished it that way or because any letter from Abert to Frémont regarding South Pass and the Rocky Mountains has vanished in the passing of time. One thing is certain. The letter of April 25, 1842, from Abert to Frémont did not contain any instructions to journey to the eastern apron of the Rocky Mountains and proceed through South Pass. Instead, Abert wrote that Frémont was to head to Fort Leavenworth, survey the Platte River as far as the Sweetwater River. Then if time permitted, he was to make a similar survey of the Kansas. Nowhere in these instructions is there anything which suggests what he was about to do, unless this letter was considered an open invitation to follow the Sweetwater, journey on through South Pass, and cross the Continental Divide.

Yet there must have been some communication between Abert and Frémont prior to the colonel's letter of April, for in his *Memoirs*, Frémont makes it quite clear that he had already started to prepare for his trek into the wilderness as early as March. At that time, he traveled to New York to purchase scientific instruments and to order a rubber boat, according to his design, from Horace H. Day of New Brunswick, New Jersey, for the price of $190.98. The boat was designed "with air-tight compartments, to be used in crossing or examining water-courses."[7] But it was not the sort of thing that was to be examined inside one's home, as Frémont discovered when he had it delivered to the Benton household.

With a flair for the dramatic, John Charles had servants carry the large packing case "to the upper gallery off the dining room where it could be displayed before dinner."[8] Everyone waited for the first glimpse of this wondrous invention. They stood, almost as though at attention, as the packing case was opened with great care. Then as the boat was freed of all covering, as its form was pulled into the open, the whole house was subjected to the odor of reeking chemicals. To Jessie, who was expecting her first child, this was the only thing which was to make her suffer nausea or any unpleasant sickness during her whole term of pregnancy. The stench permeated the air, and servants quickly began to fumigate the house by carrying ground coffee on hot shovels. This only added to Jessie's queasy stomach, and she became quite ill. The offending boat was quickly removed from the house to the barn. But the odor lingered on, and the rank fumes would forever be associated with this magnificent rubber boat.

The boat was not the only new innovation that Frémont added to his list of supplies for this expedition. Another item which he purchased from Dr. James R. Chilton, a New York physician and chemist, was a daguerreotype apparatus. The idea of taking photographs on an exploring expedition had been discussed prior to this time, but it seems quite probable that Frémont was the first man to attempt to capture the look of the West on glass plates. There is more than a passing possibility that he had a measure of success, and some unidentified lithographs in his *Reports* and *Memoirs* may be "based upon daguerreotypes or on negatives copied by Mathew Brady and others."[9]

The months of preparation moved quickly as Frémont purchased what could only be found in New York; as he wrote to Pierre Chouteau, Jr., in St. Louis to order supplies, horses, and mules and make arrangements for the hiring of a guide, hunters, voyageurs, and other workers; and as he hired Charles Preuss as his assistant and cartographer at the rate of three dollars per day. The time for leaving was drawing closer. Soon would come the day when John Charles would have to bid good-bye to his lovely Jessie. This time, at least, someone close to Jessie would be going with him on the expedition. Senator Benton had decided that it would do young Randolph—Jessie's twelve-year-old brother—a world of good to make the journey. One thing led to another, and before Frémont knew it, he had also agreed to allow Randolph's nineteen-year-old St. Louis cousin, Henry Brant, to come along. Taking the two boys did not bother him. He realized that they would be good company, and the experience of crossing that invisible line between Western civilization and the wilderness world was the kind of event that could change the future for any young man who saw the challenge of what lay in back of beyond.

## 5

On May 2, 1842, John Charles said farewell to Jessie, who was six months along in her pregnancy and definitely showing it. Jessie kissed both her husband and her brother Randolph before they left the Benton home to take a carriage to the railway station. It was a time of great happiness for twenty-nine-year-old Frémont, who was about to head his first expedition, but also it was a time of sadness as he had to leave Jessie at this important period in their lives.

Jessie did not want the parting to be unpleasant. With tender care she had assisted her husband "with his new blue and gold uniform, parting the braid and the buttons, making him blush with the glow of her own pride in his appearance. . . ."[10] She was all ready to go to the station with him to stand on the platform and wave good-bye. But this last pleasure was denied her when her mother "collapsed over the strain of parting with Randolph, and Jessie was left behind to care for her and the weeping sisters."[11] Only Senator Benton traveled to the station with Frémont and Randolph. At the station there were friends and colleagues of Benton's who were there to see the explorer off and to offer their congratulations. It was all very exciting. But after the last echo of the steam engine's departing whistle, it was Benton who had to return home and comfort both his wife and daughters.

For Frémont and Randolph ahead lay a grand adventure. They rode the train to Baltimore, where they caught a steamboat to Philadelphia. There they boarded a big mail coach that rocked along the road through the valley of the Susquehanna to Harrisburg, Pennsylvania, where they took a canal-boat to Pittsburgh. Here they caught a small steamboat down the Ohio and watched the river grow wider and wider as one tributary after another joined it. They passed through beautiful country that marked the fringe of a wilderness journey. The grass was tall and green along the banks of the river; great trees reached skyward for the sun, branched out and gave shelter to all kinds of birds that filled the air with their squawks, calls, trills, and whistles. All along this stretch of the Ohio, the country was thinly settled. No great cities broke the border of nature, and the only signs of man were the distant smoke from a farmer's log cabin, or the sight of a family waiting with all their belongings at the riverbank to board the steamer and move on with the growing tide of westward migration. Then the pastoral vista was broken as the steamboat came in sight of the growing city of Cincinnati—a city with paved streets, rows of new houses, and all the hurry-up-and-get-going of a thriving river port. At this point, where the Ohio River was wider, it permitted the traffic of larger steamboats bound up- and downriver between Cincinnati and St. Louis.

Steamboats were crowded with emigrants, land speculators, traders bound for the start of the Santa Fé Trail, drummers with goods to sell, frontiersmen headed back to the wilderness, and a mixture of Old World emigrants from England, Ireland, Germany, and any other country where the chance to get ahead in the world was a thing of the past. A mixture of languages, a collection of pioneers looking for a new opportunity in a new land, and all of them trying to find out every bit of information that might come in handy when they got where they were going.

Down the Ohio the paddlewheeler made her way, carrying a floodtide of humanity outward bound to untilled soil, to adventure and hard work; and many of these brave nomads would find only the quiet of a windblown grave at the end of their journey. Still, they put their lives down as a last stake and moved toward the far horizon.

When the steamboat reached the confluence of the Ohio with the Mississippi, the vastness of the river came upon newcomers and old-timers with a sudden jolt. This was no ordinary river. Here was a part of the continent churning seaward in a rolling, muddy, swift current—a swirling, churning monster of a river that tossed whole trees in its waves as though they were crude boats made by small children. And here was the major lifeline of the frontier, an artery that carried keelboats loaded with hides, furs, and other goods from the back country, hay boats with their floating fields of golden grass, lumber rafts that bobbed with the rushing current as the raftsmen waved and sang out to the passengers on the passing steamboats. This was the waterway to end all waterways, and the vessels bound south sped past the slower-moving ones headed upstream to pick up cargo from America's interior.

To Frémont and young Benton, the sight of this mixture of humanity on the move was a vision of excitement and wonder. This was not something that one got accustomed to seeing. This sight of Americans on the move, of people headed West, only added to Frémont's belief in the dream of Senator Benton that the future of the nation was no longer in the East. The future was even beyond the Mississippi and the Missouri rivers, and once the maps were made, once the country had been described, then Senator Benton's "road to India" would no longer be a dream; it would be reality.

## 6

TWELVE HUNDRED MILES from Cincinnati, and twenty days after boarding the train at Washington, Lieutenant Frémont and Randolph Benton reached St. Louis. Growth was the name of the city, and to both man and boy the St. Louis they had last seen must have appeared to have spread out even more as it tried to handle all the business of Mississippi trade and the growing movement of emigrants.

As Matt Field described it a year later for the New Orleans *Weekly Picayune*, St. Louis was a lively, busy city.

> The expansive Levee is so narrowed by the rising river that the boats stand opposite to the store doors, so near as to present the singular appearance of a contracted street with very queer houses, having tall chimneys all along one side. What is left of the Levee is literally piled up with produce and merchandise. It is with the utmost difficulty that drays can move about, and passengers have enough to do to elbow their way along the sidewalk.[12]

In St. Louis, Frémont and young Benton made their headquarters at one of the city's finest mansions. For they were guests of Mrs. Sarah Benton Brant. Through the Brants, Frémont was introduced to the best of the city's society. This time Frémont moved in a wider range of the growing circle of powerful Americans than during his previous visits to St. Louis with Nicollet and was not secluded among the older and more closed society of French Catholics descended from the original settlers of the city. As for young Benton, he was caught up in all the excitement of explaining to his cousin Henry Brant just what he could expect as a member of this expedition. Both boys were the envy of Henry's friends. But there was much to do and not many days in which to make all the last moment preparations, and Frémont put both boys to work running errands and checking on whatever details he believed they could handle.

Between his arrival in St. Louis on May 22, 1842, and his departure during the first week of June, Frémont checked and rechecked all the food, equipment, and livestock needed for the party. By writing ahead to Chouteau's American Fur Company, he had saved time. The workers at Pierre Chouteau's headquarters had gotten together everything the men would need on their journey into the interior except for the scientific instruments which Frémont had shipped from New York. The days in St. Louis were put to good use as John Charles interviewed men recommended for the expedition. Then as he made his selections, he had the men sign or make their marks on their individual contracts. In this manner, he hired the following men:

| NAME | POSITION | PAY PER DAY |
|---|---|---|
| Lucien Maxwell, <br> a friend of Kit Carson | Hunter | $1.66½ |
| Jean Baptiste Dumes | Cook | .75 |
| Jean B. Lefevre | Voyageur | .81¾ |
| Benjamin Potra | Voyageur | .66 |
| Louis Guion | Voyageur | .87½ |
| Basil Lajeunesse, <br> one of Fremont's best | Voyageur | .75 |
| François Tessier | Voyageur | .62½ |
| Benjamin Cadot | Voyageur | .62½ |
| Joseph Clement | Voyageur | .66½ |
| Daniel Simonds | Voyageur | .62½ |
| Leonard Benoist | Voyageur | .75 |
| Michel Marly | Voyageur | .62½ |
| Baptiste Bernier | Voyageur | 1.00 |
| Honoré Ayot | Voyageur | .83 |
| François Latulipe | Voyageur | 1.00 |
| François Badeau | Voyageur | 1.00 |
| Louis Ménard | Voyageur | .81¾ |
| Clement Lambert | Camp conductor | 1.85¾ |
| Joseph Ruelle | Voyageur | .66½ |
| Auguste Janisse, <br> the only black member of the expedition | Voyageur | .87½ |
| Moise Chardonnais | Voyageur | .75 |
| Raphael Proue | Voyageur | .75 |

This was the key party to leave St. Louis. Along with them were the two boys; Charles Preuss—cartographer and artist—and Lieutenant Frémont. Other men would be added at Cyprian Chouteau's trading post on the Kansas River (in the area of present-day Kansas City) and later at St. Vrain's Fort.

Most of the men selected for this expedition were Creole and Canadian voyageurs who knew the frontier on an intimate basis. Not all were to travel by steamboat for the four hundred miles from St. Louis to Chouteau's Landing. Only seventeen fares were paid at a total cost of $114.75 to sail upriver on the steamboat *Rowena*. The rest struck out on an overland journey to the place of meeting at Cyprian Chouteau's trading post. These men drove the horse herd and were in charge of mule teams and the Red River carts loaded with additional supplies not on board the steamboat.

As Frémont and the others boarded the *Rowena*, only one key man was missing from the party's roster. This was the guide they would need once they headed into the wilderness. Frémont had written to Pierre Chouteau and requested the hiring of the old mountain man Andrew Drips, but Drips was not in St. Louis. Instead, he was supposed to be at Westport, some five or six miles from Chouteau's Landing. Here, Frémont hoped to hire him. But there was a lingering doubt as to whether or not he would be there. Benjamin Clapp, an associate of Pierre Chouteau, had sent a letter to Drips at Westport informing him about Frémont's need of a guide, but this was not too reassuring. There was always the possibility that Drips had not received the letter or would not be available to take the job.

As Frémont strolled along and felt the roll of the boat, he met a man who appeared to be cut out of different cloth than the usual run of mountain men. He was not too tall. His shoulders were broad, and his chest was heavily muscled. But what impressed Frémont most of all was the man's manner. He looked at the blue eyes that stared straight at him; listened to his frank words; and noted his quiet and unassuming way. Frémont learned from their conversation that this soft-spoken stranger was on his way back to the mountains after having enrolled his daughter in a St. Louis convent school. He told Frémont that he could lead him to any point he had in mind.

As a result of the conversation, Frémont offered the mountain man the job as guide at the rate of one hundred dollars per month. In this casual manner, Frémont employed none other than Kit Carson.

A guide was vital. Contrary to the mythology about Frémont as a "Pathfinder," he never considered himself to be one. As the leader of an expedition bound beyond the frontier, he recognized his own limitations and knew that a dependable guide was a key factor in the success or failure of such an expedition.

7

On June 4, 1842, the steamboat *Rowena* docked at Chouteau's Landing at the mouth of the Kansas River. According to cartographer Charles Preuss, the weather was good as the party made its first camp, but the food was bad. This was only the beginning of a journey Preuss was to find uncomfortable in every conceivable way. He thought the men Frémont had hired were crude and uncouth. Clouds of mosquitoes annoyed him. Sleeping on the ground was "damned hard." And before the expedition got under way, even the good weather vanished in a steady summer downpour of rain. Two days after landing, Preuss was quite ready to go home. Writing in German in his journal, he called Frémont "foolish" and a "simpleton."

Though Preuss carped and carried on, most of his grousing was reserved for his daily journal entries. He felt like turning back from the first day, but he continued with the party twelve miles up the Kansas River to Cyprian Chouteau's trading post. Here, he pulled himself together and set to work with the others as they made their final preparations.

While Preuss complained about the food, the living conditions, and the fact that he would have to ride a horse, all the last details for moving out were taken care of as the men worked at a frantic pace.

All were occupied in completing the necessary arrangements for our campaign in the wilderness, and profiting by this short delay on the verge of civilization, to provide ourselves with all the little essentials to comfort in the nomadic life we were to lead for the ensuing summer months.[13]

The final checking and repacking of the goods took place. The eight Red River carts were loaded, and the double teams of mules were looked over carefully to make sure they were in good shape. At the same time, horses, other mules, and oxen were checked for any flaws that might cripple them in the long days of hard traveling. When everything appeared to be ready, Frémont took his final astronomical readings for longitude and latitude, checked the barometric pressure for a last reading on the altitude of their starting point, made all the notations in his journals, and gave the signal to move out.

It was the morning of June 10, 1842, and the expedition was on its way. For several miles Cyprian Chouteau traveled with them on this historic Friday until they met an Indian scout Chouteau had hired to guide the way for the first thirty or forty miles. After that, they were to make their own way on "the ocean of prairie, which . . . stretched without interruption almost to the base of the Rocky Mountains."[14] Chouteau bid farewell to Frémont and the men of the expedition, then turned back as they moved into the frontier.

On this first day the party traveled only about eleven miles from Chouteau's to the beginning of the Santa Fé Trail. They stopped for the night and made their first camp. This was a training stop to establish a pattern for setting up camp in a way that would save time and avoid the loss of supplies and animals. In the long march ahead, it was vital for each man to know exactly what his job was and how to perform it quickly in any kind of weather and on any type of terrain. The wilderness was not a place where a man could expect to get a second chance. All the seasoned men of the expedition knew this from having lived most of their lives beyond the last line of settlements.

The routine was quickly established on this first stop. While it was still daylight, the animals were hobbled and allowed to graze outside the camp circle. The eight carts were the barrier against any potential trouble, and the drivers lined them in a circle that had a diameter of about eighty yards. Tents were set up. Cook fires for the four different messes were started, and while it was still light, the men ate their first meal on the trail. Before nightfall all the animals were driven into the camp circle and were tied by individual ropes twenty or thirty feet long to steel-shod pickets driven into the ground. In this manner they were prevented from wandering away but were given enough room to do a little grazing during the night. With this done, the assignments for guard duty were passed out. By eight o'clock, the first two-hour night watch of three men took their stand. They cradled their rifles and watched for any unusual movement beyond the light of their campfires.

# The Wind of Discovery

SET UP CAMP, eat early, stand watch, roll out before dawn, hunker beside the campfire and eat breakfast, saddle up, hitch the mules to the carts, move out at daybreak and hit the trail—the routine of travel was well established within a few days. When the expedition reached the point at which they expected to cross the Kansas River late in the afternoon of June 14, they wasted no time in preparing for the crossing. But the river was not the easy stream that they had hoped to ford. Spring and summer rains, and runoff water from melting snowpacks in the high country had turned the placid Kansas into more than two hundred yards of roaring, swirling, yellow current. The sound of the fast-moving water made the horses and mules wide-eyed and skittery, and the four oxen were ready to bolt. But the hundred-mile journey from the mouth of the Kansas River to this point had hardened the men for whatever they might have to face.

Horsemen led the way through the shallows, eased the frightened horses into the deep water, gave them a loose rein and started the hard swim to the opposite shore. Riders spoke to their wide-eyed mounts as they felt the cold, swift-rushing water angle the horses downstream. Behind these first horsemen came the rest of the herd—horses, mules, and oxen—all driven by other riders. The horses and mules snorted and hesitated, then, crowded by the shouting drovers, were forced into the water. They swam with their heads held high, necks stretched out, nostrils opened wide, and tails whipping flat out on the rushing current. Like the first horses that had crossed, these animals made it to the other side without drifting too far downstream. But the oxen were another matter. The heavy, short-legged animals bawled and tried to turn back and get away from the sight and sound of the white-capped and swollen stream. The herders shouted, closed ranks, and forced the oxen into the deep water. The terrified animals drifted downstream much faster than the horses and mules. As they did, they managed to turn and make it back to the shoreline they had just left. When Frémont saw this, he ordered his men to let the oxen stay on the east side of the river for the night.

Come morning, there would be more time to round up the oxen and get them across.

Still, the animals were only one problem. The carts and supplies remained. To handle all this, Frémont decided it was time to try the rubber boat he had designed. The men unpacked the strange-looking craft; and when all of it—twenty feet in length and five feet in width—was stretched into the shallows, the wheels, body, and supplies from one cart were loaded aboard. Then, manned by three paddlemen, the rubber boat began its maiden voyage. But the unwieldy craft proved to be more difficult to handle than Frémont had expected. As it began to move downstream, almost turning around, Basil Lajeunesse—a powerful swimmer—reacted in a hurry. He grabbed a line attached to the boat, held it in his mouth, and with his head just above water, swam across, and then helped the men pull the boat over.

Fighting the icy water, Lajeunesse proved it was possible to get the carts across the river on the rubber boat. Following this first success, six more trips were made with individual carts and their loads. Then as the afternoon began to move toward the late hours, Frémont decided it was vital to get the two remaining carts across before twilight. Quickly the men dismantled both carts and loaded them and their cargoes aboard. But luck was not with them this time. The man at the helm was worried about the heavy cargo and leery of the waves that broke over the sides of the boat. In a moment of panic, he lost control. While everyone watched, the boat capsized. "Carts, barrels, boxes, and bales were in a moment floating down the current, but all the men who were on shore jumped into the water, without even stopping to think if they could swim, and almost everything, even heavy articles such as guns and lead were recovered."[1]

Two men very nearly drowned as they risked their lives to save the supplies. And even though the men endured the icy water and suffered bruises and scratches from boulders, they were not able to save everything. Sugar for one of the messes was lost, and a large bag containing nearly all the coffee for the expedition vanished into the swirling water. This was something the men would miss most of all. Other things they could do without. To lose *all* their coffee at the beginning of the journey was more than any of them cared to think about.

That night, as they ate their meal and tried to get warm next to the campfires, Kit Carson and Lucien Maxwell shivered and became ill from having stayed in the water too long. Both men suffered from exposure, overwork, and the long period of having their wet buckskins stick to their bodies. Other men also complained of the cold, and all were tired and not in the best of spirits. Realizing all this, Frémont declared the next day a stopover. This would give the men time to thaw out in the warm sunshine that was already taking on the feel of summer, and it would give them additional hours to dry the provisions, round up the four oxen, and make any necessary equipment repairs.

During their day of rest, local Kansa Indians visited the camp, and, to his surprise, Frémont found one who spoke fluent French. When he asked him where he had learned the language, the young man told him that as a boy he had lived in St. Louis. Through this man and the friendly members of his tribe, Frémont was able to add to the commissary of the expedition. He traded a yoke of oxen for a cow and calf, figuring that they could butcher the calf, milk the cow until she went dry, and then use her for camp meat. He also bartered with these Kansa farmers for pumpkins, onions, beans, and lettuce; traded for fresh butter; and even was lucky enough to trade for twenty or thirty pounds of coffee.

Mapmaker Charles Preuss did not forget the results of Frémont's trading. In his diary entry for that day, he wrote a special comment that for lunch they enjoyed such delicacies as fresh milk, good butter, onions, and even a salad. That night there was strong coffee to warm a man's insides and fresh beef to eat. This was the kind of break the men needed after their ordeal.

Three days beyond the Kansas River ford, news was received of a party of Oregon-bound emigrants who were traveling a few weeks ahead of the expedition. This word came from a hunter from their wagon train who was guiding a man and his wife back to the settlements. The emigrants, he told Frémont, were having more than their share of hardship. Several children had died, perhaps from cholera; and the man and wife he was guiding back had buried their child on the prairie. This news of death on the trail, especially the death of children, bothered Frémont. It also made him think of his own wife, who was well into her pregnancy. With this in mind, he asked the hunter if he would take some letters back to the settlements. Charles Preuss also asked the same favor as he had a letter to send to his wife.

From the hunter Frémont also learned that the emigrants were moving slowly because of their families, the number of cattle they were driving along, and the large, heavy wagons that were loaded with all their household furnishings. The oxen had hard enough going pulling such wagons on dry ground, and a terrible task when the lumbering vehicles had to be pulled across stretches of low ground where the wheels sunk into muddy bogs that were the result of underground springs and the rainfall of spring and early summer.

On the following day the clear and warm weather changed. The early morning start was dismal. A fine, driving rain came out of the north, and the touch of winter still lingered in it. The men were drenched, and they shivered and tried to keep their faces away from the cold wind that made their clothing soaking wet and clammy against their bodies. Only thirteen miles were covered during the day's march, but they did reach the Little Vermillion River and crossed over before dark. That night as they camped, the rain stopped, and the sky became clear for astronomical readings as the temperature dropped to a cool forty-nine degrees.

But wet or dry weather, cold or hot days were to be expected at this time of the year. The men griped about being too cold or too hot, but this was only the talk of a well-disciplined expedition. Each man knew his job well, did it with dispatch, and the miles of travel were tallied by Frémont at the end of each march. Then at night, while the men did their stint of guard duty and took care of their other camp jobs, Frémont retired to his tent after the evening meal to go to work. When most of the men had turned in for the night, he kept his lamp burning as he wrote his observations in his journals: the lay of the land, the longitude and latitude of their position, the altitude above sea level, the high and low temperature readings, the kinds of plants, the animal life, and attitudes and customs of the Indians they met along the way.

Frémont was well aware of the great difference between the movement of his expedition and the haphazard travel of the emigrant party that had already paid more than its share of misery as it headed for the Oregon country. But he also knew that the real purpose for his making this journey, the reason for enduring the cold nights, the hot days, the chilling rain, the swarms of mosquitoes, and the lonely nights away from Jessie was to help prevent the kind of tragedy that had befallen the wagon train of emigrants who were only trying to find a better life.

2

IN THE NEXT FEW DAYS the expedition climbed upward as they moved onto higher plains country. The nights were cool, and before daybreak there was always a heavy dew. Still, the days grew warmer and at times were quite hot. By the afternoon of the twentieth, they had crossed the Black Vermillion, and that night they made camp near a small creek not too far from the Big Blue River. The creek ran through a well-timbered valley, and the camp was pitched beside a very large spring of clear, cold water. In the area of the camp, game was quite plentiful. White-rumped antelope bounded away over the nearby rolling hills, and there were plenty of deer to be seen. In the early evening Kit Carson shot a fine buck for camp meat. But Preuss complained that it didn't make any difference how good the meat might be, the cooks always found a way to spoil it. In his diary entry for that day he wrote a long paragraph about the inability of the French kitchen crew to turn out a decent meal even with the best of food.

By morning the weather moved into summer in time with the summer solstice. At daybreak the temperature was a warm seventy-five degrees; and before the day ended, the searing wind of summer became oppressive, and the men wished for the cooler days they had experienced at the start. The warmth brought forth the blooming of wild flowers. The colors were a welcome sight that blended with prairie grass already turning honey-colored as the days grew hotter. Wild roses seemed to be scattered all over the endless view of the prairie, even between the brushy clumps of sagebrush with slim leaves that had a silver glitter whenever the warm breeze turned them skyward.

To Preuss, the country was becoming very monotonous. It looked the same as far as he could see in any direction, and there did not appear to be any startling change in view. To make things even more disagreeable, the weather was not only hot, it was heavy with water as great thunderheads filled the sky. As they made camp for the night, the lightning struck in the distance like sudden openings between the dark of night and the glare of the sun. This display of light was followed by a low rumble of thunder that gathered sound as it moved across the sky until it crashed about the camp like the sound of a million buffalo stampeding just beyond the circle of carts. Then the rain began to fall, and with the rain came hordes of mosquitoes that Preuss tried to combat by puffing steadily on his pipe and creating a cloud of tobacco smoke around his face.

By morning the sky was clear except for a vague suggestion of possible clouds at the horizon's edge. Things looked much better as the men milked the cow and had fresh milk for their coffee. As they moved onward, the soil was showing more and more sandstone that ranged in color from tawny to red. They nooned at Wyeth Creek, where they found a pack of loose playing cards that had been left behind by the train of Oregon-bound emigrants, and that night they made camp in a well-timbered ravine area not too far from the Little Blue. They were moving at a steady pace that pleased Frémont, for he knew that if they could travel from twenty to twenty-four miles each day, there would be plenty of time to achieve the goal he had set for the expedition of going beyond South Pass and into the heart of the Rocky Mountains.

The following day proved to be one of their hardest marches to date. The country became more and more sandy; prickly-pear cacti bothered both animals and men; and the journey was a dry one for twenty-eight miles before they reached the Little Blue late in the afternoon. "As fast as they arrived, men and horses rushed into the stream, where they bathed and drank together in common enjoyment."[2] But now they were in the country of the Pawnees, who were noted for causing trouble for careless travelers. The unwary were very apt to have horses stolen, at the very least; and if they were undermanned and short of arms, the Pawnees might steal their goods as well. To prevent any possibility of such a thing, Frémont ordered a full complement of men for guard duty during the night.

The next day they continued to pass through the domain of the Pawnees, and it was easy to see why these Indians defended it. The route of the expedition took them up a valley of beautiful soil where a nice stream of sweet water was bordered by groves of cottonwood, willow, and some oaks. Here the game was plentiful: elk and deer, flocks of turkey, and bounding herds of fat antelope. After a thirty-one-mile march through this splendid land, they made camp before a heavy bank of black clouds blew in from the west.

Guard-duty assignments were made for the night, and for the first time, the two boys had to stand their turn as the rain fell in torrents and was driven by a wild wind. The boys were assigned to the ten-to-midnight watch, with Kit Carson to help keep them alert and to train them. Both Randolph and Henry tried to give no indication of fear, but it was not easy for them to hide their concern for the unknown. The experienced men had insisted on telling them stories of bloody and desperate fights they had endured against the Indians on nights such as these when the only light to show any moving figure in the rain and inky darkness was either a blinding flash of lightning or the dying flicker of the campfires creating shadows that might or might not be a warrior crawling closer for a better shot with his hunting bow.

To make matters even more difficult for the young boys, the camp was situated with timbered hollows on all sides of it. With the blackness of the night, the rain, the flashes of jagged lightning, it was possible to see anything the mind could conjure. As the guard stations were several hundred feet apart, the novices were not comfortable with their first night watch. At times, twelve-year-old Randolph would call out to the sergeant of the guard that there was something outside the camp! Something moving! But there was nothing out there to be seen, and Randolph's warnings were shouted so that he could hear the sound of his own voice and the answer from the sergeant of the guard. The two hours were like two days to Randolph and cousin Henry before their first stint of night watch ended. From this night on, they were to continue to take their turn at guard duty along with the rest of the men. There was no room in the expedition to allow two boys to remain protected. Their time had come to do their share of all the work, and that included taking a stand at night watch.

The morning after the initiation of the boys to their new role, Henry Brant made a mistake he was not allowed to forget. Riding at the rear of the party, he saw what he thought was a band of Pawnees. Shouting, "Indians! Indians!" Brant rode his horse at a full gallop into the head of the moving party. He reported that he had seen twenty-seven Pawnees riding along, across the river from the expedition. Without wasting time, Kit Carson mounted his fastest horse and galloped off to check Brant's story. In a short time he returned to the alert and waiting men with a full account of the twenty-seven warriors. When he finished, the whole party had a good laugh at Henry Brant's expense. The war party of Pawnees existed only in the boy's imagination. All that Carson had found were six elk running away from the noise made by the frightened boy from St. Louis.

3

AFTER YOUNG BRANT'S FALSE ALARM the expedition reached a former Pawnee encampment. Here there were scattered buffalo bones from a big hunting party of the previous year, and the wooden frames for stretching buffalo hides were weathered but still standing. That night, as the cooks prepared meals for the four separate messes—messes which both boys felt free to visit —a fight broke out between one of the cooks and his assistant. But so long as the men did not use knives or firearms, Frémont did not interfere. This dispute was settled with two kinds of weapons: frying pans and gridirons.

No great damage was done to either man, and the battle of the cooks broke the monotony of the days of travel and gave vent to pent-up feelings. Most of all, it relieved the tension that had been building as the party moved through the country of the Pawnees, and provided a special relief after young Brant's false alarm.

The next day the party crossed over from the Blue River to the "Coast of Nebraska"—the bluffs of the Platte River. Rain squalls hit the riders at intervals. Thunder and lightning seemed to come from every direction. At one point a flash of lightning cut into the prairie a few hundred feet away and sent up a column of dust as the glare from its light almost scorched the eyes of the men.

Though the days ran together and there was much the same about each one, changes began to occur. By June 27, they reached Grand Island (near the present city of Grand Island, Nebraska), one of the largest river islands that any of the men had ever seen or heard about. Big as Grand Island was to a man crossing the prairie, it was really a band of land that split the Platte River into two channels. Reports of its size varied according to the judges of its length and width. Yet at this time it was at least fifty miles long and over a mile in width. It was a sight to behold after days of endless stretches of prairie grass broken only by an occasional rolling hill. Here, there was enough water flowing for an island to exist; and the fertile sandy soil supported groves of poplars, elm, and hackberry. That night they set up camp near the head of Grand Island, and at daybreak they moved out, taking the Platte River route to Fort Laramie.

They nooned at an open reach of river, set up their guard, gave the horses and mules a chance to graze in the tawny, tall grass, and then sat down to enjoy their midday dinner. Just as they were eating and relaxing, a warning shout of a guard that strangers were in the distance broke the peaceful scene. Men grabbed their rifles. Horses and mules were quickly driven into camp and picketed. Then Frémont's advance guard galloped forward at full speed, yelling as they rode, to meet these newcomers.

There was no danger from the fourteen men the guard encountered. Headed by John Lee and accompanied by a young Connecticut-born newspaperman, Rufus B. Sage, this motley-dressed and forlorn-looking group had their gear in packs on their backs. They were traveling on foot as they headed for the settlements. Sixty days and three hundred miles of hard traveling were behind them since they had left the mouth of the Laramie River with barges loaded with furs. Their idea had been a promising one. They had started with the spring flood hoping to make it all the way to St. Louis

with their shallow-draft barges. Luck failed them when they reached Scott's
Bluff. They found themselves dragging the heavy barges across long stretches
of sand where there was very little water or no water at all. About one hundred and thirty miles out of Fort Laramie they had to unload most of their
cargo and leave a few men to guard it until they returned with pack animals
to bring it in. They tried to carry the lighter furs and their personal goods the
rest of the way. After a hard struggle of fifteen or twenty days, they had to
give this up and cache everything except what they absolutely needed.

That noon, these worn-out men gave Frémont's party some choice pieces of
buffalo meat. In turn the weary travelers were given other supplies, and one
thing which came as a rare treat for them was a supply of tobacco, enough
that they would be able to fill their pipes for a smoke at the end of each day.
As they ate and told the news of the trail, older hands in the expedition
learned the whereabouts of friends they hadn't seen for quite a while, and the
best news of all for men who had run out of fresh meat and were eating salt
pork was that within two days they would be in the country of the buffalo.

4

AFTER LEAVING THE MEN bound for St. Louis, the expedition continued its
march until late afternoon. Camp had just been set up and the campfires for
the messes started when three figures were seen in the distance. With his
spyglass, Frémont saw that they were Indians, and two seemed to be much
larger than the other. Cautiously, all the members of the expedition watched
them move closer and closer to camp. As they came within easy view, they
were identified as two Cheyenne men and a boy of about thirteen.

When they reached the circle of carts and were invited inside the campground, it was easy to see that they had seen better times. "They were misera-
bly mounted on wild horses . . . had no other weapons than bows and long
spears, and had they been discovered by the Pawnees, could not, by any possibility have escaped."[3]

Randolph Benton and the Cheyenne boy looked each other over very
closely, as though they were two strange dogs meeting for the first time. The
young Cheyenne represented something Randolph had only heard or read
about. This was a real Plains Indian boy, a boy who rode with men on horse-
stealing raids against enemy tribes, a boy whose skin was darkened from the
sun and the steady winds that blew across the plains country. To the
Cheyenne boy, Randolph was just as much a curiosity. He had never known
a white boy, a boy who wore heavy clothing that kept the wind away from
his body, and a boy whose reddish-blond hair looked like the reflection of the
sun in the clear water of a spring.

Through Kit Carson and other men who spoke the Cheyenne language,
the adventures of these lonely travelers were translated. Young Benton was
fascinated by what he heard. There had been a small party of them—no

more than six—when they left their people about three hundred miles to the west. Four of them had split off and tried a horse-stealing raid against the Pawnees. But the raid proved unsuccessful. The Pawnees, the men said, were cowards. They did not keep their horses in the open with warriors to guard them. Instead they took the horses into their lodges each night, and it was not possible to steal horses when warriors were sleeping right next to them. Feeling disgraced by their lack of success, the Cheyennes said they had turned back and rode once again across the country of the Pawnees. When they had seen the white camp, there were only three of them still riding together. The others had taken another trail to their home. As for them, they believed they were in good fortune to have come so far through the Pawnee land without having been captured or killed.

Frémont listened to their story and felt compassion for their straits. Through his interpreters, he invited them to stay in his camp for the night and join him for supper. The Indians accepted his offer, and though the Cheyenne boy and Randolph had been wary of each other, they quickly became friends despite their language barrier.

After supper and before nightfall, Frémont asked the Cheyennes about the various watercourses that lay between their present position and their villages. He placed a sheet of paper in front of them, and they drew the locations of the creeks and rivers. As they worked, they told him that they had seen his party when they rode their horses to the summit of one of the nearby hills to look over the country. Seeing his camp, they had decided to join the large party.

This attitude on the part of the Cheyennes indicates that at this time the relationship between the races had not become one of constant fear and warfare. Though the whites were cautious as the Indians approached, this was not because they considered all Indians a threat to their security. It had been a matter of precaution because they knew that raiding bands of warriors thought that any horse herd was fair game, no matter what the color of the owners. At this time, though, many of the whites who moved across the frontier were well acquainted with various Indian tribes and did not look upon them as savages to be shot on sight. This was especially true of the men who made up Frémont's party, as many of them were part Indian, or had Indian wives, and had lived most of their lives among the Indians. These men knew the customs of the different tribes and usually spoke more than one tribal language.

As a result of this live-and-let-live attitude, the Cheyennes were welcomed as traveling guests of the expedition. This insured them their safe passage through Pawnee territory. It gave Frémont an opportunity to learn more about the country from people who knew it even better than the mountain men. And it gave Randolph and the Cheyenne boy time to know each other as they became companions on the trail.

5

PREUSS WAS AT THE REAR of the caravan. His sketch pad was on his knee, and he was drawing in the features of the land for his map. Two days had passed since the Cheyennes had joined the party, and the country was changing. The altitude was higher. The grass was tall in the fertile bottom land between rolling hills, and beside the river there were broken hills with narrow canyons—hills that could hide a small army. Then, as he viewed the whole terrain, Preuss was amazed and delighted when he saw three stands of timber in the distance. But as he began to draw the trees on his sketch pad, he noticed that there was movement. It wasn't just the wind swaying the branches. The trees were moving along the ground! Then he heard the men shout, and he knew his vision of groves of trees was an illusion.

The men riding point heard a dull murmuring that meant only one thing. Ahead were herds of buffalo, moving along and feeding on the spring grass. That night there was going to be fresh meat in camp. It meant that once again John Charles would know the thrill of a buffalo hunt. Even from his distant view, he saw the moving animals as more than just a mass. "Here and there a huge old bull was rolling in the grass, and clouds of dust rose in the air from various parts of the bands, each the scene of some obstinate fight."[4]

Now, the steady low noise of the expedition's day-to-day movement gave way to laughter and shouts of excitement. The men were anxious to ride at a wild gallop into the feeding herds and shoot fat young cows that would have sweet and tender meat. On this first hunt three young cows were killed. But in the wild chase after the fast-running animals, Kit Carson's horse fell headlong. Kit was thrown over the horse's head and slammed into the ground. While he lay there stunned, his horse got up and ran off. Right behind him, Lucien Maxwell rode at a full gallop. Without even stopping to find out how badly injured Carson might be, Maxwell pursued Carson's horse to save the bridle and Spanish bit. But tough and wiry Kit only suffered from bad bruises, and no bones were broken.

That night the camp was in high spirits. Meat—fresh, sweet buffalo meat—was consumed in quantities that would have amazed townfolk. The first course was a thick soup with chunks of meat floating in it. While the men ate this, and licked the grease from their fingers, whole rib racks were skewered on sharp sticks in front of the fire and turned around as soon as one side was seared and cooked blood rare. When the meat was warmed through, the men cut the ribs with their razor-sharp hunting knives, and ate rib after rib of the burgundy-colored meat. As they did, tongues were cut into strips and quickly roasted on sticks held over the low-burning fires. Marrowbones were placed on the hot coals to roast, and when they were done, the dark pudding of blood and fat was scooped out with knives and fingers and quickly eaten as though it were the finest paté.

After this feast of meat and more meat, men continued to eat throughout the night. Night watchers were handed chunks of roasted meat by other men who had awakened with a terrible hunger for more meat. They would eat and talk for a while, return to the fire for a tasty morsel, eat their fill, then go back to sleep. To men who were sick of a daily fare of salt pork and an occasional piece of venison or antelope, to know that they were now going to have a daily meal of sweet-tasting buffalo meat was a joy that made the hard work of the daily marches and all the routine jobs easier to endure. For they knew that at the end of each day they could hunker or sit cross-legged next to the campfires and eat their fill of hump ribs, side ribs, leg roasts, and tongue, and top it all off with fingers of bone marrow.

The whole scene was exhilarating to Frémont. This was life at its best. Man and the wilderness came together in a natural way, a way that belonged to the long history of man's ability to adapt to whatever his surroundings might be and to become an integral part of nature, a part that did not need any of the comforts of town or city living. In this atmosphere, among these men of the wilderness, and in this untamed country, John Charles found a fulfillment that was missing in the constricted roles men were forced to play in the name of civilization.

As the party moved along the next day, they reached even higher ground, and the country next to the river was better timbered. But the great scene of the day was a magnificent buffalo herd of seven or eight hundred animals coming from the river, where they had been to drink, moving slowly along the plain as they grazed. The wind was blowing away from the herd, so that the buffalo did not pick up the scent of the intruders. The country looked like good ground for a chase, and the cool wind of morning made everything just right to ride into the herd and kill some cows before the animals could run for cover among the river hills. This was more than Frémont could resist, even though he knew that as the leader of the expedition he should not risk injury. But he was young, and it had been some time since he had known the thrill of galloping his horse beside a running buffalo and making the kill. He was weary and ready for a break in routine. He joined Carson and Maxwell for the hunt.

All three riders started toward the herd at a hard gallop, closing in on them rapidly before the buffalo had a chance to break and stampede. Each rider came at the milling animals from a different direction in order to confuse them and cut off avenues of escape. Riding with his reins hanging loose, John Charles let his mount have its head and closed in on a cow trying to escape danger. He was only a yard away from the frightened animal when he fired. The ball struck down through the front shoulders and chest, and the sudden shock of death sprawled it nose first into the ground as blood spurted from the wound and out the nostrils and mouth of the dying animal. Looking around, Frémont saw that Carson had also killed a cow and was already on the ground, tying his reins to the dead buffalo's horns as he got ready to start to butcher his kill. In the distance, Maxwell neared a running animal, and, though Frémont did not hear the report of his gun, he saw the smoke curl away from the end of the barrel.

With three cows down and the herd already making a thick cloud of dust as it ran in flight, the hunters left the dead game to be butchered later, and rode after the herd. But as they neared the running buffalo, hearing their hooves pound against the plain, the dust was so thick that it was almost impossible to see them until they rode right into the moving mass that barely parted for their entrance. Above all the rest of the noise, the one thing that remained etched in Frémont's mind was the clattering of horns as the compact herd bumped against each other in their wild flight.

Before the riders saw it, their chase took them into a prairie dog village that stretched for at least two miles. In the dog town, there was a threat to the horsemen from hole after hole dotting the whole area, holes leading to underground quarters for these sharp whistling rodents. John Charles looked ahead to see how Carson and Maxwell were doing in this uncertain ground, but he saw only one rider, who was almost out of sight. At the same time, he saw the long, dark line of the caravan slowly moving along about three or four miles ahead of him. He slowed his horse to a walk and started in the direction of the faint outline of the mounted riders and the crawling Red River carts.

When he reached the moving line of the expedition, he was soon joined by his companions of the hunt. All three of them carried some meat, and they sent other men back for the remainder of the kill before the coyotes and wolves could find the slain animals and devour the rest of the meat.

That night, they made camp at the head of an island that was at least fifteen miles long. This was Brady's Island (near present-day North Platte, Nebraska), named after a man who accidentally shot himself to death at this place. His friends had buried him there, but they had not taken the precaution of covering his grave with rocks. Frémont's men became aware of this as they found human bones scattered in the open—bones bleached and dried from the ten seasons or more since a wolf pack had picked up the odor of the dead man, uncovered the grave, and eaten their fill. All that night, as the campfires burned low and carried the aroma of cooking buffalo meat in the breeze, the expedition heard the steady howling of wolves just beyond the perimeter of light, waiting on the outskirts of the circled carts for a chance to move in and pick up the leavings.

6

FOURTH OF JULY MORNING opened with the smell of smoke in the air. They were two days west of Brady's Island, and early risers and men on night watch saw the morning sunrise as a dim, reddish color. The sun was faintly visible through clouds of smoke that drifted on wind currents that swirled about as though earth and sky had joined together in a great bonfire. And while the men were safe from the distant wildfire, experienced hands knew that as the blaze raced through mile after mile of sun-dried grass, animals fled ahead of it to escape the heat that would leave a blackened wake of charred earth.

A salute to Independence Day roused the men who were still asleep. The cooks for the four messes already had hot coffee and freshly roasted buffalo meat waiting for breakfast. Before the men ate, John Charles drew something from the special supplies he had packed in addition to what was absolutely necessary. All the men stood around the compound as they were served cups of red wine to salute the day. "Red fire water," the Indians called it, and Preuss—always the grumbler—wrote that it was only some more of Frémont's "miserable red wine." Even so, Preuss did not turn down his share, and all the men toasted the day and gave a cheer to the States before they ate.

At this moment of celebration, a bawling buffalo calf darted wildly between the carts and ran through the camp. Close behind the calf, the men saw two wolves pull up short, turn, and circle around the corral of carts. This gave the frantic calf a short lead. But as the men watched this game of life and death, the fast-running wolves were joined by twenty to thirty more of their pack. Taking turns, they swiftly closed the space between them and the terrified calf before it could reach the buffalo herd in the distance. A few buffalo bulls, feeding away from the main herd, attacked the wolves in a valiant attempt to save the calf. But they were driven off by the pack, and the calf was half eaten before it died. Frémont and the men watched with the kind of interest that man always has for the doomed, but they knew there was nothing they could do to save the calf as they didn't even have a horse saddled and ready to give chase to the wolves.

After the scene of predator and prey was over, and after the men had finished breakfast, Frémont gave the order to move out. To Preuss, who thought this would be a day of rest in celebration of Independence Day, this came as a rude shock. All the time he had sipped what he considered to be an inferior wine, he had thought they would take the day off. But the day was to be like any other. Pack the gear. Hitch mules to the carts. Saddle the horses. Make sure the mess fires were put out with dirt and that no hot coals were left to give off sparks, and hit the trail in a never-ending movement across the endless plains.

The look of the country began to change as they moved along. They approached a stratum of marl-like rock, cut and shaped by wind and rain into a series of sharp cones and peaks like chimneys coming up from an undiscovered village beneath the earth. The surface of the prairie was covered with great patches of sunflowers that blazed in bright yellow and orange as they reached toward the sky.

In the afternoon, clouds of dust appeared in the distance as though a whirlwind had failed to rise into the air and spent its twisting energy on the surface of the ground. The hunters, who had seen this sight many times before, told Frémont that it was caused by herds of buffalo heading to the river for water. In a short time, the whole area was darkened by the masses of shaggy animals moving along. John Charles had never seen this many buffalo before. The herds filled the prairie bottom, covering a region two miles wide as they traveled between the river hills. The animals were no more than ten feet apart, and in this small area, he estimated there were at least 11,000 buffalo on the move. The herds seemed to be everywhere, "on every side, extending for several miles in the rear, and forward, as far as the eye could reach, leaving around us as we advanced, an open space of only two or three hundred yards."[5]

The day's march was called to a halt soon after they passed the buffalo. Camp was set up within a few miles of where the trail crossed the North Platte, and all hands got things ready for a Fourth of July celebration. St. Louis friends had provided the expedition with preserves and delicious fruitcake. Camp cooks prepared macaroni soup, choice cuts of buffalo meat, and pots of hot coffee. The Cheyennes asked what brought about this great feast, and after they were told, they wanted to know if such "medicine days" came very often.

To cap the meal, John Charles opened the brandy keg and all the men were served a stiff drink to toast the flag. Everyone was welcome to drink to the day. The Cheyenne boy had too much brandy and staggered around the camp as his head whirled and the men laughed at the boy's first experience with drunkenness.

Far from the cities and towns that had grown and flourished under the flag of the United States, this night under the floor of the sky where the stars were like illuminated trail markers in the dark of the universe, the men ate and drank their fill. Then, as they lay on the grass and had their evening smoke and the first guards assumed stations for night watch, Frémont took leave and began his evening's work.

## 7

THE MORNING after the Fourth of July, Frémont gathered the men about him and announced a change in plans. The party was to be split into two groups. The main expedition would continue to follow the North Fork of the Platte River to Fort Laramie. A smaller party would take the South Fork, travel to St. Vrain's Fort, where fresh mules might be available, and survey the country with the idea of establishing a line of outposts that would serve as a protective link between the settlements and South Pass. The group heading up the South Fork would consist of Preuss, Maxwell, Bernier, Ayot, Lajeunesse, Frémont, and the three Cheyennes, whose village lay up this river. The remainder of the expedition—twenty-five in all—would be guided by Kit Carson and headed by Clement Lambert, who could read and write. Frémont instructed them to make a cache of everything that was not absolutely needed at Ash Hollow and continue on to the Laramie River where, with luck, both parties would meet.

Before breakfast, even before the sun gave off much warmth, John Charles and his party had their supplies securely tied on a pack mule. The bulk of the scientific instruments were aboard the mule, but Frémont carried the chronometer on his person. All were armed and ready to take on a considerable force if need be. After breakfast, after John Charles bid farewell to young Benton and Henry Brant, his party rode beyond the circle of carts and soon were out of sight.

The first day they covered forty miles, and Preuss was worn out when they finally made camp. He was not accustomed to riding horses, never thought that he would learn, and was thoroughly discouraged by this turn of events. Then, to make things even worse, the cook had packed very little coffee, and failed to include sugar, flour, salt, or pepper. Even Frémont, who usually tried to overlook such hardships, never forgot their first night's meal away from the expedition. They had made a long, hard ride, and all they had to eat was a small amount of bread, the meat of an old buffalo bull, and no salt and pepper to make even that palatable. It was miserable fare, and each man grumbled about it, managed to gulp down enough to ease the hunger pangs, then in very ill humor settled into his blankets without the usual time of conversation near the fire.

In the morning, Frémont took one look at Preuss and knew that he was not cut out for this kind of journey. As long as there were the Red River carts to give him a break away from the horses, as long as the daily mileage was not much more than half of what the past day's ride had been, he was able to hold up. But this kind of traveling was far more than the city-bred Preuss could tolerate, and he was much too valuable to risk his health on this excursion away from the main trail. So, after early morning coffee, bread, and tough buffalo bull meat, Frémont called Preuss and Bernier aside and told them to ride back to the main branch of the Platte and join the rest of the expedition.

Nobody could have been happier about this new decision than Preuss. Six hours after Frémont bid farewell to Preuss and Bernier, they were back at the North Fork of the Platte. Here, they waited until the main party appeared. That night they enjoyed brandy, good buffalo cow meat, and salt and pepper to flavor it. It was the first time in his life Preuss had realized how much man depended upon salt, and he savored every mouthful of his meal.

After Preuss and Bernier had vanished from view, Frémont and the others followed a southwest course along the valley of the Platte. They passed the remains of an old fort, saw more and more sunflowers mirroring the sun, and suffered from the increasing warmth of the day. Relief from the heat came in the late afternoon when a wind-blown storm from the southwest lit up the big sky with sudden flashes of lightning that streaked in long blinding white-ness against the dark-blue thunderheads, followed by a low rumble of thunder that came rolling across the sky like a steady firing of cannon from the heights. The storm ended almost as quickly as it started; and when it was over, herds of antelope broke into a springlike movement ahead of them, and from each clump of sagebrush came countless bluish-gray jack rabbits that flicked their long ears and bounced along, shifting direction as though they were dodging invisible arrowheads.

Sunup to sundown, hour after weary hour, the days of travel formed their pattern. The major change was the weather. Mornings were cool, almost cold. By late afternoon the sun was like a red blister in the sky, and the heat closed in on the men and animals. All sweated. All slowed their movement to a crawl. Then the heat was broken by spectacular summer storms that kept smaller animals in their hiding places and sent herds of wild horses and buffalo on frantic stampedes.

On the third day after leaving the expedition, the daily pattern of events was broken. Craggy-featured Basil Lajeunesse cupped his eyes for a better look at movement in the distance. Something dark, something that wasn't a buffalo herd was out there. The Cheyennes saw the same movement, and got ready to ride for cover.

Lajeunesse passed the word to Frémont, who knew they were too far from any help and isolated on the plains. He quickly ordered the only thing that seemed possible: Ride for the clump of timber near the river, and ride as fast as the horses could go. There they would have a chance to put up a stout de-fense against the fifteen or twenty charging and yelling warriors headed to-ward them and gaining ground fast.

Beyond the oncoming warriors, though, a greater danger caught the atten-tion of Maxwell, who pointed it out to Frémont. Nearby, among the rolling hills, the main striking force of the Indians had been waiting out of sight. Now, as these hard-riding horsemen broke into the open and joined each other, the terrible truth of Frémont's position was all too clear. The odds against his party were obvious. There were at least three hundred warriors in the central striking force.

Drawing their guns and urging their horses into a full gallop for the trees, the small exploring party rode for its life. But even the trees were a false hope. The grove of timber was on the other side of the river, too far away to reach before they would be forced to fight. There was no choice. They had to fight it out in the open as the sound of hard-running ponies and yelling warriors neared their point. Maxwell raised his rifle and drew a careful bead on the warrior leading the charge. Then, just as he was about to squeeze the trigger, he lowered his weapon and shouted at the warrior in his own lan-guage, "You're a fool, God damn you, don't you know me?"[6]

Startled by the sound of his own language, the warrior swerved his horse, passed by Maxwell and the others, wheeled his mount in a tight turn that threw up a cloud of dust, and waited as Frémont and Maxwell rode toward him. He held out one hand to Frémont, as though he realized he was the leader. With his other hand, he struck his own chest and said that he was an Arapaho. Then he looked at Maxwell and smiled at his old friend, who had lived in his village as a trader. Soon the whole party was surrounded by Arapahoes asking one question after another. They stared at the three Indians who had made a fast retreat and were just now coming into view. Who were these Indians? That was the big question they wanted answered right away, but before Maxwell could answer, the Arapahoes recognized them as friendly Cheyennes. Even so, they made it clear that they were not altogether pleased. If these Indians had been Pawnees, they would have had the excitement of killing three of their old enemies.

The Arapaho chief invited Frémont and his men to come to his nearby village. Through Maxwell, Frémont told the chief that they would be honored to visit. For the Cheyennes this turned into a stroke of good fortune. As they entered the large encampment of buffalo-skin tepees, they discovered that other Cheyennes were traveling with the Arapahoes. Among them were their own families, who had joined this large party for a buffalo surround.

Except for small children and dogs, the whole camp was a scene of hard work. Even the terrible heat did not stop the activities that needed to be done as quickly as the freshly cut chunks of buffalo meat were brought in. For the temperature had risen to an oppressive 108 degrees, and the meat had to be butchered and cooked or sliced into pieces for the drying racks. Otherwise it would spoil.

Older women took care of the children and worked around the fires, while Frémont saw younger women coming in from the surround "galloping up, astride their horses, and naked from their knees down, and hips up."[7] They followed after their men to help butcher the meat before they returned to the hunt. Old men who were still able to ride at a full gallop rode back and forth between the surround and the camp and brought in more meat. The few old men who were either crippled or much too old to hunt any more chipped arrowheads and spear points. The camp was a scene of constant movement: horses, dogs, and children were everywhere, and were completely caught up in the excitement. The laughter and shouts of joy by the successful hunters and their families made the encampment a warm, friendly place—a place with the feeling of home and family, a feeling that John Charles missed as he saw the give and take of love and joy that turned the Arapaho village into a scene that only differed in culture and custom from the lively gatherings around the dinner table at the Benton home.

But the culture, before the tide of white emigration changed it, was different from any he had ever dreamed he would get to know. The lodges—he counted as many as 125—were scattered on both sides of an irregular passageway that allowed the horsemen to ride into the village without any trouble. As they rode along, Frémont saw a "tripod frame, formed of three slender poles of birch, scraped very clean, to which were affixed the shield and spear, with some other weapons of a chief. All were scrupulously clean, the spearhead was burnished bright, and the shield white and stainless."[8] This was something right out of the days of feudal chivalry; and as he rode by, he couldn't resist a sudden impulse. He reached out and touched the shield with the barrel of his rifle. Even as he did this, he knew it was not in the best of form, and he wondered if some angry warrior would take offense. Instead, he was invited to stop and eat with the chief.

A buffalo robe was spread out on the ground, and the women of the lodge placed a large wooden bowl of buffalo meat on the center of it. The chief lit his pipe, passed it to Frémont and the other men, and asked them to begin eating. As they proceeded with dinner, the chief continued to smoke. One by one, six other chiefs came to the lodge and quietly sat cross-legged on the robe. All during dinner, the chiefs remained silent. When the meal was finished, the host asked Frémont the purpose of his journey. Maxwell translated as he explained that his party had come to see the country and that they were looking for places to build forts along the trail to the mountains. All this time, the other chiefs remained silent as they listened and smoked. Each chief took the pipe as it was passed his way and, before smoking, "turned the stem upward, with a rapid glance, as in offering to the Great Spirit, before he put it in his mouth."[9]

Frémont wondered what the response to the proposed forts would be, and he considered that his frank statement of purpose might not please these plains warriors. But none of them showed any sign of surprise; none showed any sign of anger. They sat and smoked, and nodded with grave courtesy as Maxwell translated the reasons for the expedition being in their country. After the chiefs had heard everything Frémont had to say, they had nothing to say about this intrusion, nor about the plans for the building of forts. It was as though the wind and the patter of the first drops of a late afternoon storm against the tepee's skin covering had been the only sounds uttered.

Frémont looked at Maxwell, and they both got up and thanked their host. Maxwell was handed a bundle of dried meat, and the two men mounted their horses to ride to where the rest of their small party was camped near the mouth of Beaver Creek. As they rode through the driving wind and the cold shower, all that John Charles knew was that they had been treated with kindness and formal hospitality by the Arapahoes; but that did not mean the Arapahoes welcomed the idea of forts on their land. The only thing at all clear was that for the time being there would be peace, and the explorer and his men would be allowed to pass this way without worry of attack.

## 8

THAT SAME NIGHT, as Frémont and Maxwell told their companions of their experience with the Arapaho chiefs, Kit Carson and the main part of the expedition also encountered strangers on the trail. The first glimpse of the riders heading toward them gave Preuss and some of the others only feelings of doom. Surely those were Indian ponies, and the trailing pack horses were loaded with furs or buffalo robes. To the inexperienced, these buckskin-clad men had to be Indians on the move.

Carson thought otherwise, and as the riders drew nearer, he knew it was a band of trappers bound for the settlements to trade their load of furs. The man riding in the lead was an old friend. He was known throughout the Rocky Mountains and wherever there might be a good beaver stream. Kit had trapped with him, had gotten drunk on rotgut whiskey with him at the annual fur rendezvous, and had fought the Blackfoot with him when the odds were not in favor of a man's keeping his hair. For this weather-beaten man whose face was furrowed by wind and sun, by rain and snow, this man whose blue eyes had seen the grand days of the fur trade come and go, was none other than "Old Gabe" to his friends and Jim Bridger to strangers.

Both parties camped together that night, and Carson and Bridger talked of men they knew, of where they had last been seen, and of dead friends who had gone beyond the divide. The two boys—Benton and Brant—were fascinated with this legendary character who had signed on to be trapper with the Ashley-Henry Company in March of 1822. Bridger had been only eighteen years old—a year younger than Henry Brant—and he had been drawn by the same St. Louis newspaper ad that caught the fancy of what was to become the nucleus of the most famous company of American mountain men. Because he had not been able, a friend read the notice to him that began: "To Enterprising Young Men." Enterprising was respectable; but the real catch, the thing which trapped tough young men and made fur trappers out of them or sent them to early deaths, was the idea of adventure, of going up the Missouri River to the Rocky Mountains, of seeing the Indian tribes that Lewis and Clark had visited, and of giving up apprenticeships in a line of drudgery or backbreaking days behind a plow for a life of excitement in an unexplored land.

During the talk around the campfire, Kit told Bridger that he was the guide for Lieutenant Frémont. "Old Gabe" asked the key question: Where were they headed? Which way did their fork-stick point?

Fort Laramie, on through South Pass, then north into the Wind River country, Carson told him.

Even to a city man like Preuss there wasn't much doubt what Bridger thought of their journey. The mountain man had just come out of that country, and he shook his head from side to side. This was not a time to travel beyond Fort Laramie. Sioux were spoiling for trouble, and in the past autumn he and his men had been forced to fight them at the cost of lives on both sides.

When Carson asked what the trouble was all about, Bridger replied that the Sioux were upset about the whites and were not very happy about the Snake Indians either. To make things even more dangerous, the Sioux had formed an alliance with the Cheyenne and the Gros Ventre and were attacking all whites and other Indians who dared to travel through Sweetwater Valley and head north for the Wind River country. The best thing to do was to turn back, and that was his sage advice. But if they insisted in going on, he offered his services to take the party by a route he knew to the head of the Sweetwater, a route that was not so likely to have war parties traveling it.

Most of Frémont's men were ready to take Bridger's advice, and Preuss thought it the most prudent thing they could do. After all, there were only twenty-five men in the party, hardly enough to put up much of a battle; and it was hard telling what had happened to Frémont and the men with him. Maybe this mountain man was right. Maybe they should survey the Platte River and let it go at that. Better to have that information and return with it than to be killed in an attempt to carry out what even Bridger thought was impossible.

As for the boys, the only mention of their feelings about the situation was noted by Preuss. Henry Brant was all for hightailing it back to the settlements.

But Frémont wasn't there to make a decision, and the man he had left in charge, Clement Lambert, let it be known that he was determined to follow Frémont's instructions to the letter. Here was the situation, and all night long the men talked about it. When dawn broke and the campfires were covered with dirt, Lambert gave the orders to move out. They were on their way, Sioux or no Sioux, and two days later they passed Courthouse Rock and camped that afternoon at the base of Chimney Rock. Preuss was fascinated by the wind-carved form of the rock, and he took time to make a drawing of it. He also complained that it was too bad it was a formation of crumbling clay and not one of hard granite. Still, he had to admire its form even though the country around it was much drier than anything he had seen so far. As they rested around the campfires on this Sunday in July, Preuss and all the other were very conscious of one thing: in three more days they would be away from the open plains and in the safety of Fort Laramie.

## 9

THE SAME DAY that Preuss sketched Chimney Rock, Frémont and his small party reached St. Vrain's Fort, which was operated by Bent, St. Vrain & Company.[10] They were greeted by Marcellin St. Vrain and made welcome to the hospitality of the fort. They had climbed to a mile above sea level and were getting closer and closer to the Rocky Mountains. They were within viewing distance of Pikes Peak, but a forest fire that had been burning for several months cut off any glimpse of it.

But the day before his arrival at St. Vrain's Fort, the sky had broken clear enough to allow a glimpse of the snow-covered summit of Longs Peak, some sixty miles in the distance. This was the thing which thrilled him most of all, this nearness of the Shining Mountains, the great central chain looming on the horizon like a rock fence built by some ancient race of giants. There was what he had hoped to see, and his ultimate goal on this expedition. He would journey into the heart of these peaks that divided the plains and the "road to India" on the other side, the road to the Oregon country. He would see it for himself, not just hear the stories told in St. Louis and other places by trappers who had been there to trap the beaver streams and rendezvous in deep valleys they called "holes." There in the distance was what all the dreaming and planning had been about, and he would ride through South Pass and mark it for settlers following the setting sun. Then he would climb the highest peak he could find in the Wind River country, measure it, taste the wind of discovery, and return home to Jessie and tell her what it was like to journey in a land that still had the look of creation.

# Beyond South Pass

THREE DAYS OF HARD TRAVEL across a dry land of cactus, greasewood, and sagebrush—three days of heading north by northeast from St. Vrain's Fort—took Frémont and his men across Crow, Lodgepole, and Horse creeks and on through Goshen Hole, a pass between two steep ranges of hills that appeared to block the way and prevent any possibility of getting over them. Three days of using buffalo chips for fuel, enduring temperatures that started out in the seventies at sunup and reached past the one-hundred-degree mark by noon, and staring at the barren land that appeared to have been wind-burned and sunburned into a country of ash-colored soil and rocks—this was a journey around the rim of hell.

The only relief came at creek crossings. At these watering places, where melted snow water flowed seaward toward the Gulf of Mexico, there was grass along the banks, chokecherry and gooseberry bushes, and isolated groves of willows and cottonwoods. Yet in this arid land there were buffalo herds living off the protein-rich grama grass. On the third day of travel, the men headed west of north, struck the Platte River about thirteen miles away from Fort Laramie, and saw the tracks of the Red River carts and the animals of the main expedition which had passed that way just two days before.

The sun was a red glow in the western sky when Frémont first saw Fort Laramie. After days of being away from the large party, after scouting the South Platte country and seeing only St. Vrain's Fort and the big Arapaho encampment, the sight of Chouteau's American Fur Company post was highly impressive. Located on the left or north bank of the Laramie River, the fort stood twenty-five feet above the water, and it gave the impression of something the army might have built. The thick adobe walls were white-washed and picked up the reflection of the sunset. Picketed, protected by large bastions at its angles, this was not a post to be treated lightly by any potential foe.

Pitched near the walls of the fort was a cluster of skin lodges, and it was clear from the language sounds of the people who were watching the approach of Frémont and his men, that this was a camp of Sioux. Behind the Sioux tepees and the prominence of the fort loomed the background of "Black Hills and the prominent peak of Laramie mountain, strongly drawn in the clear light of the western sky,"[1] a light which gave the whole scene a striking, almost haunting appearance, as though all of it were seen as a desert vision.

Looking over the whole area, Frémont saw a familiar camp circled by Red River carts. There, a short distance above the fort and near the riverbank, was the expedition. Frémont and Maxwell rode in the lead, and they reached the camp just in time for supper. This came as a special treat after having been reduced to a steady diet of meat, and they enjoyed the chance to eat bread and have a cup of coffee. All the members of the company were in good shape—including Randolph and Henry—and Frémont relaxed and talked of his experiences during his long detour of the past ten days.

He quickly learned from Carson and Preuss, that the final part of the expedition's journey was in serious jeopardy. Jim Bridger had warned them that the Sioux were on the prod. All this was very discouraging. The plans called for an examination of South Pass—one that would give Preuss and himself time to gather data for a decent map of the area as well as information for a detailed report for Oregon-bound emigrants. This was not something that John Charles was going to give up easily. He intended to find out all that he could about this business of hostile Indians. He was too close to his goal to turn back, and he knew that if he did not manage to do all he had outlined to Colonel Abert and Senator Benton, his chances of getting support for another expedition at a later date would not be as good. That evening he would listen to all that the men had to tell him. But any decision about turning back was something he would put off until he had talked to the man in charge of Fort Laramie. He had letters to deliver to James Bordeaux,[2] the fort's bourgeois.

2

As Frémont approached the fort on the morning of July 16, he was impressed by its size and strength. Built in a quadrangular form, the adobe structure was designed to offer a maximum of protection. The walls were fifteen feet in height and were topped by a row of sharp wooden stakes. Inside the fort, he saw that the buildings were one story tall and constructed so that the back wall was against the wall of the fort. The living quarters were not overly large, and each apartment had a door and a window facing the open yard. The great entrance to the fort was topped by a square tower, and there were loopholes for riflemen. Then at diagonal corners from each other there were square bastions that could accommodate men with rifles so that it was possible to sweep all four sides of the fort with a deadly fire in case of attack.

This was a solid establishment, one that Chouteau's American Fur Company could depend upon to protect their interests. But it wasn't the first fort to occupy this strategic position. Before the construction of this adobe structure, the original post beside the Laramie River had been built of cottonwood logs in the summer of 1834. The builders had been William Sublette and Robert Campbell, who had the guts to invade the fur trading territory of John Jacob Astor's American Fur Company. When the two men and their helpers finished the post, they named it Fort William in honor of rough and tough Bill Sublette, who had never been known to turn down a fight. The builders of that first fort even had the good taste to toast the foundation log with a bottle of imported champagne they had carried along for the occasion.

Soon, Fort William was called Laramie after the nearby river; and it remained a log fort until the year before Frémont saw it. By that time it had passed into Chouteau's ownership, and, as the cottonwood logs were rotting, the whole fort had to be rebuilt. Where possible, the logs were maintained, but they were covered with a solid coating of adobe. As John Charles entered the main gate on this July morning, he saw a post which had been completely rebuilt in such a manner that it would withstand any kind of weather and any mass attack by plains raiders.

Frémont was greeted by a short, stocky man, whose round face was adorned with a black mustache. He was not dressed in the usual buckskins. Instead, he was wearing a regular business suit, even a vest. The only difference between this man and a businessman in St. Louis or New York was that his suit was badly in need of pressing and bagged at his knees. Standing alongside Bordeaux were two of his clerks, Charles Galpin and Philander Kellogg. Everyone was friendly, and Bordeaux was anxious to look over the mail Frémont had brought. But that could wait. It wasn't every day that company came to visit the fort. At Bordeaux's invitation, Frémont joined the men of the fort on a shaded seat beneath the great entrance. Here the morning breeze funneled through the open gate, across the board floor, and stirred up an occasional dust devil in the main square.

Altogether, there were about sixteen men stationed at the fort. As near as Frémont could tell, they were all married to Indian women, and there was no shortage of children laughing and playing. As he talked to Bordeaux and his men, he looked about and noticed stacks of supplies. "The articles of trade consist on the one side almost entirely of buffalo robes, and on the other, of blankets, calicoes, guns, powder, and lead, with such cheap ornaments as glass beads, looking-glasses, rings, vermilion for painting, tobacco, and principally, and in spite of the prohibition, of spirits, brought into the country in the form of alcohol, and diluted with water before sold."[3]

The sight of the alcohol disturbed him greatly. Though he knew Chouteau had to trade it in order to compete with the coureur des bois, or itinerant trader, who was willing to do anything for a quick profit, it still bothered John Charles to see Chouteau involved in this business. This was a sure way to destroy the Indian as it meant a trader could take one keg and buy every-thing from an Indian from his furs to his wife.

Though Frémont was concerned about this illicit trade in alcohol, he was more worried about the bad blood that now existed between the Sioux and the whites. From Bordeaux he learned that the trouble had started in early August of the previous summer. Henry Fraeb—one of the founders of the Rocky Mountain Fur Company—had been trapping the Little Snake River country when he and his men were jumped by a combined band of Sioux, Cheyennes, and Arapahoes. A two-day battle followed when the trappers dug in and made a rough fight of it. During the bloody affair, Henry Fraeb and four of his men were killed, but not before they had taken many of the war-riors with them. Both sides finally gave up the field of battle. The Indians re-treated with their dead, and the remainder of the Fraeb party lit out for safer ground.

Frémont's party had come this far, and they were close to their goal. Now, it seemed they would be forced to halt just short of South Pass and the Rocky Mountains. War parties were on the move ahead of them, somewhere in the vicinity of South Pass. Or, at least, so the talk went. Some reports were definite. Some were indefinite, and some were out-and-out rumors or wild stretchers. But no matter which way a man cut it, warriors *were* on the prod against trappers, emigrants, or any other tribe they didn't happen to fancy. According to Bordeaux and the other men at Fort Laramie, it was a good time to stay close to the adobe walls, to take it easy and let pressing business wait for another day, another week, another month, or even another year. There was no point in courting trouble. Trouble usually found a man soon enough anyway.

When Frémont returned to his camp, he was not at all surprised that his men had figured that, once he had heard about the Indians from Bordeaux and the others, he would tell them that they would do their exploring in an-other direction.

A party of Oregon-bound emigrants headed by Dr. Elijah White and Lansford Hastings—the same Hastings who was to write the guidebook that helped to create the disaster of the Donner party—had managed to go be-yond Fort Laramie. But they had run their string of luck as tight and as far as it would go without breaking. For if they hadn't been able to hire the white-haired mountain man Thomas Fitzpatrick—called "Broken Hand" ever since a gun had blown up in his hand[4]—not one of the White-Hastings party would have seen the other side of South Pass.

Frémont heard this story at the fort, and it was common talk that more than three hundred Sioux had set out after the emigrants. But hiring Broken Hand to guide them as far as Fort Hall had made all the difference for the lives of the emigrants. Fitzpatrick was not caught off guard, and he was ready to make the Sioux pay a high price in lives if they carried out their attack. So they talked and talked some more until the Indians agreed to let this party pass. But the Sioux sent word back to their encampment beside Fort Laramie that there would be no more whites coming that way without a fight.

Even Kit Carson didn't like the way things were breaking. He knew Bridger and Fitzpatrick from a long way back, from days and nights when the going was rough and the odds of staying alive were short. If they said the Sioux were raising hell, there was no call to think otherwise. It was easy to see that if the expedition moved ahead, they were bound to run into very serious trouble, so serious that the whole lot of them would be lucky if they ever saw the white walls of Fort Laramie again. Kit was so sure of this that he requested that someone who could read and write take down his will.[5] For while he was ready to follow the soft-spoken Frémont anywhere, there had to be provisions made for his daughter's future in case he didn't return from a journey that had all the makings of a trail to death.

Carson's attitude bothered Frémont. He feared that his desire to make out his will before going on would panic other men and keep them from leaving the fort. John Charles tried his best to ease the worries of men who were already talking about asking for a discharge. In his quiet and thoughtful approach, he spoke to the men and managed to have them postpone any hasty decisions until he found out more about the Indian situation. To investigate things as much as he could, Frémont accepted an invitation to join fur trader Joseph Bissonette[6] for dinner at the rival post of Fort Platte.[7]

3

JOHN CHARLES strolled the mile from his camp to his host's residence. As he approached it, he looked it over carefully. It had a rough, unfinished look about it. The men who had started to build it had used the local adobe, but they either didn't quite know what they were doing or simply lost interest in their task. Fort Platte was a crude enclosure with three sides that were a combination of walls and houses. The fourth side was wide open to the river and unprotected from any attack that might come from that direction. Yet this partially completed structure was the best home Joseph Bissonette had lived in since he had come to the frontier as an eighteen-year-old boy in search of adventure. Here he stayed in comparative comfort with his second wife, a Brulé Sioux, who was the mother of fourteen children. But these weren't his only children. His first wife, an Oglala Sioux, had given birth to seven other children before she died.

As they dined on the best food available at Fort Platte, Bissonette suggested that it would be wise if the expedition took along an interpreter and perhaps two or three of the old men from the Sioux encampment. There was danger, he said, only if the warriors did not see the old men and the interpreter before they charged. That was a risk that had to be taken if the expedition was to continue.

Of course, the logical man to hire as an interpreter was Frémont's host, but he made it clear that he was not willing to travel as far as the explorer wished to go. He would consent to go as far as the Red Buttes, about 135 miles beyond Fort Laramie. That far he would go because it would give him a chance to meet the returning Sioux and trade with them. Beyond the Red Buttes, though, it would not be possible to engage him because of his business; and it would not be possible to hire a Sioux to accompany them, as they would be entering the country of the Crows and that would be running too much risk. The two tribes were old enemies with a long history of hatred between them.

With no other choice, it seemed to Frémont it would be better to have an interpreter for part of the way, at least until they had bypassed the Sioux warriors; so he asked Bissonette if he would consider taking on the job. This was agreeable to the trader, but there was the matter of payment for his services. Here, Frémont was not in a position to bargain. All the factors favored Bissonette, and his pay scale as guide and interpreter for eight days came to thirteen dollars per day along with his food.

With the matter of an interpreter and guide arranged, Frémont was able to return to his camp and assure his men that the hiring of Bissonette gave them insurance against warriors. But, there would be time for any man to receive a discharge—with full pay up to this point—and there would be no hard feelings. All this was said in a quiet, almost drawing-room tone of voice by a lieutenant whose slight frame and small stature hardly made him a heroic type. Yet the quiet attitude, the calm approach to danger, and the penetrating stare of this young officer's eyes made it difficult for any man to consider disobeying him, much less to ask for a discharge. Frémont waited, and when he received no reply, he made it quite clear that there would be days of work before they departed. All the equipment and supplies had to be checked and rechecked, as they would be traveling into mountainous terrain. While the men were doing all this, they could consider what he had said to them. Then if they wished to change their minds about going along, they would still be able to do so.

During the days of preparation, John Charles, Geyer, and Preuss worked at bringing all the information they had gathered up to date. If disaster should occur, at least the results of the expedition from Cyprian Chouteau's to Fort Laramie would be completed and safely stored at the fort. This meant working on the maps for that portion of the trek, making final astronomical calculations at this point, and pulling together all their observations on animals, geological formations, fossils, river systems, plant life, and possible sites for protective forts along the trail to Oregon.

Never a day passed, though, without interruptions by Indians. They would come to the tents, step inside, ask for presents, or simply stand and watch this strange work that was taking place. Such intrusions only added to Preuss's dislike of Indians. He resented their sitting in his tent and smoking while he tried to work. To him they were like a band of ignorant, dirty children who were totally immoral. Why, they even traded women in the same fashion as a man might deal with slaves. And the whole thing was infecting Frémont's camp. Even young Henry Brant had been caught up by these barbaric customs. In a dig at Brant, Preuss noted in his journal that the stupid boy had traded a horse for a woman, but that he was not able to keep up his duties as a husband; so after three weeks the woman deserted him and went over to Fort Platte to favor another man with her love.

While Preuss tried to avoid the Indians as much as he could and made it all too clear that he did not like them, the opposite was true of Frémont. He accepted an invitation to one of their feasts, where he sat on the ground surrounded by fat, playful puppies. The entree was cooked in an iron pot suspended over hot coals, and portions were served in wooden bowls. John Charles thought the meat tasted rather like mutton, though it was a bit glutinous. Still, it was not at all bad considering that this was the first time he had ever eaten dog. The only thing which bothered him was the fact that the playful puppies around him would also end up in the pot one day.

The friendship and respect that Frémont showed the Indians was returned by their obvious feeling of friendship for him. Not only did they invite him to have a dog feast with them—and that was no small honor—but also they enjoyed watching him work and showed great respect for the sanctity of his tent.

> Here, only came the chiefs and men of distinction, and generally one of them remained to drive away the women and children. The numerous strange instruments applied to still stranger uses excited awe and admiration among them, and those which I used in talking with the sun and stars they looked upon with especial reverence, as mysterious things of "great medicine."[8]

By the evening of July 20, everything was in order. Frémont gathered the men around him. Again he discussed the dangers of the journey ahead, pointed out that Bissonette had given approximate directions to the first camp where he would catch up to them, suggested this was a good time to write any letters to loved ones to leave at the fort, and once more offered to discharge any man who had decided against this journey through South Pass and into the rugged mountain country. Only one man stepped forth and asked to be discharged and paid. This was Registe Larente, who had always complained of illness whenever there was hard work to be done. Larente would be no great loss to the expedition, and Frémont was glad to see him drop out of the party.

Then John Charles announced that there were two other members who would remain at the fort. Henry Brant and Randolph Benton were to wait for their return. To Frémont and the men, the real loss was Randolph. The boy had become a camp favorite with his questions and his good humor, and the men would miss him, as he kept them in good spirits at all times. Yet all agreed it would be too much of a risk to take him along. If it did turn out that they had to fight the Sioux, then his presence could easily cost the lives of some men. They would have their attention divided between the battle and the need to protect the boy.

That was a sad night for Randolph. He had come so far and enjoyed every moment of it, but now he was to be stopped just short of seeing the famous South Pass and the Rocky Mountains. Sensing how he must have felt, John Charles gave him a job to take his mind off the fact that he wasn't going. Each day he was to have the task of winding up the two chronometers that would be left behind.

The wisdom of leaving the boys at the fort came home the next morning after the men had struck their tents, packed the mules, saddled the horses, and walked over to Fort Laramie for a stirrup cup of home-brewed hard liquor. Just as they were taking a farewell drink, a number of Sioux chiefs intruded and presented a letter written in French, a letter that had been prepared at Fort Platte:

Mr. Fremont: The chiefs having assembled in council, have just told me to warn you not set out before the party of young men which is now out shall have returned. Furthermore, they tell me that they are very sure they will fire upon you as soon as they meet you. They are expected back in seven or eight days; excuse me for making these observations, but it seems my duty to warn you of danger. Moreover, the chiefs who prohibit your setting out before the return of the warriors are the bearers of this note. I am your obedient servant,

Joseph Bissonette,
by L. B. Chartrain.

Names of some of the chiefs:
The Otter Hat, the Breaker of Arrows,
the Black Night, and the Bull's Tail.[9]

Frémont considered the note he had been handed. Then he shared its contents with Kit Carson and the other men he relied upon. When he finished, one of the chiefs stepped toward Frémont, shook his hand, and then spoke:

"You have come among us at a bad time. Some of our people have been killed, and our young men, who are gone to the mountains, are eager to avenge the blood of their relations, which has been shed by the whites. Our young men are bad, and if they meet you they will believe that you are carrying goods and ammunition to their enemies and will fire upon you. You have told us that this will make war. We know our great father has many soldiers and big guns, and we are anxious to have our lives. We love the whites, and are desirous of peace. Thinking of all these things, we have determined to keep you here until our warriors return. We are glad to see you among us. Our father is rich, and we expected that you would have brought presents to us—horses, and guns, and blankets. But we are glad to see you. We look upon your coming as the light which goes before the sun; for you will tell our great father that you have seen us, and that we are naked and poor, and have nothing to eat, and he will send us all these things."[10]

Other chiefs followed and gave very much the same oration. Frémont listened to what they had to say, and when all were finished, he had Bordeaux ask the chiefs to have two or three of their men ride with his party until they encountered the young warriors. They declined this invitation. They were too old, they claimed, to ride so many days on horseback. It was a time in their lives to stay close to the lodges, smoke their pipes, and let the young men take care of any warfare. It wouldn't do any good if they did come along, for they had no control over the young men. If the warriors wanted to fight, they would do just that. Nothing that old men could say would stop them.

Not wishing to accept this attitude on the part of the old chiefs, Frémont spoke to them and had Bordeaux translate his speech:

"You say that you love the whites; why have you killed so many already this spring? You say that you love the whites, and are full of many expressions of friendship to us, but you are not willing to undergo the fatigue of a few days' ride to save our lives. We do not believe what you have said, and will not listen to you. Whatever a chief among us tells his soldiers to do, is done. We come here and see this country, and all the Indians, his children. Why should we not go? Before we came, we heard that you had killed his people, and ceased to be his children; but we came among you peaceably, holding out our hands. Now we find that the stories we heard are not lies, and that you are no longer his friends and children. We have thrown away our bodies, and will not turn back. When you told us that your young men would kill us, you did not know that our hearts were strong, and you did not see the rifles which my young men carry in their hands. We are few, and you are many, and may kill us all; but there will be much crying in your villages, for many of your young men will stay behind, and forget to return with your warriors from the mountains. Do you think that our great chief will let his soldiers die, and forget to cover their graves? Before the snows melt again, his warriors will sweep away your villages as the fire does the prairie in the autumn. See! I have pulled down my *white houses*, and my people are ready: when the sun is ten paces higher, we shall be on the march. If you have anything to tell us, you will say it soon."[11]

John Charles watched the sun climb toward the height he had said would determine their start. As it neared that point, he gave his last instructions to Randolph and Henry. Then he ordered his men to mount and get the Red River carts ready to roll. At that moment, Chief Bull's Tail arrived. There was a young man, he told Frémont, a man he could send to help guide them if the explorer could describe where they planned to make their evening camp.

Frémont thanked the chief, and a general description of where they planned to make camp was translated. Chief Bull's Tail understood where the young man might find them, but there was one final matter. This man was very poor. He would have to be given a horse.

That could be arranged. Bissonette had extra horses at Fort Platte. The Sioux could get his horse there, and ride to the campsite with Bissonette. Of course, the animal would cost some money as the Indian would keep it once his duties were over. Frémont agreed, but the cost of one horse from Fort Platte came to thirty-six dollars, a rather steep price for a grass-fed pony that came from a herd of wild horses and cost the fort no more than a few glass trinkets. But there was no other choice. It would not pay to insult Chief Bull's Tail, who had made such a generous offer as to send a man along. The deal was made. Frémont grasped the chief's hand for a farewell shake. Then he turned and waved good-bye to the boys and men at Fort Laramie.

Within a short ride, the party moved among the nearby hills and were out of sight of the fort. Following what later came to be known as the Hill Road between Fort Laramie and Warm Spring, the men traveled along the divide between the Laramie and North Platte rivers. An early camp was made at Warm Spring Canyon just above the spring. Here Frémont and his men were involved in trying to put up an Indian tepee he had purchased when Bissonette and the Sioux and his woman arrived.

The tepee, which was to become a Frémont trademark on his expeditions, was much better than American tents, which were too thin to offer much protection against the cold or the wind. When perfectly pitched, such a lodge gave a shelter some eighteen feet in diameter and twenty feet tall. A fire could be built in the center of the lodge to keep it dry and warm, and the smoke would funnel upward through the opening at the peak of the conical shape. The other advantage to such a dwelling was that in warm weather it was possible to raise the lower part of the skin covering to allow the breeze to pass freely through.

All of this was very well, but now as the men awkwardly tried to erect the tepee, the Sioux woman began to laugh. Then she offered her assistance and gave the men a lesson on how to put up a tepee in a hurry.

That night the men were in good spirits. But the next morning the easy road to South Pass began to turn into a rough trip through country that didn't match all the stories they had heard about the route. As they moved into the Laramie Range of the Rockies and the going became tougher mile after mile, John Charles questioned Bissonette about their trail. It was then that the truth of the trader's actual knowledge about the country came out. He admitted he did not travel around a great deal. In fact, he rarely ever got out of sight of Fort Platte. But at least Bissonette got along with the Sioux and spoke their language fluently, and this was all that Frémont could count on. Meanwhile, with the help of men like Carson, Lajeunesse, and Maxwell, they would find their own way to South Pass and educate Bissonette in the process.

4

BEFORE LEAVING the Warm Spring Canyon camp, Frémont and Basil Lajeunesse walked around the area and down to the Platte River, where they found a fine open prairie as well as some handsome groves of cottonwood trees. On the higher slopes of the small stream entering this fork of the Platte, they noticed plenty of pine trees and good building rock. All in all, it was an excellent place to keep in mind for the establishment of a military post.

The way Frémont and Lajeunesse saw it, this site was close to Fort Laramie, located near all the tribes that might cause trouble for emigrants—the Sioux, Cheyennes, Gros Ventres, and Crows—in a good location to protect the Oregon road through the valley of the Sweetwater and South Pass, and situated in such a strategic spot that a series of other posts connected by wagon roads would create a protective chain from here to St. Vrain's Fort on the South Platte and Bent's Fort on the Arkansas. This would be an ideal way to protect the mountain passes, aid the emigrants coming west, and form another line of trade with the neighboring Mexican settlements. To add to the desirability of this location, the fertile river valleys to the south would support crops, and the plains where buffalo grazed had the look of good cattle land.

As they broke camp and moved upward toward the west, the country began to change drastically. The soil was sandy and wind-blown. Here and there one could see some bunch grass hanging on, but in this high and dry plains country, the plant of survival was sagebrush. Tough, twisted, wiry clumps grew everywhere and fouled the wheels of the carts.

The whole region had the odor of sagebrush—a strong aroma like a mixture of camphor and turpentine. It was an odor to clear the congestion from a man's sinus, and the whole desolate, barren land smelled to Charles Preuss like an herb shop or pharmacy every time the wind blew.

Looking for water and grass, the party kept going hour after hour. The dried meat had run out, but one of the hunters had managed to kill an antelope which would be their supper once they reached a suitable place to camp. Bone-weary, stiff and saddle-sore from riding all day, feeling hungry and ready to make camp almost anywhere, they kept on moving as the sun set into a long glow that slowly became the first slate sky of early evening. Then at eight o'clock, after a hard trip of twenty-seven miles over country that was anything but a well-traveled trail, they reached good grass and water at Horse Shoe Creek, where they made camp for the night and tried to ease their hunger pangs by sharing one antelope.

In talking to Kit Carson and Lucien Maxwell, Frémont learned that this was a bad year, a year of drought. The snowpack in the high mountains was not as great as usual. The spring runoff was of short duration. Rivers were running much lower than usual. Some creeks were almost dry, and springs that ordinarily could be counted on for water were so dry that it was hard to believe they had ever held water.

On the next day's march, the country seemed to get even drier as they climbed higher on the plateau. Dry grass—what there was of it—crackled underfoot like ancient, brittle paper. The only exception was the sagebrush, but even that appeared as though it might not make it through the summer days of mounting temperatures and searing winds with the feel of fire.

Conditions were so bad that the Indians traveling through this area had resorted to something which they normally did only during the cold months of winter. They were cutting cottonwood boughs to feed their horses as they moved across the arid land. And when a noon halt was called at a cottonwood grove, the ground was covered with boughs Indians had cut for their horses. Having no other choice, Frémont and his men did the same thing; but as they did, he was concerned that using a source of winter feed might mean the difference between life and death for travelers moving through snowdrifts or caught in wind-driven blizzards.

Suddenly scouts galloped into the noon camp. There were Indians just ahead! Probably some of the Sioux warriors making their way back to Laramie!

Using the only defense available, Frémont ordered a move toward the river, where there was a steep, high bank. The men formed a close barricade with the Red River carts, bunched the horses and mules, hobbled and picketed them. The guns were fired to be sure they were in good working order, then reloaded; and a forward line of men took their places under cover of the bank facing the direction the Indians were expected to come from. Bissonette and the Sioux guide rode out to meet and talk to the Indians.

The expedition had just got its barricade set up and its front guard of men ready when Bissonette and the Sioux returned. With them were two Sioux warriors who were in a sulky mood. They didn't really want to give out much information but, faced with a large force of armed men, grudgingly gave bits and pieces.

They had been part of the big war party.

The one trailing the emigrants?

Yes, of that band.

Where were the others?

Most of them were in the Wind River country to attack the Crows.

But what about the emigrants? Did they attack the emigrants?

They saw the emigrants at the rock the whites call Independence Rock, but they did not fight them.

Bissonette persisted with his questioning and asked why they had not attacked the emigrants.

We belonged to a small party. Ten or twenty. Some wanted to shoot the whites. We did not wish it.

Were all the others in the country of the Crows?

No. Some were in other parties working their way down the Platte heading back to Laramie.

Some of Frémont's men were all for killing the Sioux right where they stood, but he prevented a senseless shedding of blood that would only cause trouble for the whole region. Then he had Bissonette ask the Sioux about conditions ahead. What about the water, the grass, the game?

The buffalo were not to be seen. Water was hard to find once a man rode away from the rivers. And grass was no more, not since the grasshoppers had passed over the land.

Frémont had been aware of grasshoppers ever since leaving Fort Laramie. The ground seemed to be in constant movement with flying clouds of insects that took off just ahead of their footsteps. But the news from the Sioux was even worse than he had expected. The land was without food for men and animals. It was as though the wrath of ancient gods had stricken the whole region with a triad of drought, pestilence, and famine.

When Bissonette had gotten all the information from the Sioux that they were willing to give, Frémont gave them some plugs of tobacco for their trouble. They were anxious to get on their way, suspicious about the armed whites, and in a thoroughly nasty mood.

The information obtained from the Sioux wasn't totally correct. Two days after the meeting, the expedition came into an area where the grass had not been devoured by the grasshoppers. They found some buffalo, and the hunters killed three fat cows. That night the camp had fresh meat; and when they stopped on the following day, they prepared meat for the possible lean days ahead.

Low scaffolds were erected, upon which the meat was laid, cut up into thin strips, and small fires kindled below. Our object was to profit by the vicinity of the buffalo, to lay in a stock of provisions for ten or fifteen days. In the course of the afternoon, the hunters brought in five or six cows, and all hands were kept busily employed in preparing the meat, to the drying of which the guard attended during the night.[12]

The expedition was near the present site of Inez, Wyoming. While they were fortunate in getting a supply of buffalo meat, John Charles was disturbed by the loss of one of the barometers. He had carefully watched all his instruments as they traveled the rough ground from Fort Laramie, as they were needed when he reached the mountains. But now, through an accident, he was reduced to the use of the remaining standard barometer.

Using a method discovered by sea captain Thomas H. Sumner in 1837, Frémont took a fix on the sun's meridian altitude with his sextant every day at noon. He determined his latitude by the printed mathematical tables in the *Ephemerides of the Heavens*. Then he checked the Greenwich time as kept by his chronometer, compared this against the local time as determined by the observation of a star of known right ascension across the local meridian, and calculated his longitude to give him his hour angle. With the triangulation of the sun's meridian altitude, the latitude and the longitude, he was able to ascertain the daily location of the expedition with a high degree of accuracy. The method was not a hit-and-miss affair such as one might find in most of the exploration that was taking place throughout the world—carried out by dedicated amateurs. Instead, he followed the refined scientific approach he had learned under Joseph Nicholas Nicollet. Further, Frémont brought his own curiosity and highly creative talents into sharp focus on every detail to be observed, charted, identified, catalogued, and added to the work of his cartographer. And, though Preuss put caustic remarks about him in his private journal, he never hesitated to make use of Frémont's aid, his helpful suggestions, and his concern for Preuss's own comfort and protection so that he might accomplish his vital cartographic work.

Now, the days began to run into names of the land—Box Elder Creek (Frémont called it Dried Meat Camp), Deer Creek, the largest tributary of the Platte between the Sweetwater and the Laramie. There were more meetings with Indians: Oglala Sioux, Arapahoes, Cheyennes—all of them headed home, drifting back from a drought-stricken land, no longer interested in fighting anything other than grasshopper plagues and a gut-rumble of hunger that stayed with a warrior like a wolf waiting for the weary prey to stumble and fall, to show the final sign of weakness.

Bissonette spoke to these half-starved men. Their tired words panicked the fur trader. Now, they were near the Red Buttes. This was as far as he had said he would go. There was no need for him to risk his life by going on to see country he didn't need to see. He was not going any farther than here. He rode up to Frémont and, speaking to him in French, tried to make it clear that it was not wise to keep on with this journey.

Frémont did not ask Bissonette to go the one more day to Red Buttes. But before he moved on, he wanted all his men to know what the conditions were ahead. He explained there might be lean days, but he intended to continue his march. If any man wished to turn back, he had his permission. There was enough food left for ten more days. After that, they might be in better country. He counted on a core of five or six men he felt certain would stay with him—men such as Carson, Lajeunesse, Maxwell, Lambert, Preuss. The others might turn one way or the other. He waited for those who would turn back to indicate their choice. Yet not a man moved. Then Basil Lajeunesse said, "We'll eat the mules!"[13]

That was the turning point if there was to be one. His men were not about to give up on him. Yet he did send one man back, a man who was suffering from an old leg wound, who was not a good hiker, and whose horse was giving out. Then they parted company with Bissonette and the Indians.

Once they were out of sight, John Charles and his party turned toward the river. Though it was still early they made camp. From here on the going was to be fast and light. There wasn't enough food for the men, nor enough grass for the draft mules to pull the Red River carts. The only thing that made any sense was to temporarily cache everything that was not vital.

The men unloaded the carts, removed the covers and wheels, and carried these and the cart bodies into a thicket of willows. Everything was concealed so that nothing would indicate the presence of these vehicles. All the iron work was covered with dense foliage to prevent the glitter of sunlight reflecting off the metal. All supplies they were not taking were wrapped and buried in a large hole in the sand. Then all traces of the cache were obliterated. The remaining supplies were placed in packsaddles to be carried by horses and mules.

The day was very warm, and the sky was a vast ocean of clear blue that broke against the distant peaks of the Rocky Mountains in waves of great clouds like the foam of breakers sweeping in and out on tides of air currents. The skin lodge was erected, but because the day was so warm, the anchor pins were removed so that the lower part of the covering could be raised to allow whatever air there was to circulate. Close to the tepee, Frémont put up a tripod frame that held a barometer. While he did this, Preuss was inside the lodge, where he had a small fire burning as he boiled water to observe the temperature in order to take a reading of the altitude.[14] All at once, the calmness of the day was broken by a violent gust of wind that "dashed down the lodge, burying under it Mr. Preuss and about a dozen men, who had attempted to keep it from being carried away."[15]

John Charles managed to save the barometer from the falling lodge, but the thermometer was broken. This was a considerable loss, as the other good themometer had been broken just as they were leaving Fort Laramie. The only thermometers left lacked a high graduation, going no higher than 135 degrees Fahrenheit, and this would not be of any use to measure the higher altitudes they were moving into. The only instrument that could be used to determine altitude was the one remaining barometer.

In the morning they left what they called Cache Camp, and Kit Carson took over as guide. From this point on, the party would be traveling through country he had known for many years, country he had first seen as a young mountain man trapping beaver and attending the summer rendezvous for supplies, trade, and a wild celebration of trappers and Indians who got drunk together, talked of dead friends, made love to willing women, and brawled for the plain hell of it. This stage of the journey would be a trip into the past for Kit, where landmarks were much more than trail guides. A certain rock, a mountain hole, a stretch of meadow bordered by quaking aspen, the shape of a mountain peak brought back to Carson memories of his youth and of a time when the mountain man was a loose and drifting wayfarer in search of beaver and then in search of a way to live forever in the wild and free land he could never forget, the country of the mind that was mapped in the convolutions of his brain.

Not many miles from Cache Camp, the party came to the formation known as the Red Buttes (near present Casper, Wyoming). Frémont noted that the geological composition was of red sandstone, limestone, calcareous sandstone, and pudding stone. As they moved beyond the Red Buttes, they expected to run into the area of grasshopper- and drought-ravaged land the Indians had described. Instead, grass was plentiful. Creeks were running more than enough water, and on the banks of these streams flowing down from the mountains there were willow thickets, chokecherry bushes, and fresh tracks of grizzly bears that had been feeding on chokecherries.

The warm days of July passed, but the August sun gave no relief. Hot Springs Gate, the North Platte, and Goat Island became names to enter in a journal as camp was pitched at Independence Rock.

This curious rock, this great humpback of granite Frémont described in detail; he measured it, and found that it was 650 yards long and 40 yards in height. Except for one dwarf pine growing in a pocket of soil at its summit, the rock was bare. Bare except for names, names that made it a record book in stone. Mountain men who had gathered around it one drunken Fourth of July about 1825 gave the lonesome granite monument its name. "Everywhere within six or eight feet of the ground, where the surface is sufficiently smooth, and in some places sixty or eighty feet above, the rock is inscribed with the names of travellers."[16]

Inscribing graffiti was an ancient custom, not honored by the passing of time but a flirtation with immortality nevertheless. The markings on Independence Rock ran the range from intricate carvings to crude attempts to sign a logbook of the trail. Indians made their mark. Trappers, early tourists bound for a glimpse of the fur trade and a chance to shoot wild game while taking a chance of being shot by an Indian, and even men of God, missionaries determined to convert the Indians to the white man's God, could not resist carving their names; nor could the first emigrants headed for the rich soil of Oregon's Willamette Valley—all these people of the trail tried to leave a record of their passing.

That night they camped beside the rock, and stayed there until noon of the next day as they dried the meat of more buffalo the hunters had killed. They found blood-soaked trousers that had a bullet hole in them, and a man's pipe in one of the pockets. The men speculated about what might have happened and agreed that either the emigrant party ahead of them had been jumped by Indians at the rock or one of the party had accidentally shot himself. Chances were that if it had been a battle with Indians there would have been more indications of a struggle. Yet there was always the possibility that a man standing night watch might have been picked off by a lone warrior who had slipped in close enough to fire one shot and drift back into the cover of night.

When they left the rock at noon, they followed the valley of the Sweet-water River to the granite ridge where the river had cut through and left a passage called Devil's Gate. This waterworn cut was about thirty-five yards wide and three hundred yards long. As they passed through it, they looked up at the steep granite walls towering four hundred feet above them. Here, Frémont took time to set up his daguerreotype apparatus and attempted to photograph this natural passage. Charles Preuss, in his caustic manner, wrote that Frémont spoiled at least five plates and never managed to get a picture. Whether he succeeded or not is questionable. One thing is certain. He was the first person to attempt to photograph this landmark.

Eight miles beyond Devil's Gate, the expedition made camp for the night in an open valley that was four or five miles broad and bordered on its sides by steep mountains rising abruptly to as much as two thousand feet above the valley floor. The south range appeared to be covered with timber, while the north rim was a series of broken granite cliffs where there were occasional ledges or benches that had green grass and a sparse covering of timber around the edges. The main valley had a good covering of grass and a profusion of wild flowers except near the southern boundary. There the ground was bare and white from alkali in the soil, and the setting sun reflecting off this playalike surface gave the illusion of a lake where there was no water at all. At sunset a rain squall hit the open camp. Lightning danced off the granite peaks to the tune of great thunderclaps that were like the roll of giant kettledrums. In the southern range, fires broke out in the pine forests where lightning bolts struck trees at random.

In the morning they crossed over a slight hill near the Sweetwater River and had their first glimpse of the Wind River Mountains, about seventy miles away. To Preuss, who had been looking forward to his first sight of the mountains, their appearance was a sore disappointment. He had hoped to see something like the Alps, something that would remind him of the life he had known in Europe. But when he saw the mountains, he thought they could be no more than eight thousand feet high, for like many first-time travelers in the West he was fooled by distance. The mountains seemed much closer than they were, and their altitude was impossible to judge.

During the next few days the expedition was hit with bad weather. Driving rains came out of the north and carried the first touches of winter. Temperatures dropped, and the men were cold as they rode all day long either in rain or icy wind that cut right through their clothing. All the while, they were climbing, though it was hardly noticeable unless one took time to make a barometric reading. On August 6 they left the Sweetwater Valley, passed through a rough canyon into a narrow valley, and began to follow the river to its mountain beginnings. Old beaver dams were everywhere now and the stumps of cottonwoods and quaking aspens neatly gnawed through. By evening they climbed to a high prairie and then to the summit of a ridge.

## 5

THE MORNING OF AUGUST 8 was another cold day for summer. After breakfast the men moved on under a cloudy sky and felt chilled from occasional showers and a wind that swept down from the distant snow-covered peaks of the Wind River Mountains. Frémont and Carson looked for the summit of the famous South Pass. Even for Kit it was hard to tell just where the summit was located. The upward ascent was so gradual, so prosaic and without dramatic vistas that it was hard to believe they were nearing South Pass. The grade was much too easy. It was more a broad, open plain than a mountain pass. Yet somewhere they would cross over from the Atlantic watershed to the Pacific watershed.

Six miles from their overnight camp, at an elevation of about eight thousand feet above sea level, Kit signaled to John Charles that they were crossing South Pass. This easy crossing of the Continental Divide was not so much a single place as a considerable area. Frémont thought it was between two low hills that were no more than fifty or sixty feet high. This was all there was to it. This crossing had been discovered by Robert Stuart and a party of Astorians headed back to Oregon in October 1812. Then it had been rediscovered by Jedediah Smith, Broken Hand Fitzpatrick, James Clyman, William Sublette, and a party of mountain men in the spring of 1824. Contrary to later stories that attempted to slander him, Frémont never claimed he had discovered South Pass; as he stated in his *Report*, Kit Carson guided him through it.

To both Frémont and Preuss, South Pass was a disappointment. While it was a natural route for westward bound emigrants, it lacked the dramatic qualities both men had expected. Preuss had hoped to see something resembling one of the great passes over the Alps, where there was no mistake that a man was crossing over a mountain range, and Frémont felt much the same way. He compared the crossing of South Pass "to the ascent of the Capitol hill from the avenue, at Washington."[17]

The approach to South Pass from the mouth of the Sweetwater River covered about 120 miles across a sandy plain that developed into a gradual and regular grade to the summit. At the pass, the expedition was 950 miles from their jumping-off point at Chouteau's Landing at the mouth of the Kansas River. The accuracy of the explorer's calculation of distance was extremely good, for in 1901 when Hiram Martin Chittenden measured the same route under much better conditions and with superior equipment, the figure he arrived at was 947 miles.

Beyond South Pass the expedition left the path that was to become the main wagon trace on the Overland Trail. Their goal was the Wind River Mountains, and they headed northwest.

By the next morning, there was frost on the ground and ice covered their water. While they shivered and ate their breakfast, even Preuss was impressed with the view. They were now approaching the Wind River Mountains. Not far away the first rays of the early morning sun made a lofty snow-covered peak glitter with a dazzling whiteness. As the sun rose higher, the scenery became more and more magnificent. Frémont thought the mountain peaks gleamed like silver.

Not far from their camp they left the valley and began to move upward. Following a long ravine, they came to a beautiful lake that formed the headwater for the river they called New Fork. Leading their horses down the steep, rocky ridge, they reached the shoreline and followed it to its southern end. At this point, the view before them was incredible. The mountains rose up in a series of peaks, each one higher than the other, reaching upward to the snowcapped heights that made a man's eyes squint to look at them in the bright sunlight of this August morning. John Charles stared at these grand mountains that rose above the dark line of evergreens; then his gaze came back to the yellow sands around this lake he called Mountain Lake[18] and to the shimmering groves of quaking aspen that trembled with the slightest wind. There was plenty of feed for the horses and mules, cold clear water where Preuss looked longingly at the trout swimming along and wished to catch some for the frying pan, and where he also saw wild garlic growing and noted in his journal that it would help to season the antelope meat. Once Frémont found the right place to establish a base camp, he intended to leave one party there and take another group of men with him to explore the high mountains.

Seeking a good site to establish camp, the party came to the lake's outlet, which funneled through a passage between the hills. Crossing this proved to be much more difficult than anyone figured. The rushing, waist-deep stream was about 250 feet wide and flowed over a bed of slippery rocks, jagged rock fragments, large boulders, and slick broad slabs of stone.

The swift current, the icy water, and the slippery boulders made the crossing a tough trip. Horses and mules lost their footing time and again, and Preuss decided the only safe way was to lead his stumbling mount even though it meant he would have to wade belly-deep through the cold water. But Frémont was not lucky in making this crossing, as his last barometer was broken. The men knew how much he needed it to measure the altitude of the mountains, and they did manage to save the instrument. Still, it was doubtful that much could be done with it. After they had completed the crossing and found a good campsite, Frémont looked at his broken barometer and decided he would try to repair it.

While the glass cistern of the barometer had been broken in the center, fortunately no air had gotten into the tube. He tried working with some thick glass vials he had among his supplies, but each one broke as he tried to cut it to the right length. Then, he decided to give a powder horn a try. He found the most transparent one in camp, and went to work on it.

This I boiled and stretched on a piece of wood to the requisite diameter, and scraped it very thin, in order to increase to the utmost its transparency. I then secured it firmly in its place on the instrument with strong glue, made from a buffalo, and filled it with mercury, properly heated. A piece of skin, which had covered one of the vials, furnished a good pocket, which was well secured with strong thread and glue, and then the brass cover was screwed to its place. The instrument was left some time to dry, and when I reversed it, a few hours after, I had the satisfaction to find it in perfect order; its indications being about the same as on the other side of the lake, before it had been broken.[19]

Youthful excitement at the prospect of climbing what he thought would be the highest peak in the Rocky Mountains was too much to resist. Though they were running short of food and were well out of the range of the buffalo, he did not hold back this yearning to climb the heights. Like all mountain climbers, he needed no excuse other than the fact that the mountain was there, and he was determined to climb it.

Before he left the men at Mountain Lake, he made sure they would be protected. From Carson he learned that the pass at the northern end of the mountains was one used by the Blackfeet, and there was no way of knowing when they might be coming south from their northern home to raid the Crows or Shoshonis, or to hunt buffalo on the plains along the Sweetwater River. John Charles put his men to work felling timber and digging enough dirt to form a breastwork five feet high. When they finished their temporary fort, it was then half-hidden by foliage. It would make it tough on any band of raiders who decided to attack. Baptiste Bernier was left in charge of the men detailed to remain at this fort with their animals.

For the mountain-climbing party, Frémont selected the best mules. An extra mule was to be used to pack enough food for two days as well as the cooking equipment. Each man would carry his own blanket strapped over his saddle. The instruments that were to be used were carried on their backs, and included the powder-horn barometer, a thermometer, a sextant, a spy glass, and a number of compasses.

As light was breaking, the mountain expedition rode out of the base camp. They hit a rough and rocky route just after they crossed the ridge at the head of Mountain Lake. Ahead, they saw the peaks of the first range of mountains, and below the ridge was a deep valley with three lakes in it. The surrounding ridges rose steeply. The shades of green varied from that of the deep mountain lakes to the grass of the valley, the balsam pines and the quaking aspens.

Preuss complained about the mosquitoes, but he had to admit the lakes and the chain of mountains he saw were a welcome relief from the dreary landscape he had seen day after day on the ride from Cyprian Chouteau's.

Yet, this was not like the Alps. Where were the glaciers? Where were the ice lakes?

Slowly the men and mules worked their way down the steep ridge to the valley floor and the lakes. All the wild flowers were in bloom in the open meadow, and the brilliant colors ranged from the cool blue of camas to the warm, vibrant yellows of buttercups.

Noon halt was made on the beach of the first lake, where there was good grazing for the mules. They sat under the shade of some large hemlocks and watched small brown squirrels scurry about. After an hour's rest, they rode a little inland to try to find an easier path to the ridge above the lakes. When they found one, they rode upward to a point where they could look down into the valley. Among the hills they saw lakes at different levels, connected by roaring cataracts and waterfalls. Even from the ridge, they could hear the noise of rushing water and see the white spray leaping from rock to rock as it cascaded downward.

Late in the afternoon they reached a mountain meadow completely protected by granite cliffs and pines that grew in between the rocks and even out of crevices. They made camp at this spot for the night; and while the men got the fires started and prepared supper, Frémont and Geyer wandered about through the crags and ravines and collected plant specimens. When they returned to the camp, it was almost dark.

> Our table service was rather scant, and we held the meat in our hands; and clean rocks made good plates, on which we spread our macaroni. Among all the strange places . . . none have left so vivid an impression on my mind as the camp of this evening. The disorder of the masses which surrounded us; the little hole through which we saw the stars overhead; the dark pines where we slept; and the rocks lit up with the glow of our fires, made a night picture of very wild beauty.[20]

The next day the climb became harder. They followed the course of a small stream which led them to a very small valley where there was a good meadow, and a small lake that was the source of the stream. From this location the peak that appeared to be the tallest in the range gave the impression of being close enough for them to climb to the crest and return to this lake before nightfall. Frémont selected a small group of men to make the last climb. The rest of the men were to remain at the lake and wait for the return of the climbers, who would be traveling fast and light, not taking any blankets or food, and carrying only the barometer, a thermometer, an American flag, and guns to protect themselves.

Kit Carson led the way, starting out at a fast pace, and the men moved upward through rougher and rougher country. Breathing became much more difficult; the rocks were hard on their feet; and Frémont began to feel the effects of a higher altitude as they moved to the ten-thousand-foot level. His head ached; his stomach was queasy; he became angry at Carson for moving

Mississippi River traffic made St. Louis a major city of commerce. In the 1840s it was the last view of civilization before the beginning of the American West. (*Courtesy of the Library of Congress*)

Fort Snelling and the nearby settlement of Mendota as they appeared
to the Nicolett expedition in 1838. (*The Bancroft Library*)

Prairie du Chien, Wisconsin, as Frémont saw it in 1838. (*The Bancroft
Library*)

Mapmaker, journal keeper, and a man who hated the wilderness, Charles
Preuss was a key figure on Frémont's first, second, and fourth expeditions.
(*The Bancroft Library*)

Christopher "Kit" Carson was the most famous of Frémont's guides. This rare picture was taken when he had learned to write his name. (*The Bancroft Library*)

This is the typical picture that shows Kit Carson as a handsome hero. (*The Bancroft Library*)

so fast, and the two men exchanged unpleasant words. His whole attitude was quite unlike anything he had displayed during the expedition up to this point. It was not something he could control. Quite simply, he was unable to stand the physiological stress of high elevation. His impaired judgment, fatigue, irritability, and even periods of euphoria—all of which he described in his *Report* and which Charles Preuss indicated in his journal—were definite symptoms associated with an inability to function normally at high altitude.[21]

The same sickness that bothered Frémont on this climb also took its toll with some of the other men. But they struggled upward, thinking all the time that they would soon reach the peak and then be able to return to where they had left the mules and the other men. Such was not the case. One ridge was topped only to show a higher ridge above it, and in between ridges there were many small but deep lakes. The path was one of climbing up, dropping down a steep and slippery rock face, then up the next ridge. Men stumbled and fell on the sharp or rounded rocks, cursed, got to their feet, and continued on. At one point, Lucien Maxwell lost his footing and tumbled toward the edge of a cliff but managed to keep from going over by throwing his body flat out against the rocks and ground.

In the late afternoon the climbers were worn out when they reached the shore of a little lake that had a rocky island in it. They worked their way around the lake, walking carefully on rocks that were wet and slippery from spring water that flowed over them and down into the lake. Dog weary, the men made camp at what Frémont called Island Lake.[22] Without food, without blankets, this camp at timberline was cold and uncomfortable. Basil Lajeunesse went hunting before sunset to try and kill something they could roast over the fires, but he had no luck. Frémont became ill once more, and during the cold night he suffered from the pain of a violent headache and from constant vomiting. Preuss found that sleeping on granite was like bedding down on slabs of ice, and most of the night he sat next to the fire, smoking his pipe and rotating his position so that he could keep both the front and back of his body from becoming too chilled.

In the morning, the men were up and moving at daybreak, determined to reach the peak and get back to their friends and supplies. They followed the ridges and slowly worked their way upward until they came to fields of ice and snow. Cautiously, they walked across this slippery area, trying to make sure of their footing before they advanced. But the snow was a covering for hidden ice in some spots; in such a place Preuss felt his feet go out from under him. He fell on his rear and, before he could catch himself, began to slide downhill at a rapid speed. For two hundred feet he slid as he tried to dig his hands into the ice and snow to stop his downward movement. Then he hit an area of bare rocks, rolled over twice in complete somersaults, and finally came to a halt. No bones were broken in his tumble, but as he noted in his journal, his ass and one elbow were bruised; and the pain and shock made him sit for a while before he got to his feet to climb to where his com-panions were waiting and watching.

Others became lightheaded from the higher altitude and lack of food. Once again Frémont became so ill it was all he could do to make it back to Island Lake. As he started downward, he sent Basil Lajeunesse and four men back to the mountain camp where they had left the rest of the climbing party. By sundown Basil and others had returned with mules and supplies—the men who had gone down with Lajeunesse stayed at the lower lake as they were too tired to come back. To Frémont, "Basil resembled more a mountain goat than a man."[23] Nothing seemed to diminish his endurance. And here he was with blankets, dried meat, and coffee. This was a good omen for the next day's attempt to reach the peak.

During Basil's round trip to the Camp of the Mules, the high altitude con-tinued to bother the lieutenant. His state of mind was not typical for him. In place of his usually calm, easygoing attitude, he was irritable and irrational. In this flirtation with madness, he dismissed the faithful Carson from the final group of men who would climb the peak. At daybreak, Kit was to take most of the men and their mules and return to the lower lake camp. The men who were chosen to climb the peak were Lajeunesse, Preuss, Lambert, Descoteaux, and Janisse.

Preuss knew nothing about this plan until the next morning when he awoke and found that Carson and the other men had gone down the moun-tain. At that time he learned he was to be a member of the party who would climb the peak, and Frémont told him that he hoped they would be able to empty a glass at the top and plant the American flag.

The climbers ate a hurried breakfast. Then they hid enough food for an-other meal, as they realized they would need it when they returned. Six men and five mules started the climb. Lajeunesse led the way on foot, and the others rode. They followed Basil up a defile on the right side of the moun-tain. The path was rough even for the sure-footed mules, and it was very tricky going in the shady areas where the ground had patches of ice. Slowly they worked their way upward until they were riding along the massive wall that formed the major summits. There, by their path, was a high wall of granite that terminated two or three thousand feet above their heads in a jag-ged line of sawtooth peaks.[24] Still able to ride their mules, the men continued on until they were just below the peak Frémont judged to be the highest, the one he called Snow Peak. In the shadow of this impressive mountain, they saw three small, deep lakes (Titcomb Lakes). They were able to ride the mules one hundred feet beyond these lakes to a high bench that flattened out enough to have a small meadow. From here on, they would travel on foot. They left the mules to graze on the meadow grass, piled any gear they didn't need for the climb, and started out.

Moving slowly and carefully, resting and taking time to catch their breath, the men crossed over the rocks. As they neared the snow line, the surface of the stone became very slick and difficult. Frémont removed his thick moccasins and put on a light, thin pair so that he would have better footing. Preuss found the going very difficult for his short legs, as did some of the others. He was happy when Lambert and Descoteaux managed to get over an area of slippery rock face, for Descoteaux then reached back with a ramrod and pulled Preuss and the others across. Now they came to another stretch that presented unknown difficulties—a passage across the rocks covered with snow. Again, Descoteaux helped the others by easing his way across the snowpack and breaking a path. The other men followed, stepping carefully in the tracks he had made.

The last obstacle was an overhanging buttress. John Charles worked his way around this by placing his hands and feet in the crevices between the rocks. In this manner, he inched his way around it and into the open until he was almost at the crest. Then in a burst of joy at his conquest, he leaped onto the narrow summit, halting himself just in time to keep from falling into "an immense snow field five hundred feet below."[25]

The small slab that was the highest point of the mountain only held one man at a time. But each of the climbers took his stand on the peak. Then pistols were fired in celebration; men cheered to the cold wind that blew along the crest of the Wind River Mountains, and Frémont unfurled the special American flag he had designed and had made for this purpose. Then this flag with thirteen stripes, twenty-six stars, and the bald eagle holding arrows and an Indian peace pipe in its talons was attached to a ramrod that was fixed in a rock crevice, and there blowing in the steady wind was the American flag.[26] While the flag still waved over this peak in the Rocky Mountains, Frémont got out his powder-horn barometer and measured the height of this lofty pinnacle. Even with his makeshift instrument, he came very close to the actual height of present-day Woodrow Wilson peak when he jotted down that its elevation above sea level was 13,570 feet.[27]

The exciting moment was over. Now the men were anxious to return to lower altitude. Still, the effort had been worth it. While Frémont rested, a wayward bumblebee lit on the knee of one of his men. And though John Charles alluded to the bee as a "solitary pioneer," he did not hesitate to make it part of his collection as he pressed it between the leaves of a book in the company of some specimens of flowers he had collected.

This moment at the peak of the mountain on August 15, 1842, was romantic in every sense of the word. For a while they savored the view from the heights: to the northwest they could see the snowy outline of the Grand Tetons; below them to the northeast was the beautiful valley of the Wind River country; and to the southwest were the high peaks that were the source of the Platte River. Frémont checked the various kinds of rocks he saw and tried to identify them. Then he looked over their position.

Around us the whole scene had one main striking feature, which was that of terrible convulsion. Parallel to its length, the ridge was split into chasms and fissures; between which rose the thin lofty wall, terminated with slender minarets and columns, which is correctly represented in the view from the camp on Island Lake.[28]

All that remained was to get down the mountain and, if possible, travel to the main camp where the men had built the temporary fort at Mountain Lake. But that journey took all that afternoon and until dusk of the following day.

On the night of August 16 the men were excited and happy as they sat around the campfires at Mountain Lake and talked of their adventures. The long journey from Chouteau's Landing at the mouth of the Kansas River had brought them to their goal. In the morning they would pack their gear and head out on the homeward trail.

6

TRAILMARKS, campgrounds all ran together in a weary pattern as the expedition followed the homeward trail. They moved in a hurry, for the touch of winter was in the evening breeze. By August 23—only six days after leaving Mountain Lake—they came to Independence Rock again. This time, Frémont made his mark on the great humpback of granite. With care and precision, he formed an impression of a large cross, and covered it "with a black preparation of India rubber, well calculated to resist the influence of wind and rain."[29]

Leaving this landmark behind, they moved on to the confluence of the Sweetwater and Platte rivers. That night the rubber boat was unpacked, inflated, and stowed with supplies. Frémont instructed the main party to continue overland to Goat Island. If they found no message from him there, they were to wait until he and his fellow voyagers appeared. Then he selected his crew. Preuss, Lajeunesse, Ayot, Lambert, Benoist, and Descoteaux were to crowd into the rubber boat with him for the voyage down the Platte River.

The sailors left at dawn, and they figured to reach Goat Island in a few hours. But in case things went wrong they were well supplied with the best cuts from three buffalo cows, sugar, chocolate, a camp sausage made by one of the cooks, and the last of the macaroni. They traveled in style as they paddled and drifted easily for about an hour. Then the water picked up speed, and they entered a canyon where sheer rock walls towered over a hundred feet.

As the water picked up more speed and began to shoot the boat at a faster and faster pace, the men shouted to steer this way and that to avoid boulders. All the while, they heard an ominous roar from the lower reaches of the canyon.

The boat shot near a rock wall, and some of the crew jumped overboard to pull the craft toward a small, sandy beach. The water was up to their necks, and they had a hard time beaching the boat. Then, a few men were sent ahead to reconnoiter.

The scouts returned and reported that they had seen no waterfalls but the sound that echoed throughout the canyon was coming from a series of rapids.

Was it possible to shoot the rapids?

Yes.

What about rocks?

Room to get by.

Frémont gave the order. They shoved off from the little beach, drifted into the current, and picked up speed. The water boiled through the narrow passage like a millrace. The boatmen shouted back and forth as they saw submerged rocks suddenly looming just in front of them. With sure, quick paddle strokes they maneuvered the rubber boat past the danger spots. Each time they entered another rapid, Preuss put the chronometer in his pocket and held on to his notebook in case the craft should capsize.

After they had passed through three narrows, the boat was out of the rapids and the rock-bound canyon. The water became smooth and placid, and they drifted along as the river followed its path through low, rolling hills. The men were hungry after what they had been through, and though they had planned to eat breakfast at Goat Island, Frémont gave the order to pull ashore.

The men were soaked and tired. They had not had anything to eat since the night before, and three hours had passed since daybreak.

Fires were started to dry their wet clothing. While the men got things ready to cook, Frémont walked ahead to the crest of a hill. A mile, maybe two miles beyond, he saw another canyon with more rapids. He reached the camp as Preuss passed the last bottle of brandy he had been carrying, and the men enjoyed a drink before they ate.

The men put out the fires and got ready to drift downstream to the next canyon. The water seemed to be moving faster. In a short time they neared the canyon entrance. Frémont ordered the men to head the boat for shore, and they managed to land the craft before being caught in the first of the rapids. Portage was taken into consideration, but it didn't seem like a good idea. This canyon was deeper than the first, and appeared to stretch ahead for seven or eight miles. That was too far to carry the rubber boat and all the gear. They had made it through the first stretch of rough water. The boatmen were experienced and not afraid. They would shoot through this one just as they had the other. Frémont was not so convinced of their chances that he was going to risk the remaining chronometer. He asked Preuss to take the instrument and hike along the shore, just in case anything happened.

Short-legged Preuss got out of the boat, and for the next five minutes he climbed over the broken rocks along the shoreline and looked up at the cliffs that towered much higher than the first canyon. Then he came to an

overhang where the face of the cliff jutted into the water, and where there
was no longer any possibility of walking.

While Preuss waited for the boat to ride the rough water and get to where
he was stranded, he watched it shoot over a second fall as the men shouted
with joy. But even as their loud shouts echoed upward toward the top of the
canyon walls, the boat hit a rock. Before anyone could save them, the sextant
and Clement Lambert's saddlebags had fallen into the churning water.
Frémont managed to catch the sextant as it swept by on the current. But the
saddlebags hit an area of whirlpools and before anyone could get near them,
they were lost.

The oarsmen managed to maneuver the boat to where Preuss waited, and
he boarded the rubber craft for the next run. To try to make it through the
cataract without disaster, Frémont had about fifty feet of strong rope tied to
the stern of the boat, and he put Lajeunesse and two other men ashore to
hold the rope and act as an anchor. As they entered the sheet of white water,
two of the men let go of the rope. Lajeunesse was jerked from his position
and went headfirst into the river. The boat shot forward at full speed, but
Basil held on with all his strength "his head only seen occasionally like a
black spot in the white foam."[30]

Between his swimming ability and his great strength Basil managed to
keep from drowning as the boatmen struggled to get out of the main current
and into an eddy. Here, he caught up to them; and Frémont waited until the
other two men had worked their way through the shallower part of the
stream to the boat. Once more all the men climbed aboard. As they drifted
into the main stream again, everybody rested on his knees. The stronger men
held the short paddles, and the most experienced boatmen rode in the bow to
guide the craft.

Preuss had the chronometer in a bag that he tied around his neck, and he
held his notebook in one hand. He was caught up in the excitement as the
boat picked up speed and raced through the white foam. They cleared rock
after rock, shot over falls that were four and five feet high, and became
confident that the rubber boat would take them through the rapids, through
the canyons, and all the way to Goat Island.

We became flushed with success and familiar with the danger; and, yielding
to the excitement of the occasion, broke forth together into a Canadian boat
song. Singing, or rather shouting, we dashed along; and were, I believe, in
the midst of a chorus, when the boat struck a concealed rock immediately at
the foot of a fall, which whirled her over in an instant.[31]

Frémont's first thought was that three men aboard couldn't swim, but before he could do anything to help them, his head struck a rock. He almost
lost consciousness, and he felt himself start to go under. With a last effort, he
managed to swim out of the rapids and into an eddy, where he scraped his
body against a pile of rocks. Looking around, he saw that Preuss was on the

same side of the river but about twenty yards downstream. Out in the deep water Descoteaux, who couldn't swim, was being pulled to the surface by Lambert, who had grabbed his long hair. The rest of the men had managed to save themselves. There was no loss of life, and no serious injury. In that respect they were lucky, but the luck stopped there. All their supplies, their instruments, their guns, and worst of all, their records—the journals, the notebooks, the carefully measured figures of distance, longitude, latitude, and altitude—were gone. What had not gone directly to the bottom was floating downstream, quickly drifting out of sight: oars, packs, shirts, coats, boxes of instruments rode the rough, white water of the Platte.

Lajeunesse reacted in a hurry. With the help of the half-drowned Descoteaux, he righted the boat, and they jumped into it with a paddle Basil had grabbed from the water, and headed downstream to try and save as much as they could. Men on both sides of the river worked their way along the rocky shoreline, through the shallow eddies, and searched for anything they could find.

Preuss had managed to save his notebook and a compass. As for the chronometer, it was still in the bag hanging from his neck, but it no longer worked. He looked at what could be retrieved and saw that quite by accident Descoteaux had saved Frémont's double-barreled gun because it had got caught between his legs. But everything else seemed to be in the water, and Preuss worked as fast as he could with the rest of the crew as they began to fish things out of the river. Soon they had managed to find bedding, buffalo hides, the tent, Frémont's blue coat and his bag, and a few other things. Then Preuss saw the box that had contained the books and records. He quickly got into the water and pulled it ashore, but all that was left were some of the daguerreotype plates. The rest was gone: the other compasses, the telescope, the sextant. It was a day of rotten luck, and there was no getting around it. Preuss looked at Frémont and saw that he was in a bad state. Not only had he lost his records. He had even lost one moccasin in the water. And now came a shout from Basil, yelling that the boat had burst in the middle. There would be no more drifting down the river. Ahead of all was the hard climb out of the canyon and the long walk to Goat Island.

Slowly, Frémont and Preuss worked their way up the canyon wall on one side of the river, while the other men climbed up on the other side. Without provisions, without any way to protect themselves against Indians, they walked along the ground as fast as they could in order to reach Goat Island before night. Frémont found the going very tough. His one bare foot was cut by broken rocks and punctured by thorns. But when they got off the ridge that formed one wall of the river canyon, the going became easier on the prairie. After two hours of walking, they heard a shout. There was Benoist catching up to them, and he had some good news. A book had been retrieved from the river; and as he described it, Frémont and Preuss realized the men had found the book which contained all the observations they had made. They had also found Preuss's bag containing his journal.

With their spirits lifted by this news, the men moved along at a faster pace. By sunset they topped a rise, and below them they could see Goat Island. Best of all, they saw men and horses, and smoke from campfires. They yelled to the men on the island. When they reached the camp, there was freshly roasted buffalo meat waiting for them. For once, Preuss did not complain about the cooking, and he ate more meat than he had ever consumed at one meal. All the men who straggled in from the ill-fated voyage were weary, hungry, and in need of a change of clothing. They were worn out from their wild experience, and longed for a good night's rest before they headed out in the morning for Cache Camp, where there was more food, and the hidden Red River carts.

## 7

ON THE LAST DAY of August, six days after leaving their camp at Goat Island, the expedition came in sight of Fort Laramie. It had been forty-two days since they had waved farewell to young Randolph, his cousin Henry, and the men of the post. Frémont took time to put on his worn and badly wrinkled uniform, and got out the flag they had taken to the high peak in the Wind River Mountains. This was held in the air as they came within view of the distant adobe walls and the gathering of Sioux lodges outside the fort.

The Sioux were the first to see the approaching men, and they quickly told James Bordeaux that the party was returning. Bordeaux wasted no time. He ordered his men to load the cannon and fire a welcome to the explorers. As the repeated discharges of the cannon echoed across the plains, Frémont gave the command to fire, and his men answered the greetings with scattered volleys from their rifles and pistols.

To Preuss, it was all very much what he would expect of a young lieutenant in any army. He had to admit that even in his worn and wrinkled uniform Lieutenant Frémont was at his very best and had a decidedly martial air about him. As for himself, Preuss had a growth of whiskers which he longed to shave; his own trousers were worn to the point where the only way he could cover the holes was to borrow a second pair of trousers to wear over them. After the disaster in the river, after the loss of so many items, and nearly all the good food, tonight he would be able to sit at a table—not on a rock or the ground—and eat his fill of bread and cooked meat and drink coffee, perhaps with a little brandy in it.

Randolph and Henry were happy to see the men of the expedition once again and to know that within a few days they would be heading on the long journey home. Life at the fort during the absence of the party had not been the most exciting adventure either boy wished to have. While Henry Brant had found the Indian women to his liking, his one attempt to establish himself had been a failure. Word about that got around, and he had no more luck with women. The men at Fort Laramie never let him forget about his failure to please the woman he had traded a perfectly good horse for only to lose her because he was not up to what she had expected. As for Randolph, he became bored during the long wait for the return of the expedition. He had learned something about the Indians, and that had been interesting. He had watched a fight, seen one warrior kill another, and then had seen the mourning ceremony. He told Frémont how the Indians destroyed the lodge and all the other possessions of the dead warrior, and how the wife had slashed her breast, arms, and legs with a knife. But that was only one incident during the weeks of waiting. It had been a terrible sight, yet interesting to see. After that, the days had moved by very slowly, and the daily task of winding the chronometer didn't take much time away from the passing of hours. No, he would much rather have gone along on the trip to the Wind River Mountains; and he wanted to hear all about it—what it had been like when they met the band of Sioux, and what it felt like to climb such a high mountain.

The expedition remained at Fort Laramie for three days. Frémont purchased supplies and got things in order for the return trip. Preuss bartered with a Sioux woman, and she made a pair of buckskin trousers for him. On the third morning in September, the party moved through the main gate of the fort, waved farewell to Bordeaux and the other residents of the fur post, and began the last part of their homeward journey.

Now, the men were in a hurry. The return trip was over familiar ground, but the greatest incentive for speed was the changing weather as the days grew shorter. Each morning there was the touch of winter in the air, and though it warmed up during the day and the tall sunflowers were bright yellow in the midday sunlight, by evening the temperature dropped and gave the men cause to crowd the campfires. There were short rainstorms that came out of the northwest and carried a chilling feel. This was a cold wind that would soon bring snow when storms hit—snow and a bone-chilling cold that would drop well below zero within a month, if the season happened to be one that brought an early winter on its winds.

On the second day out from Fort Laramie they camped at Chimney Rock, where Kit Carson took his leave and headed south in the direction of Bent's Fort and Taos. After Kit left, the party traveled through sandhills that were teeming with rattlesnakes, passed by Court House Rock, and dug up the barrel of salted pork at Cache Creek.

When they reached Grand Island, the yellow, muddy water of the Platte began to be a little deeper as more tributaries entered the main stream. It was a shallow river, so shallow it was hard to believe that they had very nearly lost their lives in it. These were creeks and streams of illusion—waterways

that carved lasting scars in the face of the land but held water only when it
came rushing out of the high country at the end of winter.

Though the Platte River was low, John Charles wanted to have one more
try at sailing downstream. The rubber boat was gone, but there was another
way. He would sail it in a bullboat. The expedition came to a halt. He sent
his hunters out to kill enough buffalo bulls for the necessary hides.

> Four of the best of them were strongly sewed together with buffalo sinew,
> and stretched over a basket frame of willow. The seams were then covered
> with ashes and tallow, and the boat left exposed to the sun for the greater
> part of one day, which was sufficient to dry and contract the skin, and make
> the whole work solid and strong. It had a rounded bow, was eight feet long
> and five broad, and drew with four men about four inches of water.[32]

Frémont, Preuss and two other men boarded the bullboat on September
15, and tried to drift down the Platte River. They spent more time dragging
the craft over sandbars than floating along. After three or four miles of this,
they gave up the idea. There was no point in trying to sail what the Indians
aptly called the Nebraska or Shallow River.

Seven days after the unsuccessful experiment with the bullboat, the men
reached the village of the Grand Pawnees on the lower reaches of the Platte
River. From these farmers, they purchased a good supply of fresh vegetables.
Frémont sent Lambert and two other men on ahead to the settlement of
Bellevue,[33] where there was a trading post near the confluence of the
Platte and Missouri rivers. The men were to instruct the trader, Peter A.
Sarpy, to have a boat built for the party so that when they reached Bellevue
they would be able to make the rest of their journey in a Mackinaw boat—a
boat which cost $166.00.

The grand adventure was drawing to an end. The men were as anxious as
John Charles to finish their trek. For by the time they saw Chouteau's Landing again, they would have traveled well over two thousand miles across the
Great Plains, through the country of the Pawnee and the Sioux and into the
Wind River Range of the Rocky Mountains. Now, they began to let down,
and the feeling of weariness started to set in. Then long before daylight on
the first of October, Frémont heard the first sound of civilization. Somewhere
ahead of them in the distance he heard the soft tinkling of cow bells coming
from some settlement of farmers. Another day after this, they reached
Bellevue. They sold the horses, mules, and Red River carts at a public auc-
tion. By October 4 the Mackinaw boat was ready to use, and they loaded
their supplies for the trip, boarded the flat-bottomed, ten-oared boat, and
started down the Missouri River, with enough men aboard to relieve the oarsmen after an hour's stint.

They headed for Chouteau's Landing and passed it on October 10—just
four months since they had set out from this spot. Then it was into the swift
current of the Mississippi River, and downriver for home and families. By

October 17 they were at St. Louis. The first expedition was finished, and John Charles was already thinking of the next one. Most of all, he longed to see Jessie, to hold her in his arms again, to tell her what it was like on the other side of the western frontier, and to be with her when their first baby was born.

# VII

## Western Star

OCTOBER WAS RUNNING ITS COURSE, and Jessie longed to have John Charles come home. Their baby was due within the next two weeks, and she wanted him to be there when she gave birth. She knew he was on his way, that the expedition had reached St. Louis safely. News of his return had traveled ahead of him, and it seemed that all Washington had heard that Lieutenant Frémont was on his way back from a great adventure. He had been a traveler on the Oregon Trail, a man who had crossed South Pass and then went all the way to the Shining Mountains. This was the greatest adventure in many years, and citizens of Washington longed to hear about it.

But adventure was only one reason for Jessie's longing. The months of waiting had not been easy. Her handsome black-haired husband had been gone for a short time when tragedy struck the Benton household. Jessie's mother had suffered a stroke. Three days and nights she lay in a coma. The attending physicians had to tell Senator Benton it was their considered opinion that his wife might never regain consciousness, that she might linger in a coma until her body ceased to function. Jessie's father was overcome with grief. She had never seen him so helpless. This powerful senator, this strong man who held his ground when weaker men gave way, was reduced to a humble, praying husband who remained by his wife's bed and refused to leave.

Her father's reaction was a great shock, and Jessie realized she would have to be the strong one in this time of need. All her father could do was sit by her mother's bedside, hold her icy hands, and stare at her face for some indication of consciousness. Finally, after these anxious and desperate hours and days, there was a sign of recovery. At first it was only the slight movement of an eyelid. Then, slowly, ever so slowly, Jessie's mother managed to speak a few words—words that were almost unintelligible, but they were words.

As Mrs. Benton became fully conscious, two things were quickly apparent. She had suffered a great deal of brain damage. This impaired her intelligence and left her paralyzed to the point where it was difficult for her to speak. But even in this state, she made it clear that she wanted Jessie to take care of her. Jessie took over, while her father stood by trying his best to be cheerful in front of his wife, but retiring to his room as a grief-stricken man when he was out of sight. To help Jessie, her eldest sister Eliza took over the running of the Benton household. All that summer while John Charles was somewhere along the Oregon Trail, Jessie was her mother's constant companion. But as summer turned into autumn, as September drifted into October, Jessie became larger and larger with child. Before long, it would be time for her to give birth. Where was John Charles? That was the thought ever present in her mind. He was on his way home, and she felt that the days had become longer than they had been during the first months of his absence. But then, she was not so close to her time. Now, with the baby kicking and moving about, with the changing position of the life inside her, she was impatient for his return.

In the last few days of October Jessie wondered if John Charles would arrive on time. Her father tried to assure and comfort her; and even her invalid mother, who was able to rest on the couch by the window, had regained enough of her faculties to share in the excitement of the expected return of Frémont. Then on October 29 the front door of the Benton home opened, and Jessie's happiness was so great that she began to cry. She saw the tanned and handsome John Charles standing and smiling at her. He was home! Home in time for the birth of their first child!

Two weeks later, Jessie felt the beginning of labor pains. It was going to be only a matter of hours before she would give birth. It had to be a boy, a boy she would name after his father.

On November 13, 1842, Jessie gave birth to their first child. But it was not a boy. It was a six-pound baby girl. Jessie was terribly disappointed. It was all she could do to hide her feelings, to keep her bitter disappointment locked within herself. Both John Charles and her father were aware of her feelings. They told her how much they loved the little girl, how pretty she was, how much she looked like her mother. But when Jessie and John Charles were alone, she cried and told him how sad she was that the child was not a boy— a boy who could carry his name.

To John Charles, it didn't matter. What really counted was that both Jessie and the baby were in good health. He was happy to have a daughter. There would be time enough for a boy. The birth of a daughter was very special. Now he would have another female to love and cherish—one who was part of both of them. Then Jessie's father expressed his joy about having another girl around the house, and asked Jessie and John Charles if they would consider giving his granddaughter the same name as his wife. It would make Jessie's mother and himself very happy. The parents welcomed his suggestion, and the baby was named Elizabeth, a name that became the diminutive Lily.

Realizing Jessie was still distressed, John Charles came to her room with a very special surprise. He carried it over his arm, and with a flourish spread the wind-whipped and faded American flag across her bed. "This flag was raised over the highest peak of the Rocky Mountains; I have brought it to you."[1] The time had come to stop fretting, a daughter would do just nicely. It was time to get on with their lives. Lily would have to adjust to them as much as they would have to adjust to her. There was work to be done, and in between the hours of work, they would take time to shower Lily with all their love.

2

SHOWING NO LETDOWN in the drive and energy that had carried him beyond South Pass, Frémont was anxious to put together all the information that had been gathered on the expedition. Three days after the birth of his daughter, he sent a letter to Professor John Torrey, who was a pioneer taxonomic botanist, the spearhead of the New York Botanical Garden, and the key figure of the United States Herbarium. Frémont's letter to this distinguished man of science was right to the point: Would he take the time to examine the collection of plants that Frémont had taken the liberty of sending to him? More than that, would he consider preparing a catalogue of these plants to accompany a government report he was about to prepare? Then as a tempting last piece of bait, John Charles casually mentioned that in all probability he would be heading an exploring party all the way to the Pacific during the next year, and that perhaps Professor Torrey would also be interested in whatever plant specimens he could collect during that journey.

John Torrey was hooked. He had no real knowledge of Lieutenant Frémont's identity, but he wrote at once to a colleague and friend, Professor Asa Gray of Harvard University, whose specialty was natural history. In his letter to Gray, Torrey asked about Frémont and also told Gray that the plants were identified as to the part of the country in which the explorer had found them. He went on to mention the possible expedition to the Pacific, and speculated on whether or not this lieutenant of the Topographical Engineers might consider taking a collector with him on his next trip into the West. Perhaps, Torrey suggested, he might take Melines C. Leavenworth along. After all, Leavenworth had just resigned from the army, and, along with being an experienced surgeon, he was something of a botanist. Best of all, the fellow was at loose ends, and just might be willing to take on such a job.

Frémont had more than aroused Torrey's curiosity. He had him making plans and provisions for the next expedition, if there was one. But the identification of the plants that had been collected during this first trek into the wilderness was only one part of what needed to be done.

Charles Preuss was given the assignment of preparing the maps of the country they had traversed. There was to be a general map of the country explored, and along with this, Preuss was to make "a series of maps represent-

ing, each day's journey, a guide-book in atlas form . . . for the use of the
emigration. This was the suggestion of Mr. Benton. Upon each of the maps
the places were indicated for camps where grass and water and wood would
be found."[2] The idea of a day-to-day map series was to prove extremely valuable to the tide of emigration already beginning to flow westward, and
would encourage that tide to become a flood within a few years.

The big task of summing up the results of the first expedition was
Frémont's responsibility. The government wanted a full report of what had
taken place on this trip sponsored by taxpayers' money. John Charles had no
objection to preparing such a volume, but it was his intention to write a report that would be both accurate and highly readable. It should not be a document that only the few could understand. Some way had to be found to
make the country come alive for the average reader, the possible emigrant
who might use it as a guidebook to his own future. In a very real sense,
Frémont desired to produce a work of literary merit, but one that would not
bypass the scientific and practical information that had been gathered.

Suffering the same doubts, the same moments of depression that all writers
feel to one degree or another, Frémont fretted about how to start his book.
Making charts of his meteorological observations, checking his journals for
mileage covered day by day and for the variation of weather and the places
that were good campsites was easy. The trouble with that sort of thing was
that it was much too easy and, though it gave him a sense of accomplishing
something, in his quiet moments he knew very well that it was not getting
the book written. It did not show the country as he saw it. There was no indication of what the mountain men were like or of the nature of the various
Indian tribes, and no description of the fur traders and the forts in the wilderness. What he had to do was get the vivid memories into word pictures on
paper, but how to begin was the big problem.

Everything was in readiness in the room set aside in the Benton home. His
notes were carefully laid out on the desk. Jessie had made sure that a good
supply of paper was handy and had set out the pens and ink. She even
discussed the possible style with him, and agreed it must be a narrative with
a fine literary quality. All this was fine, but three days of stewing went by.
False starts were made. Paper was crumpled and tossed into the wastebasket.
Then John Charles developed a throbbing headache and his nose began to
bleed.

The ever-resourceful Jessie suggested that maybe it would be easier for
him to dictate his report. She was quite agreeable to being his secretary. After
all, she had done this kind of thing for her father while John Charles had
been away. There was no reason why she couldn't do it again. Besides, on his
salary as a lieutenant, they could not afford to hire a professional secretary.
As for Lily, she would be taken care of by a wet nurse. They would spend
time with the baby at the end of each day of writing.

When Jessie's mother heard of this suggestion, she objected. The work would be too hard for Jessie just after giving birth to Lily. A mother's place was with her baby, not at the study desk taking dictation day after day. But Mrs. Benton's protest was to no avail. Jessie was determined that she would be the catalyst who would help her husband create a lasting narrative of exploration.

A working schedule was established, and each morning between the hours of nine and one, Jessie took her position at the desk. John Charles walked back and forth, holding his notes, and reliving the days and nights of the expedition. Jessie wrote as rapidly as she could. Her only interruptions were questions she put to her husband to encourage him to enlarge upon his subject, to clarify a scientific observation not clear to her and which she believed would not be clear to most of his readers. Beyond this, Jessie's other role in the writing of the narrative was to come to her husband's aid when he became bogged down in the natural flow of his story. At such times, she would offer suggestions as to phrasing, pacing, and all the other attributes that made his writing come alive. But at no time, did she try to distort the factual material which he knew so well and which he could describe with such clarity and vividness.

Contrary to a myth which has been sustained by detractors of John Charles Frémont, he did his own writing. Any comparison of his reports, his letters, and the one published volume of his *Memoirs* makes it quite clear that his prose style differed considerably from Jessie's. That she helped him, no one can deny. But her aid in putting together his narrative was no more than that of any good editor with an ear for the cadence and sweep of prose that brought to life an epic in exploration. As Jessie wrote in her own unpublished "Memoirs": "Mr. Frémont had his notes all ready and dictated as he moved about the room. I soon learned that I could not make a restless motion—he was (at first) constantly afraid of the motionless calm for me—it was hard—but that was lost in the great joy of being so useful to him. . . ."[3]

Once the door to the past months of travel had been opened, John Charles relived those moments. He expressed what he saw, felt, and thought in his own prose style. When the *Report* of the first expedition was completed and sent to the printers, Frémont saw to all the other details. He worked with Preuss in the final polishing of the maps, corresponded with Professor Torrey regarding the botanical and zoological specimens, and was in touch with his ill and weary mentor, Joseph Nicholas Nicollet. Then when the time came to correct the galley proofs of the manuscript, Jessie again came to his aid. She mastered "all the queer little signs that must be accurate, and behold! Mr. Frémont's first book was finished."[4]

In March 1843 Frémont's account of his expedition was published as Senate Document 243, 27th Congress, 3rd session, under the following long and involved title: *A Report of an Exploration of the Country Lying Between the Missouri River and the Rocky Mountains on the Line of the Kansas and Great Platte Rivers*. It was as though the title had been designed to give readers a preview of what was between the covers, a kind of teaser to get them interested enough to open the book and begin reading. In addition to the copies of the *Report* printed for the Senate, a motion was put before the lawmakers by Senator Lewis Linn of Missouri to have another one thousand copies of Lieutenant Frémont's *Report* printed. As the junior senator from Missouri put it, "this document would be of general interest to the whole country, and beneficial to science, as well as useful to the government. . . ."[5]

The reason for Senator Linn's pitch for more copies of this document was his own role as one of the band of congressmen from the western states, men pushing for expansion. In John Charles they had found a champion who not only was an explorer but also a writer who pictured the rich land beyond the Mississippi and Missouri rivers in such a way that it became clear that what was called a barren land not fit for anything was just the opposite. His observations proved that the country beyond the Missouri River was fertile and beautiful and "that the valley of the river Platte has a very rich soil, affording great facilities for emigrants to the west of the Rocky Mountains."[6]

The key in Senator Linn's remarks to the United States Senate was *to the west of the Rocky Mountains.* Two opposing forces were lining up for a showdown: the supporters of expansion and Manifest Destiny, and the lawmakers who were all for letting well enough alone in the country beyond the Rocky Mountains. That was too far away, too hard to control from the national seat of government, and a possible reason for trouble with Great Britain.

The expansionists were men with a vision of a national boundary that would stop at the shoreline of the Pacific Ocean. They had done just the right thing to get public opinion moving in their direction by sending Lieutenant Frémont to the Rocky Mountains and then seeing to it that his *Report* would not be buried in some committee but would be released to the newspapers, publishers, and citizens who wanted to know more about this untouched, unspoiled, virgin land.

Though Frémont's *Report* was finding an enthusiastic audience, the chance of a second expedition was still up in the air. President John Tyler's annual message in December 1842 had been one of caution as far as the West was concerned. He did not go along with the idea of granting titles to land in Oregon. The question of who owned Oregon had not been settled, and until the United States and Great Britain arrived at some workable compromise with regard to this land and the question of where the boundary line between British and American territory should be, there was no point in pursuing this will-o'-the-wisp scheme.

President Tyler had not considered the tenacity of the western bloc in the Senate, or he thought that they would be defeated and retreat and lick their wounds for a while. If he thought this, he underestimated these men. Early in 1843 Senator Linn introduced a bill on the floor of the Senate that called for the President of the United States "to cause to be erected, at suitable places and distances, a line of stockade and blockhouse forts, not exceeding five in number from some point on the Missouri and Arkansas rivers into the best pass for entering the valley of the Oregon; and, also, at or near the mouth of the Columbia River."[7] In addition, this bill provided that 640 acres of land would be granted to each male settler who would cultivate and use his section of land for five consecutive years.

The fact that this bill was passed by a vote of twenty-four to twenty-two in the United States Senate, despite the strong opposition of Senators Calhoun and McDuffie of South Carolina, should have sounded the warning bell for President Tyler. Though the bill was then defeated in the House of Representatives, the idea of Oregon was out in the open, and it was only going to be a question of time.

The key factor in pushing for westward expansion was already influenced by Senator Benton. His role as a senior member of the Senate gave him an opportunity to come to the aid of the Topographical Corps with additional government money for its projects. Of course, Colonel John J. Abert was not adverse to this kind of aid, nor did he object to the role of the army in the exploration of the American West. While it was true that he had to put up with Senator Benton, who could be difficult, it was also true that Benton's son-in-law had brought a great deal of recognition to the Topographical Corps, and Colonel Abert did not object to this.

The defeat of Senator Linn's bill was only a public setback for the bloc of expansionists. Behind the scenes, they were seeing to it that the Topographical Corps received adequate amounts of money for its future projects. President Tyler had not stopped the band of Western men. All he had accomplished was to force them to find another way to achieve what they wanted.

3

THE MACHINERY of bureaucracy was neatly bypassed by Senator Benton. He had conversations with Colonel Abert, arranged for a substantial budget, and the two men arrived at an agreement. There should be a second expedition sent to the West as soon as it could be outfitted and as soon as the weather permitted. It should be headed by Lieutenant Frémont. This time the route of travel should be different, and more of the country beyond the Rocky Mountains should be explored.

On March 10, 1843, John Charles received official notice from Colonel Abert of his next duty assignment. Along with instructions for the expedition, Colonel Abert also enclosed a reminder to Lieutenant Frémont. Laws and regulations required an estimate of the probable expenses before the actual orders for the next expedition could be issued. But to help Frémont in bringing such accounts into some kind of reasonable shape, Abert had enclosed a copy of what the expedition might embrace.

Frémont was to survey the main forks of the Kansas River to its head, and proceed to the Arkansas River. Somewhere to the south of South Pass he was to cross the Rocky Mountains, and skirt the western base of the range to explore the headwaters of the streams that flowed toward the Gulf of California. From that point on, he was to head northwest to the Columbia River. Here, he was to try and link his survey with that made by Commander Charles Wilkes,[8] who in 1841 had gone ashore and made a reconnaissance in the Oregon country as far as Fort Walla Walla. In addition, Wilkes had sent the Emmons-Eld party south into California. The result of his work was a reliable map of the Northwest. Now, what the Topographical Corps and Senator Benton wanted was an overland survey that would tie in to what Wilkes had accomplished.

On his return from the Columbia River, Lieutenant Frémont's orders called for him to come back over the Oregon Trail until he reached the Wind River Mountains. At this time, he was to make a circuit along the eastern slopes of these mountains that would take him into the headwaters of such rivers as the Colorado, the Columbia, the Missouri, the Yellowstone, and the Platte. Such a journey, it was thought, would clear up all misconceptions about the difficulties of the Oregon Trail and add to the knowledge of the country north of it. As late as March 21, in another letter to Professor Torrey, John Charles indicated this was to be the extent of his expedition. At no point in his correspondence to Torrey, Abert, or anybody else did Frémont even vaguely suggest that he might make an excursion into California.

As Congress began its recess in the early part of March, Senator Benton hurried ahead of his household to St. Louis to take care of his political fences. While he made the journey by himself, the rest of the family began to pack and get ready for their trip to St. Louis which they would make with John Charles. While they got ready for the trip, Frémont and Preuss went to New York to purchase scientific instruments and other supplies for the expedition.

Determined to take pictures of what he saw, Frémont bought another daguerreotype apparatus from H. Chilton, a New York daguerreotypist, at a cost of $68.16. From Horace Day, another rubber boat was acquired, along with such items as water bottles, a tent, waterproof clothes, and trunks. The total payment to Mr. Day came to $302.10. But the biggest expense items were to be found in the various instruments needed. From the New York firm of Frye & Shaw, Frémont bought a telescope, two artificial horizons, two pocket compasses, a barometer, and five thermometers. This bill came to $327.50, and added to that was the $200.00 Frémont paid Arthur Stewart of New York for a silver pocket two-day chronometer. The total for instruments purchased on this New York trip came to over five hundred dollars, and the real expenses for the expedition were just beginning.[9] Yet to come were all the supplies, the animals necessary to carry the men and pull the carts, transportation costs for steamboat passage for men and freight, and the salaries for the men. The total cost of this expedition would run much higher than the one to the Wind River Mountains, but they were traveling a greater distance and would be gone for the better part of a year.

When John Charles and Preuss returned from their New York shopping tour, Jessie had the Benton-Frémont household all ready for the trip to St. Louis. Everything the family would need for their stay was packed in trunks and bags. A private stage was hired, and the family and Charles Preuss were ready to go. But one other person was to join the party. This was Jacob Dodson, an eighteen-year-old free black who was one of the Benton family's servants.

Tall and strong, Jacob approached Frémont and asked if he might go along. Not just to St. Louis, but beyond there to wherever Mr. Frémont's expedition might be heading. The young man was a good worker and a person John Charles knew he could count on. The answer, to Jacob's delight, was yes. Not only could he join the expedition, but he would be placed on the government payroll as a working member of the exploring party.

All ready to depart, the family, along with Charles Preuss and young Dodson, stepped into the coach and began their two-week trip to St. Louis. The first part of the journey was along the National Road—that government-backed pike that was first begun in 1815. This road passed through Cumberland, Maryland, and into the mountains of Pennsylvania to Wheeling, West Virginia.

In the mountains of Pennsylvania, as the coach neared the summit of a grade, the overconfident stage driver gave his team the whip and tried to pass a slow-moving freight wagon. The teamster of the freighter yelled that the road was too narrow, but the cocky stagecoach driver ignored him. The outer wheels of the coach ran near the edge of a gully and slipped over. The coach lost its balance and rolled downward. Jacob, who was riding on the box atop the stagecoach, jumped clear and was the first one to reach the frightened and rearing team. Close behind him came the teamster and his men, and they helped Jacob to quiet the horses and keep them from seriously injuring each other as they kicked and jumped around.

Inside the coach, all was quiet. Then as the passengers were helped out, it was soon apparent that the only one injured was Mrs. Benton, who had bumped her head and was stunned from the blow. But her age and poor health made it necessary for the party to stop overnight at a roadside tavern.

The place resembled a hunting lodge with its abundance of freshly killed game hanging from wall pegs. To try and ease the shock for her guests, the innkeeper loaded their table with the best food she had on hand.

The buckwheat cakes were half an inch thick and porous like a sponge, capable of absorbing enough of the good mountain butter to support a man for a day; with honey from the buckwheat fields, and maple-syrup from the forest. The venison steaks were excellent, broiled over the wood-coals.[10]

After resting at this mountain tavern for the night, the party continued its journey to Wheeling. There they boarded an Ohio River steamboat that took them all the way to the Mississippi River and the busy river port at Front Street in St. Louis.

4

As IN HIS FIRST DAYS in this city, those learning days with Joseph Nicollet, the headquarters of Pierre Chouteau, Jr., and Company became the center of his activities. All the provisions they would need had to be purchased and packed.

Among the men he hired, he was happy to see one of his favorites of the trail. This was that strong swimmer, that brave and dependable mountaineer, Basil Lajeunesse. With him was his brother, François, an experienced voyageur.

Some of the others listed in the roster were inexperienced. This trip would become a turning point in their lives. Two men who were influenced in this way were only eighteen years old. They came from vastly different stations in life. At one end was black Jacob Dodson, who learned the ways of the wilderness and became a first-rate frontiersman. At the higher end of the economic range, there was Theodore Talbot of Washington, a one-time student of a Kentucky military school and the son of a former senator, Isham Talbot of Kentucky.[11] Young Talbot was considering a possible career in the military, and he had been included in the party at the request of Colonel Abert, who was a personal friend of the Talbot family.

One other inexperienced man was Frederick Dwight of Springfield, Masschusetts, a Harvard Law student. He had the notion of traveling with the expedition as far as Fort Vancouver, where he hoped he might catch passage aboard a vessel bound for the Sandwich Islands and China.

Another applicant had been with Frémont and Nicollet during their 1839 expedition, Louis Zindel, the German immigrant who had been a noncommissioned artillery officer in the Prussian Army. Here, at last, was somebody who could talk to the ever-grousing Charles Preuss in his native tongue.

Then there was the usual complement of voyageurs, hunters, and mountain men. But the key figure was missing. There was no guide. Kit Carson wasn't hanging around St. Louis or bound upriver for the back country. He had made a verbal commitment to Frémont as they returned from the first expedition to meet him somewhere along the trail if he did come westward again. But the problem with this arrangement was that Frémont didn't know where Carson might be, and Carson didn't know which route Frémont planned to take if he did manage to get funds for another journey.

Luck was with Frémont. Thomas Broken Hand Fitzpatrick was ready to get away from the confining quarters of the city, ready to head back to the big sky country. Frémont hired Fitzpatrick in a hurry, and paid him the second highest salary of all the men who signed on for the trip. The only one who drew a higher salary was Charles Preuss. He received a little over two thousand dollars for the tour of duty, and Broken Hand was paid $1,750.[12]

Fitzpatrick was an impressive man. Forty-four years old at the time of this expedition—four years older than Charles Preuss and fourteen years older than Frémont—this survivor of the early days of the fur trade had the features and ruddy complexion of a much younger man. The only thing which made him appear at all old was his full head of white hair, but the white hair was not a mark of age; it was a badge of experience that went way back to a time when Broken Hand and a party of free trappers had been cornered by a band of Blackfeet in the Wind River Mountains. All of Fitzpatrick's companions were killed. During the three days and nights that he dodged in and out among the rocks, hid behind thickets of brush, and even climbed trees to hide out, his hair had turned completely white. Even this close brush with death had not kept him from following his life as a mountain man. Now as the great days of a free trapper were over because there was no longer a demand for beaver hats, he was happy to sign on as a guide for Frémont's party. This, at least, would take him back to the country he loved and give him a chance to use the talents he had learned in such a hard way.

Altogether, thirty-seven men signed on at St. Louis to make the long march to the Pacific and back. Except for a few greenhorns, they were a tough lot, a wild band, a breed of men more than capable of holding their own no matter how rough the conditions might be. They were not men to ask for an easy time, and the most experienced always expected the odds would be against them.

To arm his party for this trek, Frémont obtained permission to secure government weapons from the St. Louis Arsenal, commanded by Captain William H. Bell. John Charles managed this through the mutual friendship of Senator Benton and Colonel Stephen Watts Kearny, who was in command of the Third Military Department at Jefferson Barracks near St. Louis. Colonel Kearny gave Lieutenant Frémont a letter of requisition for ordnance and ordnance stores to present to Captain Bell. Among the items Frémont placed on his list were thirty-three Hall's carbines and five kegs of rifle powder. But he also included a request for a twelve-pound mountain howitzer complete with a carriage and harness, and five hundred pounds of artillery ammunition.

When Frémont presented his list and letter of requisition to Captain Bell, the officer questioned the propriety of handing over these arms to a mere second lieutenant of the Topographical Corps, who was only heading a party of exploration. But the old army game of rank worked in Frémont's favor. Colonel Kearny's letter was an order for Captain Bell to issue whatever he needed, and there was no choice for the good Captain Bell. He had to follow an order from his superior officer. This he did, but, being well-trained in army regulations, he was not about to let all this pass. Two days later he wrote to Lieutenant Colonel George Talcott of the Ordnance Office in Washington. In his letter Bell pointed out that he had objected to issuing such arms but had been ordered to do so by Colonel Kearny. He hoped he had done the right thing with regard to the regulations of the Ordnance Department.

In this manner, the seed of a late-blooming discontent was sown by one letter from a meticulous captain of the St. Louis Arsenal. This wasn't the only concern gestating in the military machinery of forms, policies, requisitions, and vouchers. Colonel Abert was becoming worried about expenses, and on May 15 he sent a letter to Frémont in which he made it quite clear that he expected him to stay within the limits of expenditures agreed upon for the expedition.

The letter did not reach John Charles before he had departed from St. Louis, and it was just as well in that his expenses were quickly moving toward the maximum that Colonel Abert expected. Red tape was not standing in Frémont's way, and he was moving very fast. He had sent Fitzpatrick and eight men on ahead to travel by land to Westport (present-day Kansas City) for the purpose of purchasing horses and mules for the expedition wherever they found good animals for sale between St. Louis and Westport Landing. Then on the morning of May 13 the lieutenant and twenty-seven men boarded the steamboat *Colonel Woods* and began their voyage upriver.

To Frémont and the old hands of his party, the voyage was nothing new. But to the greenhorns who had signed on, it was a time of great excitement. This became quite evident as they left the Mississippi and entered the waters of the Missouri. Theodore Talbot saw it as part of America's moving frontier, and described the raw and new look about it and the "Go ahead" glow upon the faces of the pioneers.

As you ascend higher up the river, the clearings become fewer, it is only occasionally that you catch a glimpse of a rude loghouse just peeping out as it were from the wilderness around the humble residence of some of those hardy pioneers of the march of civilization, whose every delight would seem to be in the hardships and privations which encompass the early settler of the western wilds.[13]

Five days after sailing away from Front Street and the busy life of the St. Louis waterfront, the *Colonel Woods* docked at Westport Landing. Here, Frémont paid a fare of $150.42 for the transportation of his men and provisions.

All the baggage was gathered together, and the tents were pitched three miles below the mouth of the Kansas River and about five miles from Westport. At this busy frontier river port, Frémont made arrangements with Major Richard Cumming—a friend of Senator Benton, and the Indian Agent for the Delawares, Shawnees, and other tribes of the region—to hire two Shawnee hunters who would travel with him as far as St. Vrain's Fort.

However, the men were not to join the party until the first of June, when they would catch up to them at the Kansas crossing. The Indians were a father-and-son combination, and Talbot found them an interesting pair. James Rogers, the father, was a tall, good-looking man who wore a bright calico shirt and fringed buckskin leggings. He was a man who owned considerable property, and he had a penchant for naming his sons after American Presidents. This son was Thomas Jefferson Rogers.

One other hunter was hired at Westport. This was Lucien Maxwell, who was headed back to Taos and was more than willing to be paid for part of his homeward journey.

Two days after the establishment of this camp, young Talbot was hit with "severe bleeding of the nose, which lasted the evening and a portion of the night."[14] This was so debilitating it seemed doubtful he would be able to continue the journey. Fortunately for Talbot, the party of Sir William Drummon Stewart—the adventurer-sportsman from Scotland, who was making his last trip into the Wind River Mountains—was camped nearby.[15] In Stewart's party there was Dr. Stedman Richard Tilghman, who had recently graduated from the Baltimore Medical School.

While Dr. Tilghman worked on Talbot, Stewart and Frémont talked of their respective trips. To Stewart, it seemed only natural that the two parties should travel together as far as the Rocky Mountains. But Frémont declined the invitation. His main reason for doing so was that the route Sir William was going to follow was the one that he had been over the previous summer and there was no point in going over the same ground.

Talbot's condition was not at all good. As far as Dr. Tilghman was concerned, the young man should not be allowed to continue. To do so, he explained, would be allowing Talbot to put his life in jeopardy. This was a difficult situation. The bleeding had stopped, and he was anxious to go on. Sensing how Talbot felt, John Charles let him make his own decision. There was no doubt in Talbot's mind. Even if he died somewhere in the wilderness, he was determined to go.

There was excitement in the air at Westport Landing, the kind of excitement that was catching. It seemed as though all of America was on the move. Emigrants were everywhere. Lean, weather-beaten farmers; wives with faces burned by the sun, with expressions of concern for the long journey ahead, with a touch of sadness as they thought of leaving a former way of life and of having said farewell to relatives and friends; and children bounding about, thoroughly caught up by the excitement, and forever in the way as the last preparations were made before the wagons rolled out for Oregon's Willamette Valley or the great Sacramento Valley of California.

Men were checking wagons, talking to anyone who might know something about the country they were heading into. And there was no shortage of men who knew *something*.

Santa Fé traders were getting their big freight wagons ready for the trip down the Santa Fé Trail. Fur traders, mountain men, sportsmen, teamsters, and the Indians of the region—particularly Delawares and Shawnees were ready to head out. Then there were those who had come to this landing for the chance to make some fast money off the throng bound westward. There were authentic guides and would-be guides, anxious young men who wanted the adventure of crossing the frontier and going West, blacksmiths, traders with goods to sell or barter, roustabouts loading and unloading river steamers. There were horse traders who had the best horses, the best mules, the best oxen a man could hope to buy; but the buyer had better look out for the flaws. There was, of course, the inevitable dealer in raw whiskey, the tent saloon keeper with dreams for sale in a bottle; and there were the other purveyors of dreams—the man with a woman in a tent, and the man with a fortune just waiting for the lucky man who could call the turn of a card.

Westport Landing was a boom camp. It was a gathering by the river where all talk came down to a few things: how far was it to where a man was heading; what were his chances of making it; were the Sioux raising hell, and who knew the way once a man got beyond Fort Laramie?

On May 23 Broken Hand Fitzpatrick and his seven men arrived at Frémont's camp with a horse and mule herd of forty animals. While the animals were in good shape, it was certain the party would need more. So during the next few days Fitzpatrick and his men crossed the Missouri River and rode from farm to farm to buy more animals.

While all this was taking place, events in St. Louis had taken a turn which threatened the future of the expedition. Jessie was left in charge of all correspondence. If there was anything that Frémont had to know about, she was to make sure he got it before he left Westport Landing for the interior. Jessie opened one letter from Colonel Abert that caused great alarm. Not only was he concerned about expenditures, he was upset about the mountain howitzer. Not only had Captain Bell's letter reached Washington; it had been laid before James M. Porter, the Secretary of War.

Along with Captain Bell's letter, the Secretary of War also had copies of Frémont's requisition list and Colonel Kearny's order. None of these items were within the area of proper procedure. Without hesitation, he asked Colonel Abert for some reasonable explanation for the possession of such arms by this party.

Colonel Abert replied that this party of exploration was allowed to bear small arms—rifles, pistols, shotguns—but permission had not been granted for the acquisition of a howitzer. This was not enough for the Secretary of War. The whole affair indicated too much disregard for the regular channels of communication. It would not do to have a party of exploration taking a howitzer with them nor would it do to have the whole concept of order bypassed. Order, regularity, and system were vital to the correct operation of the military; and this irregular business of not having applied for arms through regular channels long before reaching St. Louis could not be tolerated. It made no difference if Colonel Kearny had given his approval. He had no right to ask Captain Bell to issue such arms without an order from Washington.

With this pressure applied, Colonel Abert gave in to the Secretary of War. The key item in the letter that Jessie opened, the one thing which caused great anxiety was that Colonel Abert ordered John Charles to stop the expedition and report, at once, to his office in Washington. It wasn't only pressure from a superior that influenced Abert's thinking. Two other things disturbed him very much, and he made this quite clear in his letter. He was concerned about the money that Frémont was spending, money in excess of that budgeted for the expedition; and most of all, he believed that if the threat of hostile Indians was so great as to require the use of a mountain howitzer for protection, then it was only too clear that the expedition would get very little of the geographical information it had been sent to obtain. A party under the constant threat of attack was not going to be very careful in its scientific work.

From where Colonel Abert sat, his reasoning made very good sense. But what he did not know was that if Frémont had run into the kind of hostility from Indians that required the use of a howitzer, it was doubtful that the cannon would have been very effective anyway. John Charles had decided to requisition the mountain howitzer on a completely romantic, almost Byronic impulse. Perhaps he felt that it would give his little party the look of a formidable unit on the move; or perhaps he thought that the mere firing of the howitzer—the loud noise by itself—would serve as a frightening deterrent to a large party of mounted warriors who might otherwise decide that Frémont and his men were fair game. Whatever he thought, the howitzer was of no use to him, and in the long run it only proved to be a waste of manpower to take care of it. He would have done much better had he taken along the same weight in extra food.

Jessie considered the order calling her husband back to Washington the work of somebody who did not want her John Charles to succeed. Senator Benton was out of the city at the time; so she did what she thought was the only way to thwart an obvious scheme against Frémont.

Fancy his fine, picked men, "every man a Captain himself," as Carson once said to me, under the "line and rule" control of an ordinary officer. But here "intuition" came to my aid. Behind the Chief of the Bureau who was a placid, indolent man, I saw his son-in-law who was an envious, discontented person. I ought to say here that the Report had given immediate fame to Mr. Frémont—then why not to another officer?[16]

Colonel Abert hardly deserved what Jessie wrote about him in later years. But too many things had happened over the long span of time, and even the memory of this event was colored by later disasters and tragedies that had plagued their lives. She was not about to give Colonel Abert any benefit of doubt. In her mind, he had been involved in some kind of scheme to rob John Charles of what was due him. After the passing of so many years, she could not remember it any other way. Even if she had, one thing remains true. She did take it upon herself to keep the contents of the letter to herself at that moment, and she did not send it to Westport Landing. Instead, she decided to handle this affair in a way that would protect her hubsand from any interference and send him way beyond any place where he could be reached by any official communication.

I felt the whole situation in a flash, and met it—as I saw right. I had been too much a part of the whole plan for the expeditions to put them in peril now—and I alone could act. Fortunately my father was off in the state attending to his political affairs. I did what I have always since been glad to remember. First I told no one. I knew that one of the men engaged, a French Canadian named de Rosier [Derosier] had been permitted to remain in St. Louis on account of his wife's health, gaining for her the month the party were at Kaw [Westport] Landing with Mr. Frémont. Now I sent for de Rosier and told him an important letter had come for the "Captain" and I wanted it delivered to him without loss of time.[17]

Jessie had no intention of sending Colonel Abert's letter to John Charles. Instead, she sat down and wrote one of her own. When she finished, she told Derosier that she wanted this delivered as fast as he could get to Frémont. Also, she made clear that he was to say nothing about this. Haste was the key request, and Jessie knew that Derosier could travel by land.

Derosier suggested that he take his brother with him. In that way, the brother could bring back a letter from Frémont. This would tell her how fast they had got to his camping place, and also would be an answer to her letter.

Jessie was all for this. Anything that would tell her that some duplicate copy of Colonel Abert's letter had not reached John Charles would put her mind at ease. For she feared that possibly the colonel would have done just that in case Frémont had already departed from St. Louis.

It was in the blessed day before telegraphs and character counted for something then, and I was only eighteen, an age when one takes risks willingly. It was about four hundred miles to Kaw Landing north of St. Louis as the crow flies. So I wrote urging him not to lose a day but start at once on my letter. That I could not give him the reason but he must GO. That I knew it would be bad for his animals, who would have only the scant early grass, but they could stop at Bent's Fort and fatten up. *Only trust me and go.* . . .[18]

Having sent this letter to her husband, Jessie then wrote to Colonel Abert and told him what she had done. She also pointed out that any Indians that the party might meet would never have heard of such a thing as a scientific expedition and would not hesitate to launch an attack against any party which did not appear to have the strength to defend itself. But Jessie was creating a situation out of whole cloth. Frémont's men were well-armed and more than capable of defending themselves without the use of a mountain howitzer.

No matter, the letter reached Frémont, and he took Jessie's warning to heart. If there was something that was so important that she had sent two men on a four-hundred-mile ride just to deliver a message for him to get moving, then he had better do just that.

# ·ᴥ VIII ᴥ·

## The Road to India

THE KINKS were not out of the expedition even though they were nine days on the trail and 174 miles away from Westport Landing. It was taking time to break the greenhorns of bad habits, to teach them the methods of survival beyond the frontier. Frederick Dwight was a long way from Harvard University. Law books didn't count for much. He had already lost one horse, but on this day his horse threw him and struck out for home carrying a good saddle and bridle and a pair of pistols. So that scholar of the wilderness Lucien Maxwell rode after Dwight's horse while the expedition moved ahead.

The party started to cross a tree-lined creek when Maxwell came out of the distance at a full gallop. He was riding hard. Right behind him, closing the distance, was a party of about thirty warriors in close pursuit. Experienced hands in Frémont's party quickly got ready for action. Fitzpatrick and the others shouted orders to watch out for the horses and mules. Then in a last rush, Maxwell was among them. Almost at the same time, so were the Indians who had not seen the strength of the expedition. In and out of the camp, a blur of movement, shouts to watch the horses, and the Osage warriors—their heads shaved to the scalp locks—were on both sides of the creek. But some even stopped to shake hands and talk. As they did, others waved their red blankets against the flanks of their mounts and were gone as fast as they had appeared.

After a wild ride for his life, Maxwell was safe. But now more than one horse was missing. In the wild chase in and out of the startled party, the Osage warriors had spooked the horses enough to drive off a number of the best animals. The top riders in the party pursued the Indians, and after a hard ride of seven or eight miles they succeeded in getting back the stolen mounts. This was a bad break for the expedition, and Frémont was not happy about it. It caused "delay and trouble, and threatened danger and loss, and broke down some good horses at the start. . . ."[1] The whole affair was a lesson to him. It did not pay to take greenhorns along.

By June 14 they had reached an area in the valley of the Republican River called Big Timbers by the Indians. On the south side of the river they made camp. The spring had been unusually wet, and between fording creeks and rivers and getting the carts through wet and muddy ground, the party was averaging only five or six miles of travel per day. This was much too slow for Frémont, and he decided something had to be done to speed up the expedition's progress.

> I determined at this place to divide the party, and, leaving Mr. Fitzpatrick with 25 men in charge of the provisions and heavier baggage of the camp, to proceed myself in advance, with a light party of 15 men, taking with me the howitzer and the light wagon which carried the instruments.[2]

During the cold and miserable layover at the Big Timbers camp, preparations were made for the smaller party. Louis Zindel did some target practice with the mountain howitzer. He proved to be very good at his trade, for he was able to hit a post standing four feet high from a distance of almost a quarter of a mile.

On a rainy Friday morning, June 16, Frémont and his men bid good-bye to the larger party and moved out. Still within present-day Kansas, Frémont noted the quality of the soil and the different types of grasses, such as bunch and buffalo grass. He tried to identify the profusion of wild flowers that ranged from a purplish-red wild rose to dwarf lupine, sweet William, daisy, foxglove, white flax, anemone, and the ever-present buttercup; and he listed the different trees in this well-timbered prairie country—groves of ash, elm, cottonwood, and even an occasional oak.

Now the party began to see plenty of game. There was no difficulty in killing an antelope for supper, and soon they began to see some buffalo. At first they saw only old bulls, stragglers from the main herds. But as the big herds came into view, the number of buffalo grazing in the open country was astounding. These herds ran into the thousands, and there seemed to be no end to them. By this time, Frémont and his men were at about the fortieth parallel. They saw vast prairie dog towns, so many of them that when they made their June 23 camp beside a fork of the Republican River, Frémont named it Prairie Dog River.

Bordered by stands of ash, cottonwood, and willow—trees filled with nesting birds that filled the air with musical songs—Prairie Dog River was a beautiful stream. There was plenty of grass for the horses and mules, more than enough game for the camp hunters, firewood for the cutting, and clear, sweet water. The steady singing of birds mingled with the sharp warning whistles of prairie dogs that sat bolt upright beside their holes and did a quick, diving exit as horsemen drew too near.

The next few days the men traveled through a land that had a touch of Eden about it; and as they moved farther to the northwest and began to gain in elevation, they came upon herds of buffalo that seemed to cover the face of the earth. But this grand abundance, this land of plenty vanished with a jarring surprise as they moved past the hundredth meridian on June 26 and entered a country of barren contrast. Sandhills, sparse timber to no timber at all, short grass but not much of that, sagebrush, and then the shallow water of a small tributary of the Republican River greeted them. It was wide enough as rivers go, almost six hundred yards, but it was only a few inches deep and was spread across a bed of mustard-colored sand. There was hardly any timber to be seen beside the banks of this river vanishing into its quicksand bottom. This was a river for desert country.

It was too early to make camp, and none of the men saw the stream as a great place to offer a decent drink of water much less a good place to camp for the night. When they finally located a waterhole, it was already evening. The waterhole was a buffalo wallow with buffalo standing in the middle of it. It was hardly what a man could call drinkable water, even after they had driven the buffalo out and allowed the water to settle. Buffalo had not only been standing in the water; they had rolled in it, and never bothered to move out when they felt the urge to urinate or drop a fresh stream of excrement. Added to that, the shallow pond was warm from the steady glare of the sun —warm and stinking.

Charles Preuss called it "animal water" and considered it another hardship of traveling in this godforsaken wilderness. Yet, it was water to keep a man alive, even if it was only drinkable at a time of sheer desperation.

On the last day of June, they reached the South Fork of the Platte River. This familiar sight was a great change from what they had been through, for here was a fine rolling river filled with water from the melting snowpacks of the Rocky Mountains. To Frémont and his men, this was a magnificent contrast to the parched land they had crossed. That night when "the broad expanse of water grew indistinct, it almost seemed that we had pitched our tents on the shore of the sea."[3]

2

THE MEN HAD BEEN RIDING since early morning. It was the Fourth of July, and Frémont hadn't even stopped for a rest to celebrate. He was moving fast, covering the ground with one thought in mind: to reach St. Vrain's Fort in time for a good meal. Now, as the sun neared its midday peak, the explorer and his party saw the bright sunlight reflecting off the adobe walls of the fort. They were trail-weary riders, and the sight of the quadrangular shaped post with bastions at two alternate angles and heavy main gates below the entrance tower was a welcome view, for this fort on the east bank of the South Fork of the Platte River was a place to rest without worry of raiders, a proper setting for an Independence Day celebration.

As they rode within shouting distance, they saw men standing in the main entrance. The gates had been opened, and standing there to greet the explorers were Marcellin St. Vrain, the bourgeois, and his clerk, the chief trader, and a scattering of other employees.

A year had passed since they had met, and both men were anxious to talk. John Charles wanted all the information he could obtain about the possibility of a pass through the Rocky Mountains, the present attitudes of the various Indian tribes, and any other scrap of data that would help in his job. As for St. Vrain, he wanted to know what was taking place in the States, and he wished to hear any news about trappers and traders he knew. Best of all, neither man had to converse in English except to explain something to a companion who had no knowledge of French.

St. Vrain invited Frémont and his men to join the personnel of the fort for a Fourth of July feast and celebration. John Charles was more than pleased to accept this warm hospitality. He joined his host and walked to the main dining room in one of the single-story adobe buildings that backed up against the fort's wall and overlooked the plaza. Then after the horses and mules were unsaddled, watered, and placed in the corral, the rest of the men sat at the dining table. While the dinner wasn't fancy, it was far better than the usual fare they had been eating as their supplies ran short.

When the meal was over and the men had finished exchanging news of their respective worlds, Frémont inquired about the possibility of obtaining supplies.

Well, there were a few items he could buy: some unbolted Mexican flour, a little salt, a few other things. That was about all. At the moment, the fort was short of everything.

But food was not Frémont's greatest problem. Even without bread or macaroni, his party could get by with whatever game the hunters shot. The major problem was to get fresh animals to replace his worn-out horses and mules. Frémont knew that even if he waited for Fitzpatrick, who was ten days behind him, the animals in his party would be pretty well jaded.

St. Vrain was more than willing to sell him whatever he had, but that was the trouble. All a man had to do was step into the plaza and look at the corral. It was too obvious there weren't any animals for sale.

Frémont did learn from St. Vrain that a mule herd had recently arrived in Taos from Upper California. More than likely these animals were stolen from Mexican ranchos, but still they were mules. This news offered some hope. Lucien Maxwell was planning to go to Taos, and Frémont asked him to look over these mules and, if they were any good, to buy ten or twelve. Then they could rendezvous at Fontaine-qui-bouit or Boiling Springs Creek, where it joined the Arkansas River. For John Charles planned to head southwest in his search for a possible Rocky Mountain pass.

Maxwell was agreeable to this arrangement, and on the morning of July 6 he rode out of the fort and headed south toward Taos. A few hours later Frémont and his men left the post, to follow the South Fork of the Platte River toward the mountains. One man, Oscar Sarpy, remained at St. Vrain's

Fort. This greenhorn had requested his release from the expedition as he did not think he could endure much more of this life.

During this first day away from their comfortable quarters at St. Vrain's Fort, Frémont and his men passed two abandoned posts—Forts Vasquez and Jackson—which had been used during the 1830s as trading centers in the territory of the Southern Arapaho. Beyond these posts, and only ten miles from St. Vrain's, they came to Lancaster P. Lupton's Fort Lancaster, sometimes called Fort Lupton. This post had "the appearance of a comfortable farm; stock, hogs, and cattle, were ranging about on the prairie; there were different kinds of poultry; and there was the wreck of a promising garden, in which a considerable variety of vegetables had been in a flourishing condition, but it had been almost entirely ruined by the recent high waters."[4]

Stopping for a short visit, John Charles met another young man whom he had seen during the previous trek into this country. This was the journalist Rufus B. Sage, who had been caught up by the romance of the West and had come to the Rocky Mountains to trap beaver and trade with the Indians. He then returned to the East to write a book about his life of adventure in the Wild West. Three years after Frémont saw him in this outpost, Sage brought out Scenes in the Rocky Mountains, a book which went through many printings in both hardback and paperback; one of the hardback editions even included an 1845 map adapted from Frémont's Report. But once Sage got the West out of his mind by putting it in print, that was it.

Sage was not the only man from the East that Frémont saw. In this wild and free land where the Rocky Mountains reached skyward like the hiding places of lost and mysterious gods from earlier days in the life of the earth, men from the settlements were on the move. Some like the emigrants with their wives and children were seeking a new life, a better chance. Some like the fur traders were seeking both adventure and enough profit to take care of them in old age. And others, like Frémont and Sage, were seekers of another kind. They were men who sought answers to questions about the nature of the land and about the men who made their homes far beyond the safer boundaries of settled communities.

An hour's talk, an exchange of news about the States, about mutual friends of the wilderness, about the weather, about the feelings of neighboring Indian tribes, and then the expedition was on its way again. Six miles beyond Fort Lancaster the party made camp as a cold rain began to fall—a rain with the feel of snow in it. All that night they endured the cold, but with daybreak the storm had blown past. They quickly broke camp and moved on their way, and within a few miles entered a large Arapaho encampment.

Frémont estimated that there were about 160 lodges in this camp. The buffalo-skin lodges covered a large area of level ground, and while they varied in size, most of them were about ten feet in diameter and twelve feet high. Attached to many of these were dog houses made of wickerwork and covered with cured skins. And as John Charles had noted the first time he had seen an Arapaho camp, near the entrance to each lodge there was a tri-pod of poles that held the warrior's shield, lances, battle ax, and other imple-ments of war.

The camp was filled with women and children, and the Arapaho were en-joying a season of plenty. Frémont saw the older boys taking care of the horses, smaller boys playing at various games, men sitting about discussing one thing or another, and women and older girls hard at work with their var-ious domestic duties that ranged from cooking to curing hides. As a break in the routine, now and then an old man would stroll through the camp and in a loud and eloquent voice proclaim the latest news of the day.

In great dignity, the chiefs of this camp came toward Frémont and wel-comed his party in friendship. But they were disappointed that he had only a few presents for them. Sensing their desire for more of a gift of passing, John Charles had his translators explain that the bulk of his supplies were coming in another section of his expedition, and that their old friend Broken Hand was in charge of everything. When he arrived, he would have more gifts for them.

After a talk with the chiefs and the presentation of the few gifts he had, Frémont and his men moved on. That night they camped a little above the junction of the South Fork of the Platte River and Cherry Creek—an area close to Denver, Colorado.

The next morning the party caught a momentary view of Pikes Peak. But except for this temporary view, the snow-covered landmark was hidden by a gathering of small white clouds. This was a condition that Frémont noted as part of the climate of this region. In the early morning, unless it happened to be raining, the sky would be extremely clear and the mountains were easy to see. But in no time at all, cloud formations would gather around the peaks and effectively cover them. Still, they did catch this glimpse of Pikes Peak, and then they moved along the South Fork of the Platte River until they reached a point where the river divided into three forks. They followed the easternmost branch of the river, and worked their way into higher country. By noon they were in an area of good meadow grass that was brightened by the colors of wild flowers. Timber was easily available, and the leaves of quak-ing aspen and cottonwood trees shimmered in the afternoon breeze. On the slopes of the mountains, great stands of pines gave the base of this massive range a covering of green.

To the hungry men it appeared that they would sleep another night with-out any meat for supper. But Basil Lajeunesse shot a nice deer that he found feeding in a hollow. Even though another rainstorm pelted them that night, the men were happy with their camp as they sat around "fires, girdled with *appolas* of fine venison. . . ."[5]

Direction had to be changed and Frémont knew it. On the morning of July 9, right after daybreak, the men rode eastward following the divide be-tween the Arkansas River and South Fork of the Platte as they hoped to find a herd of buffalo. The country they traveled had magnificent scenery. There were strange rocky hills with wind-eroded shapes, small valleys of green grass where clear streams vanished into sandy bottoms, and a wild range of colors from the season's first wild flowers, but with all this growth there was no sign of game. Before nightfall, as they got ready to make camp beside what is now Monument Creek, a lone buffalo bull appeared—no doubt, an older bull that had been chased away from the herd by the younger bulls—and the men had a supply of meat.

During the night there was a heavy snowfall in the high mountains. At daybreak the sky was clear, and Frémont was entranced with the beauty of Pikes Peak as the first rays of sunlight reflected off the fresh snow and gave a luminous and glittering white that dominated the skyline. And though his men were sick from the buffalo bull meat, or from the altitude, they mounted up and moved on. Heading eastward, they crossed the headwaters of the Kiowa River, and camped on the Bijou Fork early in the day to give the ill men a rest. Always curious about everything he saw, Frémont and some of his men tried to unearth the habitat of a prairie dog. The clay soil was hard to dig into, but they kept at it until dark. While John Charles never managed to catch up to a prairie dog, this excavation gave him a good idea of how the various tunnels in this dog town were interconnected.

The next day's wandering through the valley of the Bijou did not produce any buffalo. As they worked their way higher and higher until they reached an altitude of 7,500 feet, the only meat they were able to get was a large grizzly bear they surprised as the animal was digging for roots. It took six rifle balls to kill the grizzly, but as the hunters dressed their kill, they discovered the bear was in poor shape and hardly worth trying to eat.

The need for food was becoming critical, and though Frémont wanted to look the country over more thoroughly, he had no choice other than to head for the nearest place where food might be obtained. On the morning of July 12 they struck a southwest course and headed for the wagon road that ran from St. Vrain's Fort to Bent's Fort. By nightfall they were camped at Fontaine-qui-bouit, near the site of present-day Colorado Springs. The next day they moved south along an Indian trail that followed Boiling Springs Creek or present-day Fountain Creek. This was a well-used path that came out of a valley high in the mountains behind Pikes Peak, a valley or hole that the mountain men called Bayou Salade or South Park. The expedition made good time along this route, and by noon of July 14 they reached the junction of the creek and the Arkansas River. They pitched camp just below the settlement of Pueblo—a new village of adobe and log buildings that had been established the year before by the black mountain man Jim Beckwourth and other free trappers. This site of present-day Pueblo, Colorado, was hardly a prosperous village. The men were mostly American trappers, and they had seen better days during the height of the fur trade. Now that beaver hats were out of style, these men and their Mexican and Indian wives were trying to make a go of it with a little trading and some farming.

The settlers were a friendly group, and Frémont received open hospitality. But the possibility of their selling anything to the explorer was not very good. Their stock of goods and their extra horses and mules were in short supply. Their trade with Taos and other settlements of New Mexico had been severely limited—almost halted—by decrees of the Mexican government. Still, the citizens of Pueblo were willing to share whatever they had. And since they did have good milk cows, the hungry explorers were able to drink their fill of fresh milk.

From the mountain men at Pueblo, Frémont learned something that he should have heard from Rufus Sage when he met him at Fort Lancaster. The difficulties that existed between the Americans and the Mexicans were the direct result of a filibuster action against New Mexico by a band of Texans who were seeking revenge for the 1841 defeat of George Wilkens Kendall and his ragtag Texas army that had invaded New Mexico and suffered severe losses of both life and liberty from the command of Governor Manuel Armijo. Now, in this summer of 1843, as Frémont hoped to obtain supplies and mules from Taos, another unruly filibuster movement had taken place against New Mexico.

In one of the actions of this losing adventure, Colonel Charles A. Warfield and his band of freebooters—including the romantic young Sage—had drifted to the community of Mora, New Mexico. There, they had gone on a wild shooting and looting spree. When news of this reached Governor Armijo, he sent a militia unit under the command of Captain Ventura Lobata —a relative of Maxwell's father-in-law—out of Taos with his own force and a contingent of drafted Pueblo Indians, who had no wish to be involved in this struggle. While they headed after Warfield and his men, young Sage drifted back to Fort Lancaster. But the little excitement at Mora, an excitement with the stench of death about it, had been the warning battle of big troubles to come.

Colonel Warfield's small band had been reinforced by men from Colonel Jacob Snively's regiment, and this added strength had given Warfield enough of an army to inflict a severe defeat upon Captain Lobata. During this battle, twenty or more of the Pueblo Indians from Taos were killed. When news of this reached Taos, the Pueblo Indians decided it was time to run both Americans and Mexicans out of their country.

All this brought Santa Fé Trail commerce to a halt. To prevent further bloodshed and a possibility of an enlarging conflict, the United States sent a detachment of dragoons under the command of Captain Philip St. George Cooke to protect both Americans and Mexican traders using the trail. Cooke had strict orders to avoid crossing the border into New Mexico. This presented great problems for the traders. At Bent's Fort they hired Kit Carson for three hundred dollars to ride to Governor Armijo and ask him to send Mexican troops to the border to protect the caravans.

At Jim Beckwourth's village of Pueblo, Frémont picked up bits and pieces of this whole affair. All of it was quite disturbing, for he learned that Lucien Maxwell had started for Taos before news of the Pueblo Indian uprising had spread north. It wasn't only the Pueblo Indians who were raising hell. The Utes also had taken to shooting Americans and Mexicans on sight. Maxwell's father-in-law, Charles Beaubien, had been forced to hightail it from Taos to Santa Fé in order to save his life. So, somewhere out there between the mouth of Boiling Springs Creek and Taos, Lucien Maxwell either was alive and on the dodge, or was long past worrying about. Still, Frémont believed that if anyone had a chance to survive in such a situation, the resourceful and cool-headed Maxwell was just such a man. At any rate, there was nothing that could be done to help him; and this meant that Frémont could not figure Maxwell would be returning with mules and supplies.

Luck rode with John Charles at this bleak moment when the future of the expedition appeared to be in jeopardy. A lone visitor from Bent's Fort rode into Pueblo. He had made the seventy-five-mile ride, he said, just to say hello to his old friend. John Charles couldn't have been happier to see this small, familiar figure appear as though he knew he would be needed. For if any of the tough and experienced mountain men of Pueblo could have chosen only one man to go with them on a dangerous trek into the back country, the man getting off his horse and quietly greeting old friends was as good a man as anybody could ever hope to have on his side. Frémont quickly invited Carson to join the expedition as a guide and hunter for his usual salary of one hundred dollars per month. To his relief, Kit agreed to the proposition.

As they talked of the need for supplies and mules, Carson told Frémont that he had met Maxwell on his way to Taos and had tried to persuade him to turn back. But Lucien was determined to get to Taos to see how his family had fared, and told Carson that he could find Frémont somewhere around Pueblo.

The need for supplies was so very urgent that Frémont gave Carson only a few hours to rest. Then he sent him back the way he had come, for Carson had told him that supplies and mules were available at Bent's Fort. When he had secured what was needed, he was to take the shortest route to St. Vrain's Fort.

After Kit left Pueblo, John Charles got his party ready to head back up Boiling Springs Creek to visit the springs that gave the creek its name. Before he left on the morning of July 16, he hired Charles Town—a good frontiersman and a friend of the Bent brothers. Then he wrote a note for Lucien Maxwell stating he would wait for him at St. Vrain's Fort until July 26. If he did not appear by that time, the expedition would continue its trek.

Leaving Boiling Springs Creek, the expedition moved northward. A week later, on Sunday July 23, they saw the familiar shape of St. Vrain's Fort.

Fitzpatrick and the main section of the party were already there. When they spotted Frémont heading toward the fort, they fired a salute to welcome the lieutenant and his men back from their detour to the south. Best of all, Broken Hand had taken care of his animals and had been frugal with the supplies, so that he had a good outfit ready to hit the trail. Kit Carson was already at St. Vrain's Fort having made the trip from Bent's Fort with ten mules and more supplies. So, while the excursion to the south had not resulted in the discovery of any new pass through the Rocky Mountains, the delay in the forward progress of the expedition had resulted in getting what was necessary for its continuation with the added bonus of hiring Kit Carson to go along.

3

AT ST. VRAIN'S FORT, Frémont talked over all the possible crossings of the Rocky Mountains with Fitzpatrick and Carson. After consideration of all the possibilities, Frémont decided he would again take a smaller party and try to find a passage through the mountains by following the Cache la Poudre River into its source country around Longs Peak. While he was doing this, he wanted Broken Hand and the larger party with the carts and supplies to head for South Pass, cross over the mountains and strike out for Fort Hall, where they were to wait for him at this post of the Hudson's Bay Company alongside the Snake River.

Before they left the comfort of St. Vrain's Fort, the two Shawnee hunters told Frémont they had come as far as they had promised. Now they were going to return to their homes. On July 26 Theodore Talbot wrote a few hurried lines to his mother and sent it toward the settlements with the Shawnees.

The loss of the Shawnee hunters presented a problem, especially for the larger party that would be traveling under the leadership of Fitzpatrick. The mountain man Charles Town, who had been hired at Pueblo, was assigned to Broken Hand's command. This still left a need for another hunter. But there was an experienced hunter and mountain man at the fort who was willing to go. He was a twenty-five-year-old French Canadian from St. Louis. A handsome, well-built man, he was to become one of Frémont's favorites on this and future expeditions. This was Alexis Godey, a man whom John Charles ultimately considered to be cut out of the same cloth as Basil Lajeunesse, Lucien Maxwell, and even Kit Carson.

One other man was also hired to go with Fitzpatrick as a voyageur. This was a rough and ruthless French engagé who had killed a fellow mountaineer during the Fourth of July celebration at Fort Lancaster. The result of this killing was not limited to the hiring of Thomas Fallon as a worker for Fitzpatrick. For the victim of Fallon's quick thrust with a knife had left a widow, a Shoshoni woman, and two children. When she found that Frémont was heading toward her people's country, she asked if she might travel with him. He did not hesitate. He liked the children, and compared the woman's plight to that of Naomi in the Old Testament. He assigned five or six pack horses to carry her baggage and provided her with a small tent.

Altogether, counting the woman and children and himself, Frémont's party consisted of seventeen persons. Among them were essentially the same men he had taken to Pueblo. These included Charles Preuss, the Lajeunesse brothers, young Jacob Dodson, Louis Zindel to handle the howitzer, plus seven other top men. Added to this company was the one man who could find a pass through the Rocky Mountains for them if there was one to be found; and the presence of Kit Carson must have given all the men in the party a greater feeling of security than they would have had without a guide of his caliber to lead the way.

By the afternoon of July 26 the two sections of the expedition resumed their march. The South Fork of the Platte River was swollen with water from the melting snowpacks in the high mountains and a season of almost daily rainstorms. Young Talbot noted in his journal, that he and other members of Fitzpatrick's group bid farewell to Frémont's party as they crossed the river to take up their line of march. Then he wrote that later in the day they, too, crossed with the Red River carts and their supplies loaded aboard canoes. This was the last they would see of Frémont until he reached Fort Hall, for they were going to cover ground he had been over in the summer of 1842 as they made their way to Fort Laramie and headed for South Pass.

John Charles and his party swam the South Fork of the Platte River on their horses. The crossing was not an easy one for the mules carrying the supplies, and it must have taken the rubber boat or some sort of raft to get the howitzer across. But they managed it without suffering any loss of supplies or any injuries to men or mounts. Yet they were dead tired and traveled only four miles before making camp for the night at Thompson's Creek, where they were very nearly eaten alive by mosquitoes.

In the morning they headed northwest toward the Cache la Poudre and the Black Hills, the present Laramie Mountains. The party reached the Cache la Poudre below the mouth of Box Elder Creek, and the next two days were hard going. They had to climb in and out a deep ravine, and on July 29 they were forced to make river crossings eight or nine times. Each one of these fords was difficult, as the water was cold, deep, and running swiftly. Even with all the hard work, Frémont was entranced with this mountain valley and its wild scenery.

Towering mountains rose round about; their sides sometimes dark with forests of pine, and sometimes with lofty precipices, washed by the river; while below . . . the green river bottom was covered with a wilderness of flowers, their tall spikes sometimes rising above our heads as we rode among them. A profusion of blossoms on a white flowering vine . . . which was abundant along the river, contrasted handsomely with the green foliage of the trees. The mountains appeared to be composed of a greenish gray and red granite, which in some places appeared to be in a state of decomposition, making a red soil.[6]

Working their way up Poudre Canyon (above present Fort Collins, Colorado), they climbed away from the lush growth beside the creek. By the end of July, they reached the high plains along the Laramie River, and the nature of the country changed from mountain meadows to sagebrush and soil that was like ashes left over from ancient campfires.

At noon Carson returned from hunting with an antelope. The men cheered as they had been without meat since the last venison feast they had in the canyon. That night, they pitched camp a few miles southwest of present-day Laramie, Wyoming. After leaving this camp, the going was easier and faster for the party. They lined out and headed toward the Medicine Bow Range. On the first day of August they encountered a war party of Sioux and Cheyenne Indians, but the Indians were friendly, and there was no trouble.

Three days after this chance meeting with the Sioux and Cheyennes, the men allowed themselves the foolish luxury of not keeping a complete guard duty while they went about the business of erecting scaffolds and cutting slices of buffalo meat after a successful hunt—meat which they intended to jerk so that they would have a supply to fall back on if they hit lean times. They were camped in the valley of the North Platte River, after having crossed Medicine Butte Pass—a broad trail westward between the main spurs of the Medicine Bow Range and Medicine Butte (now called Elk Mountain).

The man guarding the horses happened to catch a glimpse of an Indian's head peering over a low hill. The horse guard quickly turned the herd toward the camp and gave the alarm. All hell broke loose as seventy warriors yelled and rode at a full gallop. Frémont's men coolly got into position to fire, and Louis Zindel sighted the loaded howitzer at the charging band of horsemen.

Suddenly the Indians brought their horses to a sliding halt. When the dust settled, the war party made signs for peace. As they approached the camp, Carson and other experienced frontiersmen saw that the war party was made up for both Arapahoes and Cheyennes. They explained to Frémont and his guide that they had brought their charge to a halt when they saw the party was not a band of hostile Indians. John Charles thought this was a polite story, but he was convinced his beloved howitzer had been the determining factor in ending the attack. No doubt the real reason for halting the charge was that they could see they were going to ride into a party of men who were carrying good rifles and were ready to use them. Whatever their reason, they were welcomed into camp and given tobacco and other presents.

As the warriors smoked and talked, they explained they had been on a raid against their enemies, the Shoshoni. They had surprised one of their villages located outside Bridger's Fort at the Black Fork of the Green River,[7] and managed to take some scalps and horses. But the Shoshoni men, who had not been in camp, returned in time to pursue them; and in the battle that followed, the Arapahoes had lost several of their men. Others were so badly wounded that they were coming behind the main party with a slower-moving group of warriors who were protecting and taking care of them.

The story they related wasn't a full-blown lie, but it was not quite the whole truth. They neglected to say that they had killed and scalped the man guarding the horse herd, speared a Shoshoni woman and boy who were asleep, kidnapped a girl, and stolen the horses. Unfortunately for these raiders, on their way back from their violent success they ran into a party of mountain men. Then, as they tried to put distance between themselves and these men with long rifles, they rode right into the Shoshoni warriors, who were returning from a hunt. While they managed to spear one of the Shoshoni, they also paid a high price for their raid—high enough that they lost the horses and were still smarting from what had turned into a defeat for them. Then as they talked to Frémont and his men, Preuss recorded that one of the Arapahoes expressed a desire to scalp the Shoshoni woman traveling with Frémont's party. But the strength of the expedition and the leader's attitude toward the raiders prevented such brutality from happening.

As the afternoon began to run its course, the disgruntled raiders took leave to continue their homeward journey. The excitement was over, but everyone knew extreme caution would have to be the rule as long as these warriors were anywhere around. It was going to take a victory to keep them from losing face when they reached their own camp, and men in such a mood might look upon a party of whites as fair game if the cost of victory didn't come too high. But as the jerking of buffalo meat continued and supper was prepared, Frémont did not forget to take his readings for latitude and longitude; he measured the elevation at 6,820 feet above sea level and entered in his records that the temperature at sunset was seventy degrees.

The next few days of travel was over country almost bare of everything except sagebrush. Water was in short supply. Grass for grazing was extremely sparse. They moved along the gradual grade at the lower end of South Pass. By August 9 they reached the welcome relief of water and feed at the Sweetwater River about twenty miles above Devil's Gate.

That night they camped beside the Sweetwater, and in the early morning they moved along a well-marked path. Many wagon trains had passed this way, and the sagebrush had been beaten flat by wagon wheels and the hooves of animals. On this broad road to Oregon time was taken out for a sport which Preuss found both cruel and amusing. Louis Zindel tried using his mountain howitzer as a buffalo gun.

On August 13, three days after shooting buffalo with the howitzer, the expedition crossed the Continental Divide. Frémont described this area as being "very near the table mountain, at the southern extremity of the South Pass, which is nearly twenty miles in width, and already traversed by several different roads."[8] The downward path was through an easy hollow which led them to the Little Sandy and then to the Big Sandy. For a few days they followed these streams through dry sagebrush country as they moved into the Green River Valley. This took them south of the mountains and toward Green River.

On August 15 they reached the Green and made camp on the left bank of the river, in a country altogether different from the monotonous, dull, gray region of sagebrush. This country of fine stands of cottonwood trees beside the river and on the islands in the streams was a welcome relief. The valley lived up to its name. There was plenty of grass for the horses and mules. Called the Seedskeedee Agie or Prairie-hen River by the Crow Indians, it was correctly named as there was an abundance of these tasty birds.

This was familiar country to Kit Carson as the Green River Valley often had been the site of the annual rendezvous for traders, fur trappers, and Indians. It was here that Carson had fought a duel with a French trapper named Shunar. Both men had come at each other on horseback and had fired their pistols almost at the same time. The ball from Shunar's weapon had grazed Kit's skull, digging a slight furrow and burning some hair, while Kit's shot had gone through his opponent's arm. As Kit remembered it in later years, the whole thing had taken place because of the Frenchman's bullying ways. After that, nobody had any more trouble with Shunar.

But that had taken place in the summer of 1835, when mountain men were lords of the wilderness. Now, only eight years later, it was all memory. The good times had come and gone. Those had been rough and violent years, but years to remember for the rest of a man's life. There would never be anything like them again. Some of this must have run through Kit's mind as he looked about their camp and saw the animals picketed for the night, the tents pitched, and the campfires started for the evening meal. And if he had closed his eyes for a moment, even the sounds would have been much like those wild times in the Green River Valley: horses snorting, a mixture of French, English, and Indian languages, and because of the Shoshoni woman, there was even the sound of an Indian mother and her children. But with open eyes, it was only memory of another time, another way of life.

In the morning the party made an easy ford across the river and struck out along the Oregon Trail. By late afternoon, they had covered twenty-six miles and had reached Hams Fork, a tributary of the Green River. At this campground, the indication of heavy wagon traffic bound for Oregon was plainly evident as the soil was pulverized so that even a slight breeze raised a cloud of fine dust.

Two days after the camp at Hams Fork, the Shoshoni woman and her children took leave of the party and struck out for Bridger's Fort, where she hoped to find some of her people. Then on the next day, Frémont sent Kit Carson on toward Fort Hall (in present-day Idaho) to purchase supplies that were badly needed. Two more days passed after Carson had vanished in the distance, and the men came to the Bear River Valley. Bear River flowed into the Great Salt Lake, and Frémont intended to explore this massive body of water that he had heard about. As he gathered from experienced men in his party, very little was known about this lake. There was the possibility that Etienne Provost had been the first white man to see the lake in 1824, but that was not certain. It was known that Jim Bridger and some other mountain men had seen the lake in 1825, and Bridger had thought he had reached the Pacific Ocean.

Any information concerning the lake was more in the nature of rumor than fact. As Frémont put it, "Its islands had never been visited; and none were to be found who had entirely made the circuit of its shores⁹; and no instrumental observations or geographical survey, of any description, had ever been made anywhere in the neighboring region. It was generally supposed that it had no visible outlet; but among trappers, including those in my own camp, were many who believed that somewhere on its surface was a terrible whirlpool, through which its waters found their way to the ocean by some subterranean communication."[10]

No matter how it was described, the Great Salt Lake was a thing of mystery. It was not something John Charles was going to bypass since he was in the Bear River Valley and had been told that the river flowed into the lake. The temptation was too much to resist, even though it was a detour from his route to Oregon. He was determined to find out all he could about this stranded inland sea.

4

THEY WERE ON THE OREGON TRAIL, and they followed its trace for some miles along the Bear River in a northward direction before they branched off to head south toward the Great Salt Lake. On August 25 they arrived at one of the curiosities of the trail, a sight a man was apt to enter in his diary or journal. This was Beer Springs, a name given because the appearance of the springs' effervescent and sulphurous water reminded mountain men and voyageurs of the last mug of lager beer they had sipped in a St. Louis tavern. But appearance was one thing, taste quite another when a man drank this soda water boiling up through the burnt-out lava. But Beer Springs wasn't the only sight to write home about. In this area (now under the water of the reservoir at Soda Springs, Idaho) was noisy Steamboat Spring, which shot water "out of a hole six or eight inches diameter, at intervals of half a second . . . occasionally to the height of ten feet."[11] The sound of this noisy underground bubbler was like the steady chug-chug-chug of a hard-working steamboat engine pushing the paddlewheel against a stiff current.

They camped for one day in this region of boiling springs. Frémont and Preuss examined the lava formations and the tufa that had formed around the spouting hot water, and made an analysis of Beer Springs which showed that the principal mineral in the water was carbonate of lime. The temperature of the water varied from 56 degrees in one spring to a high of 87 degrees in another.

Though they were short of food, and it would have been easier to continue on to Fort Hall, Frémont was counting on Carson to return with what they needed. Late on the morning of August 26 the explorer left the Oregon Trail at Soda Springs and headed southwest along the west bank of the Bear River. To let Carson know where to find him, he sent Henry Lee on to Fort Hall with instructions for Kit to load pack horses with whatever he could purchase and overtake the exploring party somewhere along the Bear River on its course to the lake. They found two stray calves, lost by some party of emigrants, and drove them along as a walking food supply.

The going along Bear River was not easy, and as they reached the perpendicular walls of Black Canyon, John Charles called a halt opposite a high, craggy point the men called Sheep Rock (present-day Soda Point). After a tough day's travel, they made camp near a small party of Shoshoni Indians. These people were very short of food, but were friendly and willing to share their supply of camas roots. Frémont traded goods for the roots, but his men didn't think much of this diet. That night, they slaughtered one of the calves to ease the growling in their stomachs.

Two days later, hauling the instrument wagon along, pulling the heavy howitzer on its carriage up one steep grade and down another, the weary men worked their way along Battle Creek and Weston Creek. They hacked brush until their arms ached to make a path for the wagon and howitzer carriage. While they saw great flights of ducks and geese, the men managed to shoot only a few. Fishing didn't pan out very well, and during one of the nights, a mess became desperate enough to eat a skunk for supper.

Finally they worked their way down from the rough, high ground to the valley of the Malad River. They followed this stream toward the lake, and came to an Indian village where they hoped they might be able to trade for some food. But the Indians were on the brink of starvation. When Frémont saw some of the men pull back their robes to show their lean and bony bodies, he refused to allow his men to trade with these hungry people for what little food they might have stored away.

By September 1, the party crossed the wide valley with its dark delta soil, and camped in the marshland at the junction of the Malad and Bear rivers. They were not high enough in elevation to get a view of the lake. They saw several isolated mountains ahead of them which they thought might be islands, but there was no way to prove it until they sighted the lake. Preuss was certain they were near it, as there were great flights of geese and ducks heading in that direction.

Next morning, Frémont had his men unpack the rubber boat. This craft was eighteen feet long and built in the shape of a birch-bark canoe. Inflated, it could carry five or six men as well as a good load of gear. Everything was moved to the bank of the river, and the boat made trip after trip to carry the men and equipment across the deep channel. Horses and mules had to swim, and they had a difficult time.

When everything—men, baggage, and animals—was safely on the other side, John Charles and Basil Lajeunesse got into the boat and began to paddle down Bear River. They hoped they might be able to reach the lake and return to camp before dark. But what had seemed to be a fine idea didn't work out that way. The river current moved at a sluggish pace, and the course of the stream meandered here, there, and everywhere. They passed by an Indian village, and the startled inhabitants were puzzled to see two white men drifting slowly along the river in a strange-looking craft. Frémont and Lajeunesse stopped to visit these Indians, who spoke the Shoshonean language, and were appalled at their appearance. Their hair was matted. They were very nearly naked, and they looked "very poor and miserable, as if their lives had been spent in the rushes where they were, beyond which they seemed to have very little knowledge of any thing."[12]

Leaving the Indian village, they continued their erratic voyage downstream; but as the day was getting late, they decided they would not reach the lake before sundown, and cached the boat in a willow thicket. The hike to their comrades at the camp was fifteen miles from the low salt flats and marshes where they had noticed empty univalve shells wherever the water had evaporated and left a hard, white saline, encrusted surface.

Just as the sun had dropped behind the mountains on the west side of the valley and the sky had turned a golden yellow, John Charles and Basil saw the campfire. The waiting men greeted them with a supper of ducks and geese they had managed to shoot. There was laughter and talk in the camp and the kind of feeling that decent food brings to weary and hungry men.

In the morning Basil and several other men left by horseback to retrieve the boat. They were back by afternoon, and during this time the men had even killed a pelican as well as some ducks and geese.[13] Determined to try and reach the lake as quickly as possible, they traveled down Bear River for about three miles before sunset and camped near the mouth of the river. The river was bordered with canes and rushes, which prevented their seeing the lake in full, though they did see a long arm of water that stretched to the north between them and the opposite mountains. While they didn't know it, they were at Bear River Bay, and the mountains they saw were part of the Promontory Range. Again, they had no shortage of game for food, as the hunters waded out into the marshes and shot ducks, geese, and plover for their supper.

That night was clear, but the temperature dropped and there was a considerable amount of dew. Then as they were ready to make another try to reach
the lake in the morning, Kit Carson rode into camp with the supplies he had
obtained at Fort Hall. While he had some flour and a few other items, it was
only enough to last for a few days. He had tried to get more, but Fort Hall
was short of everything. Too many emigrants had passed by, and all were
short of food.

The whole day was used in locating a fording place, and they finally
found one five miles up the Bear River. But by the time everyone was across
the river again, it was beginning to get dark and rain blew in from a distant
thunderstorm.

The next morning, they set out once again, heading down the Bear River.
They were close to the lake, but every attempt to get there had met with failure. About twelve miles to the south they could see an isolated butte—Little
Mountain—and hoped that once they reached this, the long-awaited view of
the lake would be in front of them. But before noon the ground became so
muddy they had to move toward higher ground at the base of the Wasatch
Mountains. They nooned at Willard Creek; then they struck an Indian trail
and headed around the base of Ben Lomond to the Weber Valley. In the afternoon they reached what is now called Utah Hot Springs. Typical for
Frémont, he took time to make an analysis of some of these ten or twelve
springs. He found that the water was extremely salty and contained a high
percentage of peroxide of iron and carbonate of lime. The presence of the
iron caused the ground surrounding the hot-water pools to have a reddish
stain. Time also was spent in measuring the temperature in two of the
springs. Both showed a reading of over 130 degrees.

At the hot springs they forked eastward and avoided the boggy marshland
in the area that is the present site of Ogden, Utah. But the trail appeared to
be striking directly toward a slash in the mountains from which the Ogden
River burst forth. Not wanting to go in that direction, Frémont left the Indian trail and struck out for the Weber River. They camped beside this
stream for the night, and observed that the water was clear and without the
slightest taste of salt.

Early in the morning the men were awakened by various sounds from the
nesting waterfowl as they greeted daybreak with a wild mixture of squawks,
whistles, clucks, and trills. Then as flights of waterfowl took to the air, the
flapping of their wings was like the sound of distant thunder. After a quick
breakfast, Frémont and his men walked to the summit of Little Mountain.
From this height they caught their first view of the Great Salt Lake.[14] To
John Charles, it was as though he were Balboa seeing the Pacific Ocean for
the first time. The far-reaching waters of this remnant of a giant Pleistocene
lake that once covered nearly 20,000 square miles and spread over a good portion of northwestern Utah and lapped over into both Idaho and Nevada
broke before their eyes in a bright reflection of the morning sun. Green-

tinted water mixed with the glare of white sand and salt beaches glistened and made them squint their eyes.

This was a thing of magnificence, a sublime body of water to see after all the days and nights of crossing dry plains or walking in the shadows of the sky-reaching Rocky Mountains. This was no ordinary lake. It was easy to understand why Jim Bridger had thought he had reached the shores of the Pacific. Silent and distant, not even the whitecap breakers could be heard from where they viewed it. But there it was, and Frémont saw islands that "raised their high rocky heads out of the waves; but whether or not they were timbered was still left to our imagination, as the distance was too great to determine if the dark hues upon them were woodland or naked rock."[15]

Even as they looked for a path to the shoreline, dark thunderheads gathered in the western sky. Before they realized what was happening, the storm broke with a wild fury. The islands in the lake vanished beneath the clouds and driving rain. The only place which seemed to offer decent cover for a camp and enough feed for the horses was a grove of trees along the course of the Weber River. They got there as quickly as they could. By sunset the rain stopped and the sky was clear except for a few fleecy white clouds drifting on currents of wind.

All the next day was used to prepare for their voyage of discovery. Corrals were built to hold the animals. Repairs were made on the rubber boat, and it was filled with air for the next day's sail. Frémont decided to cut the size of his party to conserve food. Seven men under the leadership of François Lajeunesse were sent north to Fort Hall to wait for the explorers. The men chosen for the lake party were Frémont, Charles Preuss, Kit Carson, Baptiste Bernier, and Basil Lajeunesse. François Badeau, Baptiste Derosier, and young Jacob Dodson were to remain at the camp and guard the horses, howitzer, and instrument wagon. These eight men watched the brilliant sunset of golden orange, and listened to the night sounds of croaking frogs, rustling birds, and coyotes barking in the distance. It was a night with the feel of early autumn. The breeze wasn't cold, but it carried enough coolness so that it felt good to sit around the campfire as the darkness came on. They had a good meal of roots and a small, fat duck that Jacob had shot with his rifle.

They spoke of the next day's adventure and wondered what they would see once they got their boat on the surface of the lake. What did the islands hold for them? Were there forests on the large ones? Was that darkness in the distance the dim outline of groves of timber? And game, what about game? There was the chance that none of these islands had ever been visited by men. If so, they would be entering places teeming with animals. All these possibilities, along with the unknown dangers, the risks that could not be calculated, were to become part of their experience sometime during the next day as they sailed the salty water of this strange inland sea to set foot where no other had walked and to see what no other had seen.[16]

## 5

THE MORNING broke calm, clear, and cool. After a quick breakfast, the men loaded the rubber boat with what they would need: blankets, cooking pots and pans, firearms, instruments for Frémont's work, and three watertight bags that held about five gallons of fresh water each. All preparations finished, John Charles and the four others pushed the boat into the river, got aboard, and bid farewell to Badeau, Derosier, and Dodson.

The rubber boat drifted easily on the slow current, and the voyage down the river had a sportsman's aspect about it. They "loitered so much on the way—stopping every now and then, and floating silently along, to get a shot at a goose or a duck—that it was late in the day"[17] when they found an outlet. Here, they ran into difficulty. The river was divided into several channels; all were so shallow that the men had to get out and wade and pull their boat along. With night coming on, they were forced to make camp. They located dry ground on a low spit where there was plenty of driftwood for their campfire. Willows were cut for their beds, and they had a surplus of ducks and geese—enough for supper and the next morning's breakfast. The evening was mild and clear, and the prevailing sound was the noise of millions of waterfowl settling down for the night.

Early the next morning, as the first glow of sunlight from the east began to lighten the slate-colored sky, the men were seated around their campfire. No clouds darkened the sky. The air was still. But Frémont's men had not slept well. They spoke of dark dreams they had during the night. Perhaps it had been the food. It might have been the strange surroundings. Their narrow camping area was almost in the water, and ahead of them was a lake which was like a sea. Yet to get to it wasn't going to be easy. The river had vanished into shallow, boggy channels that gave no promise for the boat. While they got ready to move on, they were astounded by the flapping of wings and the calls of the waterfowl leaving their nesting area to fly upstream to hunt the fresh waters, as the massive lake had no fish. The din of the birds was incredible. There were the harsh squawks of seagulls, the honking of geese, the quacking of ducks, and the screaming of plover. All of it gave the men an uneasy feeling of something not quite natural. Then as they looked ahead at the vast body of the lake, they saw bright blue in some spots and glaring white in others, where the first rays of sunlight reflected off the surface; and in other places where the water was shaded by islands or where the depth was greater, the color was a deep blue that was almost purple. Even to a man without the faintest trace of mysticism, there was something unreal, something not of this earth about this early morning view of the Great Salt Lake. To trappers who were more than a little superstitious, the prospect before them was filled with possibilities that belonged only to a world of nightmare.

Dragging the rubber boat, the men moved toward the lake. To protect their clothes from the mud, they removed them, and marched naked toward this inland sea. At each step they sank above their knees in the slimy ooze that had an odor of rottenness. John Charles tried a drink of the water. It didn't taste at all like he thought it would. There wasn't any salty quality, and though the stream still contained fresh water, it did have a disagreeable flavor that seemed to come from the fetid mud.

After proceeding in this way about a mile, we came to a small black ridge on the bottom, beyond which the water became suddenly salt, beginning gradually to deepen, and the bottom was sandy and firm. It was a remarkable division, separating the fresh water of the rivers from the briny water of the lake, which was entirely *saturated* with common salt. Pushing our little vessel across the narrow boundary, we sprang on board, and at length were afloat on the waters of the unknown sea.[18]

It was September 9, 1843, and Frémont gave the order to head the rubber boat toward a smaller island to the south. Though he was tempted by the mountainous Promontory Point, which appeared to be a large island, one of the air cylinders of their craft leaked so badly a crew member had to man the bellows at all times. Not wishing to risk a longer voyage they sailed forth in high spirits as long as they cruised in shallow water. But as the depth of the lake became greater, the men became more apprehensive. Their craft was not one to give them confidence. Some were not skillful swimmers. Though it was a calm morning, the natural swell of the lake caused whitecaps to break against the boat. The spray from the breaking waves coated their clothes, hands, and arms with a crust of common salt. All the while as they moved farther away from shore, the water became deeper and had a beautiful bright green and blue color.

Carson had been looking at the nearest island since they had shoved off. There was something about it that bothered him. There appeared to be a whiteness that bordered the shoreline, and he wondered what it might be. He asked Frémont to take a look through his spyglass. All paddling stopped while John Charles studied the distant shore. Then he reported that what Kit had been worried about was only the breaking of waves against the beach.

A strong breeze came up as they paddled their craft, and this slowed their movement. Then as they neared the halfway mark between the mainland and the island, "two of the divisions between the cylinders gave way, and it required the constant use of the bellows to keep in a sufficient quantity of air."[19] But they kept moving forward at a slow pace until they had worked their way beyond the rough open water and into the smoother surface under the lee of the island. By noon they neared a broad beach, but it was quite rocky. To protect their fragile boat from sharp rocks that might puncture the rubber, they climbed overboard into the shallow bay, unloaded and carried their gear to shore, and then lifted the boat out of the water and brought it to a higher part of the beach.

This was a strange island to the men. Without fresh water, without trees, its cliffs and rocks along the shoreline were covered with a crust of salt. An analysis was made of the salt, and it proved to be almost 98 per cent sodium chloride. After being without salt for their meat, they now had more of it than they had ever dreamed of seeing.

They climbed to the highest point on the island, a bare rocky pinnacle rising eight hundred feet above the surface of the water. From this vantage point, Frémont estimated that the island was twelve or thirteen miles in circumference. Preuss was able to sketch the general configuration of most of the Great Salt Lake. John Charles was tempted to explore more of the lake. There were distant islands, and a vast expanse of water that spread out so far that he was unable to make out what might be the extent of the lake and what mysteries existed on the faraway, silent shores.

While Frémont and Preuss looked over as much of the lake and surrounding country as they could see and worked on sketches, Kit Carson became bored with this barren and rocky land. To pass the time, he carved a large cross beneath a rock shelving at the island's summit. Then when the explorer was through with his work and ready to move to their base camp on the beach, John Charles accidentally left the brass cap to his telescope. No doubt, this cap and Kit's cross were the first signs of man's having visited this island.[20]

As they worked their way to the beach, Frémont examined the plant life. There was sagebrush, greasewood, and plenty of bunch grass. All of it grew to a tall height, but he failed to recognize that there had to be the combination of good soil and an underground water supply for such growth. Instead, he looked upon the island as an extremely inhospitable place, and called it Disappointment Island.

Before nightfall, the men gathered driftwood and built "pleasant little lodges, open to the water, and after having kindled large fires . . . lay down, for the first time in a long journey, in perfect security; no one thinking about his arms."[21] While the evening was calm, and the night sky extremely bright, a wind whirled out of the desert as they slept, and the whole island trembled as heavy waves broke against the shore. It was a strange sensation to all of them: to be in the desert, to be miles from any sea, but to be awakened by the pounding and roar of an ocean surf.

Next morning the voyage across the open stretch of the lake back to shore was very difficult in the frail craft. Bellows had to be tended to keep a supply of air in the cylinders, and the men assigned to paddle had to use all their strength to keep the boat headed for the butte that marked the point where they had first seen the lake. While Frémont wanted to take soundings, he had to give this up. It would have required stopping. Then as the water became shallower, everybody gave a shout of joy. Shortly after, the boat touched bottom on a low, muddy point. After unloading the craft and bringing it and their baggage ashore, the men built a rude camp for the night which John Charles called Fisherman's Camp. Then as he took the meridian observation at the top of the butte, Preuss and Basil Lajeunesse set off to make the nine-mile hike to the main camp to get horses to carry their gear.

Late in the afternoon, Basil returned with enough horses to carry the men and the equipment. By now the lake was rising, and they had to move camp quickly to higher ground. The following day they rode to the main camp. As they neared it, the men who had not made the voyage fired the howitzer to greet the returning explorers of the Great Salt Lake.

They stayed at this camp for one day of rest, got everything in order, and early the following morning headed for Fort Hall. Traveling back up the Weber River to First Salt Creek, they struck a northeast course. John Charles noted that this country they traveled now had very good soil, and he listed the various plants and trees that grew to a good size. This description was quite accurate and became the deciding factor in Brigham Young's mind when he selected the Salt Lake Valley as the place of settlement for the Mormons. (Still, the leader of the Latter Day Saints insisted that he had been misled by taking Frémont's *Report* at face value. There was no arm of fresh water in the Great Salt Lake as the explorer had written when he thought that the fresh waters of Utah Lake were part of the larger body of salt water.)

The great gardens of the Latter Day Saints were yet to come as the hungry expedition made camp on September 12, 1843, near present-day Plain City, Utah. That night they had to make do with a supper of seagulls Kit had shot. It was a quiet camp, and Preuss commented that an expedition of their size should have an excess of pack animals so that enough food would always be on hand. John Charles noticed the lack of spirit among his men, and it worried him that they hardly spoke and didn't even curse. If ever there was a time for Fitzpatrick to arrive with supplies from Fort Hall, that time was now; and the howitzer was fired during the evening so that if the relief party happened to be anywhere within hearing distance, they would know where their hungry companions were camped.

After the seagull supper, pickings became even leaner, and Frémont found out what life was like for the Indians of this region. Using the term of his time, he called these people "Diggers." But he soon discovered why they always carried digging sticks, as he and his men dug for yampa and camas roots to ease the pangs of hunger.

On the evening of September 14, John Charles realized things were getting crucial, and to the joy of his hungry men, he gave permission for the slaughter of a fat, young horse. Preuss didn't fancy the idea of eating horse meat, and managed to avoid it by making do with some chocolate and coffee. But the next day, he joined the others for a supper of antelope meat when they managed to purchase the animal for a little black powder and some rifle balls from a roving band of Utes.

They were camped next to Malad River as they enjoyed the antelope supper, and that night the men were startled by the appearance of a horseman. When they saw that it was Jean Baptiste Tabeau, who had been with Broken Hand, they were overjoyed.

The following morning they reached Fitzpatrick's camp and found he had brought a supply of flour, rice, dried meat, and even a little butter from Fort Hall. All the men stuffed themselves with their first good meal and Preuss was so happy to have real food again, he took time to make a shirt out of the antelope hide. It was hardly a model of tailoring, as he simply cut holes for his neck and arms and tied the skin at the back. But the temperature was getting cooler each day, and this rough shirt made a good extra cover against the raw wind.

Working their way up the Malad River, moving along at a much better pace now that their stomachs were full, the party moved away from the fertile bottom land. They entered a rough mountain ravine and climbed a steep grade which leveled off at a summit 6,300 feet above sea level. The common blue flowering flax was abundant in this region; and the slopes of the mountains were timbered with groves of quaking aspen that shimmered in gold and green, already taking on the colors of fall.

A violent, icy wind blew from the northwest and pushed massive banks of thunderheads along the windstream of the sky. Slowly the riders descended the western slope into a broad, open valley bordered by cottonwoods and aspen groves. They were at the headwaters of the Bannock River in present-day southeastern Idaho. That night, as they rested around their fires, they saw scattered campfires glimmering along the mountains—fires that marked Indian camps. So, here at the beginning of the Snake River Plain, where the mountains broke up into isolated buttes and where the land was marked by endless stretches of sagebrush and great outcroppings of lava beds that were slashed by the Snake River, it was necessary to resume night watch. Little as any man wished to leave the warmth of a campfire to stand guard on a chill night, every experienced man knew this western watershed of the Rocky Mountains was not immune to moving bands of Sioux, Cheyenne, Blackfoot, and Crow as well as Shoshoni and Bannock. These hard-riding horsemen were tough and seasoned warriors. This was reason enough to keep the exploring party on its guard.

Broken Hand gave no sign of being worried, but then he had been up against the various dangers of this land ever since he had signed on with the Ashley-Henry men on their second expedition into the fur country in 1823. While he was aware of the flickering fires that marked Indian camps, he went about his business. He explained to Frémont it was only a two-day ride to Fort Hall. All they had to do was follow the Bannock River until it reached the sagebrush plains and the valley of the Snake River. Then they would head northeast up the Snake River, for about ten miles, until they reached the junction with the Portneuf River.

Two days more, that was all. But Frémont was not a novice; like the men who had taught him about the wilderness, he would take one day at a time and watch for any slight change that might indicate something out of the ordinary, something that could mean trouble: a bird call that might not be a bird call, a crackling of brush within rifle range of the trail, the odor of smoke on the breeze, fresh tracks of a large party of mounted Indians, or a sudden change in the weather. One mile after another, was the only safe way.

6

THREE BUTTES was what they were called. These were the landmarks. Once they saw these, Broken Hand said, they would be close to Fort Hall. Three buttes just northwest of the post; one was called Big Butte—the others were Twin Buttes. These sagebrush-covered knobs were away from the fertile bottom land around the fort. These landmarks were at the edge of the Snake River Plain. Beyond them were lava beds that raised hell with man and beast, impassable canyons, thundering waterfalls where the Snake dropped over cliffs, and an endless sea of sagebrush. When they saw the distant buttes, they would not be far from the mouth of the Portneuf River. Ten miles above that Fort Hall was on the left bank of the Snake River.

The men saw the Three Buttes on September 18 as they approached the post from the dry, sagebrush foothills and "were agreeably surprised, on reaching the Portneuf river, to see a beautiful green valley with scattered timber spread out beneath us on which, about four [actually ten] miles distant, were glistening the white walls of the fort."[22]

To young Talbot, who was waiting at the expedition camp just outside the fort, the bottom land was better than desert even though the soil had some salt deposits. But the post was far from the best he had seen on this long journey. It wasn't put together very well, and while the "dobies" were whitewashed to give the place a good appearance, the overall layout simply did not impress him. Yet he had managed to pick up some of the establishment's history in between his duties and time out for reading a copy of Lord Byron's poems he carried in his gear.

Fort Hall had been built in the late summer of 1834, Talbot learned. It had been the project of a Yankee, Nathaniel Wyeth, who had tried to compete with the British Hudson's Bay Company. For two years Wyeth had managed to hang on, and flew the homemade American flag he had run up the pole on the day he opened for business. Hell, the flag was only unbleached sheeting with red flannel stripes, and a few blue patches that passed for stars, but it was an American flag. And on that August day in

1834, Wyeth and his men saluted it with a volley of rifle fire and a toast of "villainous alcohol."

But Nathaniel Wyeth's dream of empire ran out after two years. In 1836, with his funds getting low and no more money forthcoming from his merchant backers in Boston, Wyeth began negotiations for the sale of his business and fort to the Hudson's Bay Company. When the deal was completed, down came the tattered homemade American flag, and the Union Jack flew over Fort Hall.[23]

After Wyeth's departure, the command of Fort Hall passed into the quite capable hands of an experienced Hudson's Bay man, Captain Richard Grant, who had never known anything other than the fur trade after his birth and boyhood in Montreal.

John Charles rode up to the fort during a morning that had all the signs of winter. At daybreak the sky had been very dark, and by the time the men finished breakfast, a heavy snow began to fall. There is no record of what Frémont and Grant said to each other, but Grant was an easygoing man as well as a fine administrator. Like Fitzpatrick, he watched his supplies very closely so that he would not run short. This trait caused some Oregon-bound emigrants to speak harshly of him, as he would not sell them all they wished to buy. But the emigrants never considered what the situation at Fort Hall would be if Grant had sold as much as any passing wagon train wished to purchase.

After Frémont and Grant talked for a while, the factor did agree to sell a few poor horses and five good oxen, but that was all the lieutenant brought back to camp. That day they slaughtered one ox, and though the storm continued during the night, the men were in good humor as they sat around the campfires and feasted on freshly roasted meat.

The expedition remained at its Fort Hall camp for the next few days as the icy storm continued. During this layover Frémont made an analysis of the soil and found it to be good agricultural land. He also considered the region around Fort Hall an excellent place for an American military post to aid and protect emigrants bound for Oregon. He wrote nothing about the local Indian tribes—the Bannocks and the Shoshoni. The latter were often called Snakes, because their tribal sign was a serpentine gesture. Comments about the Indians, however, were made by eighteen-year-old Talbot.

Talbot did not think the Bannocks were to be trusted. He believed that, given the opportunity, they would attack any party of whites. The Shoshoni were just the opposite, and he was fascinated with these friendly people. He noticed they were smaller in stature than other Rocky Mountain Indians he had seen and tended to have short, thick legs. Many of the men and women were quite handsome, and he found that they did not indulge in thievery. When a single knife was stolen from the men of the expedition, the chief forced all the men of his tribe to take an oath and kiss a sacred bow as they proclaimed their innocence or guilt. Finally, after hundreds of warriors had passed during the day, one young man tried to avoid the ceremony. When called back and forced to perform, he turned pale and confessed that he was guilty of the theft. He returned the knife and received immediate punishment for his disgraceful deed.

With an eye for detail, Talbot even wrote about the colorful dress of the Shoshoni. The men wore deer- or antelope-skin shirts. The sleeves were open on the inner side from the elbow up, but from the elbow to the wrist the tanned skin fit very tightly. Shoulder straps were broad and carefully decorated with porcupine quills, and the shirt reached down to the thighs. Below that, the warriors wore fringed leggings, and their moccasins had a single seam on the outer edge. When they dressed for a special affair, they often wore a robe of ermine or white weasel, dragged a cured skunk skin at their heels, and carried or wore blankets and trinkets they had received in trade with the Hudson's Bay Company. The costumes for the women were very much the same as those which the men wore; the major differences were to be seen in the longer shirts for the women and the shorter leggings. To see them walking about in their finest clothing, the men carrying their hunting bows, war clubs, and circular shields made of tough buffalo hide, was a scene that remained clearly etched in the viewer's mind. Talbot wrote about what he saw with understanding and admiration for the culture of the Shoshoni.

Preuss was strangely silent about the stay at Fort Hall. Either he found nothing to interest him, or he was too concerned about what Frémont might decide to do next. Preuss was tired and looked forward to returning home before Christmas. Such was not to be his luck. John Charles was determined to move ahead, but he had decided the obvious approach of an early winter made it vital to cut the size of his party in order to support the men who would strike out across the barren sage desert on the last march to Oregon.

For some of the men, the opportunity to be paid off at Fort Hall and to return to the States was all right, as the trip ahead didn't hold much appeal. Others could see the need for a smaller party and, being old hands in the fur trade, would either head back to St. Louis or strike south to Pueblo or Taos for the winter. Altogether, eleven men dropped out of the expedition. Among them was one man Frémont hated to lose, Basil Lajeunesse, who had promised his family he would be home for the winter.

Before the two parties went their opposite directions, some of the Oregon-bound men wrote letters to be carried to the settlements. John Charles wrote to Jessie, Preuss sent a letter to his wife, and Talbot sent one to his mother. But not all the letters arrived at their destinations. As Jessie stated in a letter of December 3, 1843, to Mrs. Adelaide Talbot, a packet of letters was lost in a river crossing and among them was the one Talbot had written to his mother. One or two other letters were carried by another man, and these were not lost. And while the letter to Jessie had drifted downstream, she did talk to the man who carried the other letters, and he told her that John Charles and young Talbot were in good health.

On Friday, September 22, the dismissed men waved farewell and struck out on the backtrack. At the same time, the Oregon-bound party began its journey. Talbot wrote that it rained most of the day as they pulled the carts, the instrument wagon and the howitzer carriage through the muddy ground. They covered only ten miles on their first day away from Fort Hall as the going was very difficult. They even had trouble crossing the Portneuf River, because the storm had increased the flow of water to the point where the formerly shallow stream was often up to the axles of the vehicles. They finally made camp beside the Snake at the mouth of the Bannock River. That evening Captain Grant visited their camp, accompanied by a boy who was half Chinook and half Mexican. The Hudson's Bay man and his boy visited for a time, and no doubt were open to any questions about the route. As they departed they wished Frémont and his men good luck in their journey across the sagebrush plains.

But the expedition did not move out on the next day, as the storm increased in intensity. Until eleven o'clock in the morning snow fell steadily. Then heavy gusts of wind came out of the north, bringing an icy rainstorm that changed the snow-covered ground into a cold, slushy bog. By late afternoon the sun broke through the cloud cover, and it was easy to see that all the snow in the lowlands had melted, but in the mountains there was a heavy snowpack. They would have to move quickly in order to get to the lower country while the going was still possible. Even now, things were not at all good for the morale of the men. Preuss made this quite clear in his journal when he complained that this was a miserable sort of life. It was rain and snow, a damned cold wind, boots that were wearing out, and tents that had holes in them and offered warmth only if a man could stand smoke to the point of near suffocation.

But an icy sunrise on September 24 showed a clear sky to the west and promised a fine day. The toughest part of starting was to move out of the swampy and narrow river bottoms where they had camped. They crossed the Bannock River and moved along the uplands, but this proved to be tough going on the wet clay soil, where animals and men slipped. They had to force their way over tall clumps of sagebrush and avoid outcroppings of sharp, black obsidian. Yet they moved along at a fair pace, all things considered, and by noon they made an early camp in a willow grove about a half mile above the American Falls of the Snake River.

At this point the river began its downward course through a vast canyon that sliced through the country. Frémont noted the endless vista of sagebrush and lava that stretched ahead; the broken, snowy mountain range to the south; the white line of the snow-covered Salmon River Mountains far to the north, and the Three Buttes on the plain. He calculated that the Snake River was 870 feet wide above the falls but was squeezed into a narrow lock of jutting piles of basaltic rock to form them.

Not as concerned about the scientific data as Frémont, Talbot wrote that the American Falls were so called because "of the melancholy fate of some six or eight Americans who were drowned here some years since."[24] Talbot did estimate that the height of the greatest fall in the series of falls was about fifteen feet and that the overall height of the falls was about forty-five feet. Being young and enamored with Byron's poetry, he saw the scene as a very romantic one. Then as they made an early camp, he went hunting.

After the camp at American Falls, the days began to run together in a pattern of daily despair as they slowly worked their way through a land Frémont described as being a "melancholy and strange-looking country—one of fracture, and violence, and fire."[25] Lava boulders and sagebrush made walking or riding a slow and painful business, hard on men and animals; and the carts, the light wagon, and the infernal howitzer on its carriage became burdens that seemed almost impossible to move. To help the progress of his party, Frémont divided it once again. Ten men rode ahead with him, while Broken Hand, the remainder of the party, and the bulk of the baggage trailed behind.

Their daily view became one of extreme contrasts. To the north and south were snowcapped mountain ranges, while all around them was a desert of broken lava outcroppings and sagebrush. The Snake was a secret river that glided out of sight in a deep, palisade canyon—a river that showed itself only at those places where there was a sudden drop in the landform, a north-south fracture cutting across the rift. At such places, the mighty Snake burst into the air in spectacular waterfalls. After American Falls, the men saw Shoshone Falls, where a hidden tributary, a subterranean river, came full force out of a sheer escarpment to drop into the rushing waters of the Snake. Then the men came to Salmon Falls, or what John Charles aptly named Fishing Falls.

Food was purchased from the Indians who made their living from the great salmon runs. The economy of these people depended upon salmon. Their primary method of catching the fish was to spear them with a long spear with a loosely fitting barb on its point. Attached to the barb and the lance was a long cord. In this way neither the barb nor the lance was lost when a large fish was speared. The barb came off at once, and the fisherman would then play the salmon on the cord until it was close enough to shore to beach and kill it.

Talbot described this region in great detail, pointing out that the river was teeming with salmon headed upstream. All the Indians were hard at work, and as they were in and out of the water all day long, they wore very little clothing or no clothing at all.

Round every hut are high platforms covered with drying salmon. These present quite a gay appearance for the meat of the salmon is of a deep scarlet color. To each hut is attached a sort of storehouse in which the salmon when dried and bound into bundles with cords of grass, are carefully stored away for winter use. In their huts they have little more than their bows & arrow, fishing tackle and a few pots made of earth or of osiers lined with some resinous substance rendering them water proof. Their favorite method of cooking salmon is to roast it in the ashes.[26]

That night the weather was much warmer than it had been, and Preuss was able to sleep outside the tent and get away from Jacob Dodson, the eighteen-year-old black from the Benton household. Though Preuss liked Dodson, the moment he bedded down he was fast asleep and snoring at such a volume that unless a man were dead tired it was impossible to shut one's ears to his range of night sounds.

By October 3 Frémont and his party reached Three Island Crossing, the point near present Glenns Ferry, Idaho, where the Oregon Trail crossed the Snake River and headed cross-country toward Fort Boise. Here Frémont observed the mountain range to the south, now no more than twenty or thirty miles away, which he realized was the northern boundary of an area that nobody seemed to know much about other than the fact that it was said to be a vast semidesert region, an inhospitable land of little rain and mile upon mile of sage-covered plains.

Three Island Crossing was not an easy ford. Frémont hired an Indian to lead them across. Yet even with his help, they ran into trouble right away. Not only was the water moving at a fast pace, but there was a small bay with deep water in between the islands. The howitzer with all its weight began to pull heavily against the mules, and the men had to cut the harness quickly to keep the mules from drowning as the cannon began to pull them downstream. The men and animals retreated to shore with the howitzer. Then the rubber boat was inflated and was used to carry the baggage, carriage, carts, and howitzer to the other side. Horses and mules swam across with the help of the men. By seven o'clock that night the crossing was completed, and the party made its camp among the Indian lodges near the beach.

One more day of hard travel was needed to move up from the level of the river and cross more lava and sagebrush plains as they moved to the northwest. The following day they passed a hot spring which Frémont took time to analyze, and near the end of the day they came out of the rough lava country at the foot of the Sawtooth Mountains. About sunset they made camp next to a small stream (probably present-day Rattlesnake Creek). Here there were willows, cottonwoods, grass, and even wild roses. At last they were across the Snake River Plain and beyond the daily punishment.

Two more days of travel took them in and out of granite country, back into high sagebrush land where the soil might support a wheat crop, and on October 7 they reached the Boise River. To see something other than jagged lava and sagebrush was a sheer delight to all the men, and that night they camped under some fine old cottonwoods.

They moved along at a good pace during the next two days and covered fifty miles. On the night of the ninth they camped on the right bank of the Boise River, and early the next morning moved to the junction of the Boise and Snake rivers and followed the Snake until they reached Fort Boise. François Payette, factor of this Hudson's Bay Post, greeted them and offered the hospitality of his fort.

Payette had come to the Pacific Northwest with John Jacob Astor's Pacific Fur Company. When Frémont met him, this genial gentleman had been in the wilderness for more than thirty years. During that time he had learned the customs of the various Indian tribes, had survived the fierce competition of rival fur traders, and since his appointment to Fort Boise in 1837, had seen a steady increase in families and missionaries heading for the Oregon country. All this meant but one thing: The wild, freebooting days of the fur trade were fast coming to an end. But he had seen the best of it, and as he grew older, he was content to watch the passing parade of people on the move.

Payette had learned to live with whatever fate chose to deal him. In this post that had been built in the summer of 1834 to compete with Fort Hall, Payette made do with his French-Canadian engagés. While the factor made no real attempt at gardening and was content to get by on salmon, game, and milk from the cows of the post, he was willing to share whatever he happened to have on hand. The principal item Frémont's party obtained from the post was fresh butter.

## 7

THEY MOVED SLOWLY UP THE HOLLOW, following the gradual grade toward the crest of a ridge. Behind them, as far as a man could see, stretched the Snake River Plain. They had crossed all that, had endured the long days of sagebrush and broken lava that had been like dark rivers turned into stone. Then they topped the ridge, took one last look at what they had crossed, and dropped into a hollow between ridges.

Two men were hiking, two men afoot in the wilderness. As they drew nearer, the word was passed that they were white men. As they began to talk, the accent of the strangers gave them away. They were wandering Irishmen who had lost their horses and supplies and were headed for Fort Boise in hope of finding their mounts or securing others. John Charles had one of his animals unpacked so he could give them something to eat. Then, wishing them luck, he and his party continued on their way until they reached the Malheur River in what is now eastern Oregon.

At the shallow Malheur, a stream Peter Skene Ogden had named the Unfortunate River,[27] the expedition camped for the night. Though it had been warm during the day, once the sun went down, the temperature dropped until it was well below freezing.

Two days later the expedition was overtaken by some Cayuse Indians, home-bound messengers of a larger party of Cayuse that had been on a successful buffalo hunt near the Rocky Mountains. Frémont gave them tobacco and other presents. They asked if they could travel with his party, and John Charles welcomed them.

Higher and higher they climbed over the steep and rough ground. Then from an opening on a hogback ridge, Frémont looked to the south and west. He noticed a distinctive feature about these mountains. The range appeared to connect to what he called the California Range or the present Sierra Nevada. The mountains to the south seemed to form an "eastern limit of the fertile and timbered lands along the desert and mountainous region included within the Great Basin . . . the intermediate region between the Rocky Mountains and the next range. . . ."[28]

This was the first use of the term Great Basin to indicate the vast desert area between the Rocky Mountains and the Sierra Nevada.[29] And Frémont was the first man to make an extensive exploration of this land that is a configuration of more than ninety basins—many of former lakes—and 160 mountain ranges that run in a north-south direction and stand out like islands stranded by the long-vanished waters of ancient seas.[30]

During the next five days the travel became very difficult. They dropped into the Burnt River Valley, which looked like a dark hole as a result of more than one forest fire that had raged through the timber. All of it was up and down, down and up, and crossing and recrossing one rock-filled mountain stream after another. They had the added burden of pulling, pushing, and at times, even lifting the instrument wagon and the howitzer carriage to get them along the path. Then on October 17 they had their first good view of the Blue Mountains. Perpetual shadows from dense stands of pines and the dark soil gave the mountains a bluish hue.

They struck a fairly good trace which crossed the tributaries of the Powder River and wound its way up to the crest of a dividing ridge. In the early afternoon they first saw the Grand Ronde, or great circle valley, way below them. When they reached the floor of the valley, Frémont saw that it was ideal farming land. There was plenty of water, rich soil, belly-deep grass for livestock, and surrounding mountains with thick timber groves. At this place —now part of Union County, Oregon—the expedition camped for the night.

Though Frémont wrote a glowing description of the Grand Ronde Valley, mapmaker Preuss was more concerned about other things. The weather was getting colder each night, cold enough so that there was ice on the shallow water in the morning; and the Blue Mountains still had to be climbed. Though he knew the Pacific Ocean was somewhere beyond them, he had also heard they were heading into the wet season in a land where a man could expect to see only rainy days from November to April. Yet the next day, as they climbed into the higher country of the Blue Mountains, Preuss had to admit that the natural beauty of the land was magnificent. His only complaint was that Frémont had not allowed enough time for the beef to dry in the curing process, and the meat was too sour to eat except in case of absolute need.

To add even more hardship to their first camp, darkness arrived much sooner than anyone anticipated. This forced the expedition to halt for the night in a clearing on the top of a narrow ridge, a campground that was a long way from any water. Sour beef, no water, and a cold, windy night added up to an unhappy group of men who sat quietly around their campfires. This was too much after a hard day's march up the mountains, and wanting at least a cup of coffee to drink with their bread. "Preuss and Carson, with several others, volunteered to take the rubber buckets and go down into the ravine in search of water. It was a very difficult way in the darkness down the slippery side of the steep mountain, and harder still to climb up again; but they found water, and the cup of coffee (which it enabled us to make) and bread were only enjoyed with greater pleasure."[31]

Four more days of up and down travel through the Blue Mountains took the expedition across mountain creeks, a large branch of the Umatilla River, and through great forests of spruce, larch, balsam, and pine. The only misfortune they had in this rough terrain was the breaking of their last barometer. This meant that for the rest of the journey all readings of elevation would have to be taken by measuring the temperature of boiling water.

On October 22 the trace they had been following left the heavily timbered region and broke into the open on a high plateau. Far below, Frémont saw the Nez Percé Prairie, and the dark line of the Walla Walla River. Even from the heights, he could make out man-made clearings near the river. From what he had learned at Fort Boise, if these were cultivated openings, they had to be part of Dr. Marcus Whitman's mission settlement.

Certain that the whole party would be down off the mountain before sunset, Charles Preuss decided to give his body a rest from the saddle. He told Frémont that he would hike on ahead and meet them at Nez Percé Prairie. There was no objection to his plan, and Preuss walked ahead, reaching the Walla Walla River late in the afternoon. But as night began to come on, he realized the expedition would not manage to get off the mountain and out of the woods before dark. Having no other choice, he made a bed of leaves on the ground, built a fire on each side of his bed, and tried to keep warm during the long, cold night.

Late the next afternoon, the expedition finally made its way down. Beside the Walla Walla River, they found Preuss who was calmly smoking his pipe as he waited for his companions. Other than having an empty stomach that now would tolerate the sour-tasting dried beef, he was in good shape.

Morning broke clear and cold at the Walla Walla River camp. Men spoke in words of steam. Horses and mules snorted puffs of steam. The grass was white and wet with a heavy coating of frost, and Frémont recorded the sunrise temperature at a frigid twenty-four degrees. Little time was wasted around campfires as they broke up camp in a hurry and rode on toward Whitman's mission.

They crossed the Walla Walla River, and struck out over foothill country that had a good cover of bunch grass. From the top of one foothill, they had an "extensive view along the course of the river, which was divided and spread over its bottom in a net work of water, receiving several other tributaries from the mountains."[32] As they continued along their way, they saw horses grazing on the hills and met Indians driving horse herds out to pasture. For the soil along the river was not rich, and grazing was poor.

Within fourteen miles they reached Dr. Whitman's missionary establishment near present-day Walla Walla, Washington.[33] The mission consisted of one adobe house. But on the trail to the mission the men had noticed several other houses in various stages of construction, and there were cleared patches of soil—probably the ones Frémont had seen from the open ridge in the Blue Mountains—where crops of corn and potatoes were growing. This agricultural activity looked promising for the expedition, and they hoped they could replenish their supplies.

But when they reached the mission, Dr. Whitman was on a visit to The Dalles of the Columbia River. Yet, even if he had been at the mission, he couldn't have offered much aid as everything was in short supply, except two items—potatoes, and the word of the Lord, which had been the key drive that had taken this rural physician from Steuben County, New York, and his bride, Narcissa Prentiss of Allegany County, New York, all the way to Oregon to convert Indians and save their souls from eternal damnation.

Sermons, though, were not something trail-weary men were in a mood to hear. They went without any Holy Words, and made do with the potatoes they were able to purchase. Potatoes for breakfast, potatoes and sour dried beef to be washed down with hot coffee. Even firewood was in short supply at Whitman's mission, and the Cayuse Indians had to drag it in or load pack horses with wood from the mountains and bring it to the mission.

The Walla Walla River flowed smoothly, and ran deep over the sandy soil. This was a river that would take a boat along at a fast pace, but there was to be no sailing down the river to the Columbia. The order Frémont gave was to move out on the trail, and they struggled through a country of loose sand that stretched ahead of them and made each mile a hard trip. No grass to speak of, no timber except for isolated groves of stunted willows beside the river. All this water running beside them, and the country was a desert. A full day began and ended in the loose sand; and the morning after they plodded along, cursing the hard going, until they reached Fort Walla Walla and made camp in a grove of crippled willows beside the river. The horses had to be driven four or five miles to higher ground where there was some thin grass. A miserable country was all a man could think as the westerly winds came inland from the sea to send stinging clouds of dust and sand whirling in every direction, but here the men had their first view of the River of the West, the great Columbia.

This was no ordinary river. It was a gathering of rivers, a collector of waters from the northwest drainage of the Rocky Mountains from as far away as Jackson Hole and the Grand Tetons. And here where the Walla Walla flowed into it, the mighty Columbia was 1,200 yards wide, deep enough for ships if the problem of coming upriver through The Dalles and Celilo Falls could be solved; teeming with salmon during the spawning runs —chinook, silver, sockeye, chum, pink—and with trout and other fish at all seasons; rolling onward toward the Pacific Ocean with the drainage of more than 200,000 square miles; impressive to see and hear, and an obvious lifeline between the interior and the sea. Frémont thought it was a noble river, a "great river on which the course of events for the last half century has been directing attention and conferring historical fame."[34]

Attention and historical fame were key terms to John Charles. The two ideas belonged to each other like twins spawned in the same stream of thought. For the continuing events that were to shape the destiny of Oregon and the Far West were in full play. The ancient owners of this crossroads, this junction of trails and waterways, were the dispossessed Indians. The fur trade was coming to an end. The drive for pelts that had resulted in building such forts as the one Frémont called Nez Percé,[35] was nearing its final agony. Yet, the Hudson's Bay Company, which was responsible for reducing these Indians to a position of half-servitude and half-beggary, was to see its days run their course while Indians still fished from flimsy platforms that jutted out over the swift-moving water of Celilo Falls. Even at this season, the end was in sight for any Hudson's Bay man who observed the early movement of American emigrants making their way into Oregon. These land-hungry Yankees were to be a final blow in a series of blows to the Hudson's Bay Company, blows that would bring down their house of furs with plows, hay rakes, crosscut saws, mills, clapboard houses, churches, missions, schools, and families who would create more families and by so doing settle the Oregon question without having to petition Congress or to pick up a Hawken rifle. All the debate in Washington and London would come to an end as American farms and towns replaced British outposts and forts.

Whether Archibald McKinlay, Fort Walla Walla's factor, even thought about his dwindling future in the fur trade can be only a matter of conjecture. But this man, who had married a daughter of Peter Skene Ogden, must have sensed something akin to the end of a way of life. Still, this friendly commander did not hesitate to aid either Frémont's party or the emigrant trains bound for chosen areas selected from what they had heard or read about Oregon and the fine, rich soil of the Willamette Valley. The fateful year of decision was less than three years away, and by that time, McKinlay would have received his promotion to take care of Hudson's Bay Company's affairs at Oregon City. But on this day, late in the last week of October 1843, he invited Frémont and the heads of various emigrant parties camped nearby to join him for dinner.

Among the emigrants camped near Fort Walla Walla, John Charles was interested in the activities of a tall, lean Missourian who seemed to have the energy of three or four men. This was Jesse Applegate, who had wanted to be a mountain man but had been turned down by William Sublette. Not daunted, Jesse became a surveyor of former Indian lands, then settled down to the life of a farmer. But all this came to an end when he received a letter from a friend who had emigrated to Oregon, a letter extolling the many virtues of that country. Jesse told his brothers, Charles and Lindsay, and all agreed that Oregon was the place to be. This ended their farming days in Missouri, and when Frémont saw Jesse, he recognized him as a man filled with energy and drive. Fascinated by Applegate's ability to adapt to whatever conditions he encountered, John Charles watched him as he finished building some mackinaw boats which he and his brothers intended to use in a voyage down the Columbia. These flat-bottomed boats with a pointed prow and a square stern were between fifty and sixty feet long, and Frémont thought of how much cargo they would hold and of how easy it would be to drift along the river, but he also had heard about the waterfalls, The Dalles, where all the water of the Columbia squeezed through the narrows between high basalt cliffs, and the upper and lower rapids beyond the narrows. Past the lower rapids the boats would be fine, but in his mind a considerable risk would be taken to use them before bypassing the unknown dangers of the river.

Using excellent judgment, he decided he was too close to his goal to take such a risk as Applegate was about to take. It would be much wiser to go overland until the Columbia ran smooth and easy. He hired eight fresh horses from McKinlay's cavvy at the fort, added to his provisions with the purchase of dried salmon, a little beef, and more potatoes, and engaged the services of an Indian boy to guide the party as far as The Dalles. On October 28 they struck out and followed the Columbia River's course toward the sea. Preuss thought the decision to continue a land journey was sheer folly in that a great waterway was available. He believed this even more when Jesse Applegate's six boats overtook them and shot past as though they were a flight of arrows. The only thing worth seeing on the overland trek was the distant view of Mount Hood. Other than that, the country was one of deep, loose sand and great outcroppings of black volcanic rock that was pure misery.

Now, the days began to run together in a pattern of dull sameness. Up at sunrise, eat a breakfast that seemed to have as much sand in it as anything else, walk and ride all day through the infernal loose sand, and watch the distant cone-shaped beauty of snowcapped Mount Hood. Variations came only when they had to cross tributary rivers that flowed into the Columbia such as the Umatilla. Even firewood was hard to find, and at one point they bought some from Indians who had traveled away from the river to cut a supply, for the only firewood along the Columbia consisted of a few stunted willows and the eternal sagebrush hanging on in the constant wind.

On November 2 the path along the river was cut off by high bluffs. The Indian boy guided them away from the broad Columbia with its great black lava cliffs. They moved inland. As they did, they noticed a vast improvement in the nature of the land. No longer were they marching through sand. For a change, there were good soil, plenty of grass, high hills, and deep valleys. They forded the John Day,[36] a beautiful mountain stream that ran clear and swift over a bed of rolled stones.

The day after this crossing, they reached the Deschutes River, which Frémont called the Fall River. This stream came down from the high country and entered the Columbia with a swift rush of water that burst into the main stream and churned away from the shore for some distance before becoming part of the Columbia's sea-bound water.

Their guide took them to the regular ford of the Deschutes, where there were many Indians fishing from both banks. The fishermen hardly noticed the explorer and his men. The ford was the roughest the expedition had encountered. During the crossing, the howitzer was often under several feet of water, and some of the men were below the surface of the river almost as much as they were above it. When they finally got across, a halt was called while the cannon was wiped dry and the men took a rest.

The next day the party arrived at the Methodist mission just below The Dalles. This establishment was run by Rev. Jason Lee, an imposing figure who stood six feet three inches tall, was as broad as an ax handle at the shoulders, and wore a full dark beard. He had attended the Methodist Academy at Wilbraham, Massachusetts, and was thirty years old when he headed West in 1834 to carry the word of the Lord to the Indians. He also talked his twenty-seven-year-old nephew Daniel Lee into going forth to the wilderness with him and risking his life in the soul-saving business. Neither Lee was at the Methodist mission to greet Frémont, but one of their recruits, H. W. K. Perkins,[37] was there to welcome them to what was almost an illusion of home.

The country around the mission was quite unlike most of the land they had traveled across. Not only was there a fine valley for excellent pasture land and agriculture, but also there were oaks and other trees the men associated with the East. There were gardens, cleared fields, well-built wooden houses, stables, a barn, and a large schoolhouse. Between the mission and the river, the wooden huts of the Indians were scattered here and there. To Frémont, the whole valley had a "cheerful and busy air of civilization . . . an appearance of abundant and enviable comfort."[38]

This Methodist establishment just below The Dalles was to be the end of the land journey along the Columbia River. From this point on, now that he was safely below the rough falls and the narrows, John Charles intended to leave the majority of his party in a base camp. To make the rest of the trip to Fort Vancouver, he decided to hire boats and boatmen and take a few of his men with him to the Hudson's Bay Company's headquarters.

At the mission Frémont learned he had been quite right in his decision to come overland this far. The Applegate party had suffered a disaster in running their boats through The Dalles. As they had entered this dangerous passage, one of the boats had been lost in the fast-rushing water, and a seventy-year-old member of the party and two young Applegate boys—sons of Jesse and Lindsay—drowned before anyone had a chance to get near them.

After looking over The Dalles, Frémont was not surprised this unfortunate accident had occurred. As near as he could tell, all the water of the Columbia was compressed and forced to shoot through narrows no more than fifty-eight yards wide. "The mass of the water," he wrote, "in the present low state of the river, passed swiftly between, deep and black, and curled into many small whirlpools and counter currents, but unbroken by foam, and so still that scarcely the sound of a ripple was heard."[39]

To have come so far, to have been so near to their goal, and then to suffer such a loss in a matter of moments was more than enough to make any man consider the frailty of man against the force of the swift, dark waters of The Dalles. And while John Charles wrote that the accident was mainly the result of having an unskilled boatman, he was deeply sorry this misfortune had struck the Applegates, who were the kind of people his official reports and maps would help in their migration to the West.

The year was getting on, and now Frémont made rapid decisions in their temporary camp. First, he wrote a letter and sent it to Fitzpatrick, who would be waiting with the slower section and the bulk of the supplies at Dr. Whitman's mission. He told him to sell the carts, load the supplies in packsaddles, and come to the camp below The Dalles with the horses. Next, he put Kit Carson in command of the base camp and instructed him to employ the men in getting the gear into good shape again and to make additional packsaddles. Finally, with the aid of Reverend Perkins, he bought a large canoe from a family of Wasco Indians, an upriver branch of Chinookan-speaking people. He also hired three men from this family to man the canoe in the voyage to Fort Vancouver, where he hoped to pick up additional supplies for the long winter's journey.

8

MONDAY, NOVEMBER 6, 1843. Ten miles downriver from the mission or what the Indians called Lee House. The Chinook canoe the men put their gear into was made of a solid piece of white cedar. The tree trunk had been split with wedges; the interior had been hollowed out by the use of carefully controlled pitch fires. Then the canoe had been shaped with Hudson's Bay Company tomahawks. The final product was about thirty feet long, three feet wide, two feet deep, and tapered from near dead center to sharp prows fore and aft.

Late in the afternoon, the Frémont men boarded the canoe, and the Wasco paddlers guided the craft into the main current of the Columbia River. The first hour passed by very swiftly, and at sunset the paddlers maneuvered the canoe to shore. Supper was quickly prepared, and the men dined on salted salmon, potatoes, bread, coffee, and sugar. Then it was time to move on. Frémont thought the idea of traveling by canoe was thoroughly delightful after the day-by-weary-day treks they had been making for the past months. The craft cut through the water and shot them along at a fast rate. "We were a motley group," he wrote, "but all happy, three unknown Indians; Jacob, a colored man; Mr. Preuss, a German; Bernier, creole French; and myself."[40]

Now, as they moved along with the current, the last slate gray of sunset grew darker and darker until the color of the sky and the black waters of the Columbia River seemed to join each other. And while it had worried the explorer that they were going to travel in the dark of night, he had learned before leaving Lee House—probably from Reverend Perkins—that night travel on the river was customary in order to avoid the high winds of morning that persisted until late afternoon. But as Frémont's eyes adjusted to the darkness, he could see the waves breaking into foam as the keel of the canoe sliced into the water; and glancing toward the shores, he saw the broken and rugged shapes of dark and wild mountains.

At midnight the Wasco boatmen used their paddles to change course again, and once away from the main current, they let the canoe glide into the shallow water beside a rocky beach. Behind the shoreline there was a dark pine forest that reached upward from bluff to bluff, forming a barrier for their backs as they built large fires among the rocks—fires that gave the voyagers warmth and light as they located comfortable places to spread out their blankets to sleep until daybreak.

A hurried breakfast at rising, and they were back into the canoe and headed toward the fast-running main current. In its downward course to the sea, the river picked up more and more speed; and while Preuss found the voyage terribly uncomfortable because it was difficult for him to keep his balance in the prow of the sharp-keeled craft, Frémont was thrilled as the expert boatmen used their paddles to turn the canoe away from rocks and shoals at just the right moment. All the while, the snowcapped cone of Mount Hood stood out like a beacon to guide them on their way.

Then as they entered a region where the river cut through the high, rocky, pine-covered Cascade Range, John Charles heard the roar of cascades somewhere just ahead. But even as he caught his first view of white water tumbling over boulders and rock shelves, the Wasco boatmen maneuvered the

canoe out of the fast water and into a handsome bay which had several islands. Now, the canoe glided along toward a village of Watlala Indians, who
also spoke a dialect of the Chinookan language. The Watlala controlled the
territory from the Cascades of the Columbia River to the mouth of the
Willamette River. By so doing, they had a monopoly on the portage business
around the Cascades, and it was necessary to deal with them for assistance.

There didn't seem to be any set rate, and Frémont had to wait as the
Wascos and Watlalas discussed what the fee for portage should be. Once the
terms were agreed upon and Frémont had paid the price in goods, the
Watlalas wasted no time. They knew their trade and put their talent to quick
and vigorous use as they carried the canoe, instruments, and baggage for
about half a mile to the riverbank below the main cascade. Then everybody
in Frémont's party boarded the canoe, and the Wasco boatmen guided the
craft into water that was white with foam beating against half-hidden rocks
and swirling about in a stretch of river that appeared to have a thousand
whirlpools. But the Wascos guided the Chinook canoe "with great rapidity,
crossing and recrossing in the eddies of the current."[41]

After two miles of rough water, they reached the Lower Rapids. There was
no portage around these, and the boatmen strained every muscle and used all
their skill as they paddled, pushed away from rocks, and shifted their bodies
to change the balance and direction of the canoe in guiding it through the
last rapids of the river. When this wet journey through waves of white spray
and between ominous-looking boulders ended, they glided into the smooth
water where the Columbia broadened out and ran wide and deep without a
ripple. John Charles saw the pitched tents of emigrants on the shore, emigrants "waiting here for their friends from above, or for boats and provisions
which were expected from Vancouver."[42]

The Wasco Indians relaxed after their furious battle against the rapids and
let the canoe drift through the dark water, leaving a spreading wake behind.
Looking upward, Frémont saw high escarpments of red rock and incredible
waterfalls that dropped over cliff edges and splashed from ledge to ledge on a
dizzy path to the river. Then as he let his gaze take in the whole scene, he
saw that here the river valley widened into beautiful country that would be
ideal for farmers.

As the sun began to drop, they left the river valley and reached a high
rock wall formation—a cliff that looked as though it had been neatly cut
with a stroke of a cleaver. This was called Cape Horn, because the prevailing
westerly winds made it a navigation hazard. Whenever the wind blew, the
river became a mass of whitecaps that broke against the cliff with a loud slap
and a burst of spray that leaped high up the wet and slippery rock face; the
combination of strong current, heavy winds, and rock was a deadly threat to
anyone who relaxed his guard.

But the Wascos were alert and fully aware of how quickly the winds and the current could shift at this point, and they eased by Cape Horn with strong paddle strokes that hardly made a sound. Beyond this notorious formation, the river widened out; and as the sun went down, the boatmen maneuvered the canoe into the shallow waters along the shoreline. When they found a comfortable-looking area, they beached the canoe and stopped to eat supper. Then they pushed into the river again and moved cautiously toward the main stream in the darkness. Even though they were past any rapids, rock outcroppings, or vertical cliffs such as Cape Horn, they were faced with another problem. In the dark of night it was difficult to know whether they were in a true channel or a shallow one that might end on a sandbar in this broad expanse of water.

Great black clouds blew in from the Pacific on gusts of a warm wind that rattled branches of trees on the nearby shore. But the Wascos paid no attention to the change in the weather. Instead, they stared intently for any sign which might indicate they were not in the main channel. Within a few hours they crossed the mouth of Tea Prairie River, a small stream that entered the Columbia from the north, and they told Frémont that they were now well beyond the country of rapids and were in a region of flat land where the river was very wide. But because the river was so wide, it became even more difficult to avoid the possibility of drifting out of the main stream into the shallows where they might run aground. It was about ten o'clock at night, and the Wascos paddled across an open expanse of water that was becoming very rough as the warm, humid wind increased its intensity. Before anybody realized what was taking place, there was a sharp jolt, and the canoe rocked from side to side and almost capsized from running into a sandbar.

The men quickly backed the craft off, headed in another direction, and struck another sandbar. Realizing they had lost the main channel, one of the Wascos eased over the side and waded about until he found a deeper channel. He got back aboard, and within a few minutes the boatmen found the main stream of the river again. They paddled at a fast pace, and the canoe shot along until Frémont heard a sound he associated with settled country— the noise of a sawmill at work.

It was a strange and pleasant sensation. The sound of a sawmill, no more than that; but after all these months in the wilderness, the whirring blade and the sudden metallic ring as it worked its way through the wood became a symbol of what was behind them. They were close to Fort Vancouver. There could be no doubt about it. But wanting to appear at this headquarters of the Hudson's Bay Company at a more civilized hour and with a clean shave and a change of clothes, Frémont had the Wascos paddle in to shore.

About midnight they set up camp no more than a mile upstream from Fort Vancouver. But they had hardly settled down for the night before the fine, dry weather gave way to the increasing bank of storm clouds, and a heavy, warm rain began to fall.

## 9

It had been a little thing. Not much to ask, really not much at all, but Preuss had refused. After all the trouble to get here, Preuss wouldn't do the proper thing. Frémont was angry, and so was Preuss. They had argued while the rain fell, and now in the first light of morning, Frémont saw the bark *Columbia* lying at anchor near the landing for Fort Vancouver. But the morning had been spoiled by Preuss's stubborn attitude. All he had asked the man to do was cut off his straggly, unkempt beard, but he had refused to make himself presentable.

Preuss did not agree. Lieutenant Frémont was asking too much. Cut off his beard? If he weren't a married man, if he didn't have responsibilities, he would draw his pay and catch the English ship to get away from him. All young officers were alike. There Frémont was, all groomed and dressed in a clean uniform he had stored in the baggage. What a fool! And he still asked for the beard to be shaved. Well, the answer was no! He wasn't going to cut his beard so Frémont could say, "This is Mr. Preuss, my cartographer." He simply wouldn't do it and have to go through two or three weeks of itching while it grew out again. Then he jotted in his diary that he would rather stay in the tent with the Indians. There was plenty of good bread, plenty of potatoes, even some butter and milk.

John Charles tried to forget about the whole affair. There was too much to be done to carry on with such a petty quarrel. As he looked toward the fort and the village of wooden huts to the west and southwest of the post, his men packed the tent and the baggage and loaded them into the Chinook canoe. Then the fire was put out, and as the day became lighter, they boarded the canoe and headed toward the landing.

Located on the north side of the Columbia River at what is now Vancouver, Washington, and just across the river from Portland, Oregon, Fort Vancouver was an impressive place when Frémont saw it on the morning of November 8, 1843. For he saw it when it was nearing the height of its prosperity. More than seven hundred feet long and three hundred feet wide, this citadel of the fur trade was surrounded by a stockade of upright logs. Within the stockade was a totally self-sufficient establishment. There were twenty-two major buildings, including dwelling places for the chief factor, company officers, and clerks and such diverse structures as storehouses, an Indian trade store, two churches, a bakery, a granary, a blacksmith shop, a carpenter shop, a harness shop, a powder magazine, and even a jail. Yet this was only part of this center of command and supply for the Hudson's Bay Company.

The village of wooden huts Frémont had noticed housed artisans, boatmen, laborers, and tradesmen. For a number of miles along the fertile north bank of the Columbia River the Hudson's Bay Company had orchards, cultivated fields, and good grazing land for its livestock. Everything the company trappers and traders needed was sent from this hub of activity. These needs made an extensive list which included food, clothing, trade goods, beaver traps and other iron tools forged in the company shop, lumber processed in company mills, and gunpowder from the company magazine, as well as medicine and advice on how to treat illnesses, broken bones, and wounds. Self-sufficiency was the key to the successful operations of the Hudson's Bay Company, and even a casual visitor soon realized the extent and care that touched its far-flung empire.

This was the third central headquarters that had been built. The first had been Fort George at the mouth of the Columbia. Then in 1825 short George Simpson and tall Dr. John McLoughlin moved the operation a hundred miles upstream as they sought better farming land, a location closer to the interior Indian tribes, and a stronger British claim to all the territory north of the Columbia River. When they finished this second post, they named it in honor of the explorer Captain George Vancouver; but within five years the final site of the massive post was established one mile to the west and within easy walking distance of a deep lagoon.

Observing proper protocol, Frémont passed through the south gate and walked directly to the residence of the chief factor, Dr. John McLoughlin. Known to the Indians as White Eagle, McLoughlin was a striking figure. His hair was snow white, and when he stood to greet Frémont, he towered above him; dignified, a physician and a man of learning, Dr. McLoughlin stood six feet four inches tall. If one had set out to design a man to handle the vast empire of the Hudson's Bay Company, McLoughlin would have been the ideal answer. Though he was fifty-nine years old when Frémont met him, Dr. McLoughlin's reputation had not diminished with age. In the highly competitive fur trade, he was known as a man without mercy toward rival companies. Yet there was another side to the good doctor in that he was kind and extremely helpful to anyone in need, and even went out of his way to offer advice and credit for supplies and provisions to the new American settlers.

Frémont was greatly impressed by this chief executive of the Hudson's Bay Company. He was a rare man for any place in the world, and all the more unusual so far from the civilized society which he had been trained to serve. John Charles wrote that Dr. McLoughlin received him "with the courtesy and hospitality for which he has been eminently distinguished, and which makes a forcible and delightful impression on a traveller from the long wilderness from which we had just issued."[43]

Frémont asked about obtaining the supplies and equipment he needed. If he intended to make a winter journey back to the States, as he contemplated, many necessary items would have to be obtained from the fort. To get back upriver with the supplies would also require boats and men, and McLoughlin saw to it that he had a large Mackinaw boat, two more canoes, and enough men to help with the transportation of the goods he wished to purchase and take to his camp just below The Dalles. Among the men were Indians from local tribes as well as Canadian and Iroquois voyaguers.

Frémont fully appreciated all this help, but he explained that he was not able to pay in cash, that all he could offer were vouchers from the United States Government, which ultimately would forward payment to the Hudson's Bay Company. This was no problem as far as the chief factor was concerned; he knew he would receive payment in the future. Then he insisted that John Charles accept a letter of recommendation and credit from him which he could use at any Hudson's Bay Company post during his homeward journey. As he pointed out, there was no way that a man could foresee what his future needs might be if his party should happen to experience some unexpected misfortune.

With business out of the way, the white-haired doctor invited Frémont to take a room at the fort and make himself at home as long as he wished. After weeks and months of sleeping on the ground, of tent life and meals around a campfire in bad weather or good, and with the rainy season now at hand, the chance to sleep in a bed again, to eat at a table, and to eat something other than camp cooking was too much to resist. Frémont accepted the invitation as one of the greatest gifts he had ever received.

There were many American emigrants at Fort Vancouver, and others were just arriving or were known to be on their way. All these people had three things in common. They were near exhaustion from the long overland journey, were in need of clothing, food, supplies, and temporary shelter, and were filled with questions about the Willamette Valley or any other area that might be promising for a family willing to work from dawn to dark in pursuit of a dream of Eden.

Chief Factor McLoughlin came to the rescue of these new citizens of Oregon Territory. He gave them credit for whatever they needed in the way of food and supplies, and told them that they could pay their bill with produce from their farms when next year's harvest was over. He furnished them with temporary shelter in buildings the company owned, either at the fort or in the nearby village. Then he pointed the way to the rich farming lands and explained how to get there, what kinds of crops did well in the region, who already owned farms in these areas, and what type of dwelling held up best in a foggy, rainy Oregon winter. Finally, being concerned about keeping the peace, he gave them advice on how to treat the Indians so they could live as friendly neighbors.

Among these many emigrants, there was one man who asked Frémont if he might travel with his party on their upriver journey to Lee House just below The Dalles. He explained that he had considered settling in the area around The Dalles, as he thought this might turn out to be a key stopping place for traffic on the Columbia River. He had left his family at the mission while he traveled on to Fort Vancouver just to make sure that he had picked the right place to settle.

"Prairie Indian Encampment," by John Mix Stanley, gives a general view of a Plains Indian camp as seen by Frémont. Note the skin lodges and the strips of meat hanging from a rack to dry in the sun. (*Courtesy of The Detroit Institute of Arts, Gift of Mrs. Blanche F. Hooker*)

This scene of a buffalo hunt captures all the movement and techniques of killing these animals for meat. (*The Bancroft Library*)

Fort Laramie as it appeared in the summer of 1842. (*The Bancroft Library*)

The Wind River Mountains as sketched by Charles Preuss in 1842. (*The Bancroft Library*)

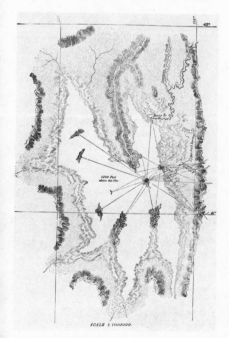

SCALE 1:1000000.

A map of the Great Salt Lake drawn by Charles Preuss from Frémont Island in 1843. (*The Bancroft Library*)

This crossing of the Deschutes Rive
shows the problems involved in such
fords. (*The Bancroft Library*)

This John Mix Stanley lithograph of The Dalles shows the geological
formation, a small Wasco Indian camp, and the type of canoe these
Indians used. (*The Bancroft Library*)

But things didn't turn out that way for this man who was destined to become the first elected governor of California. Peter Hardeman Burnett had listened to the advice of Dr. McLoughlin and his assistant and decided to settle in the lower portion of Oregon. But this was to be only a temporary stop for this Tennessee man who had been a trader and a lawyer in both Tennessee and Missouri. Peter Burnett was a man with a bounce to his gait, an itch in his feet, and a view for new opportunities. All three of these traits took him to California when the news of gold began to spread, and before his death in 1895 he had been not only governor of the Golden State but also an agent for Captain John Sutter, a judge of the supreme court of California, a banker, and a man of considerable means. However, in this early part of November 1843, he was thankful that Lieutenant Frémont was open to allowing him to travel upriver with him.

Before leaving Fort Vancouver, though, there were many things which Frémont had to be certain about. Transportation was only one aspect of his needs. To support his expedition in the long trek ahead, he purchased provisions for at least three months. These included cattle, which were to be driven to the Methodist mission, additional horses and mules, and such items for his commissary as flour, peas, and tallow. Before he was through buying what he thought he might need, his total bill at the Hudson's Bay Company headquarters ran to just over two thousand dollars.[44]

Two days at Fort Vancouver took care of everything for the backtrack of the expedition. By November 10, 1843, Frémont was ready to bid farewell to Dr. McLoughlin and head upriver to where Kit Carson and the main party were waiting for him. It would have been grand to have gone all the way to the Pacific just to see America's other ocean. But the season of fog and rain was upon them, and he had come as far toward the western horizon as was required to match the inland expedition that Captain Charles Wilkes had made in 1841. Now it was time to head homeward to see Jessie, write his report, gather his scientific data into publishable form, and help Preuss with the final versions of the maps. The great reconnaissance was completed. The long trail that had begun in conversations in Senator Benton's library or around the dinner table had come to its natural end. Senator Benton's "road to India" had ceased to be a dream, for beyond Fort Vancouver the long seacoast of the Pacific pounded the shore with an ocean that belonged to the Orient, and America.

## Strangers in a Strange Land

RAIN AND FOG, nothing but constant rain and fog, and on their third day upriver from Fort Vancouver, they arrived at the Lower Rapids of the Cascades. The Wasco Indians in the Chinook canoes shot ahead, and the boatmen used all their skill with paddles to ease the canoes through the white water. As the Wascos were almost out of sight, the Iroquois pilot spoke to his oarsmen, and they maneuvered the boat close to shore, lowered the sail they had been using, jumped into the shallow water, and began the hard job of cordelling.

The wind was blowing harder, and it drove the cold rain against the backs of the men. Frémont saw there wasn't a chance of getting through the Lower Rapids before nightfall, and he shouted to the disappearing Wascos. When they didn't answer, other men shouted and even fired their guns into the air. But the Wascos were not able to hear.

There was no point in trying to get them back. This was going to be a cold, wet, miserable night. All the men in the Mackinaw boat knew the tent, most of the bedding, and most of the provisions were in the canoes.

The riverbank was covered with large boulders and didn't look at all promising for a campground. But there was an open point of land on an island just below the last white water of the rapids. The oarsmen worked the boat to that point, and there they beached it for the night. The rain stopped, and the men hoped it wouldn't start again. Fires were built, and everyone crowded close to dry his wet clothes. As the heat from the flames drifted against their soaked clothing, there was a slight sizzling noise of steam. The supper was not what chilled men wanted, but they had to make do with salted salmon and cold bread. Soup with macaroni would have been great on such a cold night—soup, and a cup of hot coffee laced with brandy. But it was cold food and cold water. The only thing they could be thankful for was that the infernal rain had ceased. Yet a glance upward at the great banks of black clouds drifting in from the Pacific made it clear that they had better enjoy the brief interlude of dry weather.

Peter Burnett never forgot this night. Years later he wrote of what it had been like as they bedded down beside the fire after their cold supper. Frémont had one blanket, which he spread out and lay upon. He wrapped himself in his cloak, kept his clothes on, and even though the rain began to fall again, he slept as though he might have been in his own bed.

For myself [Burnett wrote], I had with me two pairs of large, heavy blankets, one pair of which I put folded under me, and covered myself with the other pair. Soon after we had lain down the rain began to fall gently, but continued steadily to increase. At first, I thought it might rain as much as it pleased, without wetting through my blankets; but before day it came down in torrents, and I found water running under me, and into the pockets of my pantaloons and the tops of my boots. It was a cold rain, and the fire was extinguished. I could not endure all this, and I sat up during most of the remaining portion of the night upon a log of wood, with one pair of blankets thrown over my head, so as to keep warm; but the weight of the wet blankets was great, and my neck at last rebelled against the oppression. I finally became so fatigued and sleepy that just before day, when the rain had ceased, I threw myself down across some logs of wood, and in that condition slept until daylight.[1]

At daybreak the hard task of cordelling the boat began once again. Slowly, the men worked it up the Lower Rapids, and they reached smooth water again in a little bay just below the Upper Rapids. Here they found the Wascos still in camp. They had pitched the lodge, and all of them were inside. When Frémont threw open the skin door, there were the Wascos "making a luxurious breakfast with salmon, bread, butter, sugar, coffee, and other provisions."[2] Furious that they were having such a great breakfast, angered that he and his men had to spend the night in the rain while they slept in the comfort of his lodge, John Charles lost his temper and ran the Wascos out.

During the next four days, the upriver journey was very hard going. The rain never ceased for any great length of time; and wet, slippery ground made cordelling and portaging tedious and difficult. But even when his own men and the hired Indians wanted to stop and take a long break, or when they wanted to take a short day's journey, John Charles would not allow them to fall behind in their duties. If the Indians stopped to build a fire, to warm themselves, he would have none of it. Hard taskmaster that he was, he quickly kicked out the fires and made it clear to one and all that the only way to keep warm was to keep working at a steady pace.

On the portage trail they passed emigrants headed down country, bound for that farming land they had heard about. But these were tired, worn-out families who were slowly stumbling along. Many had been so ill equipped for the long trek to Oregon that when Frémont saw them they were in bad shape. Their clothes were thin and tattered; hats were lost somewhere in the nightmare Snake Plains; and some were without shoes and walked the cold, muddy trail on bare feet. Their only hope was to get to Fort Vancouver, where they could be given proper clothing and badly needed supplies on credit from the Hudson's Bay Company.

Even a fellow scientist was seen on his way downstream. This was Friedrich G. J. Lüders, a botanist from Hamburg, Germany. Frémont and Preuss talked to him, but there wasn't as much time for talk as the men would have enjoyed. The Wasco Indians were ready to run the rapids with a Chinook canoe loaded with everything Lüders owned: specimens, instruments, and baggage. While Frémont would have enjoyed a breakfast halt with this fellow botanist, the Wascos were in a hurry. Lüders rushed along the trail to meet them below the roaring white water, "but he was scarcely out of sight, when by the carelessness of the Indians, the boat was drawn into the midst of the rapids, and glanced down the river, bottom up, with the loss of everything it contained."[3] Knowing what such a loss meant, John Charles named the smooth water just below the rapids "Lüders Bay."

As sorry as Frémont felt about the disaster he had seen, there was nothing he could do to help Lüders. With some luck, the man might replace his instruments at Fort Vancouver. But his specimens were lost, and the only way to gather more would be for him to follow his backtrack. While the untamed country offered a challenge to any scientist, it was not a laboratory for the timid and the weak. It was a great outdoor laboratory that was almost untapped; but to learn its secrets, to examine its specimens, required a rare breed of man who was part scientist, part explorer, part outdoorsman, and part fatalist. For what appeared to be difficult sometimes was easy, and what appeared to be easy sometimes was impossible.

Before they completed the hard journey over the portage trail, they met a Hudson's Bay crew heading downriver with two express bateaus from Montreal. With them was a woman and her daughter, emigrants from Canada. The only thing which bothered them was the wet weather, as they had just entered the rainy season. But the men of the Hudson's Bay Company were highly experienced at what they were doing and told Frémont they would be at Fort Vancouver by nightfall. As he watched them work, he had no reason to doubt their word. This was a regular run for these watermen. They carried the express for the Hudson's Bay Company on the north fork of the Columbia River. From there, overland parties carried it all the way to Lake Winnipeg, where it was divided so that part of it went to Montreal and the other part went all the way to Hudson's Bay. In this manner, the post at Fort Vancouver co-operated with the activities of even the remotest points of the trading empire. The efficiency and organization that went into such an operation struck Frémont as the key to any success in the wilderness.

During the upriver journey, Peter Burnett saw Frémont in action, and he admired his ability to lead men and to endure hardship. Even though he was only thirty years old at the time, he was a natural leader. While he was calm and gentle in manner, none of his men considered him a city man, out of his natural element. Small and slender, he had incredible endurance and a capacity to withstand cold, wet weather, to go without food, and to keep up the spirits of all. As for his relationship with the others, Burnett was intrigued.

> His men all loved him intensely. He gave his orders with great mildness and simplicity, but they had to be obeyed. There was no shrinking from duty. He was like a father to those under his command.[4]

Three days after the meeting with the Hudson's Bay men, the rain stopped and the weather was clear. That morning the Wasco Indian village came into view. The upriver struggle was over, and by afternoon all the supplies had been carried to the new camp Kit Carson had established near good grazing. Everything was in order, but Fitzpatrick and the slower section of the expedition had not arrived. That night they sat around the campfires and enjoyed a feast of roast beef cut from one of the California cows purchased at the mission.

2

SCIENTIFIC REALITY had shaped Frémont in his early years. His motto might have been: "Tell me the facts, only the facts." For he was careful in gathering data about the land, the climate, the natural life, and the Native Americans. All this had been part of his basic training under Joseph Nicolas Nicollet. But a streak of romanticism coursed through the young explorer's blood. His career had been touched with the poet's imagination many times, and in the camp near The Dalles imagination took over as he made plans for his eastward journey. Somewhere in the Great Basin there was a mythical river called the Buenaventura, a river that flowed all the way from the Rocky Mountains through the Great Basin, cut through the Sierra Nevada, and emptied into San Francisco Bay.

It appears strange that a man of Frémont's background and experience, a man so thoroughly trained in scientific exploration persisted in pursuing a river of fable. For by this late date, mountain men had crossed and recrossed the Great Basin, and not one of them ever reported a river that flowed all the way to the Pacific. Certainly Jedediah Smith would have told fellow trappers of its existence if it had been reality, and by 1843 such information should have been common knowledge to Thomas Fitzpatrick and Kit Carson as well as Dr. John McLoughlin, who had heard about much of this area from Peter Skene Ogden and other Hudson's Bay men. But the final maps weren't made. There were great regions that bore the legend "Unknown." That word was a teaser, a come-on for a man who sought the truth; and perhaps Frémont's drive to prove whether the Buenaventura River existed or not can be equated with the same quests that sent men to their deaths as they searched for the Northwest Passage, the Seven Cities of Cíbola, and the kingdom of El Dorado. At times, the thin line between myth and reality blurs in the minds of men, and nowhere is this merger of truth and fable more at home than in the deserts of the world. So, with hindsight and proper maps available, it is easy to point an accusatory finger at Frémont and say he included the Buenaventura River in his *Report* to make it a better yarn. But in a cold November of 1843, in a rough camp above The Dalles of the Columbia River, and in a situation where vague rumors and very little information were all a man could count on, the possibility that a river like the Columbia flowed out of the Great Basin didn't appear to be such a wild belief.

As the men of the camp made preparations for their homeward journey, John Charles planned the route they would follow. Moving to the south and southeast, he hoped to make a circuit that would allow him to explore the Great Basin country between the Sierra Nevada and the Rocky Mountains. By reports, maps, and conversations he knew of three principal objects he wished to locate and explore if they existed. One was Klamath Lake and what he thought would be the headwaters of the Sacramento River; another was Mary's Lake, which was reported to be in the Great Basin; and the final object of his search was the Buenaventura River. After that, the goal of his expedition was to reconnoiter the southern section of the Rocky Mountains, the headwaters of streams flowing toward the Gulf of California, and then follow the Arkansas River to Bent's Fort. At that point the grand reconnaissance would have come full circle, and the journey to St. Louis, where Jessie awaited his coming, would be like a skip and a jump compared to the long days and weeks and months in the wilderness.

In no way did Frémont fool himself about the hardships that still faced his expedition. They were heading into a strange land at the beginning of winter, and even in the spring of a good year the land before them was not noted for easy traveling. At best, they would find enough water to drink, enough forage for the animals. At worst, they might run light on both and have to make do with whatever the desert had to offer. But it was a party of hardened men, and of the twenty-five persons, most were young, a few under twenty-one years of age; and they constituted an American mix of nationalities, colors, and languages. These were wilderness men, shapers of a nation they would never understand, and they were good men to be with on such an adventure.

On November 21, Broken Hand, young Talbot, and the remainder of the expedition reached the camp above The Dalles. The Red River carts had been sold, and except for the howitzer carriage, the party was ready to travel on horseback and carry their supplies on pack horses and mules. Altogether, Frémont had 104 mules and horses. Some were left over from their past travels, but many had been purchased from the Wasco Indians around Lee House. Also, some California cattle had been picked up to drive along as a walking commissary. Then two Indians were hired to guide the party up the

Deschutes River and through the Cascade Mountains. One bore scars of wounds he had received in a battle with the Klamaths.

By November 24 everything was packed and ready to go. Then as they sat around their last campfire near the Columbia River, Reverend Perkins approached Frémont about a personal matter. One man, John Gill Campbell, had been discharged from the expedition; and as Mr. Perkins saw it, this meant there would be room for a young Chinook to go along. The nineteen-year-old boy's name was William Perkins—the latter name in honor of the missionary—and, having lived in the mission house for some time, the young man spoke a few words of English. But he wanted to see the whites, to see how they lived, and gain a better understanding of them. This did not mean he wished to live the rest of his life among them. So Reverend Perkins got Frémont to agree that once William had seen how the whites lived, he was to return to his people and friends. All this was agreeable, and that night there was a feeling of goodwill and excitement in the camp as the men looked at the brilliant stars in the black sky and talked about turning eastward to head home.

The morning broke cold and clear, with ice on the shallow water and a snowlike frost on the ground. Everyone was slow in getting started, and it wasn't until noon that the expedition headed out. By that time clouds had drifted in on the westerlies, and the men saw the last of Lee House as a muted vision through cold, stinging snow flurries. Reverend Perkins and a group of Indians rode along with the party for several miles as they worked their way along the easy road. When the road became the upward trail beside the Deschutes River, Perkins said farewell and watched the riders until they were out of sight in the uplands and bound for Fifteenmile Creek. The Indians camped with the expedition, but during the night two visitors were caught stealing. They were tied and stretched out beside the fire and watched by the nightguard. In the morning, they were allowed to go free, and they joined other camp followers bound back to the Columbia River.

All day the party worked its way upward, seeing one waterfall after another, crossing tributary streams and the Tygh Prairie, and looking back at the clear view of Mounts Hood, Rainier, and St. Helens. Camp was made that night at White River, a large tributary of the Deschutes. But even though it had been sunny during the day, late afternoon was freezing cold, and there was a wide band of ice over the shallow water close to the river-banks.

On the morning of November 27, the sky was clear, but the temperature was below zero. Trees and bushes glittered with ice and frost and made a man squint his eyes as the first sunlight reflected off the frozen forms, and the rapid White River was filled with floating ice. This was as far as Chiefs Stiletsi and White Crane wished to go. They gave Frémont and his key men some idea of the rest of the trail to Klamath Lake, and then headed out for lower and warmer country.

Now a definite pattern of travel formed. Day after day they crossed icy creeks and streams, heard the roar of waterfalls from the Deschutes River, and moved toward the rugged Cascade Range. Travel was slow, hard going, but never without a wild beauty as they worked their way through Tygh Valley, across Nena Creek, in and out of one basin or valley after another, struggling with the weight of the howitzer and its carriage, and even taking time to observe the geological formations, the fossil beds, hot water springs, and the flora and fauna of the country.

Preuss wrote that the travel was slow and hard. The guides they followed were the high peaks of the Cascade Range as they moved south by southwest. But these milestones ahead of them made their rate of progress only too clear. Twenty miles per day was an unusual day and hardly balanced the days of eight or five miles. It was a speed that just might get them back to Westport by April, if they were lucky. Sitting on a fir trunk, Preuss made his entries for December 1; and he did have something good to say, as he found the California beef to his liking, and was impressed by the waterfalls of the Deschutes River.

Days and nights, week added to week, and the tally of months on the trail began to take its toll on the men. Preuss, complaints and all, was among the sturdiest men of the party. But his diary records a tale told by a tired man, a man yearning for a clean, comfortable bed, meals at a dining table, and the company of his family. While he appreciated the beauty of the splendid waterfalls he was saddle-sore, and disgruntled that Frémont was not going to take Dr. Whitman's advice to travel by ship to Mexico, cross that country, and then catch another ship to the United States. Or, if Frémont didn't want to do that, Whitman had suggested heading south to California and going from there to the Santa Fé Trail. But no; they weren't going to do anything but head back into the miserable desert, and then make the long trek during the worst months of the year.

Signs of a trail-weary man, signs to watch for in other members of the expedition as the wind grew colder, the mornings icy and below zero, and going tougher as they slogged their way through snow and worked their way higher and higher into the mountains of the Cascade Range.

Then, as there seemed to be no end to the upward path, as the elusive pass through the Cascade Range seemed to be nonexistent, the men traveled through a beautiful pine forest and struck the divide. It was December 9, 1843, and they crossed the mountains on a fine path that Frémont called a road, and began a gentle downward ride toward the south. The day was warmer than the past days, and while they made a late camp at a place where there was poor forage for the animals, the next day's journey brought them into better country before the sun reached its midday peak. They came to a large meadow that was bordered by a fringe of timber.

Frémont was certain he had reached Klamath Lake, but there was no lake to be seen. There was some water, but not what he had been told to expect.

What the expedition had reached was not the lake but Klamath Marsh, some thirty miles north of the lake. But the change in terrain, the good pasture for the horses and mules, and the easy traveling for the men was welcome after the long upward climb from The Dalles.

Camp was established on a point of land that jutted into a deep cove of water in the marshland. Once again the routine of guard duty was established, as the reputation of the Klamaths was well known to the other tribes along the Columbia River and to the missionaries and the men of the Hudson's Bay Company. The Klamaths—or Tlamaths, as Frémont referred to them—were tough, courageous warriors, and the members of the expedition had been warned to be cautious while they were in their country. And when Frémont and the others noticed the smoke from campfires on the opposite shore of the marshland, the lieutenant ordered Zindel to fire the howitzer as a warning. The noise of the bursting shot echoed and re-echoed across the marshland, and this strange sound in this peaceful setting had its desired effect. Streamers of smoke from the Klamath village were snuffed out immediately. But while the noise of the mountain howitzer kept the Klamaths at bay, it was too successful. In the morning, no Klamaths appeared to see what the whites were doing in their country; and Frémont had hoped that they would send a delegation to visit his camp. He needed as much knowledge of the country ahead as he could obtain. Having no other choice, he selected some of his best men and had one of the Indian guides lead the way to the Klamath village.

When they were about half a mile from the village, they saw two persons walking out to meet them. Not knowing what this meant, Frémont ordered his men to ride abreast in a long line to give the appearance of more men and to ride forward at a gallop. But as they neared the Indians, it was clear that a man and a woman were coming out to meet them. This was not a sign of hostility.

Through the guide, Frémont learned that the man was the chief of the village and the woman was his wife. The chief was a tall, handsome man with high cheekbones and a large straight nose. He spoke softly in a language that neither Kit Carson nor Broken Hand had ever heard before. It did not resemble any of the speech patterns of the Plains Indians nor any of the tongues of the tribes who lived beside the Columbia River. But, by a combination of the guide's knowledge of the language, of Chinook words which were part of the trade language in this region, and of signs, they communicated with the chief of these Indians, who called themselves Maklaks. It became clear that Frémont and his men were invited to enter the village. The invitation was accepted, and John Charles described the appearance of the Klamath village —a village which was quite different than any he had seen.

The huts were grouped together on the bank of the river, which, from being spread out in a shallow marsh at the upper end of the lake, was collected here into a single stream. There were large round huts, perhaps 20 feet in diameter, with rounded tops, on which was the door by which they descended into the interior. Within, they were supported by posts and beams.[5]

The Klamaths in this area of the Williamson River of present southeastern Oregon were people who had learned the secret of perfect adaptation to what their land had to offer. And it was a bountiful land where there was plenty of deer, trout, white fish, salmon, camas roots, waterfowl of every kind during the migratory season, antelope, elk, and *apaws*—green pond-lily seeds that were parched and then ground into a fine flour that was used for mush and cakes.

To Frémont these Indians seemed almost like plants in their relationship to the environment. Small suckers and trout were plentiful; so they smoked and dried them and strung them in their lodges for handy meals during long cold spells when no other foods were available. During those periods when arctic storms blew in from the north and turned the land into snow and ice, when plants, roots, and berries were not available, when waterfowl had migrated south to warmer climates, and when all other game animals either were in hibernation or had moved to areas where food was not covered with a blanket of white, the dried and smoked fish became the difference between life and death.

Here in the midst of grass and reeds, the Klamaths had become skillful at converting grass and rushes into useful material.

> Their shoes were made of straw or grass, which seemed well adapted for a snowy country; and the women wore on their head a closely woven basket, which made a very good cap. Among other things, were parti-colored mats about four feet square, which we purchased to lay on the snow under our blankets, and to use for table cloths.[6]

Through his interpreters Frémont asked the chief if some of his people would replace the Columbia River Indians to lead them to the east. For the Indians from the region around The Dalles had come as far as they had promised, and made it clear that beyond the Klamath territory was a land they knew very little about. But the Klamaths were not interested in leaving the warmth of their lodges during such weather. The chief found many excuses not to strike out on a journey at this time. There was too much snow on the ground. He would need horses; but even if he had horses, there was yet another problem. His family was sick, too sick for him to leave them. Other men in this Klamath village also found reasons for not traveling to the east while the snow continued to fall. The only thing they agreed to do was to give information about the land, and they said that within a few days they would reach a large water.

But two days after this conversation with the Klamaths, two days of hard going through ice ponds, snow that ranged from four to twelve inches in depth, and a biting wind that carried large snowflakes which made it difficult to see very far ahead, Frémont heard galloping horses and was pleased to see the Klamath chief and some of his men. The chief apologized for his behavior at the village and for not agreeing to help the expedition find its way. Still, as they worked their way into the higher mountains, the Klamaths became uneasy about the cold and the increasing depth of the snow. They rode all of one day with the party, and part of the next. That was as far as they would travel. But before they returned to their village, the chief made it clear to Kit Carson and Tom Fitzpatrick that if they headed northeast, they would avoid a bad mountain to the south; and "would arrive at the big water where no more snow was to be found."[7]

Not long after the departure of the Klamaths, the expedition crossed a stream which Frémont thought to be the upper reaches of the Sacramento River; but, since he was still within the Klamath Lake watershed, it must have been Beaver Creek, a tributary of the Sycan River in southeastern Oregon. But no camp was made at this place, and the hard day's journey became one of crossing half-frozen swampland, then working their way upward through a thick pine forest. After seven hours of travel that was pure punishment, they stopped for the night where a few tufts of grass broke through the snow.

Saturday, December 16, started out like the day before. There were differences, though, differences that worried Frémont. The snow was getting deeper, and it was crusted enough that it cut the horses and mules as they broke through. Snow fell so thick and fast the way ahead was a white blur. The upward climb became steeper as they worked their way through the pine woods. Then near midday there appeared to be a clearing ahead.

Riding rapidly ahead to this spot, we found ourselves on the verge of a vertical and rocky wall of mountains. At our feet—more than a thousand feet below—we looked into a green prairie country, in which a beautiful lake, some twenty miles in length was spread along the foot of the mountains, its shores bordered with green grass. Just then the sun broke out among the clouds, and illuminated the country below, while around us the storm raged fiercely.[8]

As they shivered from a cold, north wind, the men looked at the lake where they would camp for the night. John Charles thought it fitting to call it Summer Lake, and he named their frigid viewing place Winter Ridge. But working their way down from the rimrock was not easy. The sun gave way to dark night before the last of the party reached the lake by heading toward the bright fires the early arrivals had built. In the long descent, the howitzer had to be left behind until the next morning; and one of the mules lost its balance and tumbled two or three hundred feet down the side of a ravine. But the hardy mule only suffered from bruises, and carrying what remained of its broken packsaddle, it followed the other animals into the Great Basin camp.

## 3

LAKES OF ROTTEN WATER, playas of cracked earth with only the illusion of water, stunted willows and blue-gray sagebrush for firewood, boggy marshes to wade through, heavy sands to march across, salt grass, no grass, and now and then a little decent forage for the hungry animals, nearby cliffs of black volcanic rock that gave the country a forbidding appearance, migrating waterfowl heading southward, blacktailed rabbits bounding a crooked path through the sagebrush, and now seven days after Summer Lake it was Christmas morning of 1843—Christmas morning in an unmapped, strange land, an Old Testament desert placed in the Great Basin. Something had to be done to revive the spirit of the men. Frémont got out the carefully guarded bottle of brandy and poured a breakfast toast to celebrate the birthday of Christ. Louis Zindel loaded the howitzer and fired one round to greet the morning, and other men fired their small arms. Coffee was poured, and there was some sugar. The lake they had camped beside on Christmas Eve at least had drinkable water. Frémont named it Christmas Lake[9] in honor of the day, and there was something right about this name applied to a lake in this remote, desolate land so much like the wilderness beyond the walls of Bethlehem.

Following a beaten Indian trail and passing obvious campgrounds, it was clear to Frémont and his men that they "were on one of the great thoroughfares of the country."[10] Still, there were no Indians in sight, only the tracks of their passing. But the Indians were there and were watching the strangers move through their country. For on the night of December 25 a horse was stolen, and when they crossed the forty-second parallel (the Oregon-Nevada line), and made camp for the night, even Kit Carson's horse was stolen. Yet the night watch had not heard any sound nor seen any movement.

Walled in on the west by a rugged mountain range, the expedition continued its southward course. They followed the Indian trail through a series of small and large basins, and on December 27 they struck a trail that turned to the southeast and led upward through a broad mountain pass. On the summit the snow was about a foot deep, and sagebrush gave way to a grove of large cedars. But the zone of trees was only in this area. As they dropped down from the pass into another basin, sagebrush prevailed once again. Here they found a dry lake bed, and the only thing which saved them from a dry camp for the night was the snowpack. By melting enough snow, they obtained water, and their tired animals grazed on green grass that poked through the snow.

With this cover of snow, Frémont decided if any more animals were stolen by unseen Indians during the night, at daybreak they would be able to track the thieves. But that night none of the animals were released from the picket lines, and in the morning there was no sign to indicate nightly intruders had been near the camp. All this worried the men. They were accustomed to seeing Indians whenever they traveled through their country. Yet, in all these days of following a well-used trail, of even having horses stolen from them, they had not seen any Indians. It was as though the tribes that inhabited this hostile world were capable of vanishing into the void of the open desert, of blending into the sagebrush and becoming part of it.

Bothered by this feeling of being watched and never seeing the watchers, the men ate a hurried breakfast, mounted up, and started out again. The hooves of the animals were muffled by the snow, and the expedition moved quietly along. They entered a region where the sagebrush resembled small trees. The trunks were a foot in diameter, and the highest limbs were as much as eight feet above the ground. Looking ahead, the men at the front of the column saw smoke rising from a camp in the tall sage. They galloped toward it, but by the time they reached the campfire, all they found were two loosely built sage huts. The inhabitants were not there. Then as the men gazed at the surrounding country, they caught sight of several Indians running over the crest of a nearby ridge. Behind them, struggling to catch up, were other members of this group of shy people.

For once they had managed to catch the Indians off guard, and Frémont looked at their belongings scattered about on grass which had been spread over the snow around a sage fire. There were a few baskets and a couple of rabbitskin robes. The weapons were not there, and it was assumed the warriors had managed to grab them before they had deserted their camp in haste.

Then the cold air carried a cry of warning from the ridge: "Tavibo!" Carson and Fitzpatrick recognized the language, and now they knew these were Indians who spoke the Shoshonean language, for the word they had shouted meant "white."

Carson and Godey, who always joined together in any risky adventure, gave their horses their heads and rode at a gallop toward the fleeing Indians. But they were not able to catch them. For these northern Paiutes were not just shy; they were afraid of these white intruders. How much they feared them wasn't realized until Carson found a woman and her two children hiding in the sagebrush. She began to scream, and she even shut her eyes as though she wished to avoid seeing him. Carson brought the woman and the children back to their deserted camp, and they attempted to give reassurance that they meant no harm. Finally the combination of gifts and the friendly attitude expressed by the men calmed her fears, and they learned that she was from a tribe that was related in language to other Shoshoni Indians.

Taking note of their language, Frémont also wrote of the life style of these Great Basin nomads:

Eight or ten appeared to live together, under the same little shelter; and they seemed to have no other subsistence than the roots or seeds they might have stored up, and the hares which live in the sage, and which they are enabled to track through the snow, and are very skillful in killing. Their skins afford them a little covering.[11]

Yet even though the explorer noticed these detailed things about these desert people, he failed to understand how brilliantly they had learned to live with the harsh environment of the Great Basin. Instead, he considered their poverty and way of life as an indication that these were human beings not far removed from the animals they hunted. He was not alone in his attitude about the northern Paiutes. The mountain men felt the same way. They were too accustomed to the culture of the Plains Indians to recognize the talents of these desert dwellers. It never occurred to them that to exist in the Great Basin required tenacity, adaptability of the highest order, an intelligence able to create something to maintain life out of the uncertain offerings of the earth, and a kind of courage that refused to give in to the extremes: the blistering heat, the bone-chilling storms, dry waterholes, seasons of drought, and plagues of insects. Even so, this first meeting between Frémont and the Paiutes was not to be the final basis for his impression of these masters of survival.

How much the Paiutes had learned to deal with their cruel world became much clearer to John Charles and his men as they moved farther to the southwest. During the remainder of 1843 their course took them in and out of various basins and across ranges of north-south desert hills covered with snow. On December 31 they arrived at the western edge of the Black Rock Desert. This was their campsite for New Year's Eve of 1844, but it was not a happy group of men who greeted the New Year. The progress of their journey had become very uncertain. Now even their animals were becoming lame from the rough terrain and were weakened by the lack of enough forage. It was not a night for celebration, and the first day of 1844 found them heading down a valley bordered by a dry-looking black ridge to the east and a high and snowy ridge to the west.

The trail dropped in and out of rough, broken gullies and took them through thick sagebrush and then on to sand hills where nothing grew. Not only was the soil a fine, powdery sand in many places, but also it was covered with a film of salt. It was a country designed to test a man's ability to survive, and the horsemen rode in silence across the dead land.

All that New Year's Day, the men rode toward a distant formation that looked like a massive black cape. At the foot of this black rock the riders could make out a thin column of smoke that seemed to be coming from hot springs. This, they decided, was a likely place for the night's camp. But the long day passed, and by nightfall they were not beside the hot springs. Not until noon of the next day, after a hard ride through a cold, driving snowstorm, did they arrive at their destination. What appeared to be a good bet from the distance became another desert trick. This was not a place to camp but a place to flee from, a place to avoid; for the rocks were volcanic, and the hills had the appearance of having been burnt in the dreadful heat of some ancient fire of creation.

Several mules and a horse gave out and had to be left on the trail before the expedition finished the long day's march and made a dry camp in an area of thick sagebrush. They hoped they had come through the worst of their ordeal. But the next morning offered something they had never expected to face. There was no storm to black out the sun, but there was fog—cold, icy fog that made it hard to breathe and impossible to see ahead for more than a few yards.

The horses were picketed a short way from the camp, where there was some grass. But in the morning the men who were sent out to get the horses became bewildered and lost in the thick fog. It was not until late in the morning that they found their way back to camp. To avoid disaster, Frémont told his men that he and all of the rest of them would have to walk and lead the animals. Not only would it give the animals a rest, but also the loads on the pack mules were to be distributed and carried by the riding stock in order to give the tired mules a lighter burden to carry. Most of all, though, it was vital to remain close together to avoid getting lost in the fog. For they were on the verge of the vast desert the Klamaths had warned them about; and if they strayed into it, their chances of coming out alive would not be very good.

Only seven or eight miles were covered during the remainder of the day, but this journey did take them away from the region of broken and sharp lava and away from the loose sands as they crossed a ridge of white granite in what is now Nevada's Granite Range. By day's end the fog had lifted enough that they could see the tops of hills standing out like extremely high peaks jutting through clouds. That night the stars were seen just long enough for Frémont to determine their latitude as 40°48′15″. Then the thick, chilling fog—the damp clouds the Paiutes called the pogonip—blanketed everything, and the men lay close to the warm orange glow of the sagebrush campfires, which allowed some limited visibility.

The next three days ran together. Fog, clammy, ground-hugging fog, during most of each day, a slight lifting at sunset, then another thick cover of cold for the night. They crossed the Granite Creek Desert, where no water filled the creek bed and there were only a few blades of grass for the hungry animals. On the day after that a mule left the herd, slowly walked to the campfire, and lay next to it to feel the heat of the flames during the last moments before it shuddered and died. If their situation didn't change soon, all of them would join the dead mule.

On the third day of fog Broken Hand explored the region ahead for some way out of this desert wilderness. While he did, Carson and Preuss joined Frémont in climbing a nearby mountain, where they hoped they could determine which route to take. From the heights they saw a column of smoke coming from hot springs they estimated to be about sixteen miles away. Near these springs there also appeared to be a channel that drained the runoff water. Frémont knew such a channel would have grass growing beside it, and he decided they would head for it in hopes that it might provide grazing for the animals.

All the rest of that day was hard going as they crossed a dry lake bed and worked their way over ground that was a combination of mud and sand. Hard as the traveling was, it turned out to be worth it when they reached the hot springs and made camp where present-day Gerlach, Nevada, is located. All around the hot springs there was a margin where the heat had melted the snow, and in that area there was green grass. Frémont measured the temperature of the largest spring, which covered about three hundred feet, and found that the water varied between 206 and 208 degrees, but that was only near the shore. In the center and down where the water bubbled and boiled out of the earth, he thought that the temperature would be much higher; but there was no way he could measure it. And though the water was salty, it was perfectly all right for cooking and was quite drinkable when snow was mixed with it.

The great concern for the party at this point was the loss of animals. Since leaving The Dalles, they had lost fifteen. A few were stolen by Indians, but most had given out, and nine had broken down in the last few days.

To cut down on such losses, John Charles decided that until they reached better country, the method of moving ahead would have to be one of exploring the route for some fifteen to twenty miles in advance of the expedition. So on January 7 he took Carson and Godey with him and they made a foray of the country ahead. By doing so, they found a ravine where there was good water and enough grass for an overnight stop. Also, there were cottonwoods for a change and a broad trail on which they saw tracks of unshod horses.

During the next two days the expedition headed southwest, following what appeared to be a well-used trail. To their immediate west, they saw a range of mountains (the Lake Range in Nevada's Washoe County) that had a fairly good covering of timber which Frémont thought might be cedar but which was really piñon pine. Pure water and a good covering of grass now became easier to find; and where there were springs, there were also groves of cottonwoods.

On January 10 Frémont and Carson reconnoitered ahead of the main party. They reached the end of the basin they had been traveling, and entered a mountain hollow where there was a good growth of bunch grass, and they left a sign for the expedition to make camp at this spot. Then while it was still daylight, while there was no fog but the enjoyable warmth of the afternoon sun, they rode upward on a trail that climbed from the bottom of the hollow. As they worked their way higher into the mountains, they noticed that the snow was becoming deeper, and at the summit of what is now Frémont Pass there was a foot of snow.

As they topped the summit of the Lake Range, they could hardly believe what they saw. Far below there was a lake, but not an ordinary lake. The color of the water was green, dark green in the deeper areas, and the size of the lake was incredible. To have come through all the desert and to top a desert mountain pass, see a lake that stretched almost beyond view and was nearly twenty miles broad at its widest place was something neither man had expected in this barren land of sagebrush and dry lake beds.

> It broke upon our eyes like the ocean. The neighboring peaks rose high above us, and we ascended one of them to obtain a better view. The waves were curling in the breeze, and their dark-green color showed it to be a body of deep water. For a long time we sat enjoying the view, for we had become fatigued with mountains, and the free expanse of moving waves was very grateful. It was set like a gem in the mountains, which, from our position, seemed to enclose it almost entirely.[12]

This night there would be good news to tell the weary men. With a body of water such as this, there would be plenty of game nearby, fish to catch, and meadows near the river and creeks that created such a majestic desert lake.

## 4

THE EXPEDITION topped the summit of the Lake Range, and the men were astounded. Frémont and Carson had told them it was a big lake, but this wasn't just a big lake. My God! There was more water sprawled out between two rugged mountain ranges than they ever believed could exist smack in the middle of sagebrush, rocks, and all the other signs of the same kind of desert country they had been struggling through.

Frémont was right. This wasn't Peter Skene Ogden's Mary's Lake they'd heard about. Any mountain man or Hudson's Bay trapper knew that lake wasn't supposed to be much more than an overflow of Mary's River, a desert sink where the river vanished into sand and mud and where the reeds and rushes stretched along the banks. But the lake they saw before them seemed out of place in this dry country, almost as though it had been set there by some mistake of nature. Maybe, just maybe, they had stumbled on to the source of the Buenaventura River that nobody could ever find.[13]

They made camp near a little stream that flowed into the great lake from the mountain on its eastern side. Then they walked down beyond the rocky shoreline to a sandy beach that reminded them of a stretch of seacoast. They tasted the water, and it was fresh. The rocks around the area were not like anything they'd seen before except around hot springs, but even then the rocks were never this size except in a place or two in the Yellowstone country north of Jackson Hole. But the rocks here took on wind-eroded shapes that resembled creatures from a nightmare. Bloated, puffed up in one place, thin in another, standing two or three horses high, and some shaped like a castle or a giant spear coming up through the ground, these were rocks that almost didn't seem to belong on this planet.

At first John Charles thought these rocks might be large granite boulders scattered around. But when he examined them and broke off a piece of one for a specimen, he discovered that they were coated with a calcareous substance which varied in thickness from a few inches to a foot. And while he lost his notes on the analysis he made of this tufa, he did recall that carbonate of lime constituted the major percentage of the minerals he was able to identify.[14]

Geology, though, was not Frémont's strongest scientific field. While he did try to identify the tufa deposits, his major interest was the lake. From the northern end of what he judged to be a body of water at least thirty-five miles long, there was no way he could determine what might be at the southern end. Even if this did not lead him to the mysterious Buenaventura River, he insisted on trying to locate it with all the drive of a romantic hero on a quest. The lake had to have an outlet or inlet somewhere. In either case, he was certain he would discover a large river.

That night they camped away from the shoreline of the lake, and as a storm came in on western winds, the men had that strange sensation of hearing wild seacoast breakers rolling across the beach and smashing over the high rocks just beyond the stretch of sand, a feeling of being next to an ocean where no ocean could exist. Then on the morning of January 13 they left their first camp beside this vast lake and followed a broad Indian trail along the eastern shoreline as they moved toward the south.

For a short distance the trail was easy going for both men and animals, but then they came to a place where the rugged mountains dropped sharply toward the water, leaving very little room for a trail along the base of the cliffs. To add to their difficulty in getting by what is now known as Howitzer Slide, a sharp, cold wind drove a wild snowstorm against their faces and whipped the surface of the lake so hard that waves five and six feet high rolled in and dashed against the rocks to make the trail almost impassable. Under these conditions, the howitzer was too much of a burden. John Charles decided to leave it on the rocks until the next day. With some luck, the storm might blow past them into the east and make it easier to retrieve the cannon.

As they moved ahead, the intensity of the storm increased, and the major concern became that of locating a sheltered place in which to pitch camp—a place that would offer some protection from the freezing wind and snow and would have some grass for the animals. But even as they searched for a campsite, the keen-eyed travelers watched flocks of mountain sheep bound across the high cliffs so quickly that they were out of range before any man could raise his rifle and take aim. Out on the rough water of the lake there were ducks that rode the heavy swells like large bobbing corks, and near the shore where there was deep water that hadn't become muddy, the men saw large fish the size of Columbia River salmon. But there wasn't time to go fishing or to try to stalk the wily mountain sheep. The storm was increasing in fury hour by hour, and it was a relief to all the men when after twelve miles they found a ravine that offered protection from the worst of the gale and also had bunch grass for the horses and mules. By the time camp was established, the snowfall was much heavier, and the whole country wore the clothes of winter.

Though it stormed during much of the night, at daybreak the sky was clear, and the fresh snow began to melt under the warmth of the sun. Time was taken to retrieve the howitzer, and the day's travel was limited to nine miles. But all during their trek to the south, one unusual formation captured the attention of the expedition. This was a large rock away from the shore, a rock that cut through the water like a massive wedge. It was opposite this unusual rock that the second lake camp was set up at sundown.

It rose, according to our estimate, 600 feet above the water; and from the point we viewed it, presented a pretty exact outline of the great pyramid of Cheops. . . . This striking feature suggested a name for the lake; and I called it Pyramid Lake. . . .[15]

Then while the last of the cattle they had driven from The Dalles were slaughtered and butchered for camp meat, John Charles estimated that Pyramid Lake was 4,890 feet above sea level, or 700 feet higher than the Great Salt Lake. He made this estimate by using the boiling point of water, but it was too high—940 feet above any high-water marks the lake had reached for thousands of years. His estimate of the height of the pyramid formation was also much too high; for when he saw it, the protruding portion of the rock could not have been much more than 300 feet above the surface of the water.

The following day the expedition made its first contact with some Indians who approached their camp. They were shy, though, and only one man was willing to come near them. He wore a rabbitskin robe and appeared to be very poor. While he seemed to speak a dialect of the Shoshonean language, it was one that neither Carson nor Fitzpatrick had ever heard. But as they could make out a few key words, they were able to learn that the man and his companions lived in nearby caves. He also indicated there was a river at the south end of the lake, but it wasn't clear to the mountain men whether the lake was the source of the river or the river was the main water supply for the lake. But from where they were camped, they could make out some kind of stream and groves of cottonwoods in the distance. The Indian went with them as they continued their march, and as they moved along, they passed by several caves in the rocky formation and noticed baskets filled with seeds, but the dwellers were out of sight.

In the early afternoon they neared the river that flowed into the lake. They met several different Indians on the trail, who did not appear to have any connection with the people of the caves. These people spoke a dialect of the Shoshonean language that was easily understood by Broken Hand and

Kit, and the guides learned that their chief was encamped just above the mouth of the river. They continued on, and when they reached the cotton-woods, they saw that the stream flowing into the lake was a large river that didn't fit any of the descriptions of Mary's River, the Sacramento River, or the Buenaventura of legend.

As they drew closer to the Indian village of basket-shaped dwellings con-structed of willow frameworks and bundles of grass tied together, the chief came out to meet them and began to speak in a loud voice. At the same time, the exploration party noticed armed Indians coming out of the thickets. Not wanting to run the risk of being taken by surprise, the expedition selected a place for their camp which offered a position of strength. It was on the grassy bottom, nearly surrounded by the curve of the river, had plenty of firewood, and was a few hundred yards down the slope from the village.

There was no need for such precaution as they soon discovered. These Pyr-amid Lake Paiutes, who called themselves Kuyuidokado or Fish Eaters, were friendly people who went out of their way to make the white strangers wel-come in their land. They shared their bountiful supply of large, cutthroat trout that looked more like Columbia River salmon than lake trout. And as the campfires were started for supper, the hungry men found that they were to be treated to a feast.

Salmon-trout, as Frémont called them, were brought in great quantities, and an orgy of eating soon followed. As the sun set, as the dark and star-filled sky made its vastness known, the weary men gathered around the campfires to eat their fill. Trout were boiled, fried, and roasted in the ashes and coals of the campfires. Whenever it appeared that the supply of pink-meated fish was running short, a Paiute would dash to the mouth of the river and spear more of the great fish for the hungry visitors. To Charles Preuss, it was something to jot down in his journal, something to keep in his memory, as he ate so much trout he felt he would gag and become ill.

While the feast went on, Frémont conversed with the Paiutes through the translations of Carson and Fitzpatrick. The major topic of conversation re-volved around the nature of the country that stretched beyond Pyramid Lake, the country that lay between this scene of plenty surrounded by the barren desert and the lush land of California that had to be somewhere to the west or southwest.

Though there was no way to be certain the Paiutes had ever seen any other whites before, John Charles did notice that one man had some brass buttons, and scattered among the other natives were articles that had been made by Europeans. Still, this did not mean the Paiutes had contact with whites. They could have picked up such items in trade with other tribes who lived closer to the settlers of California or Oregon.

Some information the Paiutes gave was not completely understood, while other things they mentioned were quite clear. They tried their best to show the men that the river (which Frémont called the Salmon Trout River—the present-day Truckee) that filled their lake came from another lake (Lake Tahoe) high in the mountains, a lake about four days away to the west and south. This was only part of what the Paiutes offered in the way of information. They also spoke of two other rivers beyond the mountains to the west and said that beside one of these rivers there were white settlers. This, Frémont thought, had to be the Sacramento River. But he wasn't certain the Paiutes meant that, or whether they were talking about what they had learned from other tribes who had crossed the Sierra Nevada in the past. Again, the communication between Frémont's two guides and the Paiutes wasn't as clear as the explorer would have wished; so he had to make do with what was understood and with the drawing of the Truckee River the Paiutes scratched upon the ground.

As the evening grew into night, he realized the way ahead remained quite vague even to Carson and Fitzpatrick. In a final effort to insure the safety of his men, he tried to prevail upon some of the Paiutes to act as guides for a few days. But they wanted no part of it and "only looked at each other and laughed."[16]

The next day was fair and clear, but the temperature in the morning was only two degrees above freezing, and even as the sun rode higher in the sky, the day did not become any warmer. The gear was loaded into the packsaddles, farewells were exchanged with the Paiutes, and the expedition followed the well-used trails along the Truckee River. To the west the men could see the snow-covered peaks of the Sierra Nevada, and along the river bottoms there were groves of large cottonwoods and plenty of meadow grass. But away from the river the land was the color of gray-blue sagebrush, endless hills and flats of sagebrush with isolated groves of squatty piñon pines, and pockets of willows or cottonwoods that marked areas of springs on benches and in mountain draws.

Eighteen miles were covered during the first day's march south of Pyramid Lake, eighteen miles along a trail that followed the river bottom land for a short distance and then moved upward to the sage-covered plateau that overlooked the clear and swift-moving stream. By late afternoon, camp was set up near present Wadsworth, Nevada, where the Truckee River channel curves west toward the Sierra Nevada. At this point the expedition could have followed the river and gradually worked its way to Lake Tahoe, and from there they could have crossed the mountains and followed the downward course of the South Fork of the American River to the Sacramento Valley. But they were not certain what lay in the direction of the snowy peaks, and they elected to leave the course of the Truckee and continue their southward path.

The next two days were easy treks for the men and their animals as they followed more Indian trails across fairly level land. On the first of these two days they reached the Carson River and followed it toward the southwest. They came to other Indian villages, but the people ran from them before they could hand out presents and ask questions about the country. Then on the second day away from the desert lake, as they wondered if the river was a branch of the fabled Buenaventura, they saw columns of smoke rising from fires on various hilltops, fires they assumed were built to signal all the Indians ahead of their approach.

The day of January 18, 1844, became one of decision for Frémont. As they passed by empty Indian lodges, which had been vacated just before they rode into sight, it was obvious that hilltop signal fires had warned of their coming. The people who lived beside the Carson River were not in any hurry to meet the men of the expedition. If these people were like the Paiutes of Pyramid Lake, it was doubtful that they would be warlike unless they were forced into a battle. Still, there was something strange, something that seemed not quite real about finding Indian villages and no Indians.

Camp was pitched in a fine meadow beside the river,[17] and though Frémont had some of the area ahead scouted, his men had not gone far enough to the south to find the Carson Valley. The report of the country ahead was that it was much the same as the region they had been crossing ever since leaving Pyramid Lake. While that presented no problems, the health of the animals was another matter. Many were lame, and most had cut hooves from the long journey over rough ground.

Supplies were checked to see if there were horseshoe nails and enough iron to forge new shoes. But the things which might have been used for this purpose had been left with the carts at Fort Walla Walla. There wasn't a chance to make horseshoes; and without them, every man in camp knew that the animals would soon be crippled.

Faced with this situation, Frémont had three options open. The expedition could winter beside this river or head back down the Salmon Trout River and winter near Pyramid Lake, where there was grass for the animals and plenty of fish and game for the men to eat. The second choice was to try to make it across the desert and the Rocky Mountains, but that wasn't an idea that could even be considered. The third possibility, and the one that had appeal to it, was to find a way across the Sierra Nevada and winter in California, where supplies would be available.

This third choice became Frémont's decision. For there was no way of knowing how long the local tribes would remain friendly once the expedition began to use their food supply for themselves and their animals. Having made his decision to seek a pass across the Sierra Nevada to the Sacramento Valley, he informed his men. "My decision was heard with joy by the people, and diffused new life throughout the camp."[18] California had a much better ring to it than more of the Great Basin, but the flaw in the plan loomed to the west and southwest in the snowy peaks of the Sierra Nevada.

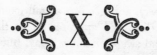

# Rock upon Rock, Snow upon Snow

THE WAY PREUSS SAW IT, they were lost. There was no other way to size up their situation. At last, though, six days since they had left the camp on the Carson River, Frémont called for a day of rest. He even got out the brandy bottle and poured a dram for each man. There was nothing like brandy at a time like this, and Preuss wished there had been more of it. He was feeling a touch of rheumatism in his hips, and his feet were cold and sore. No wonder about his feet, no wonder at all. His shoes were almost worn out, and from what everybody could estimate, they had a long way to go before they reached California.

It was January 26, 1844, and not even the local Indians they had talked into guiding them this far seemed to have much of an idea about their location. But it was hard to tell with these people, who called themselves Washo. They spoke only a few words of the Shoshonean language, and this didn't help Kit or Broken Hand very much because they had never heard the Washo language before.[1] They would have to get along as best they could. At least, the friendly Washo had fine, oily-tasting, soft-shelled pine nuts they were willing to trade for scarlet cloth and a few other trinkets. That much could be said about their good fortune in meeting the Washos, but it didn't solve the crucial questions. They didn't know where they were, and they had no real idea of how far they might have to travel to reach the sunny climate of California.

A day of rest was the minimum they needed as far as Preuss was concerned. There seemed to be no end to the hardships they had to endure, no indication that they had a chance ever to end their long march. After the camp by the cottonwoods and the Carson River, they had crossed a small range of desert hills and entered the Smith Valley,[2] crossed the Walker River,[3] and continued south to the canyon of the East Walker River and slowly worked their way up that to this camp at the lower end of what is now Bridgeport Valley,[4] California.

The last journey to the valley had been rough on everybody. They had slogged their way through deep snow drifts and cut and bruised their feet on granite boulders and outcroppings of sharp obsidian until they had reached this vast meadow that was bordered by massive granite peaks to the south, high desert hills to the east that showed only sage and piñon pines where the snow had been blown away, and a range of tall mountains to the west that reached above the timberline and appeared to be the color of snow even where the steady wind had swept all snow away. But the valley was a place to rest, to catch one's breath, and to sit around campfires of blazing piñon pines and feel all the weariness drift out of tired muscles. The high mountains around this big meadow country could wait. For the moment the sky was clear deep blue. No storm clouds were drifting on the air currents. Supplies were still in good order, and between the cracking and spitting of the burning logs and the inner warmth of the brandy, a day of rest was a tonic for aching, weary bodies.

The talk around the campfires, by men who had lived most of their lives far beyond the last smoke of settlements, was not talk of concern. At the moment things weren't too bad, and there was no need to waste a day of rest with thoughts of what might be ahead of them.

This was an attitude, though, that Preuss couldn't assume. Just the fact that there was food and warmth and they were comfortable for the day simply wasn't enough to keep him from worrying. He was a city man, who loved the pleasures of civilization, but this wasn't his first trek into the wilderness. He had learned there were certain things to be concerned about, and others to ignore. As he looked at the horses and mules, he was acutely aware of their condition. It didn't require a judge of livestock to observe that the animals were lame, sore footed, and not much more than walking skeletons. And the men weren't much better off. Their clothing was as much imagination as reality. Their faces were gaunt and burned by the wind and the glare of the sun against the snow, and Preuss knew they were halfway between starvation and freezing.

2

Preuss was not the only man worried about their situation. While Frémont kept his fears to himself, his concern about the state of his men ran deep. Perhaps he had made a mistake by coming south. No matter that it had been cold at the grove of cottonwoods six long days back; that camp had offered shelter, and there had been plenty of meadow grass beneath the snow which the animals had been able to get by pawing the cover of white away.

And there had been the possibility of simply following the Carson River into the Sierra Nevada. From the top of a ridge near the Carson River camp, Frémont, Fitzpatrick, and Carson had seen the meandering course of the river as it flowed from the west through a large valley of meadow grass.[5] The way had looked clear and easy except for one ominous threat, and it had

been that single factor which had changed the lieutenant's mind. While
there was no sign of rough weather along the course of the river, the same
could not be said about the towering mountains of the Sierra Nevada, which
dropped off in steep cliffs to the valley floor. For the high spine of the mountain range was almost invisible beneath the dark cloud covering of another
blizzard. Maybe the storm would have passed by the time they had reached
the mountains, but there had not been any way that they could be sure. So
the decision was made to turn toward the south, where the sky was clear and
where the going had been fairly easy until they had reached the river canyon
that had brought them to this camp of rest. But now, as they tried to take
their bearings, as they did their best to learn something from the Washos that
would help them find a pass across the Sierra Nevada, it was much too clear
that the choices open to the expedition were limited, difficult, and might easily prove to be fatal.

Caught in a strange country, faced with the choice either of sitting out the
winter in the Great Basin or of trying to cross the Sierra Nevada to a place
where there would be supplies and fresh animals to purchase, Frémont
elected to gamble on a winter crossing of the mountains. Accordingly, while
the men rested, John Charles and Kit rode out of the camp and headed west
across Bridgeport Valley toward what appeared to be a natural opening between the mountains.

As they rode across the big meadows, they broke ice in shallow ponds and
forded deep creeks that flowed from the granite peaks to the south. While
the day was clear, there was very little warmth. They were above six thousand feet, and the heavy snowpack on the surrounding mountains acted as a
buffer against the sun's rays. Their hands and feet were almost numb from
the cold, and they kept moving them to keep the blood circulating faster in
order to bring body warmth to the skin's surface.

When they reached the natural opening that they had seen to the west,
they followed the course of Swauger Creek[6] which flowed down from the
mountains to the northwest and cut through a smaller valley but still one
that a mountain man would call a hole. Following the creek, they worked
their way along a gradual uphill slope, and at the end of the meadow they
picked a campsite away from the deep snow, one which offered some exposed
grass for the animals. Then they rode back to Bridgeport Valley and reported
what they had seen.

The next day broke clear again, and Carson was put in charge of moving
the expedition to the new camp. While he did this, Frémont and Fitzpatrick
rode ahead to scout the country. They arrived at the point where Swauger
Creek turns almost due north into the mountains. West of this they noticed a
pass through an opening between two high rock formations. At this point
they were nearing what is now known as Devil's Gate.

They passed through Devil's Gate, and on the other side headed downhill.
Not far from the pass they saw the steam of Fales Hot Springs.[7] The going

appeared to be easier along the base of the lower mountains to the south of the hot springs, and they took this path. Continuing on toward the west, the steaming hot springs were to their left as they rode into the narrow canyon where the overflow water from the springs becomes Hot Creek and within a few miles joins the Little Walker River. But in this small canyon the horses had a very difficult time trying to plunge through the deep snow drifts. In an attempt to find an easier route, Frémont and Fitzpatrick picketed their horses and climbed into the mountain country to the northwest of Fales Hot Springs. Somewhere beyond Burcham Flat,[8] they got their first view of the West Walker River. And while the course of the river didn't appear to be an easy one to follow, it was a possible route out of this region of rough ground and deep snow drifts. The summit would allow passage across the mountains, and there seemed to be a way to get down to the river and head northwest.[9]

The snow was between four and five feet deep at the summit, but it was mainly limited to the northern side. While the men looked over the area that they would take the main party through, Frémont noticed several large snow-shoe rabbits with winter pelts of white fur. Then the two men began the long hike back down the hill to where they had left their horses, and it was past nightfall and freezing cold when they reached the campfires near Devil's Gate.

The day of January 28 was long and hard as the expedition climbed to the summit and followed the contours of the land as much as they could. But as they dropped toward the canyon of the West Walker River, the snow drifts were exceedingly deep, and the rough and rocky nature of the canyon made it much too hard to follow. Somewhere during the twelve miles they covered that day, they appear to have crossed to the west side of the river and climbed onto the high ridge that separates the West Walker River from the upper reaches of Mill Creek.[10]

Once more, as they moved through rough country where there wasn't a trail, the howitzer became a burden the men must have wished they had never seen. They struggled to pull it to the crest of the ridge west of the river and above Mill Creek. The task became so difficult they had to leave the cannon behind until the next day. Then to cap the difficulty of the climb, the last chronometer finally ceased to run, and Frémont was no longer able to calculate their longitude.

During that long day, as they worked their way through the snow drifts and broken country and made wide circuits to even higher ground in order to avoid the deep snow, they were startled by the sudden appearance of Washo Indians, who circled around them on snowshoes. As Frémont put it, they were "skimming along like birds."[11] Alexis Godey, who was ahead of the main party, "sat down to tie his moccasins, when he heard a low whistle near, and, looking up, saw two Indians half hiding behind a rock about forty yards distant; they would not allow him to approach, but, breaking into a laugh, skimmed off over the snow, seeming to have no idea of the power of fire arms, and thinking themselves perfectly safe when beyond arm's length."[12]

As the Washos vanished with a whistle and a laugh, the men of the expedition struggled along. Not a man among them had a clear idea of where they were.

In the morning, their luck seemed to take a turn. From their camp they looked to the northwest and saw yellow spots of dry grass far in the distance in present Antelope Valley. The prospect of getting to an area where there wasn't much snow and where the terrain was fairly level gave hope to everybody, even to the men who went back to retrieve the howitzer.

Leaving Preuss in charge of the camp, Frémont, Fitzpatrick, and a few others scouted ahead. They followed a trail that brought them to Mill Creek, and as they reached this tributary of the West Walker River, they came upon eight or ten Washos who had been watching their progress.

At first, the Washos would not let them come near; but as the men showed they were friendly and not hostile, the Washos came toward them and presented a gift of pine nuts. In turn, Frémont gave them a few presents, and Fitzpatrick was able to learn that their village was down at the mouth of the creek, where there was a meadow. This contact with the Mill Creek Washos was the first opportunity Frémont had to learn something about the country ahead. The Washos informed the men they would go ahead to their village and tell their people who they were and that everything was all right.

Working their way very slowly down the rough course of Mill Creek Canyon, the scouting party reached the confluence of the creek and the West Walker River at the head of Antelope Valley. Here they established camp and waited for the remainder of the men to move down the mountain and the canyon with the howitzer. Several of the Mill Creek Washos appeared, and though they were not certain about these intruders in their land, they were finally convinced it would be all right to come into their camp for a council.

At first the greatest difficulty Frémont and his men had was to grasp the language. But between signs and the repetition of certain key words in conjunction with signs, they began to build a limited vocabulary of the Washo language. In the same manner, the Washos began to understand the sounds of these strangers.

We explained to the Indians that we were endeavoring to find a passage across the mountains into the country of the whites, whom we were going to see; and told them that we wished them to bring us a guide, to whom we would give presents of scarlet cloth, and other articles, which were shown to them. They looked at the reward we offered, and conferred with each other, but pointed to the snow on the mountain, and drew their hands across their necks, and raised them above their heads, to show the depth; and signified that it was impossible for us to get through.[13]

It was possible to cross the mountains, the Washos explained, but it had to be done before the snow came. To stress their point, they told the whites that other men with white skin had crossed the high mountains south of the Washo village two years before. But these men had crossed while the sun and not the snow covered the land. Frémont thought this party had been either the one under the leadership of Joseph B. Chiles in 1843 or that of Joseph R. Walker in the same year, but the group the Washos saw was probably the Bartleson party, which crossed in the area of the Sonora Pass, not too far south of the Washos, in October 1841.

The talk continued in Frémont's camp even after sundown. Preuss and the rest of the expedition did not get through Mill Creek Canyon that day, but John Charles was certain the rough passage had held them up as they tried to pull the heavy howitzer along. He had told Preuss to leave the cannon behind if it turned out it wasn't possible to get it down to the meadowland. And as Frémont and the scouting party talked to the Washos about the way ahead, Preuss and the others were already camped in the upper meadow after having given up the struggle to get the howitzer through the canyon.[14]

Though the Washos thought it foolhardy to attempt to cross the high mountains in the winter, they had done their best to convince the white strangers. Now all they could do was offer them some pine nuts to add to their supplies, and see if one of their young men would volunteer to act as a guide for them. For both gifts Frémont was thankful. The pine nuts—which he found tasty and nutritious—would add to the scanty rations that remained. But to have a young Washo show them the way was more than he had hoped for after his first requests had been turned down.

On the cold morning of January 30—with all the party together again—the expedition was joined by the promised young man. It wasn't until late in the day that they bid farewell to the Mill Creek Washos and followed the course of the West Walker River into Antelope Valley. Some of the other Washos traveled with them during this first day's march into the broad valley, a march which covered about ten miles and must have taken them past the present Mono County, California, settlements of Walker and Coleville and to the swampy area at the lower end of the valley where the river turns northeast—an area now covered by the waters of man-made Topaz Lake.

There was no snow where they camped for the night, but the wet grass and the shallows of the river were covered with ice. The men cut piles of grass to place under their blankets, and campfires were made of the large, dry willows which lined the river.

On the last day of January, the expedition moved out of the boggy meadowland where the West Walker River turned to the northeast. The upward slope of a sagebrush plateau—where the nearby hills were covered with piñon pines—was easy going compared to what they had been through. Though the plateau was a gradual grade, there was a broad Indian trail, and the men reached the pass after a journey of twelve to fourteen miles.

Now it began to snow heavily, and the weather was extremely cold. The Washos who had come along for the adventure and for whatever gifts these strangers might give turned back. But the young guide continued to lead the way. The mountains on both sides and ahead of the expedition were half hidden by the storm, and the whole prospect before them was one of dreariness. Then, as nightfall approached, even the young Washo was dubious about continuing this march. But because he was placed between two men with rifles, he continued to guide the way until they reached a downhill ravine. This, he explained, would take the white men to the river below.

Frémont decided not to force the Washo to go any farther, for the young man was almost without clothes, and he shivered as the icy wind and the stinging snow hit his body. He was happy to give up this trek, and explained that he knew of a hut nearby where he could stay for the night. Then, without unrolling the blue and scarlet cloth he had been given for his services, he vanished into the snowstorm.

Following the directions of the young Washo, the expedition saw in the distance "a great continuous range, along which stretched the valley of the river; the lower parts steep, and dark with pines, while above it was hidden in clouds of snow."[15] This, Frémont and his men believed, was the Sierra Nevada. Somewhere beyond that, if they could get over it in such weather, the sun was shining on the great Sacramento Valley.

But the forced march of almost twenty-six miles in such cold weather had taken its toll. One man had a frostbitten foot, and three of the mules had given out. Then, as they established camp on the East Carson River, as they got fires started to fight off the cold and to prepare their meal, their camp was visited by more Washos. But like the young man who had been their guide, they were very nearly naked, and Frémont was astounded that they could stand such cold weather without heavy clothing.

An older Washo told the explorer that it was six sleeps to where the white men lived on the other side of the mountains. He did not think it wise to try to cross the peaks in such weather. His advice was to follow the river down to lower ground, down to a lake, and wait out the winter there. Frémont explained they would use the strength of their horses to break trail through the snow. All they needed was a guide. Was there one of them who would be willing to act as a guide to show them the way?

Again it was the old man who spoke. As he pointed to the cloud-covered Sierra Nevada, "Tah-ve, tah-ve," he said. Snow, snow, there was too much snow to cross the high mountains.

Time was taken by the Washos to discuss this matter among themselves. When they finished, the old man pulled a bunch of grass from beneath the snow. Then he made it clear that, if they could break through the snow with their horses, in a journey of three days they would reach country where the grass would not be covered by snow.

All this was good news, but a guide was vital. Again, through question after question, the need of these white men became clear to the Washos; and the old man told them that there was a young man among them who had seen the whites. He then presented him and swore "first by the sky, and then by the ground, that what he said was true."[16]

The young man was called Mélo—friend—and he would show them the way to where the whites lived on the other side of the mountains. But he was thinly clad, and he needed skins to make new moccasins. These were provided, along with leggings, a large green blanket, and other pieces of blue and scarlet colored clothes. Frémont wanted him to be warm in their assault on the mountains, and Mélo was very pleased with his colorful outfit.

They had a guide, and the main range of the Sierra Nevada was just ahead, looming above them with its high peaks shrouded in the fury of a wild storm. They would begin their upward climb the next day, John Charles told his men. Still, he was not as optimistic as he tried to appear. It had been snowing most of the day, and now as they sat around their campfires and made do with dried peas, some flour, pine nuts, and hot coffee with a slight touch of sugar—sugar Frémont was trying to reserve for the days when they would need all the energy they could get from their food— the snow began to swirl in great clouds that quickly covered the ground with an increasing depth of icy whiteness.

On February 1, the day that was to be their first assault against the mountains, the snow continued to fall and build up drifts in the draws and a mounting depth on the meadow. There was no starting out in such weather, and the men began to complain about their food. They needed something more substantial, something that would stick to their ribs. The remaining horses and mules had to be saved until they could no longer travel. There was no game in sight, not even a snowshoe rabbit. But there were two camp dogs, and the stray they had picked up way back in the Bear River Valley was fat and in excellent shape. What about a dog feast?

Frémont gave the men permission, and the slaughtered dog had a definite appeal once it was butchered, and the meat spread out on the snow. Then to add to their supply of meat, the Washos came into camp with a few rabbits, and these were purchased to go along with the one fat dog.

During the night the snowstorm stopped, and the morning was clear except for great white thunderheads that floated in the sky above the sawtooth peaks of the Sierra Nevada. They quickly ate breakfast, broke camp, and got under way. Crossing the river on a solid layer of heavy ice, they took a southwesterly course up present Long Valley, Nevada, and probably headed for Diamond Valley, California.[17] The going was hard in the deep snow, and as they worked their way into higher country it became necessary to break a path.

The hard work of breaking through the snow was done by a party of ten mounted men. Each man took his turn forcing his way on foot and on horseback until he and his mount became exhausted. Then the others passed by, while he and his horse took a position in the rear to recover strength as others took their respective turns. In this fashion, the party traveled sixteen miles that day, and made their first mountain camp about a mile to the northeast of present-day Markleeville, California, where Markleeville Creek joins the East Carson River.[18] They were now getting beyond the range of sagebrush and piñon pines, and here they saw tall ponderosa pines and incense cedars.

During the next two days, the expedition headed up Markleeville Creek, traveled along Charity Valley and into Faith Valley, where they camped a few miles beneath the main ridge of the Sierra Nevada. But the going had taken its toll of their energy. Men and horses were almost worn out. They had not been able to make it along the path of the creek, where the snow-pack was much too deep, and they had to take to the hillsides and break a path upward. On February 4 they saw the dark ridge of volcanic rock now called Elephant's Back, and the summit line was "a range of naked peaks, apparently destitute of snow and vegetation; but below, the face of the whole country was covered with timber of extraordinary size."[19]

Yet, the way ahead—short as it was—looked anything but promising. Almost as an understatement, the Washo guide told them that they were now entering the region of deep snow. He indicated that he was not at all sure the way ahead would be possible to get through. At this point, the expedition was strung out from Grovers Springs, down in the hollow, to Faith Valley and the imposing height of the Sierra Nevada summit.

Only the best horses had been able to make it to Faith Valley from the camp at the springs. With nightfall not far away, Frémont sent Broken Hand back to Grovers Springs to watch over that portion of the expedition for the night. There had to be a way to get the rest of the party to this point beneath the high ridge, even if it meant taking days to beat a trail in the deep snow. But the question that must have run through Frémont's mind was put into Charles Preuss's diary entry when he recorded that he wondered if the next day would not be another time when they would be subjected to illusion.

They were joined at their cold and lonely camp by two Washos. One was an old man who had much to say to them for their own good. He told them that they would perish if they tried to cross the mountains here, that if they would come back with him, he knew of a better way across the snow and tall peaks.

"Rock upon rock—rock upon rock—snow upon snow—snow upon snow," said he; "even if you get over the snow, you will not be able to get down from the mountains." He made us a sign of precipices, and showed us how the feet of the horses would slip, and throw them off from the narrow trails which led along their sides. Our Chinook, who comprehended even more readily than ourselves, and believed our situation hopeless, covered his head with his blanket, and began to weep and lament. "I wanted to see the whites," said he; "I came away from my own people to see the whites, and I wouldn't care to die among them; but here"—and he looked around into the cold night and gloomy forest, and, drawing his blanket over his head, began to lament again.[20]

There was all the reason in the world to lament, as the old Washo told them they were bound for a cold and miserable death if they persisted in their fight against the mountains. Freezing wind chilled the silent and serious men as they sat around the campfire, but more than the wind and snow concerned them. The old Washo came out of nowhere. He came like a prophet of old, and he foretold their future if they persisted in this adventure. All the cold was not limited to the outside of the listeners' bodies. As they pondered the old man's words, as they thought of their weary and sore bodies, of the vanishing food supply, of horses and mules ready to collapse in the snow, the Washo's repetitive phrases—rock upon rock, snow upon snow—became a chant of doom, a warning that struck at the heart of each man who sat around the campfire and felt the wind of winter and the nearby chill of death.

### 3

FRÉMONT SLEPT RESTLESSLY during the cold night. Long before daylight, he awoke and saw the young Washo crouched beside the fire. The man was so chilled he couldn't stop shivering even though he crowded close to the burning logs. John Charles got up, took one of his own blankets, and placed it around the young man's shoulders. Then he went back to bed, and again fell into a fitful sleep. It seemed as though he had slept only a matter of minutes before awakening once more, and he looked toward the campfire. But the young man was not in sight. This was the first sign of trouble.

At daybreak, the other Washos were gone, and all the men noticed this right away. Now the upward path would have to be found by their own scouts. The Washos had not wished to court a frozen death, and they were gone. Like something that had never been, they had left no tracks. It was as though the young guide and the old man with his dire warnings had been apparitions, ghosts of the mountains that had come in the night to chant of coldness and death.

Action was the solution, the only thing which might save them in this crisis. They had to continue their upward climb. To halt could be fatal, for the men were much too tired to turn back, too filled with doubt to wait for a better time.

Frémont sent part of the group to the lower camp to help bring the animals forward. All the other men were put to work making snowshoes and sleds. It was obvious that from this point on, the horses and mules would not be able to pack anything until they were out of the region of deep snow. The men would have to act as draft animals and break trail.

On February 6 Frémont, Carson, Fitzpatrick, and some of the others strapped on snowshoes and scouted the country ahead. Climbing upward, breaking trail, and moving on, they managed to reach the crest of a high ridge just south of where the young Washo had indicated that the pass was located. Ten miles, each one a hard journey by itself, were covered; but from the vantage point they had reached, they had a distant view of a large valley to the west—a valley without any snow. Beyond this there appeared to be a low line of coastal mountains, and Kit recognized the scene. They were looking at the Sacramento Valley, and the highest peak in the distant mountain range beyond it was Mount Diablo. All this Kit had seen when he had been in California in 1829–31 with a band of trappers under the leadership of Ewing Young.[21]

Looking at the distant view, Kit told Frémont the mountain was the one he had seen fifteen years before.

All the men were cheered by what they saw in the distance, but though the great valley appeared to be no more than a few days travel from where they stood, Frémont saw that they had many miles to go.

Having seen their destination, the men turned and headed back to camp. But as the sun began to set, the temperature dropped below zero. In this intense cold, one of the men felt his feet beginning to freeze. When he spoke about it, Broken Hand quickly built a fire in the trunk of a dry cedar; and he remained with the man to dry his clothes and to rub his feet with snow. By acting so quickly, he saved the man's feet. By nightfall, the scouting party reached the camp after a hard journey in which they had covered twenty miles on snowshoes—an experience that only two of the men had ever had before.

News of having seen the Sacramento Valley brought new life to the expedition. The men went to work with renewed vigor. They had a chance to survive if only they could get over the pass with their gear and animals. To clear a trail for the animals that were at the lower camp, the men fashioned shovels and mauls. Then they went to work shoveling snow and beating the trail so that it would be hard enough to hold the weight of the horses and mules. Under the best of conditions, what they did would have been hard work, but the men found the work almost unbearable. The lack of enough food, no salt for their diet, and the frigid weather sapped them of energy. At the end of each day it was all they could do to drag themselves back to their camp. But in two days they did clear a good path, and planned to move the animals from the lower camp on the next day. They were tired of this hard labor and tired of bringing supplies to the forward camp by loading sleighs and acting as their own draft animals.

But as the men slept on the night of February 8, as they tried to get some rest for the next day when they would return to the lower camp and move horses and mules and all the rest of the remaining gear to this camp, the wind blew at gale force as it brought in another snowstorm. By daybreak all the work on the trail was covered, and the snow continued to fall.

In an attempt to get some protection from the violent storm, the men moved forward and set up another base camp on the western side of Faith Valley just at the foot of the ridge called Elephant Back.[22] Two large trees were set on fire, and as they burned, the snow around them melted and created two deep holes which offered protection from the icy wind; and it was in these holes that they set up camp. Even under such miserable conditions, Frémont never lost his curiosity about the nature of the country. He took note of the large trees, and identified incense cedar, white pine (sugar pine), mountain hemlock, white spruce (white fir), and red pine (ponderosa or yellow pine). Then in the afternoon, he and a few men explored the way ahead. They found that the glare of light against the snow was so intense that they had a difficult time in seeing anything, and to avoid snow blindness, they wore black silk handkerchiefs over their eyes.

After two more days had passed, an attempt was made on February 11 to move the horses and mules along the trail to the forward camp. In a short time, as Preuss put it, they were faced with a damned unpleasant prospect. The first horse onto the trail sank into the snow; then others began to sink; and before anyone could stop them, some of the terrified animals left the trail and sank clear up to their ears in the drifts.

Word of the trouble was passed up the trail from one of the men with Fitzpatrick, and it became clear to Frémont and the others that they would have to build a better path.

Two more days of extremely hard labor passed, and the work nearly exhausted the men. They cleared a path with their makeshift shovels, pounded the snow with their mauls, and then placed a thick layer of pine boughs over the trail and beat this with their mauls in an effort to bind their work as much as they could. From sunup to sundown—if the sun was at all visible—the hard work went on. It continued even as the wind whirled across the high spine of the Sierra Nevada to drop more snow and to drive against the backs and faces of the men with a frigidness that penetrated their clothing and made their faces burn and sting.

By February 13 the exhausted men had to have more meat for the camp pots. As they waited for the sleds to be pulled from the lower camp with the loads of horse or mule meat, daylight began to end without the appearance of the meat train. Godey asked Frémont if they could eat the other camp dog, the one John Charles called Tlamath. Permission was granted, and Alexis prepared the dog in the same way Frémont had seen Indians go about the chore. Once he had killed it, he singed off the hair, scalded the animal in boiling water, washed the skin with snow and soap, and laid the butchered pieces of dog meat on the snow. Then, as luck would have it, the men from the lower camp arrived with a sled of mule meat. The butchered mule was none other than Preuss's favorite mount, the one he called Jack.

While Preuss refused to eat any of his faithful Jack, he, like the others, did not hesitate to eat the pet dog. And that night they had "an extraordinary dinner—pea soup, mule, and dog."[23]

On St. Valentine's Day Frémont and Preuss climbed the high peak just to the north of their camp, now called Red Lake Peak. From there they had a view of a magnificent mountain lake to the north, which Frémont estimated to be about fifteen miles in length and which appeared to be entirely surrounded by mountains. This was Lake Tahoe—though they did not realize it at the time, it was the lake the Paiutes at Pyramid Lake had described to them—and the two explorers were the first white men ever to see it.[24] When they returned to camp, Preuss found that what normally was a short hike for him had been much harder than he thought it would be, and he realized that the poor diet and the cold weather were taking their toll of his strength. While Frémont was able to leave their snowhole camp to help four men work on the trail, Preuss remained in what he called the kitchen hole and rested on his buffalo hide beside the fire. With instructions from Godey to guide him, Preuss tended the two pots and the teakettle to keep things from burning. The teakettle was filled with snow water, and periodically he would add water from this to the pot with pieces of his mule Jack floating about and to the other pot, where one half of the dog continued to stew. When he wasn't taking care of his kitchen duties, he read a copy of Byron's *Don Juan* that he carried with him.

Two days after he had made the climb of the peak with Preuss, the indomitable Frémont, who never seemed to tire, set out with young Jacob Dodson on a reconnoitering expedition to see what might be the best path over the mountains. They headed up the canyon beside the foot of Red Lake Peak and followed the downward narrow ridges where the snow was melting. In the places where trees had not shaded the snow, there were open patches of ground where grass was available, and this was something the animals would need when they reached this height.

As the afternoon sun began to drop, the two men worked their way down the western slope of the mountains. That night they camped at the headwaters of a creek that flowed west toward the Pacific. The night was extremely clear, and as they sat beside their fire, they heard a flock of geese passing overhead. There were also cries of other wild animals that had been attracted by the fire. But any sound other than the constant wind gave both men hope. If other animals were around, then there was a chance for their own survival.

In the morning John Charles and Jacob were up early, and they pushed ahead to explore the creek and its path. While trying to avoid snowdrifts in the shady region of the canyon, they attempted to cross on the ice. But they broke through and fell into the frigid water. Time was taken to build a fire, and they removed and dried their clothes. When everything was dry enough to wear, they continued to follow the creek for a few more miles, until

Frémont was satisfied he had struck a stream that would lead them to Sutter's establishment in the Sacramento Valley.

Turning back, the two men climbed to the top of the ridge again, and by using all their strength and not letting up, they reached the base camp at dark. Their return was all the better to Frémont when he was told that the remaining fifty-seven animals had reached the area and were grazing on the grassy hill he and Jacob had seen the day before. Along with this good news, the men also had salt for their meat. Taplin and some of the others had found a Washo hut, and the people inside had been willing to trade a large piece of salt for some of the goods the men had with them.

During the next two days the sun was much warmer; and as the snow continued to melt, the men worked at building a trail to the pass and at bringing all the remaining baggage up from the lower camp. Still suffering from exhaustion, Preuss continued to rest in the snow hole. He ate his fill of the lean, stringy horse meat now that salt was available, noted that his appetite was returning, and began to think of what a joy it would be if he were at a decent market with an empty shopping basket to fill.

On February 20, 1844, the expedition moved out of the snow holes, headed up the canyon, and slowly climbed toward the summit. Before day's end, they reached the crest of the ridge somewhere to the south of present Kit Carson Pass. Here, they pitched camp atop the Sierra Nevada, on a pass that Frémont thought deserved the name of "Snowy Mountain." They had come one thousand miles since leaving The Dalles, and though the way ahead did not appear easy, it appeared possible. Defeat no longer was the specter. Victory over the wilderness seemed well within reach.

4

KIT CARSON was up early in the morning. He got the fire started and roused Frémont. Soon, the other men were standing or hunkered around the campfire. A hurried breakfast of mule meat and weak coffee was the start of their first day's trek on the western side of the Sierra Nevada.

Sunrise had a beauty Frémont thought was most unusual.

> Immediately above the eastern mountains was repeated a cloud-formed mass of purple ranges, bordered with bright yellow gold; the peaks shot up into a narrow line of crimson cloud, above which the air was filled with a greenish orange; and over all was the singular beauty of the blue sky.[25]

Beauty didn't make for easy traveling, and the men found this out in a hurry as they worked their way along the high ridge between Silver Fork and the headwaters of the Upper Truckee River.[26] The day's journey covered only six miles before the expedition became so tired that they made camp on the ridge. It had been hard going all day. They had eased their way across slippery, hard-crusted snow fields, slogged over ground muddy from melting snow, and found it difficult to keep from slipping on the wide-open stretches of white granite where water from melting snowpacks ran across the rock face and dropped toward the Silver Fork. Great care had to be taken to locate the right path. A wrong turn could take them into even rougher country or bring them to draws where snow drifts were ten to fifteen feet deep.

By day's end the weather had gone through a cycle of warmth that was like the middle of April, then changed from this into a roll of thunder and a brief flurry of light snow. As they made camp, the sky was so clear they could see beyond the Sacramento Valley all the way to the last glance of the sun off a large body of water that could be nothing other than San Francisco Bay. As they built their campfires, they could see the orange glow of other fires in the distance. Though they thought these were fires in the Sacramento Valley or on some nearby ridge, they learned that they were fires among the tules beside San Francisco Bay.

Every day and a half another horse or mule was shot to supply the camp with meat, and Preuss dreaded the killing of these faithful animals that had brought them so far. Yet there was no other choice. In the draws and canyons there were remaining snow drifts the men had to cross. On the ridges there were great stands of timber, mountain misery, and buck brush to fight their way through. In all this up-and-down land, this region of granite, slate, and lava, this wild country where creeks flowed with a mad rush over water-polished boulders slick and smooth as ivory, the men needed all their remaining strength to work their way along.

Frémont and Preuss saw the natural beauty of the Sierra Nevada. Both compared the deep-blue sky and sunny climate to that of Smyrna and Palermo; and the dour Preuss even went so far as to say that the sky was as blue as forget-me-nots.

Sticking as much as they could to the high ridge, they moved to Strawberry Creek. Slowly they worked their way down, and on February 23 they reached an area that was so slippery they had to crawl across snow beds. It became necessary to use axes and mauls to beat a path through the snow for the animals.

Going ahead of the party, Frémont and Carson scouted the way down off the end of the ridge. In the afternoon they reached the South Fork of the American River. It was running fast between the granite boulders with the high water of snow that had melted during the day. Kit found a spot where the water shot between a narrow passage among slick rocks. With a short run and a leap he cleared the stream and landed on the soft soil and pine needles on the other side.

Following Carson's example, John Charles made the same leap. But he didn't reach the dark soil of the bank. Instead, he landed on one of the slick granites. The smooth soles of his moccasins glanced off the icy rocks. His feet

went out from under him, and before he had realized what had happened he
was in the swift current of the river.

> It was some few seconds before I could recover myself in the current, and
> Carson, thinking me hurt, jumped in after me, and we both had an icy bath.
> We tried to search a while for my gun, which had been lost in the fall, but
> the cold drove us out; and making a large fire on the bank, after we had par-
> tially dried ourselves we went back to meet the camp. We afterwards found
> that the gun had been slung under the ice which lined the banks of the
> creek.[27]

By late afternoon the rest of the expedition had reached today's Strawberry
Valley. But the trip had been very difficult, and in order to get through some
of the deep drifts, they had to fall back on their old method of using alternate horses and men to break the trail. Frémont was concerned that many of
his men looked as though they were on the verge of collapse. Even though
he and Preuss had endured the same daily privations and physical strain,
they were up at three the next morning to make astronomical readings to determine their latitude and longitude, and observed that the wind was blowing from the northeast and that the temperature was two degrees below freezing.

Leaving Strawberry Valley at daybreak, the men pushed themselves very
hard and managed to work their way down the south face of the mountain.
As they dropped in elevation, they left the region of deep snows and entered
a country where the only remaining snow patches were in shady areas where
the sun hardly penetrated the tall pines and the surrounding overhanging
banks of red clay soil. In the few meadows they passed, they saw the first
green grass of the coming spring; and as they continued into the canyon of
the South Fork of the American River, they saw great oak trees intermingled
among the pines.

During this day's march, Preuss noticed that some of the mules were so
hungry they had started to eat the tail of Fitzpatrick's horse, while others
were taking bites out of saddles, bridles, and anything else that might help to
give them some nourishment. John Charles also saw the condition of the
starving animals, and when they reached a creek that had an abundance of
rushes with tender, fresh shoots, he ordered a halt for the day. Then he
talked over the situation with Broken Hand, and it was agreed that Fitz and
some of the men would follow at their own pace with the weakest animals.
They could catch up to the rest of the party as the animals had a chance to
feed and regain some strength. As they did, John Charles would take Preuss,
Talbot, Carson, Derosier, Town, Proue, and Dodson and strike ahead with
the best of the horses in an attempt to push on to Sutter's Fort and then return with supplies and fresh mounts.

On the morning of February 25, the party of eight waved farewell and
started off with the hope of getting to the Sacramento Valley in no time at

all. For as they rode through this lower country, they struck an Indian trail, and the going appeared to be easy. This land had a beauty Frémont had never seen before. Oaks grew to heights of forty and fifty feet and spread out in great umbrellas of green leaves with masses of mistletoe intertwined among some of the branches. Birds filled these magnificent trees, and their various songs were a delight to hear. While the red clay soil in this foothill country was tough to cross when it was muddy, it had an unusual contrasting beauty to the thick green patches of mountain misery, the tall yellow pines, the great oaks, and the crimson—almost chocolate-colored—bark of the twisted and knarled manzanita shrub that grew to the height of small trees.

Neither Frémont nor any man with him knew the way out of this up-and-down country of steep canyons, heavy runoff water in creeks and the river, and mile after mile of thick brush and heavily timbered mountainsides that began to close in as they moved into the narrow part of the canyon.

The second day after leaving Broken Hand, the rain began to fall. At first there was just the beginning sprinkle; but as the dark clouds blew in from the Pacific, lightning streaked the charcoal sky in jagged lights and the deep roll of thunder echoed throughout the canyon. What had been a light rain became a downpour that continued all afternoon. The red clay soil became slick and sticky, and the horses had great difficulty keeping their footing. While the men became sopping wet, their clothes soaked and uncomfortable, the canyon became so narrow and steep that it was impossible to continue their way beside the rushing waters of the river. They slowly climbed upward until they reached the timbered ridge. Even this proved to be tough going, and at nightfall they dropped off the point of a spur into a ravine where there was some grass for their mounts. Here they made camp and suffered through a wet, miserable night.

In the morning they forded the river, which was sixty feet wide and rolling fast as it made white water where it struck boulders. They managed to get over the opposite hill. One mile was all they had traveled, but they were tired and hungry.

Camp had to be made on a slope, and the worn-out men needed something to give them strength to continue. A mule was shot for the mess, and Kit Carson had a request. The other messes always got to use the head, got to boil it in the kettle. Would it be all right with the captain if they had boiled mule's head?

Frémont gave his permission. Later he commented that if a mule's head was boiled for several hours, it made a passable soup. Preuss thought that if a mule's head was allowed to cook all night long, it became a delicacy.

But not even a mule's head was enough for Charles Town. Tired out from fighting the snow and now the sticky red clay mud, suffering from lightheadedness and from too little food and too much exposure to freezing or wet weather, Town disappeared the next day as the men worked their way to the heights above the steep cliffs that dropped off to the river canyon. He had been with them one moment, and before anyone even realized he had dropped back, Town was no longer in sight. While the party continued its slow trek along the timbered ridge, Jacob was sent after Town. When he found him and managed to bring him in, it was obvious that Town was in bad shape and no longer knew where he was going or what he was doing.

By nightfall the men dropped into a ravine where Kit had found some green grass. They stopped here after one of the hardest days they had experienced. The day had taken its toll. Charles Town was out of his head; three horses had given out—including Proveau, Frémont's favorite mount—and one of these horses had been carrying the cooking utensils.

On the last day of February the men remained in the ravine camp for a much-needed rest. A few were sent back after the missing horses, and Derosier volunteered to find Frémont's horse. As the day passed and the campfires were started for the night, the only man who had not returned was Derosier. All night long Frémont slept in snatches, but each time he awoke and looked about, the missing man was not to be seen.

At daybreak the party got ready to move on their way. There wasn't enough grass in the ravine camp to keep their horses for another day, and there was no sign of Derosier. Yet, for the safety of the whole party, John Charles gave the order to pull out. If the missing man wasn't dead, he was enough of a wilderness man to cut sign on their tracks and catch up to them. And if he wasn't lost in the maze of mountains, he might run into Fitzpatrick and the slower section of the expedition.

March came in like a lamb, and that was the only good thing that could be said about the day. The weather was warmer, much warmer than it had been. There was no rain, and the land of snow and rocks was far behind them. Green grass was becoming more abundant. Butterflies and wild flowers gave the country a colorful garment even if the mosquitoes were hungry. But there were serious problems that bothered John Charles.

During the day, Charles Town went for a swim. The demented man simply jumped into the river as though he thought summer had arrived. His companions rushed to his rescue and pulled him out of the icy torrent before he drowned. Then Preuss decided to walk on ahead. While this was not unusual for him, by evening he had not returned, and it was too late to search for him. When Frémont heard a man approaching their camp and thought perhaps it was Preuss, he was in for yet another shock. The lost Derosier appeared. He simply walked into the camp, sat beside the fire, and began to tell the men where he had been.

He imagined he had been gone for several days, and thought we were still at the camp where he had left us; and we were pained to see that his mind was deranged. It appeared that he had been lost in the mountain, and hunger and fatigue joined to weakness of body, and fear of perishing in the mountains, had crazed him.[28]

Things were becoming critical, and Frémont realized that time was running out for them. Two men out of their minds. Charles Preuss lost. Horses
and mules ready to drop on the trail. Gaunt-faced men who were no longer
able to do much more than make a few miles each day before they had to
rest, to sit in silence around the campfire and slowly chew the tough and
stringy horse or mule meat. This was the situation that faced Frémont. Yet,
there was no choice other than to keep moving and hope that the next ridge,
the next slope would be topped and show them the great grassland of the
Sacramento Valley.

5

PREUSS KNEW HE WAS LOST. There was no point in trying to backtrack and
join his companions. If he kept walking, if he didn't panic, sooner or later he
would reach the Sacramento Valley. Then all he had to do was continue to
follow this same river. From what he had been told, from what Carson had
told all of them, the river passed near Sutter's Fort. While that notion convinced Preuss he would soon move beyond the rolling foothills and the many
varieties of oak trees, it didn't put any food into his stomach, and it had been
two days since he had eaten anything substantial.

Using his pocketknife, he dug up a few wild onions. They were sweet tast-
ing and not at all bad, but he needed more than that to ease the hunger
pangs. Then he tried something he never thought he'd be reduced to eating.
He remembered that he had seen the poor Indians near the Great Salt Lake
eat ants. Finding an anthill, he scooped up some ants and ate them. Food was
food in lean times. But as hungry as he was, what he missed most of all was a
good smoke. He had run out of tobacco for his pipe, and that was about the
worst thing so far.

By Monday, March 4, Preuss was beginning to worry more than he ever
had before. He had thought the others would have caught up to him by now,
but they were not to be seen.

The idea that his companions might have taken another direction entered
his mind, but he didn't have the strength to head back and see if he could
find their tracks. Lack of food was beginning to tell on him. It was all he
could do to continue walking. He had to stop and take frequent rests, and
this was something new to him as he prided himself on being a good hiker.
Yet, weary as he was, he took time to write in his journal. The entries were
directed to his wife as though he considered that he might not survive but, if
he didn't, some member of the expedition would find his body and see to it
that his journal was delivered to his wife and family.

Cloudy weather carried the threat of another storm, and he wrote that he
expected to spend another wet night in the open. Then he mentioned that
his meal for this Monday consisted of raw frog legs. He had come upon a
puddle and found some small frogs. He caught as many as he could, pulled

off their legs and ate them. Even as he did, he thought that his luck was due
to change. There were tracks of bare human feet all along the trail he was
following, and he believed he would soon come to an Indian camp.

The next day started out the same as all the other days that he had been
alone. The only difference between Tuesday and the past Monday was that
after hiking for two hours he came upon mule tracks. Thinking this was a
sign that his trail mates were just ahead, his spirits picked up. It would only
be a short time, and he would see all the others.

Moving ahead, thinking he would be with the small party in a short time
and would have something to eat even if it were only a small portion of mule
meat, Preuss walked as fast as he could. He worked his way down an easy
ridge in the foothills of the Mother Lode country, and after a hike of two
hours, he saw some people ahead. They were Maidu Indians who lived in
the area, and there were five or six of them beside their huts. Some were tat-
tooing themselves with charcoal; others were beside the fire, roasting acorns
over the glowing coals. Preuss did not hesitate to walk toward these people
and by the use of signs let them know that he was hungry. At once they
served him some roasted acorns. Preuss began to fill his pockets with what
the Maidus gave him. Seeing this, they offered even more, until the mapmaker had enough acorns to stuff his pockets. Then in return for their gift,
he gave them his pocketknife and continued on his way. At least, he had
acorns to eat.

In the early afternoon he came to a place where his companions had
stopped for a noon meal. Ashes in the firepit still were warm, and he increased his pace to try to overtake them before nightfall. At sunset he had
made a tough hike of twenty-five miles and reached the present valley of
Coloma, where gold was discovered. Ahead he saw the familiar shape of
Frémont's tepee, and he knew his ordeal was over.

The men were camped beneath tall oaks and pines in this foothill valley
where the South Fork of the American River cuts a path along the valley's
northern side. The sight of the camp was a great relief to Preuss, and he
yelled to his companions of the trail. For in spite of his inward nature, he felt
a bond of loyalty and friendship for these men. Though he was unable to
show it, he was glad to see all of them gathered about the campfires.

Even though Preuss had his ups and downs and feelings of both good and
ill will about Lieutenant Frémont, and though he had written in his private
journal that he thought Frémont was a fool and an incompetent, his true
feeling for the young leader was much closer to deep friendship than he ever
let others know. And now, he was happy to see even Carson, whose backwoods behavior often rankled him to the point where he referred to him in
his writing as "Kid Karsten" as a private joke.

John Charles and the others greeted Preuss and asked where he had been.
Frémont told him he had feared for his life. A man alone was fair game, and

they didn't know about the tribes in this region. Besides, he could have strayed into some desolate canyon.

While Preuss dismissed such notions and assured everyone he knew where he was headed, Frémont told him that he had become so worried about his safety he had offered a reward to any man who would take the backtrack and try to find him. Baptiste Derosier had accepted the offer and headed toward the mountains to see if he had joined Broken Hand's section. Now, after two days, Derosier had not returned. He had seemed all right, Frémont explained, or he wouldn't have allowed him to go. Still there was time for him to appear. There was a possibility he was coming with Fitzpatrick and his men.

John Charles and the others wanted to hear about Preuss's adventures. As they plied him with questions, he told them about his hunger, the types of food he had taken to eating, even about allowing ants to run up his arm and then plucking them off to eat. The taste hadn't been too bad, just a bit on the acid side. But ants weren't enough for a hungry man. Then he had come to the Indian village, and the people gave him acorns.

The worst thing of all, Preuss admitted, was running out of tobacco for his pipe. A smoke would have helped to ease the hunger. He had tried using oak leaves, but they were much too thick, and the flavor wasn't very good. There was just nothing that resembled tobacco, and oak leaves would never do.

With Preuss in camp, the men felt better. Now there was only Derosier to worry about. If he had not lost his senses again, he probably was with Fitz and the others. If he had missed them, Baptiste was quite able to live off the land and find his way back on his own.

As Preuss told Frémont where he had been and what he had done, he stressed the point that he was never lost. To pass the time, when he rested, Preuss had observed the course of the South Fork of the American River, and he had made a sketch map of its lower reaches.

That night in the camp near present-day Coloma, California, the mapmaker ate sparingly. He was tempted by the aroma of roasting horse and mule meat, but he was afraid he would become ill if he ate very much after having been without food.

Morning was a grand change from the weeks that Preuss and the others had spent in the deep snow. The sun was warm; wild flowers filled the land with a fantastic range of colors and shapes—baby blue-eyes covered the moist flats and slopes; the dry regions were dominated by the striking red-purple of bush lupines, heart-shaped violets, fiddlenecks with curved yellow spikes hanging from twisted and hairy, yellowish-green stems; white popcorn flowers stood tall in the deep green grass; and wherever there was enough shade and dampness, there were ferns of every size and description. All this was foothill country, and in some of the tall oaks, there were the twisted and intricate webs of wild grapevines reaching upward toward the sunlight.

Then as the men moved out of the foothills, they were startled by what lay before them. The Sacramento Valley stretched to the western horizon, to the blue line of the Coast Range. To men who had seen so much desert country, this great valley was almost unbelievable. While they had seen it from the high ridges in the Sierra Nevada, they had not been prepared for this incredible prairie that spanned the gap between the Sierra Nevada and the Pacific Coast Range.

Grass was belly deep for the horses and mules, and the different shades of green moved back and forth in the light wind like waves on some long-forgotten sea. In the open, under the warm sun, wild flowers were all the colors of an artist who had become addicted to all the variations of yellow, gold, and orange that he could imagine. Wild mustard spread out in patches of bright yellow. There were cream cups with yellowish-cream flowers, but most of all, it was the California poppy that caught their attention. This flower with its bright orange petals seemed to capture the sun's rays.

As they rode through this beautiful land, they were amazed at the size of the great valley oaks that grew in groves on rolling hills or stood as islands of shade on the flat surface of the valley floor. The trunks of many of these oaks were five and six feet in diameter, and the upper limbs spread out in magnificent umbrellas of green leaves that shaded a wide area beneath. In these cool places, the men came upon herds of resting deer that jumped up and bounded away before anyone fired a chance shot. Overhead, great flights of squawking ducks and the *ha-lunk, ha-lunk* chatter of Canada geese caught the attention of the men, and they watched their V-formation flights move from one feeding region to another. Horses and mules skittered and jumped to the side as coveys of valley quail took off with a rapid flutter of wings that propelled their chunky bodies from one cover of deep grass to another.

Within a few hours they came to the junction of the combination North-Middle Fork and the South Fork of the American River. All three branches formed one large river that varied in width from sixty to a hundred yards. Then, as the men followed the riverbank, they noticed fresh tracks of cattle and horses. There was no longer any question about the nearness of Sutter's Fort.

Following the well-worn path, they arrived at a small Maidu village. It was obvious these Indians had some contact with whites, as they were wearing manufactured shirts. While they wore nothing else, their shirts were a grand sight for the weary travelers. They stopped and tried to learn the location of Sutter's from these friendly people, but they were unable to understand each other; so the party moved on.

They nooned beneath the shadow of a large oak's spreading limbs and ate a lunch of acorn meal. As they made do with this gruel, they stared at the miles of poppies swaying in the light breeze like grounded rays of the sun, and they heard the trilled songs of meadowlarks, and the harsh *queg-queg-queg* of yellow-billed magpies. But Frémont was anxious to move along. After this short break the men were back in the saddle and headed out.

Shortly after their noon halt they came to a well-built little adobe house that sat on a high knoll overlooking the river and the great valley. What caught their attention was that this house had glass windows! After all the miles since leaving The Dalles and the neatly constructed Lee House, to see a dwelling with glass windows was almost too much to believe.

But when they rode up to the house, fully expecting to find a Mexican ranchero or his family, they saw only Maidus gathered around. One of the Maidus greeted them in Spanish, and they hoped to learn the directions to Sutter's from him, but his Spanish was much too limited to help them. Then a very well dressed Maidu suddenly appeared and, in fluent Spanish, informed them that they were beside the Río de los Americanos. Ten more miles would bring them to the junction of the American and Sacramento rivers.

There was no problem about finding Sutter's Fort. He explained he was a vaquero who worked for Captain Sutter, just as did the people of this rancheria. They were not far from their destination, and he would take them there. For Captain Sutter always liked to see his countrymen.

Frémont and his men lined out behind the vaquero and began their ride to Sutter's Fort. Along the way they passed the house of another Sacramento Valley settler, the Scotsman John Sinclair.[29] But they did not stop at Sinclair's adobe. They were in a hurry now, and they watched ahead for the first view of the fort. As they did, they saw an approaching horseman.

As the rider drew near, the vaquero greeted him in Spanish. Frémont must have thought of their own gaunt and worn look. In comparison, forty-one-year-old John Sutter was trim and handsome and immaculately groomed in a finely pressed military uniform. His sideburns and mustache were neatly trimmed. Overall he had the features and bearing to capture immediate attention in a crowd. As John Charles stared at this vast landholder, this pioneer of a new Eden, Sutter introduced himself, expressed his concern for their plight, and offered them the full hospitality of his fort. They would have a roof over their heads this night, and there would be plenty of good food and wine.

Only ten years of age separated Frémont and Sutter, and they had much in common. Both were handsome and in the prime of life; both had a grasp of many languages; both loved good food and wine; both were ambitious and believed in shaping a new destiny for the West. While Frémont came as a representative of a government interested in the Far West, Sutter encouraged the settlement of Anglos in the Sacramento Valley as he dreamed of empire and courted fame.

The day was the sixth of March. The year was 1844. Frémont and his men had endured the country of rock upon rock, snow upon snow. All that remained was to take fresh horses and provisions to Broken Hand and the remainder of the expedition working their way down through the foothills. With help from Sutter, John Charles was able to return toward the mountains in the morning with all that was needed. In two more days he and his men rode into Sutter's Fort with the section of the expedition that Broken Hand had been leading. All had gaunt faces and the haunted look of despair, the look of men who never expected to live long enough to know another day of rest, another time of decent food to eat. The horses and mules that were still alive were no more than walking racks of bones.

Of the sixty-seven horses and mules they had started across the mountains with, only thirty-three remained. Frémont learned from Fitzpatrick that many of the animals had slipped and tumbled off steep canyon walls and plunged to their deaths on the rocks below. One mule that fell had been loaded with all the plant specimens that had been collected in the two thousand miles of travel since leaving Fort Hall. To John Charles this was a great loss, but he could be thankful that he and his men had survived the winter crossing of the Sierra Nevada and had not fallen victims to the wild forces of nature the old Washo had warned them about.

# XI

# The Great Valley

WHEN JOHN CHARLES FRÉMONT and all the men of his second expedition arrived at Sutter's Fort on March 8, 1844, they were following a custom that had become part of the pastoral scene in the Sacramento Valley. For the early settlers of this great valley and the travelers from far away were

> a frontier mixture of colors, cultures, languages and occupations and visions. The natural meeting place for these strangers in a new land was Sutter's Fort. Here near the Sacramento and American rivers, John August Sutter— the dreamer of personal empire—welcomes these wanderers.[1]

The men who stopped at Sutter's were from all points on the compass. Hudson's Bay Company men worked their way south from Oregon. American mountain men in search of more beaver streams found their way over or around the Sierra Nevada and stopped off to drink aguardiente, eat a decent meal, and ask about possible beaver streams. Hide and tallow traders drifted up the Sacramento River from San Francisco Bay. And men from London, Liverpool, and God knows where jumped ship, found their way to Sutter's and inquired about how a man could become a Mexican citizen and get a land grant.

Gathered at Sutter's was a true California mixture, "a rare blend made possible by distance, isolation, loneliness, and uncluttered, untouch space."[2] There were Europeans, Californios, emigrants just in from the States, Kanakas from the Sandwich Islands, and Maidu Indians from the valley and the foothills.

When Frémont first saw Sutter's Fort, it was a thriving establishment that had taken root and grown in the five years since the roving Swiss had obtained his land grant and sailed up the Sacramento River in August 1839. At that time he had hired the services of William Heath Davis, who guided Sutter upriver. Sutter chartered two schooners, *Isabella* and *Nicolas,* to carry his belongings and the people who were going to help him carve his empire out of the vast Sacramento Valley. Among these people were "four or five Germans or Swiss, who were mechanics, and three Hawaiians and their wives. . . ."[3] Along with the normal supplies he would need, Sutter had a four-oared boat, two pieces of artillery, small arms and ammunition.

To travel from Yerba Buena through San Francisco Bay and up the Sacramento River took eight days as Sutter looked the country over for just the right place to establish himself. While the days of sailing were enjoyable, the nights of stopping beside the riverbank were sheer torture as great clouds of mosquitoes swarmed about the schooners.

As the little squadron approached the junction of the American and Sacramento rivers, the banks were filled with hundreds of Indians who were curious about this intrusion into their land. Some even paddled out to the vessels in their tule-reed canoes. But there was no indication of hostility, and it was here that Sutter and his party were put ashore by Captain Davis.

> Having accomplished my purpose of landing Captain Sutter at the junction of the American and Sacramento rivers with his men and his freight, the following morning we left him there and headed the two vessels for Yerba Buena. As we moved away Captain Sutter gave us a parting salute of nine guns—the first ever fired at that place—which produced a most remarkable effect. As the heavy report of the guns and the echoes died away, the camp of the little party was surrounded by hundreds of Indians, who were excited and astonished at the unusual sound. A large number of deer and elk and other animals on the plains were startled, running to and fro, stopping to listen, their heads raised, full of curiosity and wonder, seemingly attracted and fascinated to the spot, while from the interior of the adjacent wood the howls of wolves and coyotes filled the air, and immense flocks of waterfowl flew wildly over the camp.[4]

All that had taken place five years before Frémont and his half-starved men found their way down from the snowbound Sierra Nevada. John Sutter —a former first under-lieutenant of the reserve corps of the Canton of Berne, a one-time Santa Fé trader, fur trader, a traveler who had managed to get as far west as the Sandwich Islands and as far north as Sitka—had come a long way since he had abandoned his wife and children and fled Switzerland in order to avoid debtor's prison. He had managed to get along with the Indians to the point that he was able to train them to plant crops, build a fort, herd cattle and horses, and do all the other tasks required to make New Helvetia prosperous and self-sufficient. The changes were many since he had fired a farewell salute to Davis as he sailed down the Sacramento. But there were many more changes Captain Sutter had in mind as he encouraged other Europeans and Americans to settle near him and as he participated in the political intrigue of Mexican California.

And now in March 1844, at a springtime when the great valley was experiencing unusually warm weather, Sutter welcomed Frémont and his men to share the hospitality of his fort. John Charles was happy to accept the offer.

Frémont had no idea of the vast changes that had taken place since Sutter had first settled in the great valley. The first settlement, the one quickly built by the Kanakas after Captain Davis had sailed away, had consisted of two grass houses, and a one-story adobe thatched with a tule roof. All this had been done just before the early winter rains of 1839 began. What the men of Frémont's expedition saw was something on a much grander scale.

Sutter's Fort was larger than either Bent's Fort or Fort Laramie. The only establishment that exceeded it in size in the frontier West was Fort Vancouver. But even that impressive wooden structure did not reduce the feeling of importance that any man just out of the wilderness felt when he saw Sutter's Fort. The whitewashed, thick-walled adobe structure had been built on a little knoll that gave it a few feet of elevation above the valley floor, just enough to make it appear even more imposing. While John Charles thought it was quadrangular, this structure built by Sutter's Indian workmen was actually more irregular in shape.

The walls of baked adobe bricks were eighteen feet high, and they ranged in thickness from two and a half feet to five feet at the northwest and southwest corners, where the two-story bastions had mounted cannons that could sweep an attacking force approaching from any direction. At other points along the walls there were portholes for the use of riflemen. The north-south walls were 320 feet long, the east wall was 140 feet long, and the west wall was 160 feet long.

To the north of the fort, a shallow slough emptied into the American River. Two miles below the establishment, Frémont saw a large two-masted lighter and a schooner anchored in the Sacramento River near the landing for the fort. As he approached the gate, he found a uniformed Indian standing guard beside another brass cannon. The whole place had an appearance of strength and power, and John Charles was certain it was quite capable of keeping a garrison of at least a thousand men.

Inside the compound, this citadel of the Sacramento Valley was outfitted for the care and comfort of a dreamer of empire. Sutter's private quarters consisted of three interconnecting rooms. There were barracks for the Indian troops, quarters for workmen and servants, a kitchen, a bakery, a distillery for the manufacture of aguardiente; and workshops for blacksmiths, carpenters, coopers, saddlemakers, shoemakers, weavers, and other craftsmen needed to keep this establishment flourishing. There was even a small gristmill operated by mulepower. Added to all this were the many guest rooms, storage rooms, barns, and corrals. Outside the fort, well beyond smelling distance and located near the original landing, was the tannery, where cattle, deer, and other hides were cured and made ready for trade.

That night of March 8, the weary men of Frémont's expedition joined Captain Sutter at his rough wooden dining table. They were treated to a feast of fresh trout, pink-fleshed salmon that was unbelievably tasty, ducks, geese, valley quail, plenty of beef, a smoke-cured ham, fresh vegetables and fruit, bread just out of the ovens, fresh milk and cream, newly churned but-ter, and more than enough aguardiente and white wine to drive away the last chill.

The talk at the dining table was free and easy, and it was a grand thing to hear about this land of plenty. They were served soup in china bowls com-plete with silver spoons. They ate their main courses on real dishes that In-dian servants carried back and forth to the kitchen to wash for each new entrée. The men toasted their host, and made light about their terrible ordeal in the snows of the Sierra Nevada. They also talked of the good life open to any man who had the sense to settle in this great valley; and for some of Frémont's men, the idea was to become more than talk as the time drew near for them to begin the homeward trek.

Dour Charles Preuss was in the best of spirits. After eating ants and acorns, this table of plenty was something he had never expected to see again. But there was more than food. There were men gathered around the table who could speak German. Sutter was one, but he directed most of his conversation to Frémont. Still, there were others. There was Henry Huber from Paderborn, who had come to California with the Bartleson party in 1841 and who managed Sutter's profitable distillery where aguardiente was made from corn, wheat, and wild grapes that grew in abundance along the banks of the rivers. Another German was Charles Flügge of Hannover, a man Sutter had known in St. Louis, who served as Sutter's "clerk and ad-viser." And there was Theodor Cordua from Mecklenburg in northern Ger-many.[5] Sutter had met Cordua in Honolulu and had written glowing letters to him about the future of California, encouraging him to come to the Sacramento Valley. In 1842 Cordua did just that, but unlike the other men Preuss met, Cordua did not work for Sutter. When he reached the great val-ley, he had goods to trade for land. As Preuss talked to this fat, jolly man who loved to spend an evening playing whist, he was speaking to the founder of New Mecklenburg, or present-day Marysville, California. Thirty air miles north of Sutter's Fort, Cordua had established his place on a square league of land beside the Yuba River, close to its junction with the Feather River.

But as good as it was to be able to speak his native language once again, lean times had made Preuss a poor conversationalist during his first meal at the fort. Later, during other days and nights, he would talk to his coun-trymen at length. But on this first evening Preuss was preoccupied and as-tounded by the bountiful table, and like his comrades, he ate until he must have thought he would burst.

Frémont carried on a long conversation with Sutter. Besides the talk of food and of what was taking place in the States and in Mexican California, John Charles inquired about the nature of the land: how many people would it support; what crops grew easily; what was the attitude of the Mexican government about outsiders drifting in and settling in the untapped open spaces of the great valley?

Sutter's reply was warm and open, but he did not speak for the Mexican government. He spoke for himself and for his personal vision of Alta California's future. He told Frémont that it was come one and all. He was waiting to greet them, to welcome new neighbors, and to help them get established. This was Captain Sutter's dream of a new destiny for the West, and the lean explorer listened intently to everything Sutter had to say, for Frémont also saw a future for American emigrants in this land of plenty.

2

PREUSS HAD HOPED to sail down the Sacramento River and visit Yerba Buena. Charles Flügge had talked to him about making the trip when Captain John Yates, a former Liverpool sailor and Sutter's master seaman, took the schooner *Sacramento* to San Francisco Bay and Yerba Buena to pick up supplies for Frémont that were not available at the fort. Flügge even suggested that the mapmaker shave his unkempt beard before making the voyage so that he would look his best when he met the Mexican officials at the port. But Frémont would not allow such a voyage, not for Preuss nor any other member of the expedition. They had not been disturbed by visiting Mexican officials yet, and there was no point in pushing their luck.

The explorer and his men camped outside Sutter's Fort during their sixteen-day stay, but many of their meals were eaten at Sutter's. During these meals, the lieutenant was told that Sutter had notified Governor Manuel Micheltorena of their presence in the valley, and that he had explained in his message that the Americans had crossed the Sierra Nevada to secure help for their homeward trip to the United States. Even as Sutter told Frémont about California, the Swiss was involved in a brewing revolution.

Sutter had joined forces with rancheros and merchants who were secretly rallying behind former Governor Juan Bautista Alvarado and former General José Castro in a plot to overthrow Governor Micheltorena, who had been sent to California from Mexico in 1842 as the new head of this distant outpost of empire. Micheltorena had brought some 250 unruly soldiers with him.

Many of these men were ex-convicts, bullies, and troublemakers whom Mexico had been happy to send into the wilderness. But the *Californios* did not like the look of their new protectors. Knowing this, Alvarado and Castro used the excuse of misconduct on the part of some soldiers to form a revolt against Micheltorena.[6]

While Frémont's horses and mules got fat on the native grasses, saddles and bridles were made in the fort's saddlery; the blacksmith shop kept its coals glowing, and the hammer ringing against bright orange metal fashioned

horseshoes for the animals. Clothing and all needed provisions for the homeward trek were gathered together inside the fort.

This was a very dry March in the valley, and Sutter was trying his best to
avoid an extensive crop loss. Ditches were being dug to bring water from the
American River to irrigate his lands. The Maidu girls at the fort, who were
being trained to work in a future woolen factory, had to be employed in watering the vegetable gardens. Sutter informed the lieutenant that he had to
protect his wheat crop. He was scheduled to deliver so many fanegas of
wheat to Russian ships in San Francisco Bay as part of his yearly payment
for his purchase of Fort Ross on the headlands of the Sonoma Coast, a trading center the Russians had abandoned in 1841 as they limited their sea otter
trapping to the area closer to the base at Sitka, Alaska.

Sutter had obtained building materials, cannons, ammunition, livestock,
and even the schooner Sacramento by his purchase of Fort Ross. But the
price had been much higher than he was capable of meeting. He had put
$2,000 down and promised to pay the remaining $30,000 in four yearly in-
stallments that were to be put aboard a Russian ship in San Francisco Bay at
Sutter's expense. So, this dry year that Frémont was enjoying in the
Sacramento Valley was putting a great amount of pressure on his host. For
the Russians weren't the only people to whom Sutter owed either the products of his land or outright cash. Other creditors such as the Hudson's Bay
Company and neighboring rancheros like Bernal and Suñol were tired of
being put off by Sutter, and one of them even threatened to attach the
schooner Sacramento. In a way, this might have done more good than harm.
For before that summer of 1844 came to an end, the vessel was smashed on
the rocks off the coast of Fort Ross when Captain John Yates and Supercargo
Samuel J. Hensley[7] had consumed too much aguardiente to maintain control
of the ship.[8]

Yet, even as Sutter went out of his way to help Frémont, even as he tried
to put off his own creditors, the expenses he was incurring by aiding this expedition of the United States Government would also cost him.

> I charge everything at cost [Sutter wrote] and accepted orders on the
> Topographical Bureau. No one in California would have given Frémont a
> dollar of credit and I was obliged to sell these orders at a discount of twenty
> percent. In the innocense of my heart I thought I would do the American
> Government a favor by not taking advantage of Frémont's distress, but I only
> cheated myself thereby.[9]

Unknown to Sutter, his loss to the Topographical Corps was minor com-
pared to future losses he would suffer as a result of his willingness to aid emi-
grants and to welcome all newcomers to the great valley. Even as he helped
Frémont, the explorer was calculating the strengths and weaknesses of the
Mexican government in California. He talked to Sutter at length, to other
Anglo pioneers who had been in California for some time, and to recent emi-

grants such as Joseph Chiles. From all these conversations, from what he could observe around him, Frémont could go home with only one impression. California was ripe and ready for picking. The population of Mexican citizens numbered no more than ten or eleven thousand people, and they were scattered from Sonoma in the north to San Diego in the south. Since Mexico had achieved its independence from Spain in 1821, the power of the Catholic mission system had been stripped, and the republican government had broken up the great mission landholdings, liberated the Indians, and looked with more openness upon the immigration of non-Mexican settlers so long as they embraced Catholicism and became Mexican citizens. Roads throughout the country ranged from poor to almost nonexistent, and it was easy to see that such transportation links did not offer a fast route for the movement of troops and supplies in the advent of war. Waterways, such as the Sacramento and San Joaquin rivers, were the only easy access passages to the interior of the Great Valley. As for the rest of California, the best way to get from one place to another was either to go by horseback or to trust one's life to a voyage up or down the Pacific Coast from Monterey Bay or San Francisco Bay in the north to the harbor at San Diego in the south. At these harbors, there were clusters of merchants from different countries who thrived on the hide and tallow trade, the traffic in sea otter and other furs, the importation of manufactured goods, visits from whalers, and trade in such items as agricultural crops, some lumber, and barrels of smoked or pickled beef and salmon.

The key to the culture of California were the immense ranchos. These land grants, marked by colorful diseños (maps) that relied too heavily on so many leagues from a given oak tree to a given ridge or outcropping of rock to be completely accurate, were individual kingdoms ruled by their rancheros. When John Charles first learned of the size of these ranchos, he must have thought they were like feudal states. The territory held by the Peralta family of Alta California

> included the area now covered by Berkeley, Oakland, Alameda, and part of the Santa Clara Valley. Don José Domingo Peralta's Cañada del Corte de Madera in the Santa Clara Valley was truly magnificent. It had its own chapel; a large, rambling adobe ranch house with iron grilles on the windows; a bull ring; a private dock; and a fleet of barges for transporting goods and livestock on San Francisco Bay.[10]

Men who lived in such isolated domains were not too concerned about the trickle of Anglo emigrants. These rancheros were caught up in a way of life that seemed without end. The only passion they shared outside family life, fiestas, and rodeos was political intrigue. And in 1844 such intrigue was nearing the flashpoint of revolution. Also, there was the constant presence of the British waiting on the sidelines. To the north at Fort Vancouver was the powerful Hudson's Bay Company, and their trappers ranged as far south as the San Joaquin Valley near the present city of Stockton. British warships sailed up and down the Pacific Coast and stopped in California harbors as friendly but well-armed visitors.

Seeing all this, or hearing about it, Frémont could only come away from Sutter's Fort with an impression that the future of this fertile and sparsely populated land was yet to be determined, that in this spring of 1844 the combination of unrest and internal strife was about to leave California wide open for conquest.

## 3

THE TROUBLE BEGAN over sugar that had been stolen from Frémont's supplies. He was furious about it, and he accused two of his men, Oliver Beaulieu and Philibert Courteau, of playing free and easy with what was going to be needed on the homeward journey. Sugar had to be imported in California, and it was very expensive, costing fifty cents per pound. The theft of forty pounds of sugar was not something Frémont was about to treat lightly. He made it clear the two men would pay for what they had taken by having a deduction made from their pay. Both men were to be dismissed from the party. How they found their way home was to be their problem.

To Captain John Sutter, though, the matter was not quite as clear-cut as Frémont made it out to be. In the first place, if there had been a theft—and that was yet to be proved—it had taken place within the walls of the fort or just outside. In either case, that made it a matter for Sutter's concern. It was his fort and his land, and he was the local alcalde. All this, he pointed out. Frémont did not like the idea of his men being tried in Sutter's court, but he had no other choice than to give in to his host. When Sutter listened to the complaint, considered the evidence, and dismissed the men as being not guilty, the friendly relationship between the owner of the fort and the leader of the expedition became quite cool.

Frémont objected to the decision, and he made his objections known by dismissing both men at once and deducting the cost of the sugar at fifty cents per pound from the men's severance pay. Seeing all this, Sutter immediately offered them jobs, and they were happy to accept. Almost at the same time, Samuel Neal, who was Frémont's best blacksmith, asked to be discharged in California. When John Charles agreed, Captain Sutter quickly hired Neal to work as a blacksmith at the fort.

Frémont was in no position to insult his host. He needed everything he could purchase from him, and to initiate an open quarrel would have been foolhardy. Still, the very idea that he had not been able to discipline his own men without Sutter's interference did not sit well with John Charles, and it was not something he was willing to forget.

The costs ran high on everything, and though Sutter claimed later that he was not paid enough, the total bill submitted to Colonel Abert in two vouchers amounted to $3,891.83. In addition, two other vouchers to Charles W. Flügge and Joseph B. Chiles came to $237.25 and $54.00 respectively. So the total expenditure at Sutter's Fort amounted to $4,183.08. This was not an amount Colonel Abert could brush aside as a minor expense for the expedition.

Preuss also commented on the high cost of items in California. All he wanted was a new pair of trousers. Yet the cloth alone cost him three dollars. Then when he tried to get some tailor or seamstress to make them for him, he found that the labor would cost another three dollars. That was much more than he cared to pay out of his salary, and he attempted to make his own trousers. But as good as he was sketching the lay of the land, the problems of tailoring were almost insurmountable. He cut his pattern, and it appeared to be just right. But as he began to sew, one of his trail mates pointed out that everything was fine except for one thing.

Preuss asked what was wrong, and after much laughter at his expense, the problem became all too evident. He was making a pair of one-leg trousers as he sewed both legs together. Frustrated as he was, he still refused to spend the additional money to have a skilled person do his tailoring. He very carefully undid his stitching, made sure that he had the two legs of his pattern separated, and started the whole job over.

Having to do one's own tailoring, eating too much food, and seeing the same men day after day was beginning to plague the men of the expedition. They had been on the trail much longer than anyone had anticipated, and there was a very long journey through hard country before they would once again see the first smokes of civilization as they remembered it. Cabin fever was one thing, but, by God, they had trail fever. Frémont was aware of this state of mind, for he too felt the same frustrations. He longed to be with Jessie again, to cradle baby Lily in his arms, to know the comforts of a gracious family life.

Feeling this anxiousness to get moving and still upset by Sutter's hiring three men he had discharged, and by having two other men—Thomas Fallon and Joseph Verrot—request discharges in California, Frémont decided to make his first tentative move on the homeward trip. On the morning of March 22 they rode away from Sutter's. They tried their new mounts in the short journey to John Sinclair's El Paso Rancho beside the American River. Two days were spent at this camp while the horses and mules were broken to their work and all the last-minute preparations were made for the long journey home.

Sutter had furnished Frémont with all he would need, and then some. The expedition had 130 horses and mules, about thirty head of cattle—including five milk cows—saddles, bridles, supplies, and even a young Maidu boy "who had been trained as *vaquero*, and who would be serviceable in managing our cavalcade, a great part of which were nearly as wild as buffalo. . . ."[11] The most important thing to every man was that winter had ended, the spring grass was green and tall, and they were headed for forts, settlements, towns, and cities they called home. In a festive mood, the Maidu Indians who lived near John Sinclair's place even entertained them with a dance that Charles Preuss never forgot, as one of the dancers had painted his own penis black and white—the Prussian national colors.

On the morning of March 24, 1844, Frémont and his men were ready to head out. But during the two days at Sinclair's, Baptiste Derosier disappeared. The tough métis had not regained his senses since the terrible time in the Sierra Nevada. He simply wandered off and nobody could find him. And while he was to return to his Missouri home a year later, on the day of leave-taking at Sinclair's, Frémont did not know what had happened to him.

The shortest way back would have been to recross the Sierra Nevada, but the best was to head south through the Sacramento and San Joaquin valleys until they reached the low pass over the mountains that Joseph Walker had discovered. Beyond that, they would hit the Old Spanish Trail, a trade route from Santa Fé to California. By following this trail for part of the return journey, Frémont thought he would get an even better idea of the southern extension of the Great Basin. Then they could head northeast in the vicinity of Utah Lake, find one of the fur trappers' passes through the southern Rocky Mountains, and strike a homeward course via Bent's Fort and the Santa Fé Trail.

After a cool dawn, the morning sun turned warm as Captain Sutter and several of his key men rode into camp. They greeted Frémont and told him they would ride with his party for a few miles. A farewell was said to John Sinclair, and the large calvacade moved out with Frémont and Sutter riding in the lead. They moved along the floor of the Sacramento Valley, passed groves of great oaks, startled herds of deer and antelope, and headed toward the eastern edge of the valley to avoid any possibility of meeting Mexican officials. Then after a short ride, the dreamer of empire might well have said, "Vaya con Dios." For once the expedition moved away from the Great Valley, once it struck out across the Mojave Desert and entered the Great Basin, all any man could wish them was the good fortune to have God watch over them.

4

THREE DAYS after Frémont's departure, Lieutenant Colonel Rafael Tellez, two other officers, and twenty-five dragoons arrived at Sutter's Fort. Tellez came right to the point. Where were the American invaders?

The gentle Sutter explained that they were gone. They were on their way back to the United States.

What had they been doing in California?

Sutter tried to explain that the need of supplies, the necessity to get out of the snow-covered mountains had forced the party of explorers into the Sacramento Valley.

Tellez was not at all pleased. The obvious was not good enough. These Americans had come too far to end up in California simply to rest and purchase supplies. There had to be more to it. Something else had brought them into Alta California. The officer was very curt with Sutter as he questioned him. He wanted to know why the message he had sent about these invaders had been delivered so late, and why Sutter in his role as alcalde hadn't detained these men until the soldiers arrived, until there was time to question them.

While Sutter soothed the feelings of Tellez, Frémont and the expedition moved along at a good pace. After a first camp on the Cosumnes River, they crossed the Mokelumne River and stopped overnight beside the Calaveras River in the San Joaquin Valley near the present site of Stockton. On the third day out, they approached the wide and deep San Joaquin River. They noticed that the soil was not the same as that of the Sacramento Valley. It was much more sandy, and there was not as much vegetation. This sparseness did not include the whole San Joaquin Valley. They entered a region where flowering lupine gave the ground a bright blue color as though some frantic artist had smeared the earth with a giant brush. Beyond the thickets of lupine—some standing as much as twelve feet high[12]—past the sweet aroma of the spiked flowers, there were great stands of live oaks. Then the color of the landscape changed to a rich orange as the men rode through acre after acre of California poppies.

Flowers and oaks were only part of the wild beauty of this valley. There were vast herds of wild horses and cattle, tule elk, pronghorn antelopes, and blacktail deer. Overhead there were flights of ducks and geese that passed like small storm clouds and momentarily shut out the sunlight. Instead of lightning and thunder, the waterfowl squawked, honked, and made a drumlike sound as thousands of flapping wings beat steadily against the wind.

Looking for a possible place to ford the wide San Joaquin River, the party headed toward the southeast in the direction of the glistening peaks of the Sierra Nevada. As they rode out of a thick grove of oaks, they came upon the Stanislaus River. While this stream was smaller than the San Joaquin, it was muddy, deep, swollen with water from melting snowpacks in the high mountains, and was at least fifty yards wide in the narrowest place the men could find.

During the next two days they explored the stream in both directions for a suitable ford. While they did this, some of the men roped wild horses for replacement pack animals and began the hard job of breaking them. As the horsemen did their job, the idea of fording the Stanislaus River was abandoned. Faced with this situation, Frémont decided that the only way they were going to get across was to build bullboats. He gave the order to kill several cattle, skin them, and make willow frames. All this was done in a hurry. When the boats were ready, the baggage was placed aboard, and the best boatmen ferried all the gear across the river. Then the top horsemen herded the livestock into the water and swam them to the other side.

The Maidu vaquero became very uneasy. As Frémont put it, the young man "probably had not much idea of where he was going, and began to be alarmed at the many streams which we were rapidly putting between him and the village. . . ."[13] Taking advantage of this river crossing that occupied the attention of all the men, the Maidu youth slipped out of sight, and before anyone noticed his absence, he was well on his way home.

The men were having trouble with the wild cattle they bought from Sutter. The animals had to be forced down the riverbank and into the water, but as the depth increased, they turned back to shore, with Alexis Godey—who had stripped to swim his horse—in pursuit. The last anybody saw of the fast-moving cattle was a dust cloud, and riding behind it was the naked Godey, who was determined to head them off. By nightfall, he was back in camp, cursing the fleet cattle as he stood by the campfire and put on his clothes.

Frémont gave the order to lay over for another day. In the morning they would try to run down the cattle. Though they rode back for many miles, the wild animals were nowhere in sight. It was as though the frightened cattle had never stopped running and were probably well on their way back to Sutter's rancho.

In the first two weeks of April the expedition continued its southward journey. They crossed the Tuolumne, Merced, King's, and Kern rivers, and tried to avoid any clash with the many bears that were in the area. For the large grizzlies came down to the rivers to fish and to eat wild berries that grew in thick bushes beside the banks. The herds of tule elk were much larger, but this was the season when the bucks were still without antlers. All over the floor of the valley there were scattered and sun-dried antlers from previous years of shedding. The horns were thick at the base, branched with many long points, and spread wide from tip to tip.

In this part of the San Joaquin Valley the wild horse herds were larger than any the men had ever seen. Horses roamed the grassland like herds of buffalo on the Great Plains, and it was necessary to move the expedition along the eastern side of the rivers and the valley in order to avoid them. For the stallions that herded the mares and colts along were constantly whinnying at the horses of the expedition. Everyone knew that if they allowed their spare horses to get near these droves of fast-galloping wild horses, that would be the last they would see of their extra mounts and pack animals.

Wolf packs also roamed the southern part of the San Joaquin Valley. Along with the coyotes, these predators were always on the hunt for sick, weak, or young animals in the great herds of the grasslands. To Frémont and his men, the whole valley was almost unbelievable. It was alive with game of all kinds; and the untouched, unfenced land was an open invitation for settlers. The dark soil was ideal for crops. It was so rich that any farmer or rancher would look upon it as a vision of agricultural paradise. Water was easy to come by, and the only problem it presented was that of flooding during the spring runoff, when the snow in the high Sierra Nevada began to melt. And there was no lack of building materials. The great valley oaks offered a bountiful supply of hardwood, and the natural adobe in the region was perfect for construction.

Still, as the men rode farther and farther south, they noticed changes in the land. At first these were not too obvious, but as they neared the southern end of the San Joaquin Valley, the country was quite different. The soil was sandy and not nearly as rich, and the rivers were not deep and wide. Then on April 13 they crossed a shallow stream and headed southeast into broken country where they crossed Tehachapi Creek and began to move into the mountains, where there was a mixture of pines and oaks.

When they made camp that evening, a lone Indian horseman appeared. He was dressed like a vaquero from his large sombrero to the sharp-roweled Spanish spurs strapped to the heels of his boots. Frémont greeted him and quickly discovered he spoke fluent Spanish.

It was an unexpected apparition, and a strange and pleasant sight in this desolate gorge of a mountain—an Indian face, Spanish costume, jingling spurs, and horse equipped after the Spanish manner.[14]

The vaquero said he had observed Frémont and his men from the high country. He had watched them enter the lower part of the pass and decided to visit them.

Without any prodding on Frémont's part, the man explained he had been in the mountains to visit his relatives, but that he worked for the priests of the mission at San Fernando and was on his way back. He knew the country, and since he would be traveling in the same direction as the explorer for the next two days, he offered to act as a guide.

Though the vaquero did not mention the name of the pass they were going to cross, it was not Tehachapi Pass. They were five or six miles south of that crossing and were about to leave the San Joaquin Valley and cross into the Mojave Desert over Oak Pass. In answer to Frémont's questions, the stranger gave detailed information about the nature of the country ahead, and he pointed out that if they headed directly to the northeast, they would enter a land that was barren and almost without water. The best hope for them was to strike the Old Spanish Trail and follow it to the southeast until they came to land that was not so arid. It would take them only a few days out of their way, and it would be better traveling and would offer more hope than the planned route.

Frémont was more than happy to accept his offer to guide them for the next two days. So when they moved out the next morning, the vaquero rode beside the lieutenant at the head of the column.

As they moved through the lower country of the Oak Pass trail, the men were impressed by the rare beauty of the region. The mixture of trees included various kinds of oaks, and there were sycamores, willows, and cottonwoods. From the groves of light-barked cottonwoods a gentle wind carried feathery seeds like floating cotton balls. But what caught their eyes most of all was the incredible profusion of wild flowers that formed a mad mixture of colors. As they climbed higher into the mountains, they reached an area where the slopes were covered with a yellow brightness like a reflection of the sun where acres of yellow flowers covered the ground. In and out of the flowers there was a constant buzzing of bees and the fast flicker of hummingbirds darting from flower to flower.

But the beauty on the western slope was the last touch of Eden. At the summit four companions of their guide were waiting. Beyond them, far in the distance, the color of the land was bluish-gray, the bleak mountains were dark and bare of great forests, and all the men could see that their time of easy living, their journey in a land of plenty was coming to an end.

Before sunset the party rode beyond the oaks and the groves of cottonwoods and entered the region of Joshua trees or yucca. The guide led the way into a hollow where there was some water in this dry and barren land and where they saw one last oak tree. But even the oak was out of place and barely surviving. The black bark appeared to have been scorched by the glare of sun and the heat of summer winds, and not a single green leaf could be seen on any of its twisted branches.

All the men were discouraged. After their time in the Great Valley, after traveling southward with the snowcapped peaks of the Sierra Nevada always in view, the idea of striking into the desert again was more than they wished to contemplate.

That night in camp was one of near silence except for the natural sounds beyond the light of their campfires. The men were quiet. When they spoke, they almost whispered. It was as though they feared to speak in their normal voices, as though they were concerned about the distance the sound of their talk might carry in this vast desert beyond their camp.

At dawn all the men were up and standing around the campfires. In the east the first light of the coming sun was beginning to create the horizon on this April 15, 1844. Frémont took time to buy a Spanish saddle and some long-roweled spurs from the guide's companions as mementos of the visit to California. Then it was time to mount and move out.

The faint trace of a trail cut over a low spur of hills and started downward into the endless vision of the Mojave Desert. Even in the early hours of the morning a warm and damp mist rose from the ground and moved upward as though the earth were beginning to sweat. Far in the distance there were bleak buttes, flat stretches of desert, and isolated black ridges like islands in a sea of sand.

The guide stretched his arm and pointed toward the desert and said,

"There are the great *llanos*, (plains;) *no hay agua; no hay zacaté—nada*: there is neither water nor grass—nothing; every animal that goes upon them dies."[15] But that was not where the Old Spanish Trail ran, and that was what they had to be sure about. To make certain that they would not stray into the wasteland, into the vast desert, the guide informed Frémont that he would travel with them for two more days.

# Beyond the Desert

THEY WERE HOMEWARD BOUND, but that was the only good thing any of the men could say about the journey that faced them. Everything before them was strange and out of place after their stay in the Great Valley. Beyond the desert, past the horizon that vanished in the heat of day, there was the promise of plenty and of easier traveling. The key problem was to endure, to survive long enough to stumble out of the inferno and crawl beyond the wasteland. If they were lucky, if they were careful about the dangers to man and beast, if they carried enough water from one spring or muddy creek to last to another, the day would arrive when the high snowcapped peaks of the Rocky Mountains would be within sight.

They were a strange cavalcade, almost grotesque in appearance. Around the campfires at night, four or five languages were heard at the same time. The men were all armed; their dress varied from Indian to Spanish to American to fur-trapper buckskins; and they moved along the trail with more than a hundred half-wild horses and mules.

> Our march was sort of a procession. Scouts ahead, and on the flanks; a front and rear division; the pack animals, baggage, and horned cattle, in the centre; and the whole stretching a quarter of a mile along our dreary path. In this form we journeyed; looking more like we belonged to Asia than to the United States of America.[1]

The vaquero continued to guide them until April 17. On that day he had reached the point where he would have to head southward to Mission San Fernando Rey de España, that great cattle-raising mission that now stands in the heart of a city, near Sepulveda Boulevard just a little over a mile from heavily populated San Fernando Valley. On this day in 1844 the mission was in the country, and the vaquero had plenty of work in helping take care of the range cattle since the discovery of gold on the mission rancho in 1842.

Taking time to make sure that they knew what he was trying to tell them, he pointed to a trail that was hardly visible unless a man knew where to look.

Once he was certain that they realized that here was the camino, he "pointed out a black *butte* on the plain at the foot of the mountain. . . ."[2] There, they would find water for their next camp. Frémont thanked him for his help, gave him a present of some knives and scarlet cloth, and shook hands. With that, the unexpected guide departed.

The day the guide rode out of sight, none of the men were certain about the way ahead. While the faint trace was supposed to be the trail, it hardly appeared to be the main artery between Pueblo de los Angeles and Santa Fé. That night they camped next to a small stream of cold water at the base of the ridge. There was hardly any grass for their large herd of horses, mules, and cattle. They wondered if there had been some misunderstanding, if the vaquero's instructions had been different than they had thought, or if they had taken a wrong turn. As all the possibilities were considered, one thing became quite clear: things had to change for the better, or the chances of survival were not worth much.

But there was nothing wrong with the vaquero's instructions. All the difficulty was their own fault. They had not reached the camping site until nightfall. In the darkness, the men were not able to locate any forage. The next day things were different. Camp was set up before sundown in an area where there was enough grass to feed the hungry animals. Still, one thing continued to bother the lieutenant. The trail they were following had not seen much use. He wondered whether they were on the correct path or whether they were headed away from the main artery of travel.

On the morning of April 19 the men began to see very rough ground, sagebrush, crippled trees, and scattered clumps of bunch grass. As they pushed ahead, the trace of the trail became fainter, and Frémont was concerned that he and his men might have wandered into the barren reaches the vaquero had warned them about.

For eighteen miles they were unusually silent as they stared at the endless wasteland around them. Then there was a shout from the point riders. The Old Spanish Trail had been found![3] It was what the vaquero had said. This was a well-used trail, not just faint marks on the ground. Now that they were out of the rocks and brush and were riding where many others had passed, every man was relieved. Even the horses and mules seemed to sense the change and moved along at a rapid pace. After a journey of fifteen miles, the party came to the Mojave River about six miles northwest of present-day Victorville, California. The Mojave was running a good stream of water. There were cottonwoods, willows, and grass along the river bottoms. It was a good place to rest and to get the animals in shape for the hard days ahead, and Frémont gave the order to pitch camp for a day's layover.

Between us and the Colorado river we were aware that the country was extremely poor in grass, and scarce for water, there being many *jornadas,* (day's journey,) or long stretches of 40 to 60 miles, without water, where the road was marked by bones of animals.[4]

Lacking solid information about the Old Spanish Trail, having to rely on what little knowledge of it he had picked up from men who had never traveled its length, John Charles quickly learned he could not give much credence to what he had been told. Some Californios had described this trail to Santa Fé as sandy and easy going, but it turned out to be rocky and very hard on the hooves of the livestock. It was the kind of trail where an improperly shod animal became lame in a hurry. To protect the mounts and pack animals, extra shoes were a necessary part of the regular supplies. But that wasn't the only thing to worry about. Grass was never found in great abundance. This could present a grave problem if a party should happen to hit the trail just behind a herd of several thousand horses and mules. There was the constant worry about having enough water. In such a dry country, rivers, creeks, and springs were not a sure guarantee. Then there was the threat of Indians. Mojaves, Paiutes, Utes, and raiders from the south had grown to manhood in this land of hardship. Such warriors were not apt to take pity on any stranger.

This was the route of the Old Spanish Trail. At best, it was not an easy desert crossing. At worst, it was not a crossing at all.

## 2

THE RIDERS were first seen by the men preparing the meat for the drying racks. There were only two horsemen coming out of the east, coming from somewhere in the desert, and they were headed straight for the expedition's camp.

A call to be on guard was sounded, and even the men cooking freshly slaughtered beef for the various messes stopped what they were doing and reached for their rifles.

Carson, Fitzpatrick, Godey, all the other seasoned men, selected good cover. They spread out, motioned to others to do the same, and first sightings were taken on the approaching riders. Then, it became clear that there were only two riders on jaded horses, and they weren't Indians. As they drew closer, it became obvious they were Mexicans, and one was a boy.

It didn't make sense. A man and boy traveling alone in this desert wilderness. They had no business to ride by themselves in this country. Their chances of keeping alive weren't worth a cup of spit. This was five days since they found the Old Spanish Trail; and here were a man and a boy riding along without pack horses, without extra mounts, without supplies and without water.

The riders came into camp, and men stepped forth to help them. They were covered with dust, and the boy's face was streaked with furrows of dried tears. The man said that his name was Andreas Fuentes, and that the boy was Pablo Hernandez. The boy was worn out. He was only eleven years old, and the ride had been long and hard.

Fuentes told their story slowly as he was on the verge of collapse. Six of them had left Pueblo de los Angeles, and had started out with thirty head of horses they were driving to Santa Fé. Two of the party were women. One was his wife, and the other was Pablo's mother. The other two were Pablo's father and another man.

They had intended to ride as far as the camping ground called Archilette. They knew there was a good spring at that spot and plenty of grass. There they had planned to wait for a large caravan before they ventured farther along the trail. They knew such a caravan was coming and was headed for Santa Fé. But it had many horses and mules, and they had thought to get to the grass and let their own horses feed and rest before the large herd appeared.

Everything had been all right when they set up camp. A few Indios had ventured into their camp. But they had stopped to visit, and their manner had been very friendly. When they left, everyone said that the Indios were peaceful, that there was nothing to worry about.

A few days passed, easy-going days. The horses began to get fat. The spring was cold and the water sweet. It was a good place to camp and rest while they waited. Fuentes told the men that he and Pablo were guarding the horse herd when the dust cloud was noticed, and the Indios came into view. They were riding hard and fast, shouting, and firing arrows!

There were many of them, perhaps a hundred, maybe more. They came quickly like a prairie fire in the middle of a hot summer day. Santiago—the other man—Santiago Giacome shouted to ride! The Indios came right at the horse herd, for that was what they wanted. We drove the horses ahead of us and broke their charge. Then before the warriors got their own mounts under control, we were in the open and riding as fast as we could, and the horse herd ran with us. Behind us we heard the Indios, and we rode many miles before we dared to change saddles to fresh horses. Eighty miles we rode. For sixty miles we drove the horse herd along until we were certain the Indios were no longer chasing us. Twenty miles from your camp, we left the herd at Agua de Tomaso where there is water and grass. We continued on until we saw your camp, until we knew there would be help.

And the others? What of the others?

There was no need to speak of the obvious. The men would be dead. They would have protected the women as long as they were able to fight. But after death had taken them, after they were shot through with arrows, the women would have no hope. There would be only the knowledge that their fate would not be a quick death. The Indios would take them alive. They would take them to their village where the working hands of two more women could be used.

And for the other reason?

Yes, that, too. But the children will be Indios. They will never think of themselves as anything else.

There was no question of what had to be done. The man and the boy were now the responsibility of Frémont and his men. In the morning they would ride together to Agua de Tomaso. With luck, they'd gather their horse herd.

But when they arrived at Agua de Tomaso the next day, the horses were gone. Carson and Fitzpatrick had expected this would be the case. An examination of the area showed that the Indians had come to the spring, found the horses, and driven them off.

Kit Carson and Alexis Godey volunteered to pursue the raiders, and Fuentes said he would ride with them. All three were well-armed and mounted on fresh horses. They rode out of the camp at what is now called Bitter Spring. The sun was burning hot as the men moved away from the spring and vanished into the shimmering waves of heat rising from the desert.

In the evening, as the desert wind began to get cooler, a horseman approached the camp. The first watch sounded the alarm. But only one rider passed through the line and into camp. It was Andreas Fuentes, who had come back because his horse had given out. As for Carson and Godey, they were still following the tracks of the raiders.

All that night passed without any sign of Carson and Godey. In the morning, the party remained in camp waiting for the two avengers to return. The hours passed slowly, and Frémont must have wondered if two of his key men had been waylaid by the warriors they had set out to find. In the afternoon the stillness of the desert was shattered by loud war cries. Every man got ready for action as they looked beyond the camp and saw horses coming their way. But as the animals grew closer, it was obvious that the only mounted horses were the two at the rear. The others were being driven.

Fuentes recognized some of the horses as belonging to the herd he and Pablo had been guarding when the warriors had struck. Before he could say more, the attention of the men focused on Alexis Godey. He was holding his rifle high in the air. From the tip of the barrel two bloody scalps swung back and forth. The sight made Charles Preuss sick. While the companions of Carson and Godey congratulated the men on killing some of the Indians and retrieving part of the stolen horse herd, Preuss wrote in his diary that the whole affair was nothing more than disgusting butchery carried out by whites who were no better than the Indian they killed. As the story of the raid was told, Preuss was of the opinion that the Indians were braver than Kit or Alexis.

The mapmaker was by himself in his feelings about the savagery of this wanton raid. Others in the party wanted to hear all the details. This was Old Testament vengeance to them. It was the action of two against many, of good against evil, of civilization against barbarism. Carson and Godey were champions of the wilderness, and they had taken an eye for an eye and then some.

They had not stopped tracking the Indians during the night. They had followed their sign by moonlight. Then when it became too dark in the early hours before dawn, they had rested. Before sunrise, they moved on. The sun was just lighting the eastern horizon when they neared an encampment of four lodges. They moved quietly as they eased toward the sleeping Indians. When they were thirty or forty yards from the camp, either a sudden movement among the picketed ponies, a restlessness by a warrior standing watch, or maybe a slight scratching of buckskin against brush gave them away.

After that, everything happened in a blur of movement. Giving the war cry, they charged the lodges on a fast run and were met by a flight of arrows. One arrow passed through Godey's shirt collar and barely missed his neck, but he and Carson kept moving and put up a rapid volley of rifle fire. Then the arrows stopped, and there was silence from the lodges. Looking around, the men saw two warriors on the ground, a young boy trying to escape, and an old woman scrambling up the hillside.

The boy was captured and tied so that he couldn't escape. But that wasn't the end of it. Carson and Godey had not had their fill of revenge. They were too much like their foes to be satisfied with the death of two warriors. They got out their skinning knives, made neat incisions around the heads of the fallen men, put their knees on the shoulders of the warriors and with a hand full of hair tugged until the scalps plopped loose with a liquid suction sound. The violation of the bodies gave them final satisfaction, but as the avengers held their trophies in the air, one of the scalped warriors jumped to his feet. Blood streamed from his head, and he cried out in pain and shock. From the hillside the old woman looked back and screamed as the two mountain men put final bullets into him. The woman cried out again, and they could hear her sobbing and shouting threats of vengeance. They couldn't be certain, but they thought that they had killed and scalped her son.

Then they turned to the captured boy, and he looked at them like a trapped animal. When they released him, he did not run. Once he realized that he was not going to be killed, he walked over to an earthen pot and began to tear pieces from a horse's head that had been stewing all night. While the boy ate and watched them, the mountain men rounded up as many of the stolen horses as they could find, took another look around the encampment to be sure they had not overlooked any hidden warriors, and, satisfied they had taught these Indians a lesson, rode away from the scene of violence.

Carson and Godey had told their story in a matter-of-fact way. It was as though they had gone to a trading post to purchase supplies, or had returned from a hunt for camp meat. To them, what they had done had been a necessary job, and they had gone about their work in a most efficient manner. Frémont congratulated them on the success of their raid. Then he gave the order to get ready to move out in the late afternoon, as he intended to travel in the coolness of evening and night until they reached another spring.

But Charles Preuss was not able to dismiss the raid and the killing as something that had to be done. He would remember the bloody business the rest of his life. It was a ruthless, senseless slaughter. In his journal, he wrote that he thought Frémont would have tossed away all the observations, all the field notes of the expedition to have been on this raid against these desert nomads, these Indians that the lieutenant referred to as "American Arabs." Yet, terrible as the raid had been, there were no complaints from the Indians who were part of the expedition, nor from young Talbot. Preuss remained alone in his feelings about this brutal retribution.

If Preuss ever changed his mind about this raid, certainly what he saw when they reached Archilette three days later would have been the deciding factor. They had traveled over very rough country to reach the springs where the Mexicans had been attacked. Along the way they had seen the perils of the trail marked by the sun-bleached skeletons of horses and mules.

All were silent as they rode into the camp by the spring. They were greeted by silence, and the stench of death. Pablo Hernandez's father must have fought with great courage and desperation. His body

> lay in advance of the willow half-faced tent, which sheltered his family, as if he had come out to meet danger, and to repulse it from that asylum. One of his hands, and both his legs, had been cut off. Giacome, who was a large and strong-looking man, was lying on one of the willow shelters, pierced with arrows. Of the women no trace could be found, and it was evident they had been carried off captive. A little lap-dog, which had belonged to Pablo's mother, remained with the dead bodies, and was frantic with joy at seeing Pablo; he, poor child, was frantic with grief; and filled the air with lamentations for his father and mother. *Mi padre! Mi madre!*—was his incessant cry.[5]

All the men were depressed by what they found at the springs. They camped there that night only because it was a long day's journey to the next waterhole. Before they departed in the morning, Frémont wrote a brief account of what had happened at Archilette; and he placed his description in the cleft of a pole near the graves and beside the water. He then renamed this place Agua de Hernandez[6] in memory of Pablo's gallant father.

3

AFTER LEAVING THE DEATH CAMP, the men moved at a fast pace. The weather was not too warm, and in the early morning a heavy coat was comfortable. Nothing more was said about what they had found at the springs, but the memory of it haunted them. For the horses that had belonged to the Mexicans, the horses Carson and Godey had brought back after their raid, began to give out under the hard traveling across the rough and rocky plain before the easier grassland of Pahrump Valley came into view. One by one these horses dropped. Fuentes very carefully cut off their tails and manes to use in the making of saddle girths. In this land anything that might prove useful was not wasted.

Nature was a contradiction in this desert country as April ran its course and the first of May arrived. Though water was scarce to nonexistent, it was amazing to see the varied beauty of plant life. In the rocky, sandy soil cacti bloomed as though their root systems had tapped an underground river. On the many shrubs that survived the extremes of summer heat and winter cold there was a profusion of flowers in bloom. The colors varied from white to mustard yellow, brilliant blood red, and purple that carried the muted shades of late sunset. On the steep desert hills and mountains there were tall clumps of sagebrush and groves of sturdy piñon pines that appeared out of place in this harsh land.

In contrast to the multitude of wild animals that the party had seen in the Great Valley of California, the desert was almost without game unless a man knew where to look and what to expect. Long-eared jack rabbits seemed to be the largest animal around, but John Charles knew this was not true. Every night he could hear the barking and howling of coyote packs, and in the damp ground beside springs there were deer tracks, the markings of quail and larger birds, and even the tracks of a rare mountain lion. But the major food supply for the Paiutes and Utes who called this land home consisted of insects, roots, lizards, mice, and rattlesnakes. It was a tough land, and the Indians who survived in it were a tough people.

On the third of May, the men reached the present site of Las Vegas, Nevada. The weather was clear and cool. There wasn't a cloud in the sky. The temperature in the morning was two degrees below freezing; at sunset it was a comfortable sixty-seven. After traveling over ninety miles in three days, the marshy plain, called las vegas, was a welcome relief. There was plenty of grass for the tired animals, and a good supply of water. Two small streams of clear water ran four or five feet deep from two large springs. While the water was warm, varying from seventy-one to seventy-three degrees, it was good to drink if a man let it cool in a pot. But it also provided a good bath for men who were grimy with trail dust.

Leaving the springs in the early hours of the next dawn, they headed northeast toward a gap in the distant dry ridge. The five-hour ride across the basin and through the pass in the desert mountains took them from a country of wild flowers, marsh grass, and water into a region of hot yellow sand and cacti. The air was still, and the heat of day oppressive. The appearance of more horse skeletons along with Fuentes's knowledge of the trail made it clear that they were in for a dry jornada, a tough ride of fifty to sixty miles without any water.

The hot, dull hours passed slowly as the sun reached its midday peak and began its descent toward the west. The men chewed on the inner meat of cactus to keep their mouths damp, and there was very little talk as each man tried to maintain as much body liquid as possible. Hour after hour the only sounds were the muffled beat of hooves in the yellow sand, the natural noises of animals making water or dropping hot manure, and the steady squeaking of saddle leather.

Once during the long ride a mule gave out, and Alexis Godey used his skinning knife to cut off the hooves of the fallen animal just to save the horseshoes. As they moved along, as their bodies became a solid ache from too many hours in the saddle, the warmth of the day gave way to the cold of night. Men who had been sweating began to shiver. After sixteen hours of this dead land, sixteen hours of wondering if they would have enough water to last until they reached the next spring, the extra mules suddenly found a burst of energy and began to run ahead. Old hands knew what this meant. The thirsty animals had caught the scent of water on the breeze. Within two miles the sound of moving water greeted the ears of the weary men. Just ahead was the Río de los Angeles, today's Muddy River. The jornada was over. The tired men eased off their mounts and led them to water. After the animals had drunk just enough, but not too much, the riders picketed them. Then the men gathered sagebrush and mesquite for campfires and unpacked food for the long-delayed meal.

Frémont declared the next day a layover so that men and animals could rest. But in the morning, they faced a problem they hadn't counted on. Just outside the perimeter of the camp, there was a large group of Southern Paiutes. They surrounded the camp, and their attitude was contemptuous and hostile. Carson and Godey were certain these were warriors from the same band that had murdered the Mexicans, and they passed the word to be on guard for any hostile move that might be made.

To Frémont, these warriors were "wolves of the desert."

They were barefooted, and nearly naked; their hair gathered up into a knot behind; and with his bow, each man carried a quiver with thirty or forty arrows partially drawn out. Besides these, each held in his hand two or three arrows for instant service.[7]

The arrowheads were made of a hard, translucent stone that appeared to be a kind of opal. They were deadly missiles if fired from their long bows, one that could be just as fatal as any ball a rifleman might shoot.

These Southern Paiutes had always had to fight to stay alive. The harshness of their environment was only their day-by-day problem. They were always subjected to attacks by other tribes who were feuding with them or who were out to capture women and children to sell as slaves to the New Mexicans. This infamous business dated back to the first Spanish settlements north of the Río Grande.[8] No doubt they knew that men from this party had killed two of their warriors. The chief and a few of his men disregarded Frémont's command and entered his camp carrying their bows ready for instant use.

Though the men in the expedition displayed their rifles and handguns, the chief paid no heed. Instead he pointed out that the whites were few in number, while he and his warriors were many. Then, in a show of bravado, he twanged his bow string and told Frémont that if he and his men had arms, they had theirs, and there were more of them.

Carson was insulted and angry by the chief's attitude. This was not something he was about to take. In his mind, the Paiute chief didn't know his place and didn't have the right to assert himself in such a manner. Carson was on the verge of shooting the chief when Frémont halted him as the mountain man said, "Don't say that, old man, . . . don't say that—your life's in danger. . . ."9

The moments must have passed very slowly for some of the greener men of the expedition. One miscalculation by either side could have meant a bloody battle. But the tension gradually eased. Still, the Paiutes stayed around the camp. Many walked into it carrying lizards on long hooked sticks and walked over to the campfires and roasted the lizards in the hot coals. Other Paiutes stayed in the background, just outside the camp, sometimes in sight and sometimes not. But they were somewhere out there, and they were watching every movement of the white intruders. It was not a safe place to be, and the men were on their guard all through the day and night. At dusk Frémont gave a used-up horse to the Paiutes, but the warriors who carried it off even refused to share this meat with other Paiutes who were either from different bands or who were not blood relatives.

The next day the expedition moved out and hit the trail. The country was rocky in spots and made up of heavy sands in other places, and it was tough going for the animals. No game was in sight, and the only animal tracks across the sands were those made by lizards that had crawled from shelter to shelter to avoid the warm sun. But there were also the tracks of human feet which made it clear that the Paiutes were in the area.

Twenty miles over hills and heavy sands brought the men to the Virgin River a few miles below today's Riverside, Nevada. It was a dreary river, and while it was deep and rapid, it was reddish, and became drinkable only when the mud was allowed to settle to the bottom of the bucket. Grass was sparse for the horses and mules, and firewood was limited to thickets of willow, acacia, and sagebrush. The three remaining steers gave out and were killed for whatever meat remained on their gaunt skeletons. Guards were posted to watch for any possible attack as bands of Paiutes could be seen standing on the open hillsides just out of rifle range.

During the next two days the men worked their way about twenty-eight miles upriver. They had lost the regular trail, and followed a Paiute trace. By May 9 they had traveled along the Virgin River to the vicinity of present Littlefield, Arizona. They pitched camp, and Baptiste Tabeau and a strong guard of men drove the horses and mules to an area where there was enough grass for pasture. Others found a good ford in the river, and at the same time, again found the Old Spanish Trail.

The day was very warm, and in the afternoon Frémont went to sleep. He slept soundly until sundown, when the temperature became cooler. Just as he awoke, Kit Carson approached and informed him that Tabeau was missing. Though he had men with him to guard the livestock, Baptiste had gone in search of a lame mule that had wandered off. That had been some time ago, and neither Baptiste nor the mule had been seen since.

While Frémont and Carson talked of all the possibilities, a streamer of smoke appeared from a cottonwood grove where Tabeau had been headed. To Carson this smoke meant only one thing: Somewhere downstream, the Paiutes had ambushed Baptiste. The only hope he might have, and that was slim at best, was for them to get to him before the warriors had finished with him. But even though Carson and several of the best men mounted horses and set off on a hard gallop, they did not find Tabeau. They found the mule standing in the bushes, but the animal was so badly wounded it was unable to move. Baptiste's moccasin tracks and a puddle of blood were found.

That night the men listened for any sound that might mean that Baptiste was trying to ease his way by the watching warriors. Everyone was quiet, and only the occasional soft curse, the snort of a horse or mule broke the pall of gloom.

It was a restless night, and no man slept soundly. As daylight came with its first shades of blue-gray and the distant line of yellow on the eastern horizon, a search party rode out of camp. Frémont and Broken Hand were in the lead. Behind them were Carson and a few of the expedition's best frontiersmen. They moved slowly along the southern bank of the Virgin River until they reached the spot where Carson had found the pool of blood and moccasin tracks. From the amount of blood on the ground, it was doubtful that Tabeau was alive. But the men hoped he had managed to survive.

As they combed the brush beside the river, they saw blood spattered all around the leaves. And there were places where the bushes had been beaten down as though a man had fallen, struggled, and managed to get back on his feet. There was a great deal of caked, dried blood on the ground and the brush. There was so much blood that it was the opinion of the men that their friend must have been shot through the lungs. Then they found a place where he had fallen for the last time. There were two furrows in the ground —furrows that had been made by the feet and legs of a limp body as it was dragged to the riverbank. But there was no sign of the body in the river, only the marks leading to the water's edge.

The easygoing Baptiste Tabeau, who had come so far and endured so much, was gone forever. Not even his body was found so that his companions could give him a decent burial. All the men were saddened and furious. It had to be the Indians who had been so brazen in their behavior around the camp. Those were the killers. They were probably the same tribe that had killed the Mexicans. What they needed was a final and complete lesson. All the men were anxious to ride on a hunt for vengeance. But the condition of

This highly detailed lithograph shows the Hudson's Bay Company's Fort Vancouver near the Columbia River, the nearby dwellings of workers and their families, the gardens and orchards, and the traffic bound to and from the fort. (*The Bancroft Library*)

Pyramid Lake, Nevada, as sketched by Charles Preuss in the winter of 1844. Note the howitzer beside the tepee. (*The Bancroft Library*)

Near present-day Carson Pass in the Sierra Nevada during the winter of 1844. To the right is Red Lake Peak, from which Preuss and Frémont saw Lake Tahoe. (*The Bancroft Library*)

Sutter's Fort in 1847, as it looked when Frémont saw it before the American flag flew over it. (*The Bancroft Library*)

Only ten years older than Frémont, Captain John Sutter was a dynamic and handsome man when he began to build Sutter's Fort in 1840. (*The Bancroft Library*)

Edward Meyer Kern served as an artist and a mapmaker on Frémont's third and fourth expeditions. (*The Bancroft Library*)

their horses and mules was not good, and their own dwindling food supplies for the messes no longer allowed time to avenge a killing. But there was no doubt in any man's mind, not even Charles Preuss's, that if a Paiute so much as dared show himself within rifle range, he would be killed.

## 4

MILES AWAY FROM THE SCENE of Tabeau's death, the men approached a rough draw in the mountains, one that was rocky and very tough going for their sore-footed animals. As they slowly moved upward, the desert land gave way to a country of better soil, wild flowers, bunch grass, and groves of cedars, piñon pines, quaking aspens, and cottonwoods, where birds flew about from limb to limb singing their territorial songs. The whole aspect of the land was of growth and life rather than bareness and death. Then, as they climbed higher into the present Beaver Dam Mountains, the weather turned much cooler, and it felt good to wear a heavy coat once again.

That night they camped beside the clear, cold waters of the Santa Clara River, a fork of the Virgin. This was fine country to see, and the men were glad to have sweet water and plenty of grass for their mounts and pack animals. Camp was set up close to the river, and as the fires of evening were started, a cool wind rattled the leaves of the cottonwoods that grew in large groves beside the river. The hunters of the party noticed deer tracks in the damp ground near the water, and they wanted to get some fresh meat before it became too dark to shoot. But there was to be no hunting. They were much too close to the Paiutes. That night, close watches were kept around the perimeter of the camp and the picketed horses and mules.

In the early hours of dawn a heavy cloud bank rolled in on a west wind. With the clouds came the first rain the men had seen since they had left California and entered the southern rim of the Great Basin. The rain was a relief, but like most Great Basin storms, it passed quickly. The men saddled their mounts, packed their gear, and moved out before sunlight. They rode beside the Santa Clara River until they came to Magotsu Creek. Here, they changed their route and followed this north fork of the river. They moved upward toward the headwaters of the creek, and in the distance they saw rugged snow-covered peaks. Beneath this range of high mountains, they came to a beautiful meadow called "*las Vegas de Santa Clara* . . . the terminating point of the desert, and where the annual caravan from California to New Mexico halted and recruited for some weeks."[10] They were in what is now southwestern Utah, and the beautiful area they had entered was to become the infamous and bloody ground where a group of fanatic Mormons and Indians would massacre a wagon train of Missouri and Arkansas emigrants headed for the Far West in 1857.[11] But on this peaceful May 12, 1844, what was to be known as Mountain Meadows was a welcome relief after their hard desert crossing. In the twenty-seven days since Oak Creek Pass they had traversed 550 miles of some of the most inhospitable land in the American West.

The expedition camped at Mountain Meadows for a day of rest on a ridge dividing the waters that flowed south to the Colorado River and north to the Sevier River. But they were anxious to move on, to cross the Rocky Mountains and complete their long reconnaissance. Food was becoming a crucial factor. Preuss wrote that they were having to make do with flour soup and bread. They hadn't killed any game, and as long as the horses and mules could keep moving, the men needed them for transportation more than they did for meat.

In the morning they headed northeast and descended into a broad valley where the waters flowed toward Sevier Lake. The men continued through this valley and made camp at Pinto Creek, close to present-day Newcastle, Utah. A small group of horsemen overtook them. Though the men got ready for an Indian raid, the leader of the group was a man who was more than welcome. He was tall and handsome with long black hair and fine features. His long legs gave him a loose rambling gait when he got off his horse and walked up to two old friends, Kit and Broken Hand. They were glad to see this man who knew the Great Basin country better than anybody. For Joseph Walker was the best of a vanishing breed.[12] He was a mountain man's idea of what a mountain man should be, and Walker had been there and back when the trails were not known, and had survived hard going in rough places. While Frémont and Preuss were amazed to have Walker and eight companions ride out of the desert and into their camp, none of the mountain men were surprised. Carson and Fitzpatrick had known Joseph Walker for many years. Their friendship dated back to those great times when all their companions were alive and raising hell at the annual fur rendezvous. It was typical of old Joe Walker to appear out of nowhere, to have swung through the Great Basin and slipped by the Paiutes when they were like a swarm of angry hornets.

Oh, there had been some trouble. Not much, but there had been a few fights. Walker's only regret was that some of his horses had been wounded, and he wasn't sure they would make it much farther. As for the Paiutes, well, they paid a price for the trouble. Walker said he and his men had shot two of their warriors. That slowed them down some.

Walker was bound to the other side of the Rocky Mountains, and he agreed to guide Frémont's party. This came as a good streak of luck, for they were now off the Old Spanish Trail and neither Broken Hand nor Kit knew this stretch of country. With Walker's guidance, the men headed northeast toward the distant mountains. They passed by the future sites of Enoch, Cedar City, and Parowan, Utah, skirted the southern end of Little Salt Lake, passed north of the Beaver River, and met a band of Ute Indians on May 20. The Ute chief was also called Walker (or Walkara), and he spoke fluent Spanish and some English. All his warriors were armed with rifles, and they

were on their way to the Old Spanish Trail. For one of their customs was to
rob caravans that were passing along the trail. But they avoided fighting and
killing, and took a toll for the right to pass through their territory. Like pack
rats, though, they gave something in return. The chief talked to Frémont and
the mountain men, looked over their poor stores, and quickly realized he
wasn't going to get any worthwhile booty from this party. He gave Frémont a
Mexican blanket. In return John Charles gave him a Hudson's Bay blanket
which he had carried all the way from Fort Vancouver. With this exchange
the two groups parted company on friendly terms.

Three days later the expedition reached the Sevier River. It was running
eight to twelve feet of water, and after looking the area over, the men did not
find a good fording place. Rafts were constructed of bundles of bulrushes.
Ropes were attached to both ends to steady the craft and keep them from
drifting; swimmers took the bow line across while other men steadied the aft
line. The horses and mules were forced into the water, and the best
swimmers made sure that the animals got across safely.

As the men made their trips across, François Badeau reached for his rifle,
grabbed it by the muzzle and pulled it toward himself. The hammer caught
on something, pulled back, and slipped forward against the firing pin. There
was a sudden echo of rifle fire, and blood spurted from the deadly wound in
Badeau's head. The third tragedy of the desert crossing had taken place, and
Badeau was buried beside the Sevier River.

Time was taken to carve a wooden headboard for Badeau's grave, one that
was to be seen five years later by a group of Forty-Niners bound for California. But to men who had been close to the friendly, easygoing Badeau, the
fact that his gravesite would be noticed by another traveler at another time
was not something that gave them any great belief in man's immortality. To
these men of the trail, these men who put their lives on the line every day
until the reaper picked up his claim check, the death of Badeau was a piece
of bad luck.

The next day the party reached Utah Lake, where they hoped to find the
great trout making the spawning run up the Timpan-ogo River, today's Provo
River, but such was not the case. There were some Ute Indians camped near
the lake waiting for the spawning run, but the trout had not yet appeared.

In looking over Utah Lake, Frémont made a rather curious mistake and
one that was not at all like him. Even though the lake had fresh water, the
explorer believed that it was a southern arm of the Great Salt Lake. Why he
believed this remains a puzzle. Certainly Joseph Walker knew better. Yet
Frémont stated quite clearly that while Utah Lake was fresh water and the
Great Salt Lake was heavily saturated with salt, the two lakes were connected. All Frémont said about this curious connection of fresh- and salt-water
lakes was that it was a problem to be solved.

Only a few days of rest were enjoyed at Utah Lake. Then on the cloudy
and cool morning of May 27, 1844, the men broke camp and headed into the

rough country of the Wasatch Mountains. As they climbed upward, grass became plentiful, and they were back in the zone of timber and cold mountain streams that bounded and splashed over slick boulders on a downward rush to the Great Basin. As they moved toward the headwaters of the Spanish Fork, Frémont took note of the great variety of fossil shells embedded in the limestone escarpments. But very little time was taken to examine this formation. The party was too close to the journey's end, and much too short of supplies to travel at a slow pace to allow exploration of unusual formations.

Climbing higher and higher, the men crossed a high ridge at Soldier Summit. Beyond this point they forded fast-flowing creeks as well as the Strawberry and Uinta rivers, two tributaries of the Duchesne River. The country was very rough on animals and men, and it would have been much easier if they had headed due north to South Pass and the Oregon Trail. But even though they had come this far and had endured so much hardship, John Charles wanted to explore new ground, look for new passes, and observe the nature of the country.

The first day of June proved to be a tough day of travel. Though the men had covered sixteen miles by noon, they heard a roar in the distance that had the sound of trouble. Then when they reached Lake Fork, they saw why the Indians gave it a reputation for being a stream to avoid. The water shot down from the high country with an angry roar. It rolled fast and wild, spread out in some places to a width of several hundred yards, and made a terrible sound as it swept everything along on its whitecapped current. Dead timber, limbs, brush, and even large stones rolled along the riverbed like marbles or children's broken toys. There was no chance to ford this seething and boiling stretch of water. The only hope was to find a narrow enough spot where the current ran fast and deep between rock walls and build a bridge across the river. Such a place was located and the men worked hard to build a bridge that would hold both animals and men. But when they had finished, they found that even their hard labor had not produced a foolproof bridge. One of the horses became nervous as it crossed, jumped to one side, lost its footing and tumbled off. The animal gave one scream of despair and then all was quiet as the swift water pulled the horse beneath the waves and smashed its head against the rolling boulders.

Still moving northeast and working their way slowly through the mountains, the party reached the fork of the Uinta River and White Rocks Creek on the third of June. Here they were able to purchase some supplies from Antoine Robidoux,[13] who ran Uintah Fort, a trading post in this lonely region. While Robidoux did not have a great stock of goods, Frémont was able to purchase some sugar and coffee, dried meat, one cow, and a skin boat. All this cost eighty-six dollars, which was steep but was to be expected at a remote outpost.

Before the expedition moved out of the fort on June 5, François Perrault was given his discharge, probably because he planned to do some trapping in the area, and Frémont hired two other men: Auguste Archambeault, a man whom John Charles classed with Carson and Godey, and Thomas Cowie, who had been with Walker but who did not become a paid member of the party until this date.

During the next two days the men climbed higher until they saw the Green River far below. And before the seventh of June had run its course, they dropped into Brown's Hole or today's Brown's Park of northwestern Colorado and northeastern Utah. Here they took time to make repairs on the skin boat, and the next day they were across the Green River. They passed by the remains of Fort Davy Crockett,[14] and worked their way to a sheltered little valley that had been a favorite camping ground for fur trappers during the winter months. They managed to catch a flock of mountain sheep off guard, and the hunters killed several for fresh camp meat.

The next three days was all up-and-down country. From Brown's Park, they moved up Vermilion Creek and on to the Little Snake, and on June 11 camp was pitched beside St. Vrain's Fork or today's Battle Creek. Three antelopes were shot, and as the men roasted the meat, Carson told them about a battle he had fought with Indians in this area. For this was country that saw the movement of various tribes ranging from Utes to Plains Indians.

On the following day a familiar and welcome sight greeted the men. Once again, after all the months and the great distances, there were buffalo in sight. Plenty of antelope, elk, and deer insured good hunting. But other signs indicated other hunters. Tracks of Indians in the vicinity made it necessary to be on guard and to make camp in a small aspen grove where it was possible to fort up in case raiders should spot them.

Working their way up and down, crossing and recrossing the Continental Divide, the men dropped into the buffalo country not far from South Pass and the Oregon Trail. But John Charles was anxious to explore the headwaters of the Platte, Arkansas, and Colorado rivers. Between June 12 and 17, the men traveled through North Park just below the Wyoming line and entered Middle Park, where they camped beside Muddy Creek, a tributary of the Colorado River. In the lower areas near the headwaters of the Platte River, they killed enough buffalo to hold them over as they climbed nine thousand feet above sea level and then dropped into Middle Park.

The country they were passing through was one of small broken hills surrounded by towering peaks. On the lower reaches of these great ranges were good stands of pine and quaking aspen. And while their camp was peaceful that night, the morning brought the possibility of trouble. A small party of Arapahoes stopped to talk and said that their main camp was only a few miles away. Then, as they rode away, Frémont and his men rode into the bottoms and picked out a good defensive position in case there should happen to be a war party on the move.

There was just enough time to build a rough fort, and preparations were just completed when the Indians appeared. There were more than they had expected. At least two hundred warriors, all painted and armed for battle, rode into sight.

> We planted the American flag between us and a short parley ended in a truce, with something more than the usual amount of presents. About twenty Sioux were with them—one an old chief, who had always been friendly to the whites. He informed me that, before coming down, a council had been held at the village, in which the greater part had declared for attacking us . . . but his own party, with some few of the Arapahoes who had seen us the previous year in the plains, opposed it.[15]

After a talk and the passing out of gifts, Frémont and his men were invited to come to their village. There, the Arapahoes said, was the only good ford. They could camp overnight, cross the river in the morning, and head on their way. While they were wrong about the good river crossing, Frémont really had no choice other than to go to their village. To have done otherwise would have been an open insult. When they reached the village, they camped away from the tepees, and made sure there were several sloughs between them and the Indians. They fortified their position and took all possible precautions. Still, some of the braves slipped past their watch during the night and stole a number of things from the baggage.

To put some distance between themselves and their hosts, the expedition left at daybreak. They followed the Colorado River through Middle Park for eight miles until the river became a wide and deep stream. Skin boats were quickly made, and the baggage was ferried across to the Blue River, a fork of the Colorado. From there the men began an upward climb into the mountains as they moved southeast toward Bayou Salade, or South Park.

During the next two days, men and animals worked their way along a piney ridge of mountains and climbed toward the bare peaks above where they hoped to find a crossing. As they moved into this alpine region, Frémont's memory of what it was like was not at all clear. His description of this region in his report indicates that, once again, he was having trouble with high-altitude sickness. For as the party reached what is now called Hoosier Pass on June 22, they were 11,541 feet above sea level. Once across this pass, they dropped toward South Peak and followed the Middle Fork of the South Platte River as they entered the watershed of the Arkansas River.

More Indians were encountered as the party moved along. But there were enough men and guns to discourage any attack. Yet there was always the chance of a careless man falling victim to a sudden ambush, and all the men were nervous about their situation. The Arapahoes were sending small war parties throughout the area because they had heard there were some Utes in South Park. If they had no luck raiding a Ute camp, they might be tempted to attack the whites or to ease into their camp at night to pick off a man or two. The reality of this became very clear when the expedition met a small party of trappers who had lost two of their friends just a few days before.

Bayou Salade was hardly a safe place. Indians appeared to be all over the country, and young warriors were out to count coup on somebody. Even as this threat was considered, a party of Arapahoes surrounded Carson and some of the other hunters. Carson talked easily to them, and while they caused him no trouble, they informed him that their scouts had discovered a large village of Utes in Bayou Salade and that every fit warrior was on his way to attack these intruders from the desert.

This seemed to put the expedition in the clear, and they moved ahead and set up camp beside the Middle Fork of the South Platte River in a mountain meadow. Then on the morning of June 23 they headed downhill toward the valley. As they traveled along, they set a good pace. Everyone thought that the toughest part of the trip was over, and now they were in a hurry to get to Bent's Fort and strike the trail for home. But at noon, a large party of mounted Indians appeared in sight on the point of a spur that descended into the valley. There was no thought about whether or not these were friends or foes. All the men saw that there was a very large group. It would be wise to get ready for trouble. Each man knew what had to be done, and the expedition selected the only strong defensive post available. This was a covering of willows on some islands in the river. Without hesitation, horses and mules were spurred, whipped, and driven into the water, and a temporary barricade of baggage was quickly set up.

But the rush to get into a good position for battle proved to be unnecessary. The cavalcade was a party of Ute women and children. Walker told Frémont that they had been camped on the other side of the ridge when the Arapahoes attacked, and that men were fighting. Then "they filled the air with cries and lamentations, which made us understand that some of their chiefs had been killed."[16]

The women asked Frémont and his men to join their people to ride back with them and help defeat the Arapahoes. It was not something he nor his men wished to enter into. If they had, word would have spread that they had taken a definite stand for one tribe against another. This would be bad for any future expeditions or pioneers who might return to this region. The feud between these two tribes was a very ancient one. No doubt, neither side knew how it had originally started. Any intervention on the part of the whites could only mean future trouble with the Arapahoes and their allies. Quite wisely, Frémont prevented his men from entering the contest.

Still, the scene which he saw from the ridge above the furious battle was something he never forgot. It might well have been a clash between opposing knights as "horsemen were galloping to and fro, and groups of people were gathered about those who were wounded and dead, and who were being brought in from the field."[17]

Once they were beyond the conflict, the party moved quickly. The next day Pikes Peak was in plain view, and it was like seeing an old friend. There were more days of hard traveling as they dropped out of the last of the high country and crossed the lower foothills. Then on June 29, in the late afternoon just before sunset, they reached Jim Beckwourth's small settlement of Pueblo near the mouth of Fontaine-qui-bouit River. Here they met some old friends, and that night they exchanged news of the wilderness and of men who had "cashed in their chips" and heard of the latest stories from the States that had been picked up from Santa Fé traders. Two more days and seventy miles and Bent's Fort would come into view. From there, they were as good as home.

5

ON THE PLAINS the hot winds of summer had yellowed the bunch grass, dried the small creeks, and cracked the hardened mud in old buffalo wallows. The men and their horses moved along the road beside the Arkansas River and were thankful for the shade the trees offered. Then, as they headed away from the river and squinted in the bright glare of sunlight, the steady hoofbeat of their animals was shattered by loud explosions. Horses and mules skittered and jumped. Riders were almost thrown, and Frémont wondered what had happened. But Kit and Joe Walker knew. Hell, it was a welcome home! And to Kit what he saw ahead was a good sight, a familiar place that was his second home when he wasn't in Taos.

There in the distance, standing in the open like a lost pueblo, was the adobe stronghold called Bent's Fort. From the round towers at the southeast and northwest angles of this rectangular post, puffs of white smoke rolled out of portholes like small thunderheads, and they were followed by a swishing in the air and the echoing sound of cannon fire. Then there was the ringing of a large iron bell that hung from the belfry of the watchtower above the thick-planked entry gate. Atop the belfry, the scorching summer wind whipped the oversized American flag back and forth in a dance of color that threatened to snap the ash flagpole.

Though he had heard all about it from Carson and others, this was Frémont's first view of Bent's Fort. And the size of it amazed him. The Bent brothers had not gone about things in a small manner when they had decided that this was the proper location for their post—one that would give them an advantage in dealing with Indians, fur trappers, and Santa Fé traders.

Charles Bent, the oldest brother, had sketched the plan for the adobe fort, for he had been the head of the clan since the death of his father. But it had been William Bent and Ceran St. Vrain who stepped off the lines of the structure and measured everything with a compass. What the expedition saw ahead was a fort of immense proportions. Facing eastward in the direction of the trail that saw a steady flow of freighter caravans bound for Santa Fé was the front wall. It was "137 feet long, fourteen feet high, and three or more feet thick. The northern and southern walls, of the same height and thickness, were 178 feet long. At the southeast and northwest corners rose round towers eighteen feet tall. Equipped with musketry and small fieldpieces these towers enabled the defenders to sweep with fire all four walls in event of any attempt to storm the fortress."[18] Behind the large western wall and adjoining it was a corral that was almost as large as the fort. While the corral walls were only six to eight feet tall, they did not present an easy climb for potential raiders as the broad tops were covered with a thick growth of cactus.

After all the weeks and months of riding across vast stretches of the American West, weary days and nights of trying to fill in blank spaces on maps that listed unexplored regions as the Great American Desert, the view of this establishment, this citadel of commerce on the north bank of the Arkansas River was more than arriving at another fort. This meant the wilderness was behind them. Even St. Louis was little more than thirty days away. Frémont and his weary men fired rifles and pistols into the air, shouted for joy, and coaxed their tired mounts into a trot then a gallop as they moved closer to the waving, shouting men standing beside a brass cannon outside the main gate.

Greetings were exchanged with thirty-year-old George Bent and the others even as the party slid their horses to a halt in a cloud of dust. The men dismounted, shook hands all around, and walked through the open gate. Inside they felt a sudden coolness in a tunnel between the thick walls of the warerooms that were wicketed for trade with the Indians. Then they passed through the open inner gate and into the placita. No doubt the famous black cook Charlotte Green, who claimed she was the only lady in the whole Indian country, was busy preparing dinner for the officials of the fort and any special company that might happen to arrive.

The brass cannon was pulled inside the main gate and rolled back into the breezeway as Frémont had his first view of this establishment. The place was large enough to house two hundred men, and the corrals could hold at least three or four hundred animals. There were ground-floor apartments, some second-story rooms, warehouses for goods, a main kitchen, central dining hall, blacksmith shop, carpenter shop, tailor's shop—where a French tailor from New Orleans did his best with the materials at hand—and a huge press for packing buffalo hides into bale-like bundles. Milk cows, turkeys, chickens, and even peacocks added to the fort's self-containment. There was a well of excellent water, but it tended to run low during the dry seasons, and extra water had to be brought in barrels from the Arkansas River. The biggest shortage the men faced was enough vegetables to offset a steady diet of meat. Attempts to plant crops proved to be unsuccessful in the hard soil around the fort, but Mexican traders brought corn meal and dried vegetables into the fort to trade for other goods.

To the amazement of first-time visitors at Bent's Fort, there were caged wild birds of the region scattered about: mockingbirds, magpies, and even bald eagles. Added to their color were the beautiful spreading tail feathers of peacocks, and the sharp cries of these birds never ceased to astound Indians who came to the fort to trade.

But not only caged birds gave color to this crossroads in the southwestern wilderness. There were times when Cheyennes and other Plains Indians were invited inside the placita to sing and dance in celebration of a victory over one of their foes, or to dance because Misstanstar, or Owl Woman, William Bent's Cheyenne wife, became homesick for the traditions of her people. Along with the Indians there was the open society of mountain men who came to drink, to watch a dance, or even to dance themselves in celebration of being alive for another trapping season. These men came from all the nationalities that made up frontier America. French-Canadians, métis who were more Indian than French, Mexicans from Taos or Santa Fé, a stray Irishman or German who had drifted beyond the Mississippi and found the free and wild life to his liking, black Jim Beckwourth, whose tales were only as strange and colorful as his life, Black Dick Green, who came West as Charles Bent's slave and was given his freedom for bravery but gained greater fame through the wondrous culinary talent of his wife, Charlotte, who was as famous for her dancing as she was for her cooking. Like the free and wondrous mixture of people who gathered around Sutter's Fort in Alta California, the regulars, the drifting visitors, and the men in need, all found their way to Bent's Fort. For the fort was in the right place at the right time. It was open for business, pleasure, or war; and it was prepared for any of the three or a combination of all of them.

And that night, July 1, 1844, Frémont and his men were entertained in royal fashion. A white tablecloth was spread on the dining table, and the aroma of Charlotte's cooking was enough to make a man sell whatever the Devil might require to have such a cook along on an expedition. Her bread, her pies, the things she could do with chickens or a turkey or two, the different flavor that buffalo meat took on with the right seasoning, and vegetables put together in a casserole that had the right touch of chili and wild oregano were enough to make any wilderness man wonder if he'd had anything to eat in the past months or if he'd been getting on by imagination.

But even before the meal, George Bent served what was called "hailstorms," a house specialty. Ice was brought from the ice house; wild mint came from upstream where there was enough shade and dampness, and the whiskey was a touch better than Taos lightning. Be damned, not rotgut, not aguardiente straight out of the jug, not at all, this was a mint julep, a gentleman's drink to warm a man's heart and ease his sore body. And if after dinner a man felt up to it, if he could handle a cue, above the headquarters in a second-story room there was "a billiard table hauled clear from Missouri, and chairs and a table or two, a short but hospitable bar and shelved jugs and decanters and glasses."[19]

The first evening off the trail, the first night at Bent's Fort was not something a man would ever forget. After the drinks and the dinner, there was

talk. Talk of where they had been and what they had seen. Talk of men long
dead and bones scattered somewhere in the wilderness. Talk of bad times,
good times, and the sheer joy of living long enough to cross another ridge,
find another stretch of unspoiled land, another beaver stream where a man
might plant his float stick and come up with a rich, thick pelt.

That night there was no need to stand guard duty. There was a good bed
waiting. But before that, there was another drink before saying goodnight, a
smoke beside the fireplace, and a last yarn before stepping into the night air
and breathing deeply as the moonlight outlined the Spanish Peaks to the
southwest and Pikes Peak to the northwest.

Three more days and nights were a time of rest, a time of enjoying
Charlotte Green's excellent cuisine, a time of letting go and enjoying what
was really a vacation. Only Charles Preuss was unhappy. To him, Bent's Fort
was a dreary place where swarms of mosquitoes feasted upon his blood. But it
wasn't only the mosquitoes. Scorching days with the temperature over one
hundred degrees, and a hot wind made Preuss anxious to keep moving. He
wanted to complete the long journey and get back to the company of
gentlemen again. He had hardly been able to tolerate the company of half-
civilized mountain men and voyageurs when it was vital to have them along,
but he had reached the end of his patience with such wild men. Frémont
might admire them. Well, that was all right for a foolish and romantic lieutenant. But Preuss had seen all of these barbaric creatures that he wished to
see. As for the fort, it was just another collection of primitive mud buildings.
The food was good. There was no getting around that, but the idea of a
white tablecloth on a rough wooden table, the pretension that somehow a
mint julep and a little service in such an atmosphere gave the place stature
was more than Preuss was willing to admit. Better liquor, far better food, he
was willing to grant this to anyone, but none of this changed the surroundings or the company. All of it was a bare notch above the Indians and their
half-cooked meat, their naked children, and the constant picking of lice. As
for George Bent's gracious hospitality, the grousing mapmaker simply ignored
it and assumed that anything he was getting was his by right of his station
in life.

But what Preuss thought didn't change the plan to stay until after the
Fourth of July. John Charles thoroughly enjoyed himself at Bent's Fort, and
he looked forward to the feast that Charlotte would serve on Independence
Day. And he was not disappointed. The table almost sagged with the best
that the fort had to offer. Fresh vegetables were even brought to the kitchen
from a few gardens at the settlement of Pueblo. There was plenty of buffalo
meat, a roast beef, turkeys, chickens, plenty of "hailstorms," good coffee with
fresh milk, fresh pies and cakes, and then cigars and aguardiente as the
Cheyenne dancers chanted and circled around the placita, as mountain men
let out wild yells, and as black Charlotte and her friend the half-breed
Rosalie whirled about in an American backwoods dance that was as free as

the day being celebrated. Added to all this was the firing of cannons, three cheers for the Yankees and to hell with the British, and another round of drinks to toast the glorious Fourth of July as a long-bearded fiddler stomped his foot and started another dance.

In the morning Frémont and his men thanked George Bent for his hospitality and the new life his bountiful table had put into their tired bodies. Kit Carson and Joseph Walker bid good-bye to Frémont and the others as they took their pay and headed out for Taos, where Carson's wife, Josefa, waited for him. And Kit was on his way home with a good stake, as his wages plus his mule and horse brought him a total of $1,025. Joe Walker picked up $165 for the short stint that he had served as a guide. Two other men, Charles Town and Louis Anderson, had already left the expedition at Pueblo. But all the rest pulled out of the main gate at Bent's Fort and struck the wagon road eastward along the Arkansas River.

There had been a warm, muggy shower on the Fourth of July night, but it had served to ease the midday heat. The men rode in more comfort than they had figured, but they had many miles before them when the days and even the nights would be hot; so it was enjoy whatever cool breeze might happen to drift down from the high peaks and cut into the glare of sunshine and treeless plains. During the first day away from Bent's Fort they encountered a large band of Sioux, Cheyennes, and Arapahoes who were returning from a raid against the Kiowas and Comanches. On their return they had wiped out a party of fifteen Delawares, and they asked Frémont to tell the Delawares that they wished no more trouble. He agreed to deliver their message of peace. Because the war party had lost some of their own warriors in the fight, they did not detain the expedition. To the lieutenant, the scene of this large band moving along was a colorful affair. "Dispersed over the plain in scattered bodies of horsemen, and family groups of women and children, with dog trains carrying baggage, and long lines of pack horses, their appearance was picturesque and imposing."[20]

One more day of following the Arkansas River brought the expedition to where it headed northeast toward the Smoky Hill Fork of the Kansas River. Within a few more days, they were back in the range of the great buffalo herds, and fresh meat was easily available. Summer storms broke the oppressive heat, but the heavy thunderstorms also caused the rivers to run over the banks. It was no longer a good idea to camp in the river bottoms, as a flash flood might occur just as the camp had bedded down for the night.

On July 17 trouble with the Pawnees at Big Timber Creek, near the present Ellis-Rush County line in Kansas, almost resulted in a battle. Only two things prevented a fight by the sullen Pawnees: Frémont gave them as much of his supplies as he could spare, and—as he learned later—the intervention of the Pawnee Loups prevented an attack the Pawnees planned to carry out.

Still, trouble was not behind them. They crossed one small creek after another, and sometimes these creeks were running deep with muddy water from a heavy cloudburst. In crossing one of these streams, Alexis Ayot accidentally caught the hammer of his rifle. The shot startled all the men and the animals, and Alexis—one of Frémont's best young men—was badly wounded in the leg. It was ironic after all Alexis had been through, but it was an accident common to the trail. The rifle had to be loaded in case it was needed in a hurry, but a loaded rifle was always a potential killer or crippler. All it took was a foolish mistake, a slight misjudgment, or something as unforeseen as a quick snap of brush to pull the hammer back and let it go.

Onward they moved, and they followed the Kansas River to where it heads northwest to join the Republican River. Then another twenty miles brought them to the Santa Fé Trail. From here on, the going was fast and easy. They made excellent time, and by the last day of July they were again camped beside the Missouri River in the frontier town of Kansas. Here they would take a steamboat downriver to St. Louis to come full circle.

Fourteen long months they had been in the wilderness, fourteen months beyond the jumping-off points along the Mississippi and Missouri rivers. Still, Frémont was not satisfied. There was much more to do, much more to see, to map, to examine, and in anticipation of heading another expedition, he did not sell his horses and mules. Instead, he put them out to pasture at Kansas to rest and to gain weight and strength for another journey toward the West.

Andreas Fuentes and the boy Pablo Hernandez were going on to St. Louis with him, and so, too, was the Chinook boy who had come all the way from The Dalles. The grand reconnaissance was over, and now Frémont had to think about what he had seen, examine his notes, take a close look at measurements, at sketches, at rough drafts of maps. For they had traveled Senator Benton's "road to India," and they had seen more of the American West than even Lewis and Clark.

# XIII

## Odyssey's End

MIDNIGHT, AUGUST 6, 1844. Frémont saw the dark outline of St. Louis from the deck of the steamboat. The buildings of the city were shadows in the warm, humid night. Slowly the boat chugged toward the levee. In the darkness the levee and dock were marked by lanterns to guide incoming traffic. Lanterns also indicated the position of moored scows, large cargo rafts, and other steamboats.

As the boat carrying the expedition and all its gear drew closer to the wharves, steam hissed in a rush from escape valves. Paddlewheel blades struggled against the current as the engine was put into reverse to back water and slow the speed. Sleepy dock workers came to life. Mooring lines were tossed from the steamboat, then the vessel was slowly eased into the docking position. When all was secure, the stageplank was lowered with a rumbling sound and locked into place.

Before John Charles went ashore, he made arrangements for the handling of the expedition's gear and saw to it that his men could sleep aboard the boat. It was two o'clock in the morning when he stepped onto the wharf. At that hour there were no carriages waiting to pick up incoming passengers. Except for dock hands and the steamboat crew, St. Louis was asleep. No matter. Frémont was in a hurry to get to the Benton home. He started on his way, setting a good pace. He knew that his uniform was wrinkled and worn, but he hoped to ease into the house and wash the trail dust off his body before Jessie saw him. The way he looked, she might think he was a beggar, an old army man down on his luck and reduced to a low station in life. For he was arriving home as an American Odysseus. After fourteen months in the wilderness, he walked quickly through the darkened streets of the business district, the French quarter, and then, there it was, the familiar façade of the Benton home.

He moved past the house and stopped outside the carriage house. There was no light in Old Gabriel's room on the second floor, but John Charles picked up a handful of gravel and threw it against the darkened window. He waited for a few minutes, and then he heard movement and saw the light of a lamp come close to the window. The sash slid, and through the opening he heard Old Gabriel's familiar voice asking him who he was and what he thought he was doing at such an hour. When he replied, there was a moment of silence. Wondering if the old man were going to answer at all, he told him who he was again, and asked if he would be so kind as to let him in.

Old Gabriel was very slow in answering, as though he thought he were talking to a ghost, but finally, he said, "Yes, I can let you in, but Miss Jessie is at Miss Anne's. Her husband is dying, maybe."[1]

That was all Old Gabriel had to say. Frémont saw his gray hair and black face outlined by the lamp for only a few minutes more. Then the window was shut, and the lamp went out. There wasn't any sound of footsteps on the stairs, and it was obvious he wasn't going to be allowed inside.

Not wishing to disturb the main house at this hour for fear his appearance would be too much of a shock; and realizing that the Reverend Potts, cousin Anne's husband, was suffering from tuberculosis, and that anything out of the ordinary might bring on a fatal hemorrhage, Frémont turned and walked back to the center of the city. He sat on a bench in front of the Barnes Hotel, relaxed in the summer night, and watched the stars grow pale as the first dim light of the rising sun became the line of light marking the eastern horizon. As he leaned back on the bench, he began to feel sleepy and caught himself nodding. Then one of the hotel's employees came outside, his lantern in one hand, and approached the bench. As he drew closer, he recognized the lieutenant and almost dropped his lantern.

"Great Scott! Mr. Frémont," he said. "Is that you? I thought you were far away—out west. What in Heaven's name are you doing here? Are you ill?"[2]

He assured the clerk he was perfectly all right, that he had just arrived aboard a steamboat coming downriver, and that he had not wished to disturb the family at such an early hour.

The clerk appeared to half-listen to what was being said, and when Frémont stopped, the man insisted he had to come into the hotel. There were empty rooms, plenty of beds. It just wouldn't do for Lieutenant Frémont to sit on a bench at this hour before dawn. His employer would never forgive him, not in his lifetime, if he heard he had allowed the lieutenant to sit on a hard bench in the darkness.

John Charles was touched by the man's concern. But after all he had endured, the idea of sitting on a bench was not what he considered a hardship. He thanked the clerk and told him he would wait where he was until daylight.

The clerk would not accept this decision. He insisted it was his duty to provide a room. The more the man carried on, the more Frémont thought of resting on a comfortable bed for a change. Finally he accepted the invitation and followed him into the hotel.

Once he had been given a room, he was glad he had allowed himself to be persuaded. As he looked at the waiting bed, all the weary hours, days, and weeks, caught up to him with a rush. He never even bothered to remove his clothes. He simply stretched out on the bed to rest before daylight. Later, he would take a bath, shave, and be able to greet his Jessie without the dust of the trail on him. He would be wide awake when he saw her again, and he would marvel as the glow of the morning sun captured the rare beauty of her delicate features. But for now, just for a short while, he would enjoy the luxury of sleeping on a good bed.

2

THE MONTHS had been long for Jessie, much longer than she had expected. And the waiting had grown very hard. Close friends had died, friends John Charles would miss for the rest of his life. In September of 1843 Joseph Nicollet had died in his sleep, all alone in a Washington hotel room. Later that year Ferdinand Hassler and Senator Lewis Linn died. All during this time of sorrow, there had been only one indirect message about John Charles. This had reached Senator Benton in Washington, and it brought news of Frémont's arrival at the lower reaches of the Columbia River. One message, and that was no more than the passing of a word. All the time, Jessie had to take care of her ailing mother, baby Lily, and try to keep her mind on other things.

Senator Benton became worried about Jessie when he saw her during the Christmas holiday in 1843. She was losing weight, and her spirit was low. Then as 1844 arrived without any letter or any rumor about her husband, Jessie became convinced John Charles had already started on his return journey, that perhaps he was coming through the Southwest to avoid the heavy snow and the terrible cold.

In February she decided he would be home at any moment. One day she would look out the window, and she would see him striding toward the family home. Convinced of this, she began to prepare for his arrival. Each day she made sure that she took time to fashion new clothes for Lily and herself. Then in the evenings she studied Spanish. "By March her house was in order, the new wardrobes ready. Each night a table was set for Frémont's supper and a bed made for him. Fresh wood was piled near the fireplace, and a lamp set in the window to burn till morning."[3] But the mornings would begin without any sign of John Charles, and with only worry and disappointment for Jessie.

In March word came from Washington of the disaster aboard the steam sloop U.S.S. *Princeton,* the pride of the U. S. Navy and the special pride of Captain Robert F. Stockton, who had seen to it that his ship was outfitted with a large cannon he called the Peacemaker, a mighty weapon that used fifty pounds of gunpowder to fire a 225-pound shot over a two-mile trajectory.

Captain Stockton had taken a holiday crowd of Washington's most important people for a cruise on the Potomac River. Even President Tyler had been aboard for this junket. Trying his best to impress everybody, Captain Stockton decided to demonstrate the power of the Peacemaker. But with a great blast the mighty cannon blew all apart. In the midst of its explosion, it killed and wounded many of the prominent guests, including the Secretary of State and the Secretary of the Navy. Senator Benton, who had seen his share of action on the frontier, was knocked flat by the concussion and thought he had been wounded until he realized he was one of the lucky passengers.

This near loss of her father momentarily took Jessie's mind off the whereabouts of her explorer husband. But once she was over the shock of this national disaster, she retreated to her daily concern about John Charles. When her father returned to St. Louis for the summer of 1844, he was startled by Jessie's appearance. Not the family relatives—the Brants and the Pottses—not the reassurances of the Chouteaus, not even the company of the vital and fiery members of the Blair family was enough to help Jessie in this time of waiting and wondering.

Through June and July Jessie continued to lose weight. Her mind was always preoccupied, and each night she kept her vigil. A place was set for John Charles. The lamp was lit, and she slept fitfully as each sound of a person passing by in the night made her wonder if her husband could be returning home. Then on the evening of August 6, the night Frémont finally arrived at the St. Louis waterfront, "just as she had arranged the table and lamp, word came that her Cousin Anne's husband . . . was thought to be dying."[4] Jessie rallied to her cousin's aid. Out went the lamp, and Old Gabriel got the coach ready. In a short time she stepped out of the coach and entered her cousin's home. Here she sat beside the very sick man until the first light of day. Then she retired for an hour or two of rest.

While Jessie slept at her cousin's and John Charles slept at the Barnes Hotel, Old Gabriel came into the Benton home as soon as he saw that Senator and Mrs. Benton were up. He reported his experience during the night as though he were talking about some apparition that had appeared outside his window. It looked like Lieutenant Frémont, and it had been in an army uniform; but if it really had been the lieutenant, he looked as thin as a shadow.

Senator Benton was dubious about what Old Gabriel told him, but he thanked him for the information. When the coachman was out of the room, though, the senator expressed his doubts to Mrs. Benton. Perhaps Gabriel had imagined it or had dreamed about Frémont, or there was the possibility that the old coachman had been drinking some corn whiskey earlier in the night. Yet, and the senator had to admit this to his wife, there was the possibility that Old Gabriel had seen exactly what he had described. He had always been dependable. Why not trust him now, especially with such important news? No, the senator decided, there wasn't a good reason to disbelieve

Old Gabriel. Having decided that, he went to the coachman's quarters and asked him to drive to the Potts home and inform Jessie that he had seen and spoken to Lieutenant Frémont.

At the parsonage, Old Gabriel stammered as he tried to tell Jessie what he had seen. She was excited and pressed him for more details. She wanted to know exactly how her husband had looked, what he had said, and where he had gone. Old Gabriel tried to remember everything, and he began once again when there was a knock at the door. The old coachman opened the door, and there was a gasp from Jessie as John Charles entered the hallway. Jessie was half-crying, half-laughing with joy as she ran to his open arms. Then as John Charles told of his arrival, of his brief rest at the Barnes Hotel, and of the people he had met on the way to the parsonage, there was another knock on the door. In no time at all, the house was thronged with visitors and well-wishers. The Blairs and other friends and prominent citizens stopped by to welcome the explorer, and an impromptu gathering was held before John Charles and Jessie had time to eat breakfast and be alone.

But that night was another matter. Rested and refreshed, John Charles sat beside Jessie at the family dinner table. He recounted the story of his grand reconnaissance, trying to give her the thrilling details and the color that she longed to hear, and answering the senator's questions about the country and the future it offered to American expansion.

This was a grand first night home, one he had longed to have for all the many months. Yet Jessie's delicate and fragile appearance alarmed him. Her beauty was greater than he remembered, but there was a paleness that worried him, a paleness and a lack of strength that he had never seen before. Lily, though, was a bundle of love, a child who was delighted to see her father. Senator Benton, too, was as robust as ever even though one eardrum had been shattered when the Peacemaker blew apart on the fatal cruise of the *Princeton*. But one look at Mrs. Benton showed she was a very ill woman, and that much of Jessie's strength had been sapped in caring for her.

To Jessie, her husband was as handsome as ever. Despite the hardships he had endured, he was tanned by the wind and sun and was lean and strong. She was certain that when their friends saw him, more than one woman would be enchanted by this fine-looking man, this explorer whose adventures were right out of a James Fenimore Cooper novel.

While preparations were made for the family's return to Washington, Jessie and John Charles were caught up in a constant round of receptions. It seemed that all the citizens of St. Louis wished "to do honor to the returned explorer and to hear his stories."[5] While Jessie worried that all this would tire her husband, he felt the same about her.

Away from the glitter of these parties there were moments of just being together, moments when John Charles bounced baby Lily on his knee as though she were riding a horse. There were introspective times when he thought of the friends he would no longer see. Most of all, it was Nicollet who haunted his memory. Of the men he had known, it had been the brilliant, patient, kindly Nicollet who had taught him so much about so many things; and it had been the sickly Nicollet who had stood behind their courtship and marriage when Mrs. Benton staunchly disapproved. Not that John Charles hadn't seen men die, not that he didn't know that each man would reach his end sometime; what bothered him was that Nicollet had died alone in a hotel room. After all the man had endured in his travels, to die that way didn't have any sense of justice. John Charles felt "it would have been a fitter end for him to have died under the open sky, and be buried, rolled up in a blanket, by the side of some stream in the mountains. . . ."[6]

Senator Benton traveled ahead of the family to Washington, while Frémont saw to all the final details in St. Louis. He was responsible for his men, and he made sure they were provided for until his return in the spring. He helped Andreas Fuentes secure employment. The other survivor of the Old Spanish Trail tragedy, Pablo Hernandez, became a favorite in the Benton household, and he was going to Washington with the family. William Perkins, the Chinook boy from The Dalles, was also going with them. The two California Indian boys, Juan and Gregorio, were sent to Senator Benton's farm in Lexington, Kentucky; and Frémont put them in charge of his horse Sacramento, which had been given to him by Captain Sutter.

As he took care of these last responsibilities, Jessie was in charge of packing. Her days and evenings were hectic as she directed servants in the folding of clothes, the careful filling of suitcases and trunks, and the gathering of all the other items that might be needed in the Washington home. Along with this, she also had to watch over her mother and baby Lily.

Once Frémont was certain everything was ready, he purchased stagecoach tickets for the ride to Washington. Finally the day of departure arrived. Mrs. Benton was aided in boarding the coach, and she was followed by Jessie, Lily, Pablo, William, and John Charles. When they were all aboard, they waved farewell to their St. Louis friends. Then the driver cracked his whip. With a swaying and rocking motion, the stagecoach rattled across the cobblestone streets. To the sound of horses' hooves clattering on stone, the shouts of the driver, the snap of his whip, and the creaking of well-worn wood against thick leather thoroughbraces, the Frémonts began their long ride to Washington.

## 3

BEFORE ANYTHING ELSE, there was the observance of protocol. Frémont already had a measure of acclaim as a result of the 1842 expedition. But word had spread throughout Washington that the young officer's latest expedition was the greatest American adventure since that of Lewis and Clark. Men in high places wished to talk to him, and Senator Benton proudly accompanied his son-in-law as he reported to General Scott and Secretary of War Wilkins.

The Secretary of War was impressed with Frémont's lucid answers to the many questions he asked him about his explorations in the West. Still, he was astounded by the lieutenant's youth, which he said was a good failing in that the young never see the obstacles. The observations of Secretary Wilkins were astute.

There was one duty which Frémont always found difficult and hated to consider. This was the squaring of accounts, the justification of expenses for this or that so Colonel Abert of the Topographical Corps would have something on paper that he could explain to the examiners of his department's accounts and budget. Once Frémont had satisfied such red-tape requirements, he would be ready to take on the most difficult tasks in good spirit and with a high degree of optimism.

And tasks were before him that would have made most young officers decide upon another career. But John Charles loved his work and was anxious to get back to it. There was much to do before he could plan his next expedition. The *Report* had to be written. The nature of the geological formations and the descriptions of organic remains had to be done, and for this he was to have the services of Professor James Hall, paleontologist to the State of New York. Classifications of the species of plants he had brought back was another phase of his work, and for this he was to have the aid of Professor John Torrey. The calculation of the astronomical positions Frémont had made during the journey had to be checked, and he was to work with Professor Joseph C. Hubbard in completing this. Finally, there was the monumental job of preparing the final versions of the maps, a job which Charles Preuss looked upon as congenial labor.

While all these tasks had to be completed in time for Frémont to be on his way to St. Louis and the Far West in the spring, he took time to see to the welfare of his two young charges, William Perkins and Pablo Hernandez.

Pablo was to remain in the Benton home, and though General Almonte, the Mexican minister, offered to send the boy to Mexico, Pablo decided to remain in Washington and attend school. As for William, the Chinook, he stayed in Washington for a few months. Then he went to Philadelphia to spend the winter with a Quaker family who had the time to help the boy gain some fluency in the English language. Seeing to it that both boys received an opportunity for some education was a pleasant obligation for Frémont, one he hoped would open new worlds for these frontier youngsters.

In the fall a problem of another nature confronted him, and this was something that upset him considerably. Alexis Ayot, weakened and hardly able to hold himself up on his crutches, appeared in Washington. He came to the lieutenant and presented a letter from Rudolph Bircher of St. Louis, a man who advertised himself as a hairdresser and barber with capability in cupping and leeching. In the letter, Bircher described his attempt to treat Ayot's shattered leg, but in summary he frankly admitted that he doubted the man would ever be able to get around much any more. He also stated that Ayot's bill had come to seventy-five dollars for surgical treatment and medicine. In addition, there were other expenses for his board and lodging.

The young French-Canadian was in need of all the help Frémont could give. Having an innocent faith in the United States, Ayot had come to Washington to apply for government help since he had been crippled in the service of the country. To his dismay, he discovered that because he was not an enlisted soldier, the pension laws did not apply to him.

Jessie heard his story and was distressed that nothing was going to be done for him. In her determined way, she decided that she would try to do something about it that very evening at the home of Senator John A. Dix of New York.

Using her wit and charm, Jessie convinced Mrs. Dix of poor Ayot's plight. As she told her story, it was overheard by Senator Dix and a large, bashful man who was also visiting, Representative Preston King of New York, the chairman of the Committee on Pensions. Before he departed, he told Senator Dix to have Mrs. Frémont write out briefly the story that he had heard her tell, and he would do his best to help Ayot.

As he promised, Representative King introduced a special act in the House of Representatives. It passed both houses and was signed by President Polk. All that was required of Ayot was for him to become an American resident. Upon doing that, he was to receive back pay from the date of his wound as well as a lifelong pension of ten dollars per month. This was welcome news, and Jessie told it to Ayot over a glass of sherry in the library of the Benton home.

Alexis was overcome with the news. He swayed back and forth on his crutches, tears began to run down his cheeks, and he told Jessie, "I cannot kneel to you; I have no more legs, but you are my Sainte Madonne. To you I make my prayers."[7]

With immediate personal obligations fulfilled, the time was at hand to proceed with the vital summary and analysis of what the expedition had accomplished. As far as Jessie was concerned there was no doubt as to the role she would play. She insisted on working with her husband in the final shaping of the Report. Her role, she later wrote, was that of a secretary and good editor. To carry out the work in utmost privacy and to avoid disturbing Mrs. Benton, who was still recovering from a stroke, and Frémont's mother who had come north to be with her son, John Charles and Jessie "took for a workshop a small wooden two-story house not far from the residence of Mr. Benton. This was well apart from other buildings and had about it large enclosed grounds."[8]

Senator Benton was greatly concerned about Jessie's health. It struck him that she was not strong enough to carry on her duties in the household and to assist her husband with a very difficult *Report* of the second expedition. As usual, Jessie persisted and got her way.

As she described her days with John Charles and Professor Hubbard, none of it seemed like arduous work. Yet it was difficult and consumed the energy of all associated with the project. For they were in the process of trying to put down the findings, the descriptions of almost two years of exploration in country that was largely unknown except to Indian tribes and mountain men.

In this house, no more than a block away from the Benton residence, Jessie wrote that Mr. Hubbard took the ground-floor room, where he set up his transit, while she and her husband took the upper floor as their writing room.

"Nine o'clock always found me at my post, pen in hand, and I put down Mr. Frémont's dictation until one o'clock."[9] Here they worked putting together one of the most remarkable documents in the history of exploration. Frémont paced back and forth, voiced his memories of events in the wilderness, tried to think of just how the wind blew, what the weather was like, and of his first glimpse of the High Sierra Nevada or the Eden of the Sacramento Valley. Intertwined with this were the men of the expedition, Kit Carson and Charles Preuss worrying about the rubber boat as the craft began to hit rough water in the Great Salt Lake; steady Broken Hand Fitzpatrick always bringing up the rear, always making sure that there would be enough supplies for another day of travel, another desert or mountain crossing; and the meetings with the various Indian tribes who were colorful and magnificent nomads wandering the Asiatic steppes of North America. As he recalled all of it—the good and bad times—as he remembered the wounded, the crippled, and the dead, John Charles searched his mind for the words to convey what ran deep within him, what would be part of him for as long as he was able to look up at the sky and watch the V-shaped flight of geese heading north for another summer season.

While John Charles and Jessie worked the morning hours in the upper-story workroom, young Hubbard worked on the astronomical calculations in the ground-floor room. He also served as a buffer who prevented casual visitors from just dropping in on the Frémonts. The exceptions to this rule were Senator Benton, who was always welcome, any of the other men who were working with Frémont on the various phases of the *Report*, and the one o'clock arrival of black Nancy and baby Lily. For Nancy always arrived with a basket luncheon that might consist of cold chicken, fresh biscuits, and some fruit. And while the Frémonts ate their lunch, they played with Lily. Then, when the lunch was finished and Nancy had taken Lily back to the Benton home, John Charles and Jessie would take a long walk before returning to the workshop for another two hours of work in the late afternoon.

In the evening after dinner was over, after John Charles had talked to Senator Benton, he retired to his room and went over his notebooks and tried to synthesize the material for the next day's work. During this time, it became necessary to test the accuracy of the sextant by local astronomical observation. This required setting the alarm and getting out of bed past midnight and going with Joseph Hubbard "when the streets were quiet and few passers to disturb the mercury, to a church near by where there was a large stone carriage-step near the curb on which to set the horizon."[10]

Young Jacob Dodson usually accompanied the two men, and carried a container of hot coffee. Drinking coffee to ward off the cold air, the men often stretched out against the large stone carriage-step as they watched for certain stars to come into position. As they waited, they talked, sometimes laughed about how strange they might appear to a person who didn't know what they were doing, and tried to ease the period of waiting with discussions about whatever happened to enter their minds.

Seeing the men lying on the pavement, a deacon of the church assumed they were drunk. There could be no other reason for such disgraceful behavior, and to think that one of the men was Senator Benton's son-in-law, that another was a black man, and that they were drinking was more than the deacon could tolerate. He came to the Benton home, asked for the senator, and reported what he had observed.

But the deacon received no thanks for his shocking information nor any apology for Frémont's behavior. Senator Benton heard him out, and then told him that he had not bothered to see if the men were intoxicated or if there might be some other reason for their leaning back against the step and peering into the night sky. No, the senator told him, he was only too ready to carry a rumor, to spread a falsehood, to slander without any consideration of what might be going on.

Then to add to the humiliation of the deacon, John Charles and Jessie happened to stop at the house after having taken their after-lunch stroll. Senator Benton called them into his library, turned to the deacon, and said, "There are Mrs. and Mrs. Frémont, and I wish you to repeat to them what you have been telling me."[11]

The deacon hardly knew what to do and tried to avoid what was requested of him. But Senator Benton was firm in his order. John Charles and Jessie began to laugh. Still the deacon had no idea of what the men had been doing on the pavement. This knowledge came to him in a stern lecture from Senator Benton, who accused the sanctimonious deacon of spreading slander and lacking even the slightest hint of Christian charity. Frightened and thoroughly chastised, the deacon was a shaken man as he left the Benton household with the sound of the senator's voice still ringing in his ears.

The intrusion of the deacon was only a humorous diversion from the work on the *Report*. For as the daily grind went on, Frémont was writing a book that was to become a classic in the literature of exploration. It wasn't a book limited to the narrow vision of the specialist. As John Charles tried to capture the look and lay of the land, the nature of the plains, and the Great Basin country, Oregon, and the places that offered new beginnings for emigrants willing to make the long journey West, he was writing a book for the common man. For it was the common man with his wife and family, with his short stock of provisions, with the family dog and a few head of cattle, who was going to set forth toward the setting sun in search of a better life. To this man and his companions, Frémont addressed his *Report*. These were the people on the move, the people who needed to know. For it was the common man, who was anything but common, who was going to risk everything for a new start, for a chance to be a pioneer in a new land.

And very little was left out of this classic account of the way West. Preuss's maps gave a day-by-day picture of where the wagons would have to go, what they could expect in the way of terrain, and how many miles they would have to make in order to reach a proper campground. Here, at last, was the Oregon Trail placed on a map that a man could use. But there was much more than the maps. For the reader with a sense of science, there were appendixes that described plant life, geological formations, fossils, and the changing weather patterns for the country and the seasons. Yet, important as these scientific insights were, that wasn't the heart of the *Report*. The heart, the guts, the word pictures of the West were in the masterful text that the combination of Frémont's experiences and talent made possible.

It was a best seller, a popular book, and there was no other way to put it. John Charles made it all come alive to the reader. The Platte River looked one way, but it was a far cry from the Snake River or the magnificent Columbia River. Soil at South Pass was thin and wind-blown, and even sagebrush didn't do too well. But the deep, dark soil of the Willamette and Sacramento valleys was altogether different. It didn't need a watchful eye to make things grow. It needed a watchful eye to make sure wild plants didn't overcrowd domesticated plants. Then there were the places to avoid, places like the high and dry Black Rock Desert of the Great Basin, or the high passes of the Sierra Nevada during the winter. But it was a country as big as the ocean sky that was above it. Rich, oh rich, did the emigrant say? Timber? Oregon and California mountains were dark with uncut forests of pines that stretched right to timberline; and in California's Great Valley groves of oaks stood on the valley floor like druid gods. But that wasn't all, not by the wildest guess. Grass in California grew higher than wagon wheels. Great herds of tule elk and pronghorn antelopes ranged with wild cattle and horses in unfenced vastness.

But on the way? What about the trail? Were there places a man might figure on a little help if he needed it?

The forts were listed and described. A pioneer could read the *Report* and have some idea what might be available at Fort Laramie as opposed to Fort Hall, and he would learn of the great citadels of trade at Fort Vancouver and Sutter's Fort. And he would learn about mountain men who could be hired to lead a wagon train and see it through safely. No, they couldn't all count on being able to hire Kit Carson, Broken Hand Fitzpatrick, or Joseph

Walker, but that didn't mean they couldn't find a good mountain man at one of these posts to show them the way.

But it wasn't all going to be easy going. The *Report* brought out the beauty of the land, the colors and songs of the birds, the grizzly bears eating chokecherries, and the first view of a buffalo herd moving across the plains like a dark rolling cloud. Even so, Frémont did not avoid the terrors. In vivid descriptions, he painted word pictures of mosquito-infested ponds, waterholes where only cracked mud remained, searing heat, freezing cold, stretches of land without grass for the animals, and regions where game would be short and meals would be lean. As for the owners of the land—the Indians—Frémont tried to make it clear that they could be helpful, but they might also pick off a stray cow or horse; and it was best to be prepared just in case they resented more intruders in their country. And there were all the other dangers of the trail—rattlesnakes, bad water, accidents, flash floods, steep mountains, deep canyons, heavy rains, and sudden blizzards. Frémont worked to make his vast canvas complete, tried to illustrate the way West in all its details from the smallest to the largest. Out of his labor of love came a book which was three times as large as his *Report* of the 1842 Expedition. There was no other way to describe such a grand reconnaissance.

Working steadily, as though he were possessed, he completed the manuscript by February 1845. On March 1, John Charles formally presented his epic to the War Department. Two days later there was a Senate resolution that called for a printing of five thousand extra copies. James Buchanan, shortly to become Secretary of State, moved that the number of copies to be printed be increased from five to ten thousand. This was agreed to by Congress. This was the second victory Western expansionists had won in a few days. For on March 1, 1845, Congress had passed a joint resolution admitting Texas as a new state.

Things moved quickly in Frémont's career. Not only were ten thousand copies of his *Report* printed by the government, but other publishers—at home and abroad—issued their own editions of his work. Newspapers were filled with stories about Lieutenant Frémont's adventures in the West, and he became an overnight hero. Handsome Frémont and beautiful Jessie were acclaimed by the American public. They were everything a growing nation needed for a symbol of success, and the country was not to see this combination of youth and daring again until the later cults of hero worship for George and Elizabeth Custer, Charles and Anne Lindbergh, or John and Jacqueline Kennedy.

Head of the Army, General Winfield Scott decided that John Charles Frémont should receive a double brevet of first lieutenant and captain, even though he had not graduated from West Point. President John Tyler saw to it that Frémont was given the appointment of captain by brevet.

These were days of glory for John Charles Frémont, the bastard son of a French émigré. Though there were those who still looked upon the West as a vast and barren desert and who considered Frémont's accomplishments as interesting but not very valuable, they were in the minority. The greater opinion was for expansion, for making sure that the United States was a Two Ocean Nation, that Texas was only the beginning, and that there was no sense in waiting around while the British eased into California and took over. The thing to do was to keep moving, keep reaching out, keep growing.

4

TIMING CAN BE EVERYTHING for a man's destiny, and the fall of 1844 proved to be just that for Frémont. The Democratic candidate, James Knox Polk, who had run on a promise of expansion, had won the presidential election. The Democratic plank called it "reoccupation," but one would have been hard pressed to know just what it was they had occupied and had been forced to leave. Among the most wild-eyed expansionists, the rallying call in the Oregon boundary dispute between the United States and the British was "Fifty-four forty or fight." Polk felt that this was pushing things too far. He was quite willing to draw the boundary line on the forty-ninth parallel. Still, many Americans believed the British were eternal villains and had no place in North America, least of all on the Pacific Coast. Oregon, especially Oregon, was rightfully American! Just how this was so didn't seem to matter. What mattered was that the British were there, and Americans didn't think they should be. But that wasn't all. Mexico was trying to move against Texas if there was any truth to what a man might hear. The Democratic Party was not only happy that Texas was now part of the United States; they looked with favor upon the acquisition of California and whatever else there might be in the Southwest that was worth paying or fighting for. Yet very little was known about the vast territory that was coveted, and Captain Frémont was *the* authority to consult. What he hadn't learned in his two expeditions could be taken care of by another expedition. There was no point in putting it off. To Frémont, the time was right; and he longed for a third journey of exploration.

As always, Washington was filled with rumors. The United States and Mexico would be at war in a very short time. There was talk about this, but Mexico wasn't the real worry. The nagging concern was the British. Would they use a war between the United States and Mexico as an ideal opportunity to seize Oregon and California, or would they rally to Mexico's defense and join the war against the United States? From the point of view of calm heads, nothing of this sort would take place. But the War of 1812 lingered in the minds of too many men, and to these older men, the British remained a threat.

President Polk was among those who wondered about what the British might do. A solid plank in his foreign policy was designed to keep the British from taking California. After all, California was hardly stable. Mexico's cen-

tral government was too far away and too concerned with other difficulties
to pay much attention to this distant outpost of empire. Mexico worried more
about the loss of Texas and the possible loss of other areas just north of the
Río Grande. President Polk knew from Senator Benton and from Frémont
that California was a beautiful land ready for conquest. Secretary of the
Navy George Bancroft also had made clear his thoughts about the vulner-
ability of California to the British warships that cruised up and down the
Pacific Coast.

All was not talk. While rumors of every kind could be heard at any hour,
events were shaping up for Frémont's next expedition. Senator Benton used
his tremendous influence as chairman of the Senate Military Committee,
counted on and received the backing of Secretary Bancroft, and was privy to
secret messages sent from Mexico regarding the attitude of the Mexican government. Many of these messages were translated into English by Jessie in
the Benton library. Some letters were from John Slidell, the United States
minister to Mexico; some were from William Parrott, United States consul at
Mazatlán, a man who had many connections in Mexico; and some were
from other figures in the service of the United States or in prominent business positions in Mexico and friendly to men in key government posts. Much
of this material was known to Frémont. Not that he learned about it
officially, but through Jessie, Senator Benton, and powerful friends of the
senator, John Charles was well aware of what was happening on both sides
of the border. He also was caught up with the obsession that nobody knew
just what stand the British might take in the advent of a war with Mexico.

California was only one prize. The immediate need in the eyes of expansionists was to make certain that the Oregon country became American. As
Frémont and others had reported, the Willamette Valley already had more
Americans than British. Possession was what counted. Yet the British gave no
indication of backing off, and every indication of remaining and expanding.

Something had to be done, and it had to be done quickly. This was the
best excuse in the world to send Captain Frémont on his way again. So, on
February 12, 1845, Colonel John J. Abert, of the Bureau of Topographical
Engineers, sent the captain his orders for a third expedition. But despite the
wishes of the Western advocates, there was no mention of California in
Frémont's orders.

A careful reading of Colonel Abert's letter showed no go-ahead to strike
across the Rocky Mountains and head for California. There was an implied
suggestion that part of the reason for the expedition was to check out any
probable paths Mexican troops might take if they headed north, but even this
suggestion was terribly vague and had to be read into what was written. As
for the Oregon country, the British threat, or the need to know more about
California, these items were not even indicated. If there ever was any validity
to Frémont's later claim that he had been given oral instructions to strike out
for California, if there was any validity to the secret messages from Mexico or

to President's Polk's concern about the British, then either Colonel Abert had no knowledge of these things, or he wanted his written order to appear as innocent as possible.

While the notion of Colonel Abert's not knowing about any of the machinations going on among the Western expansionists is not hard to believe, it remains suspect. There was always the possibility Abert was playing the old army game of sending out a decoy to cover the movements of the real thing. Otherwise, the usefulness of the expedition as put forth in the colonel's letter would have been dubious at best. For as outlined, Frémont was to do the following:

> . . . strike the Arkansas as soon as practicable, survey that river, and if practicable survey the Red River without our boundary line, noting particularly the navigable properties of each, and will determine as near as practicable the points at which the boundary line of the U.S. the 100th degree of longitude west of Greenwich strikes the Arkansas, and the Red River. It is also important that the Head waters of the Arkansas should be accurately determined. Long journies to determine isolated geographical points are scarcely worth the time and expense which they occasion; the efforts of Captain Fremont will therefore be more particularly directed to the geography of localities within reasonable distance of Bents Fort, and of the streams which run east from the Rocky Mountains, and he will so time his operations, that his party will come in during the present year.[12]

These instructions—coupled with Abert's request that only Frémont should keep a journal—remain curious to this day. Why waste government funds on such a limited expedition? Why state that only Frémont should write about it? None of these rules had been put down on the other journeys of exploration.

To add further confusion to Abert's instructions, most of what he was asking was already known. Frémont had seen the headwaters of the Arkansas River on his return from California. He knew about the other streams in the region from the mountain men, and none of these men had ever indicated these rivers offered any great possibilities for navigation. During most seasons of the year, these streams varied in depth from a few feet to a thin trickle of water that eased across the land so slowly that it wasn't good for more than a breeding area for mosquitoes.

In later letters to Frémont, the instructions of Colonel Abert become even more confusing. The number of men changed; a second division was to return home via a more southern route under the command of Lieutenant James W. Abert, the colonel's son, and Lieutenant William Guy Peck; also the purpose of this subgroup was to include an exploration of the southern Rocky Mountains and an analysis of the military aspects of the country. Finally, in his letter of May 14, 1845, Colonel Abert wrote that once the two lieutenants and their party had started on their roundabout way home,

Frémont should be certain he had enough remaining funds to cover his expenses for a longer time and for possible distant discoveries.

Still, there was no mention of California. Yet, when Frémont wrote his *Memoirs,* he stated that once plans for the third expedition had matured, he was given the right to proceed at his own discretion and to cross the Rocky Mountains and head west. He was, in fact, "to extend the survey west and southwest to the examination of the great ranges of the Cascade Mountains and the Sierra Nevada, so as to ascertain the lines of communication through the mountains to the ocean in that latitude."[13] Here, there was no doubt as to what Frémont thought he was ordered to do. While it can be argued that this was only aftersight, the fact remains that President Polk and other government officials, newspapers, and Western expansionists expressed no surprise when news reached Washington that Frémont was in California.

If the instructions were ever put down on paper for the expedition to proceed to California, that paper has never been found. Yet that does not mean oral instructions were not issued. When one considers all the other curious twists and turns in Colonel Abert's letters, there appears to be good reason to believe Captain Frémont had an unofficial approval to go all the way to California.

Whatever one may make of the intrigue surrounding the final go-ahead for the third expedition, there is no doubt as to the government's role in it. Financially, politically, and in every other way, this was to be a government-backed operation. To Frémont, this was all that was required. So, even as his *Report* of the second expedition went to press, he was caught up in the hectic time of making his plans for the coming spring.

Letters were sent to Colonel Abert to get all the details for the trip soundly financed. Letters were exchanged with Professor Torrey regarding the final draft of the description of plants that had been saved from the collection made during the second expedition. There were other letters to make certain that the right moves were made to outfit and hire the men for this journey. William, the Chinook boy, had to be picked up in Philadelphia; young Dr. James McDowell, a nephew of Jessie's, was going to go with them to take care of medical problems and to assist with the care and classification of botanical specimens; young Talbot was to head west with them once again; Lieutenants Abert and Peck were to travel as far as Bent's Fort with them; but one familiar face was to be missing. Charles Preuss wasn't going on this trip. Not that Preuss didn't yearn to go along, for he did in spite of his constant grousing during the previous expeditions. But Mrs. Preuss had talked him into buying a home in Washington, and she insisted he was not going back into the wilderness and leave her and the family alone once more. To replace Preuss was no easy matter, but a young artist from Philadelphia was very interested in heading to the West in the tradition of such earlier artists as George Catlin, Karl Bodmer, and Alfred Jacob Miller. More than that,

Edward "Ned" Kern looked upon Frémont as "the beau ideal of all that was chivalrous and noble."[14]

Twenty-two years old, tall, thin, red-haired, with a wispy mustache and the manners of a well-schooled gentleman, and an epileptic, Ned Kern was hardly the ideal physical model for a Frémont expedition. Yet he was determined to go. He sent samples of his work, admitted he had not yet learned to do maps but thought that he could. To follow in the footsteps of the hardy and talented Preuss was not going to be easy, but Ned was convinced that he could do justice to the task ahead. The major thing, of course, was to convince the captain. To do this, Ned Kern had Washington friends speak to Frémont about him.

> [Ned's] best hopes lay with a fellow artist from Philadelphia, Joseph Drayton, who was then busy in Washington cataloguing drawings and specimens which he had brought back from the Wilkes Pacific Expedition three years earlier. Drayton spoke with Lieutenant Henry Eld, a colleague from the Wilkes venture, and together they approached Frémont about Kern.[15]

The combination of pull and Ned Kern's obvious talent in the botanical drawings and sketches that he had sent to Frémont turned the trick. For on March 20, 1845, Ned opened a letter from the man he admired and found that he had been appointed a member of the expedition. Frémont did not try to paint anything other than a true picture of what Kern would have to face. His letter indicated that the work would be hard and constant but agreeable. For Ned Kern, this was a day of great joy.

On May 1 another letter from Frémont arrived telling Ned that he would be paid three dollars per day as of that date. He was to receive ten cents per mile for traveling expenses from Philadelphia to Independence, Missouri—going and coming. Upon receiving the letter, he was to head for St. Louis to meet the rest of the party and help in the days of organization.

Ned wasted very little time. He gathered his gear, said farewell to friends and family, and accompanied by his brother, Ben, he was off and headed down the Ohio River on a paddlewheeler. Just why Dr. Benjamin Kern went to St. Louis with him is not known, but he might have made the trip to make sure that Ned was not by himself in case of an epileptic seizure.

On the evening before John Charles was to leave, he watched Jessie as she carefully put the last stitches in a waterproof pocket she had made for his valuable documents. Realizing how much he would miss her, he lamented the fact that there was no way that she could go along. Jessie looked up at him, and between a mixture of laughter and tears that splashed on the surface of the leather, she said:

> "There! That's properly dedicated, and I must be willing to dedicate you to this service which fits you. You leave us to execute plans my father has worked for all his life. You both are part of me. My work is to let you go cheerfully. Besides," she added, archly, "you would soon tire of a repining wife, and surely you wouldn't have me a Mrs. Preuss?"[16]

But in the morning, on that day they both hated to see, Jessie gave no sign of sorrow as she saw John Charles and two black servants, Jacob Dodson and Kino, ready for their departure to St. Louis. She knew that months would pass before she would see her dark-haired husband again. Even though she had been through this kind of leave-taking before, it didn't make it any easier. She knew too much, far too much, about the wilderness her husband was headed into. While he would have the very best frontiersmen by his side, while she was aware of his great courage and strength, the fact remained that more than one good man never returned from such a journey.

As John Charles told her that he would write to her whenever there was an opportunity to send a letter, Jessie had to steel herself against a show of sadness. For she wanted him to leave home seeing her at her very best, remembering the smile, the last kiss, the little wave and farewell cheer from baby Lily, and the strong handshake and words of encouragement her father would give. These were the intangible supplies, the morale boosters for lonely moments in wild and desolate places. So the talk was about familiar things, about pleasant things. It was say hello to St. Louis friends. It was a private glance into each other's eyes. And then it was time to be on the move, time to head out again, time to fill another blank space on the map and to bring home more knowledge about the future for Americans in the West.

## ·⚜· XIV ·⚜·

# Following the Winds of Summer

THEODORE TALBOT found St. Louis a hurry-up, get-on-your-way exciting place, a westward-facing city filled with people on the move in that May of 1845. He had come on ahead with William, the Chinook. He had last seen Captain Frémont at Louisville, Kentucky. That had been for a short time before the steamboat was ready to sail on down the Ohio. The captain was on his way to Senator Benton's Kentucky farm to pick up the two California Indian boys, Juan and Gregorio, and his horse Sacramento.

Captain Frémont had talked fast as he went over his orders for Talbot. Once in the city, Talbot was to begin the first stages of pulling the expedition together. Lieutenants Abert and Peck would be there already. They would have done some of the work, but this was their first time out. Talbot would find the regular men at Chouteau's. There, he should ask about any new men who might be fit for this journey. But lay the groundwork fast. May was running into June. There wasn't time to waste.

The instructions had been issued quickly. Then the steamboat whistle blew. As he wrote to his mother from the Planters House in St. Louis, the trip down the Ohio River was on a crowded steamboat. The whole river was alive with boats and rafts of every size and description, and four steamboats were aground on sandbars.

Talbot secured quarters for William first; then he managed to get a room for himself at the Planters House. Here he made his headquarters as he followed Frémont's instructions. At the Planters House he found Lieutenants Abert and Peck, long-legged Ned Kern, and Henry King of Georgetown. All these young men hit it off at once. They were close to the same age, excited about the adventure ahead, and anxious to prove they were really worthy of the trust that had been shown them.

On May 30 Frémont and the California Indian boys arrived. But John Charles had not had such good fortune coming down the Ohio River. The steamboat hung up twice on sandbars. Yet his difficulty in getting downriver was mild compared to avoiding the many men who had heard about the expedition and wished to sign on. The regular hands—Godey, Archambeault, Proue, Lajeunesse, and Maxwell—were not only waiting; they were already getting things ready to move out. But the men who wanted to become part of this great adventure were something else. Some had a frontier background, and some were young city and town men who thought they would be able to make it in the West. They had read Frémont's *Report* of the first expedition; they had read the newspaper stories and heard all the tales in local taverns. They were filled with dreams of glory, but many were prime candidates for an early death if they ever left the cobblestone streets, the soft beds, the regular meals, the protection of a civilized community, and the luxury of knowing where they were going and how to get there by stagecoach or steamboat.

Still, no matter what Frémont told these men, no matter how bleak a picture he painted of what would face anyone who traveled with him, they crowded about him every time he stepped into the open. And though Theodore Talbot and the other young men at the Planters House were busy rounding up the many things that would be needed for the expedition, there was no avoiding men who wished to sign up for the journey. For one thing, Talbot was given the task of making out the list of applicants, of saving Frémont the time of an initial examination of them, and of issuing advance money, orders, and drafts for supplies to those men who were hired. Caught up in this, Talbot had a firsthand view of the clamor to see and talk to Captain Frémont.

Things got so bad that there was no privacy for Frémont, no way for him to have the time he needed to do his final planning. He tried to remain secluded in a small place in the French Quarter, but he was discovered. One of the clerks had a sign painted stating that Frémont wasn't staying there, but it did no good. Then John Charles placed an ad in the newspapers to notify the men who followed him about that he was willing to meet them if they would gather together at the Planter's Warehouse. There he would explain the nature of his expedition, what he was looking for in the way of men, the duties, the pay, and all the rest of it. The house was filled long before he arrived. It was so crowded that he moved outside to a square and mounted a fence in order to be seen and heard above the throng of men who were all shouting for him to speak to them.

Crowding closer to the fence, they pushed and shoved and cursed each other. Their momentum carried them forward with a rush. Frémont tried to stop them, but it was no use. They bunched together like frightened, stampeding buffalo. The fence held for a moment. Then it began to give way, cracked, snapped, and Frémont was tossed backward onto the ground.

About this time, a well-meaning Irishman, who had been standing on the corner of Second Street, not knowing what all the fuss was about, rushed up with the idea that it was a "big fight," shouting at the top of his lungs, "Fair play! Fair play! and be d——d to yez; don't you see the man's down?"[1]

Having no other choice, Frémont headed for cover in a nearby hotel. Here, he took a room, and Jacob remained with him to fend off intruders. But it was all young Dodson could do to keep men from breaking down the door. If he relaxed for only a moment, there would be a sudden surge of men. Before he could shut the door, some would be inside the room telling Frémont just why it was that they should be the chosen ones. This was too much. As a last resort, he had Jacob lock him in the room and keep the key. There he tried to have some peace while he considered the qualifications of the men he had been able to interview during the few interludes of calmness when the tide of humanity ebbed enough to give him time to think of something other than how to prevent being trampled.

By the fourth of June, Talbot was able to write to his mother that the party was shaping up. Fifty-five men were signed on at St. Louis. There were to be others selected at Westport; and when they reached Bent's Fort, they expected Kit Carson to be waiting for them.

Altogether, they were a hardy and tough lot, and they had to be for what lay ahead. Talbot knew they were bound for California, that they were going to follow Mary's River (today's Humboldt River) across the Great Basin, and that they would cross the Sierra Nevada and drop into the Great Valley. The return route was not determined, but there was the possibility that they might head home through the Southwest. No matter which trail they followed, there was little chance that the expedition would return from the field before the passing of fifteen to eighteen months.

The selection of men had been accomplished in a short time. And for the regulars, Frémont was concerned that each man should be a top marksman. To insure this, he purchased twelve beautifully designed special Hawken rifles. These were to be offered as prizes to the best marksmen. There would be shooting contests whenever possible to determine the best riflemen in the company.

As one young frontiersman, twenty-two-year-old Thomas Salathiel Martin of Tennessee, described things, this was a party that was going to be traveling fast and light. Each man's equipment was furnished by the government, and it consisted of "1 whole-stock Hawkens rifle, two pistols, a butcher knife, saddle, bridle, pistol holsters & 2 pr. blankets. For his individual use each man was given a horse or mule for riding & from one to two pack animals to care for."[2] And there didn't seem to be much doubt in any man's mind that he was bound for California.

The captain, Talbot, Ned, and a group of the men rode the twenty miles from St. Louis to St. Charles. On June 5, Talbot saw them board the steamboat *Henry Bry*. As the paddlewheeler churned the muddy water and the black smoke poured out of the stacks and drifted in the wind, Talbot waved farewell to Frémont and the men standing aboard. Then he turned and headed back to St. Louis to take care of all the last details at Chouteau's and elsewhere so that he could hurry behind and meet them at Westport or some other nearby camp. But nearly ten days were to pass before news reached St. Louis that the late spring runoff had reached the lower end of the Missouri River and raised the depth of water enough so that the *White Cloud*, the larger steamboat that Talbot had booked passage on, would be able to leave the deeper waters of the Mississippi River and head up the Missouri to Westport.

While Talbot finished his last tasks and waited for high water, Captain Frémont hadn't managed to escape applicants who wished to become part of his command. Two men who had badgered him for a position in St. Louis were aboard the *Henry Bry*. Ned Kern liked these two artists who had come all the way from New Orleans because they had heard Frémont was getting ready to head west once more. They had tried their best to convince him of their worth. But when the captain was noncommittal to blustering Alfred S. Waugh and his friend John B. Tisdale, they decided that sooner or later he was going to take them on as full-fledged members of the party. Along with many other anxious applicants, Waugh and Tisdale trailed behind the party to the outfitting camp. The westward vision was a catching disease, and most suffered acutely from it.

The men of the expedition were a mixed lot, a strange breed following the summer wind. There were the rough-and-tumble frontiersmen who never forgot the endless stretch of big sky reaching beyond the horizon. There were the whiskey-brave ones who would not be much good beyond Westport. These were men Frémont would weed out in a hurry. There were the backwoods types, such as Tom Martin, and they took every chance to sharpen their shooting eyes, to get the feel of their rifles, to put up targets and fire a few rounds whenever the steamboat had to make a wood stop. Then there were the young men from the East, all spit and polish. It was a wild mixture, a free and easy lot. It was young America on the move.

2

IT WAS A COLD, RAINY Monday morning when the *Henry Bry* docked at Westport Landing. The air had the feel of winter in it, as though there hadn't been a spring, and even though it was June 9, there wasn't any hint of summer. Isaac Cooper, a young greenhorn with aspirations of becoming a writer, noted that they got ashore as fast as they could. Each man carried his own duffle, or "possible sack," his blankets, and his rifle. But if Cooper thought there would be dock workers ready to unload the gear for the expedition, he was badly mistaken.

Orders were given. Shouts to get a move on, to hurry along, to make sure everything was put ashore became the steady sound that was heard above the fast-moving Missouri River, the thunderclaps, and the steady downpour of rain. Within two or three hours the first hard job was over, but only the first one. Supplies of all kinds were stacked in the mud: barrels of flour, sugar, and coffee; boxes of rice, macaroni, saleratus, dried meat, salt and pepper, rubber and canvas tarps, tents, iron pickets, additional rifles and boxes of ammunition, scientific instruments and a small wagon designed to carry them.

Cooper later wrote about this scene, and like Preuss, he did nothing but complain. The landing was a mudhole. The rain never let up, and he hadn't signed on to be a drayhorse. But drayhorse he was until all the plunder was moved away from the muddy landing to higher ground that wasn't trampled into a bog by men and animals. Here, the supplies were covered with tarps, and the men waited for the wagons that were to be hired to carry their goods to the first campsite Frémont had chosen as a breaking-in place for his expedition. This was at the head of Boon Creek, six miles beyond Westport.

While waiting for the wagons, the men built fires and cooked a quick meal. Ned Kern observed the wild nature of the town, and saw it infect his companions. As soon as they found their land legs, as soon as they had a little food inside them, they headed out for the nearest saloon. And like all waterfront towns, Westport of 1845 was not short on saloons, whiskey, women, gamblers, and games of chance. It was raw and wide-open. Traders bound for Santa Fé haggled with men who had mules for sale. Mountain men and would-be frontiersmen drank raw whiskey or equally raw aguardiente, and watched the women. Most of the unattached women were Indian girls, but there were Indian men standing around, and they didn't fancy a white man smiling at an Indian girl and saying something to her. The other women were either married to pioneers headed for the West, or they were daughters who had been told to watch out for the rough men. Ned Kern saw a moving panorama of color, of different faces and shapes, of a community that was half-civilized and half-savage.

There was something about Westport, something about its location at the edge of the frontier, that brought out the wildness in young men who passed that way the first time. Kern saw this in some of the men who were going to be part of the expedition. He saw it in men like Isaac Cooper who rushed to the bar for one last drink. It was almost as though it was a ritual to go through. Toss down raw, burning, rotgut whiskey. Shout and slap each other on the back. Point out the good features of a woman someone had noticed, and sing a chorus of "Old Dan Tucker" or "Lucy Neale." All these things were part of heading out, of passing across the invisible line of the frontier.

Captain Frémont and the seasoned men were waiting for the greenhorns at Boon Creek. Ned Kern saw them from the crest of a rolling hill. In back of them there was the long stretch of forever sweeping across the Great Plains toward the horizon country. Surrounded by trees, near a spring and a small stream, the camp was on a small knoll. Some of the trees had been felled for a corral to hold the horses and mules at night. But in the gray twilight, Ned could see the herd grazing on the grassland just beyond camp. Horsemen rode around the herd to keep it from wandering off and to prevent any loss to visiting Indians who might look upon the herd as a challenge for a little stealing. Most of these animals were left over from Frémont's second expedition, but they were not the thin and worn horses and mules he had left behind. Now, all were fat and in good shape.

The main problem for Frémont's experienced men was how these half-wild animals would react when saddles were cinched tight and greenhorns climbed aboard. There would be bucking and kicking, no doubt about that. More than one young man would find himself nursing a bruised body along with a bruised estimate of his ability to handle a range pony or a kicking pack mule. The task of teaching these men fell to Auguste Archambeault and Basil Lajeunesse. It was up to them to show the newcomers how to get a bit into an animal that refused to open its mouth, how to keep a horse from blowing its stomach out while cinching up and then sucking it back in just as a rider began to climb aboard, and how to ease up to a wild-eyed mule, slip on a packsaddle, and secure it with a diamond hitch. And there wasn't going to be much time to train these new men. Come morning, the fun was going to begin.

The first night in camp was the kind of thing Ned Kern had read about, but none of it seemed quite real. It was as though he were part of a tale being told or read, not as though all of what he saw, heard, felt, and smelled was happening. The whole scene was that of a nomad camp, a great tribe on the move across the steppes of Asia, bound for conquest and glory. All they lacked were families, for this group of nomads had no women or children with them. But in a quick glance, the camp was ancient and as old as mankind. The differences were in degree only. Tents were canvas, except for Captain Frémont's skin tepee. Iron pots were suspended over the coals and low flames of campfires, and the aroma of a heavily seasoned bubbling stew blended with that of hot coffee in large black pots. Men gathered around the fires as a steady drizzle fell; and even as they ate and talked, the sky became an obsidian color. Then with a suddenness that startled new men from the East, the whole sky became a brilliant glare of white as sheet lightning cracked and jumped against the clouds. Then the thunder rolled with a long echoing rumble that ended in a sharp clap as though part of the sky had exploded.

The men had been joking and singing after supper, but this violent display made them suddenly very quiet. Before they could pick up their spirits again, there was another bright streak of sky, another thunderclap, and the rain came down as though a thousand waterfalls had been sucked into the air and dropped all at once. Each man looked around for a tent, space under a wagon, or anything that would offer some shelter for the night. Ned Kern counted himself among the lucky as he rolled up in his blankets beneath a wagon, but before morning he discovered that nobody was going to remain dry in this storm, not even the men who managed to get into a tent.

After a night of heavy rainfall, a night when sheet lightning burned across the sky like the glare of a new sun, the storm blew past. The wet men got out of their soaked blankets and saw a warm sunrise. It gave them a chance to dry their gear and clothes, wipe their rifles to keep them from rusting, and to enjoy the prospect of cooking bacon and bread without feeling cold rainwater run down their shirt collars.

There was plenty of work to be done, and a day of sunshine helped to get everyone going. Supplies had to be repacked into smaller sacks for loading on pack mules and stowing into the four heavier wagons the expedition would take along. There was a shortage of tents, and men were put to work making more with the supply of extra canvas. Other men got their first baptism at saddling and riding horses and mules that did their best to put the riders out of action. The experienced men who would be responsible for supplying the party with meat took some time for target practice.

Frémont made arrangements with the nearby settlement of Delawares to hire some of their best men to go with the expedition as guides and hunters. Two of the nine or twelve who agreed to make the journey were Chief James Sagundai and his nephew Chief James Swanuck. All of these men were products of a cultural twilight zone. They had tried to adjust to the white man's ways and had become excellent farmers. Then their land had been taken away from them, and the government had moved them westward. But in moving them into the region of the Plains Indians, the whites had failed to realize that the Delawares were as foreign to these tribes as were the whites. At best, all that could ever exist was an uneasy truce that was frequently broken. Yet these men held no grudge, wasted no time on bitterness. They took things as they were, and tried to do what they could. This turned out to be considerable, for they were great warriors and natural leaders. The men Frémont hired not only were extremely loyal to him; they became a kind of personal bodyguard that would have followed him around the rim of hell if he had suggested it.

Yet the Delawares were not his only devoted followers. For John Charles had a strong personal magnetism, the kind of charisma that created great friends and enemies. He either attracted boundless loyalty or caused some kind of abrasiveness that resulted in men taking offense and breaking with him. But strong-willed men, frontiersmen and other independent characters who were quite sure of themselves, were Frémont men to the last. The captain asked nothing of them that he wasn't willing to do; he had the stamina and drive to keep moving against impossible odds; and he treated his men as equals. There was never a barrier of race, education, or family background. He gave respect to his men. In turn, they respected him.

To most of the men gathered at the Boon Creek camp during the weeks of preparation, during this time of almost daily rainfall, Captain Frémont was in charge and his orders were not to be questioned. Some greenhorns, like young Isaac Cooper, didn't care for this, even though Frémont had pointed out that this was a military expedition operating under military rules. Men such as Cooper were in the minority. The others took their orders and went about their jobs without grousing. If a man didn't want to do his job, if he didn't want to put up with things as they were, all he had to do was pick up his personal plunder and head back to St. Louis. If he wanted to go along, then, by damn, there was plenty of work to do, and it was best to get on with it.

So, when Frémont decided there were not enough tents to go around and sent the officers and artists toward Westport to look for lodging, the regular men in his party offered no complaints that he was showing favored treatment. And Ned Kern counted himself lucky to be with Lieutenants Abert and Peck as well as Tisdale and Waugh. For they found good beds and a solid roof over their heads at the farm of Linsey Lewis, just outside Westport. But the income the farmer received also had a drawback. These were lively young men who were always joking and who liked to ring the bell atop the Lewis home at any hour of day or night. And when they weren't ringing the bell, they were telling jokes, making puns, or singing the latest songs from St. Louis and points east.

This was no vacation from work for the men rooming at the Lewis farmhouse. In the daylight hours, Abert and Peck worked with Frémont and tried to pick up as much knowledge as they could. Both men knew this was a training period for them. A West Point education was one thing, but how to carry out an exploring expedition wasn't part of a cadet's classwork. Colonel Abert had made this clear to his son and Lieutenant Peck. They were to be on this journey as apprentices. No other man in the country could offer them as much knowledge about such expeditions as Captain Frémont, and Colonel Abert expected the two lieutenants to have more than a little of Frémont's know-how rub off on them. They were expected to learn the arts of surveying trails, noting botanical and geological features, observing the cultures of the various Indian tribes, and managing men, animals, and supplies. If they came home with just a portion of the captain's ability, Colonel Abert concluded that sending them along would have paid off.

While the lieutenants did their daily stint of work, Ned Kern began to learn something of mapmaking. Also, he was given time to make his first sketches of frontier types. The Delawares and the Chinook were the first Indians he sketched, and he was fascinated with their features. In remarkable drawings he captured the camp scenes. These first attempts were to lead to his later drawings, lithographs, and paintings which brought out how men and animals looked in action in this background of endless openness.

While Ned worked at his craft, the other artists—Alfred Waugh and John Tisdale—began to worry about their chances of becoming members of the expedition. Frémont hadn't said no, but he hadn't said yes. There was no other way, or so Waugh felt, than to approach the captain and ask him point-blank. The days were sliding by too fast, and it was obvious that before long the expedition would be heading out. So Waugh asked Frémont if he had decided upon Tisdale and himself.

The answer was a curious one, and it is difficult to know just what the captain had in mind. At first it appears that he was only trying to spare the feelings of the two men, but another look at what he told them gives his answer a meaning which could have been taken as one of encouragement. For he told them that he had to be careful about his selection of men, that he was directly responsible to the War Department, that he knew very little about them. Then he said that if they could produce a letter from a person of stature, he would feel justified in allowing them to come along. No more encouragement was needed. By nightfall Waugh and Tisdale had boarded a steamboat and were on their way to St. Louis to procure the desired letter.

Moving-out day for the expedition was shaping up fast. When Talbot arrived on June 15, he wrote to his mother that the camp wasn't even organized yet. But eight days later, what Isaac Cooper called the "Great northwestern-mule-wagon and pack-saddle Exploring Expedition," made its first tentative move away from Boon Creek camp.

First in the long line of the caravan was a small Yankee spring wagon with a square black top and buttoned rubber curtains. This was the most important vehicle of all as it contained all the scientific instruments: barometers, chronometers, thermometers, sextants, and telescopes. Two gentle mules pulled this wagon that young Cooper called "the Focus,—the Magnet,—the sun by day, and the moon by night to our caravan, and ever the foremost on the march, it was continually the object of our most watchful and jealous care, as the repository of the wonderful mechanism by means of which the world was to be enlightened for ages to come."[3]

After the Yankee spring wagon, the drivers cracked their whips across the rumps of four- and six-mule teams that were pulling the four larger and heavier wagons. These were loaded with supplies and stood out because of their red and white covers. Behind the wagons were the spare horses and mules and beef cattle, and the drovers calling out to watch for wild-eyed animals ready to break away, keeping the herd bunched, easing them along, and making sure swing riders watched for any signs of an animal ready to run for the open. The other men rode ahead and beside the large caravan. They helped with the herding and were ready to lend a hand if a wagon bogged in the heavy mud. Following at the rear of the long train were horsemen leading other horses and pack mules.

This was the day for finding out how ready the men were for the journey ahead, and everything could stand improvement. Greenhorns were tossed from bucking horses or had horses run away with them. Teams of mules made a habit of veering at the very right moment to pull a wagon into a mudhole where it sank to the axletree. Pack mules bucked and bolted, and in their wake supplies and provisions were scattered across the prairie. At the end of this hard day's march, only six miles had been traveled; and as the weary men made camp, they faced the job of picking up all the gear behind them, rounding up run-away animals, and putting things back into order. To add more grief to a bad first day, the light drizzle they had endured turned into another cloudburst.

Two and a half days were spent at this second camp near Westport while the expedition pulled itself together. Frémont told the men that they were traveling under military orders, that martial law was to prevail, that they were to say nothing of where they were going to any strangers, and that he was the only man who would keep a journal of their trip. To Isaac Cooper, who did not know that this was Colonel Abert's order, the rule about keeping a journal was so much nonsense. Still, he wasn't the only man bothered about the military aspect of the expedition. A number of men decided this was not their idea of a tour across the prairie, and taking advantage of the fact that one of the wagons was being sent back to Westport, they resigned, drew whatever pay they had coming, tossed their possible sacks into the wagon and departed.

Even as these men left, Frémont sent a man into Westport to hire replacements. This time, though, he took no chances. He asked for and got experienced French-Canadians. These were men who knew what they faced, knew how to handle the rough times without complaining, and knew the ways of the wilderness.

On June 26, 1845, the rain continued to make things miserable for all the men, but they moved out of the second camp at noon. Before nightfall, they had traveled ten miles and set up the third camp. This was to be the final trial march, for to cover ten miles with greenhorns and fat animals showed Frémont that even these new men were learning how to handle their mounts and take care of their assigned jobs with dispatch. The next day was to be the real farewell to anything that resembled a town or community of farmers. That night they traded with Shawnee farmers for fresh vegetables and butter, slaughtered and butchered a beef, set up meat-drying racks on which to hang strips for smoking and jerking; and ate a jumping-off meal that would seem like a feast in later times.

That last night around the fire the men talked of their days around Westport, recalled the good times they had enjoyed in trying to "buck the tiger." in a game of faro, thought about the girls they had left behind in St. Louis or even Washington, and listened to the tales of mountain men who looked upon the trip they were about to make as tame compared to what they had known when they had first headed up the Missouri to risk their lives for beaver pelts. But that was a long time ago; and now . . . hell, now, there was at least this exploring business, and it was a damned sight better than farming or trying to live in town. Even for mountain men who had seen the best of it, the thought of moving out in the morning, of seeing buffalo herds and camps of Sioux or Cheyennes made the blood course faster. There was something about heading out again, something a town man would never understand. But if a man ever got the taste for it, if he ever felt a thrill at being beyond the last settlement, there was no way to get over it. By sunup they'd be on their way, and that, by God, was what it was all about.

## 3

THE GOING WAS VERY HARD. Late rains had turned the prairie into a quagmire. The wagon traces were cut deeply into the mud, and men were always called upon to help push the three remaining large wagons until teams were able to get some traction. They were only 110 miles from Westport. But, even so, Ned was amazed when he turned and looked toward their backtrack on this first day of July.

Three riders were coming from the east toward their camp. He first noticed them in the distance when they were silhouetted on a rolling hill. Then they dropped out of sight into a draw. When he saw them again, they were on the crest of a hill just behind him. All three men were familiar, very familiar. One was farmer Lewis, the same farmer he had shared a roof with. The other two were those itinerant, never-say-no artists Alfred Waugh and John Tisdale. They had been riding hard and looked it. They were unshaven, dirty, and caked with the mud of the trail, and their faces were sunburned and windburned from the days of sunshine they had seen.

Brassy Waugh never even stopped to say a word to Kern. He got off his horse and walked briskly to Frémont's tepee, and Ned could see he was clutching some letters in his hand. Most of the men in camp were amazed to see the two artists once more and wondered what they were doing there. The answer came quickly as Waugh was in the captain's tepee for only a short time. When he came out, he looked at Tisdale and told him that they were going back.

"Tisdale said nothing, but drew from his belt a small hatchet and, like a petulant child, threw it to the ground, commenting 'I have no further use for that.' "[4]

Ned felt sorry for his two former companions, but there was nothing that he could do. For during the time the men had been away, Frémont had seen many of Ned's sketches, and had an opportunity to see how quickly he was catching on to the art of topography. The combination of Kern's remarkable talent, Frémont's personal feeling about the two romantics who wanted to go along, and the fact that one artist-mapmaker was all the expedition required added up to the sad spectacle of Waugh and Tisdale getting back on their horses and following farmer Lewis on the backtrack.

To Theodore Talbot, though, one good thing came from the ride these supplicants had made. He received mail from his mother, and the disappointed men agreed to take mail back with them.

Three days later the expedition celebrated the Fourth of July. At daybreak men were out of their bedrolls, rifles in hand, and fired a salute to Independence over Captain Frémont's tepee. Brandy was served to all hands, and Frémont announced they would remain in camp for that day. This gave the animals a rest, and the men had a chance to take a bath, wash their clothes, and do some mending. A shooting match took place; and when a Santa Fé caravan approached, the traders and their teamsters joined the celebration and brought additional jugs of whiskey. As Cooper later wrote in his secret diary, some of the men did some high drinking.

Moving on after the Independence Day break, the expedition worked its way on the Santa Fé Trail to the Pawnee Fork. They followed this until they struck the Smoky Hill Fork of the Kansas River. Then they were on familiar ground as they had come this way on their return from the second expedition. Now, as the days passed, they saw great herds of buffalo. There was no shortage of meat and no need to use their own beef. But the great buffalo herds were also followed by the Plains Indians, and there was the constant need to be on guard as well as to meet in friendship with these nomads of the plains and to present gifts for the privilege of passing through their country. At one point along this route they met a party of Arapahoes with some Comanches. These colorful and magnificent horsemen traveled with the expedition for a number of days. Talbot even had the rare chance of going on a buffalo hunt with them, and it was an experience he never forgot.

To Talbot and the others, these tribes on the move were a strange and exciting sight. There were the great horse herds, the travois being pulled by both horses and dogs, the women and children, the colorful buckskin clothing with its intricate bead and porcupine quill designs, and always the dignified ceremonial meetings. As many times as John Charles had seen this, it still impressed him; and he described a meeting with Cheyennes on the high plains as though he were writing the history of feudal knighthood.

> The men came to meet us on the plain riding abreast with their drums sounding. They were in all their bravery, and the formidable line was imposing, and looked threatening to those of our people who were without experience in an Indian country.[5]

To young Tom Martin, who was frontier stock from Tennessee, the gathering of Cheyennes was the largest band of Indians he had ever seen. The way it looked to him, there had to be at least four thousand Cheyennes, and when he heard they were on their way to Bent's Fort, he wasn't sure he liked the notion of all these Indians traveling the same trail as the expedition.

Even though Martin had not been with Frémont and his key men when they sat and smoked the pipe with the Cheyenne chiefs, he picked up the rumor that the Cheyennes were anxious to collect Pawnee scalps. When they heard that John Charles and the others had seen Pawnees a day or two back, they sent warriors on the backtrack to see if they could catch up to the Pawnees and add more scalps to help settle a long-standing feud.[6] With these instructions out of the way, the chiefs passed the pipe around again. Gifts were handed out by some of Captain Frémont's men, and a feast was held around the Cheyenne campfires.

After this July 26 meeting with the Cheyennes, the trail to Bent's Fort crossed rough ground, and the wagons slowed the progress of the expedition so much that the Cheyennes moved on ahead. By the second of August 1845, after a long dry march, the party neared Bent's Fort. Frémont called a halt. They were going to ride to the fort in style. The American flag was raised above the wagon carrying the scientific instruments. Men were told to put on the best and cleanest clothes they had. Six or seven Delawares who had been waiting for Frémont at the fort rode out to join him. Then at three o'clock the expedition rode toward the adobe walls and the great gate of Bent's Fort. The men fired a salute with their pistols and rifles. There was a cheer from the men at the fort, where the large flag whipped back and forth in the afternoon breeze, and then the brass cannon just outside the front gate fired a shot.

While the men set up camp about a mile from the fort, John Charles and some of his key men rode into the compound, where they were greeted by George Bent and Ceran St. Vrain. That night there was a big celebration for all hands. For Frémont's party wasn't the only one camped near the fort. There was a caravan of Santa Fé traders with men to guard and drive the large freight wagons.

Only a few days before the expedition reached Bent's Fort, Colonel Stephen Watts Kearny and five companies of the First Dragoons had been at the post after having worked their way down from South Pass just to look the country over in case there should happen to be a war with Mexico. Counting officers, enlisted men, and teamsters, Broken Hand Fitzpatrick had guided 280 men to Bent's Fort. Hospitality had been as good as always for Colonel Kearny and his men, but George Bent and Ceran St. Vrain were not unhappy to see this large group leave, as they put a considerable dent in the stores of the fort. So, when Broken Hand said he was staying and simply described the homeward trail down the Arkansas River to Kearny, the owners of the fort were grateful and more than helpful in seeing to it that the First Dragoons got on their way.

Now George Bent was just as anxious to aid Frémont in his desire to move along. But the expedition stayed much longer than the army. John Charles inquired as to Kit Carson's whereabouts and found that he and Richard Owens were trying to farm a piece of land near the Little Cimarron River, forty-five miles east of Taos. At once Frémont sent for Kit to hire on again.

Then he prevailed on Broken Hand to act as guide and unofficial quartermaster for the group of men he was sending back under the command of Lieutenants Abert and Peck. This unit was to head to the mouth of the Purgatory River, cross Raton Pass, strike the Red River and follow it to Fort Ceran (established in 1843–44 on Bent's Creek), leave the waters of the

Red River, cross northwardly to the Canadian Fork of the Arkansas River, and work their way back to St. Louis. Along the way, they were to observe carefully the lay of the land and make a good map of the region. Their party was to consist of thirty-four men, including Broken Hand and Dr. James McDowell, Jessie's cousin, who had decided he had seen enough of the wilderness. One other man who traveled with this group, and kept his hidden journal, was Isaac Cooper, who complained that Frémont had given them the worst horses and mules, poor stores and supplies, and kept the best for his own party. While this was not true, it would have made sense if it had been. Frémont's party was headed into a vast unexplored territory where there was no hope of finding a nearby trading post with food and extra mounts. Abert and Peck were going to travel through a region where there would be buffalo herds, where forts could be reached if necessary, and where the heavily traveled Santa Fé Trail would not be many days away.

Both parties got everything into good shape, bought additional stores and supplies, which worked a hardship on Bent's Fort, and camped until the middle of August. During this time, one of the most impressive sights any of the men had ever seen was a big Cheyenne celebration. On August 7 Lieutenant Abert wrote that Cheyenne warriors returned to their big encampment with news of a successful raid and with a Pawnee scalp to display. This called for a gathering inside the fort, and Abert was invited to come and see a scalp dance.

The lieutenant had a good position to view the dance, as he stood near the large press for bundling furs and buffalo hides. With sketchbook and notebook he captured this celebration as it actually looked and described how it affected his emotions.

I found about forty women with faces painted red and black, nearly all cloaked with Navaho blankets and ornamented with necklaces and earrings, dancing to the sound of their own voices and the four tambourines, which were beat upon by the men. I was informed that the songs were in honor of those who had distinguished themselves, holding them up for imitation, and deriding one whose behaviour had called his courage in question. In dancing they made a succession of jumps in which the feet were raised but little from the ground. When they first commenced, they were placed shoulder to shoulder on different sides of a square; they then moved forwards towards the centre, raising a yell resembling the war whoop; then they dispersed and retook their stations in order to repeat the same movements; some had lances, some war clubs, while the mother of Little Crow had the honor of bearing the scalp. I never in my life saw a happier set. The women laughed and jumped in rapturous delight, whilst their husbands and lovers were grouped around on the roofs of the Fort looking on most complacently.[7]

All was not quite as festive as this victory dance during the stay of the expedition. Frémont had Chief James Swanuck, Chief Sagundai, and other

Delawares with him. And in the prior year fourteen Delawares had been killed by Cheyennes.

To the Bent brothers and St. Vrain, the presence of the Delawares and Cheyennes offered a chance to ease the tension between these foes. It wasn't only a matter of saving lives; it came down to protecting business. Feuding Indians weren't going to spend much time bringing in furs or buffalo hides, and they also were a constant threat to anybody passing through the country. Using all the tact he could, William Bent, "persuaded Yellow Wolf and a Cheyenne delegation to sit down with the Delawares inside the fort's placita. . . ."[8] The Delawares passed around a peace pipe which had been smoked in meetings of twenty-seven different Indian nations, and young Abert observed that each man had his own form for receiving the pipe and for the ceremony that went with it. Then when each man in the council had smoked the pipe, a white interpreter, Bill Garey, translated the Cheyenne speeches for the Delawares and the whites.

The first Cheyenne chief to speak was Old Bark, and he made it clear that the Cheyennes were concerned about the Delawares as a threat to them and their way of life.

> "We have been in great dread lest you should make war upon us, and, although our women and children have been suffering for food, were afraid to venture forth, for we are now weak and poor, and our ground diminished to a small circle. The whites have been among us and destroyed our buffalo, antelope, and deer and have cut down our timber; but we are so desirous to keep peaceful that we take no notice of it, for we regard the Delawares and whites as one people."[9]

While the Delawares were willing to make peace with the Cheyennes and even invited them to attend a grand council with other neighboring nations to ratify the treaty of peace officially, it was obvious the Cheyennes agreed only to avoid any more clashes with the Delawares and possibly their white friends. For to the Cheyennes, the Delawares were more like whites than Indians. They did not understand them and saw them as people who had crossed over the line from the Indian to the white world. In this belief, the Cheyennes were not altogether wrong.

This great council was one of the last events Abert was to see at Bent's Fort. Five days later, he and Peck made their farewell visit to Frémont. Good luck was wished all around, and the young lieutenants, with Broken Hand to guide them, set out on their initial and short journey of exploration. Contrary to Isaac Cooper's report, Abert wrote that they were well supplied. They were better off than the whole expedition had been on its outward trip to Bent's Fort. Their only shortage was the lack of scientific instruments. Repeated accidents on the trip to the fort had reduced the number of scientific instruments so much that Captain Frémont was able to give them only a sextant and a chronometer to determine their latitudes and longitudes.

Despite this shortage, the young officers managed to do remarkable work. Their mapping of the southern terrain was incredibly accurate and the written report was an objective and facile account of the flora and fauna and the various Indian tribes that were seen. All this was a credit to the lieutenants as students and to Frémont as a fine teacher.

With Abert and Peck on their way, the time was at hand for Frémont to make his last preparations and to move his own party. Except for the instrument wagon, all the other rolling stock was traded at Bent's Fort for horses and pack mules. As Tom Martin remembered in later years, there were 200 pack animals in the train, and "150 loose horses and 250 head of cattle."[10] They were going to travel light and fast in order to cross the Great Basin and get to the Sierra Nevada before the winter snows.

Kit Carson and Dick Owens had arrived from their ranch on the Little Cimarron to serve as guides, and Frémont was happy to see his dependable wilderness man once again. As for Owens, it was good enough for John Charles that he was a friend of Kit's. They were major men to have on such a journey, and along with Alexis Godey, it was a trio that John Charles looked upon as men who might well have been Marshals had they served under Napoleon.

> Carson, of great courage; quick and complete perception, taking in at a glance the advantages as well as the chances for defeat; Godey, insensible to danger, of perfect coolness and stubborn resolution; Owens, equal in courage to the others, and in coolness equal to Godey, had the *coup-d'ôeil* of a chess player, covering the whole field with a glance that sees the best move.[11]

These were men who were natural leaders with a gift for survival.

But somewhere along the way, Frémont knew that Joseph Walker had promised to meet his party; and this was something that the other mountain men counted on. If they were going to make it across that desert, Walker was the man to lead the way.

By August 16 the expedition was ready to move out. Sixty men rode with Frémont, and the brass cannon at the fort boomed a farewell as the horsemen with their large calvacade headed toward the Rocky Mountains. There were two more small settlements to pass through. Then they would be on their own as they worked their way through the lower hills of the mountains until a pass was located.

Four days after leaving Bent's Fort, they rode into Pueblo. A short stop was made, and they moved on their way again. Five more days brought them to a rough settlement of mountain men located beside a tributary of the Arkansas River and in the shadow of the Wet Mountains, a spur of the Rockies. Hardscrabble was the name of this primitive gathering of log cabins where mountain men with their Mexican and Indian wives tried to scratch out a living by farming the thin soil and making horse-stealing raids that took them all the way to California.

While they stopped at this place, Tom Martin won a special Hawken rifle in a shooting contest and immediately sold it to another man for eighty dollars. But the event which Ned Kern remembered was the hiring of one of the most unusual mountain men he had ever seen. This was stoop-shouldered, yellow-haired Old Bill Williams.[12]

A loner in a lonesome trade, Old Bill Williams walked with a rolling and unsteady gait like a sailor just ashore from a two-year cruise aboard a whaler. His buckskins were so coated with grease that, at first glance, it was hard to know if they'd ever been washed or if Old Bill had fallen into a cooling kettle of bear grease. Atop his long, straw-colored hair he wore a blanket cap with its two top corners drawn upward like the points of a wolf's ears, and his face was streaked with vermilion, Indian fashion. But as wild as he appeared, John Charles decided he was the man to guide them through the Rocky Mountains. He offered Old Bill the job for a dollar per day and found. Having nothing special to occupy his time, Williams agreed to help the expedition find its way to the desert country beyond the mountains.

This was the last turning-back place for any man with a timid streak or a feeling that there might be better bets on which to risk one's life. But the men were young, in good physical condition, and ready for adventure. So it was good-bye Hardscrabble, and hello to who-knew-what-and-where, or when it might be.

# Mapping the California Trail

THE FROST OF LATE SEPTEMBER had colored the leaves of quaking aspens and cottonwoods before the expedition worked its way down the final western slopes of the Rocky Mountains. True to his word, Joseph Walker met the party somewhere in the valley of the White River. From there, he guided them to where the stream joined the Green. Then they headed northwest through the level and grassy bottom land beside the Duchesne. They crossed the headwaters of the Provo, which Frémont called the Timpanogos, and followed its course to Utah Lake. The going had not been fast, but the party had eased across the stony barrier of the Rockies. By October 10 they were camped in the Great Basin beside the lake the Franciscan friars Escalante and Dominguez had seen in 1776.

Only enough time was spent at Utah Lake to make it clear to Frémont that this body of water with a silver sheen was not part of the Great Salt Lake as he had reported. This was fresh water without any taste of alkali, and the men had a feast of big lake trout. Two days later they passed by Dry Creek. The next day they rode into the valley that was to become the Mormon stronghold of Salt Lake City. Here they met a band of Gosiute Indians under the leadership of Chief Wanship.

From the chief and his people Frémont learned this was the season of low water in the Great Salt Lake. It was possible for a man on horseback to ride to the largest island. This was not an opportunity to be missed. After the men established a camp near the southeastern shore opposite what John Charles was to name Antelope Island, the captain took Carson and a few others to ride into the shallows with him.

On their way to the island the deepest water they found was just above the saddle girths. "The floor of the lake was a sheet of salt resembling softening ice, into which the horses' feet sunk to the fetlocks."[1] On the island the men found fresh water, good grass, and several bands of antelope. As they were running short of fresh meat, they killed enough antelope to feed the camp for a few days.

When they returned to the shore, a Gosiute approached them. He complained that they had killed his antelopes. Through Walker, Frémont discovered the Gosiute claimed ownership of all the antelopes on the island and wished to be given some kind of payment for the meat they had taken. In no uncertain terms, the Indian made it clear that they had no right to kill these antelopes without permission. Realizing there had to be a payment, Frémont "had a bale unpacked and gave him a present—some red cloth, a knife, and tobacco, with which he declared himself abundantly satisfied for this trespass on his game preserve."[2]

During the two weeks at the Great Salt Lake, the explorer and his men enjoyed warm weather for the fall of the year. Completely fascinated by this great inland sea, Frémont and his party moved slowly around the southern shoreline. Camps were made at the base of the Oquirrh Mountains, and at the site of future Grantsville. At these places Frémont took note of the country and the lake. Salt was everywhere, almost beyond belief. Plants and bushes near the lake were encrusted with crystallized salt that weighted branches with a one-inch thickness. Within the water, nothing survived. There were no fish, no marine life of any kind, though the waves pushed a foul-smelling scum of insect larvae onto the beaches.

By October 25 the expedition had reached the north end of the Stansbury Mountains and established a camp in Skull Valley near present-day Iosepa. They were away from the lakeshore here, though they could see the changing colors of the water as the sun moved across the sky. But time was becoming a crucial factor. The journey to California was long and across a hard and almost unknown land. Jedediah Smith had crossed it. Before him, Peter Skene Ogden and some Hudson's Bay Company trappers had found their way through this vast high desert country, and Joseph Walker had followed the same general route. That much, Frémont and his men knew, but it didn't create a vast amount of confidence. For from the summit of the Cedar Mountains the way ahead looked anything but promising.

The flat, glaring white of the Great Salt Lake Desert stretched westward toward a sawtooth range of black mountains that appeared to be snow-covered at the heights. But to swing north or south and avoid the forbidding stretch of barrenness directly before them was out of the question. The season was late. If they had any chance of reaching the Sierra Nevada before the heavy snows of winter, that chance required marching across the blinding white salt flats.

The Gosiutes shook their heads. It was impossible to cross the salt desert. Just beyond the last foothills of the Cedar Mountains, the line of sagebrush gave way to nothingness. After that, there was the flat, white plain. Nowhere in that emptiness was there any water to drink. Nowhere was there any grass for the animals. Once a man began that journey, once he passed the halfway mark, survival depended upon the hope that the faraway black mountains might have water. If there wasn't any water, there would not be much hope of returning to the Salt Lake Valley.

While all this talk took place, Old Bill Williams checked his horses and gear. Then he approached Captain Frémont, and drew his voucher for payment against the Bureau of Topographical Engineers. He had come as far as he intended. He wasn't about to drift into that goddamned salt desert. Any man who did that was plain stupid or had lost his senses. No sir, that was one trip he had no hankering to make. So on October 27 Old Bill said farewell to men he'd known for years. Like the Gosiutes, he shook his head at the thought of such madness. Then he mounted his horse, hunched forward like he was already half asleep, and rode off toward places where a man could get a good drink of water and a jug of Taos lightning to go along with it.

With Old Bill bound for better pastures, the men remained at Skull Valley. Discussions were held about what the best chance of getting across the desert might be, and a plan of action was decided upon. From the summit of Cedar Mountains, they could see one very high peak in the mountain range beyond the salt desert. Frémont thought this would be a good marker for his men to follow. Still, there was the matter of whether or not there was any fresh water in that distant mountain range. To cross the desert with the whole party and not know if they would find water was much too risky. Another plan was the answer. A foursome of key men was to ride across the desert at night. Carson, Archambeault, Maxwell, and Lajeunesse were to take the best horses, and a pack mule loaded with water and supplies. If they found water, they were to build a signal fire. Then Frémont and the others would follow their tracks. But if there wasn't any water, enough extra water had been packed aboard the mule for these experts in survival to make the return trip to Skull Valley.

As they rode into the darkness, the men remaining behind watched them until it was no longer possible to see the vague shapes of their mounts. There was the possibility that the party would never see these men again, that they might be ambushed by Indians in the distant mountains. But Frémont had faith in the four men he had sent ahead as scouts. If anyone could survive the strange and forbidding country they had headed into, Kit Carson and the other three men were capable of it.

All during the next day, a watch was kept for some sign of smoke. While this was done, Frémont convinced a Gosiute to act as the main party's guide if it was decided to follow the tracks of the scouts. As the day drew toward its end, some of the men voiced their feeling of alarm. There had been no sign. Perhaps something had happened to their friends. Then in the late afternoon Frémont thought he saw smoke. He focused his telescope on the distant peak, and there was the signal fire he had hoped to see.

Two hours before sunset on October 29 the rest of the expedition began their trek into the wasteland of the Great Salt Lake Desert. For a few hours the Gosiute traveled with them. The dark of night became almost ghostlike as starlight seemed to be reflected in the salt flat. But his courage gave way as he got farther and farther away from Skull Valley, and he asked to be relieved of his duty. Frémont understood the man's fear, as the desert was eerie and nearly soundless except for the cracking of salt crust as hooves broke through, the snorting of the animals, and the nervous cough of a rider. The glint of salt crystals gave the illusion of the supernatural, of a land that was and was not of the earth. The Gosiute was given his payment, and he soon was out of sight as he vanished into the darkness.

All that long night the silent men rode toward the dark, shadowy outline of what Fremont named Pilot Peak. Then as the dark of night began to give way to the gray of dawn, the desert breeze became very cold. Frémont called a halt at a place where there was a growth of sagebrush. Camp was made for a short rest. Fires were started to mark their location so that Carson and the others would know where they were, and a meal was cooked over the open flames.

While they crowded close to the campfires and silently drank their coffee, a sound that was not part of the desert drifted toward them. At first it was soft and distant, but there was no wondering about what it could be. For there was no other sound quite like the jingling of spurs. Then the noise grew louder, and in the distance the shape of a rider and his horse could be seen. It was difficult to tell in the changing light of dawn how far away, and just who the man might be. But as he drew closer to the camp, entered the outer rim of firelight, and got off his horse, all the men smiled and greeted Archambeault.

There was water ahead, Archambeault told them. Water and grass. And it was not too far away. It would take some time, maybe most of the day. There had been some rain a few days before they had crossed this area, and Archambeault said that the trail from their camp to where his companions waited would be slow going. But once they rode out of the salt desert, there was water and grass. That was all the encouragement a man needed.

Late that afternoon of October 30 the crossing of the Great Salt Lake Desert was over. Carson, Lajeunesse, and Maxwell were standing beside fires next to a small stream. Camp was set up in a hurry, and the animals were turned loose to graze on the bunch grass. The gamble had paid off. It had saved the party many miles and weeks of detour. It shot them directly to the central part of the Great Basin and started them along what was to become the California Trail.[3]

2

REST WAS THE ORDER OF THE DAY. Both men and animals needed it. Yet, even as they rested, one glance to the west told the men the way ahead didn't promise any easy going. Sagebrush was the plant of the land. On the high mountains there were some piñon pines and pockets of quaking aspen and cottonwoods. But the blue-gray of sagebrush dominated the landscape, and the Toana Mountain Range did not look like any Sunday outing, not even for men on horseback.

Even though a rest was badly needed by all, Ned Kern couldn't resist climbing Pilot Peak, just for the hell of it. He became the first man to make a topographical map of this peak that was to become such an important landmark for travelers on the California Trail.

Early the next morning, during the chill of dawn, the men put out campfires and checked to make sure that they hadn't left any equipment, and then the call was given to move out. Time was running short.

Moving at a smart pace, the expedition passed just north of present Wendover, Utah. Twenty-five miles of riding brought them to the foothills of the Toana Mountains, and this barrier wasn't as difficult as they expected. There were fairly easy passes as they moved upward until they found a good spring at the north side of Morris Basin. Here, they were somewhere between 6,300 and 7,400 feet above sea level as Frémont calculated. As the sun began to set, the warmth of the campfires was welcome, for at this late season, the air had a feel of snow about it.

On the fourth of November the expedition worked its way through Jasper Pass in the Pequop Mountains. It was another day of hard traveling, another day of country that offered no great promise to life. Jack rabbits, lizards, rattlesnakes, and that was about it. Yet there was sign. The frontiersmen saw it around the waterholes. Deer tracks were plentiful—not small deer but big mule deer. There were also antelope tracks, even bighorn sheep tracks, and tracks of birds that came for water in the early morning or just at sunset if there wasn't a camp of men nearby. Now and then there were Indian signs at these places: firepits, burned rocks that had been used to heat water in baskets, chips of obsidian, an occasional arrowhead, and all the other leavings of a people on the move. But there were no Indians.

Camp was established late in the afternoon beside a small spring that eased out of the rocks and sand as though the earth were sweating. Captain Frémont named it Whitton Springs after one of the men. Here, at what is now called Mound Springs, John Charles spoke of his plan for exploring more of the Great Basin.[4]

The touch of winter was in the air, and there was a long journey ahead before they would see Sutter's Fort and the magnificent Sacramento Valley. There was no sense in staying together as one large party. If they split into two groups, arranged a rendezvous point, and fanned out, they would be able to explore much more of this central part of the Great Basin.

What Frémont was saying had all the ring of reason, but it put a great deal of responsibility on Talbot and Kern. For Talbot was to head the larger party taking the central route along Mary's River—the river Frémont was to rename after Baron von Humboldt—and Ned Kern was to be accountable for all the mapping of this region, observation notes on the flora, fauna, and geology, along with anything else that would give a picture of this stretch of territory. The saving factor for these young men was that John Charles was sending Joseph Walker along as their guide.

While the main part of the expedition took what was to become the California Trail and finally the key highway across Nevada, Frémont and ten volunteers headed southwest toward another Salmon Trout Lake that Joseph Walker had described, which Frémont was to name after Walker. This large lake near present Hawthorne, Nevada, was to be the meeting place. Whichever party got there first was to wait for the other section to appear before it moved on again. Tough Kit Carson, some of the Delawares, and two other men made up Frémont's reconnaissance group. It would have been difficult to find a hardier, more resilient party of frontiersmen.

As Ned Kern remembered it, the two parties left Whitton or Mound Springs early in the morning on November 5, 1845. Captain Frémont and his men took a southwest course and were soon out of sight in what appeared to be a great stretch of country that matched the general descriptions found on earlier maps that labeled it a "barren and sandy wasteland." But even from where the parties had said good-bye, it was possible to look toward the southwest and see that there were tall mountains capped by early snow. That didn't add up to a waterless and lifeless desert, not by any stretch of the imagination.

Keeping a south by southwest course, Frémont and his detachment drifted to the south of Franklin Lake. From there they headed into Ruby Valley southeast of present Elko, Nevada, and they appear to have crossed the Ruby Mountains by Harrison Pass. By November 8 the fast-moving party reached either present Twin or Huntington Creek, a tributary of the Humboldt River. Frémont named this stream Crane's Branch after one of his Delaware hunters, and that night they camped beside it. For the next day, they were going to have to climb the Ruby Mountains over very rough-looking ground, and John Charles thought a good night's rest would be in order.

Taking advantage of the rugged men who made up his party, he tried to gain as much knowledge of the country as possible. Early in the morning the way ahead would be determined. Then as the men moved along, hunters were sent to the right and left of the party to look for game and to keep alert for anything that might be of interest. "When anything worthy of note was discovered a shot was fired, or the horseman would make a few short turns backward and forward as a signal that something requiring attention had been found."[5]

And very little missed the sharp eyes of these men. This included a lone Shoshoni Indian who was caught off guard. The man was busy with preparations for his meal. He had a small earthen pot hanging over a sagebrush fire, and inside it were some squirrels he had killed. Nearby, there were other squirrels on the ground beside his bow and arrows. All the man's attention was devoted to the preparation of his meal. Fortunately, John Charles was traveling with some of the Delawares when the startled cook looked about and realized he was caught in the open without his weapon ready, and was being approached by strangers. Having no other choice, he did the only thing that seemed at all wise. He offered Frémont and the Delawares some of his cooking squirrels. Frémont smiled, shook the man's hand, and offered him a small gift. But the Delawares looked on this stranger as an enemy. When Frémont and Carson turned away and began to move on, the Delawares lingered long enough to take the man's bow and arrows. When John Charles saw what they had done, he looked at the well-made bow and arrows and the finely chipped arrowheads. Then he told the Delawares to return them to the man, for they had left him unarmed. He would need his weapon in order to feed and protect himself.

The days moved on as the small party crossed the rough ground of Ruby Pass and descended into Diamond Valley, where they stopped overnight on November 11 at Connor Spring, which Frémont named after another of his Delawares, James Connor. Keeping a southwestern course, the men passed to the south of today's Eureka, Nevada, drifted around the northern slopes of the Monitor Range, and then crossed the Toquima Range into Big Smoky Valley. Making very good time through this vast land, they followed the eastern slopes of the Toiyabe Mountains, rounded them at the southern end, and Walker Lake stretched out before them. At this point they were about seventy-five air miles from Pyramid Lake, and to the west they could see the granite barrier of the Sierra Nevada.

In a later letter to Jessie, John Charles wrote that some of the country he traveled through was hardly a desert.

> Instead of a plain, I found it throughout its whole extent, traversed by parallel ranges of lofty mountains, their summits white with snow. . . . Instead of a barren country, the mountains were covered with grasses of the best quality, wooded with several varieties of trees, and containing more deer and mountain sheep than we had seen in any previous part of our voyage.[6]

By November 24 the small party camped on the eastern shore of Walker Lake just where the Walker River flows into it. They had seen some Paiute Indians who lived in this region, and these Indians were a people of hunger. It seemed to Frémont that every moment of their lives was used in pursuit of food, any kind of food: seeds, insects, lizards, roots, rabbits, and if they were lucky, an occasional deer. Their only good season came when the lake trout were spawning and swam upstream. Then it was possible to kick these native cutthroat trout ashore or to impale them with spears. During those times, food was plentiful. The rest of the year was a daily effort to keep alive with whatever the country had to offer. Such conditions did not leave time to develop a great civilization, and Frémont was well aware of the plight of these desert dwellers as he and his own men began to run short of food while they awaited the appearance of the main party.

## 3

AFTER FRÉMONT AND HIS MEN had vanished into the southwest, Ned Kern kept his own journal of the route they took. They headed out for the Humboldt River when they left Mound Springs. But on November 6 the snow began to come down so heavily that they had to lay over for a day until there was some break in the weather. To make matters worse, the only firewood around was green, hard to burn, and gave off very little heat.

But there was no way to wait out the snow, no way to tell how long the storm might last. Early on the morning of November 7, the snow was falling only lightly, and Walker gave the order to move out. They headed across the sagebrush flats, struck the foothills, and began to move upward into the Ruby Mountains. The climb was steep and rocky, and long before they reached Secret Pass, the men were very nearly blinded by a wind-driven blizzard. Down from the pass and the high country, they came to a good valley where there were groves of aspen and cottonwoods. Here they made camp on a small stream that Walker called Walnut Creek because once one of his trappers had brought a twig from such a tree he had found at the head of the creek.

Two days beyond this camp the men arrived at some hot springs near present Elko, Nevada. Here, where Walnut Creek joined the Humboldt River, they met a party of Shoshoni Indians who told them about three different emigrant parties that had passed by during the fall. From this point on, the journey was one of following the Humboldt River to its sink or lake. But the travel was not easy, as the river snaked through canyons. In places Ned remembered that they had to climb high, rocky ridges to get around impassable regions. Still, there was no shortage of water, not even on the hills, as there were plenty of springs. Added to this, there was a good cover of bunch grass for the animals, and enough game to keep the supplies at a safe level.

But to Ned Kern the Humboldt River was without much variety. It was a winding, crooked stream. The water wasn't too deep, and the country that spread out to either side and to the front and rear was the essence of barrenness. It was hostile land, if land could be so described. Very little timber, maybe a few willows by the river, now and then some cottonwoods, or high up on a sage-covered hillside there might be a patch of green with shimmering golden leaves to signify the changing color of quaking aspen in the late fall. It wasn't an inviting landscape.

Mile after mile, camp after camp, the men made their way. Ned knew Talbot was the appointed leader, but it made no difference who was appointed. Walker *was* the leader, and all the men knew it. Without Joseph Walker there would have been a poor chance, slim at best, for them to find their way. Ned was convinced of this. Even as he carefully mapped the trail, he was aware of one single fact: survival depended on the difference between having Joseph Walker to lead them through this wilderness and wandering until the food ran out, the springs became dry, the rivers disappeared, and the almost invisible Indians caught them off guard.

Then on November 23 Ned Kern was able to make the following entry in his journal: "We have been fifteen days on this river, making a distance of nearly 200 miles."[7] Fifteen days, and now ahead of them was the end of the river in the Humboldt Sink, a lake about eight miles long and two miles wide.

Around the Humboldt Sink the country was sandy, barren, and short of anything that could be called a tree. The party met some Paiutes wearing rabbitskin robes, but the Indians were very shy of the whites and with good reason. Some of them may have been survivors of an earlier battle with Joseph Walker. For in October 1833 Walker was the guide for Captain Benjamin Louis Eulalie de Bonneville's party of exploration which passed through this part of the Great Basin. Having no patience with the Paiutes, who did a little stealing, Walker gave the order to his men to fire upon them whenever they saw them. The result of such an order was recorded by three journal keepers in the party: Washington Irving, Zenas Leonard, and George Nidever. According to Irving, twenty-five Indians were killed at the Humboldt Sink, Nidever put the number at thirty-three; and Leonard claimed that thirty-nine were shot.[8] Whatever the number, it was a high price in human life for a few stolen articles.

To Ned Kern this earlier slaughter of these Indians was only an interesting bit of knowledge to include in his journal. Beyond that, Ned was a man of his times. He couldn't be bothered about how many Indians had been killed, or even if the slaughter of these people had any justification. Instead, Ned gave his attention to the land around him. He noted there were a number of small streams that carried warm water into the lake, and assumed these streams came from hot springs. The main feature of the land, the thing which would be of use to parties of emigrants, was that the bottom land had good soil that offered cultivation possibilities. The other source of food for emigrants passing this way was the great number of ducks and geese that nested in the shallow waters.

Beyond the Humboldt Sink, the way ahead was anything but easy. The men found this out soon after they broke up camp and headed past the lake's outlet on November 24, 1845. They "crossed a low, gravelly ridge, mixed with heavy sand, for 4 or 5 miles . . . then struck a level plain resembling the dry bed of a lake, extending to a low range of hills on the western side 10 or 12 miles distant. . . ."[9] They were on the western portion of the Forty Mile Desert, and their horses and mules found it hard to get any traction in the loose sand or the boggy alkali flats. A whole day of hard traveling did not get them beyond this desolate land. That night they made a dry camp in some sand hills that offered no feed for the animals and only the constant sting of wind-blown sand for the men—sand that was in their food, in their clothes, and into any part of the body that was not covered.

Two more days of travel took them through more sand hills and beyond the lake which was to be named Carson, where they saw plenty of waterfowl. Finally they reached the Carson River near the future site of Fort Churchill. Here there was meadow grass by the river, sweet water, and groves of tall cottonwoods. After their long journey across the central portion of the Great Basin, this camp was a joy to behold. But Walker allowed only one night of rest. Early in the morning he had the men head southward toward their meeting place with Frémont.

After they traveled all of the twenty-seventh and most of the twenty-eighth, Walker Lake came into view. The men continued along the eastern shore of this large body of water until they reached Frémont's camp at the southern end, where he had been waiting four days. Ned Kern and Talbot had been looking forward to this lake, as Walker had told them that once they arrived there, they would have a great feast of salmon trout. But the fishing season was over, and the few Paiutes near the lake made this very clear by answering all inquiries with a negative reply of "Carro hoggi,"[10] or simply, no fish.

That night, after the men had their supper and all the details for a safe camp were assigned, Captain Frémont had a conference with his men. In the morning he was going to head northwest with Kit Carson and his small party. It was his intention to strike the Salmon Trout River, or the present Truckee River, follow it into the Sierra Nevada, locate a pass before the snow began to fall and work his way to the Sacramento Valley and Sutter's Fort.

The main force under Talbot once again would take another direction. Joseph Walker was to guide them to the south. They would follow the high wall of the granite mountains until they reached a low pass the mountain man had discovered ten years ago, a pass Frémont named after Walker. Again, Ned Kern was to be responsible for mapmaking and the gathering of other information about the land they passed through.

The meeting place of the two parties was to be "at a little lake in the valley of a river called the Lake Fork of the Tulare Lake."[11] Here, in the southern reaches of the San Joaquin Valley, the two arms of the expedition would be joined together once more, as Frémont intended to march down California's Great Valley. In this manner, two more Sierra Nevada passes would be mapped, and the whole eastern flank of the great mountain range would be described.

Mapped and described was a way of putting it. And it wasn't going to be so bad, at least not according to Captain Frémont and Old Joe Walker. But Talbot and Kern were trail-wise and trail-weary. Both young men knew that what Frémont and Walker considered a fairly easy journey might be a tough trip before it ended. Even as they sat around the campfires and talked about it, as they discussed just where they would meet, Frémont was telling them he would head northwest in the morning, then up and over the Sierra Nevada. But Joe Walker thought his men had better stay around the lake for a while just to recruit the animals. The fact that he thought this necessary didn't offer much encouragement to Talbot and Kern. All it meant was that they had drawn the wrong hole card again, and the journey southward wasn't going to be one they'd remember with fond affection. But, hell, they'd signed on for exploration and adventure, and they couldn't complain about the lack of it.

4

THE PARTING AT WALKER LAKE took place in the early morning of November 29. Captain Frémont and Kit Carson rode at the head of the smaller party as it headed northwest toward the Truckee River and the course that would take them up toward the white granite bluffs that were later to mark the Donner Pass. Yet, even as John Charles waved a cheerful farewell to the southbound men who would follow the great escarpment of the southeastern Sierra Nevada, he knew they were in for a long journey—three or four hundred miles before they crossed the Sierra Nevada and dropped into the San Joaquin Valley.

Moving at a fast pace, Frémont and his party made excellent time. By the first of December 1845 they were camped beside the Truckee River a few miles above present Wadsworth, Nevada. Three days later they had moved up the winding course of the Truckee River and made their final eastern Sierra Nevada camp on Cold Creek some two miles south of Donner Lake. All the way, they appear to have followed the traces of the Stevens-Townsend party of 1844, which had entered California via this route.

Unlike the Donners, who were to come this way the following year, Frémont and his men lucked it out. The weather was cold, and there was ice in the mornings. But the sky was clear, and there was no sign of snow. Still, there was no point in pressing their luck. So, early the next morning they moved out and began the upward climb into the white and gray granites that were ice-carved and sculptured into whatever a man's imagination might see in the humpbacked and sharply chiseled forms. By sunrise, just in time to watch the long glance of the morning sun light up the Great Basin, the men reached the summit. John Charles calculated the elevation at 7,200 feet above sea level or only forty feet less than the actual altitude of the Donner Pass.

Continuing to follow the traces of emigrant wagons, they moved along the ridge. Then as the going became tougher, they took a southerly direction and set up camp for the night in a mountain meadow. Much as they would have enjoyed a day or two of rest, this was not the season to ease along in the high country. While one day could be cold and clear, there was no way of knowing about the next day. A shift in the wind, a change in temperature, and a storm might ride in from the far Pacific on a tide of wind. Then there could be an overnight blizzard which would leave the way ahead difficult at best and deadly at worst.

Six days more was all that it took for the men to work their way out of the mountains. But those six days were long and hard as they climbed in and out of canyons, along the crests of ridges, through great stands of virgin timber, down the South Fork of the American River, and through the foothill region of oaks, yellow pines, manzanita, red clay soil and arrived in the canyons and valleys of the future gold country, where the brown cover of last season's grass protected the green shoots of new growth. Tough going was putting it mildly, but once they broke into the open, they saw the rolling hills and valley oaks. Beyond was the great open plain of the Sacramento Valley stretching far to the west to the blue line of the Coast Range.

John Charles was excited by the view of this vast land, and when his party passed by the familiar Grimes Rancho on December 9, 1845, he knew the adobe walls of Sutter's Fort would soon come into view. Following the course of the American River, the men moved at a rapid pace until they saw adobe walls in the distance. Then a halt was called about three miles upriver from the fort, and a base camp was established. Captain Frémont intended to rest and be properly attired before he rode ahead on the following day to greet Captain Sutter.

When he arrived at the fort with Kit Carson the next morning, Sutter was not there. Instead Frémont was met by twenty-six-year-old John Bidwell, a strait-laced young man who was not at all like Sutter and almost the opposite of Frémont. Still, Bidwell was Sutter's right-hand man. He was major-domo, bookkeeper, and anything else that required intelligence, good judgment, and dependability. Intellectually, this native of upstate New York, who had migrated to Missouri to become a farmer when he was only eighteen and then caught the fever to head West, was the kind of man Frémont might have found to his liking except for their differences in personality; and those differences were considerable.

Bidwell was prim, a bit on the stuffy side, and much too serious about following orders to the exact letter. The first two traits were bad enough but tolerable. It was the business of following orders so strictly that Frémont found annoying and frustrating. This attitude of following official steps one by one had never set well with him, and he had not expected to run into it at Sutter's Fort. Accordingly, he treated Bidwell with a haughtiness the young man never forgot. Years later, Bidwell remembered him as a man filled with his own importance, a man accustomed to getting anything he demanded. In this meeting with Bidwell, Captain Frémont stated he needed sixteen pack mules, six packsaddles, flour, and other provisions. Also he wanted the use of the blacksmith's shop.

Bidwell tried to explain that the fort was short of everything, that they needed their mules, and there was very little coal to heat the blacksmith's forge. Even so, he said he was willing to let the explorer have the horses and supplies he needed. Without replying to Bidwell, John Charles turned and muttered something critical about Sutter to Kit Carson. Then both men mounted and rode off to their camp without even saying good-bye.

If Frémont thought Bidwell would let things go at this, he had underestimated the man Captain Sutter had left in charge of the fort. Asking Dr. William B. Gildea, a recent arrival from St. Louis, to accompany him, Bidwell rode to Frémont's camp. Here he tried to explain he was only an employee, and that Captain Sutter was trying to patch up his political fences after an unsuccessful attempt to prevent the overthrow of Governor Manuel Micheltorena's government by Juan B. Alvarado and José Castro. But John Charles gave Bidwell the distinct impression that he believed the only reason he was being helped was that he represented the United States while Captain Sutter was a representative of Mexico. Furthermore, he said this had not been the situation during his 1844 visit to California. At that time Sutter had seen fit to give him all the horses, mules, and cattle he wanted.

The young major-domo listened to everything Frémont had to say. He didn't doubt his word, for one look at the explorer's livestock, supplies, and gear was enough to indicate that the party was in need. Yet everything was in short supply at the fort, and he did have his orders. Still, Bidwell agreed to see what he could do to help out. Overstepping his authority, he gave Frémont fourteen mules, the requested packsaddles, food, and some cattle. At that, John Charles was not thankful and hardly civil.

Finally, as a last gesture of good will, as an attempt to satisfy this visitor from the States, Bidwell allowed Samuel Neal—a former Frémont man—to shoe all the animals belonging to the expedition. But even this did not pacify Frémont. For once the animals were shod, he broke up his camp three days before Sutter returned up the Sacramento River. On December 14 the expedition headed south, and the puzzled John Bidwell was happy to see this imperious officer and his men vanish from sight.

## ·⚜· XVI ·⚜·

## A Climate for Violence

THE WARM PASTORAL LIFE, the easy-come and easy-go attitude of Californians had changed since Frémont had last crossed the Sierra Nevada and entered what had seemed to be a New Eden. Not that there hadn't been suspicion about strangers before, and even some records of putting stray Americans in jail for a while, but this last month of 1845 was an uneasy season. Mistrust was in the air, and there was a climate for violence.

Ever since the revolt against Governor Manuel Micheltorena in the autumn of 1844, unrest was the natural state of affairs. Captain John Sutter had tried to aid the governor, but in so doing he had supported a losing side. Governor Micheltorena did not put up the fight needed to defeat the revolutionaries. Sutter's ragtag army included the likes of Moses Carson, Kit's brother; mountain man Caleb Greenwood; raw-boned Ezekiel Merritt, who was all for taking California for the United States; Dr. John Marsh, who did his best to discourage Sutter's troops; and Kanakas and other assorted adventurers not committed to putting up a good fight for a dubious cause. On February 20, 1845, the Battle of Cahuenga, near Los Angeles, took place. This comic-opera conflict saw Micheltorena run up the white flag in an almost bloodless affair. Then Sutter and his troops were taken prisoners by the forces of General José Castro.

The whole business had been bad for Sutter's ego, but it had also left California even more isolated from Mexico than it had been before. Micheltorena was given his life but had to retreat to Mexico within a month. Sutter was given his life but found himself in a touchy political situation where he had to show his allegiance to the new government but was laughed at and criticized by the rough Americans, who thought that surrender had been a foolish act. If they had put up a good fight, all of California would now be theirs.

Peace was uneasy at best, a joke at worst. Independent California was divided into two ruling camps. In the south Governor Pío Pico had his headquarters in Los Angeles. In the north General Castro controlled things from his headquarters in Monterey. But there was no co-operation between the north and the south. Antagonisms were the rule of the day. Coupled with powerful personal rivalries, these antagonisms were constantly stressed by struggles over money. Governor Pico had legislation drafted that would give the largest share of money to the south, but General Castro controlled the treasury and customhouse at Monterey to the advantage of the north. Sooner or later there was bound to be another civil war. But this time there were other factors: The British were watching, the Americans were watching, and into this natural tinderbox rode Captain Frémont and his men.

Added to this unsettled question as to the force which would rule California was another internal problem that worried north and south, Mexican and American. Former Mission Indians had learned a new way of life. Padres had removed them from their native cultures to save their souls. But soul saving included much more than prayers, and the priests had been excellent teachers. Spanish became a second language for these Indians, and the ways of the conquerors were grafted to the ancient traditions of these people.

For the first time in their lives, they had learned that horses and mules were good for something other than food. They learned to ride, to break animals to the bit and saddle, and in the passing of generations they had become excellent horsemen. Along with this, they learned how to handle firearms, plant crops, and make all the things that were part of mission and rancho life. No longer were these Indians wedded to the old tribal life. They were Indians, but they possessed all the skills that the Spanish and Mexicans had taught them.

Then with one stroke of a pen Governor José Figueroa signed the proclamation of August 9, 1834, which secularized all of California's missions. Caught in another cultural shock, these Christian Indians were suddenly without the patronage of the priests. They were turned away from a life without any ties to the former tribal ways. But there was a model for them to follow, a hero whose name had been passed along. This was Estanislao, a Miwok genius who had fled the confining life in the missions, returned to his people, and taught them how to beat the invaders by using European tactics along with their own hit-and-run methods. In Estanislao's final battle in 1829, General Vallejo's well-armed force suffered many casualties before they were able to dislodge him from his fortified hill. Even artillery did not penetrate the chaparral breastworks this brilliant leader had put up, and it was only Vallejo's use of a flank attack and the ultimate chance to set the chaparral on fire that forced Estanislao out of his fortification. Yet the Miwoks were not defeated, and Vallejo was happy to ride back with something he could call a victory, even if it was far from complete.

With the memory of heroes such as Estanislao, the Mission Indians had an example for survival. While many of these Indians worked as laborers for the rancheros who took over mission lands, and some took to drink or suicide as a solution to their problem, many followed in the path of Estanislao. By 1835 the first raids were being carried out against the stock on the great ranchos. Between that time and Frémont's 1845 visit to California, the power of the so-called "Horse-thief" Indians was not limited to a few raids against isolated herds of horses and cattle. The former wards of the missions had become top-notch light horse cavalrymen, who attacked ranchos and missions, killed rancheros, and threatened the established government. In 1843 Governor Micheltorena proposed the construction of a fort in Pacheco Pass. He was formulating plans to keep all the passes clear of these wild horsemen whose most successful raid had taken place in 1840 when they ran a thousand head of stock off a San Luis Obispo rancho.[1]

2

TWO DAYS AFTER LEAVING SUTTER'S FORT, the explorer and his men pitched camp along the handsome bottoms of the Calaveras River near present-day Stockton. The weather was sunny and warm for December. The next day they arrived at the Tuolumne River, where they saw great herds of wild horses moving across the plains. That night, they rested close to Miwok villages, but it was difficult to sleep because of the constant squawks and honks of the vast flocks of ducks and geese nesting in the nearby marshes.

Shortly after sunrise the men moved on their way again. They left the San Joaquin Valley and began an easy climb into the foothill country. In the late afternoon they crossed the Merced River. As they looked for an evening campsite, they saw a band of three hundred tule elk working its way toward the river, grazing on the tall grass as it moved along.

The weather was clear but not cold when they moved on their way the following day. It was December 19, but there was no sign of winter. Within a short distance, the men came to "a beautiful country of undulating upland, openly wooded with oaks, principally evergreen, and watered with small streams which together make the MARIPOSAS RIVER."[2] Moving through this country that would one day be very familiar to John Charles when he acquired the Las Mariposas grant, the men encountered deeply worn trails that Indian raiders used when they rode out of their mountain strongholds to strike ranchos in the San Joaquin Valley.

Frémont knew about these raiders from his first trip to California and from Kit Carson, who had killed some when he had been in California with the Ewing Young party of trappers in 1829–30.[3] He took it upon himself to risk his life and those of his men to give pursuit to the "Horse-thief" Indians. He saw that the trail coming from the valley was thick with fresh tracks of a returning raiding party, and he sent Dick Owens, Lucien Maxwell, and two Delawares ahead as scouts while he and the others followed.

The whole expedition was jeopardized by this attempt to teach these raiders a lesson. There was no way of knowing how many Indians they might find, or even if the Indians had seen them and were preparing a proper ambush. Just how risky this adventure was became obvious when they reached a clearing that had been an Indian camp, and prepared to make their own halt for the night. The horses were just unsaddled, the mules unpacked, when shooting started ahead of them and they realized their scouts had run into trouble.

Leaving four men to guard the camp, Frémont and the others saddled their horses and rode at a gallop toward the sound of barking dogs and still more shooting. Within a half mile they saw a large Indian village, no more than two hundred yards ahead. Beyond the village, there was a small hill. On top of it was a good cover of brush, oak, and large rocks. Advancing toward this hill were more than a hundred warriors, who were shouting in Spanish at Frémont's scouts, who were cornered. The raiders had almost surrounded the knoll and had taken possession of the scouts' horses.

John Charles and his men shouted and began firing as they galloped toward the Indians. Then from the knoll, the Delawares gave their battle cry, and dashed down the hill to recover the horses as Maxwell and Owens kept up a steady cover of rifle fire. Dick Owens killed the Indian leading the charge, and as the man fell, the others retreated toward their village. The combination of firepower from the hill and the sudden appearance of the expedition caught the ex-Mission Indians off guard. Owens, Maxwell, and the Delawares got off the hill. The Indians regrouped at their village, and Frémont's party rode to their own camp, covering their retreat with sporadic rifle shots.

The raiders followed them to their camp. Then they took cover among the rocks and trees and began to harangue their white and Delaware foes in Spanish. *"Esperate Carrajos,"* they said—"wait until morning. There are two big villages up in the mountains close by; we have sent for the Chief; he'll be down before morning with all the people and you will all die. None of you shall go back; we will have all your horses."[4]

All that night the men kept watch. They heard the Indian women and children retreat to the mountains before midnight. Even after that hour there were occasional shouts beyond the perimeter of the camp; and the men standing watch got ready at each shout for a possible attack. During the long hours, only one shot was fired. Delaware Charley caught a sudden movement in the darkness and fired before he realized he was shooting at a wolf bounding over a fallen tree. Then, as dawn broke and the men had a better view of their position, it was obvious that during the night all the Indians had drifted out of sight.

Finally, realizing the danger he was exposing his party to by trying to run down these former Mission Indians, Frémont gave orders to move out of their country. They worked their way along the higher ridges, where there were "fields of a poppy which, fluttering and tremulous on its long stalk, suggests the idea of a butterfly settling on a flower, and gives to this flower its name of *Mariposas*—butterflies—and the flower extends its name to the stream."[5]

Staying within the rolling foothills and oak groves, the men worked their way to a small stream. Following this, they began to drop into the lower and more open country where the San Joaquin Valley and the lower hills merged. As they reached this dividing line, they saw an Indian riding at a gallop toward the open plain of the valley.

Lucien Maxwell thought the Indian was heading for the river and a possible meeting with other warriors. He shouted to Godey that they had better kill the Indian, and they were joined by two of the Delawares in pursuit of the lone rider. The chase was over open ground and across the low hills. John Charles rode with the remaining men to see what was happening. As they drew in sight of the hard-riding Maxwell, he had overtaken the Indian. Both men were already off their horses and were dueling on foot. Maxwell had two pistols, and the Indian used his bow and arrows. "They were only ten or twelve paces apart. I saw the Indian fall as we rode up. I would have taken him prisoner and saved his life, but was too late. The Delawares captured his horse."[6]

More Indians were seen ahead of the party, but they quickly hid in thickets of brush. The closeness to death in the hills may have sobered Frémont's enthusiasm for running down the raiders for he ordered his men to move along. As they did, the first rains of a dry December began to fall; and with the rain, there was a cold wind and a damp tule fog.

Following the Lake Fork, or the present King's River, the men reached Tulare Lake on a cold and windy December 22. Here, the captain expected to find the men of his main party; but all he saw was the low country around the lake shore and the thick growth of bulrushes which had dry upper leaves that rattled as the wind whipped them back and forth.

For nine more days they searched the surrounding area in the valley and the foothills. It was only in the country of oaks, yellow pines, and firs that they escaped the penetrating cold of the San Joaquin Valley. Yet, as they moved close to the snow line, they still saw no sign of their friends. Indians were always nearby, and the men had to be on their guard at all times. At that, the Indians managed to kill one of their mules. Then on the last day of December, the first snow began to fall. They worked their way upward toward the headwaters of King's River and did not turn back until they had reached an altitude between 9,000 and 10,000 feet above sea level. In this country of icy cold, they made their last high camp.

When they returned to the valley at the end of the first week of January 1846, they arrived at Tulare Lake and a favorite camping site of the Indian raiders. The Indians recognized one of their own horses that had belonged to a warrior who had been killed in the fight. Neither side, though, wanted any more trouble for the moment. Frémont was over his feeling of superiority with regard to these Indians. If he could avoid another battle with them, he intended to do just that. For the one night, the two foes camped near each other in peace. Then in the morning John Charles and his men headed away from the lake and started northward up the San Joaquin Valley, moving slowly until the thick, cold fog burned off under the late morning sun.

Frémont decided that somehow they had missed the main party. The only thing that seemed to make any sense was to ride back to Sutter's Fort. His men were more than capable of taking care of themselves.

They were too strong to have met with any serious accident and my conclusion was that they had traveled slowly in order to give me time to make my round and procure supplies; the moderate travel serving meanwhile to keep their animals in good order, and from the moment they would have turned the point of the California Mountain the whole valley which they entered was alive with game—antelope and elk and bear and wild horses.[7]

Settled back into his normal routine of following a charted course, Frémont rode at the head of his party as they hurried back through the Great Valley. By January 15 Sutter's Fort was once again in view. This time when they rode through the gates, Sutter was there to greet them. Frémont's attitude toward him was almost the opposite of his actions when he had dealings with young Bidwell. They exchanged gossip, drank wine, and ate a good meal. After four days of living in a fashion the trail never allowed, John Charles spoke to Sutter about obtaining passports for his party so that they could travel to Monterey. In the meantime, he obtained the use of Sutter's schooner *Sacramento*. Taking eight men with him, he sailed down the Sacramento River to see Yerba Buena (San Francisco) and to pay a visit to the United States vice-consul, William Alexander Leidesdorff.[8] For while he waited for the reuniting of his expedition, John Charles intended to make certain that he was on the best possible terms with any officials of the United States who were stationed in Mexican California.

Frémont and Leidesdorff hit it off in a friendly manner. And Leidesdorff took Frémont on a visit to the New Almaden quicksilver mine south of Pueblo de San José. From there they traveled on to Monterey.

3

IN THE MEANTIME, the main section of the expedition finally crossed the Sierra Nevada and reached the San Joaquin Valley on January 21, 1846. Since they had left Walker Lake on December 10, 1845, they had made the long march beside the high, southeastern barrier of the Sierra Nevada's spectacular granite peaks. At this season conditions were not good. Grass was poor; there was very little game; and meals usually consisted of boiled or roasted horse and mule meat. As they got beyond the lower end of today's Owens Lake,[9] travel became even harder because of the loose, sandy soil. For the first time, Ned Kern saw Joshua trees, which he nicknamed "Jeremiah," and wrote that the "trees have a grotesque appearance, a straight trunk, guarded about its base by long bayonet-shaped leaves; its irregular and fantastically shaped limbs give to it the appearance of an ancient candelabra."[10]

Running short of everything but the desire to survive, the men reached the downward drift of the Sierra Nevada, where the range did not present an impossible wall reaching toward the low clouds. Fighting their way through a hard-blowing snowstorm, they crossed Walker Pass on January 19, 1846. Two days later they followed King's River and reached the San Joaquin Valley. They had arrived too late to meet Frémont.

Just as John Charles had guessed, the men didn't wait for him to make an appearance. Tired and hungry for some decent food, they headed north with the idea of working their way to Sutter's Fort. By February 6 they were camped beside the Calaveras River. Joseph Walker and another of the party left the men there and walked on ahead to see if they could learn of Frémont's whereabouts. They returned in the evening with good news. With them was a very large mountain man called Le Gros Fallon. Walker had known William O. Fallon for many years during the peak of the Rocky Mountain fur trade, and he was the kind of man who could be counted on to notice the comings and goings of friends and foes alike. Not having lost this habit, he told Walker that Captain Frémont and the rest of his party were near Pueblo de San José.

Having learned of Frémont's location, the decision of whether to walk on and join him or wait for further orders was left up to Talbot. Without any notion of what Frémont's intentions might be, Talbot decided the prudent thing was to send Walker to Pueblo de San José and wait at the Calaveras camp for word. Having plenty of meat, since Chief James Sagundai had killed a large grizzly bear, the men settled down for a rest while Walker and Fallon headed for Frémont's camp.

On February 11 Kit Carson and Dick Owens appeared on the south side of the Calaveras River. They halted to make a raft of tule reeds, crossed the river, and told the men that horses were on the way, and that the trip to Pueblo de San José would not have to be made on foot. Four days later a party of men with fresh horses arrived, and the Talbot command rode south to join Frémont.

Between Pueblo de San José and the camp beside the Calaveras River, Ned Kern thought the country had a rare beauty. Even though it was only February, the signs of spring seemed to be everywhere. Wild flowers of different colors and sizes were beginning to sprout. Groves of valley oaks were showing their new shades of green. Flocks of ducks and geese were so plentiful that when they took to the air, there was a flapping of wings like the clapping of thousands of hands.

Twelve miles from Pueblo de San José, the men rode by the Mission San José de Guadalupe, but this fourteenth and richest mission, founded in 1797, was already showing signs of decline. Secularization had taken its toll.

The building is very large and built of adobes; the roof is of tiles. Long rows of adobe buildings, one story high, used as the dwellings of the native converts, are now in a most dilapidated condition, scarcely offering shelter for the few miserable Indians who still cling to those hearths, where they had been raised, by the kindness of the founders, to something like civilization. The remains of the gardens and vineyards show the care and labor bestowed on the grounds by the fathers.[11]

Even at this stage of decline, the mission was magnificent compared to Pueblo de San José. This pueblo was no more than a small village of indifferent adobe dwellings, in which many of the citizens lived only slightly better than the Indians at the mission.

Thirteen miles south of the pueblo, on the main road to Monterey, the men under Talbot's command were reunited with Captain Frémont. Camp had been established at William Fisher's La Laguna Seca Rancho, which this former Boston sea captain had purchased in 1845. Here, Frémont was refitting his expedition, purchasing horses and supplies, and thoroughly enjoying himself after having visited Monterey with William Leidesdorff. He had met Thomas Oliver Larkin, the shrewd trader and merchant from Massachusetts who had come to California in 1832. Larkin was the United States consul at Monterey, and was well on his way to becoming a rich man. Through Larkin and Leidesdorff, he was introduced to the former California governor Juan Bautista Alvarado, who owned the famous Las Mariposas grant that would one day belong to John Charles, and also met General José Castro.

To all these officials Frémont had said that he

was engaged in surveying the nearest route from the United States to the Pacific Ocean . . . being under the direction of the Bureau of Topographical Engineers . . . that [the journey] was made in the interests of science and of commerce, and that the men composing the party were citizens and not soldiers.[12]

What he had not said was that except for Ned Kern, Theodore Talbot, and himself, the men of his party had been chosen for two things: wilderness experience and expert marksmanship. Even as the whole party was reunited, the ability of his riflemen was demonstrated as one of the marksmen shot a soaring vulture out of the sky by breaking one wing just to show his talent after he had watched a demonstration of excellent horsemanship by some Californios.

4

FRÉMONT WAS IN GOOD SPIRITS now that all his men were together. The streak of self-importance he had shown to Bidwell at Sutter's Fort appeared to have vanished with the warm weather of late February. But appearances have a way of being deceptive, a way of changing with the slightest of problems. On February 20 a small problem reached John Charles in the form of a written complaint from Don José Dolores Pacheco, the alcalde at Pueblo de San José.

Don José regretted having to bother Captain Frémont, but a complaint by Don Sebastian Peralta had been lodged with his office. One of the horses in the explorer's company was a stolen animal; and when the rightful owner had come to the camp of the Americans to request the return of his property, he had been insulted and told to leave.

It was not a major problem, and there was no reason to make trouble over it. There were plenty of horses in California. Frémont could have returned the one that belonged to Peralta and replaced it at very little cost. Instead, he took it as an insult to himself and his men. It was not a question of cost but a matter of honor.

Assuming a haughty attitude, John Charles wrote a hostile letter to Don José. He maintained that the horse had been with his band since they had left the United States, that he knew about the man who had come to his camp and claimed ownership, and that indeed the man had been insulted and rightly so. Then he wrote that this intruder, this accuser "should have been well satisfied to escape without a severe horse-whipping."[13] While this was bad enough, he added more wood to the fire. In a blunt manner, he stated, "You will readily understand that my duties will not permit me to appear before the magistrates of your towns on the complaint of every straggling vagabond who may chance to visit my camp."[14]

This insulting and tactless letter to Don José Pacheco was in bad taste and showed extremely poor judgment for a visitor in another country. Then to compound this mistake, some of the men had too much to drink and took it upon themselves to insult the family of Don Angel Castro, an uncle of General José Castro. While Captain Frémont apologized for the behavior of his men, the incident only added to the suspicion of the Californios concerning the true purpose of this armed body of rude men.

Things had not reached a point of no return, but it was quite obvious that hostilities could be prevented only by the departure of these intruders to areas far away from the settlements. On February 22 John Charles and his men did move out. But instead of easing beyond the range of key Mexican towns, they took the road to Santa Cruz and pitched camp for the night on Wild Cat Ridge in the Santa Cruz Mountains.

Taking his time, Frémont rode at a slow pace through the mountains and looked over the lay of the land. He was thoroughly fascinated by the stately redwoods and the large madrones, and he noticed that in this warm climate, wild flowers were beginning to sprout even though spring had not arrived. With the interest of a possible landowner, he looked at the countryside and considered it for a future home.

By March 3 the expedition had moved beyond Santa Cruz, traveled around the southern curve of Monterey Bay, and passed by the red-tiled roofs of Monterey's adobe homes—the only elegant structures a visitor could see on the two or three unpaved and sandy streets. The town was nestled beneath the pine-covered hills and looked seaward at the Pacific Ocean that captured the changing colors of each passing day. Then the riders turned east. Their backs felt the cool western wind; their noses picked up the aroma of salt spray from the long, rolling breakers; and their ears caught the sounds of the sea world—the cry of seagulls, the deep-throated barking of seals, the thundering crash of high waves, and the steady creaking of wood from ships riding at anchor in the harbor. Twenty-five miles beyond this setting, which Frémont later compared to Italy and other Mediterranean countries, the men reached Rancho Alisal beside the Salinas River—a ranch which now belonged to William E. P. Hartnell, a former Englishman who had migrated to California and was now the administrator of the Mexican customhouse at Monterey. Here, the Americans established a camp in the Salinas Valley, where wild oats were as tall as a young boy.

Two days later, John Charles dashed off a letter, handed it to Godey, and had him deliver it to Larkin's home in Monterey. In this letter he acknowledged that his nearness to the major city of Alta California might offend Mexican officials. For that reason, he regretted not being able to visit Larkin and offered his apologies to Mrs. Larkin. In answer to a letter from Larkin about Lansford W. Hasting's account of the new route across the Great Basin, Frémont wrote that he knew nothing about this publication and was unable to judge its reliability. Then he stated that it was his intention to leave California as soon as spring arrived. No doubt he and his party would ride north toward the Oregon country.

On the same day that Frémont wrote to Larkin, the consul had received copies of two letters which General José Castro had sent to Captain Frémont. Both letters were blunt and to the point: the explorer and his men were to pack their gear and get out of Mexican territory at once. Even as Larkin read these copies, Lieutenant José Antonio Chávez had delivered the original letters to Captain Frémont.

John Charles was disturbed by this sudden turn of events. As he later described this day, he criticized Lieutenant Chávez for being abrupt and rude, and said that the young officer's behavior reflected the unfriendly attitude of General Castro. Even though he was in a foreign land, John Charles replied that he would not obey an order he considered insulting to him and to the government of the United States. But he did not take time to write to General Castro or the prefect at Monterey, instead he simply told Lieutenant Chávez what he could tell his superiors.

Saying he would not obey such an order was one thing, but Frémont must have realized that he was in no position to back up his refusal. He did not occupy a strategic piece of ground. He was greatly outnumbered by the Mexican troops, and he had not come to California with orders to start a war. Early the next day, he and his men left Hartnell's and rode to Don Joaquín Gómez's rancho at the base of the Gabilan Mountains between the Salinas and San Joaquin valleys. But this stop was only for a day.

In the morning the party followed a wood road up the mountains to the crest of the ridge on Hawk Peak.[15] Here, on a small, wooded flat, they set up camp in a position which gave them a good view of the main road, of Pueblo de San Juan, and of Mission San Juan Bautista. Grass, wood, and water were plentiful, and John Charles had his men construct a rough log fort. When that was finished, they cut a tall sapling and stripped it of all limbs so that it could be used for a flagpole. Then as the men cheered, the American flag was raised.

If it had been Frémont's intention to stir troubled waters, the raising of the flag was a good way to cause a flash flood. General Castro was incensed. His soldiers were ready to attack. Citizens were volunteering for action. All this was just the opposite of what U. S. Consul Larkin wished. For months he had been sending communications to Washington which stressed three factors that could send Mexican California into the arms of the United States without anything vaguely resembling warfare: the internal strife between Castro in the north and Pico in the south, the constant threat of the nearby British, and the gathering of influential Californios such as General Vallejo and Captain Sutter who were ready to see Alta California become part of the United States. To hasten this transformation, Thomas Oliver Larkin had been made a "Confidential Agent in California" by Secretary of State James Buchanan for the sum of six dollars per day. And now, just as Larkin was beginning to see a chance for California to fall into the hands of the United States, Frémont had upset plans that had been months in the making.

During the next few days, Larkin worked overtime as he tried to pacify the Californios and prevent an outbreak of shooting. He informed Frémont that his attitude and military posture were causing excitement and resentment and that the Mexicans were convinced that they could attack and destroy his expedition. The only solution to this situation was for him to move his men far away from the settlements, or get out of California while it was possible to do so without endangering the lives of his own men as well as the Americans who lived in California.

Even as Larkin tried to make sure that war did not break out, the situation at Pueblo de San Juan grew steadily worse. General Castro gathered his troops, marched back and forth in plain view of Frémont's hilltop camp, checked his cannons, and posted the following proclamation:

Fellow Citizens: A band of robbers commanded by a captain of the United States army, J. C. Frémont, have without respect to the laws and authorities of the department, daringly introduced themselves into the country and diso-

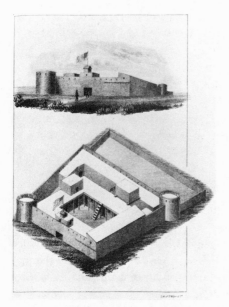

Exterior and interior views of Bent's Fort, as drawn by Lieutenant James W. Abert in 1845. (*The Bancroft Library*)

A Cheyenne scalp dance inside Bent's Fort during Frémont's stop there in 1845, as shown in a watercolor by Lieutenant James W. Abert. (*Courtesy of John Howell—Books, San Francisco*)

General José Castro as he looked when Frémont had been ordered by the general to get out of California. *(The Bancroft Library)*

Chief James Sagundai, one of Frémont's loyal Delawares. *(The Bancroft Library)*

With an eye for action and detail, Edward Kern captured the scene of what it was like to saddle up and move out. (*The Bancroft Library*)

Klamath, or Tlamath, Lake as drawn by Edward Kern. (*The Bancroft Library*)

Edward Kern's romantic concept of the expedition's battle with the Klamath Indians. (*The Bancroft Library*)

Sutter Buttes in the Sacramento Valley with Mount Shasta in the distance, as pictured by Edward Kern. (*The Bancroft Library*)

beyed the orders both of your commander-in-chief and of the prefect of the district, by which he was required to march forthwith out of the limits of our territory; and without answering our letters he remains encamped at the farm "Natividad," from which he sallies forth committing depredations, and making scandalous skirmishes.

In the name of our native country I invite you to place yourselves under my immediate orders at headquarters, where we will prepare to lance the ulcer which (would it not be done) would destroy our liberties and independence, for which you ought always to sacrifice yourselves, as will your friend and fellow citizen.

Headquarters at "San Juan."

8th March, 1846.[16]

The date was ironic, for neither Castro nor Frémont knew that at the very time this proclamation was issued, General Zachary Taylor's troops had moved out of their Corpus Christi camp and were marching toward Mexico and the first battles of the war between the United States and Mexico. Had either of these tempestuous characters known this, the first shots in the conquest of California would have been fired near peaceful Mission San Juan Bautista.

As Frémont and his men watched the activities below, as they focused a spyglass on the scene, one thing was becoming very clear. The forces of General Castro were getting stronger. Indians were being brought into the fold, and the Mexicans were giving them enough liquor to convince them that they should join Castro's army. Then Frémont counted three pieces of artillery among the weapons of the Mexican forces. On the second day of this stand-off, John Charles and his men spotted the bright-colored uniforms of cavalrymen riding up the road from Monterey.

Taking about forty men, Frémont went down the wood road where there was a good cover of brush beside the main road. There they waited for the approaching horse soldiers. They were convinced that the cover of brush beside the creek provided a perfect spot for an ambush. As they waited, the troop of cavalry came to a halt within a few hundred yards. The officers held a consultation, and then, as though they had considered the possibility of being ambushed, they turned their horses and rode back toward Monterey.

The tension was broken in the late afternoon of the third day. A westerly wind whipped the crude flagpole, and it fell across the log fort. Taking this as his cue, Frémont said they had waited long enough. The Mexicans were not going to attack. He gave the orders to load the pack horses. When everybody was ready, the expedition left the heights of Hawk Peak and dropped down the eastern slope into the San Joaquin Valley. But as John Charles wrote in a letter to Jessie, "thy retired slowly and growlingly. . . ."[17]

As the Americans rode into the valley and headed north, General José Castro celebrated *his* victory by posting another Proclamation. This one was tacked on the wall in the billiard room in Monterey:

> Fellow-citizens—a party of highwaymen who without respecting the laws or authorities of the department boldly entered the country under the leadership of Don J. C. Frémont, captain in the U.S. army, having disobeyed the orders of this comandancia general and of the prefecture of the 2d district, by which said leader was notified immediately to march beyond the bounds of our territory; and without replying to the said notes in writing, the said captain merely sent a verbal message that on the Sierra del Gavilan he was prepared to resist the forces which the authorities might send to attack him.[18]

The remainder of Castro's bombastic outburst pointed out that the Americans were cowards and poor guests. In the future these men would be repelled with force in defense of Mexican honor and independence.

Both Frémont and Castro came away from this bloodless affair with heads held high and with all their pride intact. But the sparks of violence had been struck, and the coming of conflict was only a matter of another meeting between the forces under the command of these proud officers.

# XVII

## The Turning Point

WHILE GENERAL CASTRO boasted about driving the Americans away from the territory, Captain Frémont and his men were not beating a hasty retreat. They had dropped down the southeastern slopes of the Gabilan Mountains by way of Pacheco Pass and entered the San Joaquin Valley. They did not give the appearance of being frightened or worried men. They were riding six miles per day. That speed hardly gave the impression of men in a hurry to get anywhere.

Ever so slowly the expedition worked its way through the San Joaquin Valley. They camped beside the Tuolumne River and beside the Calaveras River once again, beneath great valley oaks. As they rode along, they looked at the lush growth of green grass and heard the swishing sound as the heads of wild oats glanced against their wooden stirrups and stroked the bellies of their horses and mules.

Each detail was observed and entered in Frémont's notes. Twelve days passed in this Great Valley, days of watching wildlife, trying to identify flowers and plants, and fording the swollen creeks and rivers carrying flood-waters of melting Sierra Nevada snowpacks. On the twelfth day they were camped beside the American River across from Sutter's Fort.

At the American River camp, Frémont made plans to explore more of the valley and then head north to the Oregon country. Supplies were needed to outfit his party, and he decided he could get these by sending Lieutenant Talbot to Yerba Buena aboard one of Sutter's vessels.

Old Joe Walker and Charles Taplin[1] went down the Sacramento River with Talbot, and it was only then that the young officer learned that his friend Taplin and Walker were headed back to the States. They were tired of marching up and down California, and Frémont had allowed them to take their discharge from the expedition. All he had asked was that Taplin deliver some letters to Jessie. So, at this point, twenty-seven-year-old Taplin headed home.

While Frémont recruited his animals and gave his men a rest, word came to him that there were many Americans in northern California who were ready to take up arms and join him if he wished to launch a campaign against the government of Mexico. From the Napa Valley, mountain man James Clyman sent a letter that he could raise men, arms, and supplies for any campaign. From Captain William D. Phelps of the merchant ship *Moscow*, anchored off Monterey, came word that he was quite willing to have his ship serve as transportation if Frémont's command should need it.

John Charles expressed his thanks for their concern but pointed out he was not in California to head a military conquest. He wrote to James Clyman that if he allowed himself to be drawn into such a conflict, his forces would be greatly outnumbered and would be engaging in hostilities that would be frowned upon by the United States Government. Yet Thomas Oliver Larkin expressed his loyalty to Frémont in case of trouble when he wrote to Secretary of State Buchanan and stated he was ready to join Frémont, at once, should he become committed to a course of action.

Despite all these offers, John Charles gave no indication he had come to California on a filibustering expedition. The men who gathered around him near Sutter's Fort could talk about war all they wanted. He was not about to enter a conflict his government had not sanctioned.

2

TEN MILES beyond the mouth of the Feather River, the party struck a course a little east of north and moved toward the settlements along Bear River, a tributary of the Feather. It was a grand season to ride through the Sacramento Valley. Summer heat was almost three months away, and the sun of spring gave the men a daytime temperature in the seventies, while the nights did not drop below fifty degrees. There was no rain, and only a few great white clouds rode the tide of winds across the bright blue sky.

Following the Bear River, the men came to the rancho of Sebastian Keyser and William Johnson.[2] They stopped here for the night and the next day headed westward again to the junction of the Yuba and Feather rivers, where they saw Theodor Cordua, whose rancho was located here. His land was cultivated by Maidu Indians, and his dried beef, bushels of wheat and great loads of vegetables were sent down the rivers by launch or schooner to the market at San Francisco Bay.

All the rivers were running at the high-water level, and the Americans were ferried across by Maidus in canoes and small rafts. As they drifted on the fast-flowing water John Charles looked shoreward at the Maidu village and noticed that their huts were shaped like beehives, and many naked Indians were stretched out on the tops of these huts, taking advantage of the warm sun.

In a hurry now, the expedition followed the Feather River and pushed ahead. By March 27 the men saw a familiar face and heard a voice of welcome. The rancher on Butte Creek was none other than their former black-smith Samuel Neal. Sam had prospered since he had asked to be released at Sutter's Fort two years before. He had a good stretch of land, had become a breeder of excellent horses, and had a large herd of cattle.

Three days later they reached Deer Creek and the ranch of Peter Lassen of Denmark.[3] Here, between present-day Chico and Red Bluff, Lassen had built a smaller version of Sutter's empire. Maidu Indians worked for him as field hands, and he planted wheat and cotton and maintained a vineyard for the making of wine and brandy. Along with this, he had a good blacksmith shop and a growing cattle herd.

Lassen's Bosquejo Ranch consisted of twenty-two thousand acres of upper Sacramento Valley land, and John Charles was greatly impressed by what he saw at this outpost. Lassen and Frémont took a liking to each other, and the explorer was invited to be a guest for as long as he wished. The Dane was so impressed by the explorer that he later named a settlement (now a ghost town) Benton City in honor of Senator Thomas Hart Benton.

While the men rested at the Deer Creek camp and made short exploration trips beyond it, John Charles sent Alexis Godey, young Tom Martin, and four Delawares southward to the San Joaquin Valley to trade for fresh horses before the party continued its journey toward Oregon. As Tom Martin recalled, they bought eighteen head of horses and mules and "paid a small butcher knife and a string of beads for each horse."[4]

By the time the men had returned with the fresh animals, it was the middle of April, and spawning salmon were moving up the Sacramento and all the tributary streams. The large fish were so thick in the smaller streams that their fins rode above the surface of the water, and it was a time of feasting for the Indians, settlers, visitors, and grizzly bears.

While the horse buyers had been away, Frémont had crisscrossed the upper Sacramento Valley just to look over the country. He took special notice of trees and flowers, observed that the soil ranged between a rich, dark loam and a hard-packed red clay; and he took careful readings of the fluctuating temperature and the changes in altitude. He saw the long jagged, snow-packed range of the Sierra Nevada to his east; he was duly impressed with Mount Shasta's dominating white cone to the north, and named one of the Coast Range mountains, far to the west, Mount Linn in memory of Senator Linn of Missouri.

As they camped, newly arrived emigrants just in from the States, came to Captain Frémont and requested his help in protecting them against so-called hostile Indians. While John Charles did not take part in this sad affair, he allowed Kit Carson and most of his men to become involved in a vicious killing spree against the local Indian tribes.

As Tom Martin remembered this bloody business, they charged into the Indian village and killed twenty-four with their initial rifle attack. Then, using sabers, they cut a red path of death for three hours. When it was all over, more than 175 Indians were dead, and the survivors had taken cover in the foothill country.

The attitude of these men toward the Indians of the area was that they were only savages, something less than human. As Kit Carson put it, this "perfect butchery" would give them cause never to attack the settlements again. These men were the spawn of generations of border families that had been pushing their boundaries farther westward into Indian country year after year.

After the killing it was time for a dance! Twelve miles south of the Deer Creek camp there was a party of emigrants just in off the long trail, emigrants bound for Oregon. The men received permission from Frémont to attend a party in their honor. They took cuts of fresh bear, deer, and elk meat to the pioneers, and a festive time was had in celebration of victory over the Indians. It was a time Tom Martin never forgot as there were fifteen ladies among the party. "A place had been cleared away," he said, "and we began dancing which we kept up for two days."[5]

The stay at Peter Lassen's came to an end on April 24, 1846. John Charles thanked the Dane for his hospitality, said farewell, and struck north toward the Cascade Mountains and Oregon. His plan was to connect with the Deschutes River and to revisit the country of the Klamath Indians. He remembered this region as a land of good grass, plenty of water, and heavy pine forests on the nearby mountains.

They moved along and gained in altitude. The nature of the country changed from an agricultural paradise. Hills gave way to mountains, easy going to rough travel over broken shale; and they rode beyond the last groves of oaks and entered the elevation of pines and firs. By April 29 they were camped in Big Valley beside the Pitt River. Two days later they reached present-day Tule Lake, which Frémont named after an old friend from South Carolina, Barnwell Rhett.[6]

By May 6 the expedition reached the southern end of Upper Klamath Lake, where the Klamath Indians had a fishing station at the lake's outlet. "Up this river the salmon crowd in great numbers to the lake," Frémont wrote, "which is more than four thousand feet above the sea. It was a bright spring morning, and the lake and its surrounding scenery looked charming. It was inviting, and I would have been glad to range over it in one of the Indian canoes."[7] The Klamaths were too busy fishing to take anybody on a pleasure trip. This was the season to spear as many salmon as possible and to put the women and girls to work filleting and smoking the pink meat so that there would be a good supply for the cold months of winter.

Through Kit Carson, John Charles was able to make a deal with the Klamaths. He traded goods with them for dried trout and salmon, and they agreed to ferry the supplies and equipment across the fast-flowing Klamath River. It was strictly a business arrangement with the Indians. They had their own work to do—work that couldn't be put off—and they remembered

Frémont from the time in the snow during the 1843–44 season when they had helped guide his party toward the Black Rock Desert country of Nevada.

A sparse amount of information about the country ahead had been obtained from the busy fishermen. They had indicated that there was a major village to the north where the present-day Williamson River enters Upper Klamath Lake.

They crossed rough mountain spurs, worked their way around coves and bays, and rode up and down one hill or ridge after another. The travel was very slow, and John Charles hoped that somebody at the large Klamath village would be able to show them a better trail.

My plans when I started on my journey into this region were to connect my present survey of the intervening country with my camp on the savannah, where I had met the Tlamaths in that December; and I wished to penetrate among the mountains of the Cascade ranges. As I have said, except for the few trappers who had searched the streams leading to the ocean, for beaver, I felt sure that these mountains were absolutely unknown. No one had penetrated their recesses to know what they contained, and no one had climbed to their summits; and there remained the great attraction of mystery in going into unknown places—the unknown lands of which I had dreamed when I began this life of frontier travel.[8]

As they stood around the fires on May 8 and enjoyed the flickering orange flames that warmed their bodies, the sound of moving horses caught their attention.

Quickly all the men moved away from the campfires so they wouldn't be an easy target, and peered into the darkness. They listened and watched for some sign of movement. Two horsemen rode out of the night and into the circle of firelight. They were moving slowly, and it was easy to see that the riders and mounts were exhausted from a long, hard trip. The man in the lead was a familiar figure. He was none other than Sam Neal. His companion was Levi Sigler, who had been at Sutter's Fort and had agreed to make this journey to overtake Frémont.

Both men were stiff, and when they dismounted, they walked slowly toward the campfires, where they were offered some hot coffee. As they felt the circulation and warmth return to their cramped legs and weary bodies, Sam told Frémont they had covered almost a hundred miles during the last two days to overhaul the expedition. They had agreed to do this to let him know there was a young military officer named Gillespie about a long day's ride behind them. This fellow claimed he had important messages from the government to deliver to the captain.

They had to be damned important, Neal reckoned. The fellow had got off a ship at Yerba Buena—one just in from the Sandwich Islands—and had come up the Sacramento River in a boat. At Sutter's Fort, he had asked for guides to take him to Frémont. That was how they and the others got roped into this ride.

When Frémont asked about the "others," Neal told him that one of them didn't have much choice. He was Benjamin Harrison, the officer's black servant. The other two who had volunteered were good wilderness hands, Peter Lassen and Bill Stepp. But Gillespie and Harrison weren't the kind of men who knew how to make a go of it outside a city. The best they could hope for was that the Indians wouldn't locate them before the captain sent some help. Their chances of keeping alive depended on Lassen and Stepp, but two men couldn't hold off a whole swarm of Indians if they took a notion to jump them. There wasn't much doubt that the Indians were looking for trouble. Shortly after they picked up Frémont's trail, Neal said that Indians had tried to cut them off near the lake. The only thing that had saved them was that the horses he had brought from his ranch had enough speed and strength to outrun them.

Frémont knew that the trail back was too rough to follow at night and decided he would take a rescue party out just before daybreak. He asked Neal and Sigler if they would guide him to where they had left Gillespie and the others. Both agreed to the proposition. Then they settled down to a late supper. While they ate, John Charles selected Carson, Lucien Maxwell, Basil Lajeunesse, Godey, Dick Owens, and four Delawares to make up the rest of the party that would ride south before dawn.

## 3

LIEUTENANT ARCHIBALD H. GILLESPIE, United States Marine Corps, was determined and resolute. He was not an ordinary officer. Handsome, resourceful, brave, and very fluent in Spanish, thirty-three-year-old Gillespie possessed the kind of courage and self-pride needed for his task as a courier to carry messages from President Polk, Secretary of State Buchanan, Secretary of the Navy Bancroft, and Senator Benton to Captain Frémont.

His orders had been issued in Washington, and he had visited the Benton home in November 1845, where he talked to the senator and the lovely Jessie Benton Frémont. After that friendly visit, the lieutenant traveled by ship across the Gulf of Mexico and disembarked at Vera Cruz. There, dressed as a civilian, he caught a stagecoach that took him up the National Road and across the Sierra Madre Oriental to Mexico City.

He was not able to leave Mexico City for a month. This delay was caused by the overthrow of President José Herrera's government by the revolutionary forces of General Mariano Paredes. Turmoil and strife made any foreign traveler suspect outside Mexico City and not too safe even in the city. This hostility applied in particular to Americans, as word was out that Congressman John Slidell of Louisiana had been sent to Mexico by President James K. Polk with the authority to offer the Mexican government up to forty million dollars for what belonged to Mexico north of the Río Grande, and this included California.

Texas had been stolen. American troops were not far away from the Mexican border, and now the Americans had the gall to offer money for Mexico's northern frontier lands. Lieutenant Gillespie saw the impact of all this on the Mexican people. Newspapers called for war against the Americans. Angry speeches were a daily affair, and the central theme always came down to one thing: Mexico had to defend her honor against the aggressive Americans.

After a month of seeing all this, Gillespie was convinced that war was inevitable. Then, as he managed to leave Mexico City and travel northwest across the great central plateau, he saw the first steps toward war as Mexican troops marched northward bound for the Texas border. That action spoke much louder than all the newspaper articles or angry speeches. As Gillespie reached the Sierra Madre Occidental and the roads and trails leading to the Pacific Coast, the messages he had memorized and destroyed were outdated. The way things were shaping up, war between the two nations would be a fact and not a thought by the time he reached California.

He followed the steep roads and trails in and out of the barranca country and emerged at Mazatlán, the key Pacific port of northwestern Mexico. Here, where the great swells of the ocean broke against Olas Altas, Gillespie observed that the British fleet, under the command of Admiral Sir George Seymour, was *not* a token naval force. On the contrary, it was a power to be reckoned with should the British decide to use it either for the conquest of California or for the defense of Mexico.

As he boarded the sloop of war *Cyane* for his triangle journey to the Sandwich Islands and then back to California, he left Mexico thoroughly convinced that war between that country and his own was only a matter of time.

That had been months ago, and Gillespie had no way of knowing that on this May 9, 1846, as he and the three men traveled, General Zachary Taylor's troops were fighting and dying in the Battle of Resaca de la Palma, the second major encounter of the Mexican War in two days.

As Gillespie, Peter Lassen, and their companions camped by the Klamath River, they heard the sound of horsemen approaching, and before the marine knew what was happening, Captain Frémont and the relief party appeared out of the darkness.

4

FRÉMONT LET HIS MEN REST for the night without having to stand guard duty. Though he was too excited to sleep, all the other men were dozing in no time as he contemplated what this sudden turn of events might mean. As he considered everything and reread all the letters and instructions, he was startled by the sound of sudden movement among the horses and mules picketed near the lake, less than a hundred yards from camp.

"Drawing a revolver I went down among them. A mule is a good sentinel, and when he quits eating and stands with his ears struck straight out taking notice, it is best to see what is the matter."⁹

Seeing nothing, catching no sign of movement, he talked softly to the animals and quieted them. When they went back to grazing, he returned to the campfire and resumed reading. He knew he had a tough and reliable group of men who could serve as the nucleus for a striking force and that there were many emigrants in the Sacramento Valley and elsewhere who would join him if war between Mexico and the United States was imminent.

Between midnight and one o'clock, he grew weary. It had been a long and eventful day. The ride from the main camp had been over forty miles, and the news Lieutenant Gillespie had delivered was something John Charles had not expected. His blankets were spread beneath the overhanging lower branches of a cedar tree, as were those of his sleeping men. Except for the open lake shore, the other three sides of the camp were surrounded by low cedars, which offered shelter against the cold wind that came off the nearby snow-covered peaks and whipped across the lake.

Kit Carson and Dick Owens were sleeping near one of the low-burning campfires as John Charles drifted off to sleep. It was Kit's voice that awakened him as he heard him calling out to Basil Lajeunesse. For Kit had heard a noise that sounded like an ax striking, and it had come from the direction of the sleeping Basil. Carson and Owens were on their feet and away from the firelight at once, and they gave the alarm that the camp was under attack.

For Basil the alarm had come too late. His head had been split wide open with a tomahawk. And the half-breed Denny, who had been near Basil, was making the last sounds of life as blood spurted out of the many wounds he had received from sharp iron arrowheads. Wetowka Crane, one of the Delawares, reached for a rifle, but it was not his own and wasn't loaded. Using the rifle stock, he tried his best to defend himself but was hit by five arrows. As he fell to the ground, he was still striking at the foes even though he was mortally wounded. By this time the whole camp was firing at the raiders, and they brought down the Klamath chief who was leading the attack. Lucien Maxwell shot him in one leg, and the impact of the bullet swung him half around. At this moment Stepp fired, and his rifle ball entered the chief's back and came out near his heart, driving the man to the ground. As Carson saw him fall, he realized this was one of the bravest warriors he had ever seen.

Confusion and shock were the first reactions to this sudden and violent attack. But to men such as Carson and the other frontiersmen, the feeling of numbness was only momentary. An Indian attack was nothing new in their lives, and they automatically did what was needed to defend their position. Dick Owens ran to the lake shore, grabbed the ropes of the picketed animals, and quickly led them back to camp. Maxwell and the others kept up a steady round of fire at any sound or movement in the nearby woods. Carson directed some of the men to hang blankets from cedar boughs and bushes to act as a shield against the whirring, deadly flights of arrows; and the blankets were soon like a porcupine's hide as arrow after arrow struck them.

Then as the men watched, some braves moved into the circle of firelight and tried to retrieve the body of their fallen chief. But each time, all the men fired. They were angered to the point of hatred because of the death of their comrades, and they had no intention of letting the Klamaths pick up their dead leader.

All that night the men remained behind their line of woolen blankets, only peering over or around these shields to fire another shot in the direction of the well-hidden bowmen. Then as dawn began to break, there was silence. Easing away from their torn blankets, the men saw the tracks of fifteen or twenty Indians.

Three of our men had been killed: Basil, Crane, and the half-breed Denny, and another Delaware had been wounded; one-fourth of our number. The chief who had been killed was recognized to be the same Indian who had given Lieutenant Gillespie a salmon at the outlet of the lake. Hung to his wrist was an English half-axe. Carson seized this and knocked his head to pieces with it, and one of the Delawares, Sagundai, scalped him. He was left where he fell. In his quiver were forty arrows . . . all headed with a lancet-like piece of iron or steel—probably obtained from the Hudson Bay Company's traders on the Umpqua—and were poisoned for about six inches. They could be driven that depth into a pine tree.[10]

Angry and not yet satisfied that enough revenge had been exacted against the Klamaths, the men tied the bodies of their dead comrades on pack mules and began their journey to their main camp. After two hours on the trail, they saw many canoes on the lake. All appeared to be coming from different directions but heading for a point of land where the trail neared the shoreline. Then as the men got closer to the point, they heard the cry of the loon, and the mountain men knew this was a scout's signal that the whites were approaching.

Realizing they might be in for another battle, Frémont gave the order to bury the bodies. Shallow graves were dug in a laurel thicket, and the bodies were wrapped in blankets and placed in the graves. Then the men covered the soil with laurel and fallen logs and carefully removed the signs of their own tracks. John Charles thought this was a fitting place for these brave men, and he wrote that they were companions who deserved to have wild laurel blooming above them.

The delay in burying their comrades saved Frémont and his men from another battle on the trail. For when they reached the lake shore at the point, the canoes and Klamaths were gone. They had been waiting, but evidently thought their enemy had taken another direction.

By afternoon John Charles and his weary men rode into the main camp. As soon as the news of the deaths had been told, the Delawares blackened their faces with ashes and dirt in mourning. They were angry and hurt, and wanted more than the death of the Klamath chief to make up for the loss of Crane and Denny and their great friend Basil Lajeunesse.

In the evening the camp was quiet. The men were brooding and ready to strike out. To be ambushed was bad enough, but to lose close companions was something that had to be avenged. The men sat around the campfires, hardly talking, as they cleaned and checked their rifles and pistols. But the Delawares, with their blackened faces, struck Frémont as men who felt this tragedy more than anybody else. They were silent as they sat cross-legged around their campfire, and they seemed to be staring into the fire for some answer to what had happened. John Charles walked over to their fire and sat beside them without saying anything for a while. Then he told them he was sorry that Crane and Denny had been killed.

Chief Swanuck looked at the captain. Then he struck his breast and told him that the Delawares were sick. The Indians who had done this were still around. They knew this because they had been in the woods and saw signs that the Klamaths were not far away from the camp.

Frémont realized it was a matter of honor and revenge for the Delawares. They didn't wish this killing to be forgotten. They wanted to take some Klamath scalps to pay for the death of their own men. So John Charles asked how they wanted to carry out their vengeance. Swanuck and Sagundai discussed what they wished to do as the other Delawares listened. When they finished, Chief Sagundai told Frémont, "In the morning you go little way, stop. These Delaware stay here. Indian come in camp, Delaware kill him."[11]

An agreement for vengeance had been made, and the Delawares were satisfied that the captain realized what they had to do. In the morning, after the pack mules were loaded, the Delawares rode away from the campsite with all the others. Any watching Klamaths would assume that all the men were moving on. A few hundred yards away from the camp, the Delawares eased off their horses and handed over the reins to men heading on.

Quietly, making sure that they weren't seen or heard, the Delawares worked their way through the woods. In thickets that overlooked the past night's camp, they settled down and waited.

As the men rode along, they listened for the sound of rifle shots. Before long, they heard the stillness of morning shattered by a volley of rifle fire. Then all was quiet until the Delawares caught up to them. They were holding two fresh, bloody scalps, and they felt better about everything. Their only disappointment was that they had not been able to kill more Klamaths. But as the Indians had moved into the clearing, the snap of a twig had startled them and they had scattered for cover. Still, the Delawares had killed two and were certain they had wounded others.

This should have been the end of it, but Frémont was bitter about the death of Basil. In great measure, he blamed himself for not having placed guards around the camp. The only other time he had not had men stand guard duty was on the island in the Great Salt Lake. Before he headed south to California, he intended to make sure the Klamaths paid dearly for their ambush.

By nightfall the expedition had marched to a northwestern bay of Upper Klamath Lake. They encamped and built a log corral to hold their animals. Guards were posted, and the whole atmosphere of the camp was that of a military troop about to enter a battle. Scouts returned with the news that they were not far from the principal Klamath village. This meant that their strike against these Indians had to be planned carefully. Frémont wanted to catch them off guard. If they left in the first light of day, and kept a good pace, they should be able to attack the village before the Klamaths had a chance to get into their canoes and escape to the center of the lake.

Early on May 12 the men rode without talking, and tried to avoid pushing through brush thickets that would make too much noise. As they neared the region where the Williamson River enters Upper Klamath Lake, Frémont sent Carson, Owens, and ten others ahead to scout the exact location of the Indians and to determine the best approach for an attack. He told Kit he was not to attack until all the men had joined him.

Tom Martin was riding with Kit Carson and the advance guard. When they reached the river, there was no holding Kit back. Just across the stream was the main Klamath village, with the Indians just beginning to settle around their campfires for their morning meal. The large canoes were beached without any warriors standing guard. The Klamaths hadn't seen or heard the approaching men. When Carson gave the signal, his party started on a gallop down the ridge toward the river. Even before they neared a line of willows on their side of the river, they were spotted by Klamaths who had just drifted across in their canoes. Shouting the alarm, the warriors quickly shoved off again and headed for the other side.

The Williamson River was over a hundred yards wide at this point, and though the Klamaths began firing arrows at the charging horsemen, they had to elevate their shots and it was easy to dodge them. At Carson's signal the men opened fire and killed more than twenty Klamaths before the warriors broke and ran.

The river looked too deep to cross at this point, and Kit shouted to ride upstream to a better ford. When they reached what he thought was a good place to cross, they ran their horses at full gallop off a three- or four-foot bank into the water. But the river was almost fifteen feet deep, and men and horses went clear under, then surfaced and made it to the other side. "All of us," Tom Martin said, "had got our powder wet, and we would have been in a fine fix, if the rest of our party had not arrived at this moment."[12]

Taking some of the Klamath canoes, Martin and others of Carson's group paddled back across the river and picked up some of Frémont's section. When they returned, they had more rifles and dry powder for their own weapons. As they kept up a steady fire at the fleeing Klamaths, Frémont found a ford at a rapid upstream and came across with the rest of the men and animals.

When John Charles reached the Klamath village, he saw a dead warrior "sitting in the stern of a canoe, which the current had driven against the bank. His hand was still grasping the paddle. On his feet were the shoes Basil wore when he was killed."[13] The Klamaths were out of their village, but they fought bravely from behind brush and the first line of trees. Their weapons were no match for rifles, and they finally had to scatter into the cover of the mountains. When they did, Frémont gave orders to burn their rush and willow huts and to put the torch to their scaffolds of drying salmon. Unused arrows were found behind clumps of brush, fanned out ready to be picked up, quickly notched, and fired; and each arrowhead was made of sharp iron or steel. Frémont gave the final order of destruction; and his men smashed and burned all the Klamath canoes they could find near the lake and river.

Riding away from the scene of carnage and devastation, the captain and his men made camp about a mile beyond. While a corral was being fashioned for the animals, scouts were sent out to see if the Klamaths were moving in close again, and it was reported that they were advancing through the forest. Taking Kit, Archambeault, Stepp, Sagundai, and Swanuck, John Charles rode out to see what the Indians might be planning. As they rode into the cover of trees, one of the Klamath scouts suddenly appeared. He had his bow ready for action and drew a bead on Carson, who was riding ahead. Kit squeezed the trigger of his rifle, but it misfired. Seeing this, Frémont spurred Sacramento, and the horse jumped forward and knocked the Klamath to the ground, causing the arrow to miss its mark. Then before the man could get to his feet, Sagundai jumped off his horse, and with a powerful blow from his Delaware war club, smashed the warrior's head.

The whole affair had been bloody and without pity. Nobody even bothered to find out if this particular Klamath village had been responsible for the ambush of their camp. All that mattered was that they were Klamaths. It was believed they were guilty and deserved to pay such a brutal price. Frémont had been traveling with his mountain men and Delawares for so long, he had begun to think and act as they did. Violence and vengeance had become a way of life for him. If his men were killed, then somebody must pay for it.

That night, after the day of killing, Frémont again assumed his role as a scientist. The sky was clear, and he took observations to establish their latitude and longitude. He entered this information in his notebook, and named the stream flowing into the lake the Torrey River (today's Williamson River) in honor of the great botanist who had helped identify specimens from his expeditions.

Around the campfires there was very little sleeping that night. All the men were too keyed up from the day of battle, and they talked about each event as they relived their victory. Among all the men who had seen and heard the sights and sounds of this brutal raid, none was more taken by it than Lieutenant Gillespie. He shared Frémont's tepee that night, and he could not get to sleep. He admired these men who fought so hard for Captain Frémont, commented on their physical fitness, and kept John Charles awake as he talked over the incidents of this day. He was extremely emotional about what had happened. "By heaven, this is rough work. I'll take care to let them know in Washington about it."[14]

Captain Frémont made it clear that this was something that would not be reported to Washington, and that there was time enough to forget all about it. As for heaven's role in it, the captain said he didn't think it had much to do with the day's events.

The killing had not ended with this one battle. Before the expedition worked its way down the south side of Upper Klamath Lake and over the mountains to California, at least three more attacking Indians were shot by Frémont's men. The last warrior was shot by Kit Carson, but not before he held off the men for quite a while from his hiding place behind a rock on the side of a ravine. When they got to his body, they saw that he not only had spread arrows out on the ground for ready access but also held some in his mouth. Kit admired the bravery of this warrior and gave the dead man's bow and arrows to Lieutenant Gillespie.

By May 24, 1846, the men were back at Peter Lassen's Deer Creek ranch. Frémont wrote a long letter to Senator Benton in which he described the sudden appearance of Lieutenant Gillespie and the trouble with the Klamath Indians, who Carson considered to be even braver than the Blackfeet. Their warlike stance and their iron arrowheads and tomahawks appeared to be influenced by the Hudson's Bay Company's men—yet another indication of British influence in the Oregon country.

But the British were not the only problem. At Lassen's they also learned that General José Castro had issued another proclamation on April 17. He ordered all noncitizens out of California, and expressed his determination to put a stop to any further entrance of emigrants from the United States.

# ⁂ XVIII ⁂

## The Time of the Bear

THE STARS were on a collision course, and nothing was destined to change the path of impact. Captain Frémont and his men rode south from Lassen's Deer Creek headquarters on the morning of May 25, 1846, but John Charles was not aware of all the forces about to shape a new destiny for California. He had only seen the proclamation issued by his old foe, General José Castro, stating that Americans without Mexican citizenship were no longer welcome in California. But when Frémont reached Sam Neal's rancho, more bad news awaited him.

According to Sacramento Valley settlers, Castro's forces had been moving around the valley all during the month of May. Word was out that they had been inciting Indians to burn crops and wheat fields, put the torch to houses and barns, and kill Americans whenever they had the chance. While this information was a blend of fact and fiction, Frémont had no way of knowing what was true and what was false. Seeing no other choice he prepared for the worst.

Lieutenant Archibald Gillespie was given a requisition for supplies needed for the party's dwindling armory and stores. Included in this list were such diverse items as eight thousand percussion caps, three hundred pounds of lead, a keg of gunpowder, and a variety of stores that ranged from medicinal needs to coffee, tea, sugar, flour, salt, tobacco, soap, tent rope, and iron for horseshoes. All of these things were to be procured from the sloop of war *Portsmouth*, which was riding at anchor in San Francisco Bay. For Captain Frémont was certain that Commander John B. Montgomery[1] would not question the requisition once the marine officer had informed him of the precarious position of American settlers and squatters in the Sacramento Valley. No doubt, he would send all that was needed back up the Sacramento and Feather rivers aboard one of the *Portsmouth*'s launches.

This was hardly a small mission Lieutenant Gillespie had been ordered to carry out. But Frémont knew that the marine spoke fluent Spanish, that he had managed to come all across Mexico by himself, and that he had found his way to the Klamath Lake camp. Such a man was more than dependable. Less than a day's ride south of Neal's was Theodor Cordua's rancho. At that point Frémont assumed Gillespie could pick up a canoe to paddle down the Feather River to the Sacramento River, stop at Sutter's Fort for any additional news, and perhaps be able to travel to Yerba Buena aboard one of Sutter's vessels.

Once Gillespie had galloped on his way toward Cordua's place, Frémont got ready to leave Samuel Neal's. It was vital to know what was *really* happening throughout the Sacramento Valley. As things stood, he had no idea as to the location of any of Castro's troops—if they were on the move—and he had to be certain that the Indians had not positioned themselves for raids on the Americans. This included more than settlers, for there were emigrants coming across the Sierra Nevada, and their teams would be exhausted, the families worn out, and the men hanging on by sheer grit and nothing else.

Then to make certain that all possible trails were covered, John Charles realized he needed to know if any soldiers might be moving up the valley from the eastern side of San Francisco Bay from Monterey, San Juan or Pueblo de San José. To gain information about this route up the San Joaquin and Sacramento valleys, John Charles asked one of Neal's friends—Sutter's former supercargo Samuel Hensley—to ride south to Dr. John Marsh's[2] Rancho Los Meganos near Mount Diablo. For Marsh was located in a good spot to observe any Californios traveling the interior route up the valleys.

Moving southeast from Neal's, Frémont headed toward Bear Valley, where he thought he might find just how things were going for settlers in that area and for emigrants who would be coming through that region on their way to the Sacramento Valley. Most of all, he wished to make certain that General Castro had not set a trap for them. Here in Bear Valley on May 29 John Charles met a rough character who would have been at home with the toughest frontiersmen in his party. Tall and spare, given to stuttering whenever he became excited, this man with bloodshot eyes and with hair sunbleached and turning gray was the foot-loose old Rocky Mountain trapper Ezekiel "Stuttering" Merritt.[3] He was rugged, fearless, and a man who enjoyed taking risks just for the pure hell of it.

From Merritt, Frémont learned there hadn't been any Indian trouble yet, nor had any of Castro's brightly uniformed troopers been snooping around. But if they did, Merritt looked forward to meeting them. He didn't care too much for Mexicans in general, and one in particular that he longed to meet again was Salvador Vallejo,[4] who, it was rumored, had struck Merritt when the two of them had met three years before. The overall impression Frémont had of "Stuttering" Merritt was that here was a man to remember if anything in the way of warfare should break out. Like the other hardened men who had been with the explorer on his expeditions, Merritt was a man cut out for tough times in tough places.

Satisfied that there was no clear and present danger for the settlers and emigrants of the Bear Valley country, John Charles and his men headed back into the Sacramento Valley. From the heights of the foothills above what was to become the mining camp of Rough and Ready, the men saw four peaks that rose from the floor of the Sacramento Valley like sore boils. The tallest of these strange mountains that stood as islands in the grassland of the valley appeared to be at least two thousand feet above sea level, and their rugged terrain plus the fact that they were only some twelve miles west of the Feather River made them an ideal place to establish a protected encampment.

By May 30 Frémont's party had established its headquarters among these buttes (now called Sutter Buttes), some sixty miles north of Sutter's Fort. Here, in a protected draw near the southeastern base, the men pitched tents, took turns at guard duty, and waited for something to happen. While they waited for some indication that Castro was on the move, there was plenty of game to keep the camp supplied with fresh meat, a good cover of grass for their horses and mules, and, best of all, a natural position of strength from which they would be able to hold off a much larger force should either Castro or any of the Indians decided to move against their stronghold. Here, they would wait for Gillespie to return with ammunition and supplies.

2

DISTRUST, SUSPICION, AND FEAR were a deadly trio. As Frémont heard the tales of American settlers and squatters, it became obvious that the outbreak of hostilities would be the major summer crop in California.

Castro and the other Californios were on the move throughout the valley, or they were about to head into the valley. Castro's soldiers had been promised a free hand with the Americans. Castro was at odds with Governor Pío Pico[5] and was planning to separate all of northern California and make it into a country under his rule—a country that might well be protected by the British or the French. Castro had convinced General Mariano Guadalupe Vallejo[6] to join forces with him. Castro was ready to unleash the Indians and reward them for destroying American property and taking American lives. All these rumors and variations of them were told to Captain Frémont during the last day of May and the beginning of June.

Yet he did not move against his arch foe, Castro. Instead, he decided to attack the various Indian tribes. Still feeling bitter and resentful about the ambush by the Klamaths that had taken the life of his good friend Basil Lajeunesse, Frémont was determined to move against the Indians before they had a chance to set fire to the drying wheat fields or cause any other tragedy for American settlers. Brutal as this move was to be, even John Sutter believed the Indians posed a genuine threat.

On his trip south from Neal's, Gillespie had informed Sutter that he had seen deserted Indian rancherias, and settlers along the Feather River had told him of Indian servants who had been killed by warriors on the move. This

made Sutter leery about the Indians, but the major turning point in his attitude took place when one of Castro's soldiers gave a brand-new rifle to Chief
Eusebio so he could assassinate the genial Swiss.

Furious, Sutter raided the Maidus in the foothill along the Mokelumne
River. As they crossed the river, the current upset the rafts. Rifles, pistols,
and even the clothes of twenty-four men went downstream on the white-
capped water. When Sutter finally caught up to the fleeing Maidus at the
Calaveras River, they took cover in cellarlike holes in the riverbank. Though
Sutter and his men killed and wounded many of the Maidus, some of the
raiding party were hit by arrows. Then as the ammunition ran out, the men
retreated back to their Sacramento Valley stronghold. Still not satisfied, Sutter
offered a hundred-dollar reward for Chief Eusebio's scalp. It was collected by
Chief Pollo, who looked upon Eusebio as a renegade and considered the reward a handsome amount for killing and scalping him.

Brutal as Sutter's raid and reward for a scalp were, they were mild in comparison to Captain Frémont's "punishment" of Indians who were suspected
of getting ready to cause trouble. As he wrote in later years, "I resolved to an-
ticipate the Indians and strike them a blow which would make them recognize that Castro was far and that I was near."[7] Following this policy of creating a reign of terror in order to avoid what *might* happen, Frémont and his
men rode down the western bank of the Sacramento River. The first warm
days of June had already made the wheat fields and the wild grass turn a
golden yellow. Though the morning was cool, by midday the horsemen were
sweating through their shirts as the Delaware scouts returned with a report
of where the Maidu villages were located.

Then, without warning to these people who were simply going about their
usual fishing, winnowing seeds, chipping arrowheads, and all the little things
that made up the pattern of their days, Frémont gave the order for his men to
charge. With wild yells, the sure-shot mountain men and Delawares were
into the first village before the people knew what was happening.

Dogs ran for cover, a few ponies lit out for the open plain, women
screamed and scurried about as they tried to protect their children, and before men could even pick up their bows and notch their arrows, rifle fire
began to take its toll. A peaceful religious dance—which Frémont thought
was a war dance—came to a sudden halt. The dancers, whose faces were
painted black and who wore feather headdresses, ran toward the river; but
their make-up and feathers made them easy targets for the merciless raiders,
and only a few managed to jump into the river and swim beyond rifle range.

In this wild and savage manner the Americans rode from village to village.
At each place they repeated their pattern of death and destruction until the
late afternoon turned into twilight, and the word of their coming had
reached the last village in time for the people to run for cover in the vast
openness of the valley, or to jump into the river and swim to a hiding place
among the tules or willows on the far shore.

Barbaric and cruel beyond belief, this was a bloodbath without any semblance of sanity, and both whites and the Delawares joined in the killing with a strange and sick excitement. They had been ordered to prevent the slaughter of Americans by these Indians. Well, by all that was demonic, they had taught these Indians, these peaceful people, a lesson they'd never forget. This was the justification, the free license to kill. It was simple to these men who rode with Frémont. Kill first, and the potential enemy will not sneak up on you in the night as they did at Klamath Lake, for they will know the everlasting fear of what retaliation would be like. And there was no feeling of guilt, only the elation of having done a good day's work. As to the dead, as to the crippled and wounded, it meant nothing, nothing at all. To Kit Carson, to the Delawares, to young Tom Martin, to Dick Owens, to Lucien Maxwell, even to Ned Kern—sensitive, fun-loving Ned—to Frémont and all the rest, the California Indians were not the same as the Plains Indians. They were a lesser people, a people they called "Diggers," and a people they could not trust. But these Indians knew fear, and by God, they had given them their share of it. They would not do anything Castro wanted, not now. All this was the feeling of the raiders as they rode toward their camp at the Buttes, as they slapped the first mosquitoes of evening, and realized they were hungry from their long day of teaching the "Diggers" a lesson.

3

AFTER FRÉMONT'S RAID on the Maidu villages, the firebrands among the American settlers were convinced he would be open to their idea of striking the Californios before they had time to organize completely. Hit them hard and fast was the general opinion of these Anglos and one by one or in delegations, they made their appearance at the Buttes to talk of conquest.

They hunkered down in whatever shade was available during the warm hours of the day; and at night, they stood by the campfires, drank coffee and aguardiente, and explained all their reasons for wanting to go to war. William Hargrave from the Napa Valley spoke his piece,[8] and it all came down to one thing: If they didn't act fast, if they didn't strike first, Castro and his men would push them right out of California. William Swasey, once a bookkeeper for John Sutter, agreed with Hargrave.[9] But Swasey took it a step further: The British ship Collingwood was rumored to be at Monterey Bay, and there had been a big meeting of the Californios at Monterey. The whole thing had the smell of British intervention. Besides, Castro and Pico didn't hit it off. It was only logical that Castro—hating Americans the way he did—would ask the British to back him.

Frémont listened to what all these men had to say, heard them out to the last complaint, the smallest concern. Then when they had finished, he explained he was not in a position to become involved in an act of war without the consent of the United States. This wasn't what these settlers had come to hear, for the raid on the Maidu villages by Frémont had given them hope that he was ready to pursue a course of action against the Mexican soldiers and the fiery General Castro.

This was not the talk of a leader, a man to put Castro in his place. Frémont was dodging the key issues. All their talks with him gave them no feeling that he would rush to their aid when the ultimate attack upon them took place. Still, even as they rode away from the explorer's camp with feelings of disgust, events were taking place that would tip the scales in their favor.

On the morning of June 8, 1846, William Brown Ide who was just two years past his fiftieth birthday and who had entered California with the Grigsby-Ide party in 1845, heard a horseman approaching his new cabin in the upper Sacramento Valley, near present-day Red Bluff, California.[10] Being a man caught up in the frontier movement, he had left his New England home with a severe case of "Western fever" in 1833. He packed his wife, Susan, and their first six children into a wagon and struck out for Kentucky. Since then, this plain-looking man who had a love of learning and a talent for the written word had been on the move. Here in California, after talking to Peter Lassen, Ide had put down taproots in the rich soil of the Sacramento Valley and was ready to watch the rest of his years grow and prosper in this warm and fruitful land. But on this particular morning in June, he did not have to seek a cause for movement. It came to him as an Indian rider delivered a message from Captain Frémont.

The folded and worn piece of paper carried disturbing information. The Californios were on the move, heading into the Sacramento Valley with a force of over two hundred armed horsemen. They were burning crops, destroying houses, and driving off livestock. All this came from Captain Frémont, and he requested the appearance of every man in the valley to come to his camp at the Buttes immediately. This was a call to action that Ide couldn't ignore, and he saddled his horse, checked his rifle and pistol, picked up his powder horn and lead, and headed for the Buttes. Like all the other Americans in the Sacramento Valley, Ide had come too far and put too much of his own life and hopes on his move to California. This was not a time to turn tail and run. If it came down to a battle in order to stay, then that's the way it would have to be. So, leaving his wife and children to fend for themselves, he rode south to the Frémont camp.

On the same day that William Ide received Frémont's message, another group of horsemen arrived at Sutter's Fort. Commanded by Lieutenants Francisco Arce[11] and José María Alviso,[12] a group of Castro's men were driving a herd of 170 horses they had rounded up in the Sonoma country as a result of an agreement between Castro and Vallejo. The Californios had crossed the Sacramento River at William Knight's place,[13] and stopped at Sutter's to rest before continuing their journey south to Santa Clara. The handsome Arce, who looked more Irish than Mexican, was not one to remain silent. He boasted that Castro would put these horses to good use to drive the Americans out of California. William Knight had thought Arce was up to something and hurried to the Buttes to tell Frémont that he suspected the Californios were gathering horses and getting ready for a campaign against the Americans.

Lieutenant Arce was too much of a bragger, and the news Knight brought to the camp at the Buttes came just in time to find a hard group of men visiting Frémont. This wild bunch included Zeke Merritt; Long Bob Semple, who stood six feet eight inches tall[14]; Henry L. Ford, a deserter from the United States Army who had come to California as a stowaway aboard a whaler[15]; and Granville Swift of Kentucky,[16] another tall man—though short compared to Long Bob Semple—noted for his ability to load faster and fire with more accuracy than any other man on the Pacific Coast. These were just the leaders, but they were men Lieutenant Arce was never to forget. Once they heard the news of his pushing a horse herd southward to Castro, they needed only a slight amount of encouragement from Frémont to form a striking force and ride away from the Buttes to pick up the trail of the Californios. As these rough American emigrants saw it, they should never allow this horse herd to reach Castro. Besides, Zeke Merritt was itching for some action against the Mexicans, who offended him with their bright uniforms of blue and red and the highly polished silver decorations on their bridles and saddles.

Riding south, these rough frontiersmen stopped at Sutter's Fort just long enough to get a general notion of Arce's line of travel. Then they rode on their way again, traveling hard and fast, until they saw the tracks of a large herd of horses and the deeper hoofprints of horses carrying riders.

Following the tracks through the Sacramento Valley, the Americans stopped to eat supper at the American River. But with some twilight still left, they pushed on toward the Cosumnes River. Before they reached Martin Murphy's place,[17] it became too dark to travel, and they made camp for the night with the idea of rolling out before dawn and trying to overtake the Californios before they realized what was taking place.

Leaving their own camp while it was still dark, Zeke Merritt and his freebooters arrived at Lieutenant Arce's camp as the dawn of June 10, 1846, broke. With a wild yell, the Americans charged the camp as the Californios were beginning to awaken. Before anyone could fire a shot, Merritt and his rough riders had disarmed all of Arce's men and had secured the horse herd.

The stunned lieutenant looked at this band of ill-dressed frontiersmen and then addressed himself to Zeke Merritt, who appeared to be their leader. With disgust and contempt, he told Merritt that the only reason they had captured his camp was that they had come in the dark and caught him off guard. It was not something they should consider a victory.

Merritt wasted no time with this comment. He had been anti-Mexican ever since the incident with Salvador Vallejo, even though three years had passed. Willing to have a full-scale battle, Zeke told Arce and his men that if it was a fight they were looking for, then they'd hand their weapons back to them, ride off, and attack their camp once again.

Lieutenant Arce did not have to confer with Alviso or any of his men about this. He had made his complaint and he was still alive. That was good enough. It would not be wise to give this wild bunch of buckskin-clad savages the chance to carry out a slaughter. He was certain these barbarians were more than capable of it and probably were looking forward to it.

Considering the appearance of Long Bob Semple, Swift, Ford, Zeke Merritt, and the rest, the handsome lieutenant made a wise decision to accept defeat as gracefully as he could. But it must have galled him to have Merritt hand back his sword, allow him and his men a mount to ride, and then tell him to notify General Castro that by the time they were able to talk to him, Sonoma would be in American hands and the Vallejos would be prisoners. Then Merritt told them to hightail on their way; and as they did, the last they saw of their horses was a northbound dust cloud followed by the American bandits.

A day later, Merritt and the others drove the horses into Frémont's camp at the Buttes. If Frémont still had hopes that California would fall into the lap of the United States in a peaceful manner, the horse raid was only one thing which should have made it clear that war was about to begin. Flushed with victory, Merritt and his raiders picked up additional recruits to bring their striking force to a total of twenty. Then Zeke calmly announced they were headed for Sonoma to catch the Vallejos off guard and take over the whole place—fort, mission, cannons, rifles, horses, and anything else that might come in handy. They had won a battle, but they knew Castro would be after their hides once his two officers returned without the horses. With control of Sonoma, they'd be in a better position to make things a bit warm for the man who had threatened to drive them out of California.

## 4

DURING THE MIDDLE OF JUNE, one event after another took place. It was as though the first heat of summer had caused the long-simmering feelings of persecution to come to a boil and spill out. Americans were on the move. They had taken threats for the last time. Now they were doing something about General Castro's constant issuing of proclamations against all emigrants who had not become Mexican citizens.

Zeke Merritt and his men had just returned to Frémont's camp at the Buttes, driving Arce's horses in front of them as Gillespie left the harbor at Sausalito to sail from San Francisco Bay to Sutter's Fort and on from there to rendezvous with Frémont. Sailing with Gillespie, in a launch that belonged to the *Portsmouth*, were two of the ship's officers—including a surgeon—and eleven enlisted men. But they did not reach Sutter's Landing until midnight,

June 12, and it was then Gillespie learned that the captain had moved away from the Buttes. Nobody knew where he had gone. Facing this situation, the marine and the seamen of the *Portsmouth* took the launch a short way up the American River, dropped anchor, and set up camp to wait until they heard from him.

What Gillespie didn't know was that Captain Frémont was giving encouragement to Zeke Merritt and the growing army of Americans who had decided to attack Sonoma. Though Frémont had not offered his services nor those of his men, he had not hesitated to appoint Zeke Merritt as lieutenant of this loosely knit band who called themselves Osos or Bears, and the name was aptly chosen. If this ragtag, irregular army resembled anything at all, they had more in common with the grizzly bears that lived in California's mountains and brush thickets beside the rivers. For like these bears, the Osos were unpredictable and capable of savage violence.

In choosing Zeke Merritt to lead this attacking force, Frémont had picked the right man for action. Despite his forty years, Merritt was as lean and tough as a piece of dried-out jerky. He had been conditioned for guerrilla warfare by his long years as a Rocky Mountain trapper, and he had a personal score to settle. But the hard-riding Merritt knew he could not take the regular road to Sonoma if he wished to surprise the unsuspecting Californios. Picking up men as he traveled along, Merritt headed southwest across the Sacramento Valley. At Cache Creek, he was joined by several more men, among whom was William Todd, a cousin of Mrs. Abraham Lincoln.[18] Todd thought he'd like to take a hand in this affair, for as he had already stated in a letter to his father the previous April: "There will be a revolution before long and probably this country will be annexed to the United States. If here, I will take a hand in it."[19]

Todd's statement was an educated guess, but it was well on its way to reality as the young man followed the loose-jointed Merritt and the band of Osos. The weather was warm, and the soil was dry enough to create dust as the riders struck a course that took them away from the valley and up into the rough ground of Blue Ridge and on down to Berryessa Valley. Before nightfall they reached Pope Valley. Here they halted at the home of Elias Barnett and his wife, the widow Pope.[20] Barnett welcomed the Osos, invited them to eat at his place, and slaughtered a young steer to feed the hungry men.

Leaving Pope Valley, they rode into the upper Napa Valley on June 12 and stopped for the night. Here they picked up more volunteers and brought the size of their army to thirty-three men. After a short rest just north of the present town of St. Helena, Zeke Merritt was anxious to get on the way again. But many of the men were exhausted, and complained that more rest was needed. Long Bob Semple harangued them with a stirring speech to keep on the move and strike before they were discovered. Between the passion of his speech and his overpowering physical stature, all the men decided it was best to keep on the move.

Forging ahead was not at all easy for the weary Osos once they left the Napa Valley and began to climb the rugged Mayacmas Mountains between the Napa and Sonoma valleys. In the hours before morning the going was extremely tough. The men moved with caution to avoid falling off bluffs in the darkness, becoming entangled in thickets of buck brush or poison oak, or smacking their heads against the low-hanging limbs of oaks and pines. Then as the sun rose on June 13, they had a view of the country they had crossed in the night, and of what was ahead. Even in the light of day, it was not a country that was easy on horses or riders. There was no trail to follow, and the day ran into night before they reached the floor of the Sonoma Valley on June 14.

Once they were off the ridge, the men rested for a while; then, wanting to reach Sonoma before anyone had awakened, they forged ahead on the regular road. Dawn was almost ready to break as they neared the town, but the roosters hadn't even started to crow as the men quietly eased along and kept a careful watch for any early riser who could spread the alarm. They found only one man up and about, and took the startled citizen prisoner to keep him quiet. Then they continued into Sonoma and followed the road along the northeast side of the plaza. They quietly passed the Mission San Francisco Solano, the barracks that were no longer in use, and came to a halt in front of General Mariano Vallejo's La Casa Grande. The home was in the middle of the block and faced the largest plaza in all California. Over the main section of the house there was a second-story balcony. The spacious home also had an unusual three-story adobe tower, and a wing for the servants quarters. Impressive, rich, and unlike anything the invaders had ever seen, Vallejo's home was the essence of gracious living in a pastoral society.

Hearing the movement of horses outside, General Vallejo looked out a window to see what was taking place at such an early hour. By this time his wife had heard the noise, and she, too, stared in disbelief at what she saw. The Vallejos were stunned.

Almost the whole party was dressed in leather hunting shirts, many of them greasy; taking the whole party together, they were about as rough a looking set of men as one could well imagine.[21]

Fearing for her husband's life, Mrs. Vallejo begged him to escape while he had the chance. But the general refused to run off and leave her alone. Besides, one glance at the men outside his home was more than enough to convince him he wouldn't get very far even if he followed her advice. Having no other choice, he opened the door and asked his early morning visitors what it was that they wanted.

In no uncertain terms, the Osos told him he was under arrest. Then, as the morning sun began to light up the plaza, where there were bones and hides of butchered cattle, other residents of Sonoma began to awaken. When they saw what was taking place, they were startled and fearful for their lives.

These were Americans, but that was all they could be certain about. Whether they were bandits or men on a peaceful mission remained to be seen. Even as they watched this drama unfold, the excited and alarmed citizens saw two other Californios approach the house only to be put under arrest and escorted into the thick-walled adobe home. One of the men was the general's brother, Salvador; the other man was Victor Prudon, an emigré from France, who was the general's secretary.[22] Then shortly after these men entered the house, a servant came outside and soon returned with Jacob Primer Leese, the general's brother-in-law, and the man destined to make the necessary translation of the documents of surrender that were being drawn up in the Vallejo home.[23]

Victory had come to the Americans without firing a shot and without any injury to the residents of Sonoma. They had all that Sonoma held in the way of supplies or riches. The trouble was that it didn't amount to very much. The so-called military post had seen better days. It was run-down, infested with fleas, and hardly a place for any soldier to bed down for a night's sleep. All that seemed to be of value were the nine brass cannon, two hundred muskets, and the hundred pounds of gunpowder the men found. This wouldn't hold off an attacking force if real retribution should take place. Now that they had struck the first blow, there was no reason to think that General Castro and his troops wouldn't come looking for blood. Still, the Osos tried their best to make everything look official so that they would not be considered a band of robbers.

Written documents were exchanged between the captured and the captors. The prisoners indicated that they had been caught off guard, that the post had been defenseless under the circumstances. As for the captors, they made it clear that they were about to start a government based upon republican principles, that they would protect their prisoners, and that the families and property of the prisoners would be given proper protection. The whole affair had been bloodless, civilized, and even friendly. Only two incidents carried the potential of violence. Zeke Merritt pointed out to Salvador Vallejo that now the general was in his power, that he was a prisoner, but that he, Merritt, had no intention of striking Vallejo as Vallejo had done to him under similar circumstances. The other incident involved one man who was all for dividing the spoils until he was told in a blunt manner that if he did, he would be swinging by his neck from the nearest tree limb or rafter.

As the leading contingent of Americans carried out the official negotiations inside General Vallejo's home, the men waiting outside unsaddled their horses, bought some food from locals who had got over their fear of these strangers, and then settled down to watch for any good-looking woman who might step outside, or tried to catch up for lost sleep by bedding down under a balcony or roofline overlooking the treeless plaza. As the hours dragged by and the men began to feel the warmth of the early morning sun make their buckskin shirts into sweaty and smelly barriers that kept in the heat, they wondered what was taking so long. Finally they ran out of patience. Being very democratic, they held an election which made John Grigsby their captain and representative,[24] and they sent him into the Vallejo home to see what was happening. When he vanished from their view, one of the men found a bottle of brandy, and this made the rounds without Grigsby reappearing. Another election took place, and this time William Ide was sent into the Vallejo home to investigate.

What Ide found inside the cool adobe living room was not at all what he had expected. General Vallejo had been overly generous and had shown great hospitality to his captors. He offered them a thorough sampling of his wines and brandies, and the weary men had consumed so much of Vallejo's cellar they were hardly in condition to do anything in a hurry. Long Bob Semple kept trying to find just the right adjectives to modify his articles of capitulation. As for Zeke Merritt, he was stretched out on a chair, and his head nodded toward his chest. The newly elected Captain Grigsby sat on his chair, mutely staring into space.

Ide's sudden appearance brought a halt to the celebration of victory and defeat. The relaxed Americans brought their equally relaxed captives outside. When there was some more loose talk about retribution or reaping the spoils of victory, both Long Bob Semple and Bill Ide made speeches calling for unity and moderation. While they agreed that the prisoners should be taken to Sutter's Fort and held there, they were adamant about looting or any other behavior that would be out of line. If that was to be the nature of this affair, if that was what they had come to, then neither Ide nor Semple intended to have anything more to do with it.

Very angry and disappointed by the mere fact that anyone would dare to make such suggestions, Ide told the men not to put the saddle back on his horse if this was to be their attitude.

"I will lay my bones here [he said], before I will take upon myself the ignominy of commencing an honorable work, and then flee like cowards, like thieves, when no enemy is in sight. In vain will you say you had honorable motives. Flee this day, and the longest life cannot wear off your disgrace! Choose ye! Choose ye this day, what you will be! We are robbers, or we must be conquerors!"[25]

The combination of Ide's stirring speech and the backing of Long Bob Semple turned the trick. Most of the men sided with Ide, and they elected him leader of the Osos. Then by eleven of that morning of June 14, 1846, the trio of Merritt, Semple, and Grigsby rode away from the plaza as guards for the prisoners of war bound northeast toward Sutter's Fort. In Sonoma, the stunned citizens watched in bewilderment as William Ide and his companions in arms began to discuss the organization of a new government based on their knowledge of the structure of the United States Government. For on this warm day in June, the small, ragged band of frontiersmen and emigrants had taken their first shaky step toward the creation of a new republic. Now all they had to do was figure out how one went about the business of setting up a new government for a new country, and that was going to take a powerful amount of thinking.

## 5

FIRST, and all the men agreed to this, they needed a flag. There was the flagpole just waiting for something to take the place of the Mexican flag. But the question in the minds of all the Osos was what kind of flag they should have for their new republic. This question was still being kicked around as the second task took place, the search for materials with which to make a flag.

When the searchers had returned to the plaza, they had some unbleached cotton and a piece of red material from a petticoat. Thinking of Texas and its original flag, it was decided by all assembled that one star would do. Then they agreed that "California Republic" had a good solid ring, would be easy to see, and said all that was necessary. Yet the flag needed something to give it more distinction. Ex-dragoon Henry Ford suggested that a grizzly bear would be a good central figure to place on the flag. After all, Americans and Mexicans both respected the fighting ability of the grizzly bear; and they were nicknamed Osos. Well, why not use a grizzly bear?

Settled, by God, it was all settled. They'd have one star, a red stripe, a grizzly bear, and "California Republic" on their flag. The chore of making the flag fell to William Todd. Whether he used berry juice or whether paint was available is not known. Nor is it clear whether he used a stick or a paintbrush. But none of that mattered that warm Sunday afternoon in Sonoma.

From the petticoat material Todd cut a red star and sewed it on the upper right of the flag. Then he sewed a red stripe along the bottom border. Working carefully and under primitive conditions, Todd then printed CALIFORNIA REPUBLIC in black, though he did make an error in spelling "Republic" and had to make a correction. Finally, it came time to draw the bear. "California Republic" stood just below the star and parallel to the red border at the bottom, leaving a field of white between the name and the red stripe. It was decided that the grizzly should be just above the word "Republic," that it should be standing on all four legs, and that its head should be pointing toward the star.

Todd's artistry was not the best as he tried to draw a proper grizzly bear. His fellow Osos crowded around him, and as they watched the bear develop, it looked more like a pig trying to pass itself off as a bear. There was a good deal of laughter and joking, but nobody claimed he could do as good a job. So the grizzly that resembled a pig was finished, and no doubt a toast was drunk by all hands. Then the flag was put aside to allow it to dry for the ceremonies in the morning when it would be raised to the top of the flagpole outside the barracks to proclaim that Sonoma was now part of the Republic of California.

In the cool dawn of June 15, the Osos—some clearheaded, and some with terrible headaches and uneasy stomachs from having consumed too much aguardiente—lined up in the best formation they could muster under the leadership of Ford, who at least had some formal military training. Then, with as much ceremony as they were capable of, they watched and waited for the first light of sunrise to top the Mayacmas Mountains. When it did, men manned the halyards of the flagstaff, and everybody cheered as the Bear Flag reached the top of the flagpole and stood out in the morning breeze. Ex-dragoon Ford addressed the Bear Flaggers and quickly explained that they were now at war with Mexico, that they had a cause to defend, and that it was necessary to be disciplined and loyal and to obey the officers they elected to lead them in this conflict.

They had captured Sonoma. They had their own flag and the beginning of an army. And they had a powerful enemy in the person of General José Castro, who no doubt would soon send troops on a forced ride toward Sonoma. But the Bear Flaggers had all the confidence in the world, and as they listened to Ford's instructions on military duty, their elected commander-in-chief, William B. Ide, finished writing a proclamation which assured the citizens of Sonoma that they had nothing to fear from the troops, that they were not to be considered foes unless they were found bearing arms, and that this rebellion was to overthrow "a government which has seized upon the property of the Mission for its individual aggrandizement; which has ruined and shamefully oppressed the laboring people of California by their enormous exactions on goods imported into this country. . . ."[26] This was the stated purpose of the men under Ide's command. Finally, he brought his document to a ringing close which promised that every citizen would have the right of participation in establishing the government, that there would be civil and religious liberty, that the government would be guarded by its citizens, and that their reward would come about through the actions of the government's officers, servants, and its glory.

Stirring, lofty, well-intended, and it was a great moment for the Osos. But Sonoma was only an outpost, a sleepy hamlet beyond the main arena of action in California. True, they had captured a Mexican village and sent some of Alta California's most prominent citizens packing off to jail, and they had run up the Bear Flag. But the Bear Flag Revolt had just started. It was far from over. The Osos had made themselves known. Now, they were faced with a war to save their flag, their republic, and their lives.

## 6

THE SAME DAY the Bear Flag was raised over Sonoma, Captain Frémont arrived at Sutter's Fort and learned that Lieutenant Gillespie and men from the *Portsmouth* were waiting for him aboard a launch lying at anchor in the American River. John Charles quickly rode to where the boat was located, and found Gillespie had all the stores he had requested from Commander Montgomery. In fact there was an additional item not listed on the official invoice. This was a barrel of whiskey, and the men had knocked off its head, slung a tin cup on one side of it, and were celebrating their cruise from San Francisco Bay to the Sacramento Valley. The party had been going on all night "until there was not a soul left who had life enough to crawl to the barrel for his *tod*."[27]

Captain Frémont took one look at the men who were in different stages of recovery from their celebration, said nothing about their consumption of whiskey, and put them to work unloading the supplies when the boat reached his American River camp near Sutter's Fort. As yet, there was no news—not even a rumor—of what had happened at Sonoma. The only talk of anything out of the ordinary was the continued interest in Zeke Merritt's successful horse-stealing raid against Lieutenant Arce and his men, a raid Sutter considered highly improper. Then on the afternoon of June 16 "Stuttering" Merritt, Long Bob Semple, and John Grigsby rode into the camp with their prisoners of war. Though General Vallejo protested the treatment he and the others had received, his protests were in vain. This startling development struck Frémont as the possible beginning of war between the United States and Mexico.

Even so, he did not suggest that he and his men would come to the aid of the Bear Flaggers. The most he agreed to do was to assume the responsibility of taking the prisoners to the fort and telling Sutter to place them under guard and treat them like any other men under arrest.

Torn between his friendship and loyalty to these Californios and his personal desire to have a stable government in the country, John Sutter half-heartedly agreed to act as a jailor. Yet it was not what he wished to do, and it soon caused a rift between the gentle Swiss and Frémont. For Sutter did not guard his prisoners closely. On the contrary, he shared his meals with them, drank brandy with them after dinner, and joined his old friends for long strolls in the cool of evening.

This casual and friendly treatment of prisoners of war rankled Frémont, and he spoke to Sutter about it. What should have been a friendly discussion turned into a confrontation when John Charles lost his temper and asked Sutter if he knew how to treat prisoners. This was too much for Sutter, who said he would no longer be responsible.

Not wanting to trust just anybody, John Charles calmed down and asked if Sutter would suggest someone to replace him. Sutter suggested his clerk, William Loker, and Frémont appointed him as the new guard; but Loker did not like the job and soon quit.[28] Next Frémont appointed John Bidwell, but when he discovered Bidwell was teaching English to Victor Prudon in exchange for Spanish lessons, he dismissed him. At this point John Charles decided he would have to use one of his own men to make certain things were handled in the correct manner. Ned Kern was his choice. He could be relied upon; he got along with everybody; Sutter liked him; and Ned was the kind of man who would be able to keep things running smoothly. His sense of humor and love of life would help ease the mounting tensions around the fort.

With the matter of guarding the prisoners of war settled, Frémont realized he had better go to Sonoma and see if everything was all right. As he considered this move, the Osos were beginning to worry about their position. They were short on arms and ammunition, and they hardly had enough fighting men to withstand a full-scale attack if General Castro should launch one. To make certain other Americans would know about their serious circumstances, they decided somebody had to risk a journey to San Francisco Bay to notify Commodore Robert Stockton or Commander John Montgomery of their plight. William Todd was given this task and sent on his way.

Even as Todd headed south from Sonoma, news of the Bear Flag Revolt had reached Commander Montgomery. A protégé of General Vallejo's, José de la Rosa,[29] had reached the *Portsmouth* on June 15 with a message from Vallejo requesting the influence and authority of Commander Montgomery to insure the safety of Sonoma's citizens from anarchy and violence. Trying to remain neutral until there was an actual declaration of war between the United States and Mexico, Montgomery assured Rosa he would send a boat to Sonoma to make sure that no lives or property were in danger, that the boat would be leaving the next morning, and that Rosa was welcome to be a passenger.

Lieutenant John S. Misroon, the executive officer of the *Portsmouth*,[30] was ready to leave for Sonoma on the morning of June 16 when William Todd boarded the ship and presented Commander Montgomery a letter from William Ide—a letter which had been intended for Commodore Stockton. Todd explained to Montgomery that, as Stockton was not in port, he wished to deliver Ide's letter to him. Someone of authority needed to know what had happened at Sonoma from the point of view of the Americans.

From Ide's letter, Montgomery first learned of the Arce affair, heard the reasons for the revolt, the details of the capture of Sonoma and the subsequent handling of the prisoners of war, the proclamation stating that the Osos had formed the Republic of California and were determined to maintain their hold on Sonoma even in the face of any military force that might move against them. Also, Ide pointed out that they were short of powder for the cannon. Yet he did not request gunpowder nor anything else. Instead, he had specifically instructed Todd to refrain from asking but to accept anything that might be offered.

Todd was not as reticent in asking for help as Ide, and he did let Montgomery know that they were badly in need of gunpowder. As for the Mexican citizens of Sonoma, Todd assured Montgomery that what Ide had written was completely true, that the Californios were safe and were not faced with the loss of either life or property.

When the flag maker was finished, Montgomery told him he was free to take passage aboard the boat bound for Sonoma, and that he would only detain them a few minutes while he wrote a letter to Ide explaining that under the circumstances he had to maintain his neutrality since he was an officer of the United States Navy. This done, Montgomery gave the letter to Todd to deliver, and Todd boarded the boat from the *Portsmouth* and joined company with Rosa, Misroon and young John Elliott Montgomery, the ship's clerk and the commander's son.[31]

Lieutenant Misroon managed to take the boat from Sausalito up to San Pablo Bay at the north end of San Francisco Bay, then up Sonoma Creek, and arrived at the captured village before the warm hours of June 16 had come to an end. Young John Montgomery wrote a wide-eyed impression of what they saw in Sonoma in a letter to his mother:

> On arriving [at Sonoma] found a party of 24 men mostly dressed in Buckskins & we were met half way accross the Square by a plain man about fifty years old in his Shirt Sleeves, with a pair of pantaloons which certainly had seen better days to my eyes his Shoes looked as if they had not seen one of Day & Martin's blacking bottles for six months & his hat was somewhat more holy than rightous this man was Captain Ide he welcomed us to Sonoma & on Mr. Ms [Misroon] intimating to him that he would like to see him he called his 1st Lt. Mr. Ford a nephew of old Deacon Ford of Charlestown, & then retired after the business was settled Mr. M. & myself called on Mrs. Vallejo & he assured her of her husband's safety & she offered us beds in her house which we accepted she is a very pleasant woman indeed. . . .[32]

Lieutenant Misroon's mission accomplished two things. He was able to assure Mrs. Vallejo and Alcalde José S. Berreyesa[33] that they were perfectly safe, as Mr. Ide had given his pledge to prevent any violence, disturbing of Sonoma citizens, or the destruction of property. He was also able to return to Commander Montgomery with an intelligent report of exactly what had taken place at Sonoma and what the present situation appeared to be.

Yet the threads of peace were flimsy and not designed to stand the stress and strain of mounting tension. Two days after Lieutenant Misroon had returned with apparent good news for Commander Montgomery, the Osos decided their need for gunpowder was crucial. Lieutenant Henry L. Ford sent Bill Todd and another Bear off toward Bodega to see if they could locate what was needed; and on the same day, he sent Thomas Cowie[34] and George Fowler[35] toward the Russian River, where they were to contact Kit Carson's brother, Moses, who was major-domo at the rancho of Henry D. Fitch.[36] Hopefully, one of these parties would find what the Osos needed to defend Sonoma.

Two days passed, and neither party returned to Sonoma. This alarmed Ford and Ide. All were dependable men, and they had been sent on short rides. The situation looked anything but good. When news reached Sonoma that a force of Californios was on its way to attack, a courier was sent on a fast ride to Frémont's camp near Sutter's Fort. At the same time, Ford sent five of his best men to Fitch's Russian River rancho to learn what they could about Cowie and Fowler.

June 20, 1846, turned into a day of decision. Even as the Bear Flaggers neared Fitch's rancho and discovered that Cowie and Fowler had never been there, the courier from Sonoma arrived at Frémont's camp with news of the impending trouble for the Osos. This was the second delivery of bad news that Captain Frémont had received that day. Earlier Samuel J. Hensley and Pierson B. Reading,[37] both employees of Sutter, returned to Frémont's camp with news from Marsh's Landing on the San Joaquin River. General Castro was on the move. He was headed up the valley with a sizable force, and it was his intention to drive Frémont and his American bandoleros (highwaymen) out of the country.

The waiting was over. John Charles believed he had no options left other than to join the cause of the Bear Flaggers. It was pack the gear and get ready to move out. They were off for Sonoma before day's end.

## 7

As FRÉMONT AND HIS MEN moved toward Sonoma, events were taking place that made war between the Americans and the Californios inevitable. The men who had been sent to Fitch's rancho learned that Moses Carson had never seen Cowie and Fowler. Without hesitation, though, he gave the Osos the gunpowder they needed. Then on their way back to Sonoma, they ran into a party of Californios and were fired upon. At the end of a short battle, they had taken one prisoner—a man called Four-fingered or Three-fingered Jack.[38] From him they learned what had happened to Cowie and Fowler.

The men had not taken the back-country trails as Lieutenant Ford had advised. Instead, they had followed the regular road. Near Santa Rosa they had been captured by a band of Californios under the leadership of Juan Padilla, one of Castro's lieutenants.[39] For two days, Cowie and Fowler were prisoners. With a perverse pride in his talent for brutality and madness, Jack told the Osos what he did to the captives.

The men were tied to trees, but this was only the beginning. The game was a very old one in the history of man's inhumanity to man. The captors selected stones and took turns seeing how hard they could throw them at the men. As each stone found its mark, there were screams of pain from the men and brutal laughter from their tormentors. Bones were broken, teeth were smashed, and blood soon covered the battered and broken bodies. Then seeing that this was taking a long time, Three-fingered Jack tied a rope to the broken jawbone of one of the men and pulled it through the skin and muscles as the man screamed and then choked on his own blood. Then knives were sharpened, and the game of slicing without killing began. Slowly they cut piece after piece of flesh from the victims and threw the pieces at them or crammed them down their throats. Finally, they tired of the slow method, and finished killing Cowie and Fowler by slitting open their stomachs and ripping out their intestines.

Sickening and terrible as all this was to the Bear Flaggers, they did not kill Three-fingered Jack, though many of them would have done so with pleasure. Instead, they treated him as a prisoner of war. If he was to be executed, that would take place after a proper trial and not before. The Osos were not going to be barbarians, even if this captive and his companions had committed such an atrocity. The Bear Flaggers had taken Sonoma with motives based on high principles, and they were not going to lower themselves to the actions of murderers.

Lieutenant Ford wondered if a similar fate had befallen Bill Todd and his companion. Not wanting to wait for news, Ford called for volunteers. The Bear Flaggers had grown to ninety men as other settlers and emigrants had heard the news and drifted into Sonoma to offer their services. Ford and Granville Swift selected eighteen of the best fighting men. On the morning of June 23 they rode out of Sonoma and headed south to search for the missing men.

At Santa Rosa they picked up the trail of the Californios. On their way south they captured four men. The road was now covered with more tracks of horses, and near present-day Novato the tracks left the road and moved toward an adobe home at the Olompali Rancho. Ford and his men approached the house. They saw only a few Californios outside, and thinking these were the only men left here, Ford gave the signal to charge.

The Bear Flaggers rode at a gallop. More men poured out of the house and opened fire on them. For Padilla's party had been joined by about fifty additional men under the leadership of Joaquín de la Torre, who had been sent across the bay by Castro.[40]

Captain de la Torre and his men mounted and charged the Osos. But the Bear Flaggers were frontier-trained men. They didn't panic, gave no ground, took careful aim, reloaded, aimed and fired again and again. The charge of the Californios was broken by this cool and precise rifle fire, and they milled around for a short time, then broke and galloped south in the direction of San Rafael.

Many of the Bears wanted to give chase now that they had their foes on the run, but Lieutenant Ford decided they had no idea of what might be ahead and if they dashed off in pursuit, they might well ride into a deadly trap. They had fought their first battle and won. It was time to check for casualties. When that was done, they rode back toward Sonoma with the news. And the news was good: Not one man had been wounded or killed on their side, and they had rescued Bill Todd and his companion. As for the Californios, the Bears had killed one and wounded several. They learned from Todd that the only thing that had saved his life and his companion's was that

Todd had made it clear to his captors that if they carried out their threat of execution, they could expect all prisoners of the Bear Flaggers at Sonoma to suffer the same fate.

In the late afternoon of June 24 the Osos reached Sonoma. They were congratulated by Commander-in-Chief William Brown Ide. But even as the Bear Flaggers celebrated their first victory in their war of independence, Captain Frémont and his men were nearing Sonoma. As James Marshall, who had joined Frémont's army, remembered, it was an army that might frighten any foe.[41]

There were Americans, French, English, Swiss, Poles, Russians, Chileans, Germans, Greeks, Austrians, Pawnees, native Indians, etc. . . . Well if they whip this crowd they can beat all the world, for Castro will whip all nations, languages and tongues![42]

Dressed in buckskins, worn farmer's clothes, carrying long rifles, pistols, and sharp skinning knives, this volunteer army followed just behind Captain Frémont's force of mountain men, voyageurs, and Delawares. Spoiling for a fight, anxious to corner the wily Castro for a showdown, the men rode into Sonoma on June 25. What they heard from Ford and Ide convinced them that they'd stay overnight in Sonoma, and not another day. If the Mexicans were looking for trouble, they were more than ready.

Lieutenant Ford and a contingent of Osos rode with Frémont and his men as they left Sonoma the next morning. But on that same June 26 Captain de la Torre had heard that other Americans had joined the Bear Flaggers. Deciding his force would be no match for the American riflemen, he thought of a ruse to trick the Americans. He wrote what appeared to be a secret message indicating that he and his troops were on their way to launch a full-scale attack against the Bear Flaggers at Sonoma, gave this to a local Indian, and instructed him to head for Sonoma after the Americans attacked San Rafael. Then de la Torre and his men rode to Sausalito, where they took William Richardson's launch,[43] crossed the bay to San Pablo, where they rejoined General Castro's main army, and headed south toward Santa Clara. Not knowing any of this, Captain Frémont's force charged the mission at San Rafael only to find that the Californios were gone.

During the next two days, the Frémont men remained at the mission. Each day scouting parties were sent out to see if they could find the Californios. On June 28 three scouts—Kit Carson, Sam Neal, and Granville Swift—saw a small boat making its way across the bay toward San Rafael. As the craft drew closer, they saw that there were three men in it, and they headed toward the estuary landing to meet the incoming boat.

Just as the men beached their craft and stepped ashore, Carson turned to his companions and gave the order to shoot the Mexicans where they stood. No questions were asked. No chance to surrender was offered. Bear Flaggers, fellow Americans, had been butchered in the most savage manner possible, and as far as Carson was concerned, this was all the excuse he needed. The Mexicans were going to get an idea of what it meant to fight Americans. No more than fifty yards away, Carson and his companions must have seen that one man was old and the other two were young, that they had stepped out of the boat and shouldered their saddles to walk toward the mission in hope of securing horses. Yet he gave the order to fire. In this brutal, cold-blooded manner, Carson and his fellow scouts killed elderly José de los Reyes Berreyesa,[44] father of Sonoma's alcalde, and his twin nephews, twenty-year-old Ramon and Francisco de Haro,[45] who had agreed to make the ride to Sonoma with their uncle.

Having shot the Californios without even bothering to find out whether or not they were on a peaceful journey, Kit and his companions rode back to the mission and reported the landing of the men to Captain Frémont. When asked about the prisoners, Carson said, "Oh, we don't want any prisoners; they lie out yonder."[46] Frémont's only reply to this savage act was "It is well!"[47]

This was how Archibald Gillespie recalled the passing of news about the killings to Frémont. Yet Jasper O'Farrell,[48] who was also at the mission at the time, maintained the murders did not take place until Carson had checked with Frémont and was told not to take any prisoners. No matter how the event is interpreted, one thing remains quite clear. Captain Frémont was the officer in command. Whether he approved or disapproved of the actions of his men, there is no record of his having disciplined anyone for the senseless slaughter. To the contrary, in his *Memoirs* he wrote that the killing was done by his scouts, mainly the Delawares, and that they had shot these men because of the brutal manner in which Cowie and Fowler had been murdered.

On this same day the scouts captured the Indian who was carrying the decoy message from Captain de la Torre, but his life was spared. Here, it might have been within the bounds of warfare to kill a man who appeared to be a spy. Yet it was not done, and the news in the message had just the effect that de la Torre had hoped. Frémont immediately gave orders to get ready for a forced night ride to Sonoma to protect the Bear Flaggers from invasion.

All during the night of June 28, as John Charles and his men rode north, William Ide and his fellow Osos prepared for a coming attack by a force of men they, too, had heard was heading their way. Citizens of Sonoma were refused permission to leave. Women and children were placed in the Vallejo home for protection, and the Californio men were given shelter in the calaboose.

With civilians protected and out of the way, Commander-in-Chief Ide planned the defense of Sonoma.

The two 18-pounders, doubled charged with canister shot, guarded the main entrance, and 7 other pieces of artillery were in using order, and so arranged as to be available at short notice at any point whither an attack might be made. The 250 loaded muskets were divided among the men, and so placed as to be within convenient reach. The rifles, all fresh capped, were ready— the guards were strictly charged, the matches were always burning at night.[49]

As the night passed and dawn began to break, the Osos heard the sound of approaching horses. Ide grabbed his rifle, for his first shot was to be the signal to open fire, and he rode out to scout the oncoming men. When Frémont's party was within two hundred yards, Kit Carson saw the lighted matches swinging and all ready to light the cannons. "My God! they swing the matches"[50] Carson cried out, and his voice was recognized by the Osos. In the moments that followed, Frémont galloped his horse to cover behind an adobe house. Then, thinking de la Torre had taken the town, Frémont waited until the shooting stopped and then headed a charge toward the fort of the Bear Flaggers, only to discover that they had almost been shot by the nervous Osos.

## 8

ANGERED BY HAVING BEEN OUTWITTED, Frémont stayed in Sonoma just long enough for a little rest and something to eat. Then he gave his men orders to saddle their mounts and get ready to ride. Somewhere south of San Rafael they had a chance to overtake Captain de la Torre, who might have hidden his force in some canyon while they had been at San Rafael.

Moving right along, they reached Sausalito in good time but were too late to catch their quarry. Frémont and his weary men pitched camp at Sausalito, but John Charles was not in a good humor. Since leaving his camp near Sutter's Fort, all that his men had accomplished was the killing of an old man and his two young nephews. He had been made to appear a fool by the quick-witted Captain de la Torre.

Anchored in Sausalito's harbor was the merchant bark *Moscow*, a ship out of Worcester, Massachusetts, under the command of Captain William D. Phelps.[51] Having unloaded a cargo for trade, Captain Phelps was waiting for hides and tallow to fill his vessel for his return trip to the States. Seeing Frémont's camp from the deck of his ship, Captain Phelps went ashore to visit on June 30, imagining that he would find a tall, bewhiskered military man "looking blood, bullets, and grizzly bears."[52] But though he found a rough-looking party of American frontiersmen, he saw no leader matching what he imagined.

He was directed toward Frémont, who was:

a slender and well-proportioned man, of sedate but pleasing countenance, sitting in front of a tent. His dress . . . was a blue flannel shirt, after the naval style, open at the collar, which was turned over; over this a deerskin hunting shirt, figured and trimmed in hunter's style, blue cloth pantaloons and neat moccasins, all of which had very evidently seen hard service. His head was not cumbered by hat or cap of any shape, but a light cotton handkerchief, bound tightly round his head, surmounted a suit which might not appear very fashionable at the White House or be presentable at the Queen's levee; but to my eye it was an admirable rig to scud under or fight in.[53]

In the conversation that took place between the two officers, Frémont convinced Phelps it was vital to borrow a launch from his ship as well as some of his crew. Together with some of his own men, they would cross the open channel that Frémont named the Golden Gate. Once on the other side, they would quickly climb the hill from their landing to Castillo de San Joaquín, which overlooked the southern shore of the entrance to San Francisco Bay. They would spike the cannons of this ungarrisoned fort to prevent any possibility of having the Mexicans use them against American ships.

Captain Phelps agreed to this proposition, said he would pilot the launch, and provided all that Captain Frémont needed, even the rattail files for spiking the cannons. All the plans were made, and in the gray dawn of July 1, 1846, the launch from the Moscow picked up John Charles and his men at Sausalito. The sailors fought the stiff current running out the Gate, made it to the southern side of the entrance of the bay, and beached their launch somewhere below the location of today's Golden Gate Bridge and the remains of Fort Point. The spiking party of Captain Frémont, Captain Phelps, Lieutenant Gillespie, Kit Carson, and others from Frémont's camp and Phelps's ship, made their way up to the deserted fort. Here, John Charles had his gunsmith, Stepp, spike the ten cannons with the rattail files. The whole operation came off without any difficulty, and the men celebrated their victory. But other than restoring some of the pride they had lost to Captain de la Torre, they hadn't won anything worth the bother.

On the following day, Long Bob Semple took a small party into Yerba Buena to capture the Mexican officials stationed there and send them off to Sutter's Fort. The captain of the port, William S. Hinckley, had died the day before[54]; and it took some convincing to make his replacement, Robert T. Ridley, go to Sutter's Fort, as he wished to finish his game of billiards.[55] Once he had done this, he agreed to make the journey north, even though he considered it to be a foolish business.

As the cannons were being spiked on July 1, things were not quiet in Sonoma. Commander-in-Chief Ide had received news that other Americans living on the eastern side of San Francisco Bay and in the San Joaquin Valley had heard about the Bear Flag Revolt and were ready to join forces if arms could be supplied. Ide and his fellow Osos were not going to turn down an offer for help in their revolt. Quickly they rounded up all the weapons they could spare, outfitted a boat with a small cannon to protect the twelve men who would be in charge, and loaded one hundred muskets aboard. Before they departed Sonoma with the weapons, Captain Frémont's party returned.

Learning of Ide's plan, Frémont expressed his opposition. The arming of isolated settlers would make them foes of General Castro, and he could easily move against them with a flanking attack that would wipe them out. In such a situation, the Osos would be too few in number and too far away to offer any protection for Americans under attack. Ide listened to Frémont's argument, and agreed to hold off on sending arms to these settlers until after the Fourth of July celebration at Sonoma. This would give him two days to consider all the implications that either plan might have for the future of the rebellion, and he would be able to make his choice in an intelligent manner.

With the Bear Flag flying high, July 4, 1846, was a time for celebration in Sonoma. Cannons and rifles were fired to salute the Independence of the United States and the California Republic. An ex-navy officer, Lieutenant Selim E. Woodworth, just in from Oregon after having made the central overland crossing, read the Declaration of Independence to the assembled throng[56]; and salutes were fired once again, followed by loud cheers, and passing of the bottles and jugs. Then the rest of the day was one great fandango. Mexicans and Osos tipped the jugs together and feasted on barbecued steers, tamales, and fresh vegetables from local gardens. Then out came the fiddles, guitars, and mouth organs, and a caller stepped forth to start the dancing that lasted into the shirtsleeve summer night of the Sonoma Valley. It was a night to remember for as long as memory could recall the mixture of peoples and cultures in a celebration that represented much more than any nation's independence, a celebration that was as old as all the joy and hope that represented mankind at the peak of happiness and love.

And all of it was proper for the Bear Flaggers, the ragged Osos, who dared to take destiny in their hands, dared to risk their lives for freedom in a land of plenty that they had traveled so far to find. The next day Frémont and Ide were to meet with others from the Osos and Frémont's party to discuss the possibility of joining together, of becoming a unit under the command of the captain, of being protected—or so Frémont said—by the United States. The time of the Bear was almost over, even as the Osos celebrated their independence from Mexican rule. They looked with pride at their Bear Flag and thought of how Texas had been an independent nation before joining the Union. The idea of incorporating their fighting strength into the California Battalion under the United States flag was being considered by William Brown Ide. Though Ide was not very fond of Frémont, one thing was clear to this sober and logical man: The Osos had shown General José Castro they were not to be taken lightly; but they had not fought a real battle yet. If they remained independent, the day of bloodshed would not be far away, and Ide was not certain that he had the manpower and the necessary arms to hold out against the full strength of Castro's army. Yet if they joined Frémont, if they followed the American flag, then even the naval vessels of the United States would come to their aid if they needed help. Considering all this, Bear Flagger Ide knew that the Fourth of July celebration was the start of a new movement in California. The Osos had got things started, but now the time of the Bear was over.

## ·❧ XIX ❧·

## The Conquest of California

THE TIME OF DECISION arrived the day after the Fourth of July on a warm summer morning at Sonoma. Captain Frémont called the meeting to order inside Salvador Vallejo's adobe home. Frémont's men were present; eight or ten United States Navy officers from the *Portsmouth* were among the gathering; and the rest of the crowd was made up of what were called the Independents —some Osos and some other Americans who had not committed themselves yet.

Frémont got right to the key issue. It was vital, he pointed out, to form a compact army that would function under military discipline and would be a dependable striking force. This would require an experienced officer, and he was willing to take the responsibility for the overall command of such an army. Even as he stated this, he walked a very thin line between total commitment and a vaguely defined role as military advisor. He told the assembled Bear Flaggers and others that he was not out to conquer California. He was determined to conquer General José Castro. The fact that the defeat of Castro would mean the fall of California was not discussed in any open forum.

There were advantages, Frémont informed the Osos, if they agreed to his proposition. He would support their drive for independence according to the principles set forth in their proclamation of June 15. He offered military stores and provisions, the added strength of his own fighting force, and complete support in any military operations. For all this, he only asked three things of the Bear Flaggers: They were not to violate the chastity of women; they were to conduct their revolution honorably; and they were to pledge obedience to their officers.

Here was a curious situation. On the one hand, Frémont agreed to back the Bears and lead them into battle. On the other hand, he was extremely vague about his position. He tried to give the impression that his role was limited to the protection of American citizens from the tyranny of General Castro. The fact that Americans were in Mexican California without an invitation, that they were rebelling against the central government, and that Castro should have run them out of the country was never mentioned. Instead, Frémont assumed that Americans were in the right, Mexicans were in the wrong, and that it was his duty to protect his fellow countrymen even if they were invaders.

To William Ide and the other Osos, who had placed their lives in jeopardy while Frémont had remained in the background, his sudden offer to help them must have been very puzzling. One moment he had appeared to be sitting out the war, and the next moment he was declaring himself in but as a shadowy figure who agreed to fight Castro and his troops but would not agree to the conquest of California. To put the final touch of mystery to the whole affair, Frémont had three different pledges written by three different men so he could select the one which he thought best for future use in signing up members of the California Battalion. The three versions of the pledge were composed by William Ide, John Bidwell, and Pierson B. Reading, and of the three men, only Ide was an Oso. Lieutenant Gillespie looked over the pledges and selected Bidwell's which read like a declaration of war against the Californios.

It was agreed that all the men would sign or make their mark on this document if they wished to become members of the California Battalion and fight under the command of Captain Frémont. The compact was signed by many of the men at Sonoma on July 5, and by others at Sutter's Fort later on. Then under Frémont's direction the battalion was organized.

It was to be composed of four companies. Lieutenant Gillespie was to be Captain Frémont's adjutant, and each company was to elect its own captain. Four tough men were selected for these posts. Richard Owens was captain for most of the Frémont men, and the other companies were commanded by John Grigsby, Granville P. Swift, and Henry L. Ford.

All of this was completely illegal, and there was no escaping that fact. If the United States and Mexico had been on friendly terms, Frémont would have been throwing away his career, destroying any chance for future government service, and risking a court-martial and a possible term in a military prison. But his luck held out. Only forty-eight hours after the formation of the California Battalion, Commodore John Sloat, who had arrived in Monterey Bay aboard the *Savannah* on July 2 with solid information about the start of war between the United States and Mexico, finally got up enough courage to raise the American flag over the Customs House in Monterey.[1] He had learned of the battles of Palo Alto and Resaca de la Palma and the capture of Matamoros when he was anchored in the harbor at Mazatlán on June 5, one month before the formation of the California Battalion.

Two days after the raising of the American flag at Monterey, another naval officer, Lieutenant Joseph W. Revere, appeared at Sonoma.[2] He was carrying American flags for Sonoma and Sutter's Fort. Young John Montgomery, who was in Sonoma on July 7, 1846, wrote a letter to his mother in which he drew a picture of the Bear Flag, described the events of this time, and stated that "Cubby came down growling."

2

FRÉMONT WAS NOT AT SONOMA when the Bear Flag was replaced with the Stars and Stripes. He had returned to Sutter's Fort, but James H. Watmough, purser of the *Portsmouth*,[3] arrived at Sutter's Fort on July 10 with a letter for Frémont from Commander Montgomery. In the letter, Montgomery explained that the United States and Mexico were at war, that the Stars and Stripes was flying over Monterey and Yerba Buena, and that Frémont's presence was needed at Monterey as early as possible.

Late that same day, after the sun had gone down, William Scott rode in from Sonoma.[4] He was carrying the flag that Lieutenant Revere had brought to Sonoma for delivery to Sutter's Fort. The flag lacked the twenty-eighth star to represent the new state of Texas. This was to be taken care of later when Commander Montgomery sent some muslin to the fort to have it made. Meanwhile, plans were made to raise the Stars and Stripes the next morning at sunrise. As William "Owl" Russell recalled,[5] it was a day that none of them were to forget.

> We were out early in the morning and ready with one of the Sonoma guns right under Sutter's window, and begun firing one gun for each State. Sutter's guns in the two bastions were being fired at the same time, by men belonging to the fort. After a few shots, our gun got very warm, and threw itself on end. The charge went up in the air, breaking Sutter's windows. The General came rushing out and said: "Mein Gott, boys, you vill prake all mine vindows!" We then removed the gun; doubtless, much to his satisfaction.[6]

While Owl Russell was correct in thinking Sutter did not wish to see his windows broken, he didn't know that he was happy to see the Stars and Stripes go up the flagpole. For Sutter believed that if things had remained under the control of the Bear Flaggers, looting and plundering would have become the rule of the day.

If Sutter believed the coming of the American colors was a good omen for him, he was badly mistaken. He had not committed himself to the American cause at the beginning, at least not in any obvious manner, and Frémont had come to distrust his motives. After all, Sutter was a Mexican citizen and had many close friends among the Californios, and there was no guarantee he wouldn't take General Castro's side once again if the outcome of the war became a little uncertain. So, without asking Sutter, Frémont not only reaffirmed Ned Kern's position as commander of the fort but also changed its name to Fort Sacramento on the very day the new flag was run up to the loud booming of cannons.

As the United States flag appeared above Sutter's Fort, General Mariano Vallejo drafted a letter to Captain Frémont stating he had been awaiting this day. To Vallejo the affairs in California had been so bad for so long that the new change of government couldn't be any worse, and he hoped it would insure a better influence and a greater destiny. In this same letter he asked if the raising of the new flag meant their imprisonment had come to an end. Such was not to be the case. On the contrary, Frémont ordered Ned Kern to keep the Vallejo brothers, Prudon, Leese, and all the other prisoners under lock and key until he told him otherwise.

Then on July 12 a letter from Commodore John D. Sloat reached the fort. The ill and timid officer, in charge of the United States naval forces in the Pacific Ocean, gave Frémont an account of what had happened in Monterey, indicated that he had sent a letter to General José Castro summoning him to surrender, and closed with the following:

> Although I am in expectation of seeing General Castro, to enter into satisfactory terms with him, there may be a necessity of one hundred men, well mounted, who are accustomed to riding, to form a force to prevent any further robbing of the farmers' houses, &c. by the Indians. I request you to bring in as many men up to that number with you, or send them on under charge of a trusty person, in case you may be delayed for a day or two. Should you find any Government horses on the road, please bring them in.[7]

Sloat's letter had a ring of desperation about it. It is strange that an officer who had learned in June about the beginning of war between Mexico and the United States hesitated to carry out orders to back up any American forces if war should begin—orders which he had received from Secretary of the Navy George Bancroft. Yet Sloat had not run the flag up in Monterey until he had heard about the taking of Sonoma and Frémont's entry into battle with the Bear Flaggers. Even in this letter, he stated a need for hard-riding men and horses to quell nonexistent Indian raids against nearby ranchos. Added to this, he listed the number of strength of American ships in Monterey Bay—a powerful striking force which appeared to need no help at all.

Sloat's flagship, the *Savannah*, had fifty-four cannons. The nearby *Cyane* and *Levant* had twenty-four cannons each. There was a good supply of ammunition and a large striking force of men aboard each ship. The *Congress* was due to sail into the harbor with her sixty 32-pounder long guns. With all this, it appears strange that he was asking for additional strength.

Whatever Commodore Sloat's reasons were, Frémont had no choice other than to obey his urgent command. On the same day he received it, he left Sutter's Fort with 160 picked men. They rode south through the Sacramento and San Joaquin valleys, crossed the San Joaquin River near its junction with the Merced, and five days later, on July 17, rode past the Mission San Juan Bautista and into the village of San Juan.

At San Juan they ran up the American flag and took the arms and ammunition which General Castro had placed in hiding before he retreated south.

Two days later Frémont and his men entered Monterey and stunned most of the port's residents. Lieutenant Fred Walpole of the H.M.S. *Collingwood* was fascinated by the appearance of this rough-looking group of horsemen. To him they seemed like characters from James Fenimore Cooper's novels. Driving extra horses and a herd of beef cattle, they came out of a cloud of dust, riding in a long file. At their head was a lean, good-looking man whose clothes showed the wear of months in the wilderness. With him was a bodyguard of five Delaware Indians. All the men were colored by the wind and sun, and some were even darker than the Delawares. They rode two by two, their Hawken rifles held by one hand across the pommels of their saddles. They had pistols and skinning knives strapped around their waists, and they looked like men who would not hesitate to use any weapon they carried. As far as Lieutenant Walpole could tell, these were—except for their leader—American backwoodsmen; and most of them wore homemade buckskin clothing. Among these men was a tough, small man he had heard about. This was Kit Carson, whose reputation and stature among mountain men, Walpole stated, was the equivalent of a European duke.

Riding easily, looking from side to side, Frémont and his army of frontiersmen rode through Monterey and moved up the hillside to a point overlooking the town and harbor. Here, beneath pines and firs, they pitched camp.

To Frémont, the campsite was ideal. From this flat on the ridge overlooking the bay he had a fine view and protection against any force that might decide to attack. Below, he looked at the red-tiled roofs and large gardens enclosed by adobe walls. Beyond the thick walled adobe homes, beyond the Customs House, where the American flag whipped back and forth in the cool sea breeze, he saw the ships in the bay and heard the barking of seals and sea lions.

Among the ships in the harbor he saw Commodore Sloat's flagship—the *Savannah*—the *Cyane,* the *Levant,* and Commodore Robert Field Stockton's *Congress,* which had sailed into port just two days before his own arrival. There was one definite threat, or at least John Charles considered it so; that was the *Collingwood,* the flagship of the British admiral Sir George Seymour. Not wanting to waste any time, Captain Frémont asked Lieutenant Gillespie to accompany him on a visit to the *Savannah.*

When they boarded the ship, Commodore Sloat greeted them. At once Frémont saw he was nervous and strictly a rule-book officer. The first point of business the commodore brought up was the matter of authority. What, he wished to know, were Captain Frémont's orders? Had he received written orders, perhaps through Lieutenant Gillespie, from Washington that instructed him to take up arms against the Mexicans? When the captain answered that he had not, that he had done this in order to protect American settlers against General Castro's threats, Sloat appeared shocked. Even though he knew of the war on the east coast of Mexico, even though he had raised the flag at Monterey and had ordered Montgomery to do the same at Yerba Buena and San Francisco Bay, the commodore had taken such actions only because he had assumed Frémont had received written and official orders from Washington.

The interview was hardly a success. Frémont and Gillespie were disgusted with Sloat's attitude, and he was upset by their answers and actions. But things had gone too far along the road to war to smooth them over with apologies to the Mexicans. Like it or not, war had started.

Still puzzled by Sloat's attitude, Frémont and Gillespie returned to shore. They hardly knew what to make of their conversation with him. His letter had indicated he was ready to take action against the common foe. Now that he knew there were no specific orders for action, he was paralyzed into inaction.

Yet action was not to be denied. Commodore Sloat pleaded illness and age, turned his command over to Commodore Stockton, and prepared to sail back to the States as a passenger aboard the *Levant*. This act put the flamboyant Stockton into the kind of position he relished. An unconventional naval officer, an adventurer, a man of property and wealth, Stockton was an aggressive nationalist who believed Americans could do anything they deemed necessary. To him, whatever was good for the United States had to be good for the rest of the world.

The combination of Frémont and Stockton was one filled with energy, self-belief, and a never-say-die attitude. To both men, action was the key to success. Accordingly, on July 23, 1846, six days before the worn-out Sloat was to sail for home aboard the *Levant*, Commodore Stockton gave Frémont the rank of major and put him in official command of the California Battalion, which was to operate as a unit of horse marines. Though the major's men complained about receiving only ten dollars per month for military service and having to head for southern California aboard a ship, they were tired of the easy life around Monterey and ready for action against the elusive General Castro, who had plagued them ever since their first difficulties with him. Still smarting from having retreated from Gabilan Peak without firing a shot, they were anxious to have a go at Castro and his soldiers.

## 3

KIT CARSON WAS SEASICK for the whole voyage down the coast. Three days of rough and choppy waves did the tough mountain man in, and he wasn't by himself. Most of Frémont's men would rather have walked all the way from Monterey to San Diego. But they obeyed orders and trooped aboard the *Cyane* on Monday, July 26. Wednesday, as they reached the coast off San Diego, they broke away from the heavy swells and fought the winds that threatened to send the vessel into the shoals, managed to cross the harbor bar with about six inches to spare, and dropped anchor. This was a U. S. Navy operation until Major Frémont and the California Battalion were safely ashore. To make sure all was clear for their landing, that some kind of ambush would not be waiting for them, Captain Du Pont had his sailors lower the launch *Alligator*.[8] At 3:40 in the afternoon, Lieutenant Stephen C. Rowan, United States Navy,[9] was placed in command of a landing party of marines headed by Lieutenant William Maddox, United States Marine Corps.[10]

They reached the brig *Juanita*, which was flying Mexican colors, just in time to see the Hawaiian flag replace that of Mexico. Not wanting to take any risk of the ship getting out of the bay to aid General Castro, they prevented her from putting out to sea. Then they landed, were greeted by a peaceful crowd, and raised the American flag in San Diego's plaza. Shortly after the flag went up, Major Frémont and part of his force came ashore; but they were too late to prevent the escape of Andrés Pico and his men, who drove a herd of horses ahead of them as they slipped out of San Diego.[11]

The following day the rest of Major Frémont's men came ashore and were happy to feel solid ground underfoot once again. Don Juan Bandini, a thin, slight man whose intellectual approach to all things greatly impressed Frémont, offered his aid.[12] To Don Juan the invasion was not a bad thing. San Diego had been isolated and much too provincial for years. Now there was the possibility that a change of government might prove to be a blessing to all Californios. With one of his daughters married to the Yankee Abel Stearns,[13] Don Juan was more open to receiving Americans than Castro and his followers. Still, most of the citizens of San Diego were open to a change in government, particularly if that government promised them better conditions and more attention than they had been receiving from Mexico.

One thing was clear to Frémont. Their landing had prevented Castro's escape by sea. Rumor had it that he was in Pueblo de los Angeles with a considerable fighting force. Before they could pursue him, it was necessary to secure horses and enough supplies to see them through a campaign. From Bandini and others, John Charles learned that horses and cattle were available at the various ranchos, but these establishments were very large and not close to each other. To reach any of them, horses and guides were needed. Bandini saw to it that they had enough horses and guides to hunt for more animals.

Scouting the interior was more than a roundup to Frémont. It gave him a chance to become acquainted with the look of the land and the way of life of the rancheros. The days were warm under the clear, blue sky, but the nights were cool enough to make a campfire's heat feel good. While much of the pasture land was arid and had brush-covered hills, they found small valleys where springs and wells gave enough water that agriculture flourished. There were fine crops of pears, peaches, quinces, and pomegranates. But grapes and olives were the principal crops, and Frémont observed it was possible to get a barrel of wine just from the grapes of a single vine, and that olive trees were so loaded with fruit that branches were near the breaking point.

On August 6 Commodore Stockton sent a message to Frémont from San Pedro, where he and his men were aboard the frigate U.S.S. *Congress* along with Thomas Oliver Larkin, who hoped to be able to contact Castro and Pico and arrange a truce before there was a chance to shed blood. Before Larkin even had an opportunity to act as a negotiator between the two sides, Castro and Pico sent a message to him from Abel Stearns's Rancho Los Alamitos south of Pueblo de los Angeles, or just over fifty miles between present-day San Pedro and San Diego. All the message indicated was that they were on the move. Stockton warned Frémont to be careful as he rode north. Three days later Stockton received word that Castro's forces were located at John Temple's rancho near present-day Long Beach.[14] He quickly sent word to Frémont, but on the day before, John Charles and about 120 of his California Battalion had started for Pueblo de los Angeles, leaving Captain Gillespie and fifty men in charge at San Diego.

Peace was not out of the question, but the chances of some kind of negotiated settlement were all but gone since Commodore Stockton was determined to refuse anything other than unconditional surrender. But the night after Frémont had departed San Diego, the military force of Castro had disbanded. The general and Governor Pico left Pueblo de los Angeles and headed for Mexico. Castro took the route through San Gorgonio Pass to the Colorado River and headed from there to Sonora.

Pico went to his Santa Margarita Rancho in present northwestern San Diego County. Even in this vast domain that belonged to Pío and Andrés Pico, this stretch of land that paralleled the Pacific Ocean for twenty miles from today's Oceanside in the north to the Orange County line and San Clemente in the south, Don Pío Pico's escape to Mexico was cut off by the quickly advancing Americans. Pico went into temporary hiding at his brother-in-law's place until there was an opportunity for him to escape to Baja California, where he crossed the Sea of Cortés (the Gulf of California) to Guaymas. From there, Pico sent letters of appeal to Mexico City requesting men and arms to run the invaders out of California. His pleas were in vain. Mexico had its own troubles with American invaders, and officials hardly had time to give California a thought.

With Pico and Castro out of Alta California, there wasn't anybody able to command loyalty and support, not one leader capable of rallying any defense against the Americans.

Major Frémont and his mounted California Battalion rode north at a fast pace toward Pueblo de los Angeles from San Diego. Frémont's command was the usual mixture of mountain men, voyageurs, and Delawares, with the addition of the Osos. The major rode in front on a sorrel horse given him by Don Juan Bandini, its mane and tail decorated with green ribbons.

Meanwhile, a large force under Commodore Stockton made the march of some twenty-five miles from San Pedro to Pueblo de los Angeles. Commodore Stockton's army of about 350 men was as colorful as Frémont's in its own particular fashion. Captain Phelps of the merchant ship *Moscow* watched them as they moved away from the harbor at San Pedro. He was impressed by the appearance they made, and he had every right to be. At the head of the column marched a brass band. Just behind the band came the marines, followed by the sailors. After these units of marching men came the bullock carts, each cart pulled by four oxen. Each of the first four carts carried a quarter-deck gun, with the gun carriages secured by the breechings but ready for instant service. Following in the wake of the guns came other carts loaded with ammunition, baggage, and supplies. The carts were followed by the ship's doctor, the purser, and other officers. Some of these men were mounted on what Phelps called "rather sorry looking horses," and the others trudged along in the wake of the column's dust.

The two commands—Stockton's and Frémont's—would have looked quite normal to Falstaff, Don Quixote, or a band of small boys playing at war. Yet they were not men to make fun of, unless the joker was looking for a fight he would never forget.

Moving along at a steady pace, Commodore Stockton and his men reached the outskirts of Pueblo de los Angeles about four o'clock on the warm afternoon of August 13. They halted in the gardens just outside the town. It was here that Major Frémont and the mounted California Battalion met them.

The two commands combined into an even stranger army. Commodore Stockton and Major Frémont rode in front, and just behind them came the brass band. They were followed by all the others—the carts, the marching men, and the men on horseback. As they entered the town, the brass band began to play, and the citizens looked at their conquerors with a mixture of anxiety and curiosity. With horses dancing back and forth in the dusty streets, with uniformed marines and sailors trying to keep some semblance of order in their ranks, the invaders headed for the main plaza. Here, the men came to attention, or as near to it as some of them could manage; and as the band played "Hail Columbia," the Stars and Stripes was unfurled and run up the flagpole. The official capital of California had surrendered to a ragtag army of Americans, and not one shot had been fired, not one drop of blood had been shed.

Commodore Stockton and his men were quartered within the walls of the Government House. Major Frémont and the California Battalion picked a campground beside the river, got their fire pits dug, and settled down in the open.

Four days after the fall of Pueblo de los Angeles, Commodore Stockton issued his first proclamation. He expected loyalty from the citizens of California. Any person caught with firearms outside his home would be deported to Mexico. Thieves were to serve time at hard labor on public works. All citizens were to obey a curfew from ten o'clock at night until sunrise, and there were to be no exceptions to the rule. In short, martial law was the order of the day.

With all this stated, Commodore Stockton waited one more week as he decided what to do next, and on August 24, he sent a letter of instructions to Major Frémont. Stating that he feared the state of war between the United States and Mexico would encourage privateers to prey upon merchant vessels in the Pacific Ocean, he made it clear that he intended to withdraw his naval forces from California as soon as possible in order to protect commerce with the ships under his command.

Frémont was to command the military forces in California, and he was authorized to increase his force to three hundred men through enlistments. These men and their officers were to be used at key locations throughout California. Commodore Stockton recommended that Pueblo de los Angeles, Monterey, and San Francisco should have garrisons of fifty men; that smaller complements of troops were needed for Santa Barbara and San Diego; and that one hundred men should be kept in one garrison to be on call for any place within California.

Leaving all this to Major Frémont, the commodore then stated that if he managed to have things well in hand by October 25, he would meet him in San Francisco and appoint him governor of California and make Captain Gillespie the secretary. Then, two days after this letter had been written, Commodore Stockton prepared a report for President James Knox Polk in which he brought the President up to date. In fact, Stockton went far beyond an official report by stating that his word was the law of the land, that his person was more than regal, and that Mexican cavaliers took pleasure in shaking hands with him, while beautiful women looked upon him both as a friend and benefactor.

Letters to President Polk, Secretary of the Navy Bancroft, Senator Benton, and Frémont's beautiful Jessie were handed to Kit Carson. Kit was ordered to gather a sufficient number of men—hard and reliable men—and deliver everything to Washington within sixty days. This, Frémont thought, would give Carson and Maxwell time to stop at Taos to visit their wives. Both men and the others that Kit selected for this duty were old hands at riding long distances. They knew how to make do with limited supplies, how to get through desert country, how to avoid hostile Indians. And they showed their ability to get things ready as they picked fifteen men to ride with them and gathered a string of fifty mules that would carry supplies, baggage, and enough corn to serve as fodder in the long stretches of arid country that had to be crossed. When they reached Washington, Frémont had instructed Carson to go directly to Senator Benton, who would see to it that he met President Polk, the Secretary of the Navy, Mrs. Frémont, and all other persons of importance.

Like a messenger in a Greek epic, Carson left Pueblo de los Angeles, this distant field of battle, to ride homeward with news of victory and conquest.

John Charles envied him and "looked to his arrival at home and the deep interest and pleasure he would bring to them there almost with the pleasure I should feel in getting there myself—it was touching home."[15]

4

STOCKTON'S ORDERS were followed to the letter. Frémont left Gillespie and fifty men to control Pueblo de los Angeles. Talbot and ten men were to handle affairs at Santa Barbara, and so it went from place to place. Obviously the Californios who might have put up a fight had headed into Mexico. Frémont had tried to overtake General Castro, but his foe had too much of a lead. The only thing that was accomplished in this ride toward the desert country of the Colorado River was the discovery of cannons which Castro had buried in the sand. An ordinary party of men would not have made this find, for Castro had buried only the cannons and had gone ahead with their carriages to give the impression that the guns were with him. It was a good trick, and it would have worked if the Delawares had not noticed that there was a difference in the depth of the wheel tracks. This small difference was enough to guide them back to where the cannons were buried.

On the last day of August, Major Frémont received orders from Commodore Stockton to head north for the purpose of enlisting more fighting men to fill out the California Battalion. He suggested that the major stop at San Juan, Monterey, and San Francisco. Two days after this letter, things were shaping up rapidly, and Frémont quickly made all his preparations for his march to the north with about thirty-five men. In his last message to Captain Gillespie, which he sent on September 7, he informed him that Benjamin Davis Wilson and a force of twenty men had been placed at the Cajon Pass to make sure the Mexican soldiers did not circle back over the Old Spanish Trail and retake southern California.[16]

The day after Frémont sent his letter to Gillespie, an exhausted courier rode into Sutter's Fort far to the north. As the new commander listened to the man's wild rambling and breathless account, it became clear to Ned Kern that he was facing more trouble than he had ever planned for. One thousand Walla Walla Indians had entered the Sacramento Valley, and the messenger told the startled Ned that they had not come into California on a mission of peace.

Chief Piopiomoxmox, or Yellow Serpent as the whites called him, had come all the way from the Columbia River to get revenge for the death of his son, Elijah, who had been killed in a brawl in California and was buried in the valley. Ned tried to make more sense out of this, and he did manage to slow the excited messenger's speech enough to find that out of the one thousand Walla Walla Indians, only two hundred of them were armed warriors. But two hundred warriors carrying rifles and bent on trouble was more than he figured his small garrison could handle. To prepare for this invasion, he sent for help from Sonoma, San Jose, and Monterey.

Help came on a fast gallop. Lieutenant Joseph Warren Revere, who hated Indians, brought his garrison from Sonoma. Men began to come from throughout the Sacramento Valley, and by the time Lieutenant Revere reached the fort, preparations were well under way for a full-scale battle. Within twenty-four hours after Revere's arrival, there were almost three hundred fighters camped outside Sutter's Fort. These volunteers, Revere's garrison, and the men under Kern's command were a considerable striking force. Ned and Revere were excited and waited for the morning to come. Both were anxious for combat, and though Ned had started the expedition with a definite fondness for Indians, he had come to hate them as much as Revere, who looked upon them as some form of human insect that he liked to crush.

On the day they were ready to move their army out of the fort, the signal was given that Indians were approaching. Everything was made ready for a battle, and then Chief Yellow Serpent and a small group of unarmed warriors appeared. Kern and Revere looked on in disbelief as they saw their grand plans for victory on the field vanish before the first shot had been fired. Chief Yellow Serpent indicated he had come to the fort to speak in peace. Having no other choice, the two young officers agreed. They joined the circle for talk, and the chief began his oration:

"I have come from the forests of Oregon with no hostile intentions. You can see that I speak the truth, because I have brought with me only forty warriors, with their women and little children."[17]

What followed was a long speech in which Chief Yellow Serpent explained that he had come all the way from the Columbia River to visit his son's grave.

What the chief told them was not altogether true, but Kern's quick action in getting ready for battle had made the difference. Though the chief had considered something in the way of revenge for his son's death, his scouts had reported the build-up of troops around the fort. Rather than risk having more of his men killed, Chief Yellow Serpent put aside his feelings of wrath and ended his long trip to California with a visit to his son's grave.

This was only the first part of September, and it had the appearance of being one of those months a man would just as soon forget. Frémont had no way of knowing about the excitement in the Sacramento Valley until he and his men reached San Juan. By this time, news of the false alarm had spread south from the valley, and the talk of Ned Kern's "almost" Indian war was a bit of gossip that went well with a glass of wine. It was the kind of thing to talk about in the warmth of Indian summer while men sat on benches beneath overhangs during the midday heat.

Even as Frémont relaxed from his long ride, an official letter arrived from Commodore Stockton, who was aboard the U.S.S. *Congress*, riding at anchor in San Francisco Bay. The order was dated September 28, 1846, and Stockton wanted to know what the prospects were of Frémont's recruiting a thousand men for him, as he fully intended to sail down the Pacific Coast, land at Mazatlán or Acapulco, and march on into Mexico City. Dreams of glory on paper can be rather futile in the face of other pieces of paper with contrary facts. Three days after penning this note to Frémont, Commodore Stockton received a rude shock from southern California when a messenger brought him an urgent plea from Captain Gillespie calling for help, as the Angeleños had revolted and put his garrison under siege.

5

LIEUTENANT GILLESPIE had struck a bargain for trouble by taking a haughty attitude toward the Californios. Cocksure, convinced of invincibility—even though he had slightly fewer than fifty troopers—Gillespie continued Stockton's policy of strict martial law and kept the curfew hours posted. All of this was bad enough to the captive citizens, but insult was added to insult by an army of volunteers who were bored by occupation duty and became unruly and obnoxious as they consumed great quantities of wine and aguardiente without the ability to hold their liquor.

Rumors of rebellion against this army of occupation came to Gillespie daily, and he did become concerned when he heard that a relief party for the invaded country was on its way north from Mexico. In an attempt to protect his outposts, he sent Zeke Merritt and a small party of men to San Diego. While this helped San Diego, it weakened the force at Pueblo de los Angeles even more and made them a certain target.

Violence came without warning during the early morning of September 23. Nearly a dozen Californios launched an attack on Gillespie's headquarters. The first the marine knew of it was when he heard the sound of rifle fire coming from the front and rear of his headquarters. "Hastily he and his men armed, and took their defensive positions on the roof where they returned the enemy fire. At this moment Gillespie had but twenty-one men."[18] Yet they managed to drive off the first rebels and killed two of them in the brief but brutal fight. Still, Gillespie and his men were in no position to hold off for very long if a force of any size should attack the Government House. The attack and siege was not long in coming, and it was commanded by José María Flores.[19] His troops surrounded the Government House, forced Lieutenant Gillespie to surrender on September 29, took his artillery, and escorted the defeated marine and his men to San Pedro, where they were allowed to board the merchant ship *Vandalia* bound for Monterey.

To Thomas Oliver Larkin, who was taken prisoner by the growing army of Californios under the command of Flores, none of this came as a surprise. He had tried to warn Commodore Stockton that Gillespie wasn't the man to put in charge of Pueblo de los Angeles, but the marine was given the post. In Larkin's view, Gillespie treated the Mexicans in a manner bound to cause rebellion. People were fined and imprisoned without so much as an official hearing; requests to be repatriated to Mexico were automatically ignored; and proclamations that were insulting to the citizens were enforced with a ruthlessness that would have done credit to a Roman soldier. Larkin saw that this harshness had brought the country to its terrible state and finally drove Gillespie away in defeat and shame. It wasn't just Flores alone, as Larkin knew, for Flores had been one of the men Larkin had talked to before Commodore Stockton had captured Pueblo de los Angeles; and Flores told him that Castro would negotiate if hostilities ceased. Stockton's answer had been that immediate surrender and the raising of the American flag was all that would be accepted. So, while Gillespie was harsh, he only followed the example of his commanding officer.

Lieutenant Gillespie did manage to do one thing right before he surrendered and marched off to San Pedro. He sent word of the uprising to the north by a hard-riding courier known as Juan Flaco or John Brown.[20] Making a fast and dramatic ride, Flaco stopped at Santa Barbara to warn Talbot and his men; then he continued on to Monterey and finally San Francisco, where he delivered the bad news to Commodore Stockton.

Theodore Talbot was just settling down at Santa Barbara and finding it a beautiful place with plenty of good-looking women. He was content to take life easy in the gay and slow-moving culture of this settlement. His vacation came to an abrupt end when Flaco handed him some cigarillos containing Lieutenant Gillespie's Motto Seal that indicated he was bringing official news and not some rumor. It was all very dramatic, very secretive; and, as Talbot wrote to his mother, he remained at Santa Barbara for a few more anxious days. Then news or rumor arrived that Gillespie had surrendered and some two hundred men were marching toward Santa Barbara. Not taking any chances, Talbot and his men lit out for the mountains, where they remained for about eight days until they were spotted by the Californios. They fought a short battle, escaped without any dead or wounded, picked up a friendly guide and began the hard five-hundred-mile ride to Monterey, where they hoped to meet Major Frémont.

Even as Talbot rode north to join Frémont, even as Gillespie and his men waited aboard the *Vandalia* to set sail from San Pedro, the first week of October started in a chaotic state. Major Frémont was back in the Sacramento Valley sending notes to Ned Kern about enlisting men and branding all the expedition horses with the customary "F" (for Frémont) as these mounts and others would be needed. Commodore Stockton was sending urgent notes to Frémont restressing his need for fighting men at once in that he planned to sail the *Congress* out of San Francisco Bay, beat a southern course for San Pedro, rescue Lieutenant Gillespie and his men, and put down the rebellion.

California was in turmoil this first week of October 1846, and it was during this week that Kit Carson and Brigadier Stephen Watts Kearny met. Heading the Army of the West, Kearny and his troopers were beside the Río Grande, just south of Socorro, New Mexico, when Carson came upon them. Kit's old companion Broken Hand Fitzpatrick was guiding this army on its long march; and as they were now eight hundred miles east of Pueblo de los Angeles, they had completed half of their journey. They had come all the way from Fort Leavenworth, past Bent's Fort, through Raton Pass, and had captured Santa Fé with ease. Now they were bound for California—General Kearny, Broken Hand, and three hundred soldiers. They were following the path that was supposed to take them to the Gila River Trail, but Fitzpatrick was the first to admit he had never been through this country. The best he could do was rely upon what he had learned at Santa Fé and put to use his hard-won knowledge of the wilderness.

To General Kearny, the fact that Carson had come from California was ideal. Here was a man who knew his way across the desert, knew where the waterholes were located, knew which Indians could be trusted, and knew just how long the journey would take. To add to this bonus, Kit told the general the war was over in California. The Mexicans had surrendered, and everything was under control. Hearing all this, Kearny ordered Carson to hand his messages to Broken Hand. There was no reason why he couldn't take over that duty while Kit guided him on to California. Since everything was peaceful and California was now under the American flag, there was no need to take all the army. There was always a possibility things could change at Santa Fé. That victory had been much too easy. With this in mind, the general sent all but 110 of his troopers back to Santa Fé. The rest remained with him, and he commanded Carson to lead the way. For Kit it was so near and yet so far. He wanted to visit his wife. It wouldn't have taken long to ride north to Taos for at least a few days. But duty came first, and not knowing that all hell had broken loose in California, easygoing Kit agreed to General Kearny's order. He turned his mount and headed back into barren country between Socorro and California.

6

COMMODORE STOCKTON was in a hurry to get Major Frémont and members of the California Battalion back to San Francisco Bay as quickly as possible. He planned to sail south, and Frémont's tough army would be needed to put down the rebels of southern California. Taking a gamble on finding the major somewhere in the Sacramento Valley, Commodore Stockton sent Midshipman Edward Fitzgerald Beale[21] and a fleet of boats to look for him. What Stockton didn't know and what Beale soon discovered was that the intertwined river world of the Sacramento and San Joaquin rivers was a country of sloughs, deltas, and miles of tules. It was a riverman's territory, and the tricky waterways were not something a seafaring man was apt to know very much about.

On his second day away from the *Congress*, Beale discovered he had entered into a world both fascinating and puzzling. He had sailed out of San Francisco Bay north through San Pablo Bay, entered the Carquinez Straits, and reached the confluence of the two great rivers. As far as Beale could see there was an ocean of tules. But more than tules caught his fancy. At sunset, the red glow outlined the two peaks of Mount Diablo and cast a pink shade on the faraway white line of snowpacks on the jagged peaks of the Sierra Nevada. Then as the men made camp for the night among the tules, they were astounded by the flapping wings and the honks and squawks of massive flocks of waterfowl; the howling of coyote packs somewhere in the valley; the sudden appearance of great herds of deer, tule elk, wild horses and wild cattle coming to the river for water; and all the other animals that flew, swam, galloped, padded, or walked along through the tules, over the delta land, and on the vast plain of the valley floor.

That night, Beale slept beside the campfire and shook from the cold. He had forgotten to bring any blankets. The young midshipman was excited at the prospects before him. He was twenty years old, in charge of his first vessels—a fleet if one wanted to call these boats by such a grand name—and he was searching for the famous John Charles Frémont. To young Beale, it was as though he were "Sir Galahad going to search for the Holy Grail."[22]

The next day, as the morning fog lifted from the river and the delta, the flotilla meandered on its way until a horseman was seen. At Beale's command, all the boats made for shore while the rider watched them make their way to the riverbank. Where, Beale asked him, could they find Major Frémont?

The horseman had some idea as to Frémont's location. At least the last he had seen of the major, he was at Sonoma. Then, as though he realized these sailors would never find Sonoma, he suggested that he take them there.

To Beale this was as good an offer as he could expect, but there was a problem. They didn't have horses, and the man was proposing an overland journey. But this was easy to solve, and their horseman showed them how. Horses were rounded up from the herds grazing on the grasslands of the valley, then quickly broken to the saddle—if one could call it that—and the guide announced that they were ready to ride. To Beale and the other sailors, the idea of mounting a wild horse was something new and unexpected. But if this was the way that they were going to find Major Frémont, then they had no choice other than to mount these animals, make do as best they could, and get on with their orders.

True to his word, the guide brought them—though they were sore and stiff—overland to Sonoma. Here, where the Osos had touched off the spark that became a war, Midshipman Beale and his companions found Major Frémont and a contingent of the California Battalion. They were enlisting volunteers for duty and buying all the horses that were for sale.

Beale met Ide and a host of the others who had been in on the start of things in California. He talked to Frémont, explaining the situation as Commodore Stockton saw it, and the major agreed to go to San Francisco Bay with him by boat. That night they remained in Sonoma, but before dawn they were on horseback and bound for the anchorage of Beale's fleet of boats. Frémont joined Beale in the fastest of the boats, and they set sail for the Bay. Outsailing the rest of the fleet, they made their night camp on an island, and Beale cut some bushes to make a signal fire for the rest of the boats. Unknowingly, he cut a fair amount of poison oak. That night as the fog began to drift in and as the other boats had found the campground for the stop over, Beale began to feel chilled. Seeing his condition, Major Frémont offered to share his bed with him. Beale looked at the large grizzly hide and wondered about it, but it had the advantage of offering some warmth. Still, things were not comfortable for the midshipman, and he jotted his experience in his journal.

> I soon began to itch so much I told him there must be fleas in his bear-skin, at which he laughed. Very soon I seemed to be on fire and got up and went to where the water was lapping on the crag, but there was no balm in Gilead for me that night nor for many after. I could do nothing but swell and swear and swear and swell. Soon my head was as big as a flour-barrel and Job had no harder time than I. Howsomever, we got under way, and by the time we reached the old frigate *Congress,* I had no need to pray, "Oh, for an hour of blind old Dandolo!" for I was blind as ever he was. I remember the old surgeon, who must have got his diploma in a Sioux lodge, poured arnica over me, for which I promised him if I ever caught him ashore to pay him off with a vitriol bath.[23]

By the following morning, Midshipman Beale was a swollen poison-oaker who hardly knew that the fleet of his command was approaching the *Congress.* It was October 12, and Beale and his webfeet companions were happy to get back to their ship, to get out of the half-swamp and half-river country they had seen as an example of what the earth must have been like during the peak of the Pleistocene age.

Frémont reported for duty, and Commodore Stockton was pleased that he had 170 men with him. While they were without horses, Stockton didn't think this was anything to worry about. The men had brought their riding gear and their weapons. Plenty of horses were available on the large ranchos in southern California.

Apparently it never occurred to Stockton that rounding up horses might not be easy for men afoot. Then there was no guarantee the Californios hadn't driven the stock to the interior. But the commodore was a navy man through and through. He had no understanding of the army's need for horses if they were to have any success against the mounted lancers under the command of Mexican officers.

Seeing this situation, realizing that Commodore Stockton was nervous and impatient, Frémont agreed to go ahead. Maybe they might be lucky and find some horses close to whatever port was selected for a landing. For now, all he could do was sail and hope that Stockton's optimism turned out to be right.

Everything was agreed upon. Come morning, they would set sail. Frémont and his troops were to head south aboard the merchant ship *Sterling*. Stockton and his crew were to lead the way in the *Congress*. Meanwhile, the commodore already had sent word to Captain Mervine, who had the *Savannah* anchored at Monterey. Mervine was to be the third part of the striking force. His orders called for him to sail on to San Pedro and assist in the rescue of Captain Gillespie and his men.

But the plan fell apart before the *Congress* and the *Sterling* had completed their first day at sea. After sailing away from San Francisco Bay, the ships became separated in a thick fog bank, and the *Sterling* dropped far behind. During the next two days, she never saw the command ship even though the fog lifted. On the second day out, she did meet the *Vandalia* coming up the coast from San Pedro. In an exchange of messages with her, Frémont learned that Captain Gillespie and his troops had remained in southern California. Captain Mervine and the *Savannah* had reached San Pedro and had landed part of the crew of sailors and marines to help Gillespie with his plan to recapture Pueblo de los Angeles. But it was a valiant attempt doomed to failure. Though they had four hundred men, they were without horses and artillery, while the Californios were mounted and had one cannon. The result of this move was the loss of four men, the wounding of several more, and a hasty retreat back to San Pedro harbor and the safety of the *Savannah*.

Faced with this situation, knowing that horses were not available, that all the stock had been driven far into the interior, Frémont decided it would be foolish to go south without horses. He had the master of the *Sterling* change the ship's course, and they slowly worked their way back up the coast. Two weeks and a day after leaving San Francisco Bay, the *Sterling* dropped anchor in Monterey Bay on October 27.

At Monterey, Frémont learned he had been appointed to the rank of lieutenant colonel in the army. But he had little time to enjoy the thought of such a promotion. He needed all the horses and men he could get, and he needed them fast. He sent letters requesting both horses and men to Commodore John B. Montgomery, who was aboard the *Portsmouth* in San Francisco Bay, and to Ned Kern at Sutter's Fort. Even as he made these moves, horses were being gathered. An army of volunteers was being enlisted by Lieutenant Revere at Sonoma, by Ned Kern at Sutter's Fort, and by Edwin Bryant, the Kentucky journalist, who had asked Kern if it would be all right to travel among the emigrants and Indians to ask for volunteers.[24]

Ned Kern gave his go-ahead to Bryant's plan, and the whole thing was submitted to the commander of Sutter's Fort in very official terms:

We, the undersigned, offer to the Command of Fort Sacramento the following proposition for raising volunteers.

1st. We will separate and ride in different directions where emigrants are located and engage them as volunteers to be organized at the place of rendezvous into one or more companies, the said companies to be officered from the undersigned and others.

2nd. We are authorized to take all horses needed for said companies, to be appraised and giving receipt for same.

3rd. Such emigrants as have families and will volunteer, their families are to be furnished with flour and meat by the government, to be deducted from the pay of such volunteers. The families, if they desire it, are to be quartered in Fort Sacramento during the period of enlistment.

4th. We are to be authorized to raise as many Indians as we may deem safe to accompany us, the command of whom is to be given to some suitable person.

5th. The white volunteers to receive the same pay as those heretofore enlisted, viz. twenty-five dollars per month, with horse, saddle and bridle. Those who have ammunition, saddle and bridle will use same at expense of government.[25]

Four other men signed this document with Edwin Bryant. One of them was that outcast of the Donner Party, James F. Reed. Reed had killed a man on the trail in a quarrel he had not sought, and he had been expelled from the doomed party to go ahead by himself across the rest of the Great Basin. The other three signers were a mixed bag. Richard Jacob was a friend of Bryant's and a man who would one day marry one of Thomas Hart Benton's daughters. Andrew Grayson was already a family man and had settled with his wife and child on the upper reaches of the Sacramento Valley. The other signer was Benjamin Lippincott, a gambler by trade, but a man destined to serve as a member of the California Constitutional Convention.

Sutter's Fort became the center of enlistment activity. Emigrants just down from the Sierra Nevada, just in from their overland trek, joined the volunteer army to pick up extra money and insure their position in California after having made such a hard and long journey. Indians from California tribes, some Paiutes from the Great Basin—including Chief Truckee and his brother Pancho from Pyramid Lake—and warriors from Chief Yellow Serpent's Walla Wallas made their mark and were ready to fight with bows and arrows as well as rifles. Altogether, nearly thirty per cent of the California Battalion was enlisted at Sutter's Fort. The total of those enlisted at the fort and at Sonoma and the men Bryant's plan had picked up from camps and settlements came to between 160 and 170 men for Frémont's army—an army that would have about 400 men ready to head south before the end of November.

As this rush to enlist took place in the north, the situation in southern California had taken yet another change. Zeke Merritt and John Bidwell had been forced to abandon San Diego. Along with some Californios who were supporting the conquest, they boarded the whaler *Stonington* and sailed just off the coast until they began to run very short of supplies. In an effort to solve this problem, Bidwell and five other men sailed a small boat up the coast to San Pedro to seek aid from the *Savannah*. But Captain Mervine and part of his crew were not aboard when Bidwell got there. They were on their way to Pueblo de los Angeles with Captain Gillespie and his men.

Nobody aboard the *Savannah* had the authority to give out supplies. Faced with this problem, Bidwell and the others got what supplies they could in San Pedro. They then set sail for their rendezvous with the *Stonington* off the coast of San Diego. On their way back, they ran into a bad storm. They lost all their supplies, were nearly swamped, and reached the *Stonington* without any aid. This left them no choice. It was either starve aboard ship or go ashore and fight for survival. The opening day of battle was one John Bidwell never forgot. Captain Zeke Merritt led the way as they landed three miles away from the town. They had twenty-five men and some cannons from the ship.

> The road lay all the way through soft sand, the dragging of the cannon was very difficult, requiring most of way all the men to move a single piece. When about half way our movements were discovered. Flores came out with his men in line of battle. All were mounted. But our march continued without the slightest hesitation, one of the brass pieces being hauled a hundred yards or so was left in charge of three or four men and while they were aiming and firing, the rest went back to bring up the other and so on alternately, loading and firing till Flores fled with all his force and we entered and took possession of the town, raising the flag where it has floated from that day to this.[26]

Without additional backing, Zeke Merritt knew that he could hold San Diego for only a short time as the hilltops above the town were occupied by Californios who poured a steady fire at the Americans occupying the plaza and immediate buildings. It was a bad position to hold, and Merritt sent one of the *Stonington*'s whaleboats up the coast to San Pedro to see if Captain Mervine had returned and if he would send reinforcements.

Mervine came to their rescue by chartering the whaler *Magnolia* to take Lieutenant George Minor,[27] two midshipmen, thirty-five sailors, and fifteen volunteers to San Diego. By the night of October 16 they had landed near the mouth of the San Diego River, where they built fortifications to hold off the Californios. Contrary to John Bidwell's memory of the capture of San Diego, none of it came off in an easy fashion. As the last days of October ran their course and Frémont's army began to grow in the north, Commodore Stockton managed to slip into the harbor at San Diego with the *Congress*. Then as October ran into November, the growing force of Americans was able to take the heights above San Diego and drive Flores and his horsemen away. To make sure that they would not return, they built Fort Stockton overlooking the town. Midshipman Duvall remembered the hard work that went into the construction of the fort.[28]

> The Commodore now commenced to fortify the Hill which over looked the town by building a Fort constructed by placing 300 Gallon casks full of sand close together, 30 yds by 20 square throwing a Bank of earth and small gravel up in Front as high as the Top of the casks & running a Ditch around the whole. In the inside a Ball Proff house was built out of Plank linening the inside with Adobes, on the top of which a swivel was mounted. The entrance was guarded by a Strong gate having a draw Bridge in front, the whole fortification was completed in about 3 weeks. Guns mounted and every thing complete notwithstanding the Plank, etc. had to be carried by the men near a mile and the ditch cut through a solid strata of gravel and rock, with but indifferent tools to do it with. It is a monument of the most excessive hard Labor our forces have as yet performed notwithstanding they were on short allowance of Beef and wheat for a time without Bread Tea sugar or coffee, many destitute of shoes but few complaints were made.[29]

## 7

EVEN AS FORT STOCKTON was completed and San Diego was secured again, Captain Charles D. Burass[30] and twenty-two men of the California Battalion came south from Sutter's Fort with a brass cannon and five hundred head of horses and mules. They were bound for Monterey to deliver everything to Frémont. They rode past Pueblo de San José, came to San Juan, and pitched camp the night of November 15 on the grounds of Mission San Juan Bautista.

The same night, Thomas Oliver Larkin stopped to sleep at José and Joaquín Gómez's[31] Los Vergeles Rancho just southwest of San Juan. Larkin was on his way to Yerba Buena to visit his youngest daughter, who was seriously ill, but he never got there. During the night he was taken prisoner for the second time in the war. This time has captors were under the command of Manuel Castro,[32] a cousin of General José Castro. Politely but firmly, the Californios escorted Larkin to Castro's Salinas River camp, where he was treated kindly but informed he was being held as a hostage.

As Larkin made do with his situation, nineteen-year-old Edward Kemble was one of the soldiers camped at the mission grounds.[33] He had been in California since July 31, when he arrived in San Francisco Bay aboard the *Brooklyn*. He had been working for Sam Brannan on the Mormon newspaper Brannan was publishing in New York.[34] When Brannan said he was bringing 240 Saints to California, young Kemble couldn't resist the idea of sailing all the way. And now, only four days since his nineteenth birthday, he was involved in the destiny of California as a volunteer soldier who had only a romantic notion about a military campaign.

It was no wonder Kemble was excited. The men gathered at the mission grounds hardly would pass as a regular army. There were mountain men, emigrants, Walla Walla Indians, and two tough Delawares who had seen more than one wilderness campaign.

As the evening campfires were started, the volunteers were joined by another group of California Battalion men under the command of a loud, red-haired man known as "Hell Roaring" Thompson. A man with a knack for using foul language in a colorful fashion, a gambler by trade, and a reckless soul by nature, this was Captain Bluford K. Thompson.[35] With him was a troop of thirty-five men composed of blacks, runaway sailors on the dodge, Germans with thick accents, English drifters looking for action, and a contingent of Californios who wanted the United States to take over California. This company added to Captain Burrass's men made the whole lot as wild a mixture as ever sailed under the skull and crossbones.

Thompson and Burrass talked things over and decided there was no point in driving the herd of horses and mules all the way to Monterey until they knew where Frémont wanted to pasture the animals. By mutual agreement, they decided to leave a force of men at the mission grounds while they and a few others rode into Monterey. This was fine with most of the men who remained in camp, for the thought of laying over for a day's rest came as an unexpected gift.

The next morning was clear and cold. There was very little wind, and the streamers of smoke from the campfires drifted straight up toward a sky that resembled some vast mountain lake. There was a light frost on the grass, and the forty-five men in camp ate more than one helping of roasted meat. Then they sat back, smoked, talked, and looked at their large string of horses feeding on the grass in the vicinity of the mission. About ten o'clock a rider came into view on the crest of the hill on the Monterey road. He was riding at a full gallop and waving his hat in the air. The lounging men got up, squinted their eyes, and tried to make out the rider. Some of the mountain men checked their rifles and began to look for a good tree or rock that might serve as a temporary fort if they happened to need one. Before there was time to fire a warning shot, the courier was recognized as "Hell Roaring" Thompson, and orders were given to catch the horses and saddle up. A man riding that fast had to be bringing bad news.

Then, as the rider came within earshot, everyone could hear that he was shouting for the men to mount up, to get their rifles ready. Down the road on the edge of the Salinas plains, they had spotted a party of armed Californios waiting to ambush them where the road crossed the Salinas River. Captain Burrass and the men were scouting the area, and Thompson wasn't sure they hadn't been trapped already.

Yelling, and cursing, the buckskin-clad men, the men still dressed in sailors' uniforms, the emigrants in half-worn-out clothing, and the Walla Wallas with very little on except war paint all hurried to catch their horses, and throw on the saddles. They rode out of the mission grounds with a clatter on the hard-packed earth. The dust quickly built up behind them as they struck the road to Monterey. Young Kemble was caught up in the middle of all this frantic movement. He was so excited he couldn't be sure that he had brought everything he might need in case of a battle, but he rode with the others and heard his heart pound almost as loudly as the steady beat of horses hooves against the earth.

In one hour of hard riding the men passed through Los Vergeles Rancho and reached the boundary of La Natividad Rancho. To their relief, Captain Burrass and the others were alive. They hadn't even exchanged shots with the distant foe. From Gómez they learned of Larkin's midnight capture by a force of at least 150 men who were well mounted and armed with rifles and lances, and who were now among the oak groves and lined up as though they might attack at any moment.

Volunteers were called for to scout the position of the Californios. Joseph Foster,[36] James Hays[37] and two Delawares rode out to reconnoiter the enemy's position. As they neared the grove of oaks, they were surrounded by Californios. Puffs of smoke suddenly hung in the air, and the echo of shooting quickly followed.

As the intensity of this engagement increased, the war-painted Walla Wallas galloped out to help the surrounded men. Before they reached them, Foster was shot in the head, and Hays was down with a bad groin wound. The two Delawares were not hit. They dug into the ground as best they could and coolly took aim. They brought down a man with each shot. Suffering from his wound, all Hays could do was watch the action. After he had been rescued by the Walla Wallas, he maintained that at least nine of the enemy had been wounded or killed by the accurate shooting of the Delawares.

Young Kemble was nervous and anxious to prove his manhood, and never considered that he was in danger of being shot. With detachment he observed all that was going on. He saw "Hell Roaring" Thompson become disgusted with Captain Burrass's cautious approach and ride up to the senior officer to argue for an attack. Thompson wanted to charge while the Californios were nursing their wounds and hit them before they recovered balance or retreated out of range.

Forced into action by Thompson's bravado, Captain Burrass ordered the men to move toward the enemy formation. For a few moments the men rode at a full gallop and shouted for bravery. Then, as they neared the enemy line, as they saw the sun reflect off the long blades of sharp lances, some of them pulled their horses to a halt, turned, and began to retreat.

Seeing his command falling apart, Captain Burrass became desperate. He galloped ahead of the company, holding his empty rifle in the air as though it were a flag, and yelled for the men to follow him. Less than two miles away was the Salinas River, and the men saw the Californios in their colorful vaquero outfits. They were holding their lances upright, and their beautiful horses were pawing at the ground, nervous and ready to gallop forward. To the Indians, the movement of the battalion was much too slow. Riding their wild ponies at a full gallop, yelling loudly, they dashed in front of the line of Mexican horsemen and fired at them. This was too much to take for one of the Californios, and he charged the Indians as they were making a turn for another run. But they were much too quick for him. Before the man had retreated to his own lines, he had been hit by three or four arrows in his back and sides.

One of the Americans yelled, "Charge!" when he saw all this. The next thing Kemble knew, he was galloping straight toward the line of lancers. He and most of his companions quickly fired every shot in their rifles and neared the enemy line with useless weapons. All that saved them were the experienced mountain men and the Indians. They were prepared for a counterattack. Everything became a din of cries, shouts, and screams. Captain Burrass held his empty rifle, and a Californio rode straight at him and killed him with one shot. Hiram Ames screamed as a lance drove through his body and pulled out his last breath of life.[38] William Thorne was dead on the field.[39] And along with Hays, three other Americans were wounded in the short and vicious battle.

Stunned, shocked, unable to make another move, the men of the California Battalion did not give chase as Manuel Castro and his lancers spurred their horses and retreated down the road in the direction of Mission Soledad. Yet, even as the Californios rode away, Tom Hill, one of the Delawares, rode his horse out of a grove of oaks, gave a wild yell, and held two fresh scalps up for everyone to see.[40] The men were too dazed to pay much attention. All they wanted was to get away from this place with the stench of death about it.

It had been Kemble's first taste of war, a battle that cost the lives of four men. These volunteer soldiers were buried on the Gómez rancho, close to where they had fallen, and their final rites were a simple soldier's salute. Two other men were severely wounded, and three more suffered from minor but painful wounds.

As for the Californios, Kemble thought at least ten or eleven had been killed and a good many more had been wounded. Being young and resilient, he was still excited and full of energy when they rode into their camp at the mission grounds in the dark. As campfires were started and the cooking began, he unrolled his blankets. To his surprise, the six-shooter he had counted on using in case of trouble was safely rolled up in his blankets. "By thunder! there! my pepper-box is in my blankets!" he said. "I might have killed eleven or eight of them Mexicans!"[41]

## 8

Tom Hill and the half-breed Charley McIntosh[42] left the Salinas plains as the sun began to set. They had agreed to ride to Monterey and deliver the news of the Battle of Natividad to Lieutenant Colonel Frémont. As they rode out of sight of their companions, a group of Californios began to chase them. McIntosh had a faster horse, and he quickly put plenty of distance between himself and the men riding in pursuit. Tom Hill's horse wasn't as fast, and he heard a rider drawing closer to him. He turned in time to see the man thrust his lance at him. Leaning to one side of his saddle, he parried the lance by taking the impact of the sharp blade through one hand. As the blood spurted from the wound, Hill "seized his tomahawk, and struck a blow at his opponent, which split his head from the crown to the mouth."[43]

Nursing his badly wounded hand, Tom Hill caught up to Charley McIntosh, and they continued their journey to Monterey in the dark. Once they reached the port town, they located Frémont and told him what had taken place.

The colonel was already making preparations to march to San Juan and set up headquarters until he had enough recruits and horses to begin his trek to southern California. On the day of the battle, John Charles had written a long letter to Captain William Mervine of the *Savannah* which was anchored in the nearby bay. In the letter he had made it clear that he was bothered by the appointment of irresponsible men as officers in the California Battalion. As he saw it, many of these so-called leaders were drunk a good deal of the time and hardly capable of making sound decisions that would turn the course of a battle.

The news of the bloody affair on the Salinas plains upset him. He was convinced the charge had been disorderly and had given all the advantage to the Californios. It had been heedless, foolish, and deadly. As he put it, "A good commander spares his men. He fights to win, and to do this his head is the best weapon at his command."[44]

On the morning after learning the bad news, Frémont and his force of men from Monterey rode toward San Juan. Here he intended to wait for his new recruits and the additional horses, and to get his men ready for the march to Pueblo de los Angeles. Part of their training would be that of scouring the countryside in search of any band of Californios on the prod. He especially wanted to corner Manuel Castro and his men and put an end to their guerrilla warfare.

In a letter from San Juan he told Ned Kern to inform the Walla Walla chief that his men had fought bravely, that none of them were even wounded, and that the Delaware Tom Hill had received two slight wounds. The last bit of information would have been less than the truth for somebody other than a frontiersman such as Hill, but the tough Delaware had no complaints. He had killed the man who had attacked him, and that made up for the pain of his wound.

In closing his letter, John Charles drew a sketch of a moon and a half-moon and asked Ned to inform Chief Yellow Serpent that his men would be coming back to his camp within that time. While they were away, all Walla Wallas were to receive regular rations of beef, flour, and other food from the stores at Sutter's Fort.

The organization of the army took time. Frémont wrote to Captain Charles M. Weber, the ranchero and businessman at Pueblo de San José, about the horses and mules he had been appointed to gather.[45] He asked him to deliver the animals to Lieutenant William Blackburn of Company A of the California Battalion as quickly as possible.[46] What John Charles didn't know until later was that Weber's methods of commandeering horses, mules, and additional supplies bordered on outright theft. It became so bad, and Weber so obnoxious, that word of his behavior reached Frémont.

Before November ended the colonel wrote to Captain William Mervine about Weber's highhanded methods. As he put it, such behavior did very little honor to the United States, insulted the inhabitants, and posed the threat of driving peaceful people into the hands of the enemy for their own protection against Weber's treatment of them. In closing, he apologized for burdening him with a problem that he would gladly take care of if he had the authority to do so. But since Commodore Stockton had not yet appointed him Military Commandant of California, he believed he had to point out a potentially dangerous development to an officer of higher rank and let him take whatever steps necessary to curb a growing disenchantment of Captain Weber that could well turn into much more than bitter complaints.

As the men gathered at the San Juan camp, Frémont saw to it that they received some instruction about hanging together and waiting for commands in case of action against the Californios. He wanted no more ill-conceived charges such as that which had cost four lives on the Salinas plains. Each day as he tried to make sure that his men were ready for battle, he was faced with the arrival of more men coming in from Sutter's Fort, Sonoma, and other points to the north. The horse and mule herd increased daily, but many of the animals were in poor shape, and it was questionable whether they would last on the long march south.

Young Edward Kemble was fascinated by the variety of weapons and outfits he saw among the men at the mission grounds. They carried whatever weapons they owned or had been able to come by. Sailors had ship's carbines, and these looked like dependable weapons. Other men had muskets that might have been used during the Revolutionary War. Only two things followed a set pattern: powder horns, plain or highly polished and ornamented, and the one article of clothing issued from the United States Navy to battalion members—the common blue-flannel sailor's shirt with its broad collar and a threaded white star in the corner of each collar wing. The shirt was worn over whatever clothing the volunteer happened to own and was gathered around the waist by a broad leather belt, which also held a pistol or two and a sharp hunting knife in a leather sheath.

As for the rest of their outfits, Kemble saw a hodgepodge that belonged to a band of outlaws, not to a military unit.

Most of the men wore buckskin trousers, sometimes fringed down the outer seam with buckskin and red flannel intermixed, moccasins on their feet, and their heads crowned with the broad-rimmed Mexican hat, minus the black oil-silk cover. A narrow band of red flannel around the hat was in high favor among those men who, from a long life on the frontier seemed to have acquired the Indian fondness for bright colors.[47]

By the last day of November 1846 the camp at San Juan was ready to move out. The army had grown to 430 men, and it was a tough group made up of mountain men, Indians, sailors, blacks, emigrants, and a handful of professionals from the United States Navy. There were three pieces of artillery, an ammunition wagon, 1,900 head of horses and mules; and at the head of this army there was the only band they were to know—one single, sorry-looking bugle.

The rainy season had started, and the morning the men left San Juan there was a steady downpour. They had been wet and cold when they got out of their soggy blankets; and as they ate breakfast, they cursed the gray sky. They hadn't even managed to get half dry beside the campfires before they saddled up and rode out of the muddy mission grounds and started on the road south.

Oh, they could think about the warm weather they would have when they reached southern California. But there were more than four hundred long miles to travel before that day would arrive. It was bad enough that they might have to fight every mile of the way, but it was adding too much too ask a man to ride along with water dripping off his hat brim and down his shirt collar. Then there was the matter of food. Frémont had told them there would be plenty of cattle, but the men sent out to gather livestock had never appeared. There was no way to know what might have happened. Maybe the cattle were spread clear out into the San Joaquin Valley, or maybe the men had been ambushed by Manuel Castro.

Grumbling, looking at their horses and wondering if the thin animals would make it even for a day or two, not to mention all the way south, the men rode along in a straggling line that got longer and longer as the first day passed—a day which took them no more than ten miles south of San Juan. The second day was even worse as they worked their way through the lower end of the arroyo just south of San Juan. The road vanished into a region of slippery and sticky mud covered by loose gravel being pushed along by streams of runoff water that were like small rivers. Horses and mules mired down in the deep mud, slipped and fell, or just gave out. When this happened, the rider would gather his blankets, weapons, personal belongings, saddle and bridle, and take up the march on foot until he caught another mount from the caballada.

After a long, miserable day, in which they traveled only eight miles, the battalion pitched camp for the night. It was a discouraged lot of men who were wet, cold, and hungry. They were in no mood to joke or play a game of monte. Kemble thought it was one of the worst nights he had ever seen. What little they had in the way of provisions had been cut short by the steady rainfall on the packsaddles, rain that melted almost all the flour and sugar. As for meat, it was not available. The foraging party had not found any cattle nearby, and every man crowded near the campfires knew that it was going to be a night without much in the way of food. On top of being drenched, this was almost too much to stand.

Seeing the condition of his men, and knowing they would need plenty of meat to keep them going, Frémont decided to lay over at this camp for a couple of days. This would give riders time to head back to the vicinity of San Juan and pick up all the cattle they could find.

While they waited for the men to return with cattle, the rain continued to fall. But after two days, the riders came into view driving a herd of three hundred. That afternoon thirteen head were slaughtered, and the hungry men ate their fill. And their fill was considerable and astounded Edwin Bryant, who thought that the average consumption of fresh beef was at least ten pounds per man for each day.

With meat for their meals, the men kept up their daily march. Yet they moved along at a slow pace and without order. They were lucky the Californios had not left a striking force to pick off men who dropped behind during each day's march. Even guard duty was overlooked or performed in a negligent fashion. Kemble never saw the posting of any pickets. Still, they were not attacked, and in the early dawn "the companies would be rousted by the strains of the bugle, playing a reveille composed of such tunes as 'The Merry Swiss Boy' and 'Behold how brightly breaks the Morning,' the last being a perpetual satire upon the weather."[48]

Not many miles were traveled each day, and by December 5, 1846, the California Battalion had only reached the head of the Salinas Valley.

## 9

As FRÉMONT'S MEN cursed the weather, far to the south conditions were no better. Brigadier General Stephen Watts Kearny and his Army of the West rode their exhausted mounts out of the Colorado Desert and arrived at Warner's Rancho[49] to be greeted by a cold, driving rain that was half sleet.

Whenever the nearby mountain peaks weren't covered by clouds, the men looked up and saw a deep cover of snow.

Though Warner was in jail at San Diego, the worn-out dragoons were given meat and vegetables by Bill Marshall,[50] a deserter from a whaling ship, who had been left in charge of the ranch while "Long John" Warner tried to convince Commodore Stockton that he was not secretly assisting the Californios. From Warner's Ranch, Kearny sent a message on to San Diego through a neutral rancher, the former English sea captain Edward Stokes.[51] Stokes rode all the way to San Diego in one day and handed the letter to Stockton, who learned that Kearny was on his way with a force of one hundred dragoons and would appreciate any knowledge about the state of affairs in California.

Without hesitation, Commodore Stockton ordered Captain Gillespie to select a detachment of volunteers and ride out to warn Kearny that the forces of Andrés Pico were somewhere between him and his line of march to San Diego. Among the thirty-nine mounted riflemen who rode with Gillespie out of San Diego were Alexis Godey and Edward Fitzgerald Beale. The men carried an American flag at the head of the column, and pulled along a small brass four-pounder, a cannon that had been sent south from Sutter's Fort.

All during the night of December 4 and into the middle of the next day, Gillespie and his men were thoroughly soaked by a steady and heavy rainfall. Then at one o'clock in the afternoon the weather cleared. An advance scouting party returned to report that General Kearny was just ahead near the eastern entrance to the Santa Maria Valley. Hearing this news, Gillespie ordered the unfurling of the flag to the breeze. As they rode into the open and Kearny's men saw the Stars and Stripes flying high, the weary soldiers gave a loud cheer.

Soon the two forces were together, and Captain Gillespie told all he knew about the movements of the Californios. He pointed out it was rumored that Andrés Pico and some hundred lancers were nearby at San Pascual Valley. Commodore Stockton had made it clear that the general was free "to beat up their camp," if he wished to do so. This was news that some of Kearny's officers received as good tidings, and they immediately expressed their desire to attack.

But after hearing all Gillespie had to tell, Kearny decided it would be in the interest of keeping his men in shape if they rode ahead to the Santa Maria Valley and pitched an early camp. Both the troops and mounts were badly jaded, and a good night's rest would help them to be ready for the next day. Gillespie informed him that he and his men would stop for a few hours at this meeting place as there was plenty of good grass, and he wanted his animals to graze and rest. Later in the afternoon he and his men would join Kearny's force in the valley. The general agreed to this idea, and as Gillespie and his men unsaddled their mounts, the dragoons moved along their way.

But the clear weather didn't last for long. Another bank of dark clouds blew in, and rain began to fall again. Gillespie gave the order to saddle up and move down to the valley. Even before they got down from the mountain pass, the rain was half sleet and half water, and it came at them in stinging, driving sheets. When they finally reached the grassy and oak-covered Santa Maria Valley and located Kearny's encampment, it was obvious that the dragoons were in terrible shape.

> Almost exhausted by their long and arduous march; indeed, the whole force, save the officers, presented an appearance of weariness and fatigue. . . . The men were almost without shoes; and although we were constantly accustomed to much privation and suffering, my men considered their own condition, superior to that of these way-worn soldiers, whose strength and spirit seemed to be entirely gone.[52]

Even as the weary men of Kearny's army slept beside their campfires, the forces of Andrés Pico were not far away. Though Gillespie didn't know just where they might be, he did know that the Californios were in the vicinity. But one man with him was capable of locating them, and that was Rafael Machado, an Indian who had been part of their force until he got a chance to desert. Machado hated Mexicans for their treatment of Indians, and he was looking for a way to help in their defeat. So, when Lieutenant Thomas C. Hammond[53] came to Gillespie's camp and asked for help in a mission to locate Pico's camp before daybreak, Machado volunteered.

The scouting party consisted of Lieutenant Hammond, several dragoons, and Machado. They eased their way out of the Santa Maria Valley and cautiously approached the Indian village in the San Pascual Valley. Here, Machado told the soldiers to wait for him. He dismounted and entered the village alone. From an Indian standing guard, Machado learned that Pico and his lancers were sleeping in the village. They had come this far from San Diego because they had received word that the hated former commander of Pueblo de los Angeles, Lieutenant Gillespie, was here on a foraging expedition.

There were two trails to take from the Santa Maria Valley to San Diego, and Pico had placed part of his force at the entrance to the Lakeside route that dropped from the hills to El Cajon Valley and then on down through Mission Valley. The other route came over six or seven miles of rolling hills and dropped down into San Pascual Valley before continuing west to San Diego. Either way, it was obvious Pico was in a good position to attack during the daylight unless the men approaching knew where his force might be. The best bet that Kearny's worn-out army had was to take the San Pascual route before daybreak and catch the lancers off guard. But any chance of that vanished when a village dog began to bark, and a Mexican sentry challenged Machado as he slipped out of sight.

At the same moment, Lieutenant Hammond and his dragoons came too close to the village, and the clang of their sabers awakened Pico's men. A mounted patrol was sent out to see what was happening, and they returned and told Pico they had seen a group of American soldiers riding away in the dark. But Pico was doubtful that American soldiers had got that near his camp, and he refused to believe it until one member of his patrol rode into the village and tossed a dragoon's jacket and an army blanket stamped "U.S." on the ground. Pico gave orders to saddle up at once and get ready to ride.

By midnight, Hammond and his men were back at Kearny's camp, and he reported that any chance for surprise was gone. Despite this news, Kearny issued the order to get ready to attack. By two o'clock in the morning, the dragoons were ready to move out. The rain had stopped. The moon was almost as bright as daylight, but an icy wind blew off the snowpacks in the high mountains making it so cold that the bugler was not even able to blow reveille, and the men could hardly hold on to their reins.

Following the road over the mountains between the valleys of Santa Maria and San Pascual, the men of Kearny's Army of the West rode in front. Gillespie and his volunteers had been ordered to ride at the rear and assist with the baggage, but the tough marine protested. He pointed out that his brass four-pounder was a better cannon than anything Kearny's force had with them, and that his horses were in far better shape than the stock the dragoons were riding. But as he obeyed and got into position, Kearny changed his mind and ordered him to place his men on the left rear flank under the command of Captain Benjamin D. Moore.[54]

The whole ride from Santa Maria to San Pascual was on a fairly smooth trail that was used for carts. The men reached the top of the hill just at daybreak, and Kearny called a halt. In a short but stern speech, he told the men they were to obey their officers implicitly, that their country expected them to do their duty, and that "one thrust of a saber point was far more effective than any number of cuts."[55]

By twos, the horsemen moved away from the hilltop and began their descent into San Pascual Valley. The sound of the heavy dragoon swords echoed in the cold morning air. To the rear of Gillespie's men, Lieutenant Davidson[56] was in command of the army's howitzers—cannons which Gillespie thought to be in bad shape and quite capable of blowing all apart with the first shot.

The orders from General Kearny were to capture every man and horse in the Indian village if possible. But if there was any resistance or attempt to escape, the men were to shoot the enemy at once. Two by two, they straggled out in a long and irregular line. The worn and weary animals couldn't keep together in the march down the hogback ridge.

Hearing all the noise from the hillside, Andrés Pico and his men were mounted and ready. Dressed in their colorful and ornamented costumes, they wore leather cuirasses to protect their bodies and had serapes on to keep them warm; some even had leather shields. But the impressive part of their gear was the long and deadly lance which each rider carried. Mounted on excellent horses, the Californios waited out of sight in a gully just in front of the Indian village.

As the Americans moved lower on the ridge and neared the floor of the valley, the clear weather they had enjoyed at the start vanished in a cover of ground fog that lay across the floor of the valley. At this moment, General Kearny gave the order, "Trot!" But Captain Johnston[57] who had already reached the plain, misunderstood the command. In a loud voice he shouted to his men, "Charge!"

Forcing their worn horses and mules to gallop, twelve soldiers followed Kit Carson and Captain Johnston down the final slope of the hogback ridge, across the Santa Ysabel Creek, and straight toward the Indian village. As they neared the gully where Andrés Pico and his lancers waited, Carson's horse stumbled and fell. Kit was free of his stirrups before he hit the ground, but he was almost run over by the riders following him. He reached for his rifle, discovered it was broken, and ran toward the rear to find another. As he did, Captain Johnston rode right into the charging Californios, and was sent flying from his saddle when a bullet plowed through his forehead.

With Pico shouting to his men to fire one round and then use the lances, the Californios surrounded Johnston's men. As they did, Carson found a dead soldier and took his rifle and cartridge box just as Captain Moore and fifty men almost ran him down. Strung out in a ragged line, they shouted and rode toward the cloud of dust that marked the desperate battle. Then they saw Pico's force give way, turn, and ride off as though they were retreating. Thinking victory was within his grasp, perhaps, even thinking—as Kit Carson and Gillespie did—that the Mexicans would not stand up to American riflemen, Captain Moore yelled for his men to charge.

For over a mile, the Americans tried to catch up to the fast horses ahead. But in following, they rode into another trap as Pico's men turned, got their lances into position, and galloped at the flanks of the troopers. Out in front of his men and all by himself, Captain Moore was the first to encounter the second charge of the Californios. He rode almost into Andrés Pico, fired one shot and missed, and then slashed with his saber. Two riders closed in on Moore and pierced him with lances. As the stricken man fell from his horse, he was shot by another Mexican, and before they were through with him, Moore had been wounded sixteen times.

Riding close behind was Lieutenant Hammond, and he was speared from his horse as a lancer drove his sharp blade into his rib cage. In the wild turmoil of battle, many American rifles didn't fire because the cartridges were wet, and the men on mules were easily lassoed, pulled to the ground, and lanced.

Captain Gillespie ordered his men to dismount and use their rifles to drive the Californios away from the cover of brush by the creek. As they kept up a steady fire, they did manage to capture Pico's second in command, Pablo Véjar.[58] Seeing that Moore's men were retreating and being picked off with ease, Gillespie drew his sword, moved forward, and shouted for the tired soldiers to rally and not turn their backs to the foe. But as the marine neared Pico's men, they recognized him as the hated commander of Pueblo de los Angeles. They came at him in a wild fury, shouting his name. Gillespie tried to parry the thrust of their lances with his sword, and somehow managed to dodge the first six attempts to spear him. Then he was hit on the back of his neck. He dropped his saber and fell on it. While he wasn't cut by the blade, he couldn't move fast enough to retrieve his only weapon. As he attempted to get on his feet, the Californios closed in for the kill. They surrounded Gillespie, and though he tried to move out of the way, he was not able to dodge the thrust of the lances.

One sharp lance drove through his shoulder just above his heart and cut a deep wound open to the lungs. Seeing another blade coming toward his face, Gillespie turned and the lance slashed his upper lip and broke off a front tooth. The impact was so great that Gillespie was thrown to one side just as the horse jumped over him. Somehow he managed to get to his feet, pick up his saber, and using it to parry blows and to swing at his tormentors, he cut his way beyond the horsemen and made it to where the scattered Americans were beginning to rally and where he saw a howitzer.

What kept him on his feet must have been the will to survive. Others who saw the wounded marine were amazed that he could stand. About him the battle continued to rage, and the soldiers had taken to using their useless rifles as clubs. Everywhere there was chaos. Men cried out in fear and pain. The dead lay sprawled like punctured toy soldiers, and the wounded groaned for help. Gillespie staggered to one of the howitzers; but when he got no help from the other men, he left it just as the Californios dropped a loop around the cannon and dragged it off in a cloud of dust. As the stunned marine searched for another cannon, General Kearny was cornered by the deadly lancers. Before Lieutenant William Emory[59] and Captain Henry Turner[60] were able to rescue him, Kearny had been lanced twice in one arm and had received a deep wound in his buttocks. Emory wasn't wounded, and Turner received only a flesh wound even though his jacket had been slit in several places. With Kearny in bad condition and losing a lot of blood, the command fell to Captain Turner. But he was in charge of an army on its way to a complete defeat. Two other officers had suffered severe wounds, and one scout had been painfully wounded. Kit Carson had not been scratched. Using the tactics he had learned from years of skirmishes with the Indians of the fur country, he had taken cover behind some rocks and had kept up a steady and accurate fire whenever the lancers came within range.

Then, just as everything appeared to be lost, the incredible Gillespie stumbled toward a second howitzer. Growing faint from loss of blood, he asked some soldiers if they had a match to fire the cannon. When they told him they did not, he managed to strike fire with his flint and steel and handed his

The plaza at Sonoma, California, as it appeared just after the Bear Flag Revolt. The building with a three-story tower belonged to Mariano Guadalupe Vallejo. (*The Bancroft Library*)

An early picture of Mariano Guadalupe Vallejo as he probably looked after the Bear Flag Revolt. (*The Bancroft Library*)

An 1847 lithograph of Yerba Buena (San Francisco) as it appeared just after the American conquest. (*The Bancroft Library*)

The raising of the American flag over the Customs House at Monterey by Commodore John Drake Sloat on July 7, 1846. From left to right the ships of the United States Navy are the sloop of war *Cyane*, the frigate *Savannah*, and the sloop of war *Levant*. (*The Bancroft Library*)

A daguerreotype of Commodore Robert Field Stockton taken about 1845–50. *(Courtesy of the Chicago Historical Society)*

Major Frémont and the California Battalion on the outskirts of Monterey as pictured in an engraving. (*The Bancroft Library*)

Andrés Pico, the leader of the wild-riding lancers at the Battle of San Pascual. (*The Bancroft Library*)

burning machero to one of the men. Then as the howitzer went off with a loud explosion, he fainted.

Beale took over Gillespie's command, and held the men together long enough for them to realize the firing of the cannon had stopped the rush of Pico's lancers. The Sutter four-pounder was quickly brought into position, loaded with grapeshot, and fired. This brought an end to the battle as the Californios scattered to get out of range.

After the fury of battle, the exhausted soldiers cautiously approached the Indian village to look for more dead and wounded. But the village was deserted, as the Indians had fled into the nearby hills at the beginning of the battle to avoid becoming victims of either side. More dead and wounded were found in the Indian village, and the men lashed the bodies on mules that were skittery about the smell of dead flesh. In order to move the wounded, Kit Carson and others cut willow poles and stretched and tied buffalo robes, and the wounded were carried off the field in travois-stretchers.

Having checked the area of battle for any man they might have missed, the soldiers then headed to the north side of the valley. They worked their way to the crest of a long hill and dug in for the night. Dr. John S. Griffin cared for the wounded[61]; and as it grew dark, men got out their shovels and began to dig a grave. Into this common and unmarked burial ground, the dead soldiers of the Army of the West were laid to rest. The only salute to their valor was the constant howling and yipping of coyote packs which had caught the scent of death in the air.

Captain Henry S. Turner picked Thomas Burgess,[62] Alexis Godey, and an Indian sheepherder to make their way past the Californios and travel on to San Diego. There they were to inform Commodore Stockton of what had taken place and to request aid for the besieged troops. The men were to leave before dawn on December 7, in order to avoid a fully alert enemy camp; and though General Kearny was weak and in pain, Captain Turner read the letter to him for his approval.

During the daylight hours of December 7, the wounded but determined General Kearny decided the only safety for his men was to somehow make it to San Diego. He mounted his horse, and though it pained him very much, he sat in his saddle and gave the command to move out. The wounded men were carried in the travois, and the going was very slow. By the middle of the afternoon, they had traveled only five miles, but they did reach Rancho San Bernardo, which belonged to the English settler Edward Snook.[63] While the ranch was deserted except for a few Indians, at this place close to the north end of present-day Lake Hodges the men killed some chickens to feed the wounded and rounded up some cattle to feed the rest of the army.

Their luck seemed to be turning, and they began to think they were going to get out of this. They were sorry about the comrades they had lost, but the problem was to not join them in death but keep alive and keep moving on.

They rested for a while, then started into the valley. Out of nowhere, out of a brushy ravine, the lancers appeared again. They tried to encircle the weary Americans. When that failed, thirty or forty of Pico's men rode to the top of a rocky hill commanding the road and began to fire down. This was all Lieutenant William Emory could stand. With six to eight men he charged the hill and, by keeping up a constant and deadly fire, he and his men wounded several of the Californios and drove them off. But Pico's men had managed to drive off the cattle the soldiers had taken from Snook's rancho, and the exhausted Army of the West was trapped on what was to become known as Mule Hill, where they were surrounded by the horsemen of Pico's cavalry. Their only hope was that the couriers had managed to get through to San Diego. To protect themselves, they built rock barricades, bored holes in a low, sandy depression and managed to get some water, and slaughtered the fattest mules for meat.

After a weary night on Mule Hill, the men were greeted in the morning by the appearance of a messenger carrying a flag of truce. They allowed the unarmed man to approach, and he reported that the three couriers they had sent forth had made it to San Diego but had been captured as they were attempting to return. Andrés Pico was willing to make an exchange for any prisoners they might be holding. It would be on an even basis—one for one. Having only one of Pico's men, the army was able to exchange him for Burgess. Godey and the Indian sheepherder remained captives. The other thing Pico did for the besieged men was to send them some food and clothing that San Diego friends had sent to Gillespie by the couriers.

From Burgess General Kearny learned that Commodore Stockton had sent a return message in which he explained it would be a while before he could send help since he had very few horses in good enough shape, and lacked any means for carrying wounded men. He had understood from Godey that the army would be able to hold out or ultimately be in condition to march to San Diego. When Captain Turner asked to see the message, Burgess explained they didn't have it with them. None of them wanted to take the risk of having Pico's men discover that the commodore had written to the men on Mule Hill and had asked them to send another courier if their straits were desperate. So, wishing to avoid the capture of such a document, they had memorized it as best they could, and placed it in the hollow of an oak tree for safekeeping.[64]

This was too much for General Kearny to gamble on, and he asked Captain Turner to prepare another message. He would send three more couriers to San Diego, have them travel apart from each other, and if one of them got through, he was to make the commodore know that they were in no position to march past Pico's lancers and needed all the help they could get.

Kit Carson, Beale, and Che-muc-tah, an Indian scout, were selected for this hazardous mission.[65] They waited until it was dark, and then they eased out of camp and down the hill. As they neared the enemy line, they had to crawl over rocks and brush to get past the three lines of mounted sentinels. In order to do this without being heard, they removed their shoes and fastened them under their belts. But as they slipped by the guards, they lost their shoes, and faced fifty miles of rough country—some of it covered with prickly pear cactus—that they would have to travel over on bare feet. The men traveled all that night. The following day they lay out of sight in a gorge. When darkness set in, they split up again and headed in three different paths for the final dash to San Diego. Che-muc-tah was the first one to enter town at six o'clock in the evening of December 9. As he walked by the plaza, the band from the *Congress* was giving one of its nightly concerts. From there he went to Don Juan Bandini's home, where an evening ball was just under way, and he delivered the first news of the plight of the men on Mule Hill. Four hours later, exhausted young Beale arrived. He was in such bad shape from the journey that he had to be carried to Bandini's home to see Commodore Stockton. The last of the trio to reach the port town was Kit Carson, he had taken the longest and most dangerous route, so it wasn't until the next morning that he walked into town.

Even as the men gave their reports, another of Kearny's men died on Mule Hill from wounds. A grave was quickly dug for Sergeant John C. Cox, and his companions covered it with heavy rocks to keep animals from digging up his body.[66] Shortly after the burial, Andrés Pico made another attempt to dislodge them. His men drove a herd of wild horses through their camp, but all this accomplished was the killing of some horses by the hungry soldiers, who were happy to add the bonus of fresh horse meat to their dwindling supplies.

The men waiting on Mule Hill were in bad shape. By the time they had buried Cox on December 10, General Kearny decided he had no way of knowing whether his couriers had made it to San Diego. He did know they couldn't hold out much longer on the barren hill. The odds on lasting a few more days were not good. Running short of food, his men growing weaker each day, it was only a question of time before the lancers would make a final attack and wipe them out. To Kearny, the only solution was to try to make a break past Pico's men and head for San Diego.

Kearny asked Dr. Griffin if any of the wounded were now able to ride, and the doctor assured him that all but two men were well enough to climb into a saddle and make a dash for San Diego. That was it. They'd have to carry the two men, but the rest would make a running fight of it. It wasn't a good risk, but to remain where they were wasn't even a risk. Without reinforcements from San Diego, their camp on Mule Hill would become their last resting place if they remained much longer. Better to die in a running fight than wait until they were too weak to put up a battle. Orders were given to destroy anything that wasn't needed so Pico and his men wouldn't be able to get any use out of what they left behind. Word was passed among the soldiers that in the early morning, before dawn, they would move off the hill and try to break through the enemy lines and get to San Diego.

Resigned to whatever the next day might bring, the weary men tried to get some sleep. But an hour or two after midnight the sentinels heard the sound of marching feet moving up the hill. They called out a challenge, and the answer came back in English: "Americans!"

The sound brought new life to the besieged men behind the rock breastworks. They peered over their fortification, and coming toward them in solid formation were 120 sailors and 80 marines. They cheered the marching men on, the unit under the command of Lieutenant Andrew F. V. Gray[67] and Captain Jacob Zeilin.[68] When the rescue force that Commodore Stockton had sent out reached the camp, they passed out jerked beef, hardtack, and tobacco to the exhausted army. In turn, Kearny's men offered the best they had on hand—hot mule soup.

New life came back to the Army of the West, and early the next day, they started for San Diego without worry of another attack from Pico's lancers. Kearny's ride was painful and exhausting, and the two badly wounded men made the fifty-mile trip to San Diego on their travois-stretchers.

During a heavy rainstorm on December 12, 1846, they finally reached San Diego. But for one of the badly wounded troopers, it was the last journey.

The Battle of San Pascual had not been long, and it did not involve a great number of men. Both Kearny and Pico claimed victory, and the argument as to what constitutes victory in warfare makes anything said for either side almost meaningless. The Army of the West had twenty-one or twenty-two men killed, and thirteen or more wounded.[69] Andrés Pico claimed to have lost only one man and had twelve of his lancers wounded. But his worst loss took place shortly after the engagement at San Pascual when eleven of the Californios were captured by Luiseño Indians at Pauma Valley near the Palomar Mountains. Through the encouragement of Bill Marshall from Warner's Ranch and because of many years of mistreatment by the Californios, the Indians put all eleven to death either with arrows or with lances heated in hot coals. The only exception was one boy, among the eleven. He was executed by rifle fire.

Considering the tragic losses to both the Americans and the Californios, directly or indirectly related to the Battle of San Pascual, it is difficult to understand how either side could claim victory. They fought with honor and heroism, but the battle had no great bearing on the end of the war. All it proved was that brave men can die for a cause, for a piece of territory, or for pride alone. To these men, all three causes can be applied. To their descendants they left a legacy of courage and bloodshed. If that was worth the price, if that could be called a victory, then both sides were victorious in the face of death.

10

Two DAYS after the worn and shocked Army of the West reached San Diego, far to the north Frémont and the California Battalion were slowly approaching San Luis Obispo. This wild-looking army had endured rainy weather ever since leaving the mission grounds at San Juan. All they had in the way of food was beef, and they were eating it in great quantities as they cursed the weather. Now, as they approached Mission San Luis Obispo de Tolosa, a halt was called and a camp was established in the mountains above the mission. Beef was cooked once again, and in the late afternoon the march was resumed through mud and across deep creeks that were overflowing their banks. In the late afternoon Frémont and William Knight rode to a point of hills and looked down at the tiled rooflines and into the mission compound. There was no unusual activity, no large number of people around, but the thick adobe walls made a fine fort. Not knowing if the Californios might be waiting inside the mission, John Charles decided it would be best to approach the place during the night.

He and his men waited out of sight until about nine o'clock. All the time the rain continued to fall, but when it was very dark, the order to saddle up and move out was given. They slowly rode down to the valley, and quietly surrounded the mission. But there were no soldiers in any of the mission buildings. The battalion saw only a few alarmed and frightened people who hardly knew what to make of the armed, ill-dressed, muddy, and wet men. Most of these citizens meekly waited for whatever might happen. They crossed themselves and prayed that they were not about to be killed by these men who appeared to be thieves and murderers. A few people tried to escape by running across the roofs of the mission, but they were quickly captured.

From the prisoners it was learned that Don José de Jesús "Totoi" Pico,[70] a cousin of Andrés Pico, was in the town. The soldiers of the battalion went from house to house and captured Pico and thirty others who had fought with Manuel Castro at the Battle of Natividad. But Totoi Pico was the big prize, for he had broken an earlier parole by taking part in the battle on the Salinas plains.

Frémont made it clear to Pico that he would stand trial for his part in the battle. Then to add to the feelings that the battalion members had against Pico, they found papers in his home which indicated he had been working with General Flores. Among these documents was a dispatch from Flores about the Battle of San Pascual. The news of the success of Andrés Pico's lancers had reached San Luis Obispo in a hurry, and it was not the kind of news that made the Americans feel that they should show any pity to Totoi Pico.

As the roundup of prisoners took place, Frémont assured the terrified people in the mission that they would not be harmed nor would they be turned out of their dwellings to make room for his soldiers. Instead, the men of the battalion were quartered inside the mission church, and a guard was stationed at the altar to protect church property.

The following day, the rain came down in torrents. But this did not keep the men from looking over the mission and the town. Within the mission grounds there were several gardens surrounded by high walls and hedges of cactus; some of these plants were as much as fifteen feet tall and at the base were as thick as a man's body. There were vineyards and palm trees. Among the fruit trees the men saw fig, orange, and olive. Best of all, they were able to get a break in their steady beef diet by purchasing pounded wheat, frijoles, and pumpkins.

Two days after they had taken over San Luis Obispo, Lieutenant Colonel Frémont held a court-martial for Totoi Pico. The trial was short, and the sentence was handed down at once. Don José Pico was to be shot at the break of daylight on the next day.

At first light on December 17 the hour for Don José's execution arrived. Frémont looked out his window as the battalion marched in a tight formation to the center of the plaza. The rain had stopped, but it was a cool morning with a hazy sky. All the men were looking forward to this moment. It had been bad enough that the Californios had killed some of their friends at the Battle of Natividad. But ever since that day, they had been marching in the rain, traveling over rough country as they avoided the regular route of travel between missions. They needed something or somebody to take the brunt of their growing fury, and Totoi Pico was to be the symbol of the invisible enemy, the scapegoat for all that had happened to them.

The hour for Pico's execution had arrived, and he was ready to be taken out to the plaza to face the selected squad of riflemen. Frémont said a few last words to the condemned man. Just as Pico was taken to another room that led to the plaza, Captain Dick Owens opened the door and ushered in a striking-looking woman dressed in black, followed by a group of children. Owens introduced Colonel Frémont to Señora Pico.

She knelt before him, tears in her eyes, and pleaded with him to spare her husband's life. Behind her, the frightened children cried as she explained that her husband had no idea he had been committing a crime. He was defending his country, and he was ashamed to remain behind as others rode off to battle.

Gently John Charles raised her from her knees. Then in a soft, reassuring voice, he told her to go home. He would reconsider everything and let her know his decision.

As she left the room, he asked that Don José Pico be brought before him. "He came in with the gray face of a man expecting death, but calm and brave, while feeling it is near. He was a handsome man, within a few years of forty, with black eyes and black hair."[71] Frémont pointed out the window to the plaza where the troops were waiting. Then he told Pico that, though he had been sentenced to die, he was to be spared. For that, he had better thank his wife.

Don José dropped to his knees in front of Frémont, made the sign of the cross, and said, "I was to die—I had lost the life God gave me—you have given me another life. I devote the new life to you."[72]

Here was a turning point in the war for California. Frémont's consideration of Pico's life was to help cut short the killing. Even on the same day that this life was spared, John Charles ordered that the other captives should be given their freedom; and as the California Battalion marched out of San Luis Obispo that day, they had lost some foes and gained some friends.

Slowly, the battalion worked its way south. The weather began to clear, and traveling was much easier. But the horses and mules were badly jaded; not many miles were covered on each day's journey. Part of the country they passed had suffered from a drought, and only because of the recent storms was there any sign of new grass. A good day's travel amounted to fifteen miles, but there were other days when the column was lucky to travel three. Many of the ranchos they passed were deserted because the owners had learned of the coming of the Americans and had fled the region until the California Battalion had traveled out of the area. On December 21, the day before Brigadier General Kearny and Commodore Stockton began to make plans to march on San Luis Rey and Pueblo de los Angeles, one of Frémont's men suffered a broken leg when an unruly mule kicked him. Fortunately they were near Benjamin Foxen's Rancho Tinaquaic, and the former English sailor agreed to keep the man at his home until his leg mended.[73]

As they neared Santa Barbara, it began to rain again. Scouts were sent ahead on the regular road leading across the Santa Ynez Mountains to Santa Barbara. When they returned to the battalion, they reported that Gaviota Pass—a narrow cut between high walls of granite—was being watched from the heights by Californios. It was an ideal place for them to fire down or roll boulders upon the men if they took that route over the mountains.

To avoid a possible attack on his forces, Frémont spoke to Foxen, who offered the services of his eldest son, William, to guide them across San Marcos Pass, fifteen miles northwest of Santa Barbara. Out of use for many years, this steep pass had been one of the routes explorers and missionaries once had used as they crossed from the coast to the inland valleys.

The day before Christmas, the California Battalion followed young Foxen up the steep and slippery grade to San Marcos Pass. As they slowly worked their way along and worried about the narrow places where the hanging wall of the mountainside dropped off into deep canyons, Commodore Stockton sat in his San Diego headquarters and wrote a letter to General Kearny inviting him to join his force on its march to Pueblo de los Angeles. He pointed out that they should reach the pueblo in time to join forces with Frémont, who was approaching from the north. What Stockton didn't know was that they had not reached Santa Barbara yet, and had a rough up- and downhill climb to get there. Even then, the battalion would be a long way from Pueblo de los Angeles. Stockton was optimistic as usual. After he had drafted his letter to Kearny, he wrote another to Frémont, warning him about the excellent horsemanship of the Californios, and suggested that if there was any chance things could go against him, he should avoid any clash until he joined Stockton's force of five hundred men at San Luis Rey. Then sealing his letter, he sent it north by bearers.

From the warmth of Stockton's San Diego headquarters, everything appeared to be simple. The war was almost over, and the insurgents were on the run. But Stockton wasn't spending the night in the Santa Ynez Mountains. Though the view from the camp on the ridge was splendid, and the men could see the white towers of the mission and the great expanse of the Pacific, they also saw a steep slope that would be tough going for men and animals.

Christmas 1846 came as no gift. It wasn't until noon that the men dragging the heavy cannons reached the top of the ridge. By then the rain was falling so hard it was nearly impossible to see, and the wind whipped in from the Pacific with almost the force of a tornado. Edwin Bryant had never seen anything like it.

> Driving our horses before us we were compelled to slide down the steep and slippery rocks, or wade through deep gullies and ravines filled with mud and foaming torrents of water, that rushed downwards with such force as to carry along the loose rocks and tear up the trees and shrubbery by the roots. Many of the horses falling into the ravines refused to make an effort to extricate themselves, and were swept downwards and drowned. Others, bewildered by the fierceness and terrors of the storm, rushed or fell headlong over the steep precipices and were killed.[74]

All that day and far into the night, they battled the mountain and the storm. The cannons had to be left behind until there was a break in the weather, and slowly, by ones and twos, they reached the base of the mountains and made camp in a quagmire, where men and animals couldn't move without bogging deeply into mud with each step. Attempts to keep a campfire blazing were futile, and the wet and shivering men gave up. They found whatever shelter they could beneath trees or outcroppings of rocks, and used logs as pillows to keep their heads above water in case the runoff became too deep. The only reason they could sleep at all could be summed up in one word: exhaustion.

The morning broke clear, and they welcomed the warmth of the sun. But it was to be a day of gathering what had been left on the mountainside, of seeing how many horses and mules remained alive, and of drying out clothes, rifles, pistols, and cannons. As parties returned from the mountains with very few horses or mules, the scene of destruction was reported. In ravines, canyons, creek beds, against log jams or barriers of brush, they had found the

dead animals. Some were half buried in the mud; some were smashed by falling rocks and trees; and some were gasping their last breath of life. Only a
few were found alive, and even these animals were in very bad shape. Altogether, the number of dead horses and mules varied in the estimates from
seventy-five to one hundred and fifty. They had crossed the Santa Ynez
Mountains without having to fight the Californios, but they had paid a high
price. To make things more ironic, there had been no need to take such a detour, as the armed Californios had deserted Gaviota Pass and Santa Barbara
and headed south.

Looking more like an army in retreat, the battered, weary California Battalion reached Santa Barbara at two o'clock on the afternoon of December
27—three days after leaving Foxen's rancho for a journey of fifteen miles. To
avoid creating hostile feelings among the civilians, Colonel Frémont issued
strict orders to his men to respect the property and persons of the people, and
to secure a pass before they left camp to stroll about the town.

Taking advantage of a chance to look the town over, Edwin Bryant and
three friends discovered people were terrified that the American army would
treat them in a barbarous manner. Streets were almost deserted, and most
shops were closed. They did manage to find the dwelling of a poor shoemaker open, and were offered a meal by the man and his family, "a supper of
*tortillas, frijoles,* and stewed *carne,* seasoned with *chile colorado,* for which,
paying them *dos pesos* for four, we bade them good-evening, all parties being
well satisfied."[75]

The day after the battalion reached Santa Barbara, they marched to the
plaza and ran up the American flag. During their stay in Santa Barbara, a
period which lasted until January 3, 1847, several Californios came to
Frémont's camp and surrendered. Instead of being held as prisoners as they
expected, they were given their freedom and told no harm would come to
them so long as they did not take up arms against the Americans again. Here,
also, Frémont's pardoning of Totoi Pico proved to be of great help in starting
the machinery for the eventual surrender of Andrés Pico and his army.
Through Totoi, John Charles was introduced to the elderly Señora Bernarda
Ruíz, who wished to see the war come to an end. She informed Frémont she
could influence her people. If he would keep his army back for a while, she
would be able to arrange a meeting to bring an end to bloodshed and create a
lasting peace. All this sounded quite reasonable, and John Charles was
influenced by the woman's sound ideas about compromise and her intelligent
approach to stopping the war. He assured Señora Ruíz that he would hold
back and give her the opportunity she desired, and she could inform her
friends he would be willing to meet with them at a designated place to arrange a treaty which would be fair to both sides.

Even with this tentative peace feeler, there was yet a possibility of another
battle. Rumors had reached Santa Barbara that thirty miles to the south

Andrés Pico and his men were waiting at San Buenaventura to make a stand against the California Battalion. Frémont was convinced the battle wouldn't take place; and on January 3, 1847, he ordered his men to saddle up if they had a horse, walk if they didn't, but move out and follow the road beside the ocean, where they could hear the pounding surf and see hundreds of spouting gray whales no more than a mile offshore.

As Frémont and the battalion moved south along the beach, they were not completely on their own. Two days before the end of 1846, Lieutenant Edward A. Selden had sailed the schooner *Julia* into view; and he managed to land another cannon for the battalion's use.[76] Now he cruised just offshore, well within sight and cannon range of any Californios who might try an attack. It was the intention of Selden to keep his ship close in for as long as the men stayed beside the ocean. Once they headed inland toward the San Fernando Pass, he would not be able to come to their aid; but until then, the presence of the *Julia* was a powerful backing for the weary soldiers.

Still concerned about Frémont's situation, Commodore Stockton learned at San Luis Rey on January 3, 1847, that the battalion had reached Santa Barbara. Not knowing that they were marching south on that very day, Stockton dashed off another note of warning about the horsemanship, toughness, and the present attitude of the Californios since they had defeated Mervine and Kearny. He then employed Captain George W. Hamley, master of the whaler *Stonington*, to deliver the message.[77] Hamley agreed to the proposition, traveled by horse to San Diego, and took passage on the brig *Malek Adhel* with the intention of catching Frémont somewhere near San Buenaventura.

Six days after leaving Commodore Stockton, and only one day before the defeat of the Californios and the recapture of Pueblo de los Angeles, Captain Hamley reached Frémont's camp at "The Willows," about two miles east of present-day Fillmore. He informed John Charles that he had been guided past a group of horsemen who were observing the battalion by an Indian guide and Don Pedro Carrillo.[78] From what John Charles learned, he realized that within a day or two Pueblo de los Angeles would fall. What Hamley couldn't tell him was whether or not this would mean the end of the war, or whether it meant that Andrés Pico's lancers would come north toward his army.

Events moved very rapidly now. In two more days, on January 11, as the battalion moved toward the summit of San Fernando Pass, two bareheaded Californios galloped toward them from the south. They slid their horses to a halt, explained they were messengers, and reported the victories of Stockton and Kearny at San Gabriel and the Mesa. This was at one o'clock in the afternoon. A little later and not much farther along, another horseman approached. This was a Frenchman who was acting as a courier, and he presented a letter from Kearny to Frémont. This document had been written on Sunday, January 10, 1847, at four o'clock in the afternoon, after the

Americans had recaptured Pueblo de los Angeles and Captain Gillespie had been given the honor of running up the American flag.

Kearny's letter to Frémont was short, but to the point:

> We are in possession of this place, with a force of marines and sailors, having marched into it this morning. Join us as soon as you can, or let me know, if you want us to march to your assistance; avoid charging the enemy; their force does not exceed 400, perhaps not more than 300. Please acknowledge receipt of this, and dispatch the bearer at once.[79]

In the letter he made it obvious that he was getting over his wounds—both physical and prideful—and was ready to take over his command. This was not a letter to an officer of equal rank. "Join us" was a definite command, and all the other remarks in the message came down to one thing: Brigadier General Kearny was letting Lieutenant Colonel Frémont know that an officer of superior rank was making the decisions.

Yet the day after receiving such commands, John Charles issued a stunning proclamation to the Californios. As commandant of the California Battalion of the United States Forces, he was quite willing to meet and discuss negotiations to end all hostilities with them at the Mission San Fernando. With this offer, the end of the California conquest was in sight.

The same day that Frémont issued his proclamation and invited the Californios to treat with him for peace, Kearny sent another letter. He dashed it off at six o'clock on the evening of January 12, and a courier carried it from his headquarters at Pueblo de los Angeles. Essentially, he stressed the same points he had made in his first message, but a few things differed: He made it quite clear that the Californios had been defeated on January 8 and 9; instructed Frémont to come to him at his headquarters; and asked for an acknowledgment of receipt and a date when he might expect to see the lieutenant colonel.

While both Kearny and Stockton wondered what was taking place at the Mission San Fernando, events were moving quickly toward a treaty that would end the war. On the morning of January 12, the day that Kearny had sent off another message, Totoi Pico came to the Frémont camp at the mission with two officers of Andrés Pico's army. As Bryant recalled, they had come to treat for peace. "A consultation was held and terms were suggested, and, as I understand, partly agreed upon, but not concluded."[80]

The next day Frémont and the men he selected to accompany him rode their horses on the short stretch of El Camino Real that wound its way from Mission San Fernando to Pueblo de los Angeles. At the north end of Cahuenga Pass, no more than a stone's throw from the Río De Porciuncula (Los Angeles River), they came to a halt at a deserted ranch house, tied their mounts to the hitching rail, and walked inside. This was the first friendly meeting between Frémont and his officers and the leaders of the Californios who had waged such a successful campaign in their hit-and-run war in southern California. There was Andrés Pico, that incredible cavalry officer; and with him were his right-hand men. In turn, Frémont introduced his body of officers who were to witness the proceedings and sign the final treaty. Among them was Theodore Talbot, who was to play the role of secretary for the event.

In the seven articles drawn up for the capitulation on January 13, 1847, Frémont saw to it that the terms were of such a nature as to make it possible for the war to come to an end without rancor or bitterness.

The Californios were to hand over their arms, return to their homes, obey the laws of the United States, and not take up arms again in the war between the two countries. By doing this, they were guaranteed protection of their lives and property. They were not required to take an oath of allegiance to the government of the United States until a final peace treaty was signed between the Americans and the Republic of Mexico. They were given permission to leave California and return to Mexico if they so desired. But so long as they remained, they were to enjoy the same rights and privileges as American citizens, and the door was left open for any future arrangements for justice between both parties.

With the initial treaty drawn up and signed by the principal officers of both sides, Frémont received two more letters from Kearny. The first was written at the noon hour of that day. In this, the general made a petulant remark that nothing was known of Frémont and his men other than news of an armistice between his troops and those of Andrés Pico. Two hours later Kearny sent a longer letter. Again, he stated that he was ignorant of everything relating to Frémont's command except for news of a conjectured armistice.

John Charles looked over both letters and put them aside to answer later that night. For the moment he was more interested in one of the howitzers that Andrés Pico's men turned over to him. It was one they had roped and dragged away from Kearny's Army of the West at the Battle of San Pascual.

Time had come to answer the general's letters before riding on to Pueblo de los Angeles. And mention of the howitzers would be made. Getting his pen and paper, Frémont sat down at this place where the war had ended, today a landmark within the limits of Universal City in the San Fernando Valley.

Making his points clear, he wrote with a flourish of pride. In his short letter he stated that the Californios—Andrés Pico in particular—had surrendered to him. Then, in closing, he tossed out a bit of seasoning as he informed General Kearny that he had captured two pieces of artillery which had been lately in the possession of Pico and his lancers.

The letter was completed, a copy of the treaty was prepared, and all were handed to William Owl Russell to deliver. The courier mounted a fast horse and rode away from the ranch house at the north end of Cahuenga Pass. But like other messengers in man's history, Russell's reception at the headquarters of Brigadier General Kearny and Commodore Stockton was puzzling to a man who brought word of peace. Kearny would not receive the treaty as he claimed he was not the officer in charge; and while Stockton received it, he was angry that such a treaty had been agreed to at all. He ranted and raved about the easy terms granted to the enemy, but then he indicated to Russell that he intended to confer the office of governor upon Frémont. During the night, Russell stayed at Kearny's quarters and learned that he, too, was upset but also wished to make Frémont the governor.

In the morning, Owl Russell rode out to meet the approaching California Battalion and report what he had learned. It was January 14, 1847, and the conquest of California was a fact. The victorious Frémont rode at the head of his troops and entered Pueblo de los Angeles like a Greek hero just in from the plains of Troy.

# The Man in the Middle

IT WAS A RAINY AFTERNOON, and the column moved slowly in the sticky clay mud. Four hundred strong, they looked more like a band of mountain men than soldiers. At the rear of the procession, the men with the mule teams pulled six pieces of artillery.

Owl Russell, who had brought the signed treaty to the village on the previous day, rode out to meet the colonel and give him some news which seemed important. Kearny and Stockton were not on the best of terms, or so it seemed to Owl. Both claimed command, but Stockton was in charge. And the senior officers wished to make Frémont the military governor of California. Yet they were not happy that he had been so generous with the terms of the treaty. Of the two officers, it struck Owl that Stockton was especially upset that Pico and the rest of General Flores's men had been allowed to surrender with dignity and grace. Still, the battalion was to report to Commodore Stockton as he had already assigned quarters to them.

As for the general, Owl was convinced he was a better friend of Frémont's than Stockton. The way things appeared, Stockton was commander-in-chief over all the American forces—including General Kearny.

Frémont didn't have to ask why this state of affairs existed. Owl Russell rambled on about what the rumors were in town. The commodore had told the general he and his men would have died on Mule Hill if they hadn't been rescued by a unit of sailors and marines. Word was out that Stockton had offered Kearny the chance to command the force that retook San Luis Rey and Pueblo de los Angeles, but he had turned down the opportunity. Now Stockton claimed credit for the victories over General Flores's army in the Battle of San Gabriel and the Battle of the Mesa.

Here was news of a storm brewing, but Frémont wasn't cut out for military infighting. The way he saw it, Commodore Stockton had official orders from the Navy Department to occupy and hold on to California if war broke out. Well, war had started. He had accepted a commission in the California Battalion from Stockton, and he was still under the commodore's command.

In a curious way, Frémont overlooked the fact that he was already an officer in the United States Army and legally had no right to accept an appointment in the navy. But these were extraordinary times, and there had been no high-ranking military officer on the scene when the conquest had begun. It had appeared logical to accept the command of Commodore Stockton, and he saw no reason to change now.

Being a man committed to the pursuit of scientific truth, John Charles never considered that appearances and reality can easily reverse roles if official orders so decree. Nor did he think of the possibility of the irrational becoming rational, of the abnormal replacing the normal. In all of this, he failed to consider one major factor: he was not his own man. He was a lieu-tenant colonel in the army, and he was outranked by an angry, weary, and wounded brigadier general.

Unaware of the fine distinctions or too filled with ego to even consider his shaky position, Frémont reported to Commodore Stockton and then visited General Kearny in his quarters. The conversation between the two men was friendly, but there was a psychological barrier between them that the younger man didn't even sense. He came to the general almost like a superior officer, and gave the impression he was not only the conqueror of California but was about to become its military governor. None of this struck Kearny as fitting or proper. Yet he remained polite during their brief conversation. Run-ning deep in his mind were all the things which bothered him. Frémont was not a military man, and he had not learned the rules of the game. Twice be-fore, Kearny had run into trouble because of Frémont's acts. In 1843 he had allowed himself to be talked into authorizing a mountain howitzer for Frémont's second expedition, and this had brought complaints from Wash-ington. Then, because of information carried by Kit Carson—Frémont's close friend—Kearny had dismissed a large part of his force in New Mexico and had come west with the idea that California was already secured. That misinformation had cost him the lives of twenty-two soldiers; many had been wounded; and he himself had almost been killed by Pico's cavalry. Even though Stockton had sent Gillespie out to warn him of the Californios, the marine and Kit had assured him the Mexicans would give way and retreat under American rifle fire.

Now, after all this, here was Frémont standing in front of him—looking more like a pirate than a soldier—and going on like a schoolboy. Even as he talked, Kearny must have thought that this young explorer had taken it upon himself to sign a treaty with the very men who had taken so many American lives. He even had the gall, the unmitigated gall, to drag the howitzer the Army of the West had lost in battle behind his ragtag army of mountain men, Indians, and God-knows-what.

Kearny realized that youth and glory stood between him and his own fu-ture. After all the years of coming up through the ranks, he was about to be bypassed by this mere young officer, who was not a military man but an explorer with a flair for romanticism. So, even as this meeting ended cordially, even as the general immediately wrote to Senator Benton of how well his son-in-law looked, of how much he had accomplished, and of his desire that news of the colonel's success should be passed on to Mrs. Frémont, General Kearny was alarmed and ready to make sure that Frémont recognized his rank in the United States Army.

2

ON JANUARY 16, 1847, certain events took place in what was now being called Ciudad de los Angeles that were to play a lasting role in the history of California and in the personal future of John Charles Frémont.

Using his rank as Lieutenant Colonel Frémont, United States Army, and holding on to his assumption of the position of military commandant of California, he signed a final article to be added to the Articles of Capitulation. In a very short paragraph, all conditions for paroles affecting officers and citizens of both nations were ruled null and void, and both sides agreed to release all prisoners.

What General Kearny thought of this action was not recorded, but it is safe to assume he did not approve of it. For on that same day, he wrote to Commodore Stockton and asked by what authority Stockton was empowered to organize a civil government. He asked to see any document giving Stockton that right, and made it clear he *did* carry official letters, dated June 3 and 18, 1846, from the Secretary of War—letters approved by President Polk— which gave General Kearny the assigned duty of establishing a government in California.

Commodore Stockton replied to this challenge of his authority at once. In no uncertain terms, he pointed out that California had been conquered, a new government established by his orders, and news of these events sent by mail to the President long before Kearny ever entered California. Then Stockton bluntly informed him he would do nothing on his demand, that he was going to ask the President to recall him, and Kearny should consider himself "suspended from the command of the U. S. Forces in this place."[1]

Instead of replying, Kearny had another trick to play. Stockton had appointed Gillespie as the new commander of the California Battalion as he planned to remove Frémont and appoint him governor. Kearny had Lieutenant and Acting Assistant Adjutant General William H. Emory write to Frémont and order him to maintain his present command. "The general directs that no change will be made in the organization of your battalion of volunteers or officers appointed to it without his sanction or approval being first obtained."[2]

No claim can be made that General Kearny had not received Commodore Stockton's letter before having Emory make this move in a play for power. Most of the day had passed, and it was dusk before this order was delivered to Frémont. This was a move to undermine Stockton by placing a junior officer in a position where he would have to disobey a senior officer no matter which way he reacted.

Dusk had turned into night, and Frémont had the candles lit in his quarters as he looked over Emory's letter of command—a letter signed by Emory but composed by Kearny. Confusion was a gentle way of interpreting what the colonel read, as this was hardly a gentleman's ploy. The murkiness of unknown motives stamped this document. Yet, as John Charles pondered the curious message, he received one more official communication from Commodore Stockton. This was seemingly even more outside the bounds of reality, but it was a momentous step which took Frémont all the way to the head of the new government.

*To all whom it may concern, greeting:*

Having, by authority of the President and Congress of the United States of North America, and by right of conquest, taken possession of that portion of territory heretofore known as upper and lower California; and having declared the same to be territory of the United States, under the name of the territory of California; and having established laws for the government of the said territory, I, *Robert F. Stockton*, governor and commander-in-chief of the same, do, in virtue of the authority in me vested, and in obedience to the aforementioned laws, appoint *J. C. Frémont, esq.* governor and commander-in-chief of the territory of California, until the President of the United States shall otherwise direct.[3]

The daylight was gone, but the hours of January 16 had not been exhausted. As Frémont looked at this document, as he considered how quickly things had happened to change the direction of his future, another messenger arrived from the headquarters of Commodore Stockton. Lieutenant Colonel Frémont and his future secretary of state Owl Russell were to report to Stockton at once.

Their meeting in the adobe house was brief, friendly, and directly to the point. The commodore confirmed Frémont's position as the new governor to assume office as soon as Stockton left Ciudad de los Angeles within the next three days. At this same time, Russell was sworn in. Commodore Stockton had no instructions which specifically stated he had any right to make such appointments. And later, when faced with this very question, he replied: "My right to establish the civil government was incident to the conquest, and I formed the government under the law of nations."[4]

To Frémont it had been an incredible day. The final article of the treaty had been signed, and he had been appointed governor of California. He was only five days away from his thirty-fourth birthday, and all this had come like a gift from the gods. But the explorer was naïve once he was removed from the wilderness. He lacked the defensive mechanisms necessary for survival in a political world. He was too open to misuse by men with base motives, and he failed to suspect that the major reason for his moment of glory was a sly move by Stockton to throw the gauntlet into the face of the other devious actor in this drama, the angry and spiteful General Kearny.

## 3

THE GENERAL'S REACTION to this turn of events was deceptive and swift. Early on the morning after Frémont's appointment to high office, a messenger from Kearny arrived at his quarters. He delivered a one line note:

Dear Colonel: I wish to see you on business.[5]

The only business Frémont imagined that Kearny had in mind was the letter he had sent on the previous day—the letter ordering him to maintain his command of the California Battalion, not to turn it over to Gillespie, and to remain in that position until the general had ordered otherwise.

Realizing that he had not replied to Kearny's letter, John Charles took time to draft an answer. When he finished composing this letter, he handed it to Lieutenant Talbot, asked him to make a proper copy of it, and have Kit Carson deliver it to the general's quarters, as he was on his way to see him and would be there to sign the letter when Carson arrived.

But Frémont wasn't the only one who wrote a letter that morning. General Kearny wrote to Commodore Stockton. In this document, he informed the commodore that only since the arrival of the Army of the West could it be said that California was conquered and under control. Then in a display of displeasure at Stockton's assumption of military and political power in California, he stated:

I am prepared to carry out the President's instructions to me, which you oppose, [but] I must, for the purpose of preventing collision between us, and, possibly, a civil war in consequence of it, remain silent for the present, leaving you the great responsibility of doing that for which you have no authority, and preventing me from complying with the President's orders.[6]

As this letter was delivered to Commodore Stockton, Colonel Frémont walked to the low-ceilinged adobe where General Kearny was quartered. He entered and stood in front of Kearny's table. What followed is best presented by relying upon the testimony of the general as Frémont questioned him during his own court-martial.

Sitting ramrod straight in his chair, Kearny looked at Frémont, and asked if he had received the communication of January 16, referring to the organization and command of the California Battalion.

Frémont said he had, and that he had drafted a reply which was being copied and would arrive shortly.

As the two officers spoke of other things, Kit Carson appeared with the letter and handed it to John Charles. The colonel read it over to make sure there were no errors and, using a pen that was on the general's table, signed the letter and handed it to Kearny.

At Kearny's request, Frémont took a seat at the table while the general read the following:

CIUDAD DE LOS ANGELES,
January 17, 1847.

Sir: I have the honor to be in receipt of your favor of last night, in which I am directed to suspend the execution of orders which, in my capacity of military commandant of this territory, I had received from Commodore Stockton, governor and commander-in-chief in California.

I avail myself on an early hour this morning to make such a reply as the brief time allowed me for reflection will enable me.

I found Commodore Stockton in possession of the country, exercising the functions of military commandant and civil governor, as early as July of last year; and, shortly, thereafter, I received from him the commission of military commandant, the duties of which I immediately entered upon, and have continued to exercise to the present moment.

I found, also, on my arrival at this place, some three or four days since, Commodore Stockton still exercising the functions of civil and military governor with the same apparent deference to his rank on the part of all officers (including yourself) as he maintained and required when he assumed in July last.

I learned, also, in conversation with you, that, on the march from San Diego, recently, to this place, you entered upon and discharged duties, implying an acknowledgment on your part, of supremacy to Commodore Stockton.

I feel myself, therefore, with great deference to your professional and personal character, constrained to say, that, until you and Commodore Stockton adjust between yourselves the question of rank, where I respectfully think the difficulty belongs, I shall have to report and receive orders, as heretofore, from the commodore.

With considerations of high regard, I am your obedient servant,

J. C. FRÉMONT,
Lt. Col. U.S.A., and military commandant
of the territory of California.

To Brig. Gen. S. W. Kearny,
U. S. Army.[7]

If General Kearny's face did not indicate a normal response to this letter, Frémont should have known he had put something in writing that no subordinate officer should have done. If he had talked this over with Commodore Stockton, perhaps he would have been cautioned against such an obvious disregard for military rank. No matter how correct his case might have been,

Colonel Frémont committed a cardinal sin by telling a senior officer that he was not going to obey him until he was given a proper reason for so doing. Only one reason was needed, and Kearny possessed it—the difference in rank.

When the general had collected his thoughts and waited until his temper was under control, he spoke to the colonel with a keen edge of anger in his voice. He told him that he was a much older man and soldier, that he held Mrs. Frémont in high esteem, that he had a great friendship with Senator Benton, from whom he had received many acts of kindness. For all these reasons, he said that he wished to offer him some advice.

John Charles sat and waited, and Kearny continued. The only thing to do was to take back this letter. Destroy it. If he did that, he told Frémont, he would forget he had ever read it. As Kearny was to testify much later, "I told him that Commodore Stockton could not support him in disobeying the orders of his senior officer, and that, if he persisted in it, he would unquestionably ruin himself."[8]

Refusing to give in and make a tactical retreat, John Charles did not heed this advice. Instead he got up, stood at attention, bid Kearny good-bye, and turned and walked out of the room. It was a matter of pride, of vanity, but no matter how logical this act might have seemed in the face of conflicting orders carried by Stockton and Kearny, what Frémont did amounted to an outright act of disobediance.

What Frémont failed to understand or take into consideration was not overlooked by Kearny. Shortly after the colonel departed, Kearny wrote to the Secretary of War. He complained that Commodore Stockton was preventing him from carrying out the instructions of the President of the United States; that neither Stockton nor Frémont would obey his instructions from the President of the United States; "and as I have no troops in the country under my authority, excepting a few dragoons, I have no power of enforcing them."[9] He also enclosed copies of his instructions to Frémont, the letter of refusal from Frémont, and his own letter of complaint to Commodore Stockton. If this wasn't enough, Kearny also stated that *his* advice to march on Ciudad de los Angeles had been *reluctantly* agreed to by Commodore Stockton.

It was to be General Kearny's last day in Ciudad de los Angeles before he sailed north to Monterey, but he made it a busy day of bitterness.

## 4

IN THE GENERAL'S MIND one thing was very clear. Once he got Frémont back to the United States he intended to arrest him. Here, where the confusion of superior commanders existed, it was not possible to put the colonel in irons and hold him prisoner. But the day would come when the younger officer would discover the meaning of military discipline. Though Captain Henry Smith Turner, adjutant of the Army of the West, could not understand why Kearny didn't put Frémont in irons and keep him under arrest until the return to the States, what the loyal officer didn't know came out during the court-martial, when Kearny was asked at what time he had decided to arrest Lieutenant Colonel Frémont.

Kearny's answer was short and to the point: "I formed the design shortly after receiving his letter of January 17. That word shortly would not imply immediately. It may have been a week."[10]

Whether it was a decision made in a matter of hours or the span of a week was a minor point. What counted was the period for making such a decision was not long; and even as the general and his men marched toward San Diego to board a ship for Monterey, he must have been considering what charge or charges would best suit the case and stand up in a military trial in such bold relief that there could be one verdict only.

The fifty dragoons who traveled with Kearny were in poor shape for the march. The combination of their long overland trip, the dreadful days and nights at San Pascual and Mule Hill, and the battles to retake San Luis Rey and Pueblo de los Angeles had left the small detachment in terrible shape. Low in spirit, their clothing worn out and torn, some of the men even without shoes, they looked like the last survivors of a losing side in a war. When the general saw that one man was sick and had bleeding blisters on his feet, he dismounted and gave the soldier his own horse to ride, for ahead of them they had a march of 145 miles over rough road.

As General Kearny walked along, he was joined by Lieutenant William Emory, who thoroughly disliked Frémont. He spoke freely, and asked Kearny what was to be done about this officer. But though Kearny was angry and had plans for Frémont's future, he only hinted about them. He made no mention of a court-martial. But during Frémont's trial, Emory recalled one thing he told him before they reached San Diego. "He informed me that he should take affairs into his own hands as soon as he felt himself sufficiently strong."[11]

When questioned about the meaning of this statement, when asked if it meant that force was to be used, Lieutenant Emory replied that as far as he could recall, the general meant just that.

Plans and provisions, schemes and groundwork for the future were all part of the conversation between the general and the lieutenant as they walked along. Emory was to catch a ship at San Diego, go south, get off at Panama, cross to the Atlantic, and catch another ship to deliver messages to Washington. Kearny couldn't have selected a better hatchet man. Even Captain Turner disliked Emory and thought the man was driven by greed for immortality.

The same day Kearny marched toward San Diego, he was overtaken by

Stockton and his mounted escort of thirty sailors and marines. Both commands stopped for the night at San Juan Capistrano, but they maintained different messes and had very little to do with each other. The next day, Stockton's unit rode past Kearny and his men, gave a polite salute, and struck the road leading to the harbor at San Pedro.

Not long after Stockton and his men had vanished from view, another rider overtook the remnant of the Army of the West. This was newly elected Congressman Willard P. Hall of Missouri.[12] Hall reported to the general that Lieutenant Colonel Philip St. George Cooke[13] and the 350 men of the Mormon Battalion[14] had arrived at Warner's Ranch. To the general, this was good news. He immediately sent a messenger with orders for Cooke to march his force to San Diego, where he would be waiting for him.

The march to San Diego took General Kearny and his men five days. Once they arrived, they waited for the Mormon Battalion. During this time, Kearny again met Stockton, who had sailed into port the day before the Army of the West arrived.

The general learned that the commodore was ready to sail south along the coast of Baja California in search of a rumored French schooner that was supposed to be running guns ashore for an army of Mexicans preparing to march north and reconquer Alta California. As Kearny watched Stockton sail out of the harbor, things were beginning to break in the general's direction. Stockton and his men would not be around, and Cooke and the Mormons were on their way.

When the Mormon Battalion arrived, Kearny ordered Cooke to quarter his troops at the Mission San Luís Rey de Francia on the road to Cuidad de los Angeles. There he was to await further orders, which Kearny would send south from Monterey in due time. Then on the last day of January the Army of the West boarded the *Cyane* and made the eight-day voyage up the coast to Monterey.

As the *Cyane* entered Monterey Bay, two naval frigates were riding at anchor—the *Independence* and the *Lexington*. An old-line naval officer, Commodore William Brandford Shubrick, captain of the *Independence*, had arrived in California to replace Commodore Stockton as commander of the Pacific Squadron.[15] Shubrick was aboard the *Lexington* when he learned of General Kearny's presence. At once, he ordered the firing of a thirteen-gun salute in the general's honor. Then he sent a junior officer to invite him to be his guest for dinner aboard the *Independence*.

For General Kearny, this was a welcome change from what he had experienced in southern California. He was more than happy to join the commodore for dinner. He pulled together his worn uniform, boarded the waiting boat, and made the short voyage to the flagship. His appearance was hardly all "spit and polish." His uniform was faded from the desert sun he had endured in his march to California. He wore an old dragoon coat to protect him from the damp and foggy climate of Monterey, and his cap still carried the broad visor he had cut from a full dress hat in order to shade his eyes against the glare of sunlight in the Colorado Desert crossing.

That dinner aboard the *Independence* was like a tonic to the weary officer. Shubrick had great respect for Kearny and for the concept of rank and duty. He was outraged at what Kearny had to say about the actions of Colonel Frémont. As their conversation continued, the general showed the commodore the two letters dated June 3 and 18, 1846, that gave him the right to command troops—any troops—and to organize a civil government in California once that region had been conquered. In turn, the commodore showed him a July 12, 1846, order addressed to Commodore Sloat which Shubrick had picked up when his ship put into port at Valparaiso. This document directed Sloat to establish a civil government in California when and if it were taken by the forces of the United States.

If General Kearny wished to put a stop to the actions of this upstart Frémont, who fancied himself both a military commander and a governor, Commodore Shubrick was more than willing to help in any way possible. All this was good news to Kearny. He thanked Shubrick, said he would call upon him if and when, thanked him for the dinner, and was rowed ashore, where he was put up in Thomas Oliver Larkin's home. It had been a fine day for Kearny. He knew things were beginning to turn in his favor. Now, there was no need to hurry. All things considered, he agreed with Shubrick, they had time on their side—time to await additional, perhaps even more explicit instructions from Washington.

5

LEGAL OR ILLEGAL, right or wrong, Frémont was attempting to run a government in a conquered country. Things had to be done. Bills had to be paid in one way or another. There were debts that had been incurred for the wages of volunteer soldiers, for food and shelter, for equipment and supplies, and for livestock that had been needed in the campaign. Money was extremely short in the new government, and nothing was forthcoming from General Kearny.

Governor Frémont was too busy trying to make ends meet for a government the senior officers appeared willing to see falter and fail to satisfy their personal animosity toward him. The money needed was considerable. In attempting to take care of these financial problems, Frémont put his own future in jeopardy. He borrowed from individuals who requested interest rates that varied between two and three per cent per month. Some idea of just how much money was needed can best be realized in a deposition Frémont made to the United States Senate in February 1848.

John Charles estimated that a round figure of $600,000 would take care of all the bills—both accounted for and estimated—that had been incurred during the capture of California. In a partial breakdown, he indicated to the committee just how some of the money was spent.

From 3,000 to 4,000 horses, averaging thirty dollars
each, say . . . . . . . . . . . . . . . . . . . . . . . . . $120,000
3,000 head of cattle, averaging $10, say . . . . . . . . . . .     30,000
1,000 saddles, bridles, spurs and horse
equipment, averaging $60 . . . . . . . . . . . . . . . . . .     60,000
400 rifles, at $30 each . . . . . . . . . . . . . . . . . . .     12,000
Drafts protested and obligations,
including damages and interests, say . . . . . . . . . . . . .     50,000
Claims for provisions taken, and damages at
San Pedro and Los Angeles, examined and allowed
by a commission, before I left California . . . . . . . . . .     29,584
Provisions and supplies, to wit:
flour, grain, coffee, sugar, vegetables, and other
small items, to wit: sheep, wagons, gears,
damage to ranchos, say . . . . . . . . . . . . . . . . . . .    100,000
Services of the California battalion, say . . . . . . . . . . .    100,000[16]

These weren't all the expenses incurred. On February 5, 1847, Frémont wrote to Midshipman Louis McLane[17] and instructed him to enlist troops for a term of six months, and to fortify the entrance to San Francisco Bay against any possible foes by seeing to it that White Island (Alcatraz) had a fort and a battery established on it.[18] While the idea was a good one, the island was owned by Francis P. Temple.[19] With no money forthcoming from the government of the United States, John Charles took it upon himself to give his own signature for the debt and purchased Alcatraz Island to prevent its acquisition by any other nation wishing to control the entrance through the Golden Gate.

The purchase price of White or Bird Island, as it was then called, came to $5,000. On March 2, 1847, Frémont wrote to Temple that as governor of California he would

hereby oblige and bind myself as the legal representative of the United States and my successor in office to pay the said Francis Temple, his heirs or assigns the sum of five thousand dollars (5000) to be paid at as early a day as possible after the receipt of funds from the United States.[20]

All this was fine except for one thing. Temple was not at all sure that the United States would recognize this. The government might refuse to honor the purchase price. He refused to go through with the deal unless Frémont was willing to execute his own personal bond for the price of the island. Having heard that the French were ready and willing to buy the island, Governor Frémont did not hesitate. He signed a personal bond for the amount due, and became the owner. In so doing, he acquired another liability that was to haunt him in the future. He was forced to go into debt with Simon Stevens of New York for the purchase price plus interest. Even so, his troubles were not over. The United States would not recognize the debt due; General Kearny claimed that the act of buying the island was one of mutiny; in 1858 the government forcibly took possession of Alcatraz, and Frémont had to sue the government in 1859 to get the money he had paid.[21]

Trying desperately to get money to run the government, Frémont wrote not only to General Kearny but also to Commodore Shubrick once he learned of his arrival at Monterey. In his letter to Shubrick of February 7, 1847, he asked for any financial aid he could advance, as a large sum of money was needed to help defray the costs of operating the United States Government in California. Commodore Shubrick's letter of reply arrived six days later. If Frémont had any prior doubt that the high-ranking officers of both services were out to get him, Shubrick's letter made it clear that no officer of authority was going to help. This letter came as Frémont's drafts for such expenses had reached twenty thousand dollars and were about to be doubled. If payment was not forthcoming, he would be personally liable and open to lawsuit.[22]

Commodore Shubrick's letter not only made it clear that funds were not available; it also stated that he was awaiting the return of Commodore Stockton in order to learn from him just what had taken place in California. As things stood, Shubrick let Frémont know that as far as he was concerned the senior officer of the army in California was Brigadier General Kearny. As to the control of the government of California, it was obvious that only Kearny and himself possessed proper letters granting authority to appoint officials and run the government.

While Frémont worked long hours, wrote letters to be carried to Washington by Kit Carson and Edward Fitzgerald Beale, and tried to hold the government together by borrowing money under his personal signature, the strain began to tell on him. He suffered from headaches, wondered why all this was taking place, and waited for word from Washington that would indicate that both money and official praise were to be his for filling in when it was vital that somebody should take over. He didn't know that the biggest trouble was yet to come. While on a visit to San Francisco Bay on February 12, General Kearny received a letter from General-in-Chief of the Army Winfield Scott instructing him to muster all California Volunteers into the United States Army and to assume the position of governor of California until such time as a civil government was established.

By the first of March, Frémont heard from Kearny. But the general did not tell him about Scott's letter. Instead, he simply addressed him as Lieutenant Colonel Frémont, Regiment of Mounted Riflemen, Commander of the

California Volunteers; reminded him of his duties as commander of the Battalion of California Volunteers; and stated he was to report to Monterey and "bring with you, and with as little delay as possible, all the archives and public documents and papers which may be subject to your control, and which apertain to the government of California, that I may receive them from your hands at this place, the capitol of the Territory."[23]

Signed: S. W. Kearny, Brig. Gen., and Governor of California.

March came in like a lion named Governor Kearny—a title that came as an exclamation point, a bolt of official lightning. John Charles also received a letter from Captain Henry Turner that included five key points. Without delay, he was to muster the California Volunteers into the service of the United States Army. Lieutenant Archibald Gillespie was to be relieved of his duties and travel to Washington and report to the commander of the United States Marine Corps. All the men in Frémont's command in the military of southern California were to assume that Lieutenant Philip St. George Cooke was their commander. In addition, Cooke was to appoint an officer to receive all public property and turn it over to a senior naval officer at San Diego. Finally, Major Thomas B. Swords, quartermaster,[24] and Paymaster Jeremiah H. Cloud[25] were to ride to Monterey and report for duty to General Kearny.

As the mounting financial and emotional tensions continued to grow, rumors of possible outbreaks of hostilities became common talk. There was the persistent story that the Californios were moving north out of Mexico once again to take back what they had lost; and there was a definite anti-Mormon feeling among the Californios. Even General Kearny knew this, and during Frémont's trial, word of how much opposition there was to the presence of the Mormon Battalion came out as Colonel Frémont questioned Samuel J. Hensley. As Hensley put it, the Californios were opposed to the Mormons, even dreaded them, and "offered, if the volunteers would remain neutral . . . [to] hoist the American flag, and whip them out of the country; they said the people in the United States were fighting them, and they had a right to do so too."[26]

Isolated in southern California, receiving co-operation from the Californios and no help at all from General/Governor Kearny, Frémont decided his correspondence with the officers at Monterey was no more than a formality, a way for them to avoid responsibility for the future of California. Something had to be done in a hurry. It struck him that the only way to accomplish anything was to ride to Monterey and confront Kearny face to face. That way, there was a chance of convincing him that much more than personal feelings and positions of respective power were at stake. The government of a captured country, a new territory, a land that would eventually become another state under the American flag was much more important than the destiny of Kearny, Shubrick, or himself. Believing this, Frémont made plans to ride north.

6

IN THE COOLNESS OF DAWN three horsemen rode away from Ciudad de los Angeles on March 22, 1847. Riding alongside Frémont were Don Jesús Pico and John Charles' black servant, Jacob Dodson. Each man had three additional horses to relieve the one he was riding. The loose horses were driven along with them as the riders traveled at a steady gallop until the animals tired. Pico and Dodson roped fresh mounts; saddles were changed; and the men quickly set out again at the same grueling pace.

Their horses were not shod, and the sound of hooves striking the grass-covered earth was muffled. All that day and into evening they rode at a fast pace. Only as they rode up or down hills were they forced to slow to a trot or a walk. They passed San Fernando and El Rincon south of Santa Barbara, which they came to as the tide was out. They traveled on the wet sand and in and out of the shallow edge of breakers spreading toward the base of the high cliffs. That night they came to a halt at a rancho near Santa Barbara. They had traveled 125 miles since dawn. They were saddle-sore and weary, and Dodson's arm ached from roping mounts and using his lariat to whip the loose herd of horses along.

On the second day, they rode across the steep mountains north of Santa Barbara where the California Battalion had lost so many animals during the violent storm on Christmas of 1846. All along this route they saw the scattered and whitened bones of horses. By nightfall they had traveled 125 to 135 miles and reached Pico's home at San Luis Obispo. It was clear they would have to secure fresh mounts for the next day's journey. Word was sent out to neighboring ranchos for their best horses.

The third day, the riders got a late start. The fresh mounts did not reach Pico's home until after ten o'clock. Finally they were ready to ride again, and a young man from one of the ranchos agreed to go with them to help drive the horse herd. They were 150 miles south of Monterey, and Frémont hoped to be there by daybreak.

Hour after weary pounding hour, the men rode. By eight o'clock that night they had traveled seventy miles. But Pico had not had much sleep on the previous night, and the steady punishment of saddle leather, wooden stirrups, and the jarring movement of the horse was beginning to take its toll on him and the others as they topped a ridge and dropped toward the southern reaches of the Salinas Valley. The need to halt for a few hours could not be put off. But this part of the valley had a reputation for bands of former Mission Indians who had taken to marauding, and there were outlaws who waylaid travelers bound for Monterey. To make sure they would have a safe rest, the men rode into a canyon where there was a good cover of dense wood and plenty of grass for the horses.

The young Califomio was put in charge of the grazing horses and told to be on the lookout for anything which might mean trouble. Then, the three worn-out riders lay on the ground and went to sleep. By one o'clock in the morning, they were awakened by the shouting of the herder and the movement of horses.

At first, they thought there was an attack by Indians or bandits, but Pico heard the grunts and growls of grizzly bears. Frémont was ready to begin shooting, but Don Jesús said that would only make the bears charge. He said it would be better to try the Mexican way. Sometimes, if one spoke to the bears the right way, they could be convinced to move along. Saying this, he walked slowly toward the growling bears. When he was close to them, he shouted sharply in Spanish. The bears hesitated and then slowly moved away. But though the grizzlies were gone, the men no longer had any desire for sleep. Before daybreak, they rounded up their frightened horses, built a campfire, and cooked breakfast. As soon as it was light enough to see, they saddled their horses, and began the final leg of their ride to Monterey.

By late afternoon the riders felt a cool wind coming in from the Pacific. As they came into view of Monterey Bay, they saw banks of fog moving on wind currents toward the hills in back of the pueblo, fog that was already curling around the tops of pines and cypresses. The men had been three days and ten hours in the saddle and had traveled 420 miles.

After this long, hard ride, Colonel Frémont went directly to Thomas Oliver Larkin's house, and Larkin took him to the quarters occupied by Kearny. The general greeted Frémont with a calculated coolness. Though Kearny was now governor of California, and responsible for all its problems, he didn't believe it was necessary to talk to Frémont at that time. He would see him in the morning. Then the colonel could tell him just what it was that had prompted him to make such a ride.

On the morning of March 26, Colonel Frémont appeared promptly for his interview with Kearny. As Frémont entered the general's quarters, he realized there was not going to be a conversation with Kearny alone. Obviously, the general wished to have a witness, and there he sat in the presence of Colonel Richard B. Mason, a fifty-year-old officer of the 1st Dragoons.[27]

Frémont objected to Mason's presence, but Kearny made it clear that he was to remain. As he later testified:

> I told him [Frémont] that Colonel Mason had been sent out by the War Department to relieve me in my command in California as soon as I thought proper to leave it, and that there was no conversation which I could hold . . . on public affairs, but that it was proper Colonel Mason should be present at. He [Frémont] then told me that perhaps I had Colonel Mason there to take advantage of some unguarded expressions of his. His reply to me was offensive, and I told him that I could hardly believe that he would come into my

quarters and intentionally insult me. He made no reply; nor did he state what the object of his remark to me was.[28]

After the long, hard ride—after nearly four days in the saddle—Colonel Frémont's audience with General Kearny was being handled as something of no great matter, something a senior officer might expect of a subordinate officer getting out of line. The next remark by Kearny was that he still awaited Frémont's reply to the letter Captain Turner had sent to him concerning the disposition of the California Battalion. Was he going to obey the order?

Then even before Frémont could answer, Kearny warned him "to reflect well upon the answer . . . for his answer would be a very important one; if he wanted to take an hour for consideration, to take it; if he wanted a day for consideration, he could take it."[29]

Cat and mouse with another cat watching the game. Old-line military officers playing out the string, letting this political pup—as they saw him—this explorer who had not come up through the ranks, play out his time in front of them. Humiliation and pretended ignorance as to why Frémont had made such a trip added to the rigors of the tiring ride. But all of it came out in the court-martial. The whole rotten business was spoken again and again. It was taken down by court reporters. It was printed by the government just the way Kearny remembered—when he did remember and when he didn't forget because of convenience.

On the second day of the interview, Colonel Mason sat beside Kearny again. He sat there like some great toad awaiting the mistake of a fly in its pattern of flight. As the witness observed and listened, Colonel Frémont asked General Kearny if—in his new capacity as governor—he would assume the growing financial responsibilities of the government.

During the trial, the general couldn't remember. It was convenient to forget. When pressed by Colonel Frémont's questioning, General Kearny barely slid past perjury in his answer. He left no more than a narrow margin between truth and falsehood as he said, "I have no recollection of his having asked me. If he had, I should have answered in the negative.[30]

*In the negative.* A grand and glorious answer for a new governor. *In the negative.* Let Colonel Frémont worry about the mounting debts incurred. Nobody had asked him to run the government; nobody, that is, except Commodore Stockton, and he was an officer of the United States Navy. It was time Colonel Frémont learned he was in the army.

John Charles was faced with an impossible situation. Kearny was not interested in a reasonable discussion. To Frémont, there appeared to be only one way out. He looked at General Kearny and Colonel Mason and said it would be his pleasure to resign his commission. Again, the reply from Kearny was *negative.* "I think he did offer to resign his commission, which I refused to accept."[31]

There was not going to be any resignation. There was not going to be any monetary help from General and Governor Kearny. The hats were switched back and forth. Questions concerning the government of California required the governor's hat. To questions about anything that had to do with the army, Kearny quickly assumed the hat of a general. And before the conversation of that March 27, 1847, ended, Kearny had made it clear that he wished one thing and only one thing from Colonel Frémont: obedience.

Orders were given and made quite clear for a man who could be as foggy as Monterey's climate when he so wished. Colonel Frémont was to go back to Ciudad de los Angeles. There, he was to see to it that he followed the orders which had been sent to him by Captain Turner. Every member of the California Battalion was to be put aboard ship and sent north to Monterey, and that included Colonel Frémont. The same order also applied to archives, files, and any other government records that Frémont had in southern California.

Kearny continued to switch the hats back and forth. He gave proclamations; he gave orders; but most of all, the wearing of two hats let him get in his licks against Frémont, and he had been waiting a long time to do this. Colonel Frémont asked if he might ride north as he got seasick. This was granted, this small favor. Everything else had been taken away. But if he wished to ride all the way back to Ciudad de los Angeles and then return by horse again, that would be all right.

Two events were clear in General Kearny's memory about the interview at Monterey. At least, this was all that appeared to be clear. All the rest was conveniently forgotten. There was also a touch of wounded pride, as the two things which Kearny remembered were that Colonel Frémont had insulted him and had offered to resign his commission.

The fact that Frémont had mentioned the pressing need for funds to pay for government expenses had vanished from Kearny's mind. Nor did he remember that the main reason Frémont had given for his incredible ride to Monterey was the possibility of trouble in southern California—that armed forces were rumored to be moving north out of Mexico to recapture California, and that the Californios thoroughly distrusted the Mormons and were threatening to take up arms against them. All during the trial, as Frémont put question after question to Kearny, he exhibited an astonishing lack of memory or an incredible ability to keep a straight face while perjuring himself.

The two interviews at Monterey had made it obvious to Frémont that he was at the mercy of General Kearny and had no choice other than to follow his orders. So, without any warning of a forthcoming arrest and court-martial, John Charles rode out of Monterey and headed back to Ciudad de los Angeles. The return journey took just under four days. In less than eight days, the riders had traveled a distance equivalent to that between New York and Chicago.

7

THE DAY FRÉMONT HEADED BACK to Ciudad de los Angeles, General Kearny started a strange period of madness. Kearny had the upper hand, but he gave no impression of being a big enough man to know how to use it. Instead, he began a series of moves calculated to belittle and bedevil Frémont.

He ordered Colonel Mason to go to southern California, and gave him full instructions to issue any orders he thought necessary. When this was done, Mason was to return to Monterey. These orders were written and signed on March 27, the same day Frémont galloped out of Monterey.

The following day General Kearny wrote a letter to Colonel Frémont in which he informed him that the letter would be handed to him by Colonel Mason, who was sailing from Monterey on that day, and that he was to consider any instructions from Mason to be that equivalent of anything which the general would say. Included in Kearny's orders were three items that were to cause trouble: Frémont was to take care of unsettled accounts which he might have incurred by authenticating and putting them in proper form for the disbursing officers; Frémont was to see to it that any of the men who had come west with him as paid members of the Topographical Department were to be prepared to return home or to request a discharge in California; and, as a final command, the general informed him that he wished to see him at Monterey twelve days after he had taken care of the embarkation of the members of the California Battalion at San Pedro.

Things moved quickly now that General Kearny had decided upon his course of action. Frémont had been back at Ciudad de los Angeles for less than a week when Colonel Mason arrived on April 15, 1847, and requested his presence at his quarters that evening.

John Charles appeared at the home of Nathaniel M. Pryor just south of the Plaza between First and Commercial streets,[32] and was ushered into Colonel Mason's quarters. As in the meeting with Kearny at Monterey, John Charles again faced more than one officer. Sitting beside the stern Colonel Mason was Lieutenant Colonel Philip St. George Cooke, commander of the Mormon Battalion. The interview was short and harsh. Mason repeated the orders which General Kearny had sent concerning the volunteers, all government artillery, arms, supplies, and horses. Then he asked Frémont to go with him the next day to Mission San Gabriel to visit the California Battalion in order to ascertain how many men were willing to join the service of the United States.

The next day Frémont rode out to the mission with Mason. The men of the California Battalion were mustered and paraded in front of Mason and then ordered to stand at attention. They were asked if they were willing to continue their service in the forces of the United States. But when the volunteers learned that Frémont was not to be their commander any longer, none were willing to continue serving as soldiers. They also claimed a right to be discharged at Ciudad de los Angeles.

Colonel Mason did not take kindly to this reception, and the next day he sent a detailed letter of command to Frémont. The volunteers of the California Battalion, who had served their term of duty, were to be discharged at once. Any officers of the United States Navy serving with them were to report to Monterey for further orders. While the sloop of war *Warren* was due to sail north from the harbor at San Pedro in a short time, Colonel Mason made it clear that any volunteers taking their discharge in southern California had but a limited time to board the vessel, and that the ship could not accommodate more than one hundred passengers. As to the men of Frémont's Topographical Party, they were to ride north to Monterey with him and report to General Kearny. Horses and equipment were to be supplied to these men, but all other supplies and horses were to be turned over by Lieutenant Colonel Frémont to Lieutenant John W. Davidson of the 1st Dragoons.³³ Without directly stating it, Colonel Mason made it quite clear that Frémont was being relieved of command.

After Colonel Mason's April 7 letter to Frémont, the two men became more and more alienated. One letter after another passed between them. Colonel Mason found fault with everything that Frémont had done since he had been in California, even focusing on the role that John Charles had played in California before the raising of the flag. Time after time, Mason came back to the horses pastured in the country.

Frémont claimed he was getting the horses in shape so that he and a select group of men could ride to Mexico and join his official regiment, the Regiment of Mounted Riflemen which was serving under the command of General Zachary Taylor. As John Charles pointed out, this was one of the surprising options allowed him in the letter the Secretary of War had sent to General Kearny. Colonel Mason was contemptuous of Frémont, and he insisted that the horses be delivered at once. Twice in the same afternoon he sent for Frémont and in an insulting manner asked where the horses were and when he intended to bring them in as ordered. This was too much. Frémont resented Mason's demeaning manner toward him, and let him know that he did.

Colonel Mason's reply was immediate: "None of your insolence, or I will put you in irons."³⁴

This was more than he could tolerate. To be removed of command in this manner was bad enough, but to have Mason question his integrity and then threaten him with imprisonment was the end. Without thinking of Mason's reputation as a duelist, he said, "You cannot make an official matter of a personal one, sir, as a man do you hold yourself personally responsible for what you have just said?"³⁵

There was no question about it, Colonel Mason terminated the interview by admitting to his personal responsibility. Frémont then sent two written communications to Mason and had them delivered by Major Pierson B. Reading. In one he demanded a formal apology. In the other he wrote that if such an apology was not forthcoming, he would consider the refusal an official challenge.

Colonel Mason quickly read both notes. Then, at Major Reading's request, he wrote a refusal to Frémont's request for an apology. This was followed on April 14 by the delivery of a formal challenge from Colonel Frémont, who wrote: "An apology having been declined, Major Reading will arrange the preliminaries for a meeting requiring personal satisfaction."[36]

The choice of weapons was Colonel Mason's, and he selected a deadly weapon he was quite accustomed to using. The men would meet on the field of honor with double-barreled shotguns loaded with buckshot. Frémont didn't own such a weapon and had never used one in his life. But he had challenged Mason, and there was only one thing to do—go through with it and hope for the best. His seconds managed to find a shotgun and the necessary buckshot for him, and everything was set for the duel to take place at daybreak on the next day. But by midmorning of April 15 one of Colonel Mason's seconds appeared at his quarters. He delivered a note from Mason saying that the duel would have to be put off until they both returned to Monterey. He had private affairs to adjust before such a meeting could take place.

April passed. Mason sailed to Monterey, and on May 4, General Kearny— who was getting ready to sail to southern California—wrote the following letter to Frémont:

It has been reported here, by some of the discharged men of the Battalion of California volunteers, just arrived from Pueblo de los Angeles, that a challenge has passed between Col. Mason, of the 1st Dragoons, and yourself, the meeting to take place at or near Monterey.

As I am about leaving here for the South, in consequence of rumors of an excitement among the people in that district of country, it becomes my duty to inform you that the good of the Public Service, the necessity of preserving tranquillity in California, imperiously require, that the meeting above referred to should not take place at this time, and in this country, and you are hereby officially directed by me to proceed no further in this matter.

A similiar communication has been addressed to Colonel Mason.[37]

Six days after writing to Frémont, General Kearny completed his voyage down the coast and arrived in Ciudad de los Angeles. With him was Colonel Jonathan D. Stevenson[38] and a regiment of the Seventh New York Volunteers, who had arrived at San Francisco Bay on March 5, 1847, after a long sea voyage aboard the Thomas H. Perkins. General Kearny had ordered them to come south with him to replace the Mormon Battalion, as they were due to be discharged.

That May 10, when Frémont talked to General Kearny at Ciudad de los

Angeles, he requested permission to join his regiment in Mexico. He told the general, "he had 120 picked horses and 60 men ready to go, with *pinoli* and dried beef for their support. . . ."[39]

When Frémont asked about this during the court-martial, Kearny replied that this was true. As far as he was concerned, the whole adventure was out of the question. He indicated in his testimony that he "refused to let him go."[40]

Two days after this meeting, Frémont and nineteen of his original party left Ciudad de los Angeles and headed for Monterey. Six days after heading north, they encamped beside the Salinas River not far from Monterey.

Time was running out for Colonel Frémont. Eight days after he had set up his camp, General Kearny arrived in Monterey Bay aboard the *Lexington*. The news awaiting Kearny was that great victories had been won in Mexico by General Taylor in the northeast and by General Scott at Veracruz. By this time, the war might well be over. With that taking place, with May running its course, General Kearny made immediate plans to head back to the United States. Two days later, on May 29, he sent for Colonel Frémont and his men of the Topographical Corps.

The men were reviewed by Kearny at Monterey, and he had his orders read to them. All were to proceed to the United States under his command, and they would leave Monterey on May 31. As for the command of the military in California, that and the governorship would be delegated to Colonel Mason.

Then the orders stated precisely the names and ranks of the officers who were to march eastward, and Lieutenant Colonel Frémont's name was the first on the list. Frémont also was to discharge any men who wished to remain in California.

All this was bad enough, but General Kearny wasn't through. Until the date of departure, Colonel Frémont was to remain in Monterey and not at the camp beside the Salinas River. He was refused permission to go to Yerba Buena to get the botanical and geological specimens he had collected on his expedition, and he was to turn over all his instruments to Lieutenant Henry Wager Halleck of the Engineers,[41] who would turn them over to Lieutenant Horace Warner of the Topographical Engineers.[42] Receipts for these instruments belonging to the Topographical Department were to be carefully taken and put away.

Lieutenant Colonel Frémont had other questions for General Kearny: What about Ned Kern and Henry King? They weren't here. They might be at Sutter's Fort, or with the war over they might be at Yerba Buena. Would Kearny give him time to locate these men?

There was no charity in Kearny's heart. He had Frémont where he wanted him, and the answer was "No, sir."

Would the general help the colonel with the financial obligations he had incurred in his duties as governor?

"No, sir."

Would the general see to it that the members of the California Battalion who did not wish to join the army receive their back pay?

Again, the answer was "No, sir."

The gap between Kearny and Frémont grew wider as the hours neared for the start of the return journey eastward. They left Monterey in two different groups. General Kearny and his men marched ahead, and to the rear came Colonel Frémont and his men. It didn't matter to Kearny that the explorer had risked his life to survey a greater portion of the American West than even Lewis and Clark. All that mattered was that Colonel Frémont was out of order, had not followed military regulations, and had committed mutiny in the rule-book mind of General Kearny.

## 8

THE TRIP THROUGH THE GREAT VALLEY was one of tremendous beauty in June 1847. Winter had been long and hard in the Sierra Nevada, and the deep snowpack was just beginning to melt and flood creeks, streams, and rivers. To try crossing the Carquinez Strait was out of the question as the heavy flow of water into Suisun Bay had made the strait so swift and deep that the only chance to cross it with any safety would have been at ebb tide. Both parties—Kearny's and Frémont's—backtracked and crossed into the San Joaquin Valley over Pacheco Pass and then struck a northern course for Sutter's Fort. But the journey was not easy. The record snowfall for the winter of 1846–47 had sent incredible runoff streams toward San Francisco Bay, and the men of both parties soon found traveling extremely difficult.

While the weather was clear and warm, it had not turned into summer heat. One thing the men had to surmount was the flooded condition of the whole region. Rivers such as the Tuolumne, San Joaquin, and Stanislaus had spilled over their normal banks, and great stretches of the San Joaquin Valley looked like a lake. These rivers and their overflow had to be crossed by fording the icy water, and by using skin boats. In one such crossing a skin boat capsized, and Colonel Cooke lost everything he owned except the clothes he was wearing. In another accident Major Swords lost his baggage. One of the greatest losses was that of all the spare horseshoes and horseshoe nails.

It was slow going, and each night's camp was unpleasant because of the swarms of mosquitoes. Both parties—keeping their distance—worked their way through the San Joaquin Valley and on up the Sacramento Valley until Sutter's Fort came into view on June 13.

The parties established separate camps near the fort, and two days were spent here as preparations were made for the overland crossing. Beef was jerked. Additional horses were procured, and all the gear was checked for the long march ahead.

On their arrival at Sutter's Fort, General Kearny rode over to pay his respects to the owner of Nueva Helvetia. At this honor, Captain Sutter, who had been almost a prisoner in his own fort, ordered a cannon salute. Then the garrison that Sutter called his army was lined up for inspection. Before the day ended, Sutter invited General Kearny and his officers to join him for dinner the next evening; but Frémont was not included among the guests.

The day of the dinner at the fort was a busy one for Frémont. Chief Piopiomoxmox of the Walla Walla Indians had been making threats around Sutter's Fort that if he and his men were not paid for their service in the California Battalion, there would be trouble. It was Frémont and not Kearny who saw to it that the chief and his warriors were sent away with a herd of horses as payment. On this same day, John Charles made one more attempt to get out from under the yoke of Kearny. Referring to a letter he had received from him in March 1847, he wrote: "I am informed that you had been directed by the commander-in-chief not to detain me in this country against my wishes, longer than the absolute necessities of the service might require."[43] This was for openers. Frémont went on to point out that, since Kearny had terminated his exploring duties with the Topographical Corps, he wished to take a small party—using his own money—and travel on ahead to be with his family.

General Kearny's answer was predictable, and he had it sent from his camp to Frémont's on the same day.

Sir: The request contained in your communication to me of this date, to be relieved from all connection with the topographical party, (nineteen men), and be permitted to return to the United States with a small party, made up by your private means cannot be granted.

I shall leave here on Wednesday, the 16th instant, and I require of you to be with your topographical party in my camp (which will probably be 15 miles from here) on the evening of that day, and to continue with me to Missouri.[44]

Despite this bind, Frémont did manage to carry out one last item of business before he departed. In February 1847 he had purchased Las Mariposas from Juan B. Alvarado.[45] Larkin handled all the details for Frémont for a 7½ per cent commission, or $225 above the purchase price of $3,000. But even as John Charles was headed eastward, he took time to give the power of attorney for his property to Pierson B. Reading, who agreed to send Joseph W. Buzzell[46] with men, money, and supplies to build a house, barn, and corral for Frémont on his property near Yosemite Valley.

The guide for Kearny's party was William "Le Gros" Fallon,[47] but Frémont's party did not need a guide. It was another humiliating move on Kearny's part to hire a guide when he could have called upon Frémont and his men to lead the way across the Sierra Nevada, the Great Basin, and on to South Pass. Instead, Kearny chose to ignore his knowledge of the country.

By three o'clock on the afternoon of June 16 both units were ready to go.

The first day was short and served as a breaking-in period, but on June 17 the men traveled thirty-three miles to Johnson's Ranch on the Bear River. Here, some three miles to the east of present-day Wheatland, California, Kearny's party was joined by Edwin Bryant, who had been alcalde of Yerba Buena, thanks to the general's friendship with him. Bryant was homesick for Kentucky and had decided this was a good chance to make the overland crossing with a large and well-armed party. Kearny learned that yet another party would be following them within a month, for Bryant told him that Commodore James Biddle[48] had given Gillespie permission to leave for the States and he was coming with Commodore Stockton.[49]

Three days after leaving Johnson's Ranch, they arrived at Truckee Lake (present-day Donner Lake). The next day they came upon a scene from Dante's *Inferno*. This was the site of the cabins where the Donner Party had met with disaster. Now, as the weather had turned warmer and access to the area for coyotes, wolves, and other flesh-eaters had become easier, bits and pieces of bodies and bones were scattered all over.

Even death had to bear responsibility for the controversy between Kearny and Frémont. Captain Turner carefully noted in his journal that the general had ordered Major Swords to collect and bury everything the men could find. Another journal keeper, of the Mormon Battalion, wrote that Frémont never even stopped to help. An opposite version of this affair can be found in the recollections of William Alexander Trubody, who claimed that he had heard Frémont say, at their emigrant camp on the Big Sandy River, that Kearny had marched right on by, and that he and his men had buried the remains and burned the cabins.[50] This has been disputed on the grounds that Trubody was only eight years old at the time he heard this story. But that is not reason enough to dismiss the memory of the event. What the boy heard that night at the Big Sandy River camp was a tale of cannibalism—a major taboo in Christian culture—and he heard it from a famous explorer who had come into their camp to offer advice—which General Kearny did not do—on how to cross the Great Basin in time to avoid such a tragedy. This was precisely the kind of thing that would have remained as clear in Trubody's mind in later years as the first time he heard it beside a campfire with the shadows of night just beyond the circle of covered wagons.

Record keepers for Kearny or Frémont were bound to suffer from personal prejudice. The past friction which still remained colored the attitudes of men of both commands. On the basis of logic alone, it is hard to believe that either commander marched past the remains of the Donner Party and let the other men bury whatever they could find. The more reasonable assumption —even with the existence of an unreasonable hostility between Kearny and Frémont—is that both parties stopped and helped in this mournful task. Even at that, they didn't find all the scattered pieces of rotting flesh and bones. Over a month later, when Commodore Stockton's party passed this way, they found and buried more remains.

Space and time entered the physical and psychological movement of the
feuding commanders. Between them was the distance—apparently by
Kearny's oral order—of one party trailing the other, sometimes in view, sometimes out of sight. Ahead was the endless trek along the Truckee River, into
the vast, sage-covered Great Basin, along the Humboldt River to its junction
with the northeast trail to Fort Hall and the Oregon Trail, and then across
the Continental Divide at South Pass. From there all the familiar landmarks
were ticked off one after another as the days rolled by: Fort Laramie (where
Frémont again asked permission from Kearny to take a shorter route to Missouri than the general's plan of going by way of Fort Leavenworth, but again
the general answered in the negative), then Scott's Bluffs, Chimney Rock,
Council Bluffs, Ash Hollow, the Platte River, the Little Blue River to its
junction with the Big Blue River, and Fort Leavenworth.

Behind them came Commodore Stockton's party. Time past played its role
as all the way east on the central overland trail, Frémont was again the man
in the middle. Time present was filled with irony. It had to be there. Even
though contact between the general and the colonel was limited and infre-
quent, somewhere during the long march word would have passed, men
would have talked, and the news of Commodore Stockton's marching somewhere behind all of them would have become common knowledge. And time
past, present, and future always had to be with John Charles as he saw the
steady flow of wagon trains using the trail hard-won in his own past. But
they were using it in the present, and around campfires or at frontier forts
there was talk of how many emigrants had passed this way, how many were
waiting to move on, and how many were expected in the future.

Space and time ran together on August 22, 1847, when Fort Leavenworth
came into view at nine o'clock in the morning on a scorching summer day.
The long march from Sutter's Fort had covered 1,905 miles. The way Major
Swords figured it, this meant that the trail-hardened men had made the journey in sixty-six days at an average of thirty-three miles per day.

To General Kearny the sight of Fort Leavenworth was much like a home-
coming. Lieutenant Colonel Clifton Wharton, the fort's commander, ordered
a thirteen-gun salute in Kearny's honor. But the reception for Colonel
Frémont and the officers and men of the Topographical Corps was just the
opposite. They were not treated with dignity inside the fort, and they made
their camp outside. Here on the day of arrival, before Frémont even had time
to rest, an orderly appeared with a request for him to come to Colonel Wharton's office at once.

And here at Fort Leavenworth, uncertainty became certainty as John
Charles dismounted and walked into Colonel Wharton's office, and saw the
general and the colonel—just as in Monterey, just as in Ciudad de los Angeles—sitting and waiting.

General Kearny asked Colonel Frémont to be seated. Then without
any more talk, and with Colonel Wharton sitting as a witness, the general

read his written orders to Frémont, orders which cleared the air and explained all the general's negative responses, and his attitude toward Frémont.

FORT LEAVENWORTH,
*August 22, 1847.*

[ORDERS.]

. . . Lieutenant Colonel Frémont, of the regiment of mounted riflemen, will turn over to the officers of the different departments, at this post, the horses, mules, and other public property in the use of the topographical party now under his charge, for which receipts will be given. He will arrange the accounts of these men, (nineteen in number,) so that they can be paid at the earliest possible date.

Lieutenant Colonel Frémont having performed the above duty, will consider himself under arrest, and will then repair to Washington City, and report himself to the adjutant general of the army.[51]

It came as a shock. *Will consider himself under arrest.* He knew that he and Kearny were at odds, but he never suspected it would come to this. Angry but under control, Frémont stood up. He asked if that was all and if he had permission to leave. With permission granted, John Charles saluted both officers, turned, and walked out of Colonel Wharton's office into the glare of the blistering August sun. Without wasting time, he returned to his camp, notified the men of the situation, and immediately began to carry out the first part of Kearny's orders.

But the army game was to begin a kind of punishment at once. Whether it was suggested or ordered by General Kearny is not known; but even if he had not issued such a command or request, this was a post where Kearny was treated with great respect. So what took place may have been a reflex action on the part of the officers and enlisted men. For when Frémont and his men brought in their arms and horses as ordered, they waited five hours in the hot sun while the ordnance sergeant took his time in receiving them. All during this time, "they were not approached, spoken to, or noticed by any officer of the fort, nor offered the least hospitality. . . ."[52]

All that had been festering like a sore boil broke with General Kearny's cutting order for Colonel Frémont's arrest. At last, things were clear to John Charles. Now he could look back and realize that the turmoil in California, the puzzling, negative attitude of the general came down to one moment in the general's adobe headquarters at Ciudad de los Angeles.

But now, at Fort Leavenworth, John Charles knew that he was to become an example for any other officer who dared to challenge the rank and authority of an officer of higher rank. And as he made preparations to move on to Westport to catch a steamboat headed downriver to St. Louis, the terrible truth of his returning to Jessie and the Benton family as a man slated to stand the test of military justice in a court-martial left him with a strange report for an explorer to be bringing home to his loved ones.

## ·❧ XXI ❧·

## Prelude to Ordeal

MORE THAN TWO LONG YEARS HAD PASSED, and Jessie yearned to see John Charles. During that lonely time, she had the sadness of seeing her mother suffer another stroke and became increasingly feeble. Her only joy had been the growth of Lily. When John Charles had left, Lily was still a baby. Now, he would be amazed at how quickly she had grown. Even with Lily and her father for company, it wasn't the same for Jessie as having John Charles beside her.

She wondered how he looked, how much he had aged since she had seen him last. In one of his letters he had mentioned that his whiskers and hair were showing a touch of gray. Then when all the excitement broke, when it was learned he had been promoted to the rank of lieutenant colonel—and she knew it before he did—she had written a long letter to him. She told him how proud she was of him, and of how such a famous man as Senator Daniel Webster had mentioned his name in Congress and honored his deeds. But even that letter had been sent to him over a year ago; and now, she remembered how she tried to make it light and filled with fun. She even teased him about his age by writing, "How old are you? You might tell me now I am a colonel's wife—won't you, old papa? Poor papa, it made tears come to find you had begun to turn gray."[1] But even in teasing him, the note of sadness was there, the obvious concern and love she had for him.

Now, in August 1847, Jessie knew he might be on his way home, or he might have decided to join his regiment of Mounted Riflemen in Mexico for the last campaigns of the war. Good and disturbing information had been brought all the way from California to Washington in June by Kit Carson, dear old Kit, and young Ned Beale. She had been excited to hear about John Charles's leadership in the conquest of California, and that Commodore Stockton had appointed him governor. But Carson and Beale also had brought more than a hint of trouble.

The couriers—a party of ten that included Carson, Beale, Talbot, Stepp the gunsmith, and others—left California on February 25, 1847. They reached St. Louis the latter part of May. From there word had been sent on to Senator Benton of their arrival, and though the senator wanted Carson to come on to Washington, he had to meet him in St. Louis and talk him into coming to Washington and staying at the Benton home. At that, Kit didn't fancy the idea. As he told the senator, even St. Louis had grown too large and had too many people. The senator convinced him everything would be all right, and at last Kit had agreed.

It was upon his arrival that Jessie learned from both Kit and Beale that things were not right between Frémont and Kearny. When she asked why, Kit had told her there was a struggle for power between General Kearny and Commodore Stockton, and Colonel Frémont was caught in the middle. At least that was the way Kit saw it, and Ned Beale agreed with him.

One thing made it clear to Jessie and her father that there had to be more than just a feeling of ill will that Kit and Ned sensed. As the two men told Jessie and the senator when they left Ciudad de los Angeles, Colonel Frémont had looked upon their mission as one of public service. They were carrying messages to the Secretary of War, the Secretary of State, the Secretary of the Navy, Senator Benton, and Jessie. Frémont had offered their services to Commodore Shubrick and Commodore Stockton, but he had *not* offered such services to General Kearny.

Jessie had been deeply concerned about all this, and Senator Benton had become furious. All of it began to fit together. There had been earlier newspaper accounts—unsigned or signed with a pen name—that painted a poor picture of Frémont and Stockton, one which showed them as men willing to do anything for power. The first of these stories had appeared in the New Orleans *Picayune* of April 22, 1847; a day later the story was printed in the New York *Courier* and *Enquirer*. Then, even before the arrival of Carson and Beale, the Louisville *Journal* of May 1 and the St. Louis *Republican* of May 4, 1847, had carried versions of this scurrilous attack on Frémont and Stockton. After talking to Carson and Beale, Senator Benton was convinced that the story had been circulated by Lieutenant William H. Emory, who had been sent to the States in April by General Kearny.

There was to be no let-up until the culprits were stopped. To make sure of this, Senator Benton began to lay the groundwork at once. He talked to the Secretary of War and the Secretary of State, and made an appointment to see President Polk. But first he wanted Jessie to take Kit Carson to the President as soon as he returned to the city. All of this made Kit's head swim. He was embarrassed in his ill-fitting suit of town clothes, felt completely out of place in such a large city, and was worried that he might disgrace the Benton household because he had once been married to an Indian. This last bit of information was uncovered by Ned Beale when the senator had him talk to Kit to see if he could find out what was bothering him. With only good memories of his Indian wife, Kit told Beale, "She was a good wife to me. I never came in from hunting that she did not have the warm water ready for my feet."[2]

Kit quickly learned this was not something that bothered the Benton family. So, when the appointment with the President came on June 7, 1847, Jessie escorted Kit into President Polk's office and introduced him. Kit had a letter from Colonel/Governor Frémont to Senator Benton which explained the collision between General Kearny and Commodore Stockton, and he handed it to the President. President Polk read it, but he remained noncommittal. Jessie waited for him to say that John Charles was correct in his behavior, but he changed the subject to Carson's career. What she didn't know was that later on Polk wrote in his diary that he thought General Kearny was completely in the right.

One good thing did come out of this meeting with President Polk. Because of his interest in Kit Carson, he saw to it that Carson was given a commission of second lieutenant of the Mounted Rifles at a pay of $33.33 per month, plus $24 per month for rations, $16 per month to pay for forage for two horses, and $16.50 per month for the wages of one servant—or a grand total of $89.83 per month.

All that had taken place two months past, going on three. By now Kit was back in the wide open country, maybe even back at Taos with his third wife, Josefa Jaramillo.[3] But Jessie waited out the lonely, hot and humid days in St. Louis. Every day she hoped to hear something, some news that John Charles was on his way downriver, on his way home. Then as August neared its last days, the word arrived, and it shocked Jessie when she heard. General Kearny had come down the Missouri and Mississippi rivers ahead of her husband, and he had let the news out that at Fort Leavenworth he had placed Colonel Frémont under arrest for mutiny!

At once Jessie made up her mind. There were enough servants in the Benton household to watch over her mother and take care of Lily. She was needed by her husband and needed right now. Determinedly, Jessie booked passage on the steamboat *Martha* and set sail for Westport.

2

NERVOUS AND ANXIOUS, Jessie waited for the arrival of John Charles. She knew he would head for the landing to catch a steamboat for St. Louis. Yet the suspense was great. Two and a half years had passed since she had seen him, but the months of hardship and glory had been tarnished by General Kearny's placing him under arrest. Every time she thought about this despicable act, she became furious. And her anger grew as she waited in discomfort in a log cabin on the bluff overlooking the Missouri River, waited and suffered from the hot, stifling weather. Then one day as she fretted, she heard the sound of many horses moving along the dry and hardened ground, moving toward Westport in the last moments before sunset. She ran outside the cabin, looked toward the wide trail leading away from Westport, and there he was riding at the head of the column.

At once she saw that the hard years and the events of the past months had taken their toll. She could see it in his stern features; and as she ran toward him, she noticed the gray in his beard. But his clothing startled her. There was the tanned face of her husband, but he wore the colorful outfit of a Californio: the fancy trousers, the colorful jacket, the red sash around his waist, and a broadbrimmed hat. It was obvious he had not expected to see her waiting for him beside the Missouri River. At first he was so surprised he remained strangely silent. Then he relaxed, smiled, dismounted, and she ran to his outstretched arms. As he held her close, she began to cry with joy at seeing him and with sadness and anger about the charge of mutiny that General Kearny had brought against him.

He said nothing to her of the way he had been treated by Kearny. All this she learned from Alexis Godey. For when she realized that John Charles had to be away from the people who had recognized him, that he used the excuse of looking out for his men and the horses in order to ease away, Godey told Jessie something of what had happened during the overland march and during their brief halt at Fort Leavenworth, where Colonel Frémont was subjected to insulting treatment on the part of General Kearny, Colonel Wharton, and the other officers and soldiers stationed at the post.

Then Alexis said that things would be all right now that "we have seen the Colonel safe home—we would not trust him with Kearny. We were not under Kearny's orders—the prairies were free and we came along to watch over the Colonel—he's safe now."[4]

Here at Westport, Jessie and John Charles learned that General Kearny had sailed aboard the Amelia on August 23, the day after he had announced to Frémont that he was under arrest. But if he had gone back to St. Louis so quickly to lay the groundwork for his side of this affair, he was destined to receive a minor reception—an offer of a public dinner by a cluster of personal friends, an offer he turned down as he hurried on his way to Washington to closet himself with President Polk.

Yet as Kearny left St. Louis on August 29, not even seeing his wife, who was away from their home because of an illness in the family, Jessie and John Charles had reached St. Louis the day before on the steamboat Martha with Frémont's faithful men. It was anything but a voyage home in disgrace. Unlike General Kearny, who had the support of a few close friends, Frémont was given a hero's welcome all the way down the Missouri and Mississippi rivers. From Westport on, at each stop along the way—no matter how large or small—crowds came forth. They waved the American flag and chanted, "Frémont! Frémont! Frémont!" The news of their coming had traveled ahead of them. Crowds were at Front Street as the Martha docked and the wharf hands secured her lines. People were there to greet the hero of American exploration and the conquerer of California. To them, he was a champion for the people, a romantic symbol of a kind of wild freedom that existed in the West.

Frémont gave a brief speech to the large crowd that waited on the levee, and in turn they cheered when he and Jessie walked down the lowered stageplank.

Invitations came like an avalanche to John Charles and Jessie. Everybody who was anybody wanted to entertain the glamorous Frémonts, to show their belief in the colonel and his lady, and to put General Kearny in his place as a man who wished to smear the good name of their hero. But when he was honored by a large delegation of prominent citizens of St. Louis and asked to be their guest at a public dinner, he politely declined in a long letter of August 30 in which he stated:

> I had the pleasure this morning to receive your letter of this date, in which, with many kind assurances of welcome and congratulations on my return, you honor with the strong expression of your approbation, my geographical labors during the recent explorations in Oregon and North California, and the military operations in which sudden emergencies involved me in California.[5]

Continuing on at some length, he thanked the citizens for their interest in his scientific labors and for their favorable response to his military and political actions in California during that phase of the war with Mexico. Then he closed his letter by writing:

> I regret that, under the present circumstances, I cannot have the pleasure of meeting you at the dinner which you have done me the honor to offer me, but I beg you to accept the assurances of the high and grateful sense which I entertain of your kindness and regard, and of the very flattering manner in which you have expressed it.[6]

It was a proud day for Jessie. All her devotion and faith in her husband was not just the result of her deep love for him. This outpouring of public affection and honor—in the face of adversity—showed her how much respect he commanded. While she understood his reasons for not wishing to attend a public dinner in view of the pending court-martial, a social reception for close friends was held at the home of Colonel Joshua B. Brant on the following day between 10:00 a.m and 2:00 p.m.[7] The long and lonesome time had ended for Jessie, but even as she chatted with old friends who had come to pay their respects and to congratulate John Charles for his accomplishments, she was anxious about the days that lay ahead when his career would be put in jeopardy by a court of military officers.

## 3

WRITING from Woodford County, Kentucky, on September 10, 1847, Senator Benton let President Polk know how he felt about the arrest of John Charles. Putting things bluntly, the senator made it clear that he thought the

President should have full knowledge of what happened in California. Certainly such information should come out in a court-martial, but first there should be a court of inquiry to determine if a court-martial was in order or not. Then the senator pointed out that because of proper form, Colonel Frémont would not be able to pay his respects to the President as he normally would do. Finally, Benton made it clear that either the court of inquiry or the court-martial should take place as soon as possible. This would not only be for the good of Colonel Frémont but also for the future of California.

Six days after Senator Benton sent his letter to President Polk, Frémont arrived in Washington on September 16, and wrote to Adjutant General Roger Jones to report his state of arrest. In his long letter John Charles stressed his need for documents—all documents—for a thirty-day postponement of any trial until Commodore Stockton and his party arrived in Washington, for a complete study of newspaper stories which had smeared both his and Commodore Stockton's names, and for a trial which would not linger on and on and which would cover a wide range of topics.

In an attempt to make sure that everything would be handled correctly to insure justice, many of Frémont's statements in his letter have a redundant quality. It was as though he wanted to be sure that nothing would be overlooked. But the essence of his letter came down to the following:

> These requests I have the honor to make, and hope they will be found to be just, and will be granted. I wish a full trial, and a speedy one. The charges against me by Brigadier General Kearny, and the subsidiary accusations made against me in all the departments of my conduct (military, civil, political, and moral), while in California, and, if true, would subject me to be cashiered and shot, under the rules and articles of war, and to infamy in the public opinion. It is my intention to meet these charges in all their extent and for that purpose to ask a trial upon every point of allegation or insinuation against me, waiving all objections to forms and technicalities, and allowing the widest range to all possible testimony.[8]

Continuing at length, Frémont then stated that he had been defamed in the United States even before he knew what was scheduled to take place once he had arrived home. As he put it to General Jones:

> I was ignorant of all that was going on against me—ignorant of the charges sent from California,—ignorant of the intended arrest, and of the subsidiary publications to prejudice the public mind. What was published in the United States in my favor, by my friends, was done upon their own view of things here, and of which I knew nothing. It was only on my arrival on the frontier of the United States that I became acquainted with these things, which concerned me so nearly. Brought home by General Kearny, and marched in his rear, I did not know of his design to arrest me until the moment of its execution at Fort Leavenworth. He then informed me, that among the charges which he had preferred were mutiny, disobedience of orders, assumption of powers, &c. and referred me to your office for particulars. Accordingly I now

apply for them; and ask for a full and speedy trial, not only on the charges filed by the said General, but on all accusations contained in the publications against me.[9]

Tragedy was accumulating for John Charles as the last of Indian summer's warm days gave a hint of fall. Even as he wrote to General Jones regarding his forthcoming trial, he received sad news from South Carolina. His mother, who had been Mrs. Ann B. Hale for many years now, was gravely ill; and there wasn't much hope that she would live much longer. Without any hesitation, John Charles requested permission to visit her; and on the next day, Friday, September 17, he left for Charleston. On Monday he arrived in the nearby community of Aiken, South Carolina, where his mother lived. But he missed seeing her alive by a matter of a few hours.

The following day John Charles made the last journey with his mother as he took her body to Charleston for burial.[10] He arranged everything for this woman who had sacrificed so much for love and so much for him, and the day after her last rites, he left Charleston and headed back to Washington. As he departed, he knew that his mother had been proud of his accomplishments, and that her pride had spread out and was felt by many other citizens of South Carolina. For in the Charleston *Mercury* of September 21 there was a long article about Frémont. Without any hesitation, the newspaper proclaimed him innocent of dishonorable accusations. It then went on to point out that the people of Charleston had voted to give an honorary sword to him, and that it was backed by individual subscriptions of one dollar per person. In addition, the ladies of Charleston had purchased a gold-mounted belt to hold the sword and its scabbard. All that remained was for Colonel Frémont to receive this gift of honor once he was back in Washington and had gone through the proper period of mourning.[11]

But even a time for mourning was cut short by the necessity to prepare a defense for the forthcoming trial. The lawyers who were to be in Frémont's corner, advising him as he carried out the questioning of witnesses for the defense and the prosecution, were Senator Benton and William Carey Jones, Frémont's brother-in-law.[12] For what was shaping up when John Charles arrived in Washington was a trial that was chasing the news of the Mexican War off the front pages of the newspapers, becoming a daily topic from Washington to the towns and cities beside the Mississippi River, and taking a number-one position as an item for gossip and rumors at Washington social gatherings.

4

SENATOR THOMAS HART BENTON looked on the coming trial as a personal insult to Frémont, Jessie, and himself. He was in the same kind of mood that had thrown him into a wild shooting fray against Andrew Jackson and his cohorts years before. Time had taken its toll in many ways. Such affronts— real or imagined—to one's pride were seldom settled by duels or brawls as the new nation lost more and more of its frontier heritage. Also, the passing of years had robbed Senator Benton of the youthful strength that once would have thrown him to a physical and violent quarrel over something less important than the accusations he considered a smear against his son-in-law and all those related or friendly to him. Still, the old warrior had the power of a senior member of the United States Senate. Added to this, he was a power in the Democratic Party that had put "dark horse" James Knox Polk into the office of President of the United States. The time had come to call for payment on political debts, and Senator Benton went right to the White House to make his first collection.

It was late in October, and the court-martial was not far away when Senator Benton had his appointment with President Polk for a little talk. Like a wounded lion charging out of a thicket, Benton told Polk that Kearny was a malignant force, a destructive man determined to destroy the brilliant career of Colonel Frémont. Justice, complete and thorough, was what the senator called for. Going on at length, he stressed the great accomplishments of his son-in-law, in exploration and in seeing to it that California had an American flag flying above its harbors, cities, and towns. It was no small thing that Colonel Frémont had accomplished, not something that could be done by the run-of-the-mill officer. Frémont had made the United States into a Two Ocean Nation. As for General Kearny, he was a man who had seen better days, a man who had been defeated in California, and, worst of all, a man who wished to take out his bitterness and jealousy on a junior officer.

Warming to his topic, Senator Benton looked at President Polk as both men sat in front of blazing logs in the fireplace. The men who had scurried about from newspaper to newspaper and who had spread malicious rumors about Frémont were disreputable officers, no more than toadies for General Kearny. Before any thought of a court-martial, Benton proclaimed, there should be a court of inquiry. If a full court of inquiry were not held, then there would be no other choice than to court-martial Kearny's toadies: William H. Emory, Philip St. George Cooke, and Henry S. Turner.

President Polk listened to the senator's excited defamation of these men, and heard his praise of Frémont. Polk had very little to say. It was only after this meeting with Senator Benton that President Polk expressed his feelings in his diary. Plainly, he had not liked this conversation, which had turned into more of a lecture than anything else. For Senator Benton to carry on in such a manner was an insult to himself and to the office of the President.

He had listened to Senator Benton. But if there had ever been a chance to change his mind, Benton's roughshod approach had eliminated it. For after the senator left the White House, President Polk wrote in his diary that he saw no reason for any more interest or excitement in Lieutenant Colonel Frémont's trial than that of any other officer.

Yet President Polk was avoiding the obvious. Colonel Frémont was not the same as any other officer charged with a military offense. His government reports of his explorations were best sellers. His trouble with General Kearny—thanks to the officers around Kearny—was already well known throughout the country. But most of all, John Charles Frémont was a popular hero. To put such a man on trial for what most citizens would consider either good judgment or minor transgressions was to court public outrage. Then to compound the trouble that such a trial would cause the administration, there was the matter of public affection for Jessie Benton Frémont, the hero's wife; the solid bloc of Western-minded men who were followers and backers of Senator Thomas Hart Benton; and the fact that messages from the executive branch of the government were confusing at best, and contradictory at worst. All this would come to a head in a court-martial of Frémont, and President Polk must have been aware of it. Yet his own pride had been hurt, and he decided to avoid a court of inquiry and plow ahead with the trial. All of this was coming just as the unpopular war with Mexico was ending, just as the casualty lists were a daily reminder that the military had carried out an invasion of a smaller nation even though a great portion of the public protested such an action.

If President Polk believed he was doing the right thing at the right time, he was not very cognizant of events breaking about him. But he was determined to go ahead, and November 2, 1847, was set as the date for the start of the court-martial.

5

THE SETTING FOR THE TRIAL was announced. It was to be held at Fort Monroe, Virginia. This would be away from the tension and the pro-Frémont factions in Washington or New York. It would be quiet, isolated, and ideal for the military. There would be few civilian spectators, and there would not be the swarm of newspaper reporters that the trial would draw in a major city.

Frémont and his advisors were well aware of the basic reasons for selecting such a site. It would tend to hide the daily proceedings from public scrutiny, and make it difficult for Senator Benton and William Carey Jones to be present for each session in the court. Sensing all this, Colonel Frémont wrote to Adjutant General Roger Jones on October 11, 1847, and requested that the trial to be held closer to his means of counsel and defense.

In the same letter he wrote that he should also be tried on the basis of various allegations that had appeared in the newspapers—allegations that were on file in the adjutant general's office. By no means, Frémont pointed out, could these stories be called anonymous. The source had been revealed by the editors of the New Orleans *Picayune*, the Louisville *Journal*, the St.

Louis *Republican*, and the Pittsburgh *Gazette*. The man who had given out such information was none other than Lieutenant William H. Emory, and anything this officer made public should be included in the specifications under Brigadier General Kearny's charges.

Two days later Colonel Frémont received a short answer from General Jones. Newspaper accounts would not be added to the list of charges, and the site for the trial would remain as indicated. This appeared to be the final statement from the army, but Senator Benton and William Carey Jones refused to give up. On October 25 they sent a long, detailed letter to Adjutant General Jones. In this document they requested everything that could be of any use—no matter how small—for the defense of their client. Their request included such diverse items as all orders issued by Adjutant General Jones to Brigadier General Kearny; orders issued to Commodore Sloat, Commodore Stockton, and Commodore Shubrick; correspondence between United States Consul Thomas Oliver Larkin and the Honorable Secretary of State regarding the events leading up to the California conflict; all communications and publications about Colonel Frémont's challenge to Colonel Mason to fight a duel; and all newspaper stories pertinent to their client's case.

That was only the opening request. Getting to the heart of the matter, warming up to their subject, the attorneys for the defense wrote:

The undersigned, in looking over the charges and specifications, perceive that there are three sets of charges on the same specifications, so as to give the prosecution three chances against Lt. Col. Frémont on the same point. The first charge is "MUTINY,"—the punishment for which *may* be death, and the conviction for which is *always infamous*. The second charge is for *"Disobedience of the lawful commands of his superior officer,"*—the punishment for which *may* be trivial, and the conviction a title to honor & preferment. The third charge is for *"Conduct to the prejudice of good order and military discipline,"*—which might involve no higher point than a piece of form, of etiquette, or a punctilio. Between the degree of enormity of these three charges the difference is immense & immeasurable; and although in criminal prosecutions at Common Law a man may be indicted for murder and manslaughter on the same act, yet in Courts Martial, which concern the honor as well as the lives of officers, and where proceedings should be direct and simple, and go to convictions on the merits instead of technicalities and punctilios, every charge should have its separate specifications; and where so high a crime as mutiny is charged, no inferior charge should be predicated on the same act. But in this case the proceeding goes further than at Common Law: it goes to *three* different charges, of three degrees of enormity, for the same act, the first charge the highest, the last the lowest in the military code; while an indictment for murder and manslaughter never goes down to a conviction for some petty insult. The undersigned have deemed it their duty to notice, *and at this time,* this three fold prosecution on the same sets of acts, but they are instructed by Lieut. Col. Frémont to go into trial upon the whole—to make no objection to any thing—but to insist to the last upon a full trial—a trial upon the points of accusation against him in all the charges of Genl. Kearny,—in all the subsidiary publications,—in all the published letters from Washington City assuming the air of semi-officiality; and, in fine, upon all his conduct in California.[13]

This wasn't all that the two defense attorneys asked of Adjutant General Jones. They also requested that the trial be moved from Fort Monroe, Virginia. Here, as they pointed out, was an unjust handicap. Fort Monroe was two hundred miles away from Washington. It was not close to any metropolis, and could be said to be located in an out-of-the-way place. Such a location for such an important trial was outrageous. It meant that if last-minute information—facts which could have an important bearing upon the jury's ultimate decision—turned up in Washington, it would be impossible for the defense to get them to the court on time, even if they were fortunate enough to hear about them. Furthermore, it meant that the defense would be removed from reference documents in offices and libraries; and it would be difficult for witnesses for the defense to be brought to the scene of the trial. "Under these circumstances, the undersigned ask that the place of the trial be changed to Washington City."[14]

Finally, to prove their contention that the stories given to newspapers by both Lieutenant William H. Emory and Colonel Philip St. George Cooke were defamatory in nature and prejudiced the case against Colonel Frémont, the counsel for the defense included articles, to prove their point, from the Pittsburg *Gazette* of May 1847 and the Baltimore *Sun* of June 1847.

Adjutant General Roger Jones replied on the same day the attorneys for the defense wrote to him. He refused to give any ground on his previous rulings which eliminated newspaper articles from consideration as charges against Colonel Frémont. Nor did he agree to a change of courtroom setting. However, he did give in on official documents and papers that had any potential bearing on the trial. Yet General Jones had underestimated the power of Senator Benton. The old warrior of many political campaigns and many courtroom battles managed to see to it that the site of the court-martial was changed, and this was done in a hurry, as Benton collected political debts. The day after this exchange of letters General Jones wrote to Senator Benton and William Carey Jones to inform them that by direction of President Polk, the scene of the trial had been changed from Fort Monroe to the Washington Arsenal.

Still, this wasn't the last trick Senator Benton had in his mind. After the beginning of the trial, he gave his own letter of October 27 and the reply of Adjutant General Jones to the *National Intelligencer* for publication. But he was wise enough to wait until he had received the papers he had requested from the War and Navy Departments, as well as other pertinent documents and orders.

## Court-Martial

THE DAY WAS WARM for November 2, 1847. Indian summer lingered longer than usual in Washington. But there was an electric excitement in the air as this was the opening of the court-martial. The city was filled with visitors and regulars. Congressmen had returned from visiting their respective constituents. Visiting army officers, hoping to get a seat at the trial, strolled up and down Pennsylvania Avenue; and there was even a contingent of American Indians who happened to be in Washington as guests of the "Great White Father." But the major event, the key story in all the newspapers, was the opening of the trial for the handsome explorer of the American West and the conqueror of California.

At high noon the official opening of the court-martial began at the old Washington Arsenal—a building best described as a run-down, wooden affair about as dressy as unshined boots with holes in their soles. The chamber devoted to the trial held only two hundred persons, and it had the same twilight quality about it as the rest of the building. The ceiling was high domed, and only shadowy light from the noontime sun filtered in through the windows near the roof. It was gloomy atmosphere, but it was fitting and proper for the proceedings about to begin.

A special omnibus had carried the panel of trial officers to the building, and Brevet Brigadier General G. M. Brooke, president of the court, opened the first session of the trial. Captain John Fitzgerald Lee, the judge advocate, called the roll of those who should be present, and found that Brevet Major G. A. McCall was sick and unable to attend. All the other officers were present and accounted for as well as the defendant and the attorneys for the defense and prosecution. Contrary to Senator Benton's later accusations that the court was composed of West Point men out to get an officer who had not graduated from the Point, the majority of the officers were men who had come up through the ranks and had not graduated from West Point. Still, there was another factor involved with these men. Eleven of the thirteen officers had thirty years or more of Regular Army service, and a twelfth had twenty-nine years of service. Four of the officers from the thirteen were West Point men, and one of these—thirty-four-year-old Captain John Fitzgerald Lee—was the judge advocate or prosecuting attorney. Two other members of the court—General Brooke and Colonel De Russey—had done stints as administrators of the United States Military Academy. All in all, the court was Regular Army through and through, and that said more about its composition than any graduation from West Point.

Colonel Frémont sat at a side table with Senator Thomas Hart Benton and William Carey Jones. They were awaiting the court's decision as to whether or not the two nonmilitary attorneys would be allowed to play a role in the trial. For the moment, the lawyers were permitted to sit beside Frémont until the court decided if they were to be given permission to act as counsel for the defendant.

The audience gathered for the first day was a conglomerate of personalities. Jessie Benton Frémont had not gone along with her sister Eliza's suggestion that both of them should dress in black. With her strong-willed touch, Jessie told her sister this was not an occasion for mourning. They were not attending a funeral. So there they sat, and it was a display of faith and complete confidence that other spectators saw. Jessie's striking beauty was something no member of the audience would ever forget. Here was no grieving wife, trying to be as inconspicuous as possible. Here was a proud woman who attracted all eyes as she sat composed and controlled in her wine-colored dress and her bonnet of burgundy velvet. Beside her, Eliza was the color of a bright spring morning in her gay blue dress.

The filtered light that captured the dust and cobwebs of the old high-ceilinged room also glanced off the bright gold braid of dress uniforms, and picked up the stern features of General Kearny, who was to be the star witness for the prosecution. Beside him sat his associate from the Army of the West, Captain Henry S. Turner. Away from the uniforms, there were congressmen who had managed to get into the courtroom, reporters who were awaiting a ruling on whether or not they would be allowed to witness this trial, and a handful of Frémont men, who drew attention because of his descriptions of them in his official reports—men such as Alexis Godey and Richard Owens.

It was drama of the highest order. The curtain had been raised. The audience was seated, and the play's opening had begun with Captain Lee's calling of the roll as though the first chorus in a Greek tragedy were being recited. But the opening was brought to a halt by the absence of Major McCall. General Brooke adjourned the court until the next day, Wednesday, November 3. One thing had been accomplished during this brief meeting. The spectators and the press were introduced to the cast of characters and the stage setting. The next day they would be prepared for the first movements in this drama of age vs. youth, junior officer vs. senior officer, and rebellion vs. tradition. All of it would become a daily reminder that this new nation was now faced with its own crisis of authority, its own growth of rule-book heritage, and its home-grown challenge of youth, imagination, and irregularity.

2

ON THE NEXT DAY, the last details of protocol were the items to be covered. Lieutenant Colonel T. F. Hunt—a deputy quartermaster general—was named as the replacement for Major McCall. The proceedings of the first day were given, and the orders assembling and detailing the court were read by the judge advocate. When Captain Lee finished, he asked Colonel Frémont if he had objections to any of the members of the court listed in the orders. When Frémont replied that he did not, the judge advocate then administered the oath prescribed by law to the court. In turn, the same oath was administered to him by the president of the court.

With these steps fulfilled, Colonel Frémont was allowed to present a written document. In this paper, he stated he did not intend to base his defense on any legal or technical point. All he desired was "friendly assistance in bringing out the merits of the case in lucid and proper order, and in obtaining a full trial on the merits, in the shortest time, and with the least amount of trouble to the court."[1]

Two other requests were made by Colonel Frémont. He was willing to waive proof about the authenticity of papers used as evidence against him only if "all persons brought from California by General Kearny, for witnesses, and listed as such with the charges, and summoned, shall be sworn on the part of the prosecution, so as to save to me my right of cross-examination."[2] Finally, he asked that the court allow Thomas Hart Benton and William Carey Jones to act as his counsel.

His requests were noted by the court, but the only one allowed granted him the services of Benton and Jones as his counsel. This was subject to military rules, which meant that the attorneys could act in an advisory capacity only. They could not cross-examine witnesses or make official statements before the court as they were civilians. In the day-by-day give and take of the trial, Colonel Frémont would have to serve as his own defense attorney since he elected to have civilian counsel. With this request out of the way, the court directed the judge advocate to read the charges against the defendant.

*Mutiny.* Captain Lee carefully spelled out that Lieutenant Colonel Frémont had refused to obey the orders of his superior officer, General Kearny, beginning on January 17, 1847, when he presented his written document to General Kearny in which he declared himself to be the military commandant of California. This, as the judge advocate stressed, was open mutiny against a superior officer and against the orders of the President of the

United States. Then to back up this charge, and the only charge that General Kearny wanted to press, Captain Lee listed eleven specifications which were other aspects of the basic charge. Along with this, he submitted written orders from the general to the colonel, and a chronological exchange of letters between the two men that showed the various stages of mutiny from January 17 to May 9, 1847, when General Kearny arrived in Ciudad de los Angeles and verbally repeated his final orders to Frémont in which he told him to settle his California affairs and get ready for the overland journey with Kearny's command on their march back to the United States.

*Disobedience of the lawful command of his superior officer.* To this charge Captain Lee read seven specifications plus the documents as evidence to be submitted to the court. The time span for the listed offenses again covered the period from January 17 to May 9, 1847.

*Conduct to the prejudice of good order and military discipline.* To this, the judge advocate listed five specifications, presented various documents of evidence to the court, noted that Lieutenant Colonel Frémont had pleaded not guilty, and ended his presentation of the charges.

In the tradition of a good prosecuting attorney, Captain Lee had put forth a wide range of charges that varied from the highest in mutiny to the lowest in what might be termed a minor breach of military form. But the obvious approach of the judge advocate in issuing such a wide and disparate range of charges was to obtain a conviction of Frémont on something. It was the old legal game of put forth enough charges and present enough incriminating—or apparently incriminating—evidence to make sure that the defendant would be found guilty on at least one of the charges.

By the time the judge advocate finished with all the charges and specificacations plus the documents and correspondence, the second day of the trial was near its end. In the closing moments, the president of the court stated that an "application had been made to admit reporters into the courtroom to report the daily proceedings of the court; for publication. . . ."[3] He also read a paper from Lieutenant Colonel Frémont in which the defendant agreed to the publication of everything. All of this called for a clearing of the court of spectators, and the jury then deliberated and agreed that reporters would be allowed to attend the trial, but that the court would not sanction or approve the publication of the hearings.

But if the court thought reporters and newspapers were going to take their ruling about publication to heart, they had misjudged the ability of reporters to circle around red tape and get the essence of a story into newspapers without putting themselves in danger of being removed from the courtroom. Frémont was big news, and his court-martial was even bigger news. The ruling of the court only served as a warning to reporters to be careful. It amounted to no more than that, for things could always be attributed to an unknown source, a rumor, talk of the town, an editorial about military justice, or local color in the courtroom with some of the testimony thrown in for good measure. For if John Charles was naïve about the backroom maneuvers of the military, the officers of the court were blissfully ignorant about their lack of control over civilian newspapermen. All of this was clear as the first papers were for sale not long after the ending of the opening of the trial and the reading of the charges. No newspaper was going to bypass the chance to run a headline story on the striking and popular explorer who was faced with a charge of *mutiny*.

3

WORKING with his father-in-law and brother-in-law, Frémont prepared a defense that centered around two key objectives. First, he developed a line of questioning intended to show that the trial was basically about a dispute of command between General Kearny and Commodore Stockton. Second, his counsel advised him to discredit Kearny as a witness. Here, the plan of attack was to show that General Kearny was a man with a vindictive temper, that his memory was either faulty or that he was pretending to forget in order to avoid the truth. In short, show that General Kearny bore false witness.

By taking the offense as a defense, by aiming at these key objectives, Frémont was permitted a wide range of questions. Some of these questions appeared to have nothing at all to do with the case, but the president of the court and the judge advocate were not quick enough to prevent such miscellaneous and irrelevant material from coming to light and from being entered in the record of the trial. To make matters even more unusual in a court-martial, the combination of Benton, Jones, and Frémont made a formidable trio. The two lawyers were adroit in feeding a wide range of questions to their client, and Frémont proved to be an excellent inquisitor as he grilled the witnesses for the prosecution.

Before his first day of questioning General Kearny, Colonel Frémont addressed the court and gave the general scope of the questions he intended to put forth. He stated that the charges and specifications against him had to do with the struggle for command between General Kearny and Commodore Stockton, and that the trial was "in fact, that of Commodore Stockton of the navy, in the person of Lieutenant Colonel Frémont, of the army. . . ."[4]

After outlining the general scope of his defense, Frémont stated its second branch. It was hardly one destined to win friends among the officers who sat as members of the court. But he set the tone for the trial as he said that he intended "to impeach the motives of the prosecutor, by showing his acts and conduct towards me during a period of six months and twenty-one days of time, and over a distance of about three thousand miles of travelling, and for that purpose to avail myself of all the rights of a cross-examination of the prosecutor and his witnesses, as well as the direct examination of my own."[5]

Following this statement, Lieutenant Colonel Frémont began his first day of cross-examining Brigadier General Kearny. And the first question he asked was to be repeated time and again throughout the trial, almost in incremental repetition.

"At what time did you form the design to arrest Lieutenant Colonel Frémont?"[6]

"I formed the design shortly after receiving his letter of January 17. That word shortly would not imply immediately. It may have been a week."[7]

Here was a weak link in Kearny's accusatory chain. He was the general of the Army of the West. If he had decided to arrest Frémont—whether it had been a matter of one minute, one hour, or one week after their January 17 meeting—then why didn't he put the lieutenant colonel in irons and hold a trial in California at once? He had the power, under wartime conditions, to try and even execute any man guilty of mutiny.

Instead, General Kearny allowed this subordinate to step way beyond the mere questioning of his authority. He had stood by as Commodore Stockton appointed Colonel Frémont Military Governor of California. All Kearny did was to complain to Stockton, and even his complaint hardly carried much in the way of conviction and authority. Not until March, two months later—not until he had established his headquarters at Monterey, away from Frémont and away from the scene of any further potential rebellion on the part of the Californios—did General Kearny assert himself.

Then and only then did he remove Frémont from the position of governor, a position he then assumed for himself. At this time and place, over four hundred miles away from Ciudad de los Angeles, General-Governor Kearny began to issue definite orders to Lieutenant Colonel Frémont. But by this time, Commodore Stockton was sailing south along the Pacific Coast in search of opportunities for glory. While in Monterey, Kearny had gathered about him a small but loyal group of men who did not like Frémont and who were as anxious to see his downfall as was General Kearny. Commodore Shubrick and then Commodore Biddle took General Kearny's side in this dispute. In the army there was Colonel Mason, who was willing to fight a duel with Frémont—using shotguns loaded with buckshot—as well as Major Philip St. George Cooke and Lieutenant William H. Emory, who had already been sent to the States to spread rumors about Frémont's insurgency.

General Kearny's answer to this question, this barbed bit of logic that inquisitor Colonel Frémont asked during the long sessions while Kearny was the star witness for the prosecution, was that he did not have the men; he lacked the force of arms. It was a strange answer for General Kearny to fall back upon, and it had the ring of paranoia. Where was the great force to prevent his arresting Colonel Frémont? Was Colonel Frémont engaged in a conspiracy with the United States Navy, or at least that part of it under Commodore Stockton's command? Or was he involved in some strange way with the men of the California Battalion, or even the Californios, to take over California and prevent General Kearny from carrying out his orders from the Secretary of War and President Polk?

Time after time, Frémont baited Kearny with his reason for not arresting him at once. Time after time, he asked why he had not been told that the general had received orders which overrode—in terms of dates—similar orders which Commodore Stockton possessed and *he* assumed gave him the right to establish a civil government and appoint Frémont as the military governor of California. But General Kearny's answers fell into a strange pattern: He couldn't remember; he did remember the day after the question had been asked and when he had looked over his own written orders; but most of all, he had no reason to tell a subordinate officer the nature of any order unless so directed within the context of said order.

But what was the order? What was so important that General Kearny felt compelled to assert his superior rank and to bring on such a court-martial?

The letter to Brigadier General Kearny from Secretary of War William L. Marcy dated June 3, 1846, was ambiguous. For a key instruction within the text of the document was the foundation for General Kearny's logic that he had been ordered to assume control of everything and everybody in California.

Should you conquer and take possession of New Mexico and California, or considerable places in either, you will establish civil governments therein; abolishing all arbitrary restrictions that may exist, so far as it may be done with safety. In performing this duty, it would be wise and prudent to continue in their employment all such existing officers as are known to be friendly to the United States and will take the oath of allegiance to them.[8]

*Should you conquer and take possession* was the puzzler for Colonel Frémont and Commodore Stockton. To both officers it had been only too obvious that General Kearny and the Army of the West had not conquered nor taken possession of anything. They had been warned of trouble in California even as they had reached Warner's Ranch. Yet they had paid no heed. Instead, they suffered terrible casualties at the Battle of San Pascual—a battle that only the most jingoistic military man could look upon as a victory. Added to that, they had been rescued from Mule Hill by a combined force of sailors and marines. This was General Kearny's badly shattered force that had limped into San Diego, and it was not a force that had conquered or possessed anything. The best the survivors could claim was that they were still alive.

A second factor which Frémont drew out of Kearny in his cross-examination and in the complete presentation of documents plus the testimony of other witnesses for both the defense and the prosecution was that in the retaking of San Gabriel and Ciudad de los Angeles, General Kearny had turned down the position of commander-in-chief for the operation when Commodore Stockton had offered it to him.

Nor could the general claim that his worn and shattered troops had been of much use in either of these battles. As the testimony came out, as the documents were admitted as evidence, it was obvious that the fighting that turned the tide in these battles had been carried out for the most part by the fresh troops of the United States Marines and the United States Navy.

Even the compiled list of the killed and wounded for these two battles had been sent to Commodore Stockton by General Kearny in a manner which acknowledged the superior position of the commodore, as the general began this communication with the following: "His Excellency R. F. Stockton, Governor of California."

Yet, despite all these obvious indications of Kearny's recognition of Stockton's superior position, the moment the commodore was no longer around, the general jumped at the chance to assert his authority. He looked upon Frémont as the natural person to inherit his winds of spite.

Bad feelings were not limited to the prosecution's star witness. Pushed by Senator Benton and by his own bitterness, Colonel Frémont ranged from key topics to almost meaningless ones as he set out to interrogate General Kearny.

Who delivered the message that I signed on January 17?

General Kearny didn't remember.

Was it not the same man you met at Socorro, the man called Kit Carson, the man who guided you to California?

On the next day, Kearny apologized. It came back to him.

Yes, it had been Carson. But that had been some time ago.

Did you lose a cannon at the Battle of San Pascual?

General Kearny admitted they had, but he had been severely wounded. Events of that day were not that clear.

Did the General recall who recovered the cannon?

No.

And why not? The cannon was in front of Colonel Frémont's headquarters at Ciudad de los Angeles. Didn't the General see it?

No, I never went to Colonel Frémont's headquarters, and I didn't know that the cannon was there.

The trap was sprung. Frémont read from the seventh specification of the charge of mutiny. The general had charged Lieutenant Colonel Frémont with refusing to give up two cannons *"brought by the 1st dragoons from Fort Leavenworth, and then at San Gabriel."*[9]

In black and white. One of the specifications. There was a pause and silence in the shadowy light of the Arsenal. Then Kearny replied it had not been his charge. The charges had been changed from what he had desired.

But the general continued with his answer: "The two howitzers, however, referred to, are the howitzers which were brought by the 1st dragoons from Fort Leavenworth."[10]

Did the General give this information out so that it could be included as a specification in the first charge?

No.

Did the General recognize the fact that one of these cannons had been lost at San Pascual?

Again, the answer was no. Time after time, the General had to reply no, or I don't recall or remember. He pleaded that he had been badly wounded on the day the cannon had been lost. He couldn't remember. It was logical, but it was a specification for the charge of mutiny as the general claimed that Frémont refused to return the nonremembered cannon.

But not all the witnesses who might have been called were available. If they had been, Doctor John S. Griffin, the assistant surgeon for the 1st Dragoons, would have had another story to tell, one that was written in his diary:

> We saw the howitzer we lost at San Pascual—the only regret I had in seeing this was that the Enemy should have delivered it up, before we had an opportunity to take it, or some other piece from the Mexicans.[11]

Would not an assistant surgeon have told his wounded and recovering general about the missing howitzer that was in front of Frémont's headquarters? Or did the general forget that he had been told about the cannon? Still, it could play no role in the trial as Dr. Griffin did not testify. Yet it is a curious sidelight that General Kearny was unable to remember something which his assistant surgeon saw come into Ciudad de los Angeles with Colonel Frémont and his California Battalion and which sat in front of the colonel's headquarters in what could hardly be called a large metropolis.

Memory plays tricks, but tricky minds can play havoc with memory. Colonel Frémont came back to the howitzer more than once, but General Kearny stuck to his story of not remembering. And maybe he couldn't. Maybe the general suffered from early senility. For it wasn't just the cannon that he couldn't remember. As Frémont picked and probed, as he skillfully grilled his accuser, he found that General Kearny couldn't remember many things. Pouncing upon this as a means to discredit Kearny's testimony, he pointed out that the general couldn't remember Carson's delivering the letter to him in the general's office on January 17. The general couldn't remember Gillespie or Beale even though both men had played key roles in saving the men of the 1st Dragoons from a massacre. The general couldn't remember just why Colonel Frémont had made an incredible horseback ride of over four hundred miles in less than four days to see him in his Monterey headquarters. Item after item appeared to be lost forever to the general's memory, and his testimony became a litany: I don't remember, recall, recollect; and then, yes, now, that I see the document, the letter, the time sequence; yes it was that way; *I just didn't remember.*

The days of ordeal continued for General Kearny as Colonel Frémont appeared fresh and ready for each day's round of cross-examination. Repetition played a key role in questioning the witness for the prosecution. The general made one statement one day; then he would contradict that statement on the next day, or a day or two later. When this happened, Frémont was always ready to seize the chance to pursue inconsistency of testimony, to get Kearny to admit he had said another thing at another time. The general seemed befuddled. He was a man groping, trying to hang on, trying to keep his reserve and give the appearance of a superior officer. But the colonel was young and quick-witted, and he adroitly phrased his questions so that the general was guided to the edge of confusion and near the limits of perjury.

On one day General Kearny said that Colonel Frémont had destroyed documents before he had an opportunity to see them. But the next day, the general retracted this statement, and said:

I meant by no means to intimate that Colonel Frémont had designedly destroyed, or lost, papers. I meant merely, in presenting copies, to say that the originals were received by him, and were, of course, not in my hands.[12]

Then General Kearny accused Colonel Frémont of trying to strike a bargain for the governorship of California. But in the cross-examination, he admitted he had intended to offer Colonel Frémont the position once he left for Missouri with his troops, but all that had been before the colonel had refused to take back his mutinuous letter of January 17, 1847. A letter which the general had said would cause the colonel "unquestionable ruin."

Frémont seized this term, this damning description, and used it for its effect upon the court and spectators.

QUESTION: What did you mean by words "unquestionable ruin," as alleged to have been addressed by you to Lieutenant Colonel Frémont on the 17th of January? and did you there contemplate his arrest and trial before a court martial?

ANSWER: I meant as the words imply. I did not then contemplate at that time the arrest of Lieutenant Colonel Frémont, because I was in hopes that a little reflection would convince him of the error of adhering to the course indicated in his letter to me.[13]

The display in the old Washington Arsenal did not give a good impression of the military, and it did not promote General Kearny's public reputation. He had openly accused Colonel Frémont of a base act, of bargaining for the position of military governor of California. Then the general admitted he had warned the colonel of his *unquestionable ruin.* It was backroom day in the officers' quarters, an unknown view to the civilians in the audience, and spectacular copy for all the newspapers. But there was more as the days passed, and the general grew weary. He claimed he had not heard of the debts Colonel Frémont had incurred to run the government in California and to pay the California Battalion. He appeared to be baffled that Colonel Frémont might have offered his resignation from the United States Army when he made his long ride from Ciudad de los Angeles. Then he recalled that the resignation had been offered, but that he had refused to accept it. The list grew as each day of testimony came to a conclusion.

QUESTION: Did you leave any of the men of the topographical party behind in California?

ANSWER: Some of the volunteers asked to be discharged in California, and I directed Lieutenant Colonel Frémont to discharge them accordingly. I will explain. When Lieutenant Colonel Frémont brought his command mounted near to my quarters, I asked of them if any wished to be discharged in California. Some did wish it, and I gave the directions to Lieutenant Colonel Frémont accordingly to discharge them. Those who wished to be discharged, separated themselves from the main party, and moved to one side of the street.

QUESTION: Did you leave Mr. Kern, the artist, and Mr. King, and assistant behind, and are they not yet behind?

ANSWER: Those gentlemen were left behind in California not by my orders or directions.

QUESTION: Did you leave behind, and refuse Lieutenant Colonel Frémont permission to go to Yerba Buena for them, the geological and botanical specimens which he had been collecting in the two years of his last expedition?

ANSWER: Lieutenant Colonel Frémont expressed a wish to go to Yerba Buena, which I refused to grant him.[14]

Question and answer. Objections by the judge advocate. The courtroom cleared for deliberations on the admissibility of questions, of evidence, of the line of reason. The courtroom doors opened again, and the movement of the spectators as they settled into their seats, said their last whispered bits of conversation, and then with a rap of a gavel, the president of the court would call the proceedings to order. General Kearny back in the witness chair. Benton and Jones conferring with their client. Then Colonel Frémont would step forth, and the questions and answers would begin once again. All those days from the first reading of charges until November 18, it was the accused vs. the accuser, the junior officer vs. the senior officer. Then as General Stephen Watts Kearny stepped away from the witness chair—even though it was only for an interlude—he was replaced by Major Philip St. George Cooke, who had been held up at the last moment from rushing off to the last days of the war in Mexico. But Major Cooke was not going to be far away from the tools of war. For the very first question Colonel Frémont asked him had to do with the howitzers belonging to the Army of the West.

Wasn't it true that he, Major Cooke, had been ordered to ride over to the camp of the California Battalion and retrieve the howitzers?

I called on Captain Owens in his quarters, and, shortly after, asked to look at the artillery. He showed them to me in the court of the mission, and I observed two mountain howitzers, which I believed to have been brought to the country by the dragoons. I had received verbal instructions from General Kearny, by Captain Turner, to have them turned over to company C, of my command, and had, before I left town, ordered mules and drivers to be sent after them; of which I informed Captain Owens. He answered that I could not get them; that he had received orders not to let them go from his hands.[15]

*Verbal instructions from General Kearny* . . . , but the general didn't know about the cannons. He had testified he had never been told. Yet Major Cooke had his orders. To Colonel Frémont and his counsel this was a fine moment, a good way to close the fading moments of testimony on this November 18.

From the last hours of November 18 to the afternoon of November 27, Major Cooke occupied the witness chair. During that time, Lieutenant Colonel Frémont did his best to show that the major was a prejudiced witness and that his testimony should be disregarded.

Not giving up, continuing with the same point, Frémont introduced Major Cooke's letter of March 25, 1847, to Captain Henry Turner.

> My God! to think of a howitzer brought over the deserts with so much faithful labor by the dragoons; the howitzer with which they have four times fought the enemy, and brought here to the rescue of Lieutenant Colonel Frémont and his volunteers, to be refused to them by this Lieutenant Colonel Frémont, and in defiance of the orders of his general! I denounce this treason, or this mutiny, which jeopardizes the safety of the country, and defies me in my legal command and duties, by men too who report, and say, that they believe that the enemy approaches from without, and are about to rise in arms around us.[16]

Nor was that all of it. Major Cooke went on to say that Mr. Russell had left for the States, taking public animals with him. But, and here was the terrible implication, he had left for the States with a petition in favor of Lieutenant Colonel Frémont—a petition signed by Californios. And it wasn't only the howitzers that Captain Owens had refused to give his command. He had refused to give over any of the ordnance, and he said that the herd of horses was no longer available.

But the most damning thing which came out of Major Cooke's week of testimony was the inclusion of an article from the Missouri *Republican* of June 14, 1847, an article signed with the pseudonym of "Justice," which Colonel Frémont and his counsel believed to have been written by Major Cooke. This long, rambling piece painted a heroic picture of General Stephen Watts Kearny, and in the closing paragraphs besmirched Colonel John Charles Frémont as a man who had misused his position of power for his own glory, a man who had aroused the tempers of both Commodore Stockton and General Kearny by his insubordinate behavior, by his assuming powers that were not his, and by bargaining between Kearny and Stockton until the latter weakened and appointed him military governor of California.

All of this invective had been spelled out in a letter "From California, San Diego, Upper California, February, 1847." But after it had been read to the court, the judge advocate made a motion to have the court cleared. When the spectators were gone, the court deliberated upon the contents of the letter, and then decided that no questions should be put to Major Cooke about it, "but that the publication be entered on the records. . . ."[17]

After Major Cooke was dismissed, the next witness was Lieutenant William H. Emory. But the prosecution had refused to call him as a witness. In so doing, the only way to get him to the stand was to have him called as a witness for the defense. This meant sacrificing the right of cross-examination. Still, part of Lieutenant Emory's role as a hatchet man for General Kearny came out as Colonel Frémont managed to have newspaper articles based on correspondence from Lieutenant Emory read into the record of the trial. One of these articles, which Emory denied writing, was a letter addressed to the New Orleans *Picayune,* which appeared in that newspaper's April 8, 1847, edition. In this letter the author wrote of serious disputes between General Kearny and Commodore Stockton over command of the civil government of California, and then pointed out that "it is to be lamented, that Stockton drew Colonel Frémont on his side. It is to be hoped the President will cause the affair to be investigated at once."[18]

It was strange that the prosecution refused to call a man who had seen Colonel Frémont commit the supposed acts that had brought him before a military court. The only logical answer was that by not calling Emory as a witness for the prosecution, the defense was denied the right of cross-examination, where a series of questions plus the testimony of other witnesses might well have shown that Lieutenant Emory was guilty of slander, perjury, and illegal collusion with General Kearny.

4

IT WAS A STRANGE COINCIDENCE that on December 6, 1847, just one year after the Battle of San Pascual, the first major witness for Colonel Frémont's defense was Commodore Robert F. Stockton. Always the dandy, his rugged features clean-shaven and his wavy hair neatly groomed, Commodore Stockton was a man the crowded Washington Arsenal had been waiting to see. It had been only since the last part of October that the commodore had departed from St. Joseph, Missouri, after his overland crossing; and it was assumed by all that he had hurried to Washington to settle the bickering as to who commanded the armed forces of the United States in California during Colonel Frémont's presence in that distant field of action.

But the answer was not quick in coming. The commodore was not one to shun the limelight. He rambled on and on about conditions as he knew them in California. For when Colonel Frémont asked him to proceed in a narrative form, Commodore Stockton launched into a general and wide-ranging history of what caused the war in California, of the various battles that took place, of the formation of civil government, and of just about anything else he could remember.

Objections were raised by the judge advocate as to the point of much of Commodore Stockton's testimony. At times, even the court asked the witness to please confine his testimony to those facts which had to do with the trial of Lieutenant Colonel Frémont.

But Commodore Stockton lived up to his nickname of "Gassy Bob" during his days of testimony. It wasn't that he had reached a mutual understanding with General Kearny, as many persons thought. Quite simply, his testimony harmed Frémont's case because of Stockton's endless rambling and inability to be certain about anything. Questioned by Frémont, by the judge advocate, and by the court, the only consistent aspect of his answers was their indefinite quality. In this, he hardly varied. This was a trait that the judge advocate used to a good advantage when he questioned the commodore.

QUESTION: In your last answer, you speak of a conversation between Lieutenant Colonel Frémont and yourself, which you say you think occurred the 16th January, 1847. Do you know whether this conversation took place on the 16th or 17th of January.

ANSWER: I believe it was the 16th.

QUESTION: Look at this paper: your commission to Lieutenant Colonel Frémont appointing him governor. Have you any recollection of the day on which that was delivered to Lieutenant Colonel Frémont. If so, please state it.

ANSWER: I believe it was on the evening of the 16th that I sent for Lieutenant Colonel Frémont and gave him his commission of governor, but my recollection of it is not perfect.

QUESTION: Will you say whose hand writing that is in?

ANSWER: I think it is in the hand of my clerk, Mr. Simmons; he is not here.

QUESTION: What orders and instructions from the President of the United States or Secretary of the Navy had you in California, on the 16th January, 1847, in regard to the establishment of a civil government in that country?

ANSWER: Well, I do not think I had any.

QUESTION: Did you ever receive, and if so, when did you so receive the instruction from Secretary Bancroft to Commodore Sloat, dated July 12, 1846?

ANSWER: I think I received no other instructions, except those Commodore Sloat turned over to me, and some others, received by Mr. McCrae; afterwards the orders went to Commodore Shubrick or Biddle, and if sent to me, were only sent through courtesy. I think I have no recollection of having received these instructions of the 12th of July. My right to establish the civil government was incident to the conquest, and I formed the government under the law of nations.[19]

I think. I believe. My recollection is not perfect. I had no instructions. Then the final blow: "I formed the government under the law of nations." For young Captain Lee, it was a great day for the prosecution. For Lieutenant Colonel Frémont, the testimony of his comrade-in-arms was as damning by its vagueness as were the accusations General Kearny had filed against him.

During this last month of 1847, Jessie Benton Frémont was no longer able to keep up her daily attendance at her husband's trial. She had an extremely bad cold, verging on the brink of pneumonia. She was also expecting their second child in the coming summer. By her doctor's orders, she was forced to remain at home. But she read every newspaper account of the daily proceedings, and listened with intense care as John Charles and her father related each day's events. From everything she could learn, it appeared obvious that the evidence was in favor of her husband.

Lieutenant Archibald Gillespie testified that he had been detained in Monterey through the actions of General Kearny, who had prevailed upon Commodore Biddle to keep him there. Then to show how prejudiced Kearny was in his case against Frémont, the general tried to besmirch the character of Lieutenant Gillespie by implying that the United States marine had planned to stir up an insurrection. But when asked if he really believed this, if this had been his opinion of Lieutenant Gillespie, General Kearny replied in the negative. Still, by implication, he gave the impression that this friend of Colonel Frémont's was a seditious character.

Others who followed Lieutenant Gillespie to the witness chair related General Kearny's strange actions in California, actions that showed Kearny admitting Stockton's superiority over him, and actions which were deceptive and self-serving. Lieutenant Andrew F. V. Gray, U.S.N., testified that he heard General Kearny offer to go into the campaigns to retake Ciudad de los Angeles and San Gabriel as Commodore Stockton's aide. William H. Russell lived up to his nickname of Owl as he remembered that General Kearny assumed Commodore Stockton outranked him, and said it had been his intention to appoint Colonel Frémont to the position of governor of California. And finally William N. Loker took the stand and made it quite clear that General Kearny had bluntly refused to await the arrival of Ned Kern and Henry King before beginning the overland journey that was to result in the arrest of Colonel Frémont.

Man by man, day after day, the evidence in favor of Colonel Frémont built all during December of 1847. There seemed to be no end to it, as the steady questions showed General Kearny as either forgetful, senile, or a man flirting with perjury for his own personal vendetta.

Yet, as the trial continued, six days each week, some newspapers, and some public opinion began to turn at the sight of this overkill on the part of Frémont and his counsel. "Enough!" was the cry. Kearny also was human, and he had made his mistakes. But stop the steady onslaught of questions and answers that were destroying the general's career and aging him before the eyes of the spectators. He had been vindictive. That was granted. He had been wrong. That was granted. But there was no need to follow in his footsteps, no need to hit the man again and again when it was obvious he was finished, and all but destroyed.

5

BRIGADIER GENERAL KEARNY was absent from the courtroom on January 3, 1848. The record for the third day of the new year indicated that the general was ill. There was whispered conversation about this among the spectators, but all noise was brought to a halt by the sharp rap of General Brooke's gavel. The day was one of the shortest in the case. Colonel Frémont let the court know that he had no more witnesses to examine. However, there were some he should like to have summoned for the defense, just in order that the judge advocate should have the opportunity to examine them. On the next day he would submit a list of names. With that, the court adjourned for the day.

The following day Colonel Frémont submitted fourteen names of witnesses. Two among the fourteen were Richard Owens and Joseph B. Chiles.

The reply of the judge advocate was that "he had no questions to ask these witnesses, and did not think it necessary that he should swear them in the case."[20] The court also noted that it had no questions to ask these witnesses, and saw no reason to summon them to testify. Instead, Major Swords was sworn in, and he was questioned and requestioned about an implication that he made regarding the methods Colonel Frémont's men had used in gathering horses and mules for the California Battalion. All of this seemed rather meaningless in relationship to the trial, and it gave a distinct impression that the judge advocate was using up the day as though he wanted to be certain the trial would not come to an end.

Wednesday, January 5, 1848. Brigadier General Kearny returned to give more testimony. During that day and for the next few days, Colonel Frémont insisted that General Kearny had sent forth written questions for Captain Lee to consider while he had been away from the court on the pretext of being ill. Each time the colonel rephrased his question or statement, the court was cleared and the colonel was told he could not ask such a question.

The sparring, the coming back to small points went on from January 5 to January 8. The only other witness called during this period was Owl Russell, who took the stand briefly on Saturday, January 8. Again Russell said that General Kearny had told him he was outranked by Commodore Stockton, who was commander of the Pacific Squadron.

Back on the stand again, General Kearny denied he had said such a thing to William Russell or anybody else. Then he went on to explain that while he recognized Commodore Stockton as acting governor and commander-in-chief, he only worked in co-operation with Commodore Stockton. In no manner did he consider his position to be lower in rank than that of the commodore. As Kearny went on, he said that Stockton had "the relative rank with a colonel in the army; if he had been a lieutenant in the navy, with the relative rank of a captain in the army, I would have treated him with the same courtesy."[21]

As for the matter of appointing Colonel Frémont to the post of governor of California, the general denied he had ever said anything of that nature to Russell or any other person. Yes, he had spoken openly and freely to Russell about Colonel Frémont. But all he had done was compliment the work of the colonel. At no time had he suggested that he intended to appoint him governor of California.

But the interplay in the courtroom, the daily exchanges of questions and answers, the barbed and caustic remarks that Colonel Frémont sometimes let slip, and the obvious favoritism the spectators and the newspapers had for Frémont and his cause had driven General Kearny right to the limits of his temper. As the session of Saturday, January 8, 1848, came to a close, he asked the court if he would be allowed to make a statement. Permission was granted, and General Kearny let his feelings come into the open.

> I consider it due to the dignity of the court, and the high respect I entertain for it, that I should here state that, on my last appearance before this court, when I was answering the questions propounded to me by the court, the senior counsel of the accused, Thomas H. Benton, of Missouri, sat in his place, making mouths and grimaces at me, which I considered were intended to offend, to insult, and to overawe me. I ask of this court no action on it, so far as I am concerned. I am fully capable of taking care of my own honor.[22]

Stunned. Silent. Astounded. Baffled. The reporters didn't have the words. Nobody had expected this from Brigadier General Kearny. But everything had been building up for an explosion, and he couldn't hold it back any longer.

Senator Benton stood, his great figure looming above the counsel table. In a voice accustomed to booming out in the Senate, he launched his counterattack. It came so fast and with such power that the court didn't know what to do. But as they recovered from the initial shock of having a civilian speak out at a court-martial, one of the members of the court pointed out that any remarks reflecting upon the proceedings of the court were not admissible. Obviously the officer had not seen Senator Benton in action. In a few words Old Bullion Benton made it clear that it was the duty of the court to punish but only after they had heard. Plain and simple, they had not heard, and they were about to hear.

It was nearing three o'clock in the afternoon, and the court was ready for adjournment. Not one spectator moved. Not one member of the court suggested adjournment until Senator Benton had finished with a flourish of melodrama.

> When General Kearny fixed his eyes on Colonel Frémont, I determined if he should attempt again to look down a prisoner, I would look at him. I did this day; and the look of to-day was the consequence of the looks in this court be-

fore. I did to-day look at General Kearny when he looked at Colonel Frémont, and I looked at him till his eyes fell—till they fell upon the floor.[23]

After this Senator Benton expressed his respect for the court. General Brooke, president of the court, said that he thought General Kearny had looked upon Colonel Frémont only with kindness, with politeness. Then as three o'clock arrived and General Brooke called for adjournment, General Kearny stood and said, "I wish in the presence of the court, to say, that I have never offered the slightest insult to Colonel Frémont, either here as a prisoner on this trial or any where, or under any circumstances.[24]

With this, the gavel struck the hour for adjournment on one of the last days before statements were to be made by the judge advocate for the prosecution and by Colonel Frémont in his lengthy defense summary—a summary that would take from January 24 to January 27, fill eighty-one pages of the official proceedings, and conclude with a stirring plea for recognition of his services to his country.

My acts in California have all been with high motives, and a desire for public service. My scientific labors did something to open California to the knowledge of my countrymen; its geography had been a sealed book. My military operations were conquests without bloodshed; my civil administration was for the public good. I offer California, during my administration, for comparison with the most tranquil portions of the United States; I offer it in contrast to the condition of New Mexico during the same time. I prevented civil war against Governor Stockton, by refusing to join General Kearny against him; I arrested civil war against myself, by consenting to be deposed —offering at the same time to resign my place of lieutenant colonel in the army.

I have been brought as a prisoner and a criminal from that country. I could return to, after this trial is over, without rank or guards, and without molestation from the people, except to be importuned for the money which the government owes them.[25]

The speech was not without exaggeration and some stretching of the truth. For there had been bloodshed in the taking of California, and the threat of a civil war under the instigation of General Kearny simply wasn't true. As for Frémont's high motives and scientific labor, here he was on solid ground. Yet, as a dramatic summary of his defense for a court-martial that should not have taken place, his words caught the emotion and turmoil of his ordeal. It was good copy for newspapers, and Colonel Frémont was compared to Columbus, who discovered a new world only to be rewarded by arrest and disgrace.

6

THE COURT read the testimony in the latter part of January. Then for three days, they deliberated on the charges. On Monday, the last day of the month, they reached their verdict. The old Arsenal was jammed with spectators and reporters. Any gambling man would have bet on Colonel Frémont. The accumulation of evidence showed that he had committed some minor acts which should have been disciplined at the time by Brigadier General Kearny, but there was nothing in the great mass of testimony that indicated Colonel Frémont should have been forced to endure a military court-martial. By all odds, there was no reason to think that even a court of military officers would find the accused guilty of anything that required severe discipline.

Brigadier General George M. Brooke called the court to order. The members of the court "after full and mature consideration of all the testimony, find the accused, Lieutenant Colonel John C. Frémont, of the regiment of mounted riflemen, United States army, as follows. . . ."[26]

The audience was stunned as they heard the verdict. They had found Colonel Frémont guilty! He was guilty on all three charges and on each specification under those charges!

"And the court does therefore sentence the said Lieutenant Colonel John C. Frémont, of the regiment of mounted riflemen, United States army, to be dismissed from the service."[27]

But it didn't stop with the initial shock wave. There was more to follow, and what came out next was strange and contradictory in light of the verdict. Six of the twelve members of the court recommended Colonel Frémont to the clemency of President Polk because of his distinguished personal services for the United States. Then in the "Remarks by the Court," the officers who had sat through day after day of the court-martial and who had read all the written evidence came up with a most peculiar statement.

Under the circumstances in which Lieutenant Colonel Frémont was placed between two officers of superior rank, each claiming to command-in-chief in California—circumstances in their nature calculated to embarrass the mind and excite the doubts of officers of greater experience than the accused—and in consideration of the important professional services rendered by him previous to the occurrence of those acts for which he has been tried, the undersigned members of the court, respectfully commend Lieutenant Colonel Frémont to the lenient consideration of the President of the United States.[28]

The whole affair was hard to believe. Frémont was guilty. But it was not his fault. Frémont was dismissed from his rank as an officer of the United States Army. But it was suggested that the President of the United States offer clemency. In short, the whole thing had a rigged appearance, and the newspapers wasted no time in pointing this out.

Suspicion that the trial had been a way of putting Frémont in his place came home to haunt all of John Charles's supporters within two weeks after the end of the trial. For on February 16, 1848, President James Knox Polk issued the following proclamation:

Upon an inspection of the record, I am not satisfied that the facts proved in this case constitute the military crime of "mutiny." I am of the opinion that the second and third charges are sustained by the proof, and that the convic-

tion upon these charges warrants the sentence of the court. The sentence of
the court is therefore approved, but in consideration of the peculiar circumstances of the case, of the previous meritorious and valuable services of Lieutenant Colonel Frémont, and of the foregoing recommendations of a majority
of the members of the court, the penalty of dismissal from the service is
remitted.

Lieutenant Colonel Frémont will accordingly be released from arrest, will
resume his sword, and report for duty.[29]

This was too much. Though Senator Benton encouraged Frémont to accept the pardon, telling him that within the ranks of the service he could get
at those who had pulled off this miscarriage of justice, John Charles
adamantly refused. It was a matter of honor. He was not guilty of anything
as far as he was concerned. To accept clemency would be the same as recog-
nizing the verdict of the court. By no means would he be talked into this. He
would prove his worth on his own and without the backing of the United
States Government.

Yet there were last items that required government backing, and through
the influence of Senator Benton, Frémont got financial help for the preparation of his *Geographical Memoir upon Upper California, in Illustration of
His Map of Oregon and California*. Still, even as he worked on it with the
help of Jessie, trouble struck again. One night as she neared the end of her
pregnancy, she startled John Charles by saying, "Do not move the lamp. It
makes it too dark." Then before he could react, she fell to the floor in a deep
faint. The family physician was called. He ordered that Jessie was to remain
in bed until she gave birth, and not to exert herself in any way.

To John Charles, this was almost the last straw, the final outcome of the
court-martial. He forged ahead, but his heart was not in his work any longer;
and he referred to what he was doing as "the cursed memoir." He was robbed
of his drive to turn out a full report of his third expedition. Even so, what he
did accomplish was not to be overlooked. The *Geographical Memoir* was extremely valuable. Here, for the first time, was a clear picture of the nature of
the Great Basin, the Sierra Nevada, and the Pacific Coast Range. The idea
that the Great Basin was only a region of deserts was eliminated as he described the interior mountain ranges which contained meadows, forests of
piñon pine, streams, and small lakes. He stressed the importance of the central route along the Humboldt River as the natural overland crossing for emigrants bound for California.

Added to the *Memoir* was the large, detailed map which Charles Preuss
drew from his own surveys as well as those of Frémont and Kern. It was,
without question, the most accurate map that had been made of the Far
West, and it was to be of great value to wagon trains headed west.

The map and the *Geographical Memoir* were completed by June 8, 1848,
and the United States Senate ordered twenty thousand copies for distribution. But this wasn't the last need of government help. The matter of set-

tling the California debts remained. Here, Frémont was aided in his financial difficulties by Senator Lewis Cass of Michigan, who shepherded a bill through the Senate that appropriated $700,000, and named Frémont, Reading, and Hensley as commissioners to adjudicate the claims. But when this bill reached the House, the sum of money was reduced to $500,000, and other commissioners were appointed.

Through all this bickering and infighting, there was a noticeable change in the personality of John Charles Frémont. The lightheartedness gave way to a shield of bitterness that hid the hurt feelings of this man who had explored so much of the American West for the sheer intellectual joy of it. All he saw in the way of happiness was the birth of his son, Benton, on July 24, 1848. Yet even the baby boy seemed hurt by the months of the court-martial, and the family doctor was concerned about his fragile health.

The sores of disappointment and neglect began to fester and poison John Charles's state of mind. This incredible explorer of lands beyond the far horizon was too young to rest on past laurels. Yet the glory years were all behind. Ahead were trails without guides, expeditions without backing. Not a quitter, he was determined to find his own way.

# ᔕ XXIII ᔓ

## Snows of Disaster

The court-martial was over, but John Charles Frémont felt as though he were still on trial. Admired by the many and hated by the few, he found himself an outcast from any opportunity to head a government survey. His luck had vanished, and he appeared to be doomed to wander the wastelands of the soul.

But proud and powerful Senator Benton would not stand still for this abuse of his son-in-law. Railroads were the coming thing, railroads all the way to the Pacific. Even the government was talking about the possibility of making a survey for a route to the West. The senator wasted no time. He talked to St. Louis businessmen, convinced them St. Louis should be the hub of an all-year railway route—one that would follow the Santa Fé Trail to Bent's Fort, cross the Rockies, and streak on to California. It was a dream of glory, and once Frémont proved it was possible, St. Louis would be the center of all railroad traffic bound westward.

Three key businessmen agreed to the senator's proposition. They would furnish the supplies, the horses and mules, and some money. But they could not pay the wages and stand the expenses of a government-backed expedition. Perhaps Frémont could hire a few key men and tell the others that they would share in profits once the government saw that the route they had explored was the natural one to back.

Frémont was back in his element. Wasting no time, he contacted men who might be willing to make the journey. He explained they would cross the mountains in the middle of the winter. They would travel light and fast. No wagons or Red River carts would encumber them. When they reached Bent's Fort, they would pick up a guide and head over the mountains to California.

To men who had been with Frémont on other expeditions, the proposition sounded like a good bet. They were bored with town and city life and rest-

General Stephen Watts Kearny, commander of the Army of the West.
(*The Bancroft Library*)

San Diego, three years after the conquest of California, as pictured in a lithograph based upon a sketch by H. M. T. Powell. (*The Bancroft Library*)

Los Angeles about 1853, six years after the American conquest, as pictured in a lithograph by Charles Koppel. (*The Bancroft Library*)

The terrible winter in the San Juan Mountains during the disaster of 1848–49, as pictured by Edward Kern. (*The Bancroft Library*)

Alexis Godey, the hero of Frémont's fourth expedition. (*The Bancroft Library*)

Kit Carson and John Charles Frémont, a daguerreotype taken at Taos just after the tragedy in the San Juan Mountains. (*Courtesy of the Denver Public Library, Western History Department*)

less to move into the wilderness again. The colonel told them that he was going to California to stay, that Jessie would make the Panama crossing and come to California, and that they intended to live on his Rancho Las Mariposas and had already shipped farming equipment around the Horn. But there was another pull to get men to go. News of a gold strike near Sutter's Fort had filtered into St. Louis. If that was true, then California might be even more than they figured on. Twenty-two seasoned men signed on. Among them were Alexis Godey, Charles Preuss, Ned Kern, and rough Tom Martin.

Added to the veterans were the greenhorns. Ned Kern's brothers—Richard, an artist, and Benjamin, a physician—had decided to make the trip. Captain Andrew Cathcart of Prince Albert's 11th Hussars was at loose ends since the death of his friend Frederick Ruxton, and Cathcart agreed to make the journey. Others among the new men were Frederick Creutzfeldt, a botanist; Saunders Jackson, an ex-slave who went along as Frémont's personal servant and chef; and fourteen-year-old Theodore McNabb, a nephew of Alexis Godey.

All the members of the party boarded a steamboat and started upriver from St. Louis on October 4, 1848. With them was Jessie, baby Benton Frémont, and Jessie's black servant, Aunt Kitty. Still upset by the verdict of the court-martial, Jessie wanted to go as far as possible with John Charles before she had to wave farewell.

Two days later, as the steamboat's paddlewheel worked against the current of the Missouri River, the sickly baby Benton, who was not even three months old, gasped and died. Jessie and John Charles were crushed by this tragic event, and the mother immediately placed the blame for the death of their first son on General Kearny and the members of the military court. If it had not been for them, if they had not caused the ordeal of court-martial, Benton Frémont would have been a healthy baby. John Charles tried his best to comfort his grief-stricken wife, but he felt that the daily sessions of the trial, the events leading up to it, and the final result had taken away from Jessie's strength; and because of this, the baby had been weakened.

Determined more than ever to make the expedition a success, Frémont was ready to endure any fury nature might throw at him. But his first concern was for Jessie. Accompanied by Aunt Kitty, she went beyond Westport to Boon Creek. Here they stayed as guests of Major Richard Cummins and his wife. Indian Agent Cummins even provided a log cabin for the Frémonts to spend their nights in as final preparations were made for the expedition. After the tragedy aboard the steamboat, Jessie needed these eleven days with her husband and his men. And the men were very attentive and concerned for the colonel's lady.

Each day, Jessie left the agency and went with John Charles to the camp where his men were getting things ready.

I occupied a Sibley tent in the camp [she wrote], and Mrs. Cummins, the wife of the venerable and good agent for the Delaware Indians . . . sent out there a daily luncheon—the men kept me supplied with quail broiled on sticks by the fire, which the October weather made very welcome.[1]

The day for parting came on October 20. It was Friday, and the weather was clear and pleasant. That much could be said in the way of a possible good omen. But for Jessie and John Charles the parting was not right. Too much had happened to mar the beginning of anything. Once the men were out of sight, Jessie spoke to Major Cummins, and he took her to the deserted campsite for one last look. That night she was startled by the sudden appearance of John Charles, who had made the ride from their first camp five miles out on the trail. He remained for what Jessie called an "early tea for a stirupp cup." Then he held her close, told her not to worry, but to take care of herself in her long journey to California across the Isthmus of Panama and up the Pacific Coast. She watched him mount his horse, and waved farewell as he galloped into the darkness to begin a journey toward the snow-covered barrier of the Rocky Mountains.

2

By NOVEMBER 15 the expedition was camped beside Bent's Fort. They had traveled 560 miles beyond Westport, had been through cold rainstorms, and had endured a prairie fire that some of the party had started through carelessness; now the weather had turned extremely cold and snow was falling. They remained here for two days as the snow storm continued and the temperature dropped to twelve above zero. Frémont took time on November 17 to write to Senator Benton. In his letter he mentioned that they had met Broken Hand at Big Timbers, where he was giving out supplies to a gathering of Apaches, Comanches, Kiowas, and Arapahoes as he fulfilled his new role as Indian Agent. The major items in this letter had to do with the weather. Both Indians and whites warned him that this was a bad winter, that the snow was deeper in the mountains than it had been for a very long time. In closing, he indicated he did not yearn to head into the snows of the high mountains:

I think that I shall never cross the continent again, except at Panama. I do not feel the pleasure that I used to have in those labors, as they remain inseparably connected with painful circumstances, due mostly to them. It needs strong incitements to undergo the hardships and self-denial of this kind of life, and as I find I have these no longer, I will drop into a quiet life.[2]

The idea, as the colonel put it, was to cross the Rockies between the Arkansas and the Río Grande. They would strike a course that would "ascend the Río del Norte to its head, descend to the Colorado, and across the Wah-satch mountain, and the Great Basin country, somewhere near the 37th parallel. . . ."³ It was unknown country, a land few trappers had bothered to penetrate. It was enough to look upward and see the Spanish Peaks, Wha-to-yah, the Breasts of the World to the south; and Pikes Peak to the north. They were covered with snow when the clouds shifted enough so that they could be seen. The tents of the expedition were white with snow, and sheets of ice formed on the water of the river during the night and broke away dur-ing the day. But the orders were to push on toward the settlement of Pueblo. There they might find a guide, for no man at Bent's Fort had looked on this trip as promising anything more than a cold way to cash in his chips. Thirty-five days, that was what Frémont had said, thirty-five days and they'd all be enjoying the sunshine beside Sutter's Fort in California's Sacramento Valley. Well, there was a long, steep climb before then, snow and ice to freeze a man's blood; and if they got through that, the Great Basin wasn't going to be easy going with worn-out men and animals. Thirty-five days to California? To the men around Bent's Fort it was more like thirty-five days to freeze to death.

At Pueblo, Old Bill Williams agreed to guide the party across the moun-tains. Most of his companions shook their heads in disbelief, and figured they'd never see Old Bill again. On November 22, the men rode out of Pueblo, and headed toward the mountains, stopping at the rough settlement of Hardscrabble, twenty-five miles upriver. Here, they bought all the corn the old mountain men would sell to carry along as additional food for the horses and mules. They rested at Hardscrabble for a couple of days, ate chicken and baked pumpkin, and got everything ready for the assault against the mountains.

This was the jumping-off place, and here one man said to hell with it and turned back. But Frémont had a way of talking to his men, a way that said follow me and we'll ride to glory. Everybody knew it was crazy. The Indians shook their heads. The mountain men figured they might find the bones and the plunder once the snow melted, but following a trade that was every bit as romantic as exploration, they wished Frémont the best of luck and thought it would be a damned fine trick if he pulled it off. When they rode out of Hardscrabble, the sun was shining off the distant Wet Mountains as though the first day of spring had dropped by for a visit. By God, the citizens of Hardscrabble thought, they just might pull it off.

The plan was to cross the Wet Mountains, then go up the eastern flanks of the Sangre de Cristo Mountains and cross them through Robidoux Pass, drop into the area of the Great Sand Dunes, follow the Río Grande's headwaters up San Luis Valley, and then cross the San Juan Mountains and the Conti-nental Divide at either Williams Pass or Cochetopa Pass. On a map the going seemed possible. But the route they were going to follow was a hard trip in the summer, and they were going to have to face deep snowdrifts, temperatures that would drop way below zero, blizzards that would freeze a man standing upright, and blinding, driving snow that had the feel of the Arctic about it.

By December 17 the men knew that their ascent of the mountains was almost over. According to the recollections of Micajah McGehee as printed in *Outdoor Life* in May 1910, mules were starving to the point that the animals kept falling down every fifty yards or so, and the men would have to unpack and repack them. Then the animals began to eat ropes, the pads and rigging of the packsaddles, blankets, and then each other's manes and tails until they were even nibbling into the flesh.

As for the men, they were not much better off. Weakened by the terrible cold and by the lack of food, they could not make more than a half mile to a mile each day; and even this required the beating of a trail with spades and mauls. When they reached an elevation of almost 11,000 feet, the cold became intense, the labor difficult; and at this altitude they suffered from lack of oxygen. The temperature dropped to twenty degrees below zero, and the snow ranged in depth from four feet in the open and on windy rock faces to as much as a hundred feet in the sheltered draws and canyons.

At this altitude, Frémont's judgment was impaired as he suffered from mountain sickness just as he had in the Wind River Mountains. He tried to make decisions, but he seemed incapable of deciding just what to do. Finally, on their twenty-sixth day out of Hardscrabble, he admitted they were defeated. They had lost more than half of the mules, and the remaining animals were almost ready to drop. The men were not any better off. The steady upward movement, the daily battle against the blizzards, the bone-chilling cold, and the terrible effort to move forward had taken their toll of the party's strength and reduced men on the brink of starvation close to the point of madness. The glare of the snow and the smoke from their campfires reduced their vision so that it was difficult to see what might be ahead. Time and again, men fell and rolled in the snow, cutting themselves against brush, trees, and rocks, and became so discouraged they were ready to give up, lie down, and drift into the long sleep.

To avoid freezing to death, they slept together in deep snowholes. As for food, they were reduced to a steady diet of mule meat. Tom Breckenridge was able to look back upon their experience with sardonic humor long after it was over, and in August 1896—a nice warm month—he published his version of what happened to the men of the fourth expedition in *The Cosmopolitan*. Among the many things that he described of their season in a cold hell was a mock menu for December 25, 1848, at what he rightly called Camp Desolation:

BILL OF FARE. CAMP DESOLATION
December 25, 1848.

---

MENU
MULE.

---

SOUP
Mule Tail.

FISH.
Baked White Mule.
Boiled Gray Mule.

MEATS
Mule Steak, Fried Mule, Mule Chops,
Broiled Mule, Stewed Mule, Boiled Mule,
Scrambled Mule, Shirred Mule,
French-fried Mule, Minced Mule

DAMNED MULE
Mule on Toast (without the Toast),
Short Ribs of Mule with Apple Sauce
(without the Apple Sauce),

RELISHES
Black Mule, Brown Mule, Yellow Mule,
Bay Mule, Roan Mule,
Tallow Candles.

BEVERAGES
Snow, Snow-Water, Water

Humor in retrospect only; a bitter laugh for old survivors, it was no more than that. By Christmas Day, there wasn't a man among them who didn't realize that their chances of getting out of the mountains alive were not worth betting on. They had walked into a white death, a freezing and chilling death, and any way they put it, things came down to one thing—in the summer they would be picked clean by carrion eaters, and that they could count on.

John Charles wasn't going to give up without a fight. He selected Henry King—newly married Henry—Old Bill Williams, Creutzfeldt, and Breckenridge to walk out of the mountains and head for the nearest settlement for help. Hopefully, they would reach some small village before they had to make the 160 mile journey to Taos.

After the four men left, Frémont decided that all of the others should move down the canyon of Embargo Creek to its junction with the headwaters of the Río Grande. With dogged determination, even with a possible hope that once the rescue team returned they might yet overcome the mountain heights and cross into the Great Basin, Frémont pushed ahead. But he was leading men who were frostbitten, starving, and almost ready to give in. It was only between fifteen and twenty miles from the mountain camp to the Río Grande. But it took the men twenty days to reach the river.

During this downward journey, New Year's Day of 1849 arrived and passed. For a while, the weather was cold but clear; and the spirits of the men picked up. Then another storm hit them. The last of the mule meat was consumed, and there was no game in sight. The party began to string out in twos and threes as they staggered slowly along. They boiled rawhide ropes, rawhide bags, and anything else that gave the illusion of food. For ten miles the men were strung out along the mountain slope. At the very end of the line were the Kern brothers, who carried more personal belongings.[4] Traveling with them were Captain Cathcart and the three California Indians—Manuel, Joaquin, and Gregorio.

At the head, and already at the Río Grande was Frémont's group, which included Charles Preuss, Alexis Godey and his nephew, Theodore McNabb, and Saunders Jackson. The third group in the middle of this straggling and weakened party consisted of the remaining men.

On January 9, 1849, the first death was recorded. Raphael Proue, a French engagé, a veteran man of the plains and mountains, told others his legs were frozen. With that, he lay down in the snow. Though Lorenzo Vincenthaler covered Proue with blankets, it was no use. The man drifted into a deep sleep and froze to death. Frémont was furious. The day was one of sunshine; Proue was an experienced man. Yet he gave up. He let the will to live go out of him without fighting to the last. This was not what the colonel had expected of Proue. He felt that the dead man had betrayed him. Now death was in their midst, and others might well give up. Two days more, that was all Proue had to wait, just two days more. By then Old Bill Williams would be back with a rescue party. To give up this way was not something Frémont could understand. It was not part of his fiber, not something that had ever entered his mind.

3

BUT THE RESCUE PARTY was in terrible shape. They had reached the San Luis Valley, and had traveled just a little over half of the 160 miles to Taos. Still, the gaunt and hungry men did well to move four or five miles during a day. They had eaten the last of the candles, had shared a small hawk they had killed, and were suffering from frostbite and the beginning of snow blindness.

Their feet were inflamed and covered with sores, and it was so painful to move along they took off their boots, wrapped their feet in torn pieces of blanket, and carried their boots to roast over the fire. Boots, belts, and knife scabbards became food. Anything that would ease the pangs of hunger was cooked and eaten. For eight days they continued this way, until Old Bill shaded his eyes and looked toward the east. His companions were certain he had seen something or somebody, but it wasn't until that night around the campfire that he told them he had seen distant smoke from a Ute village.

Thinking they were saved, the men believed that all they had to do was move on to the village. Old Bill had lived among the Utes. He had lived with a Ute woman. Just as they thought salvation had come their way, Old Bill told them he could not take them to the village. He had done something terrible to these trusted friends. He had gone on a drunken spree in Taos and had agreed to guide the soldiers on a raid against them. Ever since that raid, every Ute was on the lookout for him; and if they ever caught him, they would lift his hair and rightly so.

The help the men had hoped for was not to be. Instead, the next day they would have to leave the course of the river and strike out across the plain in order to dodge the Utes. This was the final blow to endure. Out in the open there would be no possibility of game and no wood for building fires. They were between the rock and the hard place. To go ahead to the Ute camp would mean certain death, and to move onto the open plain would mean a slim chance to avoid freezing or starving to death before they had completed the detour around the Indian village.

But the men forged ahead. They fought snow blindness, hunger, and the pain of frostbitten feet. By January 11, the day they were to have returned with help for their companions, Henry King ceased to stumble along. Though they were almost across the open country, he was too exhausted to continue and stopped. They were no more than a quarter of a mile from the river and a stand of timber. Yet he could not continue. He told the others he had to rest. Then he would follow when he regained his strength.

None of the men could help him. The best they could do was make it to the river, where there was wood, and get a fire started. Then with luck they might even find something to eat. The distance was short, but it became a long and terrible trip. It took them over two hours to make this short distance. They crawled on all fours, fell flat, gasped for air, and slowly raised themslves up to crawl on until they reached the river, where they made a fire of driftwood.

When Creutzfeldt had regained enough strength and his benumbed body had become warm again, he returned for Henry King. But he was too late. He had wasted his energy on a dead man. When he got back to the river camp, it was obvious to the others that King's death was almost the last thing the botanist could endure. He could not dismiss it from his mind, and he became so despondent his companions wondered if he would continue to fight to stay alive. As Breckenridge remembered, it wasn't only Creutzfeldt who was ready to give up. The next morning they broke camp and moved along the bank of the river, not really caring if they lived out the day.

4

WHEN RELIEF did not reach the expedition by January 11, all hope left the men who were barely hanging on. To John Charles, the situation called for a desperate move. Old Bill Williams and the others should have been back if they had made it. The only assumption was they had died in their attempt to get out of the mountains. Believing this, Frémont divided the last of the remaining provisions. Half the food was given to twenty-four men who were too weak to make a forced march; the other half was for the relief party he would head in an attempt to save the lives of the other men. His group consisted of Alexis Godey, his nephew, Theodore, Charles Preuss, and Saunders Jackson. All five were in better shape than the others, and they would try to make it to some settlement.

Before departing, Frémont left the rest of the expedition under the command of Lorenzo Vincenthaler. Of all the men he might have selected, he couldn't have chosen a less dependable man. Vincenthaler was not a mountain man and had not been a leader. He was a cunning, fawning man who had played up to Frémont. Perhaps this made him seem capable and trustworthy. Whatever Frémont's reasons were for choosing such a man in this desperate situation, those reasons were not based on a sound appraisal. For not long after Frémont's departure, this petty and immoral man proved his worthlessness by his callous treatment of the men under his command.

He insisted they should try to keep moving, to follow the direction Frémont had taken. He failed to recognize their condition. Most of the men were walking skeletons whose eyes were bloodshot and swollen. Scratches and cuts did not heal and became running sores; but Manuel, the California Indian boy, was in the worst shape of all. His feet had frozen, and the flesh had rotted from his soles and sloughed off. He begged Vincenthaler to shoot him. When he refused, Manuel said good-bye to his companions and managed to make his way back to a brush hut beside the river with the help of Juan and Gregorio, who started a fire for him, cut enough extra wood to last him for as long as he should remain alive, and left him after spending a last night with him.

Manuel wasn't expected to live. Proue was dead. But it was only the beginning. The day after Manuel had crawled into the brush hut, Henry Wise of Missouri, a veteran of the third expedition, couldn't take another step, sprawled in the snow, and gave up. The next day Carver lost his senses, wandered away, and was never seen again.

While one disaster followed another among the bickering men under Vincenthaler's command, Frémont and his small rescue party moved along at a
good pace. Two days after they had started out of the mountains, they
crossed the tracks of Indians and horses. They followed sign for three days,
and on their fifth day away from their companions to the rear, they reached a
Ute camp. Here, John Charles met the son of a Ute chief he had known.
Giving this small band his own blankets and a rifle and promising other re-
wards, he convinced the young Ute to guide them to the small village at the
Red River which is present Questa, New Mexico. They stayed overnight at
the Ute encampment, and in the morning set out with their guide and four
Indian horses that were so poor from lack of food that they were only able to
move at a slow walk.

During their sixth day on the move, they traveled only six or seven miles.
As the sun set, they saw the smoke of a campfire in a grove of timber not far
from the river. The guide wasn't sure about riding toward it as it might be a
camp of hostile Indians, but Frémont thought it might be the relief party returning to help them. With caution, they moved ahead. When they reached
the camp, they could hardly believe what they saw. Breckenridge, Creutzfeldt, and Old Bill Williams were alive, but that was all that could be said.
The men were in the last stages of starvation, badly frostbitten, and barely
recognized Frémont and the others.

King was not with the starving and half-frozen men. When Frémont asked
about him, the answers were confusing and almost incoherent. Frémont and
his men searched the area and found Henry King's body at another campsite. Not only was his body frozen, but it was obvious his companions had
been so desperate that they had eaten parts of King's body. But Breckenridge
and the other survivors denied that they had indulged in cannibalism.

The sorry-looking horses were used to carry Old Bill, Breckenridge, and
Creutzfeldt. From the Red River settlement, Frémont and Godey hurried on
to Taos for help.

5

THE MEN waiting to be rescued ceased to watch out for the safety and survival of everybody. Part of this was due to Vincenthaler's poor leadership,
but the major factor in the collapse of co-operation came down to two things:
starvation and a penetrating cold that eroded the will to live.

Instead of pulling together, the men broke into small groups. They fought
among themselves, and what little game they managed to kill was not divided
equally. The weaker men got very little, while the stronger men took most of
the food.

Even as Frémont and Godey rode to Taos, the two veteran engagés—Antoine Morin and Vincent (Sorrel) Tabeau—gave up, sat down, and remained together until they perished. Then in a show of a desire to live at all

costs, Vincenthaler selected the strongest men remaining in the party, told the others to break into smaller groups that could keep up with each other, and on January 21, at midnight, they sneaked out of camp and started moving toward the Red River settlement. With him were Tom Martin, a veteran Frémont man from Tennessee; Julius Ducatel, a greenhorn from Baltimore; George Hubbard, an experienced wilderness man from the Iowa border country; John Scott, a professional hunter; Billy Bacon, a greenhorn from Missouri; Benjamin Beadle, a veteran outdoorsman from St. Louis County, Missouri; Josiah Ferguson, a frontiersman from Missouri; and Joaquin and Gregorio, two California Indians who had no desire to risk becoming food for the men remaining behind.

On the same Sunday Vincenthaler deserted his command, Frémont and Godey arrived in Taos. They had left Preuss and fourteen-year-old McNabb back at the Red River settlement while they made a forced ride to pick up supplies and additional horses and mules for the men left in the mountains. When they entered Taos, it was already dark, and they rode directly to Don Carlos Beaubien's store. They tied their mounts to the hitching rail, entered the dimly lit room and saw Kit Carson, Dick Owens, and Lucien Maxwell. Owens was nearest to them, and Frémont spoke to him first. But Dick Owens didn't recognize the bearded, half-starved, gaunt man he had traveled and fought beside. Then Maxwell realized it was the Captain and Alexis Godey. In no time, they were surrounded by old friends who offered all the help needed to get the remaining men out of the mountains. But one thing was certain to all of them, Frémont was not in any shape to return. He was exhausted, sick, near collapse, and one leg was badly frostbitten. The only thing to do was to put him to bed at Kit Carson's house, feed him warm soup, and let Godey—who was still in good shape—lead the way back to the trapped men.

## 6

HARDLY TAKING TIME TO REST, Alexis formed a relief party, and early on Monday morning, January 22, he started back into the snows of disaster. At the Red River settlement he picked up some more horses and, using all his strength and knowledge of the wilderness, left that place the following morning, moving at a rapid pace. Now time was the key factor, and Alexis knew it.

Hubbard dropped out of Vincenthaler's band of deserters. When Godey found him, his corpse was still warm. Next Alexis came upon Scott, and though he was in bad shape, he was alive. But in taking a short-cut to avoid the bend in the Río Grande, Godey bypassed the camp where the Kerns, Cathcart, Taplin, Rohrer, Andrews, McGehee, and Stepperfeldt were hanging on. He did come upon Ben Beadle and Josiah Ferguson, who had dropped behind the Vincenthaler group. Ferguson was almost gone, and Beadle was stiff and without life. Now the problem was to find the others.

Doubling back, the tough Alexis and his relief party scoured the area for some sign of the missing men. There had to be smoke hanging in the air if anybody was still alive or strong enough to keep a fire going, and Alexis watched the skyline for the white and black streamers.

Even as he searched, things became desperate in the Kern camp. Men who weren't snow blind tried to hunt, and they did kill two grouse. But that was hardly enough for them to eat. Taplin brought in part of a dead wolf he had found, and they ate that even though it was rotten. They ate bugs, roots when they could find them, moccasin soles, and even a lodge skin bag. Yet they continued to get worse. Andrews dropped in his tracks, and they helped him back to the campfire, where he lingered on for a few days before his eyes became fixed.

The day after Andrews had perished, Henry Rohrer, a millwright from Georgetown, began to panic. The other men tried to calm him and to keep up his will to live. But even as they talked to him about his wife and children, Rohrer got worse. He began to rave and thrash about, and before the night came to an end, the last of his strength was gone. At this, one of the men suggested what had been the unspeakable. He pointed out that there was no use in allowing the man's body to be consumed by wolves. The flesh was fresh. Terrible as it sounded, it would be better to eat their dead friend than sit by his body and starve to death. He even offered to cut up the body out of sight of the others so that they would not have to endure the scene. His suggestion was turned down. The men couldn't face the thought of it, at least not yet. They agreed to avoid the fate of the Donner Party and to hang on. Surely, the relief party would reach them before long.

Three days after the death of Henry Rohrer, the men were on the verge of giving up. Their bodies were not much more than skeletons, and their clothing hung loosely. Their vision was very bad from the constant glare of light against the glistening white snow, and their long hair and beards were matted and framed their gaunt faces and sunken eye sockets, making them look like a gathering of mummies. But on this day, January 28, Alexis Godey found them and gave them a mare to kill for food while he rode on up the river to search for more survivors.

Tougher and stronger than any man of the expedition, Godey made his way on up the river. He found the bodies of Morin and Sorrel. But he kept on the move, covering fifty more miles upstream from the Kern camp. In his brush lodge, he found Manuel, the Consumne Indian, and the badly injured man was still alive. He asked about any others, and Manuel told him that Carver had gone out of his mind and started back into the mountains, following Embargo Creek.

Leaving food for Manuel and telling him that he would be back for him, Alexis tried to make it up Embargo Creek to recover the baggage that had been left behind. But some of his mules froze to death, and he had to quit his march back into the mountains. He did find a trunk that belonged to Frémont and a small amount of other baggage which he packed on mules. Then he headed back downstream. On the way, he picked up Manuel, the men at the Kern camp, and all the others along the way. By February 11 he had brought the last survivors into Taos, and had made a remarkable round trip of about 320 miles through rough country and deep snow in twenty days.

The fourth expedition was over, and it was a disaster the survivors would never forget. Bitterness developed over what had happened, and blame for poor leadership was attributed to Frémont by the Kerns and some of the others. In turn, John Charles thought Old Bill Williams was at fault. He had hired him for their guide because he was supposed to know more about this region than any other mountain man, but he was not able to avoid the trap of the high country and did not seem sure about where he was taking them.

Alexis Godey defended Frémont by stating in a newspaper article that Old Bill and he were at fault; that Colonel Frémont had not wanted to take the Carnero Pass route which they had insisted upon but had suggested that they cross the mountains by way of Cochetopa Pass. Yet this really wouldn't have made that much difference. While Cochetopa Pass might not have had quite as much snow as Carnero Pass, the fact remained that long before the men and the animals reached the heights, they were in serious trouble. Ultimately the blame had to fall upon Frémont, as he was the leader and it was up to him to take decisive action and either follow Old Bill and Alexis or state that he did not wish to take the path they had chosen. The real mistake was in trying to cross these high passes in the midst of one of the worst winters the Indians or mountain men had ever seen, and it was a mistake that proved to be very costly in suffering and the loss of life.

Ten men, essentially one-third of the expedition, had not made it out of the mountains. As for the survivors, many suffered from the painful burns of frostbite. Yet not one man had to have so much as a limb or even a finger amputated. They had enough clothing for freezing weather and worked so hard in trying to get over the mountains and then in climbing down out of them that the red cells in their blood were not affected long enough to cause permanent damage. If there had been long enough periods of no circulation, fingers and toes—even hands, feet, and noses—would have suffered from a lack of blood for the tissues, and this would have resulted in gangrene. Fortunately, the heroic Godey got to the survivors in time to prevent a total disaster. But when the men at the Kern camp insisted that a special providence had directed him to them just in time, he smiled and said, "Providence, hell. 'Twas good management."[5]

And good management plus Alexis Godey's bravery and strength had made the difference between life and death for the men he saved. But though he brought them out of the mountains without any major injuries, the survivors still suffered from the psychological shock of their ordeal. The Kern brothers remained hostile to Frémont for what had happened. Stepperfeldt, the gunsmith, lost his senses for a while and vanished into the desert, but was finally found and brought back to Taos, where he recovered.

Still, Frémont was not a man to quit. From men he knew at Taos and Santa Fé, he borrowed enough money to purchase horses and supplies. Then, he invited any of his party to ride to California with him, where he intended to meet Jessie at San Francisco. From there, he let the men know that he was headed for his new ranch in the foothill country near Yosemite Valley.

Except for Cathcart, Old Bill Williams, and the Kern brothers, all the other survivors indicated a trip to California would be a good tonic after their time in the snows of the San Juan Mountains of the Rockies. All told, twenty-five men rode out of Taos with John Charles and headed south toward the Gila Trail. All their past suffering was only a nightmare memory as they drifted across the border into Sonora, Mexico, and passed through Apache country and such devastated Mexican pueblos as Santa Cruz before they made a wide horseshoe turn that took them north to the rough settlement of Tucson. From there they rode to the Gila Trail and followed it to its junction with the Colorado River. Here Frémont met 1,200 Mexicans—men, women and children—from Sonora. They were bound for Alta California, and verified the discovery of gold. He asked twenty-eight of them to join him and come to Las Mariposas to mine. He would grubstake them, and they would share in any of the profits. They agreed to his proposition, and joined Frémont's party to strike out across the Colorado Desert on the trail to El Dorado.

# ·❦· XXIV ·❦·

## Life in El Dorado

THE ASPINWALL STEAMER rolled at anchor eight miles away from the mouth of the Chagres River. As Lily was handed down the ship's ladder to the waiting boatmen, Jessie thought she was going to be ill. The air was hot and humid, and it carried the stench of rotting fish, the heavy and sweet aroma of cinnamon and other spices, the mixture of body sweat, engine oil floating in a skim on the surface of the water, and the pungent odor of decaying plants from the thick green jungle that grew right down to the distant shoreline.

The captain of the Pacific Mail steamer warned Jessie and her brother-in-law, Richard Taylor Jacob, of the many dangers in crossing to the Pacific port of Panama; and he particularly stressed the need to boil all drinking water. Then Jessie, Lily, and Richard Jacob were crowded into small boats to make the voyage to the river. Richard was encouraging and assured Jessie he would watch out for them all the way to California, and Lily was all bounce and excitement as they reached the shore. Here was a world that astounded Jessie. Scarlet flowers seemed to burst from the tangled green jungle like strange tongues. And lined along the riverbank were rows of narrow bongos, or dugout canoes, with palm-thatched shelters to cover the passengers to be taken upriver by half-naked blacks and Indians who were the boatmen for the forty-mile river trip to Gorgona. As Jessie waited for Richard to make arrangements with the boatmen, Captain Tucker stepped forth and introduced himself.

He explained that Colonel Aspinwall had told him to be on the look out for her. There was no need to make any arrangements. He had seen to that. She and her party were to make the trip in one of the Aspinwall bongos. He assured her that the crew was very reliable, that they would make overnight stops at the camps for the Panama Railroad survey, and that he often brought his own wife upriver in the hollowed-out log craft of these bongo boatmen.

All the baggage was quickly loaded, and Jessie's party boarded the narrow and rocking bongo. For the next three days, the boatmen poled and paddled their craft against the heavy river current. Along the banks and even overhead Jessie saw a lush growth of green plants, creeping vines, and magnificent flowers of brilliant warm colors. Birds with rainbow plumage squawked and flew off in a blur of colors and gave the impression of Japanese fans suddenly come alive with the gift of flight. The crew laughed and sang their own versions of "Oh, Susanna," and other popular Gold Rush songs. At times they had to halt and get out their sharp machetes to cut away a thick growth of vines that had blocked the passage almost overnight.

During the trip to Gorgona, Richard became ill. When they went ashore, he had to be put to bed at once. There was no possibility of his going on; and as soon as he regained some strength, he was to be sent back to Chagres to board a steamer for home. Jessie refused to allow this to halt her journey. She had come this far, and she was determined to forge ahead. Instead of wondering what to do next, she accepted an invitation from the local alcalde to have breakfast at his home. It was unlike any dwelling she had ever seen:

> The stilted house with its wattled sides, thatched roof, and inside walls of unbleached sheeting looked more like a magnified vegetable crate than a human habitation. At breakfast the chief dishes were baked ringtailed monkey and boiled iguana, a large lizard. Both dishes were tasty, once you forgot the monkey's resemblance to a child burned to death.[1]

After this experience, the next stage of Jessie's journey was a long and hard day's mule-back ride. Indians were in charge of this overland trip, and they were experienced hands who made sure their animals followed the winding trail that was about four feet wide and snaked in and out of groves of towering palms and clusters of mangrove trees as it followed the downward course of the mountains and passed through the lush jungle regions where sunlight barely filtered through the covering of rain forest. Sudden downpours drenched riders, baggage, and mules and turned the trail into a slippery line of mud that dropped in and out of canyons and crossed swollen streams that roared through deep cuts in the mountainside. At these places there were no bridges, and it was up to the riders to hang on and keep a tight seat as the sure-footed mules jumped the narrow, rushing streams.

This jarring downhill ride seemed endless until Jessie had her first view of the Pacific Ocean. The wide expanse of endless sea reminded her of what it must have been like when Balboa first sighted this unknown ocean. The excitement of history coming alive made a full impact on her as she saw the walled city of Panama that had been established in 1519. It seemed almost unreal as she looked ahead and noticed the roof and spire of the cathedral all inlaid with mother of pearl and glistening in the late afternoon sun. Then the full feeling of a mass of men on the move, of Argonauts in search of the Golden Fleece, struck every fiber of her imagination as she got her first glimpse of the thousands of forty-niners camped in the plaza or any other spot they could find to await passage aboard some ship bound for California.

Jessie and Lily were taken to lodgings that had been reserved for them at

Madame Arce's balconied and red-tiled home. For the first time since leaving New York, Jessie enjoyed the luxury of clean sheets on a good bed, of something to eat that was better than ship's fare or baked monkey, and of having the chance to use a bathhouse. While the bathing place was without lights, it had open slats near the ceiling for ventilation. On the slate floor there were ceramic jars that held from a quart to a gallon or more of water. The bath attendant poured the contents of the smallest jar first for her to become accustomed to the shock of cold water after having been in the tropical heat. Then when the final large jar had been poured, Jessie learned there were no towels, and she had to dry herself in the sun inside a sheltered court.

In this warm and comfortable place, she received a letter from John Charles that he had sent from Taos, New Mexico, on January 27, 1849, not long after he had got away from the snows of disaster. While he described some of the ordeal he had endured, he was very sketchy about details. But by reading between the lines, she could tell that things had been far worse than he indicated.

Seven weeks went by at Madam Arce's before there was a chance to book passage on a California-bound ship. It came during the night, and Jessie was awakened by the loud booming of a signal cannon as a steamer entered the harbor and dropped anchor. She looked out her window at a scene of wild excitement. Men were gathering their gear, yelling and singing, and lining up to try and get aboard the ship before it was too loaded.

Two ships had entered the harbor. The *Panama* had rounded the Horn and sailed up the Pacific Coast, and the *California* had sailed south from San Francisco with a shanghaied crew. Even before Jessie finished dressing Lily and herself, Madam Arce rapped on her door. Jessie opened it to be greeted by the captain and lieutenant of the *Panama*. The younger officer took one look at her quarters and said, "God! What a crib for a lady!"[2] But Jessie would have none of his criticism. She quickly told him it had been her home for seven weeks, and that she had been treated with utmost kindness.

Yet her quarters in Madam Arce's home appeared palatial compared to what she was given aboard the *Panama*. Outfitted with good accommodations for about eighty passengers, the ship had almost four hundred aboard before she sailed out of the harbor. Spaces were parceled out on the deck, and Jessie made a shelter "by throwing the folds of a large American flag across the spanker boom. Here, they slept on iron cots padded with blankets."[3]

Even with such rude quarters, the voyage was not bad until they encountered a storm just south of San Diego. Soaked by the driving rain, Jessie caught a severe cold, developed a high fever, and hemorrhaged from her congested lungs. The concerned captain appealed to passengers with cabins, and one man gave his up so she could be protected. Even in this condition, she was more concerned about John Charles; and the first news she received about him came at San Diego, where the *Panama* stopped to land some passengers. There was a loud knock on her cabin door, and a fellow passenger shouted, "Mrs. Frémont, the Colonel's safe, riding up to San Francisco to meet you. He didn't lose his leg, only a bad frostbite."[4]

This was a tonic to help her regain her health, and on June 4, 1849, the *Panama* sailed through the Golden Gate and fired a cannon to announce her arrival. When Jessie heard the steady beat of the steam engine halt, when there was the metallic rattle of the anchor chain and the splash of metal striking water, she knew her long wait was over. Now, it was get ashore, and somewhere in the crowd of people along the waterfront, somewhere in the cold, foggy air, John Charles would be waiting.

2

TOO ILL TO HELP HERSELF, Jessie was carried ashore. Through the help of concerned passengers, she was put up at the Parker House just off Portsmouth Square. Here she remained in bed while others watched out for Lily. Ten days after her arrival she heard a loud shout from Portsmouth Square. It carried above the other noises of this bustling Gold Rush city, and it was a name that made her weep. The man who called out said that her husband had arrived and was on his way to her room. Before she could even thank the bearer of such good news, John Charles entered the room, and she began to sob as he knelt beside her chair.

> Then we both spoke at once, each wanting the other to begin at the moment we had parted over a stirrup-cup of tea. . . . Suddenly he looked at me closely with fear in his eyes. "You have been ill, you are ill now, my darling." I was about to deny it when Lily came in. . . . She looked at her father gravely as he knelt beside me. As he rose and hugged her, then drew a chair up close, and took her on his knee, she said bluntly: "You didn't come. Mother almost died. A lady downstairs says she will die."[5]

Though Jessie tried to dismiss her illness by asking about his terrible time in the San Juan Mountains, John Charles insisted that they would have to find another lodging in San Francisco that would be warm and comfortable. Then there was the need of servants, as Jessie was not strong enough to take care of things by herself.

Jessie said that this was pointless. She had not made such a long journey to stay inside a house in San Francisco. She was going to Las Mariposas. The warm summer climate of the Sierra Nevada foothills would be just what she needed. Besides, she wanted to be with him and to see their new home.

John Charles would have none of this. San Francisco was to be home until a proper house had been built at their mountain ranch. Then and only then would he agree to her living so far away from civilization. With this said, he proceeded to rent the home of the late U. S. Vice Consul Leidesdorff, and he looked for servants to aid Jessie while he was away. But in the mad rush of San Francisco in the summer of 1849, servants were not easy to find. Nor did Jessie show signs of regaining her health in the foggy and chilly climate. Realizing that she needed warmer weather, John Charles packed Jessie, Lily, and all their baggage into a six-seated surrey that had been built for him in New Jersey and then shipped around the Horn. When everybody was ready, including Juan and Gregorio—the California Indian youths—the Frémonts left San Francisco and made a slow journey to Monterey, where Jessie could get away from the cold westerly winds and the eternal banks of fog that rolled through the Golden Gate.

At Monterey, the Frémonts rented a wing of the former governor's mansion, a large adobe home that belonged to Señora José Castro, whose husband was in exile in Mexico. Though he refused to return to California, Madame Castro held no hard feelings about Frémont. War was one of those things over which the individual had very little control. She believed that once the killing had ceased, there was no point in carrying hatred in one's mind like a festering growth. To her, the Frémonts needed a home, and there was plenty of room in her mansion.

To make their wing of the Castro home even more comfortable, John Charles told Jessie he was going to San Francisco to purchase household goods. When he returned, the unloading of the surrey was an eventful time. He had purchased bales of French damask and Chinese satins to be used for draperies and hangings. And he brought out bolts of cloth that could be used to make new clothes, for he had to tell Jessie that her trunks of garments that had been stored in a San Francisco warehouse had gone up in flames when it burned. Jessie was startled to hear such news, and she shuddered at the idea of making new clothes. But the choice had been made for her.

There seemed to be an endless procession of goods. There were rolls of cloth and matting to cover the floors, an assortment of Chinese and English porcelain, two English china punch bowls that were to serve as wash basins, East Indian wicker chairs, New England bedsteads that had been shipped around the Horn, sheets and blankets, intricately inlaid and carved teak furniture from China, spermaceti candles, and candlestick holders made of tin. And while these weren't the most co-ordinated household items, Jessie had to admit they would help turn their rooms in the Castro home into more than an inn for the night.

With a house full of possibles, as a mountain man would have put it, John Charles told Jessie he had some good news. In San Francisco he had seen their old friend Lieutenant Ned Beale. And Beale had a letter for him from the newly elected President Zachary Taylor. President Taylor had asked John Charles to head the Boundary Commission surveying the new border between the United States and Mexico.

While Jessie waited to see if this meant that her husband would be away from her again, John Charles quickly put her mind at ease. He had no intention of giving up his mining activities in the Mother Lode country. But he had accepted the position with the intention of resigning as soon as someone else could be found for the task. He had done this for two reasons. First, the fact that President Taylor offered him the position made it clear that the hero of the Mexican War had confidence in him despite the verdict of the court-martial. Second, it would be a good thing to have on his record if he should accept the invitation of others and become one of the first candidates for senator from California once statehood was granted.

## 3

AFTER JOHN CHARLES'S TERRIBLE TIME in the snows, after Jessie's hard trip across the Isthmus of Panama and her struggle to regain her health, the streak of bad luck ran out for the Frémonts. Las Mariposas became something that Thomas Oliver Larkin had never considered when he purchased it for Frémont. It became a bonanza of the southern Mother Lode when the Sonoran miners struck it rich in this foothill country, only forty miles away from Yosemite Valley.

It was a long ride from Bear Valley on the Las Mariposas grant to either Monterey or San Francisco. In the summer months, all travelers dropped down from the yellow pine country and passed the red-clay, bull-pine, and poison-oak region. Then they rode alongside the Mariposa River to the San Joaquin Valley, where the summer heat reached beyond one hundred degrees. The golden-colored grass and the dying wild flowers of spring no longer kept the dust of the valley floor from rising upward from the hooves of horses to cover men and riders with a fine coat of rich, delta soil. In the winter months, the same journey took them down the slippery red-clay trails and beginnings of wagon roads to rain-swollen rivers. Once across these icy waters, the remaining journey was over the vast flood plain of the San Joaquin Valley, which was as much a shallow lake as it was land, until they crossed the Pacific Coast Range to the Salinas Valley.

Throughout the summer and winter months, Frémont made this journey to bring one-hundred-pound buckskin sacks of gold to put into the adobe storeroom behind the Castro home. Each sack, Jessie wrote, was worth as much as $25,000. And while the Frémonts had entered California not knowing how they were going to pay their daily bills, now a fortune was being amassed from the rich vein on their estate of over forty thousand acres. Altogether, twenty-nine ore-bearing veins were discovered. But the most valuable ledge was on Mount Bullion, named in honor of Senator "Old Bullion" Benton. "It outcropped on the grant for over eleven miles, and the belt of mineral veins tributary to it was often over two miles in width."[6]

Enough gold was taken from these placer diggings to send the Sonorans back to Mexico with a richer stake than they had dreamed about. When they asked to go home, Frémont simply gave them the key to the storage room and told them to take what was theirs and leave the key. Not one man betrayed the trust he had shown, but there was trouble in the wind.

Las Mariposas was a "floating grant." This meant it had no set boundaries and no clear title. The former owner, Alvarado, had run into trouble with the Miwoks when he tried to survey the land, and he had never been able to fulfill the terms of the survey and settlement to make the title clear and legal. Another problem destined to plague Frémont was that the original terms of the grant did not allow Alvarado to sell the property. Finally, as news of the rich gold strike on the land filtered out of the Mother Lode, Frémont had to contend with claim jumpers who did not care that he had paid for the land. As far as they were concerned it was anybody's gold.

Before all this trouble reached a peak, John Charles enjoyed a period of peace and privacy. He saw to it that a two-story frame house was constructed in Bear Valley so that Jessie and Lily could come and spend time at Las Mariposas.

Wearing his sombrero, ranchero jacket and trousers, and riding boots with large-roweled Spanish spurs, John Charles and his men rode beside the surrey as it took Jessie and Lily across the San Joaquin Valley and up into the red-clay country. Along the way they stopped and camped. While the men slept on the ground, Jessie drew the cushions together in the surrey and slept there, and Lily curled up in the boot. It was a life of movement and excitement, of discovery and riches. Then along with their homes in Monterey and Bear Valley, Frémont added another in San Francisco when he purchased a ready-made house. The whole thing was like some magnificent, giant-size cabinet made by a master craftsman.

Life was going well for John Charles and Jessie. He was no longer somewhere in the wilderness, and she saw more of him than ever before. She didn't have to be concerned about taking care of her mother day and night. It was a life style that Jessie could have enjoyed forever. But rumors of politics floated in and out of family conversations, and she wondered how much longer this idyllic life would last.

4

As 1849 NEARED ITS END, Frémont was testing the political waters. The move was on for California statehood. And even as John Charles argued against the use of slave labor in mining claims, it was obvious that a major issue for California's future was the national debate over slavery. The proslavery faction thought that Frémont—a Southerner by birth, married into a prominent Border State family—would side with them. This was not the case. For, as he was asked about his political leanings and was sounded out as a candidate for the United States Senate once California was admitted to the Union, John Charles made it clear that he was a member of the Free-Soil wing of the Democratic Party and was absolutely opposed to the spread of slavery into the western territories. Furthermore, he was a staunch supporter of a central national railroad to the Pacific, and promised he would do his best to see that it was constructed.

The idea of a railroad was one thing acceptable to all sides. But Frémont's stand against slavery was opposed by the proslavery faction of the party. Still, his name and national recognition made him a natural prospect for a political candidate. The obvious solution to this problem was a compromise between the antislavery and proslavery groups. The idea was agreed upon. In the meeting of the self-styled California legislature at San Jose in December of 1849, John Charles Frémont was elected as the antislavery senator from California, and William M. Gwinn was elected to represent the proslavery people (though the election, would not be valid until California was a state). Straws were drawn to determine which man would have the short term and be forced to campaign for re-election in the fall of 1850, and Frémont lost. Still, he was going to return to Washington as a senator, and the idea of erasing the disgrace of the court-martial in such a manner was something he wanted to share with Jessie right away.

Though the weather was calculated to keep most men inside any shelter they could find, John Charles mounted his sorrel horse and rode south from San Jose in a downpour of rain. With only an occasional flash of lightning to show him he was on the road, he rode seventy miles to Monterey. When he entered the house, he saw Jessie carefully explaining the pictures from the *Illustrated Times* to Lily. Jessie was startled to see him standing there, all drenching wet and afraid to move onto the rugs. But he smiled and told her that he had just been elected a senator from California.

Far into the night, long after Lily was asleep, they sat and talked after a supper of cold beef, biscuits, and cup after cup of hot coffee. It was a life that had come full circle for them. They had left Washington without knowing their future. Now the mines at Las Mariposas had restored their money and added a fortune to their name, and the disgrace of the court-martial had been wiped clean by two things: his temporary acceptance of the position as head of the Mexican Boundary Survey, and his forthcoming return to Washington as Senator Frémont of California. Then, as the night drew near its close, John Charles left Jessie and made the ride back to San Jose. For the rest of the convention would determine the future of California—a golden kingdom by the Pacific that was due to enter the Union at a time when the key issue among the states and the territories was slavery. To Frémont and Jessie, there was no question as to what was right; and as he rode away and vanished into the storm again, she knew he would fight to make sure no man could ever hold another in bondage.

5

WITH MIXED FEELINGS of regret and happiness, the Frémonts left Monterey on a rainy New Year's night of 1850. John Charles carried Jessie along the streets that had become creeks, and Gregorio carried Lily. At the wharf, they boarded a large rowboat loaded with their baggage. Another Indian manned the oars and slowly made his way through the choppy waters of Monterey Bay to where the steamer *Oregon* was riding at anchor.

As they boarded the ship, the weeping of Gregorio made Jessie and Lily cry, and John Charles assured him they would not be gone forever. But he continued to sob until John Charles told him he would send for him once they were settled in Washington, D.C. Yet, though Gregorio stopped his lament, Jessie kept it up as she thought of the life she was leaving behind. All of it had been a holiday existence for her.

But as the *Oregon* sailed down the coast, Jessie and John Charles talked to other passengers. Their thoughts turned toward Washington. And they began to long for a return that would bring them to the Benton family home.

At Mazatlán, just south of the Tropic of Cancer, the *Oregon* put into the harbor to take on a load of coal for the engines. Guns boomed from an English man-of-war riding at anchor to salute the newly elected California senators. The United States Consul, John Parrott, invited the celebrities to spend the day at his thick-walled adobe home; and the Frémonts, who had changed from their woolens to lighter clothing, were chilled in the coolness of Parrott's home.

When they sailed away from Mazatlán, both John Charles and Jessie came down with serious colds and fever. Frémont's frostbitten leg began to bother him greatly, and he walked with a decided limp. But it was Jessie who became worse as her fever remained high. When the *Oregon* steamed into the harbor at Panama, the Frémonts were so ill that they had to be carried ashore on stretchers and were put up at Madame Arce's. Only Saunders Jackson, the free black who had found enough gold at Las Mariposas to buy his family from slaveholders, was well enough to see that the Frémonts were watched over day and night.

Madame Arce turned her ballroom into a hospital ward for the sick couple. She saw to the care of Lily, who had not caught the fever. John L. Stephens, who was now vice-president of the Panama Railroad Company, had the couple visited by the company physician, and nuns acted as volunteer nurses. Stephens, who had endured Arabia, Yucatan, and the work in Panama, was not in good health; but he was more concerned about Jessie's condition and told Frémont, "Pioneering is hell on women. That child is all eyes and grit. Nothing else left."[7]

Despite his failing health, short and stocky Stephens did his best to bring some cheer to the sick couple. "He would put a chair between our linen cots and say, 'I have come to take my chill with you'—and talk on with wit and charm as he shivered and shook. . . ."[8]

Finally, the day arrived to move across the Isthmus. John Charles had recovered enough to ride a mule again. But the difficult part of the trip to Gorgona and the start of the bongo voyage down the Chagres River to the Atlantic presented a challenge as Jessie was not strong enough to sit astride a mule. The problem of getting her to Gorgona was solved by an officer from an American man-of-war anchored in the harbor.

It was his device to have a ship's hammock put upon stretchers which were prolonged into shafts and an awning with curtains rigged over it on light strong supports. The sailors brought this up into the great ball room which had been made into a hospital for us, and I was fitted into my fresh looking large palanquin, Madame Arce putting one of her own crimson silk lace trimmed pillows under my head and the flat canvass pocket by me filled with pocket handkerchiefs and a cologne flask. The four picked Indian bearers—answered for by Mr. Stephens—were drilled a little by the sailors, and started off two at a time between the shafts—resting them on crotched supports when they changed to fresh bearers. Mr. Frémont on a mule on one side and my little girl also riding—well and fearlessly—keeping close, with Saunders bringing up the rear with our baggage packed on mules. . . . And so the rough mountain journey was made and my hammock palanquin comfortably placed in an open boat to descend the Chagres.[9]

At Chagres, now Colón, the Frémont party boarded the *Georgia* for the voyage to New York. As the steamer made her way across the Gulf of Mexico, Jessie suffered from a terrible case of Chagres fever. She became delirious, and thrashed about so much that she had to be lashed to a sofa for her own protection. And while John Charles suffered from an attack of this fever, his was not so severe as Jessie's. Yet by the time they arrived in New York, pale and thin as she was, Jessie was able to walk down the gangplank.

Frémont wired Senator Benton that they had arrived and would be staying at the Irving House. It was here, in a suite of rooms that had just been vacated by Jenny Lind, that Jessie looked at herself in a full-length mirror and realized how ill she had been. Her eyes were deeply sunken, her pale skin had turned a jaundiced yellow, and she seemed to be nothing more than skin and bones. Standing beside her was fat and rosy-cheeked Lily, whose skirt was much too short and who wore buckskin moccasins that had been given to her by Gregorio just before they left Monterey.

But good food and a nontropical climate soon made the difference as they rested in the familiar surroundings of the Benton home. By the time California was admitted to the Union on September 9, 1850, Jessie was her usual striking figure, and she sat in the gallery on the following day and watched Senator Frémont admitted to his seat. The full circle had been completed from that day in the Washington Arsenal when he had been found guilty on all counts by the officers of the court-martial. Now he was back on top again. A bit grayer, a little older, but a man of means, of fame, and a senator from California, the thirty-first state admitted to the Union.

## 6

SENATOR FRÉMONT had a short but busy tenure of office. Still suffering from attacks of Chagres fever and from rheumatism in the leg that had been severely frostbitten, Frémont was in the Senate for only twenty-one working

days. Even so, during this short time he introduced eighteen pieces of legislation. Of these bills, the most important were a bill to grant the state of California public lands for educational purposes; a bill to grant it six townships in
order to found a university; a bill to set aside land for asylums for the insane,
the deaf, dumb, and blind; a bill designed to regulate the methods for working mines in California; and a bill to have the government back the opening
of a transcontinental wagon road.

Along with all these measures, Senator Frémont spoke openly against the
institution of slavery, voted for the abolition of the slave trade in the District
of Columbia, and voted against the bill which provided a stiff prison sentence for any individual who encouraged slaves to run for freedom. At this
moment when the forces for and against slavery were on a collision course,
Senator Frémont's open support of any antislavery measure was not the mark
of a scheming politician. During one session on the floor of the Senate, he almost got into a fight with the half-drunk Senator Foote of Mississippi, who
disliked his antislavery attitude and accused him in turn of putting forth a
bill regarding California mining that was to his own advantage. Before all
this ended, Senator Frémont sent Senator Foote a letter in which he
demanded that he retract his statement and apologize or meet him on the
field of honor. While the duel never took place, the mere fact that one senator had challenged another became the talk of all Washington.

Then, as the fall session drew to a close, word reached Frémont that a
strong proslavery party was in full swing in California. If he expected to be
re-elected, he had better come home and do some political fence mending.
Without hesitation, he left and made the crossing of the Isthmus of Panama
once again. He was back in California before the end of 1850. But he came
back to more trouble than he had anticipated. Not only was he in political
difficulty, but also he had more squatters on his Mariposa property than
before—squatters who ignored his first claim to the land and its mineral
rights. He became ill again and was put to bed with neuralgia, rheumatism,
and sciatica.

When Jessie learned of this in one of his letters, she did not hesitate even
though she was pregnant. Taking Lily with her, she hurried from the East to
take care of John Charles. This time her tropical crossing did not result in
Chagres fever, but she arrived to find that John Charles had been defeated in
his bid for re-election by the slavery faction.

There was no time to waste on what might have been. There was too
much trouble at Las Mariposas. Men had come from all over the world, and
each gulch in the Mother Lode country had become an overnight tent and
shack city. Many of these prospectors thought nothing of taking another
man's belongings, paid no attention to claims that were being worked by
others, and were thoroughly despicable to the Mexicans, Chileans, and Chinese. Some of the worst offenders were the convicts who had managed to get
out of Australia's Botany Bay and Sydney. These Sydney Ducks and other

criminals roamed the Mother Lode. Their behavior in San Francisco resulted in a call for vigilantes.

Despite such conditions, Frémont did his best to make a go of things on his Mariposa property. Along with mining, he contracted with the Federal Government to supply beef to Indians who had been pushed off their hunting grounds and who were on the verge of going to war against these intruders who were destroying their land. As he worked all during the winter and spring of 1851, he left Jessie and Lily in a home on Stockton Street in San Francisco, not far from Portsmouth Square.

Here, on April 19, 1851, Jessie gave birth to John Charles Frémont II. He was a sturdily built baby, and Jessie said: "He is strong as a native son should be, and as a son of Colonel Frémont he is already well traveled."[10]

Then on May 4 the fire bells clanged, people shouted and screamed. The first great San Francisco fire began to burn downhill from the Frémont home. John Charles and Gregorio quickly hung soaking wet carpets and blankets on the sides of the house. A friend carried boxes of legal papers and other valuables to his house on Russian Hill. Jessie, the baby boy, and Lily were helped to get ready to move at a moment's notice. But the fire stopped its uphill rush before it reached their home. Still, this was not the last of the fires to plague San Francisco. A month later, while John Charles was back at Las Mariposas, a second fire broke out on a Sunday morning in late June. This time there was no stopping it. Gregorio carried Jessie in his arms as the blaze neared the home, and baby Charley was carried in the arms of a nurse as Lily scurried alongside. Then from a neighbor's house, Jessie watched her home burn.

When Frémont returned from the Mother Lode, he was frantic when he found only the blackened remains of the house. But Gregorio had seen to everything. Other neighbors had even saved some of the household goods for the Frémonts. Not far from their previous dwelling, Gregorio had located another house among the sand dunes. It was here that John Charles found all of them waiting for dinner as Gregorio tended a fire and cooked a kettle of soup hanging from a tripod over the hot coals.

Jessie's fragile condition, and the nightmare of two fires so close together had affected her greatly. At night, she frequently awoke, got out of bed, and wildly groped for an open window or door as the memory of fire bells in the night haunted her. This, and the fact that his agents for the Mariposa property—David Hoffman and Thomas Denny Sargent—could not agree on how to organize the mining companies so that money could be raised through leases, caused John Charles to consider a change. The easy placer gold was gone. Capital was needed for hard rock mining. The legality of his claim was not yet clear. All this convinced him he had endured enough business for the time being.

One foggy evening in December 1851 he looked at Jessie as she tried to make do and prepare for a Christmas holiday in their temporary quarters. He asked her how she would like a trip to Paris for a New Year's gift. She looked up at him and smiled. Then she suggested Charley might enjoy a closer peep at the man in the moon. Even as she teased him, he opened his wallet and pulled out a brightly colored packet of steamer tickets. One look was all she needed. The journey was well marked from San Francisco to Panama to Chagres and across the Atlantic to England and France. For once they were going to do something for pleasure alone. Life in El Dorado would have to take a back seat.

# XXV

## The Last Expedition

POLITICS WAS THE NAME OF THE GAME, and Frémont realized this when they reached England in the spring of 1852. News awaited him about Congress ordering five surveys for a potential railway route to the Pacific. Yet there was no invitation for him to head any of them.

Secretary of War Jefferson Davis was in charge of appointments. He was a West Point man and proslavery. Both institutions made him anti-Frémont. To Davis, it did not matter that Frémont had the best training and experience for the task. Nor did it matter that he was honored by such a prominent body as the Royal Geographical Society. John Charles was on the wrong side in the growing feud between North and South.

Even in London, where he enjoyed the limelight, John Charles suffered another indignity. He was arrested and thrown in jail. Friends bailed him out. All this was because of the failure of the United States Government to honor four drafts he had drawn in 1847 to purchase supplies for the California Battalion. English creditors, who held these worthless notes, planned to get their money back by having Frémont arrested. But their maneuver was circumvented by testimony taken from former Secretary of State James Buchanan in Philadelphia and sent to the British court to clear Frémont's name.[1]

Only this one thing marred their stay in London, but as they sailed across the English Channel to France in May, the couple laughed at what had happened. When they reached Paris, Jessie and John Charles felt very much at home. It was like being back in the French quarter of St. Louis once more, and the flavor of Gallic life was a welcome change after California and England. Parisian society enchanted them, and they received a warm reception from men and women who admired Frémont's explorations and claimed him as one of their own. Nor was Jessie overlooked as her beauty and wit attracted all.

Feeling thoroughly at home in Paris, the couple rented an Italian-style mansion on the Champs Elysées, just between the Place de l'Étoile and Rond

Point. Lily and Charley were kept at home, and a governess was hired to take care of them and see to it that they learned as much proper French as time would allow. Jessie's and John Charles's lives were filled with great joy as they attended balls and dinner parties, and were invited by royalty who were fascinated with Frémont's experiences in the American West.

Yet, as the couple enjoyed themselves and Jessie grew larger with child again, news of another nature arrived from Senator Benton. Twenty-one-year-old Randolph, who was just due to enter St. Louis University, had been stricken with a disease that had all the virulent effects of cholera. According to Jessie's father, Randolph became extremely bilious, ran a high fever, and in a matter of a few days passed from a delirious and painful state into sudden silence and death. It was difficult for Jessie and John Charles to accept. Happy-go-lucky Randolph, the boy who had been so much fun for the men of Frémont's first expedition, was gone forever. Jessie didn't think she could stand it. She cried and cried until she was near a state of collapse, and her eyes became so sore she could hardly see.

For Jessie's health, Frémont decided they would remain in Paris until the birth of the baby. Then, when Jessie was able, they would sail for home. For, along with the bad news, Senator Benton had suggested it would be possible to get private backing for Frémont to make his own railroad survey. In this way, he would be in his element again; and as amateurs stumbled around in the wilderness, he could point the way for a future railroad line.

Then on February 1, 1853, Jessie gave birth to a baby girl, who was named Anne Beverly after Frémont's mother. Now it was only a matter of a few months before she would be ready to return home. The European holiday was coming to an end, and it was time for John Charles to get back to the business of exploration.

2

Washington, D.C., in June of 1853 was worse than John Charles and Jessie had remembered. There was no let-up in the humid, hot weather. The days began with a stifling and pervading warmth and got worse as the hours passed. The only good thing they could comment upon was that they were home again. They had rented a house not far from the Bentons, and as Jessie took care of Anne Beverly and watched over Charley and Lily, John Charles began to consider what he wished to accomplish on his next expedition. The more he thought about it, the more he was determined to show that the San Juan Mountains would be the best all-year route for a central overland railroad. To prove his point, he again decided to cross the region in the middle of winter. But even as he made his plans, the baby girl became ill with a digestive ailment that was runing rampant throughout the city. Not wanting to risk Anne Beverly's life, Jessie accepted the invitation to stay at the Frank

Blair estate at Silver Springs, Maryland, until the epidemic had run its course.

Their personal physician assured the Frémonts this was the best thing they could do, as Washington was hardly a healthy place for such a frail child. But the move did not help. On July 11 Anne Beverly died in her mother's arms. News of the tragedy reached Washington quickly. The grief-stricken John Charles hurried to be at Jessie's side, to comfort her as best he could, and to make the sad return journey with her as they brought the tiny coffin to Washington for burial.

Jessie's reaction was just the opposite of her behavior when Randolph had died: She remained calm and almost impassive about Anne Beverly's death. It was as though she was in a state of shock and failed to realize what had happened. When Senator Benton commented on her ability to withstand such an ordeal, Frémont said, "It was she who remained dry eyed to comfort me, for I was unmanned over the cruelty of this bereavement. Her calm stoicism, so superior to mere resignation, soon shamed me into control."[2]

The death of tiny Anne Beverly pushed Frémont full force into preparations for his fifth expedition. If he didn't drive himself, he knew he would become more and more despondent over the tragedy. He talked to his father-in-law about all possible aspects of this journey. They considered the two expeditions already in the field and noted they were following the route John Charles failed to complete in the winter of 1848–49. One party was headed by Gwinn Harris Heap and Lieutenant Edward Fitzgerald Beale. The official government expedition, the one Frémont had hoped to lead, was in the charge of Captain John W. Gunnison. It also included two men who had been with Frémont on his ill-fated fourth expedition—Richard Kern and the botanist Frederick Creutzfeldt. Both expeditions were headed for the San Juan Mountains west of Bent's Fort, but they were going to make their crossings in the summer. This seemed pointless to Frémont. He was certain the route could be used in the summer. The questionable factor was its value during winter.

As these parties worked their way into the mountains, Frémont was busy in New York. He purchased all the needed scientific instruments, including a daguerreotype camera. Then to make certain that the camera would be used correctly, he hired a handsome, talented artist and daguerreotypist who was living in Baltimore. Thirty-eight-year-old Solomon Nunes Carvalho was a descendant of a Sephardic Jewish family.[3] He had been born in Charleston, South Carolina, and he jumped at the opportunity to go on a Frémont expedition. John Charles was pleased to find such a qualified daguerreotypist. For ever since his own 1842–43 attempts at taking pictures of the West, he had been anxious to follow Alexander von Humboldt's advice and become the first explorer to make a photographic record of an expedition.

Now, all he needed was the service of a first-rate topographer. Though he had written to Charles Preuss from Paris, the sturdy German had turned him down. Mrs. Preuss would have none of it. Her husband had survived the terrible fourth expedition. She did not want to see him head back into the wilderness with Frémont again. Instead, she allowed him to sign on as a draftsman with that section of the Pacific Railway Survey assigned to exploring and mapping a potential southwestern railway route.

To replace Preuss, Frémont hired twenty-nine-year-old F. W. von Egloffstein, a Prussian immigrant. For, like Preuss, Egloffstein was a skilled topographer, talented artist, strong, and quite capable of enduring the hardships of the trail.

With these key men hired and sent on their way to St. Louis, where the final preparations for the expedition would be made, John Charles returned to Washington. He stayed as long as he could with Jessie and the children, for he was well aware of Jessie's concern about the danger of this winter exploration. Then, before August had run its course, Frémont was on the National Road in a stagecoach and headed for the nearest steamboat landing on the Ohio River to book passage for St. Louis. His concern was that the right men would still be available at Chouteau's. With luck, Kit Carson just might be in the city, but the chances were not very good. But perhaps there would be some experienced hands. For he had to have more than dedicated amateurs with him, or the chances for survival would not be great.

When he reached St. Louis, his concern about not finding too many experienced hands was justified but for one notable exception. Much to his joy and relief, Alexis Godey was in the city and willing to hire on for the journey.

Other men were hired at St. Louis, including Oliver Fuller, who signed on as an assistant to Egloffstein, and W. H. Palmer, who came along as a "passenger" willing to work his way just to be in on such an expedition. Frémont was still concerned about the matter of pictures, and he decided to give another photographer, a Mr. Bomar, a chance to compete with Carvalho. Willing to take the risk of being let go before reaching the frontier, Bomar boarded the steamboat *Francis X. Aubrey* along with the rest of the party, and they started upriver for Westport at the beginning of September. Even as they did, news had already reached St. Louis that the Heap-Beale expedition had crossed Cochetopa Pass in good shape. It was obvious, now, that all that remained was to prove that the pass could be crossed in the dead of winter.

By September 15 the Frémont party had arrived at Westport, where other members of the expedition were already in camp awaiting their appearance. One other task was to determine whether Carvalho or Bomar was to go along. To do this, a contest was held. Success was speed, and Bomar's process took far too much time to be anything other than a handicap on a field expedition. The matter was settled, and Carvalho was the official photographer of the party.

By September 20 the men were ready to move out. All were armed with rifles, Colt pistols, knives, and anything else that might come in handy once they were beyond the last settlement. By writing ahead to Major Cummins, Frémont managed to obtain the services of ten Delawares, including Captain Wolf who, according to Carvalho, was a very large and imposing man.

Two days later, moving slowly to get accustomed to the trail, the party of twenty-one arrived at the Shawnee Mission. Here, Frémont hired Max Strobel as another assistant for Egloffstein. But the possiblity of the expedition ending before it got beyond the Shawnee Mission suddenly became apparent as Frémont became very ill. Leaving Palmer in charge and telling the men to move ahead with Captain Wolf as guide, the colonel and Strobel headed back to Westport.

Five days after they had vanished, the expedition saw a lone rider coming from the east and hoped it was the colonel. As the horseman drew closer, they saw that it was Max Strobel. When he dismounted, he told them Colonel Frémont had gone on to St. Louis for proper medical advice. Yet he had issued instructions, according to Carvalho's journal entry, for the men "to proceed as far as Smoky Hills and encamp, where there was plenty of buffalo, and to send back 'Solomon,' the Indian chief, who had accompanied him in a former voyage to Westport, to conduct him to camp. He thought he would be with us in a fortnight."[4]

A fortnight passed without any sign of the explorer. Then, as October 30 neared its late afternoon, the sun was blotted from view by dense clouds of smoke from a vast wildfire raging through miles of dry grass. As the fire drew closer to the camp, the men, wondering if Frémont had survived this blaze, followed the lead of the Delawares and carried all the camp gear down to the bank of the creek. They picketed the nervous horses and mules in the groves of cottonwoods beside the water. That night passed in a strange red glow that appeared to stretch in all directions for endless miles as though some last fire of destruction was burning the floor of the sky.

By morning the area around the camp was a smoldering, blackened scar. The men spoke of moving to a better area, where the fire had bypassed the grass and the trees beside the river, but they had to remain where they were so Frémont would be able to locate them. Their eyes burning from smoke, they had just started to eat breakfast when one of the Delawares gave a loud shout and pointed toward the burning plains. Coming out of the fire and smoke, riding at a full gallop were four horsemen. In the lead was Colonel Frémont; behind him was an incredibly large man on one of the biggest mules any of them had ever seen; and beside him rode Solomon, the Delaware chief, and one other man who had been hired as a camp cook.

Without hesitation and with great joy, the men in camp fired their rifles and pistols into the air to greet the returning men. As the admiring Carvalho put it, "No father who had been absent from his children could have been received with more enthusiasm and real joy."[5] The four riders—Frémont; Solomon; Lee, the black cook; and the big man, who was Dr. Ober—had traveled nearly fifty miles across burned ground where all signs of a trail had been turned into miles of ashes. But the leader was back, and though he had brought a physician with him to make certain he was ready to travel, Frémont was anxious to head out for Bent's Fort and the high country of the Continental Divide just beyond it.

3

THIRTY MILES before Bent's Fort came into sight, the expedition reached a new stone fort beside the Arkansas River. Here, east of the great adobe citadel, Frémont found William Bent at a place that was still under construction. The new establishment was solid, but not nearly as large as the old fort. As John Charles and William talked of old times, the story of what happened to the famous fort came out in a jumbled and sad story.

Cholera, it had been the damned cholera. It had come the year after Bent had warned Frémont about trying to cross the mountains in the heavy snows.

John Charles waited, and slowly the rest of it came out. Forty-niners on their way to California had brought the fever with them. It had killed both of Bent's brothers and wiped out half the Southern Cheyennes. There was nothing Bent could do. The whole fort was lousy with the fever. He packed his wife, Yellow Woman, and their children, into one of the twenty wagons he used to take away those things that weren't rotten with fever or the stench of death. And he had moved out—just up and left the place.

He had to talk about it, and Frémont listened as he continued. Bent had tried to sell the stricken fort to the United States Army, tried to get them to buy the shell. They wouldn't touch it, and he wasn't going to let it go to the first set of drifters or raiding tribe that found it empty. He went back to it, passed through the great opening where the big American flag used to bend the heavy pole whenever the wind blew, and it was like going into a haunted house. The voices, the sound of Spanish, Cheyenne, and other Indian languages, the talk of mountain men just in with a load of fresh beaver pelts—it had all echoed there in his mind. But the job had to be done. He rolled powder kegs into the key rooms and spilled a trace of powder from the kegs to the doors. This done, he lit a torch and ran from room to room and touched off the spasms of flame that burned to the kegs and set off one wild explosion after another. Then it was silent and dead, as long gone into memory as his brothers, his wife's people, and all the friends who burned to death with fever.

It was the death of a way of life, and Frémont heard all of it. He heard it, and knew that his own way of life was also dying, going away right before his eyes. Even now, even during this week he stayed at William Bent's new fort, John Charles realized that the very things he had done, the thing he was now doing had opened the way for more and more people who would change the face of the land, the way of wilderness living. Yet, like Bent, he couldn't stop. It was what he did best, and even on this last expedition, he was going to give it all he had left in his body.

And Bent helped Frémont as much as he could. He supplied him with extra mounts and pack mules, and sold him jerked meat, coffee, a little sugar, tobacco, buffalo robes, and gloves and overshoes made of buffalo hide. Finally, he found a small buffalo-skin lodge for Frémont and a larger one that would protect the rest of his men during a heavy blow. Then on November 26, as Dr. Ober headed back for the settlements, John Charles and his men waved good-bye to William Bent and began their trek toward the cloud-covered heights of the Rocky Mountains.

4

THREE DAYS INTO DECEMBER the men passed out of Huerfano River Valley and entered the mountains. While the weather was cold, the snowpack was very light. They followed the tracks of the Gunnison party, which had taken wagons over the mountains and had cleared a good path wherever timber blocked the way.

Up and over the Wet Mountains, across the steep sides of the Sangre de Cristo Mountains by way of Sand Hill Pass, they bore to the north of the sand dunes and moved into San Luis Valley at an easy pace. Frémont and Egloffstein, with the help of Fuller and Strobel, made all the necessary readings and sketches for a map. Carvalho took as many pictures as time would allow, and they headed along the course of Sawatch Creek and reached Cochetopa Pass on December 14, 1853.

At the pass they had their first real touch of winter. Cloud banks moved in on fast-drifting air currents, driving snow stung their faces, and mountain fog made it difficult to see the trail. On the ridges the snow was over two feet deep, but at Cochetopa Pass, a light covering of four inches was all they saw. At this pass they were over nine thousand feet, and the wind whipped through the area with an Arctic blast that drove the snow off the level summit. Cochetopa Pass, or El Puerto de los Cíbolos (the Gate of the Buffaloes) was rightly named by both the Indians and the Mexicans. For it was possible for buffalo to cross through here at almost any season of the year. Frémont had found the right place for a railroad line, for the iron horse and its trailing herd of freight and passenger cars.

High on success, the men looked behind at the rough country they had traveled over. Then they stared ahead, and quickly realized that crossing the Continental Divide was only a stage in their journey. Ahead lay the task of working their way down the mountainside, climbing in and out of canyons, and making their way over other mountains that remained between them and the Great Basin. Carvalho was excited by this momentary success, and the expedition waited as he made a daguerreotype panorama of the continuous mountain ranges ahead of them.

Heading out again, the men worked their way westward down the mountainside, following the course of Cochetopa Creek until it reached what is now the Gunnison River. They followed this river until canyons prevented their going any farther. They then cut across country along the course of White Earth Creek to the Uncompahgre River, and followed it until they reached the meandering Gunnison River once again. They followed it to Grand River and the Green River to reach present-day Gunnison Valley, Utah. Directions for a city of the wilderness. Go so many miles beside one river. Take a right turn on another river. Follow that until you hit this other river. Take another right turn, and keep going. Simple, easy as can be if you know your way around in the wilderness; and Frémont and Godey knew their way. Yet it was anything but simple. It was hard every mile of the way, and the cold weather and driving, stinging snow made the going that much tougher on the men and their animals.

At one point, they worked their way through the Grand River Valley and had to climb a mountain that caused more trouble than Frémont had wished to see. To greenhorn Carvalho, it was something to put in his journal, something he would talk about later, but at the time, it was touch and go for survival.

When we were about half way up, the foremost baggage mule lost his balance and fell down, carrying with him nearly all the party, who might have been seen tumbling head over heels down the mountain, a distance of several hundred feet. I was thrown from my horse, and remained up to my head in the snow, but my horse was rolled over to the very bottom, where I found him unharmed. One horse and one mule were killed on the spot.[6]

The journey became worse day by day. Food grew short, and the men were cold and weary. Soon horses and mules would have to be killed for food, for the jumbled land of canyons, steep mountains, and deep ravines was taking its toll from the caravan. The Delawares managed to track and kill a fat, young wild horse, and this helped ease the hunger pangs. Then when they reached the Uncompahgre Valley, they came to a camp of Utes and managed to barter for fresh venison. Yet a battle with the Utes almost took place when one of them discovered that Frémont's party was eating his woman's horse. Payment was demanded and given. Then the Utes decided they wanted a share of everything in camp, including a keg of gunpowder. John Charles bluntly refused their demands. At the same time, he told his men the Utes wouldn't start a fight because they had their families with them.

While he was right about their unwillingness to start a pitched battle because of their families, Frémont and his men had a restless and wary night. At daybreak they moved out in a hurry and traveled over thirty miles before they pitched camp beside the Grand River. They had just made camp when an armed party of warriors appeared. They wanted more payment for the horse. The white men had paid the wrong person. The horse had belonged to them. Having said this, they held their rifles and bows in the air, made threats of starting a fight, and insisted they were going to be paid for their horse.

During all this, Frémont remained inside his lodge. Periodically, Carvalho brought him information about the state of affairs with the fifty or sixty braves who threatened to kill everybody in camp unless they were given what they wanted. To all this, the colonel sent forth negative replies. He instructed Carvalho to set up a paper target on a nearby tree and give the Indians a demonstration of the kind of power each man had in his Navy Colt revolver.

Puzzled and leery about the chief in the buffalo-skin lodge who never appeared, wondering if some kind of magic was taking place, the Utes felt better when Carvalho set up his target and fired one shot and hit it. That was not unusual. Any man could hit a target so close. But their attitude changed as Carvalho fired a second and third shot without taking time to reload. This was a magic gun. They had never seen anything like it before. Then Carvalho, who was one of the best shots in camp, invited the chief to try his luck with the pistol. Not quite certain about this gun that didn't have to be loaded, the chief dismounted, held the pistol and fired at the paper. Again, there was the sound of a shot.

> The fifth and sixth times two other Indians exploded it; having discharged the six, it was time to replace it in my belt. I had another one ready loaded which I dexterously substituted, and scared them into the acknowledgment that they were all at our mercy, for we could kill them as fast as we liked, if we were so disposed.[7]

The Navy Colt solved the dangerous moment, but the Utes did ask if they could stay at the camp overnight. Again Carvalho went to Frémont's lodge and reported this information. The colonel was agreeable, but to protect their goods and animals, he insisted that eleven men remain on guard for the night.

Not once during the whole time the Utes were in camp did Frémont come out of his lodge. To the Indians, this was strange medicine, a magic they should not disturb. The Great Captain of the whites had sent forth magic guns that fired without reloading. There was no way of knowing what other powers he might have. In the cold of dawn the warriors rode out of the camp and nothing had been taken. All that had been given up was the sleep of eleven men who had remained on guard all night.

What the Utes didn't know as they rode out of sight was that the Great Captain often remained inside his skin lodge by himself. As Carvalho put it:

> Col. Frémont's lodge was sacred from all and everything that was immodest, light, or trivial; each and all of us entertained the highest regard for him. The greatest etiquette and deference were always paid to him, although he

never ostensibly required it. Yet his reserved and unexceptionable deportment demanded from us the same respect with which we were always treated and which we ever took pleasure in reciprocating.[8]

With the threat of an Indian attack out of the way, another danger soon made itself felt. The weather became so cold that only water running fast and deep didn't freeze. This presented terrible problems in river crossings. Men had to plunge into the frigid water, and then stop and get a fire going before they lost the circulation in their limbs. Food was running very short, and they couldn't afford to take time to hunt. All they could do was rely on the slaughter of their own horses, and this had to be done on a ration basis. Every animal killed had to be food for all the men for six meals. Then as more horses were killed, it became necessary to take turns walking, as there were not enough horses to ride.

With obvious memories of what had happened on the disastrous fourth expedition, Frémont called the men together just before they reached the Green River. It was a solemn moment as he asked them to swear that no matter how difficult times became, no man would eat the body of a fallen comrade. Every man took an oath, and all promised that they would shoot any man who fell back on his word.

Day after day they moved through canyons, circled around cliffs, climbed up and down pinnacles and buttes, forded icy rivers, and picked off any game they happened to see. One day they killed and consumed a porcupine; another day a beaver was brought into camp, but more and more it became a matter of eating their own horses and mules as the animals began to drop from lack of forage. As each animal was slaughtered, the men ate every part they could. Entrails were boiled in a strange soup; "hide was roasted so as to burn the hair and make it crisp, the hoofs and shins were disposed of by regular rotation."[9]

Barely hanging on to life, feeling the pain of frostbite, the men fought to keep alive as they worked their way along the southern reaches of the Wasatch Mountains and the rim of the Great Basin. The days seemed endless, and the bitter cold grew worse. Yet there was no let-up in moving ahead, no giving in to despair. Each night when camp was made and the men clustered around the fires to slowly thaw their numb bodies, Frémont continued to work. He stood in the deep snow for hours, endured the penetrating cold, made astronomical readings, and carefully jotted all the information down so that a proper map could be fashioned of this region.

With their horses and mules giving out or being killed for food, each member of the party now found himself walking most of the time. Frémont and his men saw that their boots were wearing out. Some of the men were completely barefoot, while others made do with "a piece of raw hide on their feet, which, however, becoming hard and stiff by the frost, made them more uncomfortable than walking without any."[10] Freezing, always hungry, and becoming exhausted, the men collected cactus leaves, burned off the spines, and consumed the leaves as though they were potato peelings.

As they entered deeper snowdrifts, it was all they could do to force themselves ahead. They were nearing fifty days in this wilderness, and it was already the first part of February 1854. There was no possibility of turning back. The only hope was to forge slowly ahead. As Frémont led the way he suddenly felt his strength begin to leave him. It was a moment when he realized he might not make it.

> Going up a long mountain slope, I was breaking my way through the snow a little way ahead of my party, when suddenly my strength gave out. All power of motion left me. I could not move a foot; the mountain slope was naked, but it just happened that near by was a good thick grove of aspens, and across a neighboring ravine, the yellow grass showed above the snow on the hill side. Saying to Godey as he came up, that I would camp there, I sat down in the snow and waited. After a few minutes, strength enough came back and no one noticed what had happened.[11]

In the morning, he felt stronger. The men lined out behind him, and slowly they continued their upward climb toward the summit of the range. When they reached it, Carvalho looked ahead at more ranges of snow-covered mountains. Though Frémont assured him that the Mormon settlement of Parowan was no more than fifty miles away, Carvalho looked at ranges of everlasting snow, and was convinced they would never get away from the cold death that surrounded them. But John Charles took a compass reading, pointed ahead as though there were a well-marked trail through the maze of canyons and mountains, and began to move down the mountain slope. As he did, he noticed deer tracks, and offered a rifle to any man who could bring in a deer. A few hours after his offer, as they neared a valley, Weluchas—one of the Delawares—caught up to the party. He had a buck slung across his shoulders. The rifle was his, and there was fresh meat for the starving men.

Now, though, the party was strung out in a ragged line. Lack of food, constant freezing weather, worn-out boots or no boots at all, and clothes tattered and torn, had reduced the strongest of the men to the verge of giving up. Carvalho and Egloffstein dropped far behind as they tried to help Oliver Fuller. Even though they were now out of the up and down country that makes up today's Canyonlands National Park and Bryce Canyon National Park, Fuller was not capable of going on. He told his friends to leave him. He wasn't going to make it even with their assistance. With great reluctance, the men agreed. They wrapped Fuller in a blanket, told him that they would get help back to him, and started out to catch up to the main party. By ten o'clock that night, they reached the campfires, reported on Fuller's condition and location, and then ate some meat that had been saved for them.

Frank Dixon, a Mexican worker, volunteered to go after Fuller. John

Charles gave him a horse to ride, another to carry the disabled man, and some cooked meat. That was all that could be spared. As Dixon rode into the dark, a blizzard began to rage.

At daybreak there was no sign of Dixon or Fuller. Trying to save his men, Frémont sent three Delawares out. At midmorning one of them returned with Dixon, who had been lost and had never found Fuller. The men kept the fires going and waited. At nightfall, the other Delawares rode into camp with Fuller. The assistant engineer was almost dead. His feet were frozen, and his skin was black from his feet to his ankles. The men took one look at their companion and shook their heads, but Frémont decided they would stay in this camp until Fuller regained enough strength to make the trip to Parowan. Yet three days passed and the man didn't seem any better. Two Delawares agreed to walk alongside his horse and hold him in his saddle. In this way they started ahead. Still, even as they walked and tried to keep up Fuller's spirits, he died in the saddle on February 7, 1854. They took his body off the horse, wrapped him in a rubber blanket and placed him beside the trail. If they reached a settlement in time, a party would return to bury him. It was the first death, and it was not something to talk about.

They had traveled only a short distance from where they had left Fuller's body when they struck visible traces of wagon ruts that marked the road along the west side of the Wasatch Mountains. The road served the isolated Mormon settlements and headed southwest to California via the Virgin River route. Suddenly they met a band of Utes under the leadership of Arapeen, Chief Wakara's brother. He recognized Frémont from the time they had met in May 1844, and gave him a dog to slaughter for his hungry men. In exchange, Frémont gave Arapeen some flour he had among the remaining provisions.

That night they camped beside the wagon road, and the following day they straggled into the small Mormon community of Parowan. The settlers saw their terrible condition and offered all the help they needed. But the first thing John Charles requested was the aid of some men to go back with part of his group to bury Oliver Fuller beside the trail. The Mormon families saw to it that the survivors of the expedition were put up in their homes, treated their frostbitten hands and feet, and fed them slowly so that they would not become ill from eating too much at once.

Here in this isolated community of four hundred pioneers, Frémont may have learned of the death of John Gunnison, Richard Kern, Frederick Creutzfeldt, and three others who had taken a short survey away from their large expedition only to be killed by a band of Paiutes. As bad as it had been for Frémont to see Fuller die a short distance from help, he had lost only one man. Considering that they had endured fifty days in the wilderness, that they had crossed some of the roughest country in the American West in the middle of one of the coldest winters the Mormons had seen in this raw land, the men of the fifth expedition had been fortunate.

That night, Jessie had a strange experience in their Washington home. She had been worried about John Charles, and as she stepped into a room beside the parlor to get more wood for the fireplace, she thought that something lightly touched her shoulder. Then, there in the darkness, she was convinced she had heard John Charles whisper her name in a playful way. At once, she realized that something very strange had taken place, something which told her that John Charles was out of the wilderness and safe.

## 5

THE MEN OF THE EXPEDITION remained with the hospitable Mormons of Parowan until February 21, 1854. In the meantime, Frémont send word home by Territorial Secretary Babbitt, who departed on February 9 to journey to Salt Lake and Washington. In his letter, John Charles reported on the success of the expedition. He pointed out that this crossing would serve very well as a railroad route, and stated that he noticed good stands of timber as well as vast deposits of coal and iron in this southwestern corner of Utah Territory.

Even as Frémont and a party of stronger men left Parowan on February 21, Carvalho and Egloffstein were too used up to continue to California until later. Instead, they rode as wagon passengers to Salt Lake. As for John Charles, he wanted to prove that his idea for a railroad line was the most suitable. In order to complete his survey, he and his party followed the wagon road south to the new Mormon community of Cedar City, eighteen miles from Parowan. From here they struck out into the unexplored Escalante Desert. They crossed the present Utah boundary, entered Nevada south of today's Pioche, and kept moving through a series of snowstorms until they reached the granite barrier of the Sierra Nevada at the thirty-seventh parallel, a little south of present-day Bishop, California.

Hoping to cross the mountains over Walker Pass, Frémont ran into heavy snow and had to turn back. Then he followed the southeastern flank of the Range of Light until he saw a hollow that presented a gradual upward climb to an almost snowless crossing. On the other side, they worked their way down to a fork of the Kern River and followed it into the southern part of the San Joaquin Valley. Here, there was no sign of winter, and wild flowers were already beginning to bloom.

The trip to San Francisco was easy, but to John Charles it meant the end of a way of life he had enjoyed for many years. This last expedition and the one before had taken their toll. He no longer found any pleasure in combating the forces of nature. This time it had been all he could do to survive. Even as he arrived in San Francisco, even as he was cheered for his accomplishment, he knew his days as an explorer were over. Younger men would have to follow in his path. Life on the trail had turned sour. It had robbed him of friends whose bodies were markers for roads and railroads, men who passed that way and gave everything. They had paid the steep price, and all of this was in Frémont's mind as he wrote:

> It seems a treason against mankind and the spirit of progress which marks the age, to refuse to put this one completing link to our national prosperity and the civilization of the world. Europe still lies between Asia and America; build this railroad and things will have revolved about; America will lie between Asia and Europe—the golden vein which runs through the history of the world will follow the iron track to San Francisco, and the Asiatic trade will finally fall into its last and permanent road. . . .[12]

The golden vein, the cinch across the wide belly of the continent, the difference between a single coastline and a Two Ocean Nation—all this had been John Charles Frémont's dream. Now, the last challenge had been met. The trails, roads, and routes were mapped. The youthful glory of exploration had reached its culmination. He had followed the winds of discovery as they blew across the vast and lonely land. Now it was time to put away the tools of exploration, time to discover fulfillment in other dreams of glory. The maps were made. He had finished his last expedition and had known for the last time the thrill of moving out, of crossing the frontier to explore the wilderness of the American West.

# XXVI

## Peaks of Glory, Valleys of Despair

THE TRIP BACK TO WASHINGTON was a sample of things to come, of the rapid changes that were taking place since he had first learned the art of exploration. His late mentor, Joseph Nicolas Nicollet, would not recognize the methods of travel that had once been wild dreams but now were working realities. John Charles departed by ship from San Francisco Bay in April to make the journey to Panama. This time, though, he did not face the horse and bongo crossing to the Atlantic port but traveled as a passenger on the newly completed Panama Railroad. And even though he left California in April, by the first part of May he was back in his Washington home telling his lovely and large-with-child Jessie all about his adventures.

All the conversation was not limited to talk of the forthcoming baby. His father-in-law was deeply concerned that the nation was nearing the flash point of disaster, and it all came down to one thing: slavery. Let there be no doubt about it. Something had to be done quickly to end the abominable trade in human beings or there was bound to be a clash between North and South over the issue. The course of the stars made it clear that the destiny for the United States would be one of outright war if the mounting tensions were not halted.

Frémont couldn't deny the inherent dangers that the nation faced. All of it was much too obvious. Because of his own antislavery stance, he had suffered defeat in his attempt to be re-elected as a California senator. Even Benton, who was strongly opposed to slavery, had lost his long-held seat in the United States Senate in 1851, the same year that Harriet Beecher Stowe's *Uncle Tom's Cabin* became a runaway best seller in the North and a hated book in the South. In 1852 Benton had won a seat in the House of Representatives, and now he was due to run for re-election in the fall. He admitted his chances of losing were very good indeed. Most Missouri voters were all for slavery and believed Benton was betraying his southern heritage. Then there was the attack on the Missouri Compromise of 1819, which had allowed Missouri to enter the Union as a slave state and Maine as a free state but had prohibited any extension of slavery north of the latitude 36°30′ in the territory acquired by the Louisiana Purchase. If Senator Stephen A. Douglas of Illinois managed to get his Kansas-Nebraska Bill passed, then Nebraska would be a free state and Kansas a slave state. This would effectively repeal the Missouri Compromise, and the fires of conflict between the North and South would move westward. Bloodshed would follow into this setting, and Kansas would become the testing ground for things to come.

Day after day, John Charles heard the bad news. Even the dangers of exploration seemed tame compared to the Old Testament warnings Benton issued as though he were an ancient prophet who had come forth from the wilderness with a terrible vision. While all this took place, Jessie gave birth to a healthy baby boy. The joy of life entered the family with the new baby, who was named after Jessie's favorite cousin, Frank Preston. Then on May 25, 1854, the thing they dreaded took place. The Kansas-Nebraska Bill passed and the Missouri Compromise was repealed. This made it clear that the antislavery faction had lost in its bid to prevent the spread of slavery into the West.

September became the cruel month. First, it was Charles Preuss they heard about. He had returned from the Railway Survey in the Southwest in very poor health as he had suffered a sunstroke. He didn't improve with the passing of time. On September 1, he left his Washington home, apparently for a stroll, but didn't return by nightfall. A search party was sent out. They found him a few miles outside the city at Clark Mills' farm. The tough mapmaker, who had endured so much hardship for the sake of science, had made his last journey. He had hanged himself from a tree limb. Eight days later, on September 10, Jessie's mother asked for help to walk into the library. Slowly, she touched her husband's desk, looked at the book-lined room, and asked to be helped back to her couch so that she might take a nap. Then as Jessie noticed she was sleeping longer than usual, she walked over and discovered that her mother had died in her sleep.

Benton, who had gone into the country for a few days rest, was grief-stricken that after all these devoted years he should have been away when his wife died. Letters of condolence came from all over Washington and points outside the capital. For the devotion of Senator Benton—and he would always be called Senator—had been one of the great love stories of the time. But once the services had been read, it was back to politics; and that fall Congressman Benton lost even his seat in the House of Representatives because of his strong stand against slavery. Then as the New Year arrived and the Old Warrior worked on his manuscript for the second volume of *Thirty Years' View*, the Benton house caught fire and burned to the ground. This was all he could take. He had endured enough of Washington. He accepted an offer to travel on the lecture circuit throughout New England and the West to speak on the growing national crisis.

To the Frémonts, the Washington scene had also become intolerable, and they moved to New York in the spring of 1855. They were hardly settled when news arrived of more squatter trouble at Las Mariposas. Not wanting to risk the health of the baby and Jessie, John Charles saw to it that the family was sent off to Siaconset, Nantucket, for the summer with a nurse to help with the children. Then he headed back to California to straighten matters out in the Mother Lode.

2

Upon his return from California, politics were nearing Frémont's door. He was approached by the Democrats to be their presidential candidate, but he turned their offer down because of their support of slavery. It made no difference to him that his father-in-law remained a loyal Democrat despite his antislavery stance. John Charles felt the time had come to take a definite stand on the great moral issue of the time. In no way, he told the Democrats, could he support the party that backed the repeal of the Missouri Compromise and refused to speak out against slavery.

Frémont was an attractive possibility as a strong contender for the presidency, and though he had rebuffed the Democrats, the newly formed Republican Party approached him about running for office under their banner. They stood forth against slavery, against the repeal of the Missouri Compromise, against the Kansas-Nebraska Bill, and against the Fugitive Slave Law.

Once again, there was great excitement in the Frémont home. It was almost as though he were planning for another expedition. This time, though, he was dealing with the wilds of the political world—a world that was alien to him. It would require speeches, public appearances, and an exposure to the public that he had never enjoyed. For John Charles was basically a quiet, introspective man, a shy, nongregarious individual, not the type cut out for political campaigning. In many ways his personality was defined by his joy in the lonely path he had followed as an explorer. There, in the new country of the trans-Mississippi West, he had been very much at home. To be alone in his own tepee, to sit around a campfire with the men who made up his expeditions had been more than the necessity of a task; it had been a way of life which he had cherished. Now he was to enter a country of public exposure, of rumor and gossip, of half-truth, of grand-sounding statements of purpose which when rendered of all the fat boiled down to one key goal: win the office for the party and worry about what had been said later.

Political meetings were held during the late fall of 1855 and the winter of 1856. Northern liberals and the new Republican Party backed Frémont all the way. The call for a ticket based upon free men and free soil was sounded, and the backing began to grow for this romantic American hero. Francis P. Blair and his son Frank rallied behind him, as well as such public figures as John Bigelow and the poet John Greenleaf Whittier. The missing man of power was former Senator Thomas Hart Benton. Though Frémont was his son-in-law and the man who had carried out many of his own dreams of empire and exploration, the Old Warrior remained a true Democrat even after Frémont became the official candidate of the Republican Party on June 19, 1856, during its convention at the Musical Fund Hall of Philadelphia. His running mate for Vice President was Senator William L. Dayton of New Jersey, who beat out Abraham Lincoln for second position on the ticket.

While this was to be the first try for the White House by the newly formed Republican Party, their chances of winning were not impossible. They knew things would come down to the major issue of slavery, and they were going to be hurt by their strong stand against it. Still, the Democratic front runner, James Buchanan, was not unbeatable. But a third party was in the election. This was the remainder of the Whigs plus a splinter faction of the Know-Nothings. The election promised to be close, dirty, and hard.

From the beginning, the Republicans created a legendary figure in Frémont. Using the catch title of "Pathfinder," they made him into something he never claimed to be. His great contributions as a scientific explorer were overlooked for the best that the promotional men of politics could come up with. "Frémont and Victory" became a slogan. Popular songs were written. John Bigelow, with Jessie's help, dashed off a campaign biography that sold for one dollar. Charles Wentworth Upham published another biography glorifying Frémont. John Greenleaf Whittier wrote a poem of his exploration days called "The Pass of the Sierras." The New York *Evening Post, Times,* and *Tribune* carried editorials urging voters to back Frémont. Colored lithograph posters of the "Pathfinder" sold for a dollar each. Horace Greeley and the New York *Tribune* issued a pamphlet life of Frémont. Torchlight parades were held. Speakers spoke. Talkers talked. Through it all ran the feeling of a kind of revival meeting as audiences cheered and chanted and sang for victory in what one supporter said was "a bugle call of liberty."

The campaign of 1856 was not what Frémont had hoped a presidential election would be. Solid issues were bypassed in favor of catch slogans. He was taken from rally to rally in much the same manner as a show horse making the circuit of county fairs. All this was without meaning and pointless to him. He was accustomed to mapping out campaigns which had definite objectives. If the wind blew, it was real and carried the feel of the seasons. But in this political campaign, nothing that blew his way appeared to be touched with reality. Then the smell of dirt began to catch the false breeze fanned by the opposition, especially by the Know-Nothings. Cartoons depicted Frémont and Jessie as belonging to the lunatic fringe of Republicanism, and then John Charles was attacked for being a Catholic. Though he quickly proved he was an Episcopalian, it was difficult to dispel the rumors. He had to admit he had put a cross on Independence Rock, and though he pointed out this was a Christian symbol for all branches of Christianity, it made no difference. After all, his father had been a Catholic; his niece Nina attended a Catholic school; and Frémont and Jessie had been married by a Catholic priest.

Nor was his religion the only smear used by his opponents, who supported Millard Fillmore for the Know-Nothings or James Buchanan for the Democrats. There was the matter of Frémont's illegitimate birth, and that was used for all it was worth. Then they attacked him for claiming to have discovered South Pass—a claim he had never made. They made as much out of the disastrous fourth expedition as possible. Other scurrilous charges were hurled at him, and the range of filth seemed endless. He was accused of being a hard drinker, of being a slaveholder himself, of shady financial dealings and of terrible brutality in California. Of these charges, the only one which had any substance to it was the last because of his treatment of the Indians in the Sacramento Valley and his failure to halt the senseless murder of three unarmed Californios near San Rafael. Yet the smear campaign continued right up to the election, and its major theme became the danger of Frémont to the slave economy of the South, a danger which was summed up by one slogan: "Free soilers, Frémonters, free niggers, and freebooters."

Election day came and passed. Lily cried because she had set her heart upon living in the White House. Frémont, who had been a gentleman throughout the campaign, took all of it rather stoically and without apparent rancor. Jessie accepted defeat without much in the way of emotion, as though she had not wanted to be first lady from the beginning. But the Whig Party was dead. The Know-Nothings had lived up to their chosen name. And the Republican Party had enjoyed a respectable first run at the White House, as their candidate had done exceedingly well despite his forthright stand against slavery. Democrat James Buchanan carried nineteen states; Republican John Charles Frémont carried eleven states; and Whig Millard Fillmore carried eight. Of the popular vote, Buchanan polled 1,341,264; Frémont only 500,000 less, and 500,000 more than Fillmore.

The loss was nothing to be ashamed about. On the contrary, if the Whigs and Know-Nothings had not been in the race, and if Thomas Hart Benton had backed him, Frémont might have become President of the United States. Whether that would have been good or bad, whether that would have resulted in the Civil War four years earlier is something historians can only speculate about.

3

THE FRÉMONTS; their niece Nina; a French servant named Mary; young Douglas Fox, son of the English mining authority Sir Charles Fox; and two free blacks, Isaac and Lee, were living at Las Mariposas in Bear Valley, California, by the spring of 1858. The party of eleven had sailed from New York aboard the steamship *Moses Taylor* in March, crossed the Isthmus by train, and sailed up the coast from Panama to San Francisco as passengers on the *Golden Age,* which passed through the Golden Gate on April 12.

During the trip to California, Jessie had been despondent and worried about her father. His health was not what it had always been. Though he said it was nothing to worry about, Jessie remembered the haunted look in his face and the large body which had become shrunken and frail. She had hated to leave him, but he had assured her he would be all right. He had his work to finish on his *Digest of Congressional Debates*, and he insisted on their leaving. What he didn't tell Jessie or John Charles was that he was dying of cancer and had to take opiates in order to get any relief from pain.

Not knowing Benton's condition, the Frémonts happily went on a shopping tour in San Francisco. Household furnishings and a multitude of supplies were needed for the whitewashed frame dwelling they laughingly called their "White House." Once the purchases were made, they were shipped upriver by paddlewheeler to the Great Valley, and then loaded into spring wagons and taken to the red-clay foothills of the southern Mother Lode.

Here, in what was now Mariposa County, the Frémont holdings covered 44,386 acres.[1] There was the home at Bear Valley, the two-story Oso House hotel and its convenient saloon. Near it was another two-story building that served as a company store. At the bottom of the Merced River Canyon were the Benton stamp mills. Then there were three gold mines in operation: the Josephine, the Pine Tree, and the Princeton. One other mine, the Mt. Ophir, and its stamp mill were leased to Biddle Boggs.

The combination of these various industries plus the rental of town lots in Bear Valley and Mariposa, the rental of ranches and flumes, and the collection of a monthly four-dollar permit tax from foreign miners brought in a total monthly income of about $39,000. Large as the sum seemed, operational expenses were very high. The monthly payroll was $10,000. Then there were other mounting costs for construction work on shafts, tunnels, and a short-line gravity railroad that dropped four miles into the Merced River Canyon to carry ore to the Benton Mills. In addition, money went out at a steady rate to pay the Chinese railroad workers, miners, mill hands, mining engineers, lawyers, taxes, interest on debts, and wages for a Viennese baker and an Italian restaurant-keeper who fed the workers and other customers.

Here at Bear Valley in April of 1858, news reached the Frémonts of Senator Benton's death. The shock was hard for Jessie to bear, and John Charles did his best to comfort her. Yet both of them knew that a great influence had passed from their lives, an influence that Jessie stoutly maintained should be cherished and kept burning.

They carried on, as Senator Benton would have expected of them. Then, as the foothill spring gave way to the stifling heat of summer, trouble of another kind developed. Squatters and claim jumpers had moved onto some of the Frémont property, and a group called the Merced Mining Company had taken advantage of John Charles's absence to develop the Pine Tree, Josephine, and Mt. Ophir gold mines. But when he returned from the East, he had come back to Las Mariposas armed with an 1856 patent that made clear his ownership of any and all mines, lots, or structures on his grant. Without hesitation, he claimed that which belonged to him and began to work all but Mt. Ophir, which he leased out. A particularly violent group of miners, called the Hornitos League, decided to defy Frémont. They bribed a watchman and jumped the rich Black Drift, another of the colonel's claims. As soon as he learned of this, John Charles went to the aid of his men at the Pine Tree Mine. Even as they fortified their position, the claim jumpers besieged them, with the idea of starving them out. As they carried out this part of their plan, some of the worst of the gang threatened to burn the Frémont home and issued a threat to Jessie, giving her just twenty-four hours to clear out.

Jessie refused to be intimidated. When John Charles heard of her position, he tried to reason with the squatters, but they were in no mood to talk. Frémont's main concern was for his family. He feared the bullies would begin to drink, and with enough liquor in them, they might resort to anything. Still, even as he tried to talk to them, Jessie played her own hand. Eighteen-year-old Douglas Fox volunteered to make the ride northeast, in and out of the Merced River Canyon, to Coulterville, where there was a home guard and where others could ride the eighty miles to Stockton to obtain more aid. The whole affair was exciting, dangerous, and potentially violent. But it turned out to be bloodless as the Coulterville home guard marched from Tuolumne County to Mariposa County and made the Hornitos League think twice about carrying out their threats. As they delayed the outbreak of gunfire, the state marshal and five hundred men arrived from Stockton to put a final end to such lawlessness.

All of this was fun to tell such famous literary visitors as Horace Greeley and Richard Henry Dana in the late spring of 1859, but the summer heat was beginning to tell on Jessie along with the nervous strain of living in a community that resented the presence of the rightful owners of most of the land, including the site of Mariposa, the county seat. To remove her from this frontier gold camp, John Charles purchased some twelve acres and a cottage in San Francisco from banker Mark Brumagim. The property was two miles away from the Golden Gate and opposite Alcatraz Island. Originally called Point Médanos and then Point San José, (the site of today's Fort Mason), it had come to be known as Black Point because of the dense growth of dark-colored mountain laurel on it.[2] Just to the west of the property was a bay that was later known as Washerwoman's Lagoon, as it was used as a laundry site for many of San Francisco's residents. A mile away, on the thirty-five acres of Alcatraz Island Frémont had once owned, was a fortification containing three batteries of cannons: thirty-five faced San Francisco and the Presidio; nineteen faced the Golden Gate; and forty faced the direction of Sausalito. Along with the batteries, the island had magazines for cannon balls, a barracks, a guardhouse, furnaces for heating the cannon balls, a fog bell, and a lighthouse. This was a touch of irony as during

Frémont's court-martial one of the specifications under the charge of mutiny was that he had purchased White Bird or Alcatraz Island to protect the Golden Gate and San Francisco Bay.

The cost of the Black Point acreage and cottage came to $42,000 in gold, and John Charles saw to it that the deed was taken out in Jessie's name in 1860. Improvements were needed for the cottage, and these ran up an additional bill of between $10,000 and $15,000. Yet it was a delightful location for a view of the Bay, the Gate, and the hills, east and north. On this jutting point, Jessie took full advantage of the scenic vistas.

The Frémonts had a windowed veranda with a three-sided view, and Jessie often sat and read in this pleasant place. At other times she and John Charles talked to such friends as Ned Beale, who was moving up in rank in the army, to a promising young writer called Bret Harte, and to the popular lecturer Rev. Thomas Starr King. Here in this atmosphere of beauty where the view of the Bay and the Golden Gate was magnificent on bright, clear days, or possessed a quality of mystery on foggy or stormy days, the Frémonts and their circle of friends and admirers talked of the world of culture as they listened to the tolling fog bells and the distant sound of breakers smashing against the rocky headlands of the Golden Gate.

At Black Point, in what they called "The Porter's Lodge" at the suggestion of Reverend King, the Frémonts enjoyed an interlude of peacefulness in their lives. It was a time when they were leaders in the growing cultural life of San Francisco, when their home saw the comings and goings of the famous, the would-be famous, the to-be famous, and all the others who looked upon Jessie and John Charles Frémont as special people at a special place in the drama of California.

This peaceful period was a dream come true after all the years of expeditions, political battles, and tragedies that cut down family members and men who had traveled with John Charles on the dangerous and lonely treks into the wilderness of the American West. It was a time for reflection, a time to enjoy the finer things of life, and a time to sit by a fireside without posting a guard or planning the next day's march.

Money was coming in at a grand rate from the holdings in Mariposa County. Still, things were not as smooth as Frémont would have wished. As fast as money came in, it went out at an even faster rate to pay operational expenses and the two per cent per month interest on mounting debts. New resources had to be tapped, and John Charles and his attorney, Frederick Billings, decided to sail to Europe at the beginning of 1861 to seek additional capital. Facts and figures about the various aspects of the business were assembled. Projected possible earnings were charted, and an expensive series of photographs was taken of everything that contributed to income and possible future income from Las Mariposas.

When this was all completed, John Charles asked Jessie if she would like to go along with them. The combination of business and a European holiday seemed like a good idea. Jessie couldn't think of a better gift for having stood firm against the Hornitos League. Yes, by all means, she would enjoy a trip to Europe. Besides, she could obtain a new wardrobe, visit old friends in Paris, enjoy the museums, and get her fill of opera and the theater.

All of it was grand, and Jessie began to pack as the end of 1860 drew near. Then, on a Sunday morning as Jessie and Lily were coming down Russian Hill in a carriage, the horses suddenly bolted. The coachman was unable to control them, and the rocking and rolling carriage sped down the hill until the tongue broke and drove into the cobblestones. The impact threw mother and daughter out of the careening runaway vehicle. And while Lily suffered no injury, Jessie wasn't as fortunate. An arm and a leg were badly injured, and she was forced to give up the trip she had been longing to take.

Disaster piled upon disaster in a short period. By February, John Charles wrote to Jessie to tell her he had met the newly elected President Abraham Lincoln at New York's Astor House. They had talked about many things, but the main topic was the growing fury between North and South, a fury which John Charles saw as the first sign of a war between brothers. As he wrote: "With the inflammatory press and inflammatory conversation on every hand, I am convinced that actual war is not far off."[3]

His sense of the temper of the times was highly acute, and he heard of the inevitable while he was in Europe. Ironically, it began in his own home state of South Carolina with the bombardment of Fort Sumter in Charleston harbor on April 13, 1861. To John Charles, there was no other choice than to sail home immediately and volunteer his services for the defense of the Union. Until the safety of the United States was assured, all personal business at Las Mariposas would have to wait. Upon his return, he was given a commission of major general in the Union Army and assigned the command of the Department of the West, with headquarters at St. Louis. He sent word to Jessie to bring the family and meet him in the East. From there they would return to St. Louis, where he would prepare for a campaign that was quite different than his wilderness expeditions.

4

JESSIE WASTED NO TIME in hurrying to John Charles's side.

> In eight days after getting that letter I was at sea with my little family, and a trained nurse, for my arm and one foot were still in splints and only my hand was useful. The lovely home was indefinitely broken up and a friend rented it and bought the furniture and horses and carriages.[4]

The friend she referred to was none other than Edward Fitzgerald Beale.

Jessie and the family sailed out the Golden Gate aboard the steamer *Sonora* bound for Panama and the Pacific terminal of the Panama Railroad that their late friend John Lloyd Stephens had headed during the crucial time of construction, a time when he shook from fever and made jokes about the fires of the flesh that were burning out his life. In her hand, Jessie carried a going-away gift from Rev. Thomas Starr King—violets from his garden and a copy of Emerson's *Essays* which Starr King had given her as he said, "Smell, read, and rest."[5]

Once the *Sonora* was beyond the Golden Gate, which John Charles had named, once the last glimpse of Black Point and San Francisco had blurred and vanished, the sadness of another farewell was over, and Jessie looked forward to the happy hello and glance of love that would pass between John Charles and herself when she reached New York. For all their years had been touched by partings and reunions, by sad good-byes and happy hellos.

After meeting John Charles in New York and seeing him in the uniform of a major general, Jessie had little time for pleasure. While in California the War of Rebellion was an exciting topic of conversation, on the eastern seaboard it was a reality that had put young men into uniforms, brought out the best and worst in individuals, and was the subject of wild rumors that had the Confederate troops marching on Washington. And there was more truth to the rumors than the North ever suspected, for on July 21, 1861, as the Frémonts boarded a train for St. Louis, the South routed the forces of the North in the First Battle of Bull Run.

Panic was in the air as the train moved along toward Missouri. There was no guarantee that Southerners had not cut the line and captured the Border States. While none of this had taken place, the arrival at St. Louis was unlike anything John Charles or Jessie had ever seen before in this city which had meant so much to them in past years.

Steamboats swung idly at their wharves, the streets were practically deserted, a Confederate flag flew from secessionist headquarters, and business houses stood gloomily behind their iron shutters.[6]

Even as horses hooves echoed in the deserted streets, Frémont had plans in mind. Quarters were going to be established at the Brant's home by invitation. There he was to work from five in the morning until midnight or later as he prepared his troops for a long campaign that would clear Missouri of all rebels and open the way to move his forces along the course of the Mississippi to attack Memphis and eventually capture New Orleans.

From the beginning, though, he was faced with almost insurmountable problems. His forces were short of arms and ammunition. Other supplies were badly needed to equip and move a large army. If this wasn't enough trouble, there was the strong group of open secessionists in Missouri that he had to contend with. They became stronger each day as a succession of Confederate victories brought more men to their side. Then there were the foreign officers Frémont had in his command—including the Hungarian Major Charles Zagonyi—who were not looked upon with favor by Missourians. Nor did the local citizens consider the isolation of Frémont in the Brant mansion—an isolation which did not allow them to drop by for a visit whenever they felt like it—the American way of doing things.

Frémont's greatest difficulty was caused by the Blair family. They were extremely powerful in the politics of the Border States, had the ear of President Lincoln, and frowned upon Frémont's turning St. Louis into a fortified city where citizens were not allowed to come and go at their will. Then when the general declined to give a friend of the Blair family the exclusive contract to outfit forty thousand soldiers, Francis Blair was furious. Because of his close relationship to the Bentons and the Frémonts, however, he got over this. It was only when the general refused to give Frank Blair the commission of major general that an open feud developed. For the elder Blair had high hopes for a political future for his son Frank. In fact, he saw him as a potential candidate for President of the United States, and this was the final blow to the Blair pride. The Blairs did not consider Frémont a good general. He was openly antislavery in a state that was closer to the South than to the North. He refused to be copartner with the family and issue the proper rank to the son who was Francis Blair's hope and pride. This was the final split between the two families who had been close friends for so many years. It meant Francis Blair would do his best to have Frémont removed from command just as he had managed to remove his predecessor, General William S. Harney.

The greatest insult to the Blairs and to many other Missourians came about on August 30, 1861. On that day General Frémont not only declared martial law but also issued the first emancipation proclamation. To the Blairs, to most Missourians, and even to President Lincoln, this was hardly a wise move at the moment. Border States were being held in the Union by a very thin thread, and this was the knife that could easily cut that thread of loyalty to the Union. Nevertheless, Frémont's language was quite clear as he stated:

> The property, real and personal, of all persons in the state of Missouri who shall take up arms against the United States, or who shall be directly proven to have taken an active part with their enemies in the field, is declared to be confiscated to the public use, and their slaves, if any they have, are hereby declared freemen.[7]

This sent a shock wave throughout the country. Up to this point in the conflict, the idea of freeing the slaves was not the key issue of the war. In fact, to President Lincoln and his cabinet, it wasn't even an issue. The primary order of business, the reason for fighting such a bloody war of brother against brother, was to preserve the Union. To jubilant abolitionists, though, Frémont's proclamation was sensational. President Lincoln had remained so silent about the slavery question that many abolitionists considered him to be a quiet supporter of the dreadful institution.

By September 2 President Lincoln had sent a special messenger to St. Louis to deliver his personal objections to Frémont's proclamation of August

30. The gist of what the President wrote came down to two things: It was too early for such a proclamation as it would drive away any Southerners who believed in the preservation of the Union, and it would cause Kentucky to join the Confederates. In light of this, Frémont was asked to greatly modify his emancipation proclamation to remain in line with the August 6, 1861, act of Congress regarding the confiscation of property used for insurrectionary purposes.

General Frémont wrote to President Lincoln and stated his objection to such a move. He asked that, if it had to be done, written orders from the President should be sent to him. The order was sent in a hurry, and Frémont had no choice other than to obey it. To Jessie, things were not that simple, nor was she going to give up without a fight. She could see the devious hand of old Francis Blair and his son Montgomery, the Postmaster General, behind the whole affair. They considered Missouri and the other Border States their private political territory. The fact that Frémont was not giving them key roles in his plans for the Department of the West had turned them from friends to enemies. Taking time off from her volunteer work with the Sanitary Commission, an organization similar to the present Red Cross, Jessie packed a bag, took her maid with her, and caught a train for Washington on September 8. Maybe men could take such things with detachment and a philosophical demeanor, but she was going right to President Lincoln's office and tell him just what she thought of the whole business.

The weary President found time to see Jessie at nine o'clock in the evening. They met in the Red Room, and Lincoln paced back and forth as he spoke to her. He was so tired he never thought to offer Jessie a seat, but he lectured her as a schoolmaster might talk to some child who had overstepped heɩ bounds. He pointed out that he had told Frank Blair to act as an advisor to Frémont, to make certain that he understood his position in holding the Border States. If he had listened to Frank Blair, there would be no trouble. Abrupt and angry, Lincoln told Jessie, "The General should never have dragged the Negro into the war. It is a war for a great national object and the Negro has nothing to do with it."[8]

If Frémont had trouble before, Jessie only compounded things. Rumors of the rift between Frémont and Lincoln were spread throughout the North. Then, when a committee was sent to St. Louis to investigate Frémont's operation and his serious losses in the battles of Springfield, Missouri, and Wilson's Creek, it was clear to all that his days were running out as commander of the Department of the West. Though Major Zagonyi and 150 handpicked cavalrymen made a romantic and successful charge on the Confederate garrison at Springfield, even this worried President Lincoln. He feared the loss of men in such engagements and seriously doubted their value to the winning of the war. There was only one thing to do, and President Lincoln did it. On October 24, 1861, he drafted an order relieving General Frémont of his command—an order which reached Frémont on the outskirts of

Springfield on November 2 and brought to an end his one hundred days as commander of the Department of the West.

The whole affair was humiliating to General Frémont. Not only was he dismissed, but also many of his officers were sacked without so much as pay for their services. The latter was done on the grounds that they had been given commissions on an irregular basis. But it was clear that the real reason for their dismissal was that they were loyal to Frémont. This was only the beginning of trouble for President Lincoln. Abolitionists took up Frémont's cause and pointed out that he had been fired because he had opposed slaveholders. Flags flew at half-mast over the buildings and homes of Frémont's St. Louis supporters, and liberal Northern newspapers rallied to his defense with stirring editorials. Nobody on Frémont's side ever questioned his ability as a military man, a natural tactician on the field of battle. If they had, his ability as strategist in war would not have stood close scrutiny. Equally as bad, those who were against John Charles did not examine his record as a military man but insisted on playing up the fact that he was only interested in freeing the slaves. Somewhere in between was the truth, but it was obscured by emotion and plays for political power.

The wrangling and investigations continued into 1862. Then President Lincoln realized that for political reasons alone he would have to give General Frémont another command. In March 1862 it was off to war again for John Charles as he was appointed head of the Mountain Department, which included western Virginia, eastern Kentucky, and part of Tennessee. Jessie went with him to present-day Wheeling, West Virginia, where he set up his headquarters at the McLure Hotel.

These were uncertain days for any officer in command in the Union Army. Too often commands were issued from Washington, and Washington was seething with ambitious, discontented men who gave President Lincoln a great deal of bad advice. The turnover in generals had almost become a Washington joke, but to the officers in the field it was hardly humorous. They were short of arms, ammunition, and supplies. They were given orders by men who placed pins in maps and drew grand schemes without any actual knowledge of conditions. Nor did they realize the talent of the Southern generals who were fighting a campaign on their own ground.

General Frémont soon realized the full extent of this situation when he received orders from President Lincoln to march his troops from western Virginia across the mountains to Tennessee, seize the railroad at Knoxville, and rescue any Union soldiers or sympathizers in that region. All this called for was making a march across one hundred miles through the Alleghenies, trying to make do off land that offered little support, and arriving at Knoxville in good enough shape to fight the forces under the command of Stonewall Jackson. Yet General Frémont did try the impossible. It was a disaster from the start, but it had not been Frémont's plan. He tried to follow out impossible orders, tried to coax men along who were short on clothing, sometimes even without shoes, hungry most of the time, and much too exhausted to put up a strong battle against a rested and waiting foe.

President Lincoln finally sensed his own fault in the defeat of General Frémont's Mountain Department, but not until he had sent Carl Schurz to investigate. Schurz returned to Washington with praise for Frémont's attempt to do what Lincoln had ordered. He pointed out the impossibility of the task under existing conditions. Lincoln then consolidated the forces of Frémont, Banks, and McDowell into the Army of Virginia under the command of General John Pope.

Frémont got along with Pope just about as well as he did with Frank Blair, and the fact that Lincoln saw fit to put this younger officer in charge, this man who Frémont believed had been disloyal and insubordinate, was more than he could endure. He requested that President Lincoln relieve him of his command. When the request was granted, Frémont returned to New York. For he was convinced that so long as Lincoln and the Blairs were around, there was no chance for him to play a role of any importance in the war. He left just in time. For as the summer of 1862 drew toward its end, General Pope suffered one of the worst defeats of the Civil War at the Second Battle of Bull Run.

## 5

FOR THE REMAINING MONTHS OF 1862, Frémont tried to keep his mind on his personal business. He flatly refused to be part of a growing antiadministration campaign. His disagreements with the President were minor compared to the terrible struggle between North and South. Then on January 1, 1863, President Lincoln issued the Emancipation Proclamation. Jessie was relieved that the man in the White House had done this, but she believed it should have been done earlier. Still, she kept this in the family, and expressed her feelings about it in a letter to her sister Eliza.

> Well, my dear Eliza, the Emancipation Proclamation has brought England to our side, and emancipation has proved a pivotal term after all. A few of us felt this in '61. War-politics—hyphenated heartache. My one hope is to see the end of both in our lives. At fifty the General is gray, worn, and in poor health. At thirty-nine my heart, played upon by joy and bereavement, pride and humiliation, longs only for the privacy of a real home again. . . . I am no prophet, though the daughter of one, but I forsee the fall of the House of Blair. I still have filial affection for father Blair, but Frank and Montgomery will soon betray to the long-suffering President that the Blair soul is with the South.[9]

The year had just started, and it looked promising after the past two years. That was all that could be said about it as a series of events turned the world upside down for the Frémonts. The first tragedy was the death of Jessie's sister Eliza Benton Jones. This sad time was followed by more financial difficulties over the Mariposa property. Way over his head in debt, unable to handle business with any great success, John Charles was completely out of his element. His debt on Las Mariposas was over two million dollars, and the interest and legal fees were mounting daily. In an effort to get out of this growing problem, he sold his estate to a group of New York business sharks. He came out of this affair with only a small portion of his former fortune. But the year was hardly over. While Jessie wrote of Frémont's Civil War experience and sold it to a publisher as *The Story of the Guard*, news reached them of the death of Thomas Starr King just as her book came out in October. Then to cap a year best forgotten, they received news of another event in October. The United States Government confiscated all the Black Point property, leveled "The Porter's Lodge" to make room for a battery of artillery, used other homes for barracks and offices, and refused to send any payment for what they had taken. Ironically, they named the post Fort Mason.

As 1864 began, the radical wing of the Republican Party, the war Democrats, and the Unionist Germans began to beat the drums for a third party. It was their contention that Lincoln was a Northerner who sympathized with the South, and that the candidate for freedom and free soil was John Charles Frémont. But in conversations the larger cause became their topic. Though it was pleasing to his pride to be asked to run for the presidency again, this was not the time. Then in a clear statement of purpose, John Charles turned down the backing that was his for the taking. "Offered patronage to my friends and disfavor to my enemies, I refused both. My only consideration was the welfare of the Republican party."[10]

On June 4, 1864, Frémont resigned his commission in the Union Army. Following his belief that the future of the United States was more important than any one man, he removed himself from any political contention. Less than a year later, at Appomattox on April 9, 1865, the South surrendered to the North; and the deadly war of brother against brother came to an end.

Politics and the military were gone. So, too, were the days of exploration. Yet, despite tremendous financial losses, Frémont had managed to remain a millionaire. He was not content, though, to be a host in their brownstone mansion at present-day 21 West 19th Street, between Fifth and Sixth avenues in New York. He needed something to occupy his mind, some grand plan. He found it when he became involved in the construction of the Memphis & El Paso Railroad. Once again he was westward bound in his mind's eye; and as his own money poured into this venture, he sought other backers to help promote this all-year route that would cut through the Southwest on its way to California.

Trips to Europe were taken to interest potential investors, and more of Frémont's money went out for these excursions. Then there was the need for a summer home, a place to escape New York's heat and the confinement of city life. Pocaho, Jessie called it, for she believed that the Webb place, about two miles north of Tarrytown, deserved its Indian name. Here, in a stone house that sat on an estate of more than a hundred acres of trees, lawn, and open country, the Frémonts were at home during the summer. On this promontory, which would one day become part of John D. Rockefeller's estate, John Charles and Jessie "looked down on Tappan Zee, that expansion of the Hudson where early Dutch navigators shortened sail and implored the protection of St. Nicholas before they crossed."[11]

The pleasant years passed much too quickly. Before John Charles and Jessie realized it, the children had become young adults. Lily was a close companion to Jessie. John Charles, Jr., was enrolled in Annapolis, and Frank was a cadet at West Point. Then in the summer of 1873 the good life was brought to a halt by a sudden turn in fortune as the Memphis & El Paso Railroad fell into financial collapse.

With this "railroad panic" John Charles was subjected to a loss of most of his fortune as well as extensive legal expenses. He had not been one for keeping good books when he was an explorer for the Topographical Corps, and he was slated for disaster in his business ventures. When all this came to an end, even Pocaho and all its furnishings had to be sold. Horses and carriages went; so did art works—including Jessie's favorite painting of the Golden Gate. Still, Jessie held back the tears. When a potential buyer of the property commented upon the beauty and size of the rooms in the house, Jessie stated: "The rooms are large. They have held much happiness. The new owners will find few shadows on the walls."[12]

6

FRÉMONT WAS HEADED WEST AGAIN IN 1878. With him were Jessie, Lily, and Frank, who had dropped out of West Point because of tuberculosis. They were bound for Arizona Territory, as John Charles had been appointed territorial governor by President Rutherford B. Hayes. Frémont's name had been submitted to the Senate on June 8, 1878, and four days later he received the official appointment with a salary of $2,600 per year according to the Federal Register.[13] It wasn't much. But it was much more than he had coming in, and the Republican Party believed it was time for them to do something for the man who had launched them into the glare of national politics.

At points along the way West, General Frémont was greeted at station stops. Both Chicago and Omaha invited him to attend banquets in his honor, but he politely refused. As he pointed out, he had to get to Arizona Territory to take office. But the real reason was his desire to move along the tracks that followed the old trails, to move as quickly as possible, and to see companions of the days of exploration if any were still alive. Passing by the smaller towns, the white-haired Frémont waved to the people who crowded the station platforms for a glimpse of the legendary figure who had been in the trans-Mississippi West long before the coming of railroads, towns, and multitudes of settlers. In San Francisco John Charles was given a reception by the

Pioneer Association of California. Then a familiar face came out of the crowd, a strong and faithful smile greeted him. At once, all the years seemed to vanish. The crowds were gone, and he was back in time talking to Alexis Godey of what it had been like before. Nothing else would do. Alexis boarded the train to Los Angeles with John Charles,[14] for there was much to talk about, old times to catch up on, old friends to remember from hard days in hard places.

From Los Angeles, the Frémonts rode the train to the end of track at Yuma. At that point, they boarded the best the army had in the way of vehicles and made the journey to the higher elevation of Prescott, the territorial capital of Arizona. Here, they rented a house from Tom Fitch, a local attorney, and settled down to life in this frontier community. It wasn't as raw as many might have thought. They had the services of Ah Chung, a Chinese cook they had hired on their way to Prescott because of his knowledge of the problems of putting forth a good dinner despite the limitations of Arizona's markets. In no time, Ah Chung located a place that sold various meats—including venison and wild turkey—an Italian farmer who could supply the household with butter and fresh eggs, and some Chinese farmers who delivered vegetables "to the door in the regular paniers on a stick we are used to on the five cent fans.[15]

John Charles was happy to have an opportunity to dream of big projects once more. He made recommendations regarding a possible railroad that would run from Tucson into Mexico and terminate at Point Lobos on the Gulf of California. He became interested in various mining claims in conjunction with Judge Charles Silent, helped in the relocation of the Pima Indians, suggested a home guard to protect ranchers and communities from Apache raiders—not knowing that the best troopers in the army were not having much luck at controlling the Apaches—and tried to obtain the San Juan del Río Rancho in Sonora, Mexico. The biggest project he had in mind was to turn the Colorado River water into the region that is now the Imperial Valley of Southern California to form a great inland sea, change the desert climate of Arizona, and have an endless supply of water for irrigation. All these activities kept him on the move, sometimes as much as twelve hours a day in the saddle as he rode across deserts and mountains. At other times he was away from Arizona for weeks and months as he traveled back and forth to the East to try to raise money for promising enterprises.

Never a man to give up, Frémont tried one thing after another with the hope that somehow he might restore his lost fortune. While he did all these things, the high and dry climate of Prescott cleared up Frank's lungs, but the climate did not agree with Jessie. Much as John Charles hated to have her leave him, her health came first, and in the fall of 1879 she returned to the East, took a house on Staten Island, and continued with her literary career.

Realizing how much he missed Jessie, Governor Frémont moved his office to Tucson so that she might rejoin him. She planned to do just that, but the situation in Arizona was becoming very shaky for him. Many of the citizens sent complaints to Washington about his continued and sometimes lengthy absences from the territory. With a change in the office of the President, pressure was applied to effect his resignation. This was too much to endure again. On October 11, 1881, he wrote a letter of resignation to President Chester A. Arthur.

Sixty-eight years old, his hair turned white, his days of glory gone forever, Frémont left Arizona and headed East to join his beloved Jessie. Now, the years were marred by poverty. Only the memories maintained the glint of gold. Jessie worked hard at her writing, and John Charles tried to get some money from the government in payment for the Black Point property. Then, as nothing was forthcoming, he decided to write his memoirs. They moved to Washington so that he could be near the repositories of official papers, and he found a publisher in Belford, Clarke & Company of Chicago and New York. The old excitement returned once again as he relived his life up through the third expedition and the conquest of California in the first volume, which came out in 1887. He and Jessie waited for a great sale such as President Ulysses S. Grant had enjoyed with his *Personal Memoirs*, but Frémont's luck seemed to have vanished. The nation was no longer interested in men who had mapped the trails and opened the wilderness. His potential audience was made up of children of pioneers. They were interested only in escaping the hard work of pioneering and joining the brave new world of cities and the industrial age.

Six years had passed since Frémont had left Arizona, and he felt all those years as he reached seventy-four. He was worn out and poor. Then he became very ill with a severe case of bronchitis. A physician was called, and he recommended getting the general to a warmer climate. Yet there was no money for such a move. Jessie overlooked her pride and approached an old friend, the railroad baron Collis P. Huntington. His reaction was immediate. He bought them tickets that would take them to Los Angeles, and gave them enough money to get themselves established once they reached California. Though Frémont objected to all this, Huntington would have none of it. It was not a matter of charity so much as it was a little something for mapping the way for wagons, stagecoaches, and railroads to follow. Or as Huntington put it: "You forget our road goes over your buried campfires and climbs many a grade you jogged over on a mule; I think we rather owe you this."[16]

## 7

THEY SETTLED IN A COTTAGE on Oak Street in a warm but quite different community than Frémont had first seen in 1846. It was no longer Californio in feeling, and it was hardly Pueblo de los Angeles. It was an Anglo city with growing pains, but the climate was pleasant and helped Frémont to regain his health.

For two years the Frémonts lived a quiet life of poverty. All the time, Jessie was fully aware of how helpless John Charles felt, and she secretly encouraged friends to start a movement to have him restored to his highest military rank and be given a pension at that level. This movement restored his self-confidence. Once again, he made plans. He would make another trip to Washington and point out the proper form the government should follow with regard to the Black Point property. At the same time, he would follow through on the idea of receiving a pension at the rank of major general.

He arrived in Washington at the beginning of 1890, and it was hardly the city he had first seen many years before. It was all get-up-and-go, and it had the look of stability about it rather than the impression of something that had barely been started. Even here, tragedy followed him as though he were King Lear caught by the furies of fate. There was a letter from Jessie, and in it she wrote of Alexis Godey's death at seventy-one from illness, and told him of the young Californio girl who was his widow. But as one generation passed beyond the divide, another was in the saddle, and Frémont saw this as he stayed with his son Charley and his new family. For the young officer was enjoying a stint of shore duty in the District of Columbia Navy Yard.

By April, Congress had acted on a petition to restore Frémont to his rank of major general, and with this he was given a six-thousand-dollars-per-year pension. But the Black Point land was not taken into consideration, and he received no compensation for it. Still, he did have his pension, and he was happy that he and Jessie now would have enough to live out their lives without the constant specter of poverty at their doorstep. At once, he sent a wire to her about his restoration of rank and told her that he would be home soon.

One more errand had to be carried out. He had promised a family friend in Washington that when he was in New York in July, he would visit a Brooklyn cemetery and place fresh flowers on the grave of her son in honor of his birthday. But by the time he reached New York, it was already caught up in a terrible heat wave. Even so, he made the long streetcar ride in the broiling sun, returned to his hotel room, where he wrote to the boy's mother and to Jessie, and then retired for the night. Tired and weary, looking forward to returning home to Jessie and California, seventy-seven-year-old John Charles Frémont felt a sudden drop in the temperature as the heat gave way to a cold ocean wind. He became very chilled, and sent for his physician and close friend Dr. William J. Morton.

By the time Dr. Morton arrived, he realized that there was more than a chill bothering Frémont. He had severe cramps, a high fever, and a rapid pulse, and his abdomen was as rigid as a drum skin. Dr. Morton realized that John Charles had peritonitis, either from a ruptured appendix or gastric ulcer. In either case, there was very little chance he would live out the night. He quickly sent a telegram to John Charles Frémont, Jr., and Charley arrived later that night.

All night his father battled the poison in his system. At midnight he seemed to be coming out of it. Improvement continued until morning was near, until it was the usual time to break up camp and hit the trail. Then Frémont began to vomit. Just three hours before, Charley had sent a telegram to his mother stating, "Father is ill." Now, as he watched him throw up the poison in his body, as he saw him suddenly become peaceful, he heard him tell Dr. Morton, "If I continue as free from pain, I can go home next week." Then his eyes closed, and the doctor leaned over him and asked which home he meant. As Charley watched his father half smile, he heard his last words: "California, of course." The end had come, and Charley sent another three word telegram, stating, "Father is dead."

The burial was simple, the way Frémont wanted it. There was no line of military men and politicians, no mountain men because they had crossed the range before him. He had requested to be dressed in a plain black suit and to be put into the earth in a plain pine coffin. Other than this, Charley placed a miniature of Jessie as she had looked in her youth and her last telegram to him in his crossed hands. The great love affair had ended, and the explorer of a wild land was faced with another world to survey. Two days later, after he had lain in a Trinity vault, his body was transferred to the Rockland Cemetery at Piermont, New York, which had donated a burial plot that would accommodate John Charles and Jessie Frémont. Here, Charley selected a site his father had admired, a site not far from the home he had enjoyed at Tarrytown. This became the explorer's final campground.

Jessie lived on in genteel poverty for twelve more years. Congress voted her a widow's pension of two thousand dollars per year. Along with this, the women of Los Angeles raised enough money to have a cottage built for her at the corner of Hoover and Twenty-eighth streets. She called it her "Retreat," and she lived there surrounded by portraits, books, and furniture that she and John Charles had enjoyed together. These were the material links to the past, but the important things were all the memories that she clung to until her death on December 27, 1902. When she was gone, her ashes were taken to Piermont, and there she was buried beside John Charles on the brink of a steep bluff overlooking the Hudson and the happy home they had named Pocaho.

Before her death, she continued to play the role of Frémont's staunch defender. She saw to it that his story was told over and over again, and she made certain that those who saw fit to attack him in print got a well-deserved public scolding. For his critics were men who had come along too late for the time of giants. Their steel had not been cured in the valleys of despair and on the peaks of glory.

# Notes

## CHAPTER I

1. Thomas Hart Benton's vision of a road to India (Asia) was stated first in a speech before the United States Senate in 1825. He spoke in favor of a military occupation of Oregon and stated: "There is the East; there lies the road to India." It was a dream that remained a part of his thinking for the rest of his life. For an excellent study of this topic, see Henry Nash Smith, *Virgin Land: The American West as Symbol and Myth* (Cambridge, Mass., 1950).
2. John Charles Frémont, *Memoirs of My Life* (Chicago and New York: Belford, Clarke & Company, 1887), Vol. I, p. 21.
3. *Ibid.*
4. *Ibid.*, p. 23.
5. *Ibid.*
6. *Ibid.*, pp. 23–24.
7. *Ibid.*, p. 24.
8. *Ibid.*
9. *Ibid.*

## CHAPTER II

1. Frederick Marryat, *A Diary in America* (London: Printed for Longman, Orme, Brown, Green, Longmans, 1839), Vol. II, p. 1.
2. In 1826 John Jacob Astor's American Fur Company formed an alliance with Bernard Pratte and Company of St. Louis. When Astor quit in 1834, the Western Department became Pratte, Chouteau and Company; while the Northern Department, under Ramsay Crooks, was called the American Fur Company. In 1838 Pratte dropped out, and the Western Department became P. Chouteau, Jr., and Company. Then in 1843 Crooks left the business, and Chouteau picked up the fur trade of the Upper Mississippi and Missouri rivers. Yet people continued to call the firm the American Fur Company. In the interest of clarity, I have elected to call it Chouteau's American Fur Company.
3. Charles Geyer was hired by Nicollet at his own expense as he did not have time to wait for government approval.
4. Colonel Joseph Snelling had selected the site for Fort Snelling, and on September 10, 1820, he had laid the cornerstone. And stone became the building material for this bastion; good timber was too far away and too expensive to bring to this site, but there was plenty of limestone and no shortage of boulders to use in the construction of a solid post. After pacing off the terrain to be covered by the fort, Colonel Snelling decided that it called for a diamond-

shaped structure. Once the plans were drawn, four years of hard work followed as the men of the command cut blocks of limestone, gathered fieldstones, and slowly put together an impressive fort that commanded both rivers and all four directions. When the work was completed, Fort Snelling crowned St. Peter's Bluff like some medieval castle.

5. Evan Jones, *Citadel in the Wilderness: The Story of Fort Snelling and the Old Northwest Frontier* (New York: Coward-McCann, Inc., 1966), p. 188.

6. Named after the Red River of the North, these carts were made of wood and rawhide. The spoked wheels were about five feet in diameter, and the rims were usually covered with rawhide. See Ramon F. Adams, *Western Words* (Norman: University of Oklahoma Press, 1968 edition), p. 246.

7. Donald Jackson and Mary Lee Spence, editors, *The Expeditions of John Charles Frémont* (Urbana: University of Illinois Press, 1970), Vol. I, p. 23.

8. Frémont, *Memoirs*, p. 35.

9. *Ibid.*

10. *Ibid.*

11. *Ibid.*, p. 36.

12. *Ibid.*, p. 37.

13. *Ibid.*, p. 39.

14. *Ibid.*, p. 40.

15. *Ibid.*, p. 42.

16. *Ibid.*, p. 48.

17. *Ibid.*, p. 49.

18. *Ibid.*, p. 51.

19. *Ibid.*, p. 53.

## CHAPTER III

1. Frémont, *Memoirs*, p. 59.

2. *Ibid.*, p. 67.

3. John R. Howard, "Memories of Frémont," Frémont Papers, The Bancroft Library, University of California, Berkeley.

4. Catherine Coffin Phillips, *Jessie Benton Frémont: A Woman Who Made History* (San Francisco: Printed by John Henry Nash, 1935), pp. 50–51.

5. Jessie Benton Frémont, "Memoirs," MS., Frémont Papers, The Bancroft Library, University of California, Berkeley, p. 5.

6. Phillips, *op. cit.*, p. 51.

7. *Ibid.*

8. Jessie Benton Frémont, *Souvenirs of My Time* (Boston: D. Lothrop & Company, 1887), pp. 37–38.

9. Two versions of where the wedding took place appear in print. I have elected to use the one from Phillips, *op. cit.*, p. 57. Allan Nevins, in his *Frémont: Pathmarker of the West* (New York: Longmans, Green and Company, Inc., 1955 edition), states that the Frémonts were married in the Gadsby's Hotel. This information appeared in the New York *Tribune* of June 23, 1856, during Frémont's campaign as the Republican Party's candidate for President; but it is a dubious story, for it seems unlikely that the couple would have been married in such a public place when they were eloping, and it is even more unlikely

that this information would have come to light after the Frémonts had been married for such a long time.

10. There are two versions about visiting Nicollet. Some have Frémont going alone; others have the newlyweds making the journey to Baltimore together. I have elected to use the latter story.

11. Phillips, *op. cit.*, p. 57.

12. *Ibid.*, p. 58.

13. *Ibid.*

14. *Ibid.*

15. *Ibid.*

## CHAPTER IV

1. Frémont, *Memoirs*, p. 70.

2. Phillips, *Jessie Benton Frémont*, p. 61.

3. *Ibid.*, p. 62.

4. Thomas Hart Benton, *Thirty Years' View; or, a History of the Working of the American Government for Thirty Years, from 1820 to 1850* (New York: D. Appleton and Company, 1856), Vol. II, p. 469.

5. *Ibid.*

6. *Ibid.*, p. 478.

7. Frémont, *Memoirs*, p. 71.

8. Phillips, *op. cit.*, p. 62.

9. Donald Jackson and Mary Lee Spence, eds., *The Expeditions of John Charles Frémont* (Urbana: University of Illinois Press, 1970), Vol. I, p. 146.

10. Phillips, *op. cit.*, p. 63.

11. *Ibid.*

12. New Orleans *Weekly Picayune*, May 8, 1843.

13. John Charles Frémont, *Report of the Exploring Expedition to the Rocky Mountains in the Year 1842 and to Oregon and North California in the Years 1843–44* (Washington, D.C.: Gales & Seaton, 1845), p. 9.

14. *Ibid.*, p. 10.

## CHAPTER V

1. Frémont, *Report*, p. 11.

2. *Ibid.*, pp. 14–15.

3. *Ibid.*, p. 18.

4. *Ibid.*, p. 19.

5. *Ibid.*, p. 23.

6. *Ibid.*, p. 28.

7. *Ibid.*

8. *Ibid.*, p. 29.

9. *Ibid.*, p. 30.

10. St. Vrain's Fort was first named Fort Lookout. Later it was called Fort George, but the name that stuck was St. Vrain's Fort. Built in the summer and fall of 1837, it was said to have been designed by George Bent. Located about thirty-eight miles north of present-day Denver and six miles northwest of present-day Platteville, Colorado, it was about halfway between Bent's Fort to

the south and Fort Laramie to the north. For a history of the fort, see LeRoy R. Hafen, "Fort St. Vrain," *Colorado Magazine*, XXIX (Oct. 1952), pp. 241–55.

## Chapter VI

1. Frémont, *Report*, p. 36.
2. For a good account of Bordeaux's life, see John Dishon McDermott, "James Bordeaux," in LeRoy R. Hafen, ed., *The Mountain Men and the Fur Trade of the Far West* (Glendale, Calif.: The Arthur H. Clark Company, 1968), Vol. V, pp. 65–80.
3. Frémont, *Report*, p. 39.
4. Thomas Fitzpatrick (1799–1854) was an Irish immigrant who became one of the most famous of the mountain men. Along with Jim Bridger, "Broken Hand" had been one of the founders of the Rocky Mountain Fur Company in 1830. When the fur trade ended, Fitzpatrick became a guide for emigrant trains and expeditions including Frémont's 1843–45 expedition. In 1846 he became an Indian agent for tribes of the upper Platte and the Arkansas. See LeRoy R. Hafen and W. J. Ghent, *Broken Hand: The Life Story of Thomas Fitzpatrick, Chief of the Mountain Men* (Denver: The Old West Publishing Company, 1973 ed.).
5. At this time, Kit Carson could make his mark. But the most he ever learned was how to sign his name. He never learned to read and write. See Harvey Lewis Carter, *'Dear Old Kit': The Historical Christopher Carson* (Norman: University of Oklahoma Press, 1968), pp. 188–91.
6. See John Dishon McDermott, "Joseph Bissonette," in Hafen, *The Mountain Men*, Vol. IV, pp. 46–60.
7. Fort Platte was built in 1841 by Lancaster P. Lupton, who had come west with Colonel Henry Dodge's 1835 expedition to the Rocky Mountains. Lupton took his discharge to enter the fur trade, built the fort, and sold it in the spring of 1842 to Sibille, Adams & Company.
8. Frémont, *Report*, p. 43.
9. *Ibid.*, pp. 44–45.
10. *Ibid.*, p. 45.
11. *Ibid.*, pp. 45–46.
12. *Ibid.*, p. 51.
13. *Ibid.*, p. 53.
14. The boiling point of water is 212 degrees Fahrenheit or 100 degrees Celsius at sea level, but it is lower at higher altitudes. By measuring the temperature of boiling water, it is possible to obtain a measurement of altitude.
15. Frémont, *Report*, p. 54.
16. *Ibid.*, p. 57.
17. *Ibid.*, p. 60.
18. This appears to have been present-day Boulder Lake east of Pinedale, Wyoming.
19. Frémont, *Report*, p. 63.
20. *Ibid.*, p. 65.
21. See Paola S. Timiras, "Neurobiological Studies," in *25 Years of High Altitude Research: White Mountain Research Station* (Berkeley: University of California, 1973), p. 33. This publication contains an excellent bibliography of

the work done at the White Mountain Research Station between 1950 and 1973.

22. Island Lake is about eighteen air miles northeast of Pinedale, Wyoming. See Orin H. Bonney and Lorraine Bonney, *Guide to the Wyoming Mountains and Wilderness Areas* (Denver: Sage Books, Alan Swallow, Publisher, 1960).

23. Frémont, *Report*, p. 68.

24. According to Bonney & Bonney, *op. cit.*, p. 98, what the climbers saw was a western wall made up of Frémont, Sacagawea, and Helen Peaks.

25. Frémont, *Report*, p. 69.

26. This flag is in the Southwest Museum, Los Angeles, California.

27. They climbed Woodrow Wilson Peak, not Frémont Peak. It was not the highest peak in the Rocky Mountains as Frémont thought, nor even the highest in the Wind River Range.

28. Frémont, *Report*, p. 70.

29. *Ibid.*, p. 72.

30. *Ibid.*, p. 74.

31. *Ibid.*, p. 75.

32. *Ibid.*, p. 78.

33. Located at the mouth of Papio, or Papillion, Creek, this settlement is now at the southern edge of Omaha, Nebraska. See Merrill J. Mattes, *The Great Platte River Road* (Omaha: The Nebraska State Historical Society, 1969), p. 121.

## CHAPTER VII

1. Jessie Benton Frémont, "Memoirs."

2. Frémont, *Memoirs*, pp. 162–63.

3. Jessie Benton Frémont, "Memoirs," pp. 41–42.

4. *Ibid.*

5. Benton, *Thirty Years' View*, Vol. II, p. 479.

6. *Ibid.*

7. *Ibid.*, p. 469.

8. Commander Charles Wilkes headed a naval expedition between 1838 and 1842. His voyage and overland marches included such areas as Antarctica, some of the islands of the Pacific, the coast of the Pacific Northwest, the Columbia River basin, and south to part of northern California. See Charles Wilkes, *Narrative of the United States Exploring Expedition During the Years 1838–1842* (New York: G. P. Putnam, 1844).

9. For a good breakdown of the expenses connected with this expedition, see Jackson and Spence, *The Expeditions of Frémont*, Vol. I, pp. 378–90.

10. John Charles Frémont, *Memoirs*, p. 166.

11. For a good biographical sketch of Theodore Talbot, see Theodore Talbot, *Soldier in the West*, ed. Robert V. Hine and Savoie Lottinville (Norman: University of Oklahoma Press, 1972), pp. XI–XX.

12. For a list of wages paid to the men, see Jackson and Spence, *op. cit.*, pp. 378–90.

13. Theodore Talbot, *The Journals of Theodore Talbot*, ed. Charles H. Carey (Portland, Oreg.: Metropolitan Press, Publishers, 1931), p. 4.

14. *Ibid.*, p. 5.

15. Sir William Drummon Stewart made his first trip to the Rocky Mountains in 1832. On his 1837 trip he took the artist Alfred Jacob Miller with him, and

Miller's paintings of the last days of the fur trade are a remarkable visual record of the times. While Stewart was not an explorer, he always took artists and men of science with him. His 1843 expedition was no exception. In his party were Charles Geyer, the botanist who had been with Nicollet and Frémont in 1838, as well as three other plant collectors: Friedrich George Jacob Lüders of Hamburg, Germany; Alexander Gordon, an immigrant from Scotland; and Karl Friedrich Mersch, a professor of chemistry from Luxemburg. For more about Stewart and this expedition, see Mae Reed Porter and Odessa Davenport, *Scotsman in Buckskin* (New York: Hastings House, Publishers, 1963).

16. Jessie Benton Frémont, "Memoirs," p. 43.

17. *Ibid.*, pp. 43–44.

18. *Ibid.*, p. 44.

## CHAPTER VIII

1. Frémont, *Report*, p. 107.

2. *Ibid.*, p. 108.

3. *Ibid.*, p. 110.

4. *Ibid.*, p. 111.

5. *Ibid.*, p. 113.

6. *Ibid.*, pp. 121–22.

7. This was the second of three forts Jim Bridger built. The first was built in August 1841 beside the Green River. When it was threatened by raids of Sioux and Cheyennes, Bridger gave it up and built a post at Black's Fork in 1843. But he abandoned this after the raid by the Arapahoes and Cheyennes that Frémont met. Bridger moved farther west, and on December 10, 1843, he sent a letter to P. Chouteau & Company, announcing the opening of the post that stood at the present location of Fort Bridger, Wyoming, also on Black's Fork. The fort was abandoned in the 1850s and destroyed by fire. Then in 1858 it was rebuilt as a military post. See J. Cecil Alter, *Jim Bridger* (Norman: University of Oklahoma Press, 1962 ed.).

8. Frémont, *Report*, p. 128.

9. Daniel Potts, an Ashley-Henry man, publicly named the lake in a letter that was published in the Philadelphia *Gazette and Public Advertiser*, Nov. 14, 1826. Claims of having circumnavigated the lake in a skin canoe were attributed to James Clyman and other mountain men. See Dale L. Morgan, *The Great Salt Lake* (New York: The Bobbs-Merrill Co., 1947), pp. 80–82.

10. Frémont, *Report*, p. 132.

11. Talbot, *Journals*, p. 46.

12. Frémont, *Report*, p. 148.

13. Migratory waterfowl are now protected in this area at the Bear River Migratory Bird Refuge northwest of Ogden, Utah—one of North America's outstanding waterfowl reserves.

14. The Frémont party was at an altitude of 4,673 feet. Today there is an historical marker at this spot to commemorate Frémont's having been there on September 6, 1843.

15. Frémont, *Report*, p. 151.

16. While Frémont thought his party were the first non-Indians to sail the waters of the Great Salt Lake, this was not true. In the *Missouri Herald*, Nov. 8,

1826, there was a report of four of William H. Ashley's trappers having sailed around the lake in canoes during the spring of 1826. They noted that the lake was salty, and their estimate of its size was considerably larger than the figures which Captain Howard Stansbury made when he explored the lake in 1850, for he found it was roughly seventy-five miles long and fifty miles wide. See Morgan, op. cit., pp. 19, 80-82, 224-49.

17. Frémont, Report, p. 153.

18. Ibid.

19. Ibid., p. 154.

20. When Captain Howard Stansbury was on this island in 1850, he thought Carson's cross indicated that an early Spanish explorer might have been there. As for the brass cap to Frémont's telescope, it was found in the 1860s by Jacob Miller, who had pastured his sheep on the island. For though Frémont had not found it, there was a seepage of fresh water—enough for sheep—near the north shore. For the best history of the island, which Stansbury named Frémont Island, see Morgan, op. cit.

21. Frémont, Report, p. 156.

22. Ibid., p. 161.

23. The original location of Fort Hall is now on Idaho's Fort Hall Indian Reservation. All that can be seen here is a stone marker with a bronze plaque. A replica of the fort can be visited at Ross Park in Pocatello, Idaho.

When Nathaniel Jarvis Wyeth built Fort Hall, he thought it was the beginning of his career in the West, and that he would never have to return to the ice business at Fresh Pond, Massachusetts. In 1831 he had come under the influence of Hall Jackson Kelley, a Boston visionary who had organized the American Society for Encouraging the Settlement of Oregon Territory. But Kelley's idea of sending three thousand colonists from the East vanished as Boston backers became more interested in a series of fur trading posts and a Pacific Coast fishery. Their final plan called for the regular shipment of furs and salted salmon from the West to the East.

Wyeth built a wooden fort, not the adobe structure that Frémont saw, as the adobe was added later by the Hudson's Bay Company. The fort was named after Henry Hall of Boston, the oldest man in Wyeth's company. But the backers began to bicker about everything. Even Wyeth's cousin John published a book in which he ridiculed Nathaniel's efforts. Sale became the only solution. When this was done, Wyeth returned to Fresh Pond, where he became well known for innovations in the ice business. He even had successful experiments with frozen fruits and vegetables. See William R. Sampson, "Nathaniel Jarvis Wyeth," in Hafen, ed., The Mountain Men and the Fur Trade, Vol. V, pp. 381-91. For an account of Fort Hall, see Frank C. Robertson, Fort Hall: Gateway to the Oregon Country (New York: Hastings House, Publishers, Inc., 1963).

24. Talbot, op. cit., p. 51.

25. Frémont, Report, p. 167.

26. Talbot, op. cit., p. 54.

27. Peter Skene Ogden gave this stream the name of Unfortunate River in 1825-26 because Indians plundered a cache of the Hudson's Bay Company at this spot.

28. Frémont, *Report*, p. 175.

29. The nearest thing to this name was the Great Sandy Plain on Charles Wilkes's 1841 map. Wilkes had not explored the Great Basin, but he did have access to the general cartographic material of that time, and made use of a legend that read: "The Country is extremely Rocky and rough, the Rivers running through Clift Rocks," a description of the land that had been put down on a map drawn by Jedediah Smith before he departed for Santa Fé and his death on the trail in 1831. See Dale L. Morgan and Carl I. Wheat, *Jedediah Smith and His Maps of the American West* (San Francisco: California Historical Society, 1954).

30. For a good history of this country, see Gloria Griffen Cline, *Exploring the Great Basin* (Norman: University of Oklahoma Press, 1963).

31. Frémont, *Report*, p. 180.

32. *Ibid.*, p. 182.

33. The site of Whitman's mission is seven miles west of Walla Walla, Washington.

34. Frémont, *Report*, p. 183.

35. In 1818 the Northwest Company carried its rivalry with the Hudson's Bay Company all the way to the junction of the Walla Walla and Columbia rivers. Here Donald McKenzie built Fort Nez Percé. Three years later the Northwest Company and the Hudson's Bay Company merged. By 1832 most trappers and early emigrants called the post Fort Walla Walla.

36. This river enters the Columbia from the south above The Dalles. It is named for John Day, a Virginian who was a hunter for the Astorians. While it is often assumed that Day died beside this stream, it is more likely that he died at Little Lost River and that at one time that stream was named after him and not the one that Frémont crossed. See Francis D. Haines, Jr., "The Lost River of John Day," *Idaho Yesterdays*, 2, No. 2 (1958–59), pp. 6–10.

37. Rev. H. W. K. Perkins was a member of the second party of recruits for Jason Lee's work. It was Perkins and Daniel Lee who established the mission near The Dalles.

38. Frémont, *Report*, p. 187.

39. *Ibid.*

40. *Ibid.*, p. 188.

41. *Ibid.*, p. 189.

42. *Ibid.*

43. *Ibid.*, p. 191.

44. This bill included food and supplies purchased at two other Hudson's Bay Company posts—Fort Boise and Fort Walla Walla. In addition there was a bill for supplies purchased at Fort Hall. Two other items were not accepted by the government. One was the sum of $500 paid to Frederick Dwight, an unofficial member of the party. The other was a bill of $175.40 for private items.

## CHAPTER IX

1. Peter H. Burnett, *Recollections and Opinions of an Old Pioneer* (New York: D. Appleton and Company, 1880), p. 133.

2. Frémont, *Report*, p. 193.

3. *Ibid.*, p. 194.

4. Burnett, *op. cit.,* p. 135.

5. Frémont, *Report,* p. 204.

6. *Ibid.*

7. *Ibid.,* p. 207.

8. *Ibid.*

9. Located in southeastern Oregon, in the present-day Frémont National Forest, this was one of the Warner Lakes, either Hart Lake or Crump Lake.

10. Frémont, *Report,* p. 211.

11. *Ibid.,* p. 212.

12. *Ibid.,* p. 216.

13. Mary's Lake is the present Humboldt Sink in Nevada, and Mary's River is the Humboldt River. For a full account of the confusion that existed with regard to both of them, as well as the fabled Buenaventura River, see Cline, *Exploring the Great Basin;* and Dale L. Morgan, *The Humboldt, Highroad of the West* (New York: Farrar and Rinehart, 1943).

14. Tufa formations are mainly calcium carbonate deposits. For a description of the ways in which they are formed, see Sessions S. Wheeler, *The Desert Lake: The Story of Nevada's Pyramid Lake* (Caldwell, Idaho: The Caxton Printers, Ltd., 1967), p. 90.

15. Frémont, *Report,* p. 217.

16. *Ibid.,* p. 219.

17. The camp at Carson River was at the future site of Fort Churchill, which was built in 1860 to protect the Overland Trail from Paiute raids. See Ferol Egan, "The Building of Fort Churchill," *The American West,* Vol. IX, No. 2, Mar. 1972; and Ferol Egan, *Sand in a Whirlwind: The Paiute Indian War of 1860* (Garden City: Doubleday and Company, Inc., 1972).

18. *Ibid.,* p. 220.

## CHAPTER X

1. The language of the Washo Indians is of the Hokan linguistic family, and it resembles the dialect of California's Chumash tribe. See John R. Swanton, *The Indian Tribes of North America* (Washington, D.C.: Smithsonian Institution Press, 1968), p. 383.

2. The valley is named after Jedediah Strong Smith, who passed through it in 1827 after his west to east crossing of the Sierra Nevada in May—a crossing he made in the deep snow near present-day Ebbetts Pass, California. See Francis P. Farquhar, *History of the Sierra Nevada* (Berkeley: University of California Press, 1965), p. 26.

3. Frémont named the river and its branches after mountain man Joseph Reddeford Walker, the guide for the 1845 expedition.

4. First called Big Meadows, this valley is now called Bridgeport after the town established there in the 1850s—a town which became the seat of Mono County, California, in 1864.

5. This valley, the river, and the capital of Nevada are all named after Christopher "Kit" Carson.

6. Swauger Creek is named after Samuel A. Swauger, who patented some land here in 1880. See Erwin G. Gudde, *California Place Names* (Berkeley: University of California Press, 1969 ed.), p. 326.

7. The hot springs were named after Samuel Fales, a native of Michigan, who had settled first in Mono County's Antelope Valley sometime before 1868. In 1877 Fales developed the hot springs. At one time there were a hotel, cabins, enclosed hot baths, and an enclosed swimming pool of warm water. While there is still a resort at Fales Hot Springs, the original hotel burned, but not before this author had enjoyed its hospitality as a boy and a man.

8. Burcham Flat is named after James Burcham, a Confederate deserter who grazed cattle here in the 1860s. See Gudde, *op. cit.*, p. 42.

9. If Frémont and Fitzpatrick had followed Hot Creek to its junction with the Little Walker River, they could have followed this stream to its junction with the West Walker River and then continued along the sides of the river canyon. The other choice would have been to head almost due west and try to cross the Sierra Nevada near present-day Sonora Pass. But this would have taken them to an elevation above 9,000 feet; and it is doubtful that they could have made it across such a high pass at this season.

10. I have hunted the country on both sides of the river, and I believe it would have been easier to follow the ridge above Mill Creek and work one's way to where the creek joins the West Walker River at the head of Antelope Valley. For the high ridges of the Sweetwater Mountains to the east of the West Walker can be very difficult to take horses and mules along even when there isn't any snow. As for following the length of the river canyon, that remained a difficult journey, even in the summer, until the modern Highway 395 was built.

11. Frémont, *Report*, p. 225.

12. *Ibid.*

13. *Ibid.*, pp. 225–26.

14. Though it appears obvious that the howitzer was left in Mill Creek Canyon, the search continues. Arguments for other resting places for the cannon include the East Walker River and Lost Cannon Creek. The first can be eliminated in that the party had the howitzer with them long after they left the East Walker. The second is doubtful in that Lost Cannon, or Canyon, Creek is west of the Mill Creek Washo village. Finally, a howitzer like Frémont's was brought to the Nevada State Museum at Carson City, Nevada, by a local rancher many years ago. Unfortunately the museum records are not complete for this relic. Though it may be the missing howitzer, no doubt the hunt will continue.

15. Frémont, *Report*, p. 227.

16. *Ibid.*, p. 228.

17. There are a number of theories as to the route the expedition took to cross the Sierra Nevada. For the most part, I tend to agree with the one in Vincent P. Gianella, "Where Frémont Crossed the Sierra Nevada in 1844," *Sierra Club Bulletin*, 44, no. 7, 1959, pp. 54–63.

18. *Ibid.*, p. 55.

19. Frémont, *Report*, p. 230.

20. *Ibid.*, p. 231.

21. Born in Washington County, Tennessee, about 1792, Ewing Young became a fur trapper at an early age. By 1822 he was in Santa Fé, and he trapped beaver in the streams of New Mexico and Arizona. Kit Carson learned much of his trade from Young and went to California with him on a trapping expedition. In 1834, Young guided Hall J. Kelley to Oregon. Young took a liking to

Oregon and stayed to become a cattleman, lumberman, and wheat farmer. When he died in 1841, his son, Joaquin, came up from Taos to take over his father's estate. See Harvey L. Carter, "Ewing Young," in Hafen, *Mountain Men and the Fur Trade*, 1965, Vol. II, pp. 379–401.

22. Again, I agree with Gianella (*op. cit.*, p. 58), for this appears to be the logical place to have established a base camp for the final push over the mountains.

23. Frémont, *Report*, p. 234.

24. On some of the maps in the early editions of Frémont's *Report*, this is called Mountain Lake. Later, he named it Lake Bonpland in honor of Aimé Bonpland, the French botanist who went to South America on Alexander von Humboldt's expedition. In the early 1850s the name was changed to Lake Bigler in honor of Governor John Bigler of California. But as Bigler was an outspoken secessionist during the Civil War, the lake was given the name Tahoe— a Washo word that means "lake water." But the official changes on the maps were not made until 1945. See Gudde, *op. cit.*, pp. 328–29.

25. Frémont, *Report*, p. 236.

26. This country is northwest of present-day Silver Lake, California. I have hiked the area to trace Frémont's possible route, and even during the summer this is rough country to travel through.

27. Frémont, *Report*, p. 237.

28. *Ibid.*, pp. 240–41.

29. John Sinclair was a former employee of the Hudson's Bay Company in Oregon. Also, he had been editor of a newspaper in Honolulu. He came to California in 1839. When Frémont saw him in 1844, Sinclair was taking care of Eliab Grimes' ranch to the north of New Helvetia. See Hubert Howe Bancroft, *California Pioneer Register and Index* (Baltimore: Regional Publishing Company, 1964 ed.), p. 329.

## CHAPTER XI

1. Ferol Egan, Introduction to John Yates, *A Sailor's Sketch of the Sacramento Valley in 1842* (Berkeley: The Friends of The Bancroft Library, 1971), p. 1.

2. *Ibid.*

3. William Heath Davis, *Seventy-five Years in California*, ed. Harold A. Small (San Francisco: John Howell—Books, 1967 ed.), p. 15.

4. *Ibid.*, p. 16.

5. See Erwin G. Gudde, ed. and trans., *The Memoirs of Theodor Cordua, California Historical Society Quarterly*, Vol. XII, No. 4 (Dec. 1933).

6. Egan, *op. cit.*, p. 4.

7. Samuel J. Hensley came to California from Kentucky as a member of the Chiles-Walker party of 1843. He worked for a time for Captain Sutter as supercargo aboard the *Sacramento*. He took part in the revolt against Micheltorena, served as a Bear Flagger, testified at Frémont's court-martial, tried gold mining, opened a store in Sacramento in partnership with Pierson B. Reading, and was among the founders of the California Steam Navigation Company.

8. The *Sacramento* was wrecked on the rocks off the coast of Fort Ross on June 30, 1844. On November 30, 1844, Captain John Yates and Supercargo Samuel J. Hensley signed an affidavit at New Helvetia admitting their responsibility. See George P. Hammond, ed., *The Larkin Papers*, Vol. II, 1843–1844 (Berkeley: University of California Press, 1952), p. 298.

9. Erwin G. Gudde, *Sutter's Own Story* (New York: G. P. Putnam's Sons, 1936), p. 101.

10. From "Twilight of the Californios" by Ferol Egan, *The American West* magazine, March 1969, copyright © 1969 by the American West Publishing Company, Palo Alto, Calif. Reprinted by permission of the publisher.

11. Frémont, *Report*, p. 248.

12. It is not unusual to see bush lupine five feet in height, but in the rich soil of the San Joaquin Valley it has sometimes grown to a height of ten or twelve feet.

13. Frémont, *Report*, p. 250.

14. *Ibid.*, p. 254.

15. *Ibid.*, p. 256.

## Chapter XII

1. Frémont, *Report*, p. 257.

2. *Ibid.*, p. 258.

3. For a good account of the trail's history, see LeRoy R. Hafen and Ann W. Hafen, *Old Spanish Trail* (Glendale, Calif.: The Arthur H. Clark Company, 1954).

4. Frémont, *Report*, p. 259.

5. *Ibid.*, p. 265.

6. Today, Agua de Hernandez is called Resting Springs. It is about 92 miles west of Las Vegas, Nevada, in Inyo County, California. It was named Resting Springs in the 1850s as it became a camping place for Mormon emigrants bound for San Bernardino, California.

7. Frémont, *op. cit.*, p. 267.

8. For a full discussion of the slave trade in this region, see Hafen and Hafen, *op. cit.*, pp. 259–83.

9. Frémont, *Report*, p. 267.

10. *Ibid.*, p. 270.

11. As any persecuted minority develops its share of militants, the Mormons followed a typical pattern. One of the final results of the invasion of their land by the United States Army in the Utah War of 1856 was the massacre of the Fancher party at Mountain Meadows by the Sons of Dan in 1857. See Juanita Brooks, *The Mountain Meadows Massacre* (Stanford: Stanford University Press, 1950).

12. Joseph Reddeford Walker was a native of Roane County, Tennessee. By 1819 he was in Independence, Missouri. A trapper and trader, Walker served as a guide for Captain Bonneville's 1832 expedition, saw the Great Salt Lake in 1833, pioneered the central Nevada crossing, discovered Yosemite Valley, guided Frémont's 1845 expedition, and in later years became a rancher in Contra Costa County, California. Walker Pass, Walker River, Walker Lake, and Walker, California, are named after him. See Douglas S. Watson, *West Wind: The Life Story of Joseph Reddeford Walker* (Los Angeles: Johnck & Seeger, 1934).

13. Antoine Robidoux was a naturalized Mexican citizen. He was in the fur trade in the Southwest from 1825 until the last years of his life, when he returned to his native Missouri. He established Uintah Fort in 1837 or the early 1840s. The fort may or may not have been burned by the Utes in a winter raid during

The Frémont "White House" at Bear Valley. Photograph by Carleton E.
Watkins. *(The Bancroft Library)*

Jessie Benton Frémont on the enclosed porch of "The Porter's Lodge" at
their Black Point home just south of the Golden Gate on the west side of
San Francisco Bay. *(The Bancroft Library)*

Jessie Benton Frémont in her middle age. (*The Bancroft Library*)

Major General John Charles Frémont at the time of the Civil War.
(*The Bancroft Library*)

John Charles Frémont as he looked during his last years, when only the memories of glory remained. (*The Bancroft Library*)

1844–45. For more about him, see William S. Wallace, "Antoine Robidoux," in Hafen, *Mountain Men and the Fur Trade*, Vol. IV.

14. For more information about this post, see LeRoy R. Hafen, "Fort Davy Crockett, Its Fur Men and Visitors," *Colorado Magazine*, 29 (Jan. 1952), pp. 17–33.

15. Frémont, *Report*, p. 283.

16. *Ibid.*, p. 286.

17. *Ibid.*, p. 287.

18. David Lavender, *Bent's Fort* (Garden City: Doubleday & Company, Inc., 1954), pp. 136–37.

19. Edwin L. Sabin, *Kit Carson Days* (New York: The Press of the Pioneers, Inc., 1935), Vol. I, p. 289.

20. Frémont, *Report*, p. 288.

## Chapter XIII

1. Phillips, *Jessie Benton Frémont*, p. 82.

2. Jessie Benton Frémont, *Souvenirs of My Time*, pp. 164–65.

3. Phillips, *op. cit.*, pp. 81–82.

4. *Ibid.*, p. 82.

5. *Ibid.*, p. 83.

6. Frémont, *Memoirs*, p. 412.

7. Phillips, *op. cit.*, p. 98.

8. Frémont, *Memoirs*, p. 413.

9. Jessie Benton Frémont, "Memoirs," p. 46.

10. Frémont, *Memoirs*, p. 413.

11. Jessie Benton Frémont, "Memoirs," p. 48.

12. Jackson and Spence, *The Expeditions of Frémont*, p. 396.

13. Frémont, *Memoirs*, p. 422.

14. Solomon Nunes Carvalho, *Incidents of Travel and Adventure in the Far West* (New York: Derby & Jackson, 1857), p. 18.

15. Robert V. Hine, *Edward Kern and American Expansion* (New Haven: Yale University Press, 1962), p. 7.

16. Phillips, *op. cit.*, p. 94.

## Chapter XIV

1. St. Louis *Weekly Reveille*, June 9, 1845.

2. Thomas Salathiel Martin, "Narrative of John C. Frémont's Expedition to California in 1845–46, and Subsequent Events in California Down to 1853, Including Frémont's Exploring Expedition of 1848," MS., The Bancroft Library, University of California, Berkeley, p. 3.

3. Isaac Cooper (pseud., François des Montaignes), "The Plains," St. Louis *Western Journal and Civilian*, Vol. IX, No. 1 (1852), p. 222.

4. Hine, *Edward Kern*, p. 18.

5. Frémont, *Memoirs*, p. 425.

6. The Cheyennes and Pawnees had been foes since 1833. At that time, when the Lonid Shower took place—a time the Cheyennes called The Year the Stars Fell—the Pawnees managed to steal the bundle of Sacred Arrows, talismans of the Southern Cheyennes. See George Bent, *Life of George Bent Written from*

*His Letters by George E. Hyde*, ed. Savoie Lottinville (Norman: University of Oklahoma Press, 1968), pp. 48–54.

7. Lieutenant James W. Abert, *Through the Country of the Comanche Indians in the Fall of the Year 1845*, ed. John Galvin (San Francisco: John Howell—Books, 1970), p. 2.

8. Lavender, *Bent's Fort*, pp. 245–46.

9. Abert, *op. cit.*, p. 4.

10. Martin, *op. cit.*, p. 8.

11. Frémont, *Memoirs*, p. 427.

12. William Sherely Williams was from Rutherford County, North Carolina. From 1802 to 1825, he was a Baptist missionary among the Osage Indians. But he left his Osage wife and two daughters to join General Champlin Sibley's surveying expedition to Santa Fé. Then he became a fur trapper and one of the strangest mountain men of all. He had a reputation for being eccentric and a loner. But he was a wild free gambler and spender whenever he returned to Taos with a catch of beaver pelts. He was with Frémont for part of the third expedition, and he was the guide for the fourth expedition. He was killed by Ute Indians or Mexicans in March 1848 along with Dr. Benjamin Kern when they tried to recover equipment that had been left behind in the San Juan Mountains of New Mexico. See Alpheus H. Favour, *Old Bill Williams, Mountain Man* (Norman: University of Oklahoma Press, 1962 ed.).

## Chapter XV

1. Frémont, *Memoirs*, p. 431.

2. *Ibid.*

3. Lansford W. Hastings met Frémont at Sutter's Fort in January 1846. He learned about the central crossing of the Great Basin and included this information in later editions of his book *The Emigrant's Guide to Oregon and California*. In the spring of 1846 Hastings crossed Nevada over this route with James Clyman and James H. Hudspeth. While Clyman went on to St. Louis, Hastings and Hudspeth waited at Fort Bridger to pick up emigrants and send them along this new shortcut. Among those whom Hastings advised were the members of the Donner Party, and one of his suggestions was that they cut a road through the Wasatch Canyon. This took too much of their time, and combined with their other mistakes, they reached the foot of the Sierra Nevada far too late in the year. For the best account of their tragedy see George R. Stewart, *Ordeal by Hunger: The Story of the Donner Party* (Boston: Houghton Mifflin Company, 1960 ed.).

4. My source for Frémont's trail in the region between Pilot Peak and Mound Springs is Charles L. Camp, ed., *James Clyman, Frontiersman* (Portland, Oreg.: The Champoeg Press, Inc., 1960), pp. 330–31.

5. Frémont, *Memoirs*, p. 435.

6. *Ibid.*, p. 452.

7. Edward M. Kern, "Journal of Edward M. Kern of an Exploration of the Mary's or Humboldt River, Carson Lake, and Owens River and Lake, in 1845," Appendix Q in Captain James Hervey Simpson, *Report of Explorations Across the Great Basin of the Territory of Utah for a Direct Wagon-Route from Camp Floyd to Genoa, in Carson Valley, in 1859* . . . (Washington, D.C.: Government Printing Office, 1876).

8. For greater detail about this event, see Washington Irving, *The Adventures of Captain Bonneville, U.S.A.* (New York: G. P. Putnam, 1868); Zenas Leonard, *Narrative of the Adventures of Zenas Leonard,* ed. Milo Milton Quaife (Chicago: R. R. Donnelley, 1934); and George Nidever, *The Life and Adventures of George Nidever,* ed. William Henry Ellison (Berkeley: University of California Press, 1937).

9. Kern, *op. cit.*

10. *Ibid.*

11. Frémont, *Memoirs,* p. 439.

### CHAPTER XVI

1. Sherburn F. Cook, *The Conflict Between the California Indian and White Civilization* (Berkeley: Ibero-Americana: 22, University of California Press, 1943), Vol. II, pp. 30–37.

2. Frémont, *Memoirs,* p. 444.

3. See Charles L. Camp, "Kit Carson in California," *California Historical Society Quarterly,* Vol. I (October 1922).

4. Frémont, *Memoirs,* p. 446.

5. *Ibid.,* p. 447.

6. *Ibid.*

7. *Ibid.,* p. 451.

8. William Alexander Leidesdorff had been appointed United States vice-consul by Thomas Oliver Larkin in October 1845. Leidesdorff was born in 1810 in the Danish West Indies. His father was a Dane, and his mother was a mulatto. Leidesdorff came to California in 1841 as master of the *Julia Ann.* He became a Mexican citizen and was known as a prominent businessman and land owner. See Robert E. Cowan, "The Leidesdorff-Folsom Estate: A Forgotten Chapter in the Romantic History of Early San Francisco," *California Historical Society Quarterly,* Vol. 7 (June 1928), pp. 105–11.

9. Frémont named the lake, river, and valley after Richard Owens. See W. A. Chalfant, *The Story of Inyo* (Bishop, California: Piñon Book Store, 1964 rev. ed.), p. 98.

10. Kern, "Journal."

11. *Ibid.*

12. Frémont, *Memoirs,* p. 456.

13. "Documentary," *California Historical Society Quarterly,* Vol. 4 (Dec. 1925), p. 374.

14. *Ibid.*

15. Colonel Fred B. Rogers maintained that the log fort was not built on Gabilan Peak (now called Frémont Peak). He claimed that it was two miles away, outside present-day Frémont State Park, on Hill 2146 at the head of Steinbach Canyon. See Gudde, *California Place Names,* p. 114. For another view of what might have taken place on this peak, see Richard Dillon, "Gabilan Peak Campaign of 1846," *Historical Society of Southern California Quarterly* (March 1953).

16. *Fort Sutter Papers,* ed. Seymour Dunbar (New York: The DeVinne Press, 1921).

17. Frémont, *Memoirs,* p. 460.

18. *Fort Sutter Papers.*

## CHAPTER XVII

1. Charles Taplin was from New York. He was a member of Frémont's third and fourth expeditions. In 1853 he was a wagon master for Captain Gunnison's railway survey. Taplin died on March 14, 1855, at San Antonio, Texas. There is some confusion about his being a member of the California Battalion, but in one of Theodore Talbot's letters to his mother, he indicates that Taplin left California before the war began. See Robert V. Hine and Savoie Lottinville, eds., *Soldier in the West: Letters of Theodore Talbot* . . . (Norman: University of Oklahoma Press, 1972), pp. 41-42.

2. A native of Austria, Sebastian Keyser had been a trapper and had come to Oregon with John Sutter in 1838. By 1841 he was in California. His associate, William Johnson, was a Boston sailor who settled in California in 1840. By 1845 Johnson had purchased the Bear River land from Don Pablo Gutiérrez. See Bancroft, *California Pioneer Register and Index.*

3. Peter Lassen came to the United States from Denmark in 1819. In 1839 he came to Oregon. During the summer of 1840 he sailed aboard the *Lausanne* to Bodega, California. From there he hiked inland to Sutter's Fort. In 1840-41 he worked as a blacksmith for Sutter. Then he tried a succession of ventures: operating a sawmill near Santa Cruz, being a professional hunter and trail blazer, owning a steamboat, ranching, and mining. The latter was his downfall, as he joined the silver rush to Utah Territory and in 1859 was killed by whites or Indians at Black Rock Canyon, northeast of Pyramid Lake.

4. Martin, "Narrative," p. 13.

5. *Ibid.,* p. 15.

6. Robert Barnwell Rhett was from Beaufort, South Carolina. He served as that state's attorney general for five years. Then he was a congressman for ten years. It was Rhett who had the honor of presenting an ornamented sword and belt to Frémont from the citizens of Charleston, South Carolina, in August 1848.

7. Frémont, *Memoirs,* pp. 483-84.

8. *Ibid.,* p. 486.

9. *Ibid.*

10. *Ibid.,* pp. 491-92.

11. *Ibid.,* p. 493.

12. Martin, *op. cit.,* p. 20.

13. Frémont, *Memoirs,* p. 494.

14. *Ibid.,* p. 495.

## CHAPTER XVIII

1. John Berrien Montgomery was a descendant of a naval family. He commanded the *Portsmouth* from 1844 to 1846. He retired in 1861, but returned to active service as a rear admiral during the Civil War. See Fred B. Rogers, *Montgomery and the Portsmouth* (San Francisco: John Howell—Books, 1958).

2. John Marsh came to California by way of New Mexico in 1836. He owned Rancho Los Meganos near Mount Diablo and was noted for his poor treatment of other emigrants. See George D. Lyman, *John Marsh, Pioneer* (New York: Charles Scribner's Sons, 1931).

3. Ezekiel Merritt came to California in 1841 or earlier. Those who knew him described him as a tough, raw-boned man at least forty years old. John Bidwell reported that Merritt died during the winter of 1847–48. See Bancroft, *California Pioneer Register and Index*, pp. 246–47.

4. Salvador Vallejo was a brother of Mariano Guadalupe Vallejo (see note 6 below). Like his brother, Salvador lived in Sonoma, where he was a ranchero and militia captain. Rough, brave, hard-drinking, and noted for his cruel treatment of Indians and Americans, he was very popular among his fellow citizens. See *ibid.*, p. 367.

5. Pío Pico was the last Mexican governor of California. He controlled southern California and was sympathetic to the English rather than the Americans, but he could not control José Castro.

6. Mariano Guadalupe Vallejo secularized Mission San Francisco Solano, founded Sonoma, owned many large ranches—including Rancho Petaluma—dominated Mexican affairs north of Monterey, favored the formation of an independent Alta California, and looked more favorably upon the Americans than the British or other possible future rulers of California. See Myrtle M. McKittrick, *Vallejo, Son of California* (Portland, Oreg.: Binfords and Mort, 1944).

7. Frémont, *Memoirs*, pp. 516–17.

8. William Hargrave moved to California from Oregon in 1844. He settled in the Napa Valley, joined the Bear Flag Revolt, and served as a lieutenant in Company C of the California Battalion. See William Hargrave, "California in '46," MS., The Bancroft Library, University of California, Berkeley.

9. William F. Swasey emigrated to California in 1845 as a member of the Grigsby-Ide party. He worked as Sutter's bookkeeper for two months, worked as a clerk for William Davis in Monterey for a short time in 1846, worked as a consular clerk for Thomas Oliver Larkin, served as a commissary assistant for the California Battalion, served as clerk of election and secretary of the council in San Francisco in 1847, tried his luck in the trading business in 1848, and was involved in various political affairs during his life. For his own view of the conquest of California, see William F. Swasey, "California in '45–'6," MS., The Bancroft Library, University of California, Berkeley.

10. For a good account of Ide, see Fred Blackburn Rogers, *William Brown Ide, Bear Flagger* (San Francisco: John Howell—Books, 1962).

11. Francisco Arce was eleven years old when he came from Baja to Alta California in 1833. He held various government positions in Monterey, owned the Santa Ysabel Rancho beside the Salinas River, and left California with José Castro to fight the remaining period of the Mexican War in Mexico. Here, he was almost executed by the Americans who captured him and thought he was one of the Irish deserters who comprised the San Patricio Battalion. See Bancroft, *op. cit.*, pp. 39–40.

12. José María Alviso was the son of Ignacio Alviso who came to the San Francisco Bay region in 1776 with the Anza expedition. At one time, José María Alviso owned the Milpitas land grant between present-day Oakland and San Jose, California. See *ibid.*, p. 35.

13. William Knight was from Indiana. He came to California via New Mexico with the Workman-Rowland party in 1842, but he returned to get his family. In 1843 Knight settled beside the Sacramento River in today's Yolo County at a

place that came to be known as Knight's Landing. He was active in the Bear Flag Revolt, and later on he established Knight's Ferry on the Stanislaus River in Tuolumne County, where he died in 1849. See *ibid.*, p. 210.

14. Robert Semple came to California with the Lansford W. Hastings party of 1845. A dentist and a printer, Semple was a friendly man who was well liked by all who knew him. He and Chaplain Walter Colton of the U. S. Navy began publication of *The Californian*, the first newspaper in California. See Rogers, *William Brown Ide*, p. 34.

15. Ford's real name was Noah Eastman Ford, but when he deserted from the U. S. Army, he assumed his brother's name. He arrived in Monterey in 1843. He worked as a hunter and trapper for Sutter, fought with Sutter in the revolt against Governor Micheltorena, served as an officer in the Bear Flag Army and the California Battalion, and later served as an Indian agent at the Nome Lackee and Mendocino Indian Reservations. See Fred Blackburn Rogers, *Bear Flag Lieutenant: The Life Story of Henry L. Ford* (San Francisco: California Historical Society, 1951).

16. Granville Perry Swift of Kentucky came to California from Oregon in 1844. He was not an educated man and worked as a hunter and trapper. During the gold rush Swift made a fortune. Then he became a cattle rancher in Colusa, Tehama, and Sonoma counties. Harvey J. Hansen and Jeanne Thurlow Miller, *Wild Oats in Eden: Sonoma County History in the 19th Century* (Santa Rosa, California: Harvey J. Hansen and Jeanne Thurlow Miller, 1962), p. 41.

17. Martin Murphy, Jr., came to California with his father—a native of Ireland —and his brothers and sisters in 1844 with the Stevens party. See Bancroft, *op. cit.*, pp. 257–58.

18. William Levi Todd of Edwardsville, Illinois, emigrated to California in 1845. Twenty-eight-year-old Todd had been trained as a druggist. He served as a Bear Flagger and as a member of the California Battalion. He left California in 1879 and eventually died in Italy. See Rogers, *William Brown Ide*, p. 35.

19. *Ibid.*

20. Elias Barnett came to California with the Bartleson party in 1841. For a time he shared a place with George C. Yount in the Napa Valley. In 1843 Barnett married the widow of William Pope. He fought as a member of the California Battalion. After the war he returned to the Napa Valley, where he died in 1850. See Bancroft, *op. cit.*, p. 51.

21. *The Californian* (Monterey), Sept. 5, 1846.

22. Victor Prudon emigrated from France to Mexico, and came to California in 1834. He was noted for his flowery prose, and many of Alvarado's and Vallejo's papers were written by him. See Bancroft, *op. cit.*, pp. 292–93.

23. Jacob Primer Leese was from Ohio. He had been a Santa Fé trader from 1830 to 1833, when he emigrated to California. In 1837 he married Rosalia Vallejo, a sister of Mariano Guadalupe Vallejo. He became a prominent businessman in early California. See *ibid.*, pp. 218–19.

24. John Grigsby, of Tennessee, came to California from Missouri in 1845. He was active in the Bear Flag Revolt, served in the California Battalion, lived in Sonoma and then Napa after the war, and then moved to Texas. See *ibid.*, p. 170.

25. See Rogers, *William Brown Ide*, p. 44.

26. *The Oregon Spectator* (Oregon City), July 23, 1846.

27. Joseph T. Downey, *Filings from an Old Saw*, ed. Fred Blackburn Rogers (San Francisco: John Howell—Books, 1956), p. 33.

28. William Loker came to California from Missouri with the Hastings party in 1845. He went to work for Sutter in January 1846, served in the California Battalion, testified at Frémont's court-martial, and eventually became a St. Louis broker. See Bancroft, *op. cit.*, p. 225.

29. José de la Rosa was a printer, tailor, tinsmith, musician, alcalde at Sonoma in 1845, and owner of the Ulpinos Rancho. See *ibid.*, p. 313.

30. Lieutenant John S. Misroon purchased a lot in San Francisco and invested money with Thomas Oliver Larkin for the purchase of land and cattle before he sailed home. See *ibid.*, p. 250.

31. John E. Montgomery and his brother William Henry were murdered in 1847 during a mutiny aboard the *Warren*. See Rogers, *Montgomery*, pp. 87–92.

32. See Rogers, *William Brown Ide*, p. 48.

33. José de los Santos Berreyesa was the son of José de los Reyes Berreyesa, who was killed by Frémont's men near San Rafael on June 28, 1846 (cf. note 44 below). See Bancroft, *op. cit.*, p. 58.

34. Thomas Cowie migrated to California with the Chiles-Walker party in 1843. He was killed near Santa Rosa in June 1846. See *ibid.*, pp. 110–11.

35. George Fowler is not identified in the literature.

36. Henry Delano Fitch was a sailor by trade. He became a Mexican citizen in 1829, married Josefa Carrillo, and lived a long and prominent life in California. See Bancroft, *op. cit.*, pp. 142–43.

37. Pierson B. Reading was from New Jersey. He came to California in 1843 with the Chiles-Walker party. He worked for Sutter, participated in the Bear Flag Revolt, served as a member of the California Battalion, owned Rancho Buenaventura in Shasta County, and ran in 1851 as an unsuccessful candidate for governor. See *ibid.*, p. 297.

38. This was Bernardino García, an infamous killer and thief. He was not executed for these crimes, but he was hanged in later years for others. See *ibid.*, p. 155.

39. Juan N. Padilla was a barber in San Jose in 1843. In 1844–45, he ran a saloon at Yerba Buena. He served as a lieutenant in Castro's command; and for a time, he owned Bolsa de Tomales Rancho in present Marin County. See *ibid.*, p. 273.

40. Joaquín de la Torre was born in California in 1812. A man of great courage and energy, he disliked the Americans and fought to the last against them. He owned Arroyo Seco Rancho, and he was killed in 1855 while trying to arrest Anastasio García. See *ibid.*, p. 155.

41. James Marshall is best remembered for having discovered gold at Sutter's sawmill at Coloma, California, in 1848. See Theressa Gay, *James W. Marshall: The Discoverer of California Gold* (Georgetown, Calif.: The Talisman Press, 1967).

42. San Jose *Pioneer*, June 7, 1879.

43. William A. Richardson, a native of England, came to California in 1822 as a mate on the whaler *Orion*. He became a Mexican citizen in 1823; married María Antonía Martinez; taught navigation to local citizens; served as a pilot

on San Francisco Bay, and owned Sausalito Rancho. See Bancroft, *op. cit.*, pp. 302–3.

44. José de los Reyes Berreyesa was born in California in 1787, served in the military, taught school, and owned Rancho San Vicente near Santa Clara. See *ibid.*, p. 58.

45. Ramon and Francisco de Haro were the sons of Don Francisco de Haro, who came from San Blas, Mexico, to California in 1821. In 1846 the twin brothers were militiamen stationed at Yerba Buena. See *ibid.*, p. 179.

46. Werner H. Marti, *Messenger of Destiny: The California Adventures, 1846–1847 of Archibald Gillespie* (San Francisco: John Howell—Books, 1961), p. 60.

47. *Ibid.*

48. Jasper O'Farrell came to California in 1843 by a sea voyage around South America and up the Pacific Coast. This Irish surveyor served with Sutter in the Micheltorena campaign of 1845, lived at San Rafael, and made the permanent street survey for San Francisco. See Bancroft, *op. cit.*, p. 265.

49. Rogers, *William Brown Ide*, p. 53.

50. *Ibid.*

51. William D. Phelps first saw California in 1840–42 when he was master of the *Alert*. He explored the Sacramento River, served as master of the *Moscow*, and eventually published *Fore and Aft*, a narrative of his experiences. See Bancroft, *op. cit.*, pp. 283–84.

52. New York *Tribune*, Aug. 14, 1856.

53. *Ibid.*

54. William Sturgis Hinckley was a nephew of William Sturgis of the Boston trading firm of Bryant & Sturgis. Hinckley became a Mexican citizen, and he married Susana Martinez, the daughter of Yganico Martinez. In 1844 Hinckley became alcalde of Yerba Buena (the future San Francisco) and was captain of the port. See Bancroft, *op. cit.*, pp. 188–89.

55. Robert Ridley was employed by the Hudson's Bay Company at Yerba Buena. For a time, he commanded Sutter's launch, headed Fort Ross in 1841, married Juana Briones of North Beach, and, after Hinckley's death, became captain of the port. See *ibid.*, p. 303.

56. Selim E. Woodworth, ex-lieutenant of the U. S. Navy, was a native of New York. He emigrated to Oregon in 1846 and then drifted south to California. He was among the men who volunteered for the relief party to rescue the Donner Party. He owned lots in San Francisco, served at sea again aboard the *Warren* and the transport *Anita;* participated as a prominent member of the Vigilance Committee of 1851; served as a commodore in the U. S. Navy during the Civil War, returned at war's end to join his wife and children in San Francisco, and died at age fifty-five in 1871, leaving his widow and five children. See *ibid.*, pp. 388–89.

CHAPTER XIX

1. John Drake Sloat was appointed commander of the Pacific Squadron in 1844. His orders were stated in such a way that there was no doubt that he was to act in case of war between the United States and Mexico. Yet, even though he knew about the war as early as June 1846, he did not assume his responsibility until a month later.

2. Joseph Warren Revere published *A Tour of Duty in California* in 1849. In this book he described his role in the conquest of California. He resigned from the navy in 1850 and became a rancher. During the Civil War, he served as a brigadier general of the 7th New Jersey Volunteers.

3. During the conflict, James H. Watmough commanded the garrison at Santa Clara, campaigned against the Indians along the Stanislaus River, and then became a landowner with a San Francisco lot and a ranch in Sonoma County, which he purchased from Vallejo in 1853. In later years he resumed his career in the U. S. Navy. See Bancroft, *California Pioneer Register*, p. 377.

4. William Scott came to California in 1845 as a member of the Grigsby-Ide party. After the war he ran a store at Sonoma and appears to have worked for Sutter on the sawmill at Coloma until the discovery of gold. See *ibid.*, p. 322.

5. William H. Russell, also known as "Owl," came to California in 1846 with the same party as William Bryant. Russell served in the California Battalion, helped frame the treaty of Cahuenga on January 13, 1847, served as Frémont's secretary of state, acted as a major witness for Frémont during his court-martial, returned to California in 1849 and had a law practice at San Jose and elsewhere. He was appointed U.S. consul at Trinidad, Cuba, in 1861. See Dale L. Morgan, *Overland in 1846* (Georgetown, Calif.: The Talisman Press, 1963), Vol. II, pp. 460-61.

6. William Russell, "Reminiscences of Old Times," ed. Fred Blackburn Rogers, *Historical Society of Southern California Quarterly*, Vol. 33, No. 1 (March 1951), p. 11.

7. Frémont, *Memoirs*, p. 531.

8. Samuel Francis du Pont was a nephew of E. I. du Pont, the munitions-maker for the American Revolution. Thomas Jefferson secured him an appointment in the U. S. Navy.

9. Stephen Clegg Rowan served as a major in the march of Stockton's battalion from San Diego to Los Angeles. He was slightly wounded at the battle of the Mesa.

10. William A. T. Maddox captured and paroled José de Jesús Pico and other officers near San Luis Obispo; and he was given the rank of captain in the California Battalion.

11. Andrés Pico was Pío Pico's brother. He was a top-notch horseman and an excellent cavalry officer who commanded the Mexican lancers at the Battle of San Pascual.

12. Juan Bandini came from Lima, Peru, to California as a young man. In addition to his land holdings, he was active in politics. He was Governor Pico's secretary and a member of the Assembly. He thought California would do better under American rule, and he aided Frémont in securing horses and supplies.

13. Abel Stearns from Massachusetts came to California after he had lived in Mexico and had become a citizen. He married Arcadia Bandini, a beautiful daughter of Juan Bandini; and he became a large landholder.

14. John Temple came to California from Massachusetts in 1827. He acquired his land through marriage and purchases. Later he opened the first general store and market in Los Angeles. Then he and his brother, Francis, built the first office building in the city. See Bancroft, *op. cit.*, p. 353.

15. Frémont, *Memoirs*, p. 567.

16. Known in California as Don Benito Wilson, this native of Tennessee emigrated to California in 1841 as a fur trapper and trader with the Workman party of New Mexico. Wilson married Ramona Yorba, daughter of Don Bernardo Yorba. He bought land throughout southern California, became a rancher and an excellent Indian subagent, served as a state senator three times, and was mayor of Los Angeles when it was no more than a cow-town. See Richard Dillon, *Humbugs and Heroes: A Gallery of California Pioneers* (Garden City: Doubleday & Company, Inc., 1970), pp. 352–56.

17. Joseph Warren Revere, *A Tour of Duty in California* (New York: C. S. Francis & Co., 1849), p. 157.

18. Marti, *Messenger of Destiny*, p. 77.

19. Captain José María Flores came to California in 1842 as Governor Micheltorena's secretary. Flores also was the commissioner that General Castro sent to treat with Commodore Stockton. After the final defeat of the Mexicans, Flores returned to Mexico where he served in the army. See Bancroft, *op. cit.*, p. 144.

20. Juan Flaco, or John Brown, emigrated from Sweden to California in 1828. He often served as a courier. After 1853 he was a vaquero and caretaker of the Edward W. Howison ranch near Stockton, California. See *ibid.*, p. 72.

21. Edward Fitzgerald Beale was a hero at the Battle of San Pascual. He carried the first official news of the discovery of gold in California to Washington, served as a Superintendent of California Indian Affairs, commanded the U. S. Army Camel Corps, explored a central railroad route to the Pacific, aided Juarez in overthrowing the French, owned Tejon Rancho near present-day Bakersfield, California, served as surveyor general for California and Nevada in the 1860s, and served as minister to Austria-Hungary in the 1870s. See Stephen Bonsal, *Edward Fitzgerald Beale: A Pioneer in the Path of Empire, 1822–1903* (New York: G. P. Putnam's Sons, 1912).

22. Frémont, *Memoirs*, p. 574.

23. *Ibid.*, p. 575.

24. Edwin Bryant was born in Massachusetts in 1805. When he was eleven years old, his family moved to Lexington, Kentucky. As a young man, he studied medicine, but gave it up to become a newspaperman. By 1832 he was co-owner of the *Kentucky Reporter* and *Lexington Observer*. Suffering from poor health, he decided to go to California in 1846. During the war in California, Bryant enlisted men and served as the captain of Company H of the California Battalion. In 1847 General Stephen Watts Kearny appointed him alcalde of San Francisco. He purchased San Francisco property, but gave up California to return to Kentucky. He traveled with General Kearny's men to Washington, where he was a witness against Frémont during his court-martial. After that, Bryant returned to Kentucky. But in 1849 he came back to California, where he dabbled in real estate until 1853, when he returned to Kentucky. In 1869 he made one last trip to California and returned home again just before his death. He is best remembered for his 1848 classic, *What I Saw in California*.

25. *Fort Sutter Papers.*

26. John Bidwell, "California in 1841–1848," MS., The Bancroft Library, University of California, Berkeley.

27. Lieutenant George Minor was placed in command of the garrison at San Diego. In 1847 he was assistant quartermaster in Stockton's battalion; he was a

member of the first jury at Monterey, and he was a witness at Frémont's court-martial. See Bancroft, *op. cit.*, p. 249.

28. Midshipman Robert Duvall served as an acting lieutenant in Stockton's battalion. See *ibid.*, p. 127.

29. Robert Carson Duvall, "Extracts from the Log of the USS *Frigate Savannah*," *California Historical Society Quarterly*, Vol. III, No. 2, (1924), p. 122.

30. Charles D. Burrass came to California from St. Louis in 1846. He was the senior captain at the Battle of Natividad on November 16, 1846, where he lost his life.

31. José Joaquín Gómez was a friend of the Americans and favored their cause.

32. Manuel de Jesús Castro was a cousin but not a supporter of General José Castro. After the Flores rebellion in southern California, Manuel Castro was placed in command of the northern division. When the war ended, he went to Mexico with Flores. Later, he returned to California. See Bancroft, *op. cit.*, pp. 93–94.

33. Edward Cleveland Kemble was a New York State man whose family had been in the newspaper business. When the war ended in California, young Kemble worked for Sam Brannan on the *Star*. In time, Kemble became the owner of the *Star*, the *Californian*, the *Alta California*, and the *Placer Times*. He worked as a staff writer for the *California Chronicle*, was assistant editor of the *Sacramento Daily Union*, served as a lieutenant colonel during the Civil War, served as Inspector of Indian Affairs, and returned to newspaper work before his death as a writer for the Associated Press. He also published an excellent *History of California Newspapers*.

34. Samuel Brannan was a printer, newspaperman, Mormon elder, and a firm believer in the future of the West. He is best remembered for his famous announcement in San Francisco on May 15, 1848, that gold had been discovered at Sutter's sawmill on the south fork of the American River at present-day Coloma, California. For an interesting account of his life, see Paul Bailey, *Sam Brannan and the California Mormons* (Los Angeles: Westernlore Press, 1943).

35. Bluford K. Thompson came to California in 1846. He was captain of Company G of the California Battalion. A professional gambler, Thompson was noted for his profanity and recklessness. After the war he settled in Stockton, California. Here, he murdered a man, but he was acquitted in a trial at Sutter's Fort. But it was made clear that he was no longer welcome in California. In 1848 he crossed the Sierra Nevada and headed for the Sweetwater, where he was killed in a fight. See Bancroft, *op. cit.*, pp. 354–55.

36. Joseph Foster was from Missouri. He served as captain of Company F of the California Battalion.

37. James Hays served as a member of Company F of the California Battalion.

38. Hiram Ames was an 1846 emigrant from Missouri. He was buried on the Gómez rancho, and his belongings were sold at Sutter's Fort in September 1847. See Bancroft, *op. cit.*, p. 36.

39. William Thorne was an 1846 emigrant to California. Sometimes his name is mistakenly given as Cooper because he was a cooper by trade and hence was called "Billy the Cooper."

40. Tom Hill had been a fur trapper with Kit Carson in 1834. But by 1839, as

the great days of the fur trade neared an end, Hill joined a band of Nez Percé Indians who were in Montana for their annual buffalo hunt. He returned to the Oregon country with them, and remained there until 1846. When the Walla Walla Indians started for California in 1846, Hill went along to look the country over. He joined the California Battalion with the warriors from Chief Yellow Serpent's band. After the Battle of Natividad, he became a scout for Frémont and went with his army all the way to Los Angeles. See Francis D. Haines, "Tom Hill—Delaware Scout," *California Historical Society Quarterly*, Vol. XXV (June 1946), pp. 139–48.

41. Edward Cleveland Kemble, *A Kemble Reader: Stories of California, 1846–1848*, ed. Fred Blackburn Rogers (San Francisco: The California Historical Society, 1963), p. 82.

42. Charles McIntosh was half Cherokee or Delaware. He came to California with the Walker-Chiles party in 1843. See Bancroft, *op. cit.*, p. 232.

43. Edwin Bryant, *What I Saw in California* (New York: D. Appleton & Company, 1848), p. 363.

44. Frémont, *op. cit.*, p. 595.

45. Charles M. Weber came to California in 1841 as a member of the Bartleson party. He was a native of Germany, and had first arrived in New Orleans in 1836. In the winter of 1841 he worked for Sutter. By 1842 Weber had settled at Pueblo de San José, where he was a trader, miller, baker, shoemaker, salt merchant, and then a rancher in partnership with William Gulnac in 1844 when they acquired Rancho Campo de los Franceses. Weber was active in the revolt against Governor Micheltorena, and he became a captain in the California Battalion. But his highhanded methods of gathering horses, mules, and supplies from other citizens caused hard feelings. In 1847 he settled at French Camp, outside the future location of Stockton, which he planned and laid out as a town and a San Joaquin Valley riverport. During the gold rush he struck it rich on Weber Creek in present-day El Dorado County, California. To mine his claim, he hired Indians for a small sum and reaped a high profit. In the later years of his life he was generous to his friends and to the city of Stockton, but as he grew old, he became mentally disturbed and avoided most people. For an excellent account of his life, see George P. Hammond and Dale L. Morgan, *Captain Charles M. Weber. Pioneer of the San Joaquin and Founder of Stockton, California, with a Description of His Papers, Maps, Books, Pictures and Memorabilia Now in the Bancroft Library* (Berkeley: University of California Press, 1966).

46. William Blackburn was a cabinetmaker from Virginia. He came to California with the Swasey-Todd party. He served in Company A of the California Battalion, than settled in Santa Cruz, where he was active in politics, became a popular judge, and was noted for his farm, which produced premium crops and which had an orchard that was a Santa Cruz attraction. See Bancroft, *op. cit.*, p. 61.

47. Kemble, *op. cit.*, p. 92.

48. *Ibid.*, p. 95.

49. Named after Jonathan Trumbull (Juan José) Warner, this stopping place in present San Diego County, California, was as important to emigrants coming along the southwestern route to California as Sutter's Fort was to emigrants tak-

ing the central overland route. Warner had come to California in 1831. He became a Mexican citizen; and in 1844, he was granted Rancho Agua Caliente or Valle de San José. See Joseph J. Hill, *The History of Warner's Ranch and Its Environs* (Los Angeles: privately printed, 1927).

50. William Marshall deserted the *Hopewell* at San Diego in 1845. He was in charge of Warner's Ranch when General Kearny entered California in 1846. He was the instigator of the Pauma massacre in which the Luiseño Indians killed eleven Mexicans. For his role in this sordid affair, Marshall was hanged in 1851. See Bancroft, *op. cit.*, p. 239.

51. Edward Stokes was an English sailor who came to California aboard the *Fly* in 1840. He married Refugio Ortega, and in 1843–44, he was granted the Santa Maria Ranch, or Valle de Pamo; and then the Santa Ysabel Rancho. The total number of acres in these grants came to 35,427. See Richard F. Pourade, *The Silver Dons* (San Diego: The Union-Tribune Publishing Company, 1963), p. 64.

52. Marti, *op. cit.*, pp. 94–95.

53. Thomas C. Hammond was a lieutenant of Company K, 1st United States Dragoons. He died of the wounds he received during the Battle of San Pascual. See Bancroft, *op. cit.*, p. 177.

54. Captain Benjamin D. Moore was an officer of Company C, 1st United States Dragoons. He was killed during the Battle of San Pascual. See *ibid.*, p. 252.

55. Marti, *op. cit.*, p. 96.

56. Lieutenant John W. Davidson was with the 1st United States Dragoons at the Battle of San Pascual and in the other battles of 1846–47. Later he became a colonel and then a brigadier general. He served on the Pacific Coast until 1859, and he died in Minnesota in 1881. See Bancroft, *op. cit.*, p. 115.

57. Abraham R. Johnston was a captain of Company C, 1st United States Dragoons. He was killed during the Battle of San Pascual. See *ibid.*, p. 202.

58. Pablo Véjar was born in California in 1802. In 1821 he was a soldier at San Diego, but he was sent to Monterey for attempting to desert. In 1828–29 he was a leader in a revolt against the government. For this, he was sent to Mexico in 1830. By 1833 he was back in California. In 1846 he was second in command at the Battle of San Pascual. See *ibid.*, p. 369.

59. Lieutenant William H. Emory, United States Topographical Engineers, fought in the Battle of San Pascual, acted as Commodore Stockton's adjutant-general in recapturing lost positions in southern California, planned the fortifications of Los Angeles, testified against Frémont at the court-martial, published *Notes of a Military Reconnaissance in 1848*, took part in the Mexican Boundary survey, and rose to the rank of major general during the Civil War. See Bancroft, *op. cit.*, pp. 130–31.

60. Captain Henry S. Turner was General Kearny's right-hand man in the Army of the West. He fought with distinction at the Battle of San Pascual, testified against Frémont during the court-martial, and served as a banker in San Francisco from 1852 to 1854. For a detailed account of his life, see Dwight L. Clarke, ed., *The Original Journals of Henry Smith Turner* (Norman: University of Oklahoma Press, 1966).

61. Dr. John S. Griffin was an assistant surgeon in the United States Army. He was in the Battle of San Pascual, took part in the final campaigns in southern

California, served at San Diego and Los Angeles as head of the military hospitals, visited the Mother Lode country in 1849, served at Benicia, California, until 1852, traveled to the East in 1853, and returned to California and settled in Los Angeles in 1854. See George Walcott Ames, Jr., ed., "A Doctor Comes to California—The Diary of John S. Griffin, Assistant Surgeon with Kearny's Dragoons, 1846–47," *California Historical Society Quarterly*, Vols. XXI (1942) and XXII (1943).

62. Thomas H. Burgess was an emigrant from Kentucky who came to California in 1845 with the Grigsby-Ide party. He was with the Osos at Olompali when they had a brush with the Californios just north of San Rafael. See Bancroft, *op. cit.*, p. 76.

63. Edward, or Joseph Francisco, Snook was an English sailor who became a Mexican citizen in 1833. In 1838, he purchased a ranch at Point Reyes or Tomales. At this time he was married to María Antonia Alvarado of San Diego. By about 1840 or 1842 he was back at sea as commander of the *Jóven Guipuzcoana*. In 1842 he was granted Rancho San Bernardo, where he died in 1847. See *ibid.*, pp. 333–34.

64. Many years after the siege of Mule Hill, one of Juan Bandini's vaqueros found this message in the hollow of an oak tree. Now, it is in the Gaffey Manuscripts, the Huntington Library, San Marino, California.

65. See Dwight L. Clarke, *Stephen Watts Kearny: Soldier of the West* (Norman: University of Oklahoma Press, 1961), pp. 224–26.

66. John C. Cox was a sergeant of Company C, 1st United States Dragoons. See Bancroft, *op. cit.*, p. 111.

67. Lieutenant Andrew F. V. Gray from the *Congress* headed the relief expedition sent to save Kearny's command. Gray was Stockton's aide in the final campaign of 1847. He then went overland with messages, and testified at Frémont's court-martial. See *ibid.*, p. 167.

68. Captain Jacob Zeilin was a United States Marine stationed aboard the *Congress*. See *ibid.*, p. 392.

69. The number of men killed at this battle varies from one report to another. General Kearny's report to the War Department lists nineteen dead, but this does not include one or two more who died from wounds they received in the battle. Dr. Griffin lists eighteen dead. Captain Gillespie lists twenty-one who were killed. Twenty-one is the total listed by Arthur Woodward, "Lances at San Pascual," *California Historical Society Quarterly*, Vols. XXV (Dec. 1946) and XXVI (March 1947), while twenty-two is the total listed by Dwight L. Clarke, *Stephen Watts Kearny*, p. 218.

70. José de Jesús "Totoi" Pico was born in Monterey in 1807. His father had come from Mexico as a soldier about 1790, and he established the northern California branch of the Pico family. "Totoi" Pico once owned the Piedra Blanca Rancho, which later became part of George Hearst's San Simeon. Pardoned by Frémont, Pico became an important ally in the march south, and he helped to arrange the surrender of Andrés Pico and assisted in the Treaty of Cahuenga. In 1852–53, he served as a member of the state legislature. See Bancroft, *op. cit.*, pp. 285–86.

71. Frémont, *Memoirs*, p. 599.

72. *Ibid.*

73. Benjamin Foxen was an English sailor who arrived in California aboard the *Courier* in 1826. Two years later he jumped ship. He was baptized as William Domingo, became a Mexican citizen, married Eduarda Osuna, and obtained Rancho Tinaquaic to the northwest of Santa Barbara. See Bancroft, *op. cit.*, p. 149.

74. Bryant, *op. cit.*, p. 380.

75. *Ibid.*, p. 383.

76. Edward A. Selden had been a midshipman aboard the *Columbia* earlier, but was promoted to lieutenant and given command of the schooner *Julia*, once called the *Julia Ann*. See Bancroft, *op. cit.*, p. 323.

77. George W. Hamley carried messages to Frémont, acted as a witness at Frémont's court-martial, and in 1853 was a claimant for Güejito Rancho. See *ibid.*, p. 177.

78. Pedro Carrillo was a son-in-law of Juan Bandini. He had been educated in Honolulu and Boston. In 1838 he had been arrested by José Castro. Carrillo supported the Americans; owned Álamos y Agua Caliente and Camulos ranchos; became port collector at San Pedro, San Diego, and Santa Barbara; served as alcalde of Santa Barbara; surveyed the site of Santa Barbara; served as a justice of peace at Los Angeles; and was elected to the California legislature in 1853. See *ibid.*, p. 86; and see Roland C. Rieder, "Pedro Carrillo and the Los Angeles Land Office," *Pacific Historian*, 6 (Nov. 1962), pp. 179–80.

79. *Message of the President of the United States, Communicating the Proceedings of the Court Martial in the Trial of Lieutenant Colonel Frémont*, Senate Exec. Doc. 33, 30th Cong., 1st sess., Washington, D.C., 1848, p. 73 (hereafter cited as *Court Martial Proceedings*).

80. Bryant, *op. cit.*, pp. 391–92.

CHAPTER XX

1. *Court Martial Proceedings*, p. 118.

2. *Ibid.*, p. 5.

3. *Ibid.*, pp. 175–76.

4. *Ibid.*, p. 198.

5. *Ibid.*, p. 76.

6. *Ibid.*, p. 80.

7. *Ibid.*, p. 36.

8. *Ibid.*, p. 39.

9. *Ibid.*, p. 95.

10. *Ibid.*, p. 41.

11. *Ibid.*, p. 165.

12. Willard P. Hall had enlisted as a private in the 1st Missouri Cavalry under the command of Colonel Alexander W. Doniphan. On the Santa Fé Trail, Hall heard that he had been elected to Congress. He continued on to New Mexico, then cut over to California, joined General Kearny's force, and returned to Missouri.

13. Philip St. George Cooke was one of the youngest men ever to graduate from West Point. He came to California in 1847 as commanding officer of the Mormon Battalion. For his account of his Mexican War experiences, see *The Conquest of New Mexico and California* (New York: G. P. Putnam's Sons, 1878).

14. Short of money for the emigration to the Great Salt Lake Valley, Brigham Young seized the opportunity offered by the United States for the formation of a Mormon Battalion to fight in the Mexican War. He ordered young men to sign up so that they could earn money for the Mormons, hold on to their firearms and ammunition, and keep the horses and mules given to them for use in the campaign.

15. William B. Shubrick had been sent to California as a senior officer to replace Robert F. Stockton. Shubrick remained until March 1847. After that, he commanded a squadron blockading Mexican ports.

16. *California Claims*, Senate Report 75, 30th Cong., 1st sess., Serial 512.

17. Louis McLane was an acting lieutenant of the U.S.S. *Levant* who had been assigned for duty with the horse marines stationed at San Juan Bautista to guard the lines of communication between north and south California. See George Walcott Ames, Jr., "Horse Marines: California in 1846," *California Historical Society Quarterly*, Vol. XVIII (March 1939), pp. 72-84.

18. *Court Martial Proceedings*, p. 8.

19. Francis Pliny Temple, brother of John Temple, came to California from Massachusetts aboard the *Tasso* in 1841. He became a prominent businessman. See Bancroft, *California Pioneer Register*, p. 352.

20. *Court Martial Proceedings*, p. 12.

21. Frémont, "Great Events During the Life of Major General John C. Frémont . . . ," MS., Frémont Papers, The Bancroft Library, University of California, Berkeley.

22. *Court Martial Proceedings*, p. 107.

23. Bigelow, *John Charles Frémont*, pp. 200-1.

24. Major Thomas B. Swords served as chief quartermaster of the Army of the West. He returned east with Kearny in the summer of 1847. During the Civil War, he was breveted brigadier general and major general in the Quartermaster Department.

25. Jeremiah H. Cloud came to California as a member of the Mormon Battalion. He died on August 4, 1847, at Sutter's Fort as a result of injuries he sustained when he fell off his horse.

26. *Court Martial Proceedings*, p. 233.

27. Colonel Richard B. Mason arrived at San Francisco Bay on February 13, 1847. He came as a passenger on the *Erie*, a navy storeship commanded by Captain Henry S. Turner's brother. Mason carried messages from Washington which made Kearny both the civil and military governor of California, and which indicated that Mason was to succeed Kearny in June 1847.

28. *Court Martial Proceedings*, p. 104.

29. *Ibid.*

30. *Ibid.*, p. 107.

31. *Ibid.*

32. Nathaniel M. Pryor came to California from Kentucky in 1828. He was a silversmith and clockmaker by trade. He had been with James Ohio Pattie's men when they were captured in California. After Pryor's release from prison, he became a Mexican citizen. He lived in the area around Los Angeles, worked as a clockmaker, hunted sea otters, owned a vineyard, married a Sepúlveda, joined the revolt against Micheltorena, commanded a group of citizen artillerymen

against the forces of General Flores in 1846 until he was captured and put under arrest for helping the Americans. He died in 1850. See Bancroft, *op. cit.*, p. 293.

33. Lieutenant John Wynne Davidson had been in charge of the two howitzers of the Army of the West. Later he became acting assistant quartermaster at Los Angeles.

34. Bigelow, *op. cit.*, p. 205.

35. Frémont, "Great Events," p. 42.

36. *Ibid.*

37. Bigelow, *op. cit.*, pp. 208–9.

38. Colonel Jonathan D. Stevenson was commander of the military district in southern California until his regiment was mustered out of duty in 1848. He became a San Francisco real estate agent, was a claimant for Los Médanos Rancho in present-day Contra Costa County, California, and held the position of U.S. shipping commissioner at San Francisco. See Bancroft, *op. cit.*, p. 342.

39. *Court Martial Proceedings*, p. 103.

40. *Ibid.*

41. Henry W. Halleck resigned from the army in 1854. He became well known as a member of the San Francisco law firm of Halleck, Peachy & Billings. During the Civil War he was a major general, and he followed Frémont as commander of the Department of Missouri. From 1862 to 1864 he was military adviser to President Lincoln.

42. William Horace Warner came to California as a member of the Army of the West. He was killed by Indians during a surveying expedition in the Sierra Nevada in 1849.

43. *Court Martial Proceedings*, p. 281.

44. *Ibid.*

45. Juan Bautista Alvarado was born at Monterey in 1809. He served as revolutionary Governor of California in December 1836 to July 1837. Then he was the official Governor from 1837 to 1842. In 1844, he helped overthrow Governor Micheltorena. Alvarado was the grantee of several large ranchos, including Las Mariposas which Larkin purchased for Frémont on February 10, 1847.

46. Joseph Willard Buzzell came to California about 1841, when he deserted the whaler *Orizaba* at Halfmoon Bay. He spent some time with Isaac Graham at Santa Cruz; then he became a trapper for Sutter until 1843. That year he went to Oregon, where he married one of the Kelsey daughters. In 1844 he returned to California with the Kelsey party. He served with Sutter against Micheltorena, worked for Leidesdorff, served in the California Battalion, settled in Stockton as early as 1848, and drowned at Halfmoon Bay a few years before 1879. See Bancroft, *op. cit.*, p. 78.

47. *Ibid.*, p. 137.

48. Commodore James Biddle arrived in California at Monterey Bay in March 1847. Biddle was the replacement for Commodore Shubrick as naval commander of the Pacific Squadron.

49. Before Commodore Stockton left Monterey for his overland journey, he published a long article in the July 17, 1847, issue of the *Californian* in which he pointed out that he had been commander-in-chief of all military operations in the conquest of California, and that General Kearny had been *second* in com-

mand. Stockton had submitted his article much earlier, but publisher Robert B. Semple refrained from printing it at that time because General Kearny informed him that he would hold him accountable if he printed it.

The members of Stockton's overland party were a mixed bag. They started from Yerba Buena; worked their way to Sonoma, where they gathered livestock; and on July 20, 1847, they left the Sacramento Valley from Johnson's Ranch. For a time Edward Kern and Henry King were with them, but both men became ill and returned to California. Among the party were Archibald Gillespie, Samuel J. Hensley, and about forty-six other men. The four guides were Joseph B. Chiles—the head guide at $2 per day—James Beckwourth, Garrett Long, and Francis Drake Brown.

The mysterious Brown has often turned up in relationship to Frémont and the California Battalion; but in that there were other Browns in California, this man's identity remained a blank until recently when Glenn Housh traced his origin. Francis Drake Brown walked from Platte County, Missouri to Council Bluffs in 1846. Here, he met a wagon train headed by Buffalo Jones, and Brown was offered a job as a teamster. The party was just three weeks ahead of the Donner Party, and they crossed the Sierra Nevada in the latter part of September and the first of October 1846. During the conquest of California, Brown served in Company B of the California Battalion under the command of Captain Henry L. Ford. At the end of the war Brown refused to sign up in the Regular Army, and took a job as one of Stockton's guides. For additional information about Francis Drake Brown, see his obituary in the August 1903 issue of California's Colusa Sun.

On the way east, the Stockton party had a battle near present-day Reno, Nevada, with a combined force—according to Brown—of 1,500 Paiutes and Pit River Indians. After the battle, the party followed the Humboldt route across the Great Basin as far as the cut-off to Fort Hall. When they reached Fort Hall, they headed east to South Pass. They had more Indian trouble along the way, and during one battle, Stockton received an arrow wound through both thighs. They reached Independence on October 14, 1847. When they learned of Frémont's arrest, Stockton and Gillespie left for Washington to testify in Frémont's behalf.

The total cost for this expedition came high for an overland crossing. The final bill submitted to the government reached $7,000.

50. Charles L. Camp, "William Alexander Trubody and the Overland Pioneers of 1847," California Historical Society Quarterly, Vol. XVI, No. 2 (June 1937).

51. Court Martial Proceedings, p. 115.

52. Ibid., p. 282.

CHAPTER XXI

1. Phillips, Jessie Benton Frémont, p. 106.

2. Frémont, Memoirs, p. 74.

3. Carson's first wife was Waa-nibe, an Arapaho girl. She died in 1841. In 1842 he married Making-Out-Road, a Cheyenne woman, at Bent's Fort. This marriage lasted only a few months. In 1843 Kit became a Catholic and married

Josefa Jaramillo, the fifteen-year-old daughter of Francisco and Apolonia Jaramillo, a prominent New Mexican family of Taos.

4. Frémont, "Great Events," p. 52.

5. Bigelow, *John Charles Frémont*, p. 215.

6. *Ibid.*, p. 216.

7. *Missouri Republican*, Aug. 31, 1847.

8. Bigelow, *op. cit.*, pp. 218–19.

9. *Ibid.*, p. 220.

10. Frémont's mother had been married a third time to a Mr. Hale. Apparently he was not at the funeral. There is no indication in the Frémont Papers or the published writings of John Charles and Jessie Benton Frémont as to this man's identity.

11. Frémont received the sword and belt from the citizens of Charleston, South Carolina, through one of the state's representatives to Congress. "The sword was a splendid piece of workmanship, silver and gold mounted. The head of the hilt, around which is coiled a rattlesnake belonging to the old arms of the State, is formed to represent the summit of the Palmetto tree. On the guard is a map, with the word 'Oregon,' partly unrolled, to display the coast of the Pacific Ocean. On the scabbard, which is gold, are two silver shields hung together, with the words 'California' and '1846,' respectively. Below them is the following inscription: Presented By The Citizens of Charleston, To Lieutenant-Colonel JOHN CHARLES FRÉMONT. A Memorial Of Their High Appreciation Of The Gallantry And Science He Has Displayed In His Services In Oregon and California.

"Still lower down on the scabbard is a representation of a buffalo hunt.

"An elegant and costly gold-mounted belt, having the present arms of the State on its clasp, presented by the LADIES OF CHARLESTON, accompanied the sword." Bigelow, *op. cit.*, p. 222.

12. William Carey Jones worked with Senator Benton as Frémont's legal counsel. Jones had married Eliza Benton, Jessie's older sister. In 1849, because of his legal background on Spanish land titles and his fluent command of Spanish, Jones was given the position of special investigator of California land titles. Because he had to investigate all titles—including Frémont's Las Mariposas—by 1850 bad feelings developed between Jones and the Frémonts, so much so that Jessie even suggested that Jones had caused her father to lose much of his admiration and regard for John Charles.

13. *National Intelligencer*, Nov. 6, 1847.

14. *Ibid.*

## Chapter XXII

1. *Court Martial Proceedings*, p. 4.

2. *Ibid.*

3. *Ibid.*, p. 27.

4. *Ibid.*, p. 40.

5. *Ibid.*

6. *Ibid.*, p. 41.

7. *Ibid.*

8. *Ibid.*, p. 30.

9. *Ibid.*, p. 64. This entry is italicized in the *Court Martial Proceedings.*
10. *Ibid.*
11. Ames, "A Doctor Comes to California," *California Historical Society Quarterly*, Vol. XXII, p. 41.
12. *Court Martial Proceedings*, pp. 34–35.
13. *Ibid.*, p. 101.
14. *Ibid.*, pp. 113–14.
15. *Ibid.*, p. 122.
16. *Ibid.*, p. 125.
17. *Ibid.*, p. 133.
18. *Ibid.*, p. 166.
19. *Ibid.*, pp. 197–98.
20. *Ibid.*, p. 298.
21. *Ibid.*, p. 322.
22. *Ibid.*, p. 326.
23. *Ibid.*
24. *Ibid.*, p. 327.
25. *Ibid.*, p. 446.
26. *Ibid.*, p. 337.
27. *Ibid.*, p. 338.
28. *Ibid.*, p. 339.
29. *Ibid.*, pp. 340–41.

CHAPTER XXIII

1. Jessie Benton Frémont, "Memoirs," p. 73.
2. Bigelow, *John Charles Frémont*, p. 360.
3. *Ibid.*
4. Ned Kern even carried the Fort Sutter papers with him, as he wished to take them to California. The original papers are in the Huntington Library in San Marino, California.
5. The fate of some of the survivors of the fourth expedition seemed cursed. Two weeks after Godey had rescued the men, Benjamin Kern and Old Bill Williams hired Mexican packers and their mules and headed back into the mountains to pick up the baggage they had left at the Embargo Creek camp. They never returned. All that was ever found of the two men was some of the clothing they had been wearing on a few Mexicans. But whether they killed Kern and Williams was never learned. Other theories state that the men were killed by Utes or Jicarilla Apaches.

Richard Kern, Charles Taplin, and botanist Frederick Creutzfeldt joined the Gunnison Expedition of 1853 that made a summer trip through Cochetopa Pass in search of a railroad route. Gunnison, Dick Kern, and Creutzfeldt were killed by Utes or Paiutes near present-day Seiver Lake, Utah. The only thing that saved Taplin was that he got sick at San Luis Valley and had to turn back. Yet his health was broken, and two years later he died.

Ned Kern finally became friends with Frémont again. During General Frémont's period of command in St. Louis at the time of the Civil War, Captain Edward Meyer Kern served as an officer of the topographical engineers.

Then in 1863, when he was only forty years old, Ned Kern died in Philadelphia.

Even the sturdy Charles Preuss was not immune to the run of bad luck for the men of the fourth expedition. He suffered a bad sunstroke in 1850 and never fully recovered his health. In a mood of deep depression, he committed suicide by hanging himself from a tree limb on a farm not far from his Washington, D.C., home in September 1854.

For a detailed study of the fourth expedition, see William Brandon, *The Men and the Mountain: Frémont's Fourth Expedition* (New York: William Morrow & Company, 1955). For a collection of original documents by men of the fourth expedition, see LeRoy R. Hafen and Ann W. Hafen, eds., *Frémont's Fourth Expedition: A Documentary Account of the Disaster of 1848–1849 with Diaries, Letters, and Reports by Participants in the Tragedy* (Glendale, Calif.: The Arthur H. Clark Company, 1960).

The quotation is from Brandon, *op. cit*, p. 270.

CHAPTER XXIV

1. Phillips, *Jessie Benton Frémont*, pp. 136–37.
2. *Ibid.*, p. 140.
3. *Ibid.*, p. 141.
4. *Ibid.*
5. *Ibid.*, pp. 142–44.
6. Frémont, "Great Events," p. 110.
7. Phillips, *op. cit.*, p. 170.
8. Frémont, "Great Events," p. 129.
9. *Ibid.*, p. 130.
10. Phillips, *op. cit.*, p. 175.

CHAPTER XXV

1. By an act of Congress on March 3, 1854, the major debts and interest—amounting to $48,814—were paid. This did not include $15,000 that Frémont had borrowed for the California Battalion, a sum which Congress apparently never paid.
2. Phillips, *Jessie Benton Frémont*, p. 191.
3. Born at Charleston, South Carolina, on April 27, 1815, Solomon Nunes Carvalho was the son of David Carvalho and Sarah D'Azevedo. His parents were Sephardic Jews with a Spanish-Portuguese ancestry. Solomon's father had served in the American volunteer force during the War of 1812. By 1828 he was living in Baltimore. During these years away from Charleston, David Carvalho developed various business interests in Baltimore and Philadelphia. He introduced the manufacture of marble paper, and according to tradition, he served as a member of the Philadelphia Court of Arbitration. Coming from such a prominent and affluent family, young Solomon received a classical education, and he was encouraged to develop his artistic talent. A curious and highly intelligent young man, Solomon moved with ease from one field to another. Perhaps a mutual respect for learning and discovery led to his joining Frémont's fifth expedition. Whatever the cause, a major result of his joining the party as official artist and photographer was the only full report of the jour-

ney. For as Frémont became involved in politics and business, Carvalho published a book about the expedition in 1857, and he dedicated it to Jessie Benton Frémont. For a complete study of Solomon Nunes Carvalho, see the following: Solomon Nunes Carvalho, *Incidents of Travel and Adventure in the Far West* (New York: Derby & Jackson, 1857); Bertram Wallace Korn, Introduction to the Centenary Edition of Carvalho's book (Philadelphia: The Jewish Publication Society of America, 1954); and Joan Sturhahn, *Carvalho: Portrait of a Forgotten American* (Merrick, N.Y.: Richwood Publishing Company, 1975).

4. Bigelow, *John Charles Frémont*, p. 431.
5. *Ibid.*, p. 433.
6. *Ibid.*, p. 436.
7. *Ibid.*, p. 439.
8. Carvalho, *Incidents of Travel*, p. 133.
9. *Ibid.*, p. 125.
10. Bigelow, *op. cit.*, p. 441.
11. Frémont, "Great Events," p. 185.
12. *National Intelligencer*, June 13, 1854.

## CHAPTER XXVI

1. The complications surrounding Frémont's holdings in present-day Mariposa County, California, are explained in detail in the following: C. Gregory Crampton, "The Opening of the Mariposa Mining Region, 1851-1859," unpublished Ph.D. dissertation, University of California, Berkeley, 1941; Frémont, "Great Events," Frémont Papers; Jessie Benton Frémont, *Far West Sketches* (Boston: D. Lothrop and Company, 1890); and Jessie Benton Frémont, *Mother Lode Narratives*, ed. and annotated by Shirley Sargent (Ashland, Oreg.: Lewis Osborne—Book Publisher, 1970).

2. For the complete story of Black Point, see the Frémont Papers; and Lois Rather, *Jessie Frémont at Black Point* (Oakland, Calif.: The Rather Press, 1974).

3. Phillips, *Jessie Benton Frémont*, p. 234.
4. Frémont, "Great Events," p. 218.
5. Phillips, *op. cit.*, p. 235.
6. *Ibid.*, p. 237.
7. Frémont, "Great Events," p. 253.
8. *Ibid.*, p. 271.
9. Phillips, *op. cit.*, p. 259.
10. *Ibid.*, p. 271.
11. *Ibid.*, p. 274.
12 *Ibid.*, p. 293.
13. Bert M. Fireman, "Frémont's Arizona Adventure," *The American West*, Vol. I, No. 1 (Winter 1964). This article corrects many errors about Frémont's years in Arizona.

14. Elizabeth Benton Frémont, *Recollections of Elizabeth Benton Frémont*, comp. I. T. Martin (New York: Frederick H. Hitchcock, 1912), p. 136.

15. Elizabeth Benton Frémont, Letter to Nellie Haskell, Frémont Papers, The Bancroft Library, University of California, Berkeley.

16. Phillips, *op. cit.*, p. 311.

# Bibliographic Essay

A BIBLIOGRAPHY in the normal sense has not been included in that the basic information consulted for this biography can be found in the notes. All the primary and secondary sources used would make a sizable book. However, there are trails for readers who wish to follow the exploration of the trans-Mississippi West and the acquisition of Oregon and California.

Two earlier biographies of John Charles Frémont contain notes and indications of sources that were as complete as the authors could make them at that time. Frederick S. Dellanbaugh, *Frémont and '49* (New York: G. P. Putnam's Sons, 1914), and Allan Nevins, *Frémont: Pathmarker of the West* (New York: Longmans, Green and Company, 1939 and 1955) are pioneer attempts to capture the life of Frémont. Both books are limited in that the authors did not have all the material which has become available.

An extensive bibliography of the events surrounding Frémont's five major expeditions can be found in a remarkable work of documentary scholarship by Donald Jackson and Mary Lee Spence, *The Expeditions of John Charles Frémont* (Urbana: University of Illinois Press, 1970 and 1973), Vols. 1 and 2, and the supplement: *Proceedings of the Court-Martial*. The third volume of this study will cover Frémont's *Travels from 1848 to 1854*. This chronological collection of annotated materials forms a backbone for any writer who wishes to capture the essence of Frémont's life and times. This author admits a great debt to the thorough scholarship of Donald Jackson and Mary Lee Spence.

The key manuscript collections dealing with John Charles Frémont are to be found in The Bancroft Library, University of California, Berkeley; the California State Library, Sacramento, California; and the Henry E. Huntington Library and Art Gallery, San Marino, California. As for government documents, these are available from the National Archives and the Library of Congress. Many of these have been reprinted and annotated in the works of Jackson and Spence.

Other sources for primary material about Frémont and his times can be found in the collections of the California Historical Society, San Francisco, California; the Society of California Pioneers, San Francisco, California; the Yale Western Americana Collection, Yale University, New Haven, Connecticut; the Southwest Museum, Los Angeles, California; and the Missouri

Historical Society, St. Louis, Missouri. In many cases, materials from these institutions have appeared in edited and annotated articles and books.

Some of the important documents from The Bancroft Library and the Huntington Library have been published. For me, two published versions of original material in the Huntington Library were very helpful: *Fort Sutter Papers*, edited by Seymour Dunbar (New York: The DeVinne Press, 1921); and *Frémont's Fourth Expedition: A Documentary Account of the Disaster of 1848–1849*, edited by LeRoy R. Hafen and Ann W. Hafen (Glendale, California: The Arthur H. Clark Company, 1960).

The early work of Hubert Howe Bancroft in his seven volume *History of California* is vital for any scholar. But Bancroft was anti-Frémont, and his study reflects that attitude.

A clear picture of the various activities in California before, during, and after the conquest can be found in the outstanding work of one man: George P. Hammond, editor, *The Larkin Papers*, 10 vols. (Berkeley: University of California Press, 1951–64).

A major reference work for all scholars of the American West is the classic by Henry R. Wagner and Charles L. Camp, *The Plains and the Rockies: A Bibliography of Original Narratives of Travel, Exploration and Adventure 1800–1865*. A fourth and greatly expanded edition of this book was completed by the late Charles L. Camp, and I had the opportunity of reading it before it was sent to the printers. The book is scheduled for publication by John Howell—Books of San Francisco.

The published works of John Charles Frémont are extremely valuable to any biographer. His government reports were done with a master's touch and maintain their freshness. His *Memoirs* are vital for the early years of his life; but since only one volume was printed, the story is not complete. Jessie Benton Frémont's articles and books add another dimension to her husband's life. However, she had a flair for drama, and her works must be used with care.

The bulk of unpublished material by John Charles and Jessie Benton Frémont is in The Bancroft Library. Here, there are manuscripts, letters, and papers. In general, this collection can be found in the Frémont Papers. Included among the manuscripts is the unpublished second volume of Frémont's autobiography, "Great Events During the life of Major General John C. Frémont. . . ." Along with his work, there is the unpublished "Memoirs" of Jessie Benton Frémont. All these documents help to fill out the total picture of John Charles Frémont.

Finally, The Bancroft Library is a Mother Lode of manuscripts, narratives, interviews, and letters by or about persons who were involved with Frémont and his times. Included in this gathering are such items as papers and letters by and about John Augustus Sutter, Thomas Oliver Larkin, John Bidwell, Pierson B. Reading, General Mariano Guadalupe Vallejo, and many others who played major or minor roles in the history of California and the American West. In addition, there are microfilms of journals by Charles Preuss and

Theodore Talbot, an outstanding collection of early California newspapers, and files of interviews with early California figures. Among the latter items is the "Narrative" of Thomas Salathiel Martin, which I edited and annotated under the title *With Frémont to California and the Southwest 1845–1849* (Ashland, Oregon: Lewis Osborne—Book Publisher, 1975). Here, in The Bancroft Library, was the rich vein to be worked in tracing the life and experiences of John Charles Frémont.

# Index